GW00361845

Who Can Tell
A Learning Experience

Who can tell a young man when or where or how
He should live his life when what he knows is now
Who can tell when all we learn is best in things we do
Not telling then but challenge, choice
And problem solving new

Who can tell that loving life so much depends
On facing consequence while despair descends
Who can tell that learning's best in liking what we do
Not pleasing self but pleasing friends
And growing wiser too

Who can tell from whence we learn or how or where
We should listen, open doors, try new ways, and share
Where is hope in those we choose to teach the other well
Not ever can we know its source
And neither who can tell

Who can tell you what to think or tell you what to do
Who can tell you when to blink or tell you who are you
Where is wisdom to decide what is right or wrong
Not ever choose the easy way
And other just too long

Who can tell how others live and who can feel their pain
Who can tell when not to give so others live again
Who can tell when all we learn is best in things we do
Not telling then but challenge, choice
And problem solving new

Contents

Better Belize It

The National Express coach left South Molton Square 'on the dot' at 12:30pm on 5th September 1997. It was a Friday and the end of two weeks in which the door had been firmly and perhaps finally closed on life as I knew it. My house, my home, had already been let and the tenants had wanted to move in, so I had stayed with friends in a busy and ancient farm since two Saturdays before, 23rd August and had been dropped off in time for the coach along with two suitcases filled with what effectively were all my worldly goods. What had I done? It had all seemed perfectly natural really. My wife had departed suddenly ten years before after 27 years of marriage and I already had plenty of experience living on my own. Despite this, life had also been full. The demands of primary teaching and leading Cub Scouting in Devon County left little time for other pursuits and none for sitting around moping, so Voluntary Service in Primary Education in the tiny Central American country of Belize, formerly British Honduras, just sort of happened; now was the moment of truth, so, as is my habit, 'Let's get on with it!' But it was not quite like that. The present life would never be completely left behind and the new one would not arrive in an instant. The moment of truth now seemed essentially a collapse of time. I would still have to be patient. Also, I had always reflected a great deal on what was happening around me and I had lately noticed that habit was getting worse.

The coach was almost full, which was unusual for this stage of its journey. Working my way between bodies spilling over from their seats into the aisle space I could see only two seats free, each with a single occupant sitting by the window. The first was a well-dressed, middle-aged woman who looked up as I approached but remained fixed with her baggage filling the empty space. Seeing this, the youth further on picked up his bag and placed it on his knee. I thanked him and sat down. I supposed that we might never know what another is wrestling with in their mind but knew that I would more than ever have to have care about how others see us in another land. It wasn't made any easier when the woman unpacked a huge picnic for herself and was rude to the stewardess when she brought her tea. "If it's not strong enough there's a red button up there" was all that the stewardess would say, beating a rapid retreat. I wondered if the red button would make the tea stronger, which helped me at least. 'How others see us' was in a way the subject of conversation I had with a past pupil while waiting for the coach. Christine was a bright girl both intelligent and perceptive. She had told of her present progress with languages and her love of Japanese in which she was fluent and which no doubt would be of great value in the changing world. Part of my enthusiasm for her interest had to do with the social politeness of the Japanese and I had illustrated that with a story of them also waiting for a bus…

That bus stop was at Trummelbach in the Swiss Alps, heaving with tourists who were there for the beauty as well as maybe a loose connection with the demise of Sherlock Holmes at Reichenbach. As our bus pulled in I saw from my seat immediately behind the exit that there was a long queue headed by a group of Japanese. The entrance at the front remained closed while the driver called up another bus on his radio, as our bus was already crowded. The exit door at the side opened to let passengers out. Two elderly and loud Germans got on through the exit, pushing past the Japanese who had stood back and proclaimed loudly that they had tickets and were to be followed by others. The driver spotted what was going on and promptly shut the side door, separating the two elderly Germans and leaving the large group standing outside in their proper place in the queue. Unfortunately, a single walker who had got on the crowded bus earlier at Schilthornbahn and had to stand in the exit well was unable to get back on! He had stepped out to make it easy for others to get off and left his rucksack inside. The walker waited patiently at the closed door. As he was waiting an 'informed' English woman announced that it was not fair that anyone waiting couldn't get on and had a train to catch. With typical Swiss efficiency an empty bus arrived in minutes to take up the rest of the queue. Our alert driver then opened the exit door. The walker collected his rucksack and got back on the bus again but at the entrance. It must have happened before! At the end of it all the loud (and separated) German who was now standing by the exit door, rang the bell when he wanted to get off. The bus sailed on to the next stop regardless and the driver must have done something else because the bell only rang the one time however many times the irate German pushed the button. Yes, it must have happened before. That and many other thoughts in leaving behind a whole way of life meant that the present journey was soon over and I found myself pitched out into the bustle of Victoria Coach Station.

When I arrived in London, I went straight to the Regents Palace Hotel, Piccadilly where I was booked in for the night. It hadn't been possible to obtain a booking at Heathrow so the next best thing was to be on the end of a tube line straight to the airport. Even so, the next day was the funeral of Princess Diana and I was concerned about the lines being busy. Logically they should only be busy on the way in to London but you never know. After settling in I went straight down to the tube station and asked. There seemed to be no problem but I nevertheless decided to be early next morning. I certainly wasn't prepared for the atmosphere in London that night.

I had determined to walk some of the funeral route and spent the rest of the evening doing just that, first making my way directly to Parliament Square so that the last part of my walk took me along behind Horse Guards, between there and St James' Park. The air was electric. I could feel the presence of huge numbers of people although the route I had chosen was strangely quiet for a fine, early September evening in the Capital. Somehow, I wasn't surprised to meet the Bishop of London, the Archbishop of Canterbury and a female member of the clergy whom I didn't recognise coming towards me. They were engaged in quiet conversation in a quiet street and I made no indication of having recognised them. Parliament Square and the funeral route were far from quiet. People were bedded down for the night two or three yards deep on the pavements and verges and all other available space was covered with flowers. It was a very moving sight in its own way but I strongly felt a sadness that such a great sum had been spent on the flowers, the travel to London and all the incidental expense that would probably not have been donated to the causes Princess Diana undoubtedly supported by her work and patronage – and certainly wouldn't be now! Was it a blinding light that now flashed briefly in the mind or a little worm that would remain to question understanding, compassion and faith? So many contrasts shouted out from tragedy: the outpouring of love by many for the loss of an icon, a heroine, and the desperate need of millions of disadvantaged people across the World.

The return took me back along Whitehall, across Trafalgar Square, negotiating a crowd of women looking for a taxi in the rain naturally oblivious to all around them, and Leicester Square. Then wandering about a strangely quiet Soho, feeling ever more detached, before finding a KFC for the Kentucky Fried Chicken I had promised myself before leaving the country. Unfortunately, I broke a tooth on a bone whilst eating the chicken which wasn't a good start and remained as a discomfort and a reminder of this day until the tooth was repaired while on holiday back in the UK some eighteen months later.

There was no delay going to the airport next morning after all, despite a heightened state of anxiety and feeling of remoteness at the direction I had taken in life: dragging two cases behind me from Victoria to Piccadilly, across roads, busy pavements to Victoria Station, heaving on and off the escalator, waiting in the ticket queue; Victoria Line North one stop, Piccadilly Line East one stop, two escalators, one up, one down; two more escalators, nineteen steps then nine steps; crowds; banging cases. Underground from Piccadilly to Terminal 4 direct cost three pounds twenty, a very clean way to arrive; easy rolling for cases, baggage and trolleys with smiles at the check in. Boarding at gate 8 at 11:45am. This last part of the journey only took about three quarters of an hour and the train was not crowded. It was interesting, maybe just watching people going about their early morning business, but my mind was all over the place wondering how we each see the other and where I fitted in.

Two minutes silence at 11:00am polarised perception: lives apart, lives in contrast; in death exaggerated for all as Heathrow froze. A prostrate man across three seats woke to be silent.

The shock of return to airport normality seemed to mark the beginning of a shift at last on to a new plane, both physical and spiritual. Boarding was called almost immediately but slow so that I was greeted by fellow volunteer Jayne, embarked upon the same adventure and with whom it turned out I would be working in a new life. The Boeing 747-400 was ten seats wide seeming to me like an elongated cinema, having otherwise travelled only in Europe and once to Kenya but that had been long ago in a Super Constellation of BOAC! My seat, 36H, was by the starboard gangway and being on my own again there was plenty of time in a long flight for observation and to further wonder how and why? Plenty of time also through delay in take-off, first due to congestion then someone's baby was sick so that passenger left and their luggage had to be found from the hold; an hour late, an announcement of departure and re-starting the engines and another saying "We are now delayed in the queue."

My seat companion remonstrated with her child, a boy, who wanted to go to the toilet, "See what you have done now - wanting drink then chips. You will have to wait until we take off." Cocktail biscuits were brought and received with a great sigh. I, also bursting but with amusement, could think of no way to share even those thoughts that might be helpful.

Stewards distributed sweets as an aid to pressure balance in the ears, common practice then; Werthers' Original, much advertised also at the time. Imagine: we were late, "Give them all a sweet!" The boy resorted to opening and shutting the window blind, "No we haven't moved." One hour and fifteen minutes late. "The sick child's probably better by now. They could have stayed perhaps." Then we were moving; an hour and a half late; next in line.

The Boeing accelerated and rotated steeply, climbing fast into a clear blue sky. 09:14, "Unfasten seat belts." The drinks trolley appeared, blocking the aisle; the boy trying to get to the toilet, jigging up and down. 09:45, Lands End heading for Miami five hours behind, taking a southerly route so we were told, to take advantage of a tail wind and make up time.

The boy was fine now but the mother was not a happy bunny at the point where all were settling down, because of the knees pressing through her seat from behind; the knees belonging to a big man whose small space was further restricted by some sort of bulkhead to his side and behind him. She launched herself as a knight into battle while he, claiming to be an Albanian with no English, hid his face behind me and was defended by the much younger woman beside him. I kept quiet although getting a bit tired of it, sustained only by the knowledge that he spoke English perfectly well, having heard him at the check-in; also when asking for food (in a quiet voice) from a stewardess. The flight BA 293 was ten and a half hours but it was very comfortable, the view was good for the short time we were over land and we were very well fed.

Tony, Bernadette, Jayne, Jan, Caroline, Ann, all fellow volunteers, and I met up at the Best Western Hotel after we had made our separate ways in smaller groups. We spent the evening very pleasantly, getting to know each other over a meal and a few drinks in the hotel and a walk. A circus coming to town added to the colour of surreal Downtown Miami. Only the room toilet hauled the seeming suspension of life in limbo temporarily back to earth: blocked; no splash and floating; not a nice sight. The following morning, Sunday, was spent largely wandering round the waterfront in the vicinity of the Hard Rock Hotel, named after Elvis and sporting a huge revolving electric guitar over its roof, not very attractive to my mind but definitely spectacular.

We arrived at Belize International Airport at about half past three in a much smaller 'plane from Miami, which didn't hang about. That flight was about an hour and a half and the total time difference was now seven hours but this would increase to eight hours with the end of British Summer Time. We were met by Chrissie, the Field Director for VSO, and Henry, the Programmes Officer and travelled by road from there via Belize City to Belmopan, taking about an hour and a half. When we arrived we were introduced to our host families. There were two of us staying with Mr and Mrs Sosa plus a coming and going of a family that I wasn't able to work out. We sat down to local cuisine for dinner at 7:00pm.

In the evening I started the first film to be sent to year 7 at South Molton Community College with Mr & Mrs Sosa making an introduction after shots of a map of Belize and stills of a George the Snail soft toy that was made for me and promoted echoes of many stories shared with the students in the Junior School there in another life.

So it began. What, I wondered, could be the consequences, the outcome of any activity, any decision, any experience, and any new life? The life and death of Diana, Princess of Wales, surreal in juxtaposition seemed to whisper 'How' and 'Why' and 'To what effect'. And there had been adventure already; expect the unexpected. And what of the learning in this new role as Curriculum Coordinator for the Ministry of Education, Government of Belize; how does that fit? What had I done? Who can tell?

Orientation

Voluntary Service Overseas (VSO) properly places great value in their Orientation Programme. In most countries this takes three weeks but Belize is English speaking and small both in area and population and a week would suffice, mostly covering culture, geography and services; all very cosy, but that could be misleading for reality afterwards was the work to be done and the newness of life and living to come. On

Monday we were given ID cards and an overview of VSO in Belize. British High Commission Registration Cards also had to be filled in. Much of this was done in a nice little café behind the Angelus Press building in the capital, Belmopan, over which the Field Office was located. We then went walkabout to find the Banks, the Post Office and the Market; all of which were located close by. The open air space of the market was most interesting, full of fruits, vegetables and many items of local crafts. I made a mental note to return but also that there would be many such places and pleasant hours in prospect. Unlike most markets in developing countries there was no pressure to buy and an easy relationship with vendors always willing to chat and curious to know what is going on to aid progress in their country, close to the sixteenth anniversary of independence from British colonial rule.

At 11:00am we travelled to Xunantunich (pronounced Shunan Tunish) in Cayo District, where we had a hearty packed lunch in the shade from Caribbean sunshine with the afternoon's presenters Inez Sanches, Roy Cayetano and Myrna Manzanares. They led sessions on Mayas, Creoles and Garifunas, the three main ethnic groups, in a simple shelter in the rainforest close by this ancient Maya site where the towering El Castillo gazes out over the hills and forests of Western Belize. An armed policeman attended our little group, as we were only half a mile from the Guatemalan border. I didn't know what to make of that at the time, a rumble in the jungle perhaps, although there were many dark suggestions of threat over the years to follow. My main interest in the presentations focussed on the great variety of culture and colour of peoples in such a small country and this seemed at once reflected in the land itself. I saw my first toucans at Xunantunich - and trees that have buttresses, roots that spread wide over and above the ground, and parasitic plants growing on them; too much for the senses and already a surfeit of memory to look out for later. Take it as it comes. On the way out we had seen some Mennonites, a smaller but significant ethnic group important to the country's economy, a religious sect almost refugees and welcome in the country although withdrawn from open society and therefore largely overlooked by the general population who seemed not to notice them. There were not many of the Mennonites about but they were easy to recognise by the very plain way they dressed without colour and by their carts with iron rims on the wheels. Comfort and convenience were denied them. It was almost a relief to indulge in simple social chatter when later that afternoon we travelled to San Ignacio, the principal town also in Cayo District in Western Belize, and had a restaurant dinner with three local volunteers already there.

Early on Tuesday we travelled to a place called Clarissa Falls where there are lush green pastures as well as rainforest not too far from Xunantunich. The wildlife was incredible. There was also accommodation so I determined that at some time I should stay there or at least somewhere like it; one of the many plans already, to be saved for later. The falls were something of a misnomer being only a few feet high but the Mopan River was beautiful. Dinner was again excellent, certainly exotic, and taken in company with more toucans that had come in from the forest and perched on the roof beams of an open outdoor dining shelter beside the river. This was the venue for a session on Development Education! Back in Belmopan we had a session of medical tips (in the Bullfrog Inn) and a tour of the local hospital.

Wednesday was one of the many Public and Bank Holidays, 'National Day'. I spent the day exploring Belmopan, choosing and sending postcards of the amazing splendour of Mayan sites and unspoilt rainforest and being chased by the celebration parade - which was small but lively and colourful. Thursday morning was spent in Belmopan on local issues; employers' perspective - by one who employs VSOs; and British funding by the British High Commissioner, Gordon Baker, with whom we had lunch. After lunch we had a session on safety in Belize and travelled to Belize City for a tour around before dinner with two more local volunteers and an evening session on survival skills (to cope with culture shock?). Then back to Belmopan.

The session on survival skills had something of an unexpected effect. For one thing I couldn't quite see what difficulties needed to be overcome in order to survive. Being far away from family and friends at home is a big issue for many and food, shelter, clothing (perhaps) and weather (the heat and humidity) might need some getting used to. Also there were some very obvious differences in attitude and tradition that easily surfaced but getting about was a happy experience and home with the Sosas couldn't have been better. No, the tension for me had more to do with the little bubble of home that was the comfort of our little group of newcomers to Belize, great companions but a distraction, a distortion even, of a glorious new life to be savoured, shared and learned about; a new place to be and part to play; in the words of George Herbert (1593-1633)…

'A man that looks on glass,
On it may stay his eye;
Or if he pleaseth, through it pass,
And then the heaven espy.'

The next day, Friday 12th September, six of us departed for Belize City where the morning was spent on Moho Caye - a nice little island just offshore - with sessions on Politics, Culture and Socio-Economics before having lunch there, after I had been found, for this was where I first became properly known for 'wandering off'. Although Moho Caye is small, it is easy to lose sight of a group of ex-pats and this was a first experience of the edge of Mangroves and their weird and twisted tree roots exploring the warm surface waters of the sea; too much to miss and a world away from the sessions soon forgotten. A comfortable gateway into this fusion of fantasy and strange reality was provided by the tiny wooden landing stage and I was lost; lost until the sound of gentle rise and fall of water and sighs in the trees was broken by voices and only an enduring vision of crabs remained; crabs with multi coloured claws, little and large, waving above the surface as they danced in time with their world.

In the afternoon we were taken to our new host families. Jayne, Bernadette and I were staying with the Leiva family for a week during which we were to find our own accommodation.

I had sent off a clutch of cards, 'Ancient places, modern faces', and received my first letter which emphasised the life change so far… 'By now it is a week since you left England for your exciting adventure in Belize and therefore time to sit down and write a quick letter to say 'Hi!' When I was 18 I went to live in the USA for a year and stayed with cousins for a few days before transferring to my 'host family'. After just two or three days I received a letter from my Mum and I'll always remember how good it was to hear from her amongst the mixture of wonder, excitement and homesickness that I was feeling at that time. You are probably not homesick but I still hope that you will be glad of a letter from time to time! You left Britain on such a difficult day, a shattered country grieving badly. You will be glad to know that we are pulling together and life is starting to get back to normal. Princes William and Harry have gone back to school and work has begun at Buckingham Palace and St James' Palace to remove the flowers and sort them (for distribution to hospitals or compost). You will be pleased to know that Scouts are involved in this and that – miracle of miracles – the media showed a very positive profile of Scouting in action. The Scouts in question were a great asset to our Movement and even wore mushroom trousers, which I think must be very rare these days. 'My' Cub Scouts have sent a card of condolence to Prince Charles and his two sons and we said The Lord's Prayer as the Archbishop of Canterbury asked us to do at the Princess of Wales' funeral.' …I wasn't homesick but would certainly write – to share.

Being fully independent for the first time that weekend I started some exploring, mainly along the route to the Education Development Unit on the site of the Teachers' Training College and along to the end of the same road - University Drive - which was not too far. At the end there was a speedboat mooring; the ferry to Moho Caye, the offshore island where I first wandered and wondered. This route to work also went by some mangrove swamps, home to thousands of land crabs of all sizes; some pelicans; lots of storks, cranes and herons - different from ours; different species of lizard - iguanas three or four feet long and more delicate, colourful lizards up to eighteen inches and small ones which run very fast; many frogs, very noisy at night, and crickets you never saw but only heard. There was even an iguana about two feet long living in a building by where I was to work and I saw my first snake there - very beautifully marked.

Wider exploration of Belize City, north of the river, revealed colonial buildings mixed with modern concrete shops and a whole range of living conditions for peoples of different ethnic origin all the way to the city waterfront with its almost ancient swing bridge and bustling water taxis. Returning around the edge of the Caribbean Sea and University Drive, I had my first really good sight of storks and pelicans, lots of them in flight over the water: soaring, gliding, turning with tremendous control; ten of them at one point, gathered together for formation flying; changing places so that at times it was difficult to see which was the leader. A pelican flew over very high; wonderful wing shapes, wonderful indeed, with wings in the shape of the letter W.

So much was new and different and happening so quickly and, looking back, it was the walk back to the Caribbean and the park beside Lindbergh Landings among so many others enjoying the late afternoon sunshine by the sea that marked my adoption into the Leiva family.

Monday was a different day. We were to be introduced to work at nine o'clock that morning. At 8:15 I was standing looking across at the Stationery House, painted several shades of purple and blue and standing six storeys high - not looking like a six-storey building but rather more squat; standing dressed for the first time in long trousers and white shirt with short sleeves, socks and shoes, ready for the office. I got up just after six which was late for people round there, and had a leisurely breakfast of rice and beans - well flavoured - and a kind of flapjack, together with juice, coffee and water. The young children around had gone off to school but the High School students appeared to start a little later. Generally speaking, school started at eight o'clock.

Walking to work could never be dull: a large green lizard about three feet long which turned out to be an Iguana, waddled quickly off into the bushes while smaller, slimmer lizards, brown with yellow stripes along each side and down the middle of the back and about two feet long, hung about longer, appearing frozen in immobility until disappearing almost without disturbing the undergrowth. Land crabs emerged crazily and at random from holes in the ground, waving their multi coloured claws before disappearing en mass ready to emerge again and again; a silent symphony in the sunshine, echoes of Moho Caye; inspirational…

A Lesson for the Day

It was not your usual, run of the mill sort of lesson, thought George, it was more your 'University of Life' although it wasn't really intended to be. In all the best lessons we find ourselves learning something that hadn't been planned. So it was for George!

Oh yes, the 'proper' lessons were interesting and the 'teachers' had gone to a lot of trouble to make the whole thing a happy experience with interesting people and wonderful surroundings. But those surroundings provided much, much more.

Now, as you know, George is a rather slow sort of fellow - slow even, for a snail. He doesn't run about making a lot of noise; well, you don't when you're a snail; it's difficult running about with only one foot and George doesn't even try (you should see him dance but that's another story).

No, George likes to watch. He waves his tentacles about and 'feels' - trying to work things out in his mind. He does like to chat but only with one or two people at a time because that is a good way to test ideas, look more closely and learn from others who notice things. He doesn't like being part of the crowd too much because it is often noisy and then you miss things when there is so much to see. And there was the sea: the Caribbean Sea; warm and beautifully blue; tiny, choppy waves stretching out to the horizon, interrupted only by the bright green tropical islands beneath a clear blue, brightly-sunlit sky. Birds called back to the laughing water and storks and pelicans soared overhead - occasionally skimming down for fish.

This was the spot where the whole group that George was with, waited for the speedboat which was the 'ferry' to take them out to one of the islands for lessons! But that too, is another story. That was what the trip was for. This was the unplanned learning - not to be missed!

Even though it was only the sixth day in this part of the World, the others had already noticed that George had a tendency to wander off on his own - not too far, yet - and this was what he was doing now! The landing stage was empty except for George and two men moving about occasionally; talking to each other in an unusual way. That was interesting. They were different and yet very much the same: tied together by the same job - for the walkway was sinking into the sea. Their job was to work out how to repair it and one was telling the other what to do. It worked like this: First, there was their appearance. One was clearly a boss man. He was dressed for the office and he waved his arms about - "We'll have this bit here and that bit there!" The other was dressed for work and he hadn't brought anyone with him to boss about. He wished he had! He waved his wooden ruler about, then his pencil. But what were more interesting were the movements. The Boss Man waved one arm much more and much wider than the other. And the fingers of that hand opened and shut as if they were grabbing at something.

The other waved the arm with the ruler much more and much wider than that with the pencil. And the ruler was a folding one. It opened and shut as if it too, was grabbing at something.

A kind of dance!

George had heard of a kind of dance that was called a ritual. This was performed on special occasions or at certain times of the year. A Ritual Dance! "Wow!" thought George.

The movements were fascinating. Not so much moving around as moving about, mainly rooted to the spot; one arm seeming much smaller than the other - a mere echo of its larger brother:

> Waving in time with gentle breeze,
> Pointing lazily at an evening sky,
> Opening, closing, almost
> Laughing at the sun
> Changing in colour with reflected light,
> Answering gently, clouds passing by,
> Reaching, grasping, almost
> Dancing for the sun
> Responding as one with sudden alarm,
> Each, as the other, dropped his arm.
> Sighing, sinking, almost
> Shrinking, they had gone...

Something had drawn them away. George's attention changed.

The landing stage surrounded a tree which grew out of the water. He was amazed, for he had never seen such a tree before. It had its branches as all trees have but there were those beneath it as well as those on top. The roots came right up out of the ground, right up out of the water. They grew as branches might but upside down, a solid reflection of the tree above the water.

George gasped. And he thought,
"We haven't even got into the speedboat yet!" And that too, is another story.

George knew that when you look at something new, you see the whole thing first and then the detail (If you are still interested!). But even so, he was not prepared for what he saw next.

Crabs!
Lots of them!
All over the roots of the tree and out of the water!

Few were in the water; most were out. Of those that were in at all, most were in the ground - in holes; beautifully round holes; sunk into the soft soil around the edge of the sea.

George's attention was caught by two crabs in particular. And one was bigger than the other, more bossy.

"Familiar!" he thought.

But what were more interesting were the movements. Each waved one arm about much more and much wider than the other and the pincer on the end of it was much bigger. And the bigger pincer on that arm opened and shut as if it were grabbing at something. A kind of dance!

"Wow!" thought George, again.

The movements were fascinating. Not so much moving around as moving about, mainly rooted to the spot; one arm much smaller than the other - a mere echo of its larger brother:

> Waving in time with gentle breeze,
> Pointing lazily at an evening sky,
> Opening, closing, almost
> Laughing at the sun
> Changing in colour with reflected light,
> Answering gently, clouds passing by,
> Reaching, grasping, almost
> Dancing for the sun
> Responding as one with sudden alarm,
> Each, as the other, dropped his arm.
> Sighing, sinking, almost
> Shrinking, they had gone...

George's movement had startled them. But then, he too, was startled out of his thoughts:

"George!"

His name echoed as members of the group called, for it was time to join the speedboat and the other lessons of the day. But George was not to forget this lesson - although he was still caught unawares when the time came to remember...........

It was some days later, as George was dawdling along - along University Drive as it happens - thinking about things. He was supposed to be going somewhere but he wasn't in any hurry - and we needn't go into that again.

It was HOT! The air throbbed with heat, ninety-five degrees of heat (It should really be called temperature but George said it was heat), ninety-five degrees of heat and no wind; but it so happened that University Drive, which had buildings down one side, gave way to a mangrove swamp on the other side where George was slowly moving. It was said that crocodiles lived in that swamp. Of course, George hoped to see one but there were other things attracting his attention just now. In the heat of the day, vultures circled lazily overhead but the shade of the mangrove trees provided cover for a variety of other creatures of much more interest.

A pair of white egrets strutted slowly, with measured step matched by the movement of the head and beak; multi-coloured birds of many sizes, flitted and screeched among the leaves and branches; huge butterflies, red on black, orange and sulphur coloured, flapped heavily on their way. But the most amazing sight was the flowers.

George stopped...

On a bare patch of ground surrounded by green grass, what George saw was hundreds of beautiful flowers. The patch was not large - perhaps three metres around - but it was packed with hundreds of delicate flowers. Each flower appeared to have two stems, one much bigger than the other. On the end of each stem, the flower opened out in a riot of yellows and oranges - even a little red - reflecting brightly, the light from the sun.

"Odd 'though," thought George, "to have no green at all!"

But what were even more interesting were the movements. Each flower waved one stem about much more and much wider than the other and the bloom on the end of it was much bigger. And the bigger bloom on that stem opened and shut as if it were grabbing at something. A kind of dance!

"Wow!" thought George again, and moved forward for a closer look.

Immediately, all the flowers disappeared!

George stopped. And, as he stopped, all the flowers appeared again, almost at the same time but not quite. It was like a carpet spreading out once more before him. Once again, the movements: Each flower waved one stem about much more and much wider than the other and the bloom on the end of it was much bigger. And the bigger bloom on that stem opened and shut as if it were grabbing at something. A kind of dance!

Crabs!
Hundreds of them!
Each one a perfect 'flower'
Its arms reaching up from the hole it occupied, beautifully round, sunk into the soft soil
alongside a swamp fed by the sea.

The movements were fascinating. Not so much moving around as moving about, seemingly rooted to the spot; one arm much bigger than the other - a mere echo of its larger brother:

Waving in time with gentle breeze,
Pointing lazily at an evening sky,
Opening, closing, almost
Laughing at the sun
Changing in colour with reflected light,
Answering gently, clouds passing by,
Reaching, grasping, almost
Dancing for the sun
Responding as one with sudden alarm,
Each, as the other, dropped his arm

Sighing, sinking, almost
Shrinking, they had gone…

"Well, I never did!" thought George.

Thus was born the first piece of writing for children back home who were well used to 'George the Snail' stories.

The first day at work began with an interesting and highly entertaining tour of Belize City in a small, open bus colourfully decorated in Caribbean style, the first part of which, the Fort George area, is in transcript…

'I'm not sure if you are all Belizean but I'll say welcome to Belize. I don't know how long you have been here but I'll say welcome to Belize and Belize City in particular. Er… My name is Captain Nicholas Sanchez and I was born right here in Belize City some sixty - odd years ago and Er…. Right down the street down there… Er, Oh and I lived in Canada for forty years, I lived in Vancouver, British Columbia - So how am I doing the… OK. And Er… how come I'm doing the Belize City Tour? Well Er… No-one else is doing it so I guess I find a need and fill it.

Er… This is a very intense course and I talk quite rapidly because sometimes I'm passing places, two or three of them at a time and I can't stop because of narrow streets or a line-up behind me and so on so you have to see the places too carefully. Er… Please ask any questions you want but… there… remember now about - just before you ask that question - just two blocks or two minutes away and I'll be answering it for you. But go ahead; ask! May I ask where you folks are from, please?

….de fire station where you were waiting in de rain. Dis Er, Dat was built in 1900 as the Customs shed - the Customs Bond - in 1923 it was converted to the Fire Station and that's where de… All de doors and so on you see there are just the em, where de fire engines dey be backed in. By 1918 de plant had de chain drive with big valves and hand boom and sirens and so on.

Across the street is the Belize Store. Dat store dere was built by the people who own this building here - The Belize Estate and Produce Company. It was built in 1920 and it is the largest wooden building in the country. It houses the Post Office and some ministries - The Ministry of Land and so on of course, and erm… during the war, because the erm… Collaborators that were caught down here in Belize er in British Honduras were interned upstairs. I think they thought they could get away with it because dere ain't nobody down dere in British Honduras. But the OSS, they came down and looked around maybe a week or two and went around - pick em all up, put em upstairs! From dere dey were sent to Jamaica to de concentration camp over dere…

…Dat store was one of the largest shoe stores in Belize City. You could buy a pair of shoe' in there for three dollars. Er… Not much but a person working get two dollars a week. It was tough. My Dad was an electrician here and he work for ten dollars a week in dose days. But three bucks was for a pair of shoes was a lot of money.

This is the Belize Tourist Board and The Belizean Consulate is right upstairs here. And over here is The Jubilee Library. The Jubilee Library was opened here in the Jubilee of King George V on de third of December 1935. Er Mr Carnegie gave all the books and Mr Turton, Robert Turton, gave the land and the buildings for it. As long as it is being used for a Library they can keep it but the day the last book leaves then….

The Palace Hotel or what's left of it - not much anyway: no roof; no floors; no windows; no doors. But you can see the trees growing on it. Those are the Strangular Tree. The Strangular Tree always starts from the top growing down. Always go…. Never starts from the ground. On a structure, on a hillside, on another tree - a Cahoon Tree like this - never from the ground up…

This is the City Hall… At one time the Town Hall… Belize at one time was about the largest town in the world I should say. In 1912, Belize Town, St. George's Caye nine miles away, Caye Caulker twenty one miles away and San Pedro thirty six miles away. That's quite a lot of territory for a small town. Here's a temporary market. It has been temporary now, for eight or nine years. How long's a temporary market? The big green tank is one of the three reservoirs we have for the water for the washing and cooking and whatever. It was a yellow tank when I was a kid and I've called it the yellow tank ever since, in my mind.

The Department - the Ministry of Education; the Department of Housing and Planning… You see a lot of carryings in the streets of Belize and so on because… …a guy walks along with a box on his shoulders… That's from that tree there - the Cerecote; very hard wood, very heavy. The Cerecote, the

Sapodilla, Logwood, er Lignum Vitae, Ironwood - they sink. They will sink right now. You throw them in the water - you won't see them anymore.

Now… em… there's two things I like to say now about Belize… I see people writing about Belize and they miss the truth. First of all they say that Belize is south of Mexico's Yucatan Peninsula. That's not so at all (shows map). Here's Belize right here and here's the Yucatan Peninsula right here. So we are very much a part of the Yucatan Peninsula. We are not south of anybody's anything. Not south of Mexico's Yucatan. This is the State of Yucatan. The river is on the eastern seaboard of the Yucatan Peninsula - Right? From here right down… OK, that's number one! And number two is the one that… Oh! They gave me heck for that one because I told them that Belize does not have the second longest Barrier Reef in the World… If you do buy one of these maps, I'll autograph it for you. I'll also give you one of my photographs…

But they wouldn't buy the map because it said that Belize had the fifth longest Barrier Reef in the World. You have Australia which is 1600 km. The South West Caledonian Barrier Reef is 600km. The New Caledonian - er, North East is 450km and the Great Sea Reef of Fiji is 260km.

The Belize Delta here was very swampy, very, very low lying, and it was all filled in. It has been filled in over the years. This was an island right out here - George Island, but then in 1926, Baron Henrik, Ernest, Victor Bliss. Er came on our shores. He came on his boat the Sea King and he anchored his boat, the Sea King, right over there, four or five hundred feet off. And he was crippled from the waist down and he and his friend Willoughby Bullock, the Solicitor General of the time, and Douglas Jones, our Colonial Secretary… They believed in the internal combustion engine and instead of buying in to the people who made engines, they bought in to Shell Oil. It didn't matter who make engines, you buy my oil! And he makes quite a bit. When he came in to the coast of Belize in 1926 on the third of January, he was very ill. He had food poisoning. He suffered in Trinidad and Tobago. So he said, "Where can he go?" and we said, "Come to British Honduras because the folks here are very loving and kind and giving and they don't want to take anything from you." Well, that was true except that we did accept the one million, six hundred thousand pound which he gave us in a Trust Fund and… He was buried in a garden over there, just beyond that swing… When there was enough interest from the Trust Fund, he was buried as near as possible to he sea….'

A flavour of the tour of Belize City which was to last for some two and a half hours without any let up in either the flow, confusion or the speed of Captain Sanchez' commentary.

Later, Ernest Raymond, the Chief Education Officer, outlined the organisational structure of the Education Service and a tour of the premises was followed by an overview of the History of Education and Curriculum Development in Belize given by Alexander Bennett who had led the curriculum development thus…

17th Century. There was only a small settlement of loggers, mainly men. A town grew at the mouth of the Belize River to produce wood for making dye.

18th Century. The market for logwood declined and logging for mahogany grew. However, there were very few people up to 1800 and even fewer were white, so there were no schools.

1708. The Battle of St. George's Caye.

1816. A school for 10 -12 children, funded by public subscription, was put in the charge of an Anglican Rector. This was called the Honduras Free School which grew to 150 children by the mid-nineteenth century. A school for girls was added and then one for infants.

From 1820, The Methodists and the Baptists both opened schools.

1847. The Indians rose up against the Whites in Mexico which resulted in an influx of Mestisos and Mayan Indians from the rest of the Yucatan. A population of 8,000 in Belize rose considerably by 1860. Schools grew and the Roman Catholic Schools grew out of all proportion to the rest.

1850. First Education Act for the Church and State System. Education was open to all, regardless of race or belief. Even so, it was the churches who would tell the Board of Education where the schools should be and the Government which paid for them. The system put in place was an imitation of the Jamaican/ UK system (payment by results).

1892. Act passed which revived the Board of Education with a stronger code of rules called the Board Rules. In the nineteenth century the curriculum imitated the English model with, for example, the monitorial system; the content of the Primary Curriculum consisted wholly of the 'three Rs' and needlework for girls. The method comprised rote learning and memorisation.

A study was made in the late nineteenth century and later, the geographic location of places and English

History were introduced into the syllabus. Also in the late nineteenth century, Secondary Schools were established, first by the Wesleyans, then the Roman Catholics and then the Anglicans. It was still a British system and a British curriculum.

1900 -1930. Introduction of compulsory schooling

1926. Revision of Ordnance to include compulsory education.

1928. The Colonial Secretary wrote a critical review of education in Belize. A practical Primary Curriculum was proposed because most children would not go to Secondary School. The World Depression hit Belize very badly and the education budget was cut.

1931. Severe hurricane damage added to the ravages of the Depression.

1932. A serious fire in the area of Albert Street hit the economy further. The British Government sent in advisers with the result that further cuts were made in the Education Budget.

1934. B H Easter was sent in to find ways of making the best use of funds. He criticised the cuts in the Education Budget and recommended that the share of GDP be restored to 10%. Wide changes to the system were also recommended:
Rote learning should be dropped and new subjects added to build on children's own interests.
Teachers should be trained properly.
The report was not implemented in its original form but was studied and developed even through depressed times: A Pupil Teacher School was set up; Jean's Teachers were facilitating change; Exchange visits were organised; and new subjects were introduced.

1940s. Teachers were sent overseas to train.

1944. Colonial Education and Welfare Development Act. English Language and Arithmetic became the curriculum. There was no formal curriculum development until the 1950s.

1950s. A new constitution led to policy proposals that the curriculum should be more Belizean.

1954. The first Teacher Training College was set up. A Pupil Teacher system was introduced with First and Second Class Teachers.

1960. CEO programme to re-write the syllabus (curriculum).
Committees were set up for the subject areas: Arithmetic became maths; English became Language; History/Geography became Social Studies - giving rise to Integrated Learning. A need was identified for a focus for the committees.

1974. A co-ordinator (Alexander Bennett) was appointed.

1975. The Curriculum Development Unit was established in a room in St. Mary's School with a budget for its operation. Messrs' Raymond/Aspinal/Tulin started working on the Senior Guides to a) bring them up to date b) provide orientation for teachers and c) provide a resource centre.
Performance objectives were set (There was still conflict between cognitive and behaviourist theories.).
By 1984 all levels had been covered in all core areas but not beyond that. The Rural Education and Agricultural Project (REAP) was instituted. The Primary Education Project (PEP) was instituted. Curriculum Development remained unfinished.

1992. It was decided that the Belize Primary Education Project (BPEP) needed a written policy.

1995. Mid-term review. Previous work was halted and the building of a new curriculum began, based on integration.

Tuesday began with a meeting on domestic and task arrangements by Ellajean Gillette, the Director of the Education Development Unit (by which we were known), who in common with many others seemed to use a language register which was very stilted and formal and not very efficient in conveying either ideas or information. A timeline had been set but the deadline to be ready for field-testing of the New Curriculum had been brought forward to 17th. October although this was not to be with children but rather a discussion process with teaching staff who would eventually carry out the trials. Teacher Training, Curriculum Development, Text Books, Assessment and School Facilities were all needing improvement. A Staff Appraisal Report had identified a need to revise four core areas based on the Pillars of Learning identified by UNESCO: Learning to live together, Learning to be, Learning to do and Learning to know. The documents to support the revision would be Philosophy, Goals for Education (the National Curriculum), Schools' Curriculum (the syllabus) and a Teachers' Handbook that would be given another name to avoid prescription.

 David Leacock outlined the role of the Assessment Unit (established in 1992) as Primary Certification and Scholarship and the Unification of Belize National Certification Examinations. Only 60% of Primary leavers went on to Secondary Education. There was an access problem for many young people and the data from tests used for selection had not previously been used to inform development. Junior Achievement Tests had been introduced in 1994.

Wednesday's meeting gave an update on the coming month and a start on work to begin the next day. The team - Ellajean Gillette, Ernest Raymond, Katherine, Jayne, Max, Chris, Rachael, Geraldine, Margarita Vandley and Corinth would be completing the outcomes, editing and reviewing by 17th October target. There would be a funding review at the end of October.

The afternoon was spent on a 'bus stop tour', visiting schools in Belize City but this was of very limited value giving the poorest of impressions of any learning which might be taking place even in well-equipped schools, which these were not. Only five Primary Schools in Belize had (incompatible) Apple-Mac computers under the Michael Ashcroft Project.

By the end of the first week staying with the Leivas, Jayne, Kathryn, Bernadette and I were to have our own accommodation arranged. Mine turned out to be different because Jayne nipped in where I had expected to go and this emboldened me to ask the family if I might stay with them until I was able to move to my permanent placement in Orange Walk 54 miles north. It was a joy to be accepted which has been reinforced ever since as an adoptee.

All change again at the weekend with the parade celebrating the Battle of St. George's Caye. I found myself perched on the roof of a shop owned by a friend of the family I was staying with beside the only roundabout in the whole of Belize. (There were three sets of traffic lights in the country and seven lifts - three of the lifts being in one building). The roundabout was one of the many developments going on which made progress only when money became available. Houses were often built the same way - with reinforcing rods sticking out of concrete ready for the next bit to be added on. The shop I stood on had such rods conveniently placed that I could hang on to while I was filming the amazingly colourful and lively Caribbean festivity; an addition, along with a commentary, to a parcel being prepared for year seven back home and concerning the adventures of George the Snail in Belize. The heat, for three hours however, was intense.

The Battle of St. George's Caye was when the local British Settlers drove off the Spanish - decisively. There is much argument about the detail, as the Spanish seem to have turned tail, unaccountably, although they had much stronger forces. Much the same (it seems to me) as happened with the Armada. The historical evidence that it happened, however, is very clear.

The carnival parade was a long time coming but when it did arrive, it was extremely lively. Huge crowds showing support and enthusiasm; lots of movement in dance, bands, music and costume; interpretation of Folk Lore; highly decorated floats with lots of people joining in to hang on to the vehicles and move along with the procession. Loud speakers were very loud; the 'throb' of the beat and the life in the rhythm. Huge and mysterious was the presence of Anansi the Spider who is very important in Belizean Legend and Folk-Lore, coming as he did originally, as stories from West Africa; Anansi surrounded as were many other characters and floats by the current 'Jump-Up', 'Follow de Leeda', over and over with band after band

All ages and organisations seemed to join in and a lot of groups showed a great deal of teamwork and togetherness in their presentations; people there having the natural rhythm which is both joyful and social. Some of the costumes attached to just one individual, were huge and must have been extremely difficult to manage even though the breeze was very slight; unusual because there seemed not much in the way of 'little wind' or 'little rain' in Belize City. It was HOT and/or windy and/or wet. Mostly it was just HOT. And, boy was it hot on that day!

The film I took didn't do justice to the length of the carnival procession either, which was in fact about two hours long: often a throbbing, heaving mass of bodies and costume moving in time with the beat and the rhythm of the music. Junior bands were just as good as the older ones and of course, every bit as enthusiastic. It was difficult to do justice to all that was going on, even from the vantage point that I had. There was a great deal of movement and lots of people also jostling for position but there was no doubt what a joyful occasion it was, even including a steel band and what a steel band, with no gaps in the procession for two whole hours; continuous stream of joy and enthusiasm. And so ended, from our vantage point at least, the carnival procession to mark the anniversary of the Battle of St. George's Caye with a group of excellent tumblers working on a hard surface; a performance repeated for several hours in 90+ degrees!

Relations as a budding member of the family grew apace in just one week and on Sunday I went to communion with Mrs Leiva to a lovely Downtown Anglican Church, also St Mary's as is our church at home. A neighbour who happened to be a churchwarden there took us in her car and as the regular minister was on holiday the Bishop of Belize took the service. The theme was 'The first shall be last' and this was linked to the Belizean experience where the people must expect to have a large part to play in the future of their country and not to expect too much or leave it all to the Government (about which the Bishop was scathing).

The Bishop welcomed us at the door where I was treated as something of a celebrity - a good way to have conversation which one might otherwise not have. At the 'Peace', birthdays were called and many other matters of interest to the congregation. At each stage, the appropriate person stood up and beamed round amid enthusiastic clapping. Then I heard Mrs Leiva's name mentioned. This was strange, I thought, as Mrs, Leiva is Catholic and she had really come to accompany me. More strange when I heard VSO! Then, somehow, I was standing beside Mrs Leiva, the only white face in the place, beaming round to more enthusiastic clapping. When the clapping died down, I was asked my name. Max was okay but no one could manage to pronounce my surname so I was addressed as Mr Max and a further burst of enthusiastic clapping broke out. A Bishop has never clapped me before, let alone by a Belizean congregation and from then on I have been known as Mr Max, always in Belize and in other places since.

The Bishop's vestments were cream and white with colourful Belizean tapestry to mark the country's Independence. The fact that it was the 16th anniversary of independence next day was part of his address: the coming of age of Belize.

We went to a food festival at the Anglican Cathedral in the afternoon where we met the Canadian High Commissioner with whom I had a long chat about Scouting, a contact I had hoped to develop as a link with Devon Scouts. It turned out that the Anglican Cathedral had an interesting history. I was fascinated that it was built of brick and more so that the bricks came from England. Apparently, the bricks had been used as ballast in the ships empty of cargo, returning to Belize for the next lot of logwood; huge quantities, for example, of mahogany. Sitting, or wandering around talking and eating is a much-favoured Belizean pastime and the pleasant hours were also spent with musical entertainment given by a group of young people forming a steel band from Wesley College nearby; players communicating their contribution with each other much as happens in jazz bands. Briefly, the sight of the only other ex-pats present jarred in my mind. A group of Peace Corps and VSOs occupied a whole table for eight - all to themselves and looking inward – such a pity, I thought, and another thread in personal orientation was formed, linked strongly with the tendency to 'wander off', at least from my own!

Monday was a public holiday and an opportunity to gather another video and more material to send to year seven…'The next film is of a different kind of procession; very much more formal and intended to celebrate Independence Day two days after the last one… …several schools have gone by already but you can see how well turned out the young people are - showing a great pride in themselves and in their country… This procession lasted for about an hour which gives some idea of the number of people who took part. Music seems to play an important part in school life here. I have been to another event where the same musicians from the Wesleyan College have been playing in a steel band which sounded absolutely fantastic. I seem to have captured, in the film, rather more girls than boys but their numbers are about equal. Although schools are mixed, they do not walk in this procession together - rather as separate units. It is also noticeable that the groups of boys walk after the girls. There are lots of those conventions here. Perhaps this is something you might like to debate for yourselves…'

There were street parties and 'jump-ups' in the afternoon, mainly centred in one huge conglomerate around Regent Street, Albert Street and in-between. I separated from the three girls I went with and was mostly the only white around for three hours. In the middle of the afternoon I bought a storybook from Myrna Manzanarez, a local writer whom I had already met in orientation and who came to be known as friend, and sat down to read it between two Belizean families on a seat on the landing stage on the South side of the Swing Bridge over the Belize River. When I made room for two children, I was completely sandwiched. They didn't stay long so I felt rather like the smelly tramp in the comedy sketch. I carried on reading and was soon joined by one of the 'pains' starting his hard luck story. "No good asking me, I'm English" resulted in an odd laugh and silence. I made out to finish the book and went. Not the best part of the city, I learned, to stop in one place for long.

Progress was made at work on Tuesday by my producing a diagrammatic representation of the structure of the curriculum adopted by all which made it easier to understand and we started making plans for selecting trial schools.

Slipping out at lunchtime I visited Hilberto Riverol the National Commissioner at Scout HQ close by and made myself known. Evidently a Trainer was needed to train both Leaders and the Trainers in Orange Walk, which happened to be the centre for my posting and I was put on the mailing list. It was agreed that the time in Belize City could be used to familiarise and observe. Hilberto knew the Leiva family through Lions International. He also came from Corozal which was an area later added to my official activities. Two Belizean Scouters, one from Orange Walk and one from Corozal, were staying with the Leivas during the week and the Scouter responsible for Training, Alma Ailey, was on the radio that morning being interviewed about a National Beach Clean-Up to be undertaken by Scouts the next Saturday. She was a supervisor at Belize Teachers' Training College next door to the Curriculum Unit where I worked.

Completing plans and making contacts continued through the week, punctuated by an interview with the Chief Education Officer on Thursday. That interview and the fact that Ellajean had gone on holiday soon proved to be as providential as many other apparently random events already noted as it led to my earlier departure for Orange Walk than Ellajean had planned.

On Saturday 27th September, just one month after my arrival in Belize, I set off for Orange Walk at six o'clock in the morning with Mr and Mrs Leiva, Antonio, their second son, Bernadette, Jayne and Katherine on the Express bus. There were wonderful views of the Belize River. Abundant wild life drew my attention including many white storks or egrets maybe, perched on bushes and small trees. Rich vegetation appeared steadily greener as we approached Orange Walk where it was very green indeed on the outskirts of the town. What looked like huge termites nests bulged crazily on some of the trees where we crossed over a bridge at the New-River. The bus was a second hand version from the USA, very comfortable and fast, covering almost sixty miles in an hour and a quarter to Orange Walk before it continued on to Chetumal beyond Corozal, across the border in Mexico. It was air-conditioned and with on-board entertainment in the form of a video. Refreshments were provided on longer, 'Premier' journeys.

Arriving in Orange Walk, we first visited Mr Leiva's father who had been ill, and then spent some time walking around the town where everyone seemed to know everyone else and very friendly with a population of about 15,000. Everywhere was clean and tidy with plenty of space and no rush; life moving at a very tolerable pace. Excellent shops were extremely clean, both for food and for other consumable goods and the New River running alongside was beautiful. I knew already that I couldn't wait to move there and fully take up my posting.

There wasn't time to explore Orange Walk further as I soon discovered that we were off to the homes of Mrs Leiva's family in San Estevan some six miles of sugar cane interspersed with a few orange trees distant and where we were driven in the local bus by her brother-in-law. Again, there was so much to see and I had started to use a small dictation machine as an aid to writing letters to individual students in the projected schools' link who had taken the trouble to write to me as well as the more general material being prepared and sent…

'San Estevan is six miles away. Mrs Leiva's brother-in-law drove the bus which he runs himself. The six miles is pretty-well solid sugar cane and orange trees but it should be remembered that most of this country has not been given over to cultivating single crops but has been left alone. Also, the sight is in no way monotonous for it is broken up and it is all very green. The sugar is harvested twice - next in 'spring'. There are seasons and they are at the same times as in England but, being much closer to the Equator they are much less defined. It doesn't get cold, just less hot. It doesn't get wet (for long) although when it does rain it makes a proper job.

The flowers on the trees are amazing. Some of the trees about forty feet high have huge brilliant red, scarlet flowers on them in great numbers. Massive blue butterflies with black-bordered wings spanning about four inches flutter about. The water in the river seems almost still, reflective and with very little apparent flow. I wonder where the crocodiles are today.

There are some thatched roofs close by; luxuriant vegetation, especially at the water's edge, purple flowers and lizards, about 10 inches (24cm) - black with a yellow stripe down each side and one in the middle of the back. I come upon a ferry crossing where the hand-operated, wooden boat operates only from Monday to Friday so it must be used to serve work and school.

In the village, coconut trees and orange trees abound - both heavily laden. Chickens wander freely. There are many Palm Trees and other species of trees with exotic flowers - mostly brilliant crimson. The occasional hut has a thatched roof but most homes have corrugated iron roofs. The older buildings are constructed with timber but almost all newer ones are made with concrete. These are built using a reinforced concrete frame and filled in-between with blocks, often leaving the bottom part open to allow the passage of air underneath and to exclude uninvited guests. A tiny jet-black bird, little bigger than a wren, inhabits the gardens. Many butterflies of a wide variety of size and colour - through the reds, yellows and blues flutter by on butterfly business.

At 12:00 midday, my shadow is about 40cm long. The temperature is 95 degrees in the shade. There is little breeze, so the heat is intense; the air throbs with it. Only the local children are moving about outside - seeming to enjoy the spectacle of my doing so as well. I am about to go and have lunch and at 2:00pm I am due to leave on the bus back to Orange Walk Town where I shall meet a Venture Scout called Ricardo and the Scout Group he belongs to, returning to the village at about 4:00pm. The family are visiting a Mennonite Community at Little Belize.

The Scout Group were busy on a National Beach Clean-up Campaign but, because Orange Walk Town isn't by the sea, the clean-up took place where people go down by the river. This involved collecting rubbish, bagging it and recording the type of material to take full part in the National campaign. I was given the opportunity to introduce myself to the Group, showed my Scout shirt and its badges including the eighty years of Cub Scouting - and my four training beads which is the most you can get and created the greatest impression. I met the Group Scout Leader and also a young Leader who is about to go to Edinburgh for an international youth conference, representing the Belizean Government and, of course, Scouts. He is going to spend a fortnight there. I was given a great welcome from the youngest Cub Scout to the oldest Leader.

A lot of concern was shown for Princess Diana and the effects that her death may have had in the UK. The Scouts wanted to know as much as I could tell them and it was good to have been in London on the night before the funeral. Sunday (at four o'clock in the morning!) was the killing of the pig but that will appear among the adventures of George the Snail because I expect he will have something to say about it. Down by the river, later on, there was silence (almost). Pipefish with iridescent blue tails swam lazily in the water, occasionally interrupted by much larger fish; a huge variety of butterflies and dragonflies fluttered, darted and hovered above; small deer peeped from the forest; an open canoe, dug out of a single tree trunk, glided by, low in the water with two Belizeans in it. All was peace and the pig was forgotten - almost!

The family at home in Belize City are very interesting. The house is made of concrete with a wood and corrugated iron roof. There is a large main room upstairs, with three bedrooms and what they call a washroom which has a shower in it. Downstairs, there is another main room with three bedrooms and two washrooms. There is also an extension on the back with another three bedrooms. The wide, deep and slow Belize River is about 100 metres away.

Apart from Mr And Mrs Leiva, there is their eldest son and his wife and three grandchildren aged 4, 2 and 1, who live downstairs. They also have a younger son who lives with them, sometimes upstairs and sometimes down. When I arrived it was with two other Volunteers. One of them moved to a place of her own after a week and the other moved to her District after a fortnight. I decided to stay until I go to Orange Walk. I get very well looked after. I have my own room and washroom downstairs. Meals are put in front of me and all my washing is done for me. As I am here to get to know Belizeans and the family know so many people at Orange Walk as well, I see no reason to move in-between there and my placement - even though I do want a place of my own. What is really interesting is the number of other people who live there - wider family, friends and students who live away from the city and come in for the weekdays, all Belizeans. In each of most rooms there are three or four beds, mostly occupied! Young people don't get a lot of privacy here, so be thankful for yours!

I haven't really worked out how many there are altogether but I have met an awful lot of other people and I'm getting to know most of them…'

Also, in setting the scene…

'My job title is Primary Curriculum Co-ordinator. A bit of a mouthful! What it means is that I am to look after the introduction of a new curriculum in Primary Schools, in two of the six Districts of Belize. The new curriculum (this is what children are supposed to learn) has to be tested in a sample of schools, assessed, revised where necessary, and then launched in all schools, starting with a series of workshops. When I arrived, it was to find that the curriculum to be used wasn't finished. This meant that the first part of my time would be spent helping to finish it in Belize City, and that task was expected to take until the end of the year. In fact, it has now been finished and I will be moving to Orange Walk shortly, as I said.

Anyway, working here has been interesting. There are four Volunteers on the team including me, who will be going out into the Districts. The team also has two consultants, one of whom is Belizean, the other English, and two Belizeans who have come from local Education. These last four will remain here to work on the rest of the curriculum. This first part is for the first three years (age 5, 6 and 7). Up to now, the eight of us have been working together to produce all that is needed to take into schools. That is now finished and arrangements are being made for it all to happen. One of my main concerns now, of course, is to find a home for myself (not living with a family) in Orange Walk Town.

I have an office which I share with another volunteer. It is ten feet square so it is a very comfortable size, and has large windows on the outside wall. The windows are fitted with wrought iron security bars on the outside - as most places are. They do not have glass in them. There is no need of glass. Instead, they have fine mesh screens to keep out biting insects and metal shutters which open and shut horizontally, using a handle which you turn for each section. Inside, we each have a large wooden desk and a fan which works all the time we are in. The fan, which is a big, freestanding one which turns from side to side, is necessary for us to keep cool but all papers on the desk have to be weighted down! Along one side of the office is a large bookcase full of books. Through the door, the space opens out into the general office where the secretary and typist work. At one end of there are the washrooms and the Director's office, and in the opposite direction there are five more offices either side of a corridor which leads to a large meeting room. This whole space is on the ground floor of a two-storey building and is called the Curriculum Development Unit. Concrete steps at each end of the building lead up to a full-length veranda and a similar, slightly smaller arrangement (because of the veranda) which houses the Assessment Unit. Assessment is all about how well children are doing, including examinations. The building is made of concrete as most of the new buildings are, and is located on the site of the New Teachers' Training College in Belize City. All the buildings on the site are constructed in the same way and the whole space is about the same size as the Senior School in South Molton - if you include the school playing field and car park in South Molton as well.

The site is made up from a mangrove swamp so it is not unusual to see the heavy iguana lizards up to seventy centimetres long and other, lighter, more colourful lizards up to 50cm: also water snakes, perhaps 50cm, and a huge variety of colourful birds and butterflies; not to mention the small gecko lizards which have 'sticky' feet to climb walls, frogs, crabs and the fish which breed in the various waters about the place. (You don't really want to know about the biting insects! - I certainly don't!) Across the road, outside of the compound, there is a large mangrove swamp area where there are claimed to be crocodiles and where I have seen many kinds of storks, herons and wading birds - and vultures circling overhead! Yes, working here has already been most interesting…'

…Thus the whole adventure was to be shared with children at home and soon to be joined with a direct link with children in Belizean schools.

Transition

With all the excitement, change and promise, especially promise of intended placement, the focus was on making the move to Orange Walk as soon as possible. This was reinforced by reluctance on the part of the Director for Educational Development to make the necessary arrangements. The intention to keep volunteers in Belize City at department headquarters and expect them to commute had become obvious, together with the direct control to be exercised over all activities: no way! The corner of my mind permanently engaged on this problem was continually bombarded with new and greater interest and challenge and the need to get away from the office. The killing of the pig on the Sunday in San Estevan was one such.

The pig weighed 160lbs and took five men to despatch it in some way: I didn't see how because the whole performance started unannounced to me at any rate, at four o'clock in the morning and I was still in bed. It was brought from a neighbouring house, weighed and eventually dispatched outside my window. Aroused by the sounds of voices and a brief, shrill squeal I was quickly dressed and in time to see the hide being singed and then large quantities of hot water used to soften skin and hair, over and over again while the skin was scraped clean before the carcase was butchered. The whole operation took until about 10:00am - by which time it was very hot outside where it was taking place. It took over an hour just to get all the hair off. The skin was fried right away to make what we used to call scratchings and which are eaten with great relish out here.

I can't say I felt anything for the pig. It was already dead of course and the teamwork, energy, enthusiasm and banter were intoxicating; all helped along with seemingly endless bottles of Belikin, the local brew. The meal taken informally with tortillas outside and washed down with more Belikin was wonderful; men and women grouped slightly apart with no restraint on continued banter such that reflection on the fate of the pig and the manner of its passing didn't take hold until much later as I took a lone walk in near silence by the New River: wide, flat calm, almost still and reflecting bright white clouds in the hot sultry afternoon. Pipefish darted, flashing their iridescent blue tail fin. A huge variety of butterflies and dragonflies fluttered and hovered and many fish swam lazily in the water. A small deer appeared briefly in the forest edge at the river bank and a dug out open canoe with two people in it, passed low in the water.

I found my way around Word Perfect at work on Monday, using a free standing computer in the Assessment Unit upstairs from our office. The notebook I had brought with me especially to help with writing and not expecting to find personal computers was already proving wholly inadequate; time consuming in the face of all the writing to be done. Some twenty letters and cards had been sent already, as well as the journal writing and sharing with year seven at home in the evenings; also increasing curriculum demands during the day. These were the early days of PCs of course and my experience had been with the Archimedes and the BBC micro. I didn't get on with Word Perfect as well as with Word for Windows and transferred my first tape commentary and transcript to the Microsoft version using up all my spare time on Tuesday. Tuesday was also the day when the Chief Education Officer agreed to all requests for next curriculum stage including travelling and working out in the Districts. My good friends Kathryn a Peace Corp volunteer, and Corinth a Belizean educationalist and I had made great effort to achieve this: a useful time for the Director (who also became a good friend) to take a holiday.

The first parcel was made ready to send to the Head of Year Seven at home in South Molton: the beginnings of a link with Belize and hopefully with Belizean schools (all extracts of communication with the school as distinct from students, being recorded here in *Garamond Italic font in place of the usual Garamond Regular*)…

'Herewith, your first tape and commentary… I have some ideas for developing interest (Some hinted at in the text) but I would welcome whatever dialogue as soon as possible… When I move to Orange Walk we can start to work towards young people communicating. I have already met the Scouts at both National level and in Orange Walk/Corozal Districts… Greetings to Year7…

In that same week I started a monthly arrangement to stay with the Leivas until I left for Orange Walk, went to the bank to check my account for payment of bursary, obtained a cash card and checked its use. There would be no Barclays Bank in Orange Walk which was likely to be a bit of a pain. Quite apart from the growing friendship with the family, my staying with them was fortuitous. I already didn't want to move until my place was permanent. Letters were arriving such that communications were becoming established both ways; a Belize Telecom refund and a bank statement gave even more security to a feeling of having arrived and I found a supply of padded bags at Angelus Press close to the Pallotti roundabout from where the Battle of St. George's Caye Day parade had been witnessed. 'Outcomes' for the new primary curriculum were finished at work: these as a set of bullet points in each goal/area as 'Pupils should…' They were now ready for development, field testing and for the World Bank. At 3:00pm on Friday a Welcome Party was given by the original members of the curriculum group. The programme consisted of the welcome, a cameo of 'ourselves', a video of Belize, Punta, party time and presentation of visitors' guides in a pack. No surprise other than Punta which was an entirely new experience: Garifuna rock music, danced by Belizean women; a shuffling step, twisting torso enhanced by hands and elbows and dominated by rapidly undulating and ample buttocks. I went with Bernie and Susan to Jayne's new home in the evening. Bernie was due to go to Punta Gorda right down south in Toledo District at the end of the week so I would be the only one left with the family.

It was a family weekend starting with a 5:30am walk to the market and returning with Mr Young, the Canadian Consul in good time for the start of Mr Leiva's birthday celebrations from 10:00am-10:00pm (and on into the night with family time): an all-day (and night) drinking of rum and Coke and canned Mexican Beer. Mr Leiva cooked barbecue chicken, lots of it, which was eaten with rice and beans. Mr Leiva's brother and two others came down from Orange Walk and stayed until about 5:00pm. Others came and went throughout the day. Sunday was planned as a visit to the Baboon Sanctuary with the Lions Club but heavy overnight rain prevented this and having got up early to go it was good to enjoy a quiet day, walk out with Bernie in the afternoon, take a look at a computer that Marco had for sale that turned out not to be working and use his machine to catch up with writing. By the end of the next week the date was fixed for the move to Orange Walk as 1st November and on Saturday the whole family went shopping in Chetumal.

As with all other stories, 'Shopping in Chetumal' was sent in the next package to Year Seven students back in South Molton. It was a great weekend and being a national holiday we returned to Belize City on the 2:00pm Premier, I having found lots of tee shirts to send off as gifts.

<u>Shopping in Chetumal</u>

'Belizeans from Belize City and north through Orange Walk and Corozal escape when they can, across the border into Mexico where the shopping is much cheaper and easier to do. This is an account of my visit to Chetumal with the family I am staying with in Belize City. We stayed for two nights in the Hotel Ocum which is right in the centre of things…

The journey began at 6:00am on a 'Batty Bus' (yes that is the name – Batty Brothers!) The buses are bought second hand from the United States but they are very comfortable with on board toilet, video, air conditioning and food provided. The air conditioning is very efficient so travelling is in no way hot. Our bus was a 'Premier' which calls only at Orange Walk Town and Corozal Town in the whole one hundred mile journey. Even so, we did have to wait for a very long time at customs to get across the border - an hour and a half in the sun because so many Belizeans were crossing into Mexico even that early in the morning! I didn't go shopping (or in my case, looking at shops) right away but went to visit the Maya Museum which is a new one close to the hotel. Unfortunately I was not allowed to take any kind of camera in so there is nothing for you to see, and I only took a short piece of video film for the whole weekend.

The museum is well laid out on three levels: the underworld, the living world and the heavens. It is also made as a series of walkways to the floors on three levels which are suspended in an artificial rainforest. Right up through all the floor parts there is a full size model of the carved column which in Mayan art, represents the three states. Throughout the museum there are examples of Mayan culture; numbering systems; calendars; trade; animals and plants; buildings; sculpture etc. with plenty of touch sensitive displays as well. Outside the main building there was a display of children's work so local children must go there. Also, quite a lot of rooms which appeared to be some sort of study rooms surrounding a central 'garden'. This was planted as a tropical rainforest and contained typical Mayan buildings. The following is the text of two descriptions of the houses and the house on view which I did film and which will appear on your next tape:

'Modern Maya homes are built by their owners who practise Maya culture and who maintain ancestral customs in the construction of their houses. These houses, in turn, demonstrate Maya values of intelligence, rationality, economy and functional design. The region's hot climate influences its architecture and the Maya, to protect themselves, create a micro-climate inside their houses. The hot air rises to the upper part of the house and escapes through the palm roof, maintaining the cool air below. The apse shaped, or semi-circular design of the floor, walls and roof is ideal for resisting hurricane winds - and the rainy weather requires a roof that allows for the rapid run-off of water. A traditional house measures approximately 8m long, 4m wide and 5m high. This structure is secured by four main posts of OKOMM. The roof is put together from a framework of poles that carry, each one, its respective Mayan name. Forked boughs, wedges and rattan fastenings are used throughout the construction. The walls are made of thin wood poles. When these are set vertically, the walls are called CHUYCHEE. But when the poles are set horizontally, they are called KOLOLCHEE.

The Maya house has two doors for cross-ventilation. There are no windows. The roof is made of a palm called GUANOO or XAANN which can last up to thirty years thanks to the waterproofing properties of the smoke produced by wood cooking fires. There are two spaces inside the Maya house. A large area that serves as both the living room and sleeping area and a kitchen called the KOBENN. In the living room/sleeping area of this house one finds an altar, hammock, baskets or boxes of clothing, various tools, a rifle and several products derived from maize. The kitchen is one of the most important spaces of the Maya living area. The furniture is quite unique. Note the three stones of the cooking fire, KOBENN on which the COMAL XAMACHH is placed, the small, circular table for making TORTILLAS, the low benches K'ANCHEE and the long table for spreading recently milled maize. Numerous utensils aid the Mayan woman in food preparation. Among them a large variety of gourds or vessels made from plants, the indispensable MATATEKA'A and a more modern corn mill.'

After visiting the museum I went off to explore the old indoor market. The first effort was to walk around the outside which was packed with stalls where a wide variety of goods were being sold. Although none of the people selling actually got up and tried to sell anything in particular, which can be a bit irritating, I could feel eyes following me everywhere. Also, I am always aware of how conspicuous my camcorder is. Even so, it wasn't long before I ventured inside. The maze of passages, the jumble of stalls, the variety of goods on sale, the huge stock that must have been around, was absolutely amazing. Aggressive selling was much more open - more in proportion to the closed, claustrophobic effect of being almost entombed among a huge variety of goods and a heaving mass of people trying to sell them. The main concerns seemed to be that I should need a hammock and a Mexican hat. I didn't stay inside very long but before I did emerge, I explored the meat selling area - briefly! I'm afraid I couldn't stand the atmosphere, especially the smell, for long and moved out to the open air again. Then I walked around the outside once more.

From there, I took a taxi and met up with the family at a pre-arranged eating house. The chicken was delicious but not quite as my family expected. We were supposed to have had one whole chicken and tortillas, onion and chilli-pepper sauce between five of us. A small part of the order wasn't delivered. Objections and rejections in Spanish are very interesting indeed. Then it was across the road for shopping in San Francisco de Asis which is a large store much like a supermarket in England except that the foods are different and the car park is very small, with few cars in it. Most people walk or take a taxi. The average taxi fare is five pesos, about 45p.

After the supermarket, we took another taxi to shoe shops and a textile retailers which also sold haberdashery and women's clothes - during which time I wandered about instead with the sixteen year old son Antonio and looked at watches, bicycles, stereos, binoculars and airguns etc. - listening all the time to how good they were in his opinion!

Another taxi took us on to a restaurant and entertainment spot. This was a largely wooden building of fairly considerable size and traditional construction, with a roof thatched with palm leaves but extended in the more 'modern tradition' with corrugated iron! The tables were nicely laid out and the beer was excellent and well served: twenty-four pesos for a round for four of us and entertainment and five plates of bites/dips thrown in - to be eaten with the usual segments of fried tortilla. These included liver and octopus as well as the traditional dips. The entertainment too, was great. A keyboard player and small group provided the music which accompanied a number of soloists, both male and female.

We returned to the hotel via numerous shops which were beginning to close but which would be open again in the evening until 9:00pm as is also the custom in Belize City.

The current exchange rate of pesos to $BZ is 3.60 pesos to the dollar. Belize dollars exchange rate with sterling is roughly 3.20 dollars to the pound. Thus the present value of the pound is about 11.52 pesos. The rooms in the hotel are 50 pesos per night for the single room that I had. That is the equivalent of just four pounds, thirty two pence (There are no pound signs on these keyboards - only $). More people cost less for each one. A room for three for example, costs only 90 pesos. Of course you must remember that incomes are much lower here too.

Just at the moment of recording this I am lying on the double bed, dressed now but not long since. It is very comfortable just to lie under the fan for a few minutes. There is plenty of space and absolute privacy. The room is bare of course but I have my own washroom, toilet and shower, all completely tiled. And showering, I can assure you, is a very pleasant experience here - with no limit, no curtain and no screen; all within a very generous space, as I said, completely tiled. And as it is so warm, there is no need of the usual trappings such as we have in England although the fan is necessary – the fan which is fully six feet in diameter, whizzing furiously above, creating most pleasant conditions. The windows when open are screened to fully protect against mosquitoes and any other biting insects that fly. All points of access are covered with ornate wrought iron screens for safety. The door is glazed steel fitted with a triple deadlock too, but I must say that the 'feel' in Chetumal is extremely safe.

We all left the hotel on Sunday morning, walking along Heroes (avenue), looking for somewhere for breakfast. This was taken at another hotel as the restaurant the family had planned to use was closed. Surprisingly, I thought, breakfast there which for me consisted of a very generous omelette, unlimited coffee and toast, cost 20 pesos and was served in pleasant and fully air conditioned surroundings. Bearing in mind that current daytime temperatures are over ninety! After breakfast I spent some time in a large bookshop which was housed in a building which must have been some sort of meeting place or museum perhaps. It was about the size of our Junior School hall (housing 280 children and a stage) and had an arched ceiling which was completely covered with a huge and colourful mural (part of which defies description here).

It started to rain but that almost never seems to last long. The postcards were extremely disappointing. I bought a few but they were not of Chetumal even though they were part of the 'Chetumal Collection'. I finished up with all the same cards which just showed three storks in silhouette, perched on leafless trees which might be anywhere. It soon stopped raining and we were zipped away in another taxi to the new market by the bus station. This is even more huge and just as complicated as the old market although there is a little more space to move around. I hadn't any particular intention of buying anything other than a tee-shirt to use as a prize for year seven but I did buy a reinforced shopping bag which seems to make more sense for carrying things backwards and forwards to the office than using a plastic SavU carrier bag (SavU is the local supermarket in Belize City). There is a tendency for things to be snatched at times. At 10 pesos that was good value (87p). An organiser which can be worn on the belt, for money and personal belongings was priced at 20 pesos but when I wrinkled my nose it was 15 which at one pound thirty was extremely good value: zipped pocket for money and small items; zipped pocket for papers; zipped internal pocket for larger items such as a small camera, binoculars or the recorder that I am using, glasses case, sunglasses and hat. Not that I would ever carry that much. Extremely strong material, security flap with 'click' fasteners, belt fastening, a handle and carrier strap (if one should wish to use such a thing). Finished in black with a 'Boy London' logo!

Local Mexican/Mayan/Chetumal tee-shirts of a small size proved difficult to find. Most tee-shirts bear a heavy American influence in their design. I did, however, eventually find a local tee-shirt and a Mayan tee-shirt but which are XXL and XL. I later found a medium Mexican/Chetumal tee-shirt with a parrot design and a small size with a Cancun logo (more about Cancun when I have been there). A local, highly coloured print shirt which I am now wearing outside my shorts would amaze you all!

From the bus station, I then walked back down Heroes to the old market again, where I looked round for a short time and then returned to the hotel to take a shower. There I found that the room had been cleaned, the whole washroom and shower washed out, fresh bed linen fitted and a clean towel, and new soap and toilet roll provided - not to mention the pleasure of taking a short rest towards the end of a hot Sunday afternoon.

The rest didn't last long. Can't stay still, have to go out. So the walk took me along Heroes again, all the way down to the park, the sea and the obelisk. From there, left was turning East with the sun beginning to drop behind. It was a lovely walk: hot, bright sunshine but a cool breeze coming in off the sea immediately alongside; choppy little waves as I passed the statue of the fisherman just offshore, which is lit up and is the centre of a water spray at night; past a little kiosk and the people just enjoying the breeze; past the point of the waterslide where a little crowd of locals of all ages were enjoying a dip in Chetumal Bay not quite as clean being so close to the city, as I would like it; watching the water birds in the quieter spots.

Then circling round a tree-lined area with many different varieties of trees, all of which I don't recognise; past the lighthouse where the sea is much livelier and there is evidence of rocks further offshore. Looking straight down the bay is towards Corozal and down the coast of Belize, looking across the bay towards Ambergris Caye and the start of the Barrier Reef. On past a large marble floored, indoor meeting place to the University until turning left, I took a straight road which eventually came back to Heroes, turned right for a short distance and returned to the hotel, five or six miles on, for yet another shower.

Off out to dinner in the evening and then to the concert in the park. I had intended taking some video of the concert but it is not always convenient to carry the camera. It would have been good! The whole of the park by the sea was lit and thronged with people. Many stalls and other vendors sold food and drink, sweets and candy floss. Others sold souvenirs, small items attractive to the eye. No traffic; just many people of all ages enjoying an evening out. At the edge of the park and beside the sea, there is an obelisk/monument with a large, paved, open space in front of it. It was here that the open air stage, lights and batteries of speakers had been set up for the concert - with control console down among the seats.

The sound, not at all to my taste, had natural acoustics which made it an impressive experience whether one was walking around or sitting down. And the groups were local, lively and much appreciated by the crowd. How long it went on I don't know. Young families certainly didn't stay too long and I returned to the hotel for a good night's sleep by 11:30pm to be ready to return home the next day - except that I found lots of tee-shirts just before setting off back!'

It was a surprise to find a letter waiting after work that week in response to a forgotten enquiry... Dear Mr

Grantham, I refer to your letter to Mr and Mrs Clark, dated 5th August 1997. I would be very interested in offering you a teaching post at Ariel in 1998. My only worry is that if you are a non-Zimbabwean, a Temporary Employment Permit would have to be obtained and in your particular case I do not believe that the Immigration Department here would be forthcoming. If you are a member of the VSO organisation, is it possible that they could assist you in any way? If you wish to pursue this matter, please contact me at your earliest convenience. I had to decline of course, although Africa had always been my dream.

Most on my mind outside work was now the pressing need for accommodation from day one of the move. I certainly didn't want to commute the 54 miles daily on the regular bus over two hours each way so the next excitement was to set off for Orange Walk Town to have a look at a potential house on Saturday, 18th October with Mr and Mrs Leiva, Tabo and Neria, on the 6:00am express (non-stop) bus. They had made enquiries of their many friends on my behalf, helpful as always. Buses were at least hourly but Neria didn't believe in doing anything or going anywhere without making full use of the day or wasting time on the regular bus. We arrived in Orange Walk Town and stopped at Landy's and Sons garage who's owner was also the owner of the house that I was going to look at - and possibly, to look at some others. We were driven to the house to meet the owner who lived next door to the house for rent. The two properties were surrounded by high walls with a high fence on top. Two pit bull terriers patrolled the area and the whole place looked very secure and was in a reasonably good district. There were two apartments: one, the complete ground floor; and the other, the complete first floor which was much bigger. It had a very large veranda which faced east - with a lovely aspect across other properties and beyond into the country and the rainforest across the other side of the New River. There was one bedroom, a huge living room with a big dining table in it, a very large kitchen with a serving hatch, bathroom, washroom and an additional large space inside at the top of the stairs which led from the apartment below. There was a door at the bottom of these stairs which would remain permanently locked. At $Bz375 it was rather expensive even though it did have a lot of practical and aesthetic advantages so I would have to give it some more thought.

We walked down through the cemetery which could be part of the route to the District Education Office but I would not do that regularly (so it was suggested). The route round the main road was probably only a couple of minutes longer - taking under ten minutes altogether so it seemed hardly worth the risk. However, we did cross the cemetery that day and went to visit Mr Leiva's relatives before going to a large general store in order to buy a wedding present for the wedding they were going on to in San Estevan. I had been invited to the wedding but rather mucked up the arrangements by not understanding what was going on. I bought a half set of crockery and cutlery ready for when I moved - just two of each item, the cutlery at $8-50 and the crockery at $21-25. After that I had a look to see where the District Education Office was and found it to be easy to get to.

We all waited for Ricardo Alcoser at the bus station at roughly the time he might have expected me to arrive in Orange Walk. Mrs Leiva's brother-in-law came by on his motor bike and he was despatched to give Ricardo the message that I was there. Mr and Mrs Leiva moved off to go to San Estevan to go to the wedding and I waited, not very long. I saw the brother-in-law go by, back in the opposite direction on his motorbike and supposed that the message had been delivered. A few minutes later a huge Dodge Shooting Brake with dark tinted windows, pulled up alongside and I wondered why such a vehicle should stop at the bus station. The great side door slid back to reveal great big armchair seats inside and a grinning Ricardo, Richard, sitting behind with his mum and dad whom I hadn't yet met in the front. I was duly taken to their home to meet the family: six children, several dogs and cats, puppies and kittens. Their house was in the area where the employees of Belize Sugar Corporation live. We had a very interesting conversation about young people, children, society and Belize - helped along with a couple of beers and followed by lunch which was fried rice and beans with all the trimmings and chicken. After that I joined the local Scout Group for a short while and came in to town again. Richard and I had a walk around some of the shops and waited for a bus. I arrived back in Belize City just after five o'clock.

In the evening I went to Jack's party. It was good to meet with so many volunteers and a few Peace Corps but it really wasn't my scene and I left as soon as I decently could, just after midnight. It finished at 4:00am. Jack, a volunteer from Canada, had begun working in Belize about a year earlier and had also found his place in the family: grandparents Tabo and Neria, sons Marco and Antonio, daughter in law Miriam and grandchildren Miguel, Mariami and Martin aged 4, 3 and 2. Marco and Miriam lived on the ground floor of the house while everyone else lived up the outside stairs on the first floor although I soon came to have a room with the family downstairs.

I went to Mass at St. Joseph's with Mrs Leiva who took Miguel with her. It was World Mission Sunday on the 19th. Most people are Catholic in Belize. The sermon was on 'Witness' without looking for status or reward. I was able to take communion in which the biscuit represented both the body and the blood. The process was very much quicker than at home - even quicker than the Catholics in England - and I found that rather inhibited the spiritual feeling of the occasion (should it?). I managed to follow the service in Latin American Spanish but the content and especially the words were not at all clear from the book. Large pieces were left out to my experience. Words were repeated and chorused to fit sung versions without warning. There was a lively choral group with guitars and a drum. The singing was good from a very substantial congregation and there was a powerful presence of Spirit.

A meeting after work with Hilberto Riverol the National Commissioner followed by a meeting with National Scout Executive went well and I left with a copy of the current Annual Report and the Development Plan up to the year 2002, feeling that a link with Devon Scouts and Cub Scouts especially was looking very promising.

On 22nd October, Wednesday, standing at the bus stop waiting for the seven o'clock bus to Orange Walk in plenty of time at quarter to seven, I was filled with anticipation both for the journey and for the purpose: more house hunting.

Tilletts to Let
<u>The Arrival of 'Mr Max' in Orange Walk</u>

A milestone of my living in Belize: that is how I view the move to Orange Walk from Belize City. The city is an interesting place but I have not been comfortable with it because of the severe restrictions on my movements in the interests of safety. Living with the family is great but I am really looking forward to finding my own place in the two Districts for which my VSO assignment gives me some considerable responsibility.

I arrived in Belize on 7th September, 1997. The first week was spent as in-country orientation and work started at the Education Development Centre in Belize City on Monday 15th September instead of the promised Orange Walk Town. Soon after, it became clear that I was expected to be there until January. Already that was not an attractive thought and my mind was immediately bent on improving that! So here I am, in the early morning of 22nd October, on my way to look at a house or to be more precise, at houses. This is in the plural because I have already found the house I would like. That was on 18th October but at $Bz375 the rent is high for my limited budget. What a tangle of thoughts chase through my mind, unfinished, inconclusive, unsatisfied, as I try to concentrate on the buses approaching the one and only roundabout in Belize at the start of the Northern Highway. The Northern Highway! I'm told that this dual carriageway mudflat has been an alternating single carriageway for months and the bus stops at a different place every day, changing sometimes more than once. Still, I concentrate because I am neither sure which bus operator is right at this time of day nor which of each operator goes in what direction or stops where. All the cues and clues seem alien and too many other thoughts chasing each other through my head prevent the formulation of an appropriate question to anyone standing nearby. Even the right question will probably produce a reply in Creole for which I can barely discriminate the sounds.

The thoughts roll on. Can I afford the house I want? What about the computer I'm negotiating for which will help with the schools' 'linking' - my own pet project? How is all that going anyway? The mail is so frustrating. Whenever I write I find myself answering a thought I had a month ago and trying to anticipate one a month ahead! What will the other houses be like? My mind drifts off again to the chain of events from which I came by the list of houses to let which is slowly disintegrating in a sweaty trouser pocket. My goodness, it is hot! Did I think Hot? No, I mean HOT!! Is it ever any different? What time is this bus due? I was told seven o'clock so I arrived at a quarter to just in case. I suppose this is the right bus stop. What time is it now? Ah! Here it is. Move forward. Just in time, spot the board jammed in the front window. Some place called Ladyville... Lord's Bank... That sounds a good bet,

"Orange Walk?"

"No man!" But now I have spotted where they put the board. What on earth do they mean by Express, Premier, and Regular?

Now it must be right. At seven fifteen I'm standing at the back end of a queue which has suddenly materialised from nowhere, as far away as you can get from the single entrance at the front of the bus. I'm sure there was no-one here when I arrived! I wonder whether I should nip round to the front of the bus and check the board. It did say Orange Walk; a Batty Bus? But I certainly didn't see anything about what kind it is: Express, Premier, or Regular? Whatever! It took a long time for my tail of the queue to reach the steps up into the dim interior, hotter than outside and filled with sweating bodies with whom, at least, I could relate in that respect. It was packed!

I hesitate. This is not what I expect. There are seats either side of a gangway. Okay. But they are not the same size. I remember an experiment, years ago, with a single seat on one side and three seats on the other: still more in the dim and distant past, no seats on one side and four on the other. This is neither of those. This is two and a half seats on the off-side, the left hand side where the driver sits, and one and a half seats on the near side! I wonder. If this is to accommodate the natural anatomy of most Belizeans who don't need a great deal of height but are generally one and a half seats wide? Yes, that must be it - two on one side and one on the other. I count: no, that's not it. The seats are crowded. Many people are cheek to cheek even across the gangway. Standing room only? No way!

Halfway along the bus, I spot a woman sitting on her own in a one-and-a-half seat. I make for the spot, easing my way between ample thighs, bags and feet. A small strip of seat is showing under the curve of her leg and I ease myself down and locate my right quarter along it. There is a voluminous shuffle, a sigh and a hitching of dress and I am perched, balanced at least, on the edge - locked in position by a left leg hooked around the right leg of the man opposite (well, against really!) to gain support from the edge of his seat. How long? I wonder. Oh Lord! Here comes the conductor. I haven't got my money out. My wallet is in my hip pocket, on the right hand side of course. My change is in my trouser pocket on the same side. Both lost in folds of something or other which certainly isn't mine.

Fascinating! In a trance I watch the conductor approach. He seems to have his eye fixed on me. There must be others - Please let there be others! How does he do that? Without effort, bodies slide one on the other as he advances until he slips one hip back against the seat opposite and comes to rest, hand outstretched, eye fixed on gringo, expectant.

Panic... I fumble... The woman moves but as a gesture of some sort - not to make room. I slide myself upwards. "Orange Walk" I say, to gain time.

"Four fifty" and still the hand outstretched, fingers twitching. Has everyone on the bus turned round? Are they all looking? By some action for which I seem not consciously responsible, a five dollar bill finds its way into my hand. The change and ticket are received and I keep them in my sweaty palm for fear of further disturbance.

If it was hot outside what is it now? Surely all these bodies must fuse under the basic laws of physics? I need a distraction. Much too hot: can't see outside. All the windows are open but if there is any breeze I can't feel it: too many obstructions.

All too slowly the crush is eased: Ladyville, Lord's Bank, Sandhill, and there is room to see. Better still, I stand to let my large lady friend get off the bus. I smile, hopefully into the withering look. The smile fades but only long enough to realize that I have a whole seat (well, one and a half actually) all to myself, a window to look out of, breeze coming in, and a view up the bus clear enough to see what is going on.

My eye is caught by strange and challenging behaviour at the front of the bus. A mime; a slow ballet of threatening gesture; thrust and counter thrust; a battle of wills being played out by two men each apparently intent on outwitting the other: two men who were not on the bus earlier and who must have boarded when my attention was wholly concentrated on the departure of my companion and the relief of pressure on my right thigh.

The pair is sitting in the second seat back on the left hand side (which gives them an extra half space to share). In front, between them and the driver, a woman on her own is disturbed by the activity behind her. The guy nearest the window, dishevelled, distant seeming, in bearing and expression, giving off a body language which is definitely not of normal travellers, is thrusting his upper body back and forth and side to side in a slow and deliberate manner as a caged animal might, pressing against the back of his own seat, the seat in front and the other man at his side. Clearly restrained, he gets up; he sits down; he turns round; he ducks between the seats and stands, bottom-up in the small space between; all at the same deliberate pace measured against each obstruction, almost all! Punctuating the movement is a rush into space, over the seat behind; over the seat in front; over the man next to him. I wonder if he might try the window. At each movement, the woman understandably becomes more and more agitated, the man raises a warning arm and the guy moves on to another tack. Certainly a ballet if put to music.

How long will it go on? Two stops have gone by and people have got off and on, spaces still filled as before, but now we are stopped again and the woman sees with obvious relief that a seat is free further back, away from the contest. Round two perhaps or the second act? The two front seats on the opposite side of the gangway are also free of passengers since the last stop. Mute gesture; rhythmic pressure towards the gangway; a silent heaving duo until the man gives some way, grabs the guy's arm, propels him across the gangway and he is in a seat on his own (or one and a half seats which is even better now!) Round three follows in almost unbroken movement. The man has slid into the front seat behind the driver, let the guy go free but is sitting with his arm across the gangway, hand firmly gripping the seat opposite. The guy, just as trapped, sits as if in triumph and glares around the bus as all the passengers strive to avoid his eye. I wonder if they got on at Ladyville. I know that men are restrained there and they must have to travel at some time, somewhere, somehow, but not much fun for some others.

It is 8:45am as the bus arrives in Orange Walk. Can that really have been an hour and a half! Perhaps it was an age of discomfort and extraordinary behaviour. Perhaps it was a brief glimpse of fascinating new experience. Either way, could it really be an hour and a half. I wonder how the return journey will compare. What will I be thinking then? The mood of uncertainty over housing is both exciting and uncomfortable; a reflection, perhaps of the suspense on the bus. But we are here and in my pocket a list of hope and just maybe one attractive house might not be so expensive.

My first instructions are to find a Mr Tillett who drives a Tillett's bus and the only clue as to his whereabouts is that the bus will be parked by the Fire Station at different times through the day. I feel that my confidence at finding the right bus has taken a great leap forward in getting to Orange Walk in one piece and the Fire Station shouldn't be too difficult to find. I look around, taking in a new scene; a bustle of activity and inactivity which I wouldn't have thought possible until now. I take some time to explain my quest to locals sitting in the shade of a tree in the middle of the road who say they will point him out when he comes. There is no bus at the moment. Then, as I move up the road towards the Fire Station, just in sight, a shout drowns the sound of traffic "Mr Max!" and the men were pointing.

Mr Tillett was due to go out at 10:30. He used his radio unsuccessfully, to try to contact his father. Then he radioed for another bus in which I was taken specially to see the house via his home. He couldn't find the key of the house to let but picked up a parcel which had to be delivered - part of the service. Discussion on the need for the population of Orange Walk to grow to fill the buses led to the discovery that old Mr Tillett had eight sons, all of whom drove the buses. This was nothing like a regular bus route - being extremely bumpy and narrow. Lots of people looked hard to see what was going on. No wonder with a full size Bluebird commandeered as personal transport by Mr Max, newly arrived, in the back streets of the town. I was only able to look at the house from the outside. It looked nice and had a veranda. He said it would cost $250. We returned to the Fire Station to discover that old Mr Tillett had got the message and arrived.

We went in old Mr Tillett's pick-up back to the house as he had the key: two bedrooms, large bathroom and kitchen; huge living room and balcony at $300 but... much of it was very tatty; badly fitting screens, dirty bathroom and kitchen and a huge outside which would need a lot of upkeep and attract mosquitoes. The downstairs was even worse (That is what he offered for $250). I couldn't possibly invite anyone to stay there in those conditions. I said I would get back to him either way, later in the day. Undeterred as to which way I might decide, old Mr Tillett was just as chatty and I was taken back to the Fire Station by a different route for the welcome and the ride.

There were more possibilities and I set off to find the house of Gina Baize who worked at the Orange Walk Technical College. To let was a 5 bedroomed house in centre of town belonging to people who had gone to the US, $300, the only additional cost being water and electricity. The route from the Fire Station: four blocks West on San Antonio Road to a white house opposite Aquarius, arriving for Gina's lunchtime 12:00 - 1:00pm. Gina wasn't there but I met with the husband who was not the husband yet - why did he tell me that? Instead of my waiting he took me to see the house right away, in his car. The description was largely correct but the condition was even more depressing. Large outside grounds which would need a lot of attention and attract mosquitoes. Dilapidated bungalow; broken screens; no bars (it had been broken into); dreadful bathroom; foul kitchen; dark and dismal. Huge space which could never look lived in by one person. I was offered the key to be able to go back and look on my own during the day. Eventually, I accepted it because it seemed churlish not to honour his trust.

At the Pharmacy near the market, De La Fuente, I was told that there were no apartments left but that the owner has a friend with one, whom he would call at the end of the day if I hadn't found anywhere. Everyone had been so helpful but my spirits were very low by this time and I determined to pull myself together and negotiate with them, which was sure to be okay but which I find difficult and to be avoided if at all possible.

Landy Burns was just as helpful. He offered the ground floor at $300 (my VSO ceiling) but it must have been obvious how attracted I was to the top floor and balcony. He asked if I was prepared to move at all. How far? $325; he obviously wanted a difference in order to let the ground floor. Long let was emphasized and the rent agreed.

I knew I would be very happy there.

I returned the key which had been lent to me at lunch time at the appointed time. Again, I was treated with both courtesy and hospitality - meeting the family of three girls, given a drink and offered food, even though I wasn't going to take the bungalow.

After walking around to find the actual entrance to Mahogany Drive and South Main Street to look at the house again that was to be my home, I walked across the churchyard back into town to find Mr Tillett and talk to him. It was a friendly encounter but Mr Max departed rather less spectacularly than he had arrived.

Before catching the 3:30pm regular bus back to Belize City with the children going home from school I took the opportunity to visit to the District Education Office in the square where I found confusion over who is the District Education Officer and which is his office. This was not entirely a puzzle as I had already heard mutterings about political appointments and there had been an election but the degree to which this would be a problem had yet to be revealed.

So many things were coming together, often set out in letters, and now I had an address. One such in reply to a year 7 pupil who agreed to illustrate a 'George the Snail' story…

'…When you next write please address the letter as above. It does need my Christian name because people here know me as Mr Max and it will speed up delivery. Also, Belizeans find it difficult to pronounce my surname… Tell Mr Berry that I think I may have found a school to work with and I should have a better idea before Christmas. There is a lot to do because schools have nothing like the resources that you have, but it is not impossible and I am finding support for the idea of schools linking with each other.
Enclosed, is the only copy sent to England of my first 'George the Snail' story set in Belize. Like the other, it is a 'true' story and I have more in mind. I hope you enjoy it. You will see that I have acquired some use of a computer. Actually, I'm negotiating to buy a second hand computer and that will help a lot with the huge amount of writing I have set myself as well. Please would you sort out your illustrations? I intend to publish the stories when I get back and if you would like to be part of that you will need to have collected your ideas together. Size doesn't matter; the material (drawings and writing) does. We can desktop publish for presentation later…'

In the evening, Volunteers were to meet the new VSO Programme Director, Mark Wright, at 7:00pm at the Calypso night club in Belize City where I arrived with about ten minutes to spare, to find the place closed. I enquired in the Fiesta Inn next to it (part of the same complex) but they knew nothing of a meeting or even of VSO! I met Jayne (on her bike) outside the Lindbergh Landings - thinking they might have gone there - and we continued to search to no avail. At 7:30 we gave up and returned to the family's house pausing on the way to buy $3.00 chicken to eat when we got there. At about 8:15 Henry and Jack turned up to fetch us in the vehicle. I finished my chicken first! They had all met without checking the Calypso just after we left and moved even further up the road to have a meal there. Otherwise, the evening was quite pleasant. The food was expensive but of good variety and very tasty - so was the only wine I have had here. Not a lot of use in terms of meeting Mark (except for Jane who sat next to him with Chrissie Gale on the other side) but pleasant nonetheless.

David Eck in the office had a computer for sale at $1,500 so I went with him and Margarita Gomez after work to look at it. It was a 486 with CD and speakers. Also, there was plenty of software including a comprehensive DTP, Word Perfect and Microsoft Office. It seemed a good buy and I expected to do so within a month by continuing my frugal habits and since David was happy to wait. It was a rush to be back for an evening meal and then at 7:00pm, meet Katherine for a drink at Lindbergh Landings. It was very pleasant under the palm trees, by the Caribbean Sea and under a clear, starlit sky; the sound of the sea and a gentle breeze - interspersed with karaoke, some of which was good, some not so good, some blooming awful. This was to celebrate my going to Orange Walk at the end of the month.

My Dad died six years ago, Friday 24th October, early in the morning. It had been hard to come to terms with the circumstances of his death and all that went before, since I was twelve years old. In a way, being so far away from home as he so often was, must have helped for I had thought much more about him in coming to Belize than in past times when the memory had been buried; possibly because people here ask questions.

During Principals' Day at work, they were endeavouring to produce a programme for an outcome over three years of Division One, sequence it and note some of the things children will do. They weren't very good at it. Listening was prime and actually doing, well..!

There were other celebrations to mark my being established in my own right as it were. Drinking and drinking and eating had already presented as a national sport and it was certainly undertaken with great enthusiasm, goodwill and togetherness, ten of us, extending into the larger end of the small hours when sleep overtakes naturally into the daylight. Marco discovered my fondness for lobster which I so rarely had in England and that was on the menu as well as chicken as an especially memorable all-day first; then…

"Dis Is Where De Action Is...."

Not really your ordinary day. It was a day with the Lions. At least, it was with the Lions Club from Belize City. Just like home really - or was it? We're in the wrong continent for real, animal lions but these were just as wild in their own way. Double Head Cabbage and Bermudan Landings really are places which I did visit (there was Burrell Boom as well). As for the Community Baboon Sanctuary: the Community is the people living in Bermudan Landings who made and maintain the sanctuary, not the baboons; and baboons are not the rather bad tempered creatures with big red bottoms that you find in Africa, but gentle and very beautiful Howler Monkeys, black, shiny and shy. And this is the only sanctuary for them in the World!

I was very much looking forward to the outing. It had been postponed once, on Sunday, 5th October, because there had been torrential rain during the night and the road was rough at the best of times. Now it was Sunday, 26th October. The day dawned clear and the ground was dry. The outing was to go ahead.

My connection with the Lions Club, like so many things since coming to Belize, was through the Belizean family I have been staying with and become a part. Mrs Leiva is an active member of the club and the whole family were to join in on the outing, from the youngest grandchild at under two, right through to the grandparents; nine altogether, including me. "Not surprising," I thought when the outing was first mentioned, "Seeing the Howler Monkeys was going to be of great interest to everyone". And that was what we were going for: that and some sort of meeting of the Lions Club.

It did seem odd that Double Head Cabbage kept being mentioned by the Lions. I had looked at the map and found that it was quite a bit further on than Bermudan Landing, where the sanctuary was centred. But there seemed no reason to question the matter. It probably had something to do with the meeting (I was right about that) and I put it out of my mind. Certainly, **this** morning there was nothing much more in my mind beyond the outing, getting there, and the monkeys themselves.

"Neria Leiva always likes to be in plenty of time!" I thought benevolently at the appointed starting place. We were the only ones present and ready to get on the private hire bus - which **was** there! And it was hot, very hot. It is always hot, even standing in the shadow of the bus, for it was cooler there than inside. One by one, and over what seemed a considerable time (this is Belize and time assumes a very different priority here), vehicles arrived, people emerged; boxes - lots of boxes of many different kinds - were loaded on to the bus and the expeditionary party grew. I supposed that the number of boxes and things was a bit odd too but, again, there seemed to be no reason to question the matter. People do carry a great deal with them when they go on a picnic and I knew there was to be a picnic. So I continued to wait, quite content watching the families organise themselves, ignoring the 'wants' of children in a most impressive manner.

There were several false starts involving getting on and off the bus to avoid the heat, as more boxes had to be sent for and it was realised that 'so and so' hadn't yet arrived, but we did eventually move off and I had still managed to sit where I wanted to be - at the front of the bus so that I could see where we were going. Each time I had travelled with the family on a bus so far, it had been a Premier Batty Bus with air conditioning and tinted windows. I never had a window seat and Belizeans seem to like to travel with all the curtains drawn. This one was a joy: a regular bus with no tinted windows, no air conditioning and no curtains on the windows. It didn't matter that the bus heaved and swayed over a short piece of unfinished road leading out of Belize City (the work is taking so long that it has become a joke). I could see - and I did want to see. Neither had I noticed that all the men were at the back of the bus and I was sitting with women and children only. That hadn't yet come to my notice..... **Yet!**

"Mr Max!" A voice bellowed from the back of the bus. There was no surprise in the title. Belizeans are very polite and like to be formal when using a name out loud which accounts for the 'Mr' bit. Also, my Christian name has come to be used in this way because Belizeans are not taught to put their tongue between their teeth. There is no need to in Creole which they often speak. So my surname is difficult for them to say and it has become quite the thing to be known as 'Mr Max'. No one forgets it and everyone delights in using it. Makes for good friends! Some time must have passed while all those thoughts crossed my mind although I was not aware of it then and had so far not turned round.

Not so any longer...

"Mr Max!
Come back here! Dis is where de action is!"

A chorus of voices joined in perfect unison, like a herd bellowing from the back of the bus; and again...

"Mr Max!
Come back here! Dis is where de action is!"

I turned to see arms waving in the air, beckoning urgently. Some of the arms held cups aloft while others pointed to them. Slowly, it dawned on me what was happening. I should have known. I have been in the country long enough to know. All thought of the view outside faded as I made my way down the rocking bus to find a complete bar open; a Belizean bar which served rum and coke with lots of ice. It was all there - even the ice, broken not made, in convenient chunks to fit in the cup which was thrust into my hand and filled, as the seat I was to occupy was shown to be ready.

Thus it was a very sociable occasion; a pleasant journey; good conversation becoming increasingly lively. A machine well-oiled always runs well. Never mind it was the passengers who didn't notice how rough the road was. No-one noticed that the bus bounced and slewed as it normally does over the hard, potholed, mud road! But I was quite alert enough to notice when we passed through Burrell Boom; quite alert enough to take note as we crossed the new bridge where the ferry used to be, over the Belize River. I had studied the map and I knew that Bermudan Landing was not very far.

Imagine my surprise when the pace of the bus and the pace of 'The Action' slackened not at all; when a brightly coloured painted sign slipped by, proudly proclaiming 'Bermudan Landing'; when another even more attractive and informative sign not only announced the 'Community Baboon Sanctuary' but also described it - if only one was to pause long enough to read it. It is not a big village. It came and went unsung. "Oh well," I thought, "There is still Double Head Cabbage. That sounds interesting! Perhaps we are going there for the meeting and the picnic and will visit the sanctuary on the way back. As I comforted myself with that thought, I was further consoled (although my generous friends couldn't have known that it was a consolation) as my cup was refilled - again! How could I, given such hospitality, draw the attention of my hosts to the oversight of the howler monkeys?

I have tried to find out how these places got their names. Bermudan Landing is on the river and it is a mighty river, slow flowing, ideal for transport in difficult country. Burrell Boom is also quite close to the river but Double Head Cabbage! Well! I haven't been very successful. All the Belizeans I have spoken to so far don't even seem to have considered the matter. One did venture to suggest that a newcomer to Double Head Cabbage had found one there but I can't see that being the true story. A double head cabbage isn't unusual... Is it? Anyway, no joy in that direction either - nor much when we arrived! There were no houses that I could see; not even the lovely Mayan ones built with straight vertical logs side by side and roofed with palm thatch. There must have been some somewhere though, because there were two large concrete buildings, quite close together, with - and this was a surprise - an orderly queue of Belizeans patiently waiting (as Belizeans do - already told you that!) outside each of them; but what for?

The two buildings turned out to be a school and a high school at that. Not very old but obviously without the resources for maintenance: rotted timber windows which are not replaced; the only equipment inside, the desks and a blackboard; no evidence of any materials at all, not even a cupboard in which things might be stored. Outside there is a basketball pitch (that's good anyway); loos which look most uninviting - and the only distinction borne by the staff loo was that it was separate. As if to emphasise the dreary aspect a large but dilapidated pig sty housed a tall looking boar, a sow and some piglets, all emaciated. I couldn't see any reason for that because the whole area around was rich with vegetation and therefore roots, which they like to browse. They had a brief feast that day anyway!

Returning from looking around I found that the reverse of the packing on the bus was taking place. There didn't seem to be any way in which I could help so I started to unpack myself - taking the cameras out of my backpack. "Might as well make some sort of record of events," I thought. No-one had been at all concerned; they were all busy with their various tasks - whatever they may be. Too busy to be concerned with what I was doing until now that is...

"Mr Max!
Mr Max has a camera! Mr Max has a *video* camera!"

Once again a chorus of voices joined in perfect unison, like a herd bellowing from behind the bus; and again...

"Mr Max!
Mr Max is camera man! Mr Max can do the filming!
Dis way, Mr Max, to where de action is!"

"Well, fine," I thought, "But what action?" (I had discarded my cup). That was when it finally dawned what this was all about. There was a dentist and his team and an oculist with her team. There would also have been a GP but he had an emergency to deal with that day in Belize City. I was to film and take pictures of the whole proceedings so that they could be used for their fund-raising evenings. The service was given free and the friends in the Lions, and their families were making a day of it.

It was back to the action then alright. Another cup was found (It was a sin to lose the first one. I got away with that only through my ignorance) and filled - repeatedly. It is quite difficult filming and taking pictures with two cameras while drinking rum - fun though! This led straight in to the picnic which was the only break in the main action: rice and beans and chicken, standard fare but with all the trimmings; all well organised when the truth is known. Very relaxed, I ventured to make mention of the Community Baboon Sanctuary.

"No probl*em*!"

Now, I know that expression has spread far and wide but no one I have heard emphasises the em quite like the Belizeans do! Come to that, the emphasis is often on the last syllable and quite fascinating to listen to. Something to do with Creole, I wouldn't doubt; so, "No problem!" Three people in the immediate conversation echoed the assurance. "We'll stop in Bermudan Landings. We'll stop so that you can look in the museum there as well!" I made sure that I would be ready.

I suppose that no one could have told the driver. The action went on alright but "No problem!" was forgotten. Still in the action, my desire to stop was greater and watching carefully through the window was maintained. I saw the sign as we passed the museum. Bermudan Landings came and went. I carried on looking up in the trees in the vain hope of seeing monkeys from the heaving bus which made as much noise from its passengers inside, as the engine and groaning chassis made from the outside. Disappointed, I hadn't the heart to fuss - until...

"Monkeys!
Mr Max! - Monkeys!
Stop de bus! - Stop de bus! Back-up! - Back-up! Stop de bus! - Stop de bus!
Mr Max! - Monkeys!"

The bus reversed at great speed and lurched to a stop several times, each to its own excited command. Somewhat overcome but still, I had thought, much more sober, I was nevertheless slow in response compared with my friends - and not a little ashamed at thinking they had forgotten. I gathered my wits and the camera as the next shout came...

"Mr Max! - Monkeys!
Come back here! - Where's your camera?
Get Out! - Get Out! Get out of de bus! Dis is where de action is!"

I did get out. I did film the monkeys. But it was not easy. It was not easy because the light of the sky above the trees was very strong. It was not easy because the trees were very dark. It was not easy because the monkeys were so black. It was not easy because of the rum. Most of all, it was not easy because of the **Howling** that came from the bus behind me. **This is where the action is! This is the way to party! This is the Pride of Lions!**

Quite a day! The monkeys were as amazed as I was. So amazed that they were sat still in the branches of the trees, quiet - watching! - listening!

We saw some more a little further on, including some babies but they were impossible to film. I didn't mind. We saw them. We saw the monkeys. Let's party...

Dis is where de action is!"

Moving day came at last to Orange Walk. Henry from VSO arrived at 8:30am to take me there and collect some used VSO household items and equipment to be passed on to me. We had discussions on the way up about the slow pace of work; my story writing; the links I was trying to set up for schools and Scouts with the UK; and my final hepatitis inoculations. We seemed to have plenty of time so we turned back down the Old Northern Highway to have a look at the Maruba Resort and Jungle Spa. I thought that would be the only time I would ever go there. It was very nice but very expensive.

There were problems finding the key-holder to pick up the things that were in store from the previous VSO. The equipment and linen was disgusting but it had to be moved and I was in my new house by 5:30pm when Henry had to go!

I had long since lost count of the number of new lives beginning in my experience but this one had surely achieved an identity all of its own. I felt much as a cork might as flotsam in a turbulent sea a mere seven weeks after leaving the UK. But as always in learning, here is where I am and this is where it starts: what are the problems and what are the resources? Get on with it! There was plenty to do and occupy my mind apart from domestic issues and belonging; as I preferred it, finding my own way in a completely new society. Keeping a journal and sharing the experience with people left in the UK since this was now home was already well established; now there was a whole new chapter in work; development of the new Primary Curriculum, setting up Schools' and Scouts' links and learning, so much learning about people, their children, their culture and their country. I had responsibility for both Orange Walk and Corozal Districts, two of the six districts in Belize. Corozal was another thirty miles or so to the north and since I already knew for certain who was the District Education Officer there it seemed to make sense to leave next morning at 7:30am for Corozal Town to meet up with Pedro Cucul. I also managed to visit Principal Orvin Rancheran at Calcutta School and Principal Ismael Vallejos at San Antonio School in the morning as well as Principal Valerie Rogers at St. Paul's Anglican School in the afternoon, returning by 5:30pm to spend the evening cleaning the fridge and the cooker! Both San Antonio and Calcutta are somewhat out of Corozal town, Pedro's office was in the centre and St Paul's Anglican School was in town and right on the beach – a Caribbean beach! The visits were great. Friendly conversation rather than direct questions helped in trying to understand some of the expectations of the new curriculum in schools and their management and see for myself both some of the difficulties and what might become positive resources and attitudes. More especially, the children were wonderful. It is such a pleasure and a privilege to have full and immediate attention to be able to launch straight into puzzles, challenges, group contests, stories and games; and a good way to express a firm belief that learning should be FUN.

Back in Orange Walk, the last day of the week, also the end of October was spent waiting for a telephone to be activated and cleaning all morning, especially the cooker and fridge. Thanks to the good offices of Landy Burns, a lady came in to clean the floors and bathroom and took away the disgusting linen to wash. Landy had also arranged to have bars fitted on the balcony windows – a VSO requirement. By early evening the cooker was working and I had my first cup of coffee at 5:15pm using boiled tap water.

I had written to year 7 at the end of last week and all was good…

'It is my last day here in the central offices of the Curriculum Development Unit of the Ministry of Education here in Belize City. The first part of the work is done and I am ready to take it out to selected schools in Orange Walk and Corozal Districts. So I have some free time which I am using to write to you. I'm sitting at the desk in my office (The desk is mahogany which grows here - a big ecological issue for you to find out about). The fan works full time: the sun is shining from a brilliant blue sky and the outside temperature is just over 90 degrees. Very few buildings have glass in the windows. Only banks and places like them (and some stores) have air conditioning and glass in their windows. The rest, including this one, have fine mesh screens to keep out mosquitoes and louvered metal or wooden slats which can be closed at night (a bit like venetian blinds only more solid). As a result I can hear the birds singing outside. The whole complex is built on a mangrove swamp, the edge of which is barely 20 metres from where I am sitting. Just round here, I have seen huge butterflies all different colours, many species of brightly coloured birds, herons, storks, egrets; pelicans and vultures overhead; huge iguanas and more colourful lizards (a mere 50cm); water snakes, frogs and crabs - but, as George says, that's another story!'

Chapter Two

Orange Walk

The move to Orange Walk in no way lessened either belonging in my Belize family or being included in family life. At 7:00am on this first Saturday I was due to meet Marco, Miriam and Miguel to go to Chetumal for the weekend…

At five past seven, two Express buses have come in ready to go and the Premier isn't due to leave until 7:30am. Maybe the Express bus is a better bus to go on as it would probably mean being further ahead in the queue at the Customs Post at the border. The first bus pulled out at five past seven. There is the inevitable queue at what is referred to here as the bathroom which is simply a lavatory with one pan and a wash basin which costs 25 cents a go - otherwise you don't get in. It is a beautiful morning with the birds singing and Orange Walk is really waking up very quickly, even on a Saturday; although it was certainly quiet where I live near the cemetery at six o'clock. The first bus has actually gone round the back for no apparent reason and is presently parked on the bus stop for the regular bus route, Victoria Avenue which is part of the Northern Highway as it passes through the town. Main Street runs roughly parallel, two blocks to the East. The bus set off to pass the bus station again at 7:12am on its way out to Chetumal via Corozal.

The second Express bus left at 7:15, just as a Premier pulled up. This was not the one I was waiting for and it didn't come in to the bus station. There are a lot of extra buses this morning. Not only is it the Fair in Chetumal but it is also the end of the month when people go shopping for cheaper goods in Mexico. My bus pulled in shortly afterwards. Marco, Miriam and Miguel were on the bus. Tabo, Neria and Mariami had travelled up the previous day. Miguel had occupied my seat from Belize City where it was booked.

We waited an hour at Customs, out in the hot sun, but that was only half the previous wait. I must remember to fill out the required forms before getting there in future; also, not forget my glasses or leave my bag on the bus. In the queue, I was spotted by Kathryn who came for a chat, and Christine who was going on to a beach resort for the weekend with another VSO from San Ignacio. We passed the showground on the edge of Chetumal and arrived in the bus station by the New Market from where we took a taxi to the Hotel Ucum where we met up with the others. Neria had obtained her hospital results the day before and was pleased that they were clear as well as leaving the weekend free. My room had been booked but had cost 72 pesos as a double instead of the single rate of 50 pesos. There were no single rooms for this weekend.

We went out separately and agreed to meet up at three o'clock but I haven't yet decided whether to go to the show today or tomorrow, or both. I went for a walk and had something to eat and drink – having a very happy wander around in the old market. Then I went off to buy some rum and some coffee. Kathryn and two Peace Corps, who also came up on the bus, went off to the museum first, intending to go to the show tomorrow. I had great fun trying to buy a sink plug. Few sinks have them as I discovered. Here it is evidently called a tapox p-lavabo. A second shopkeeper wrote 'boxito' on the same piece of paper. Well, a name is a start, assuming it is the right name! (I later got what I wanted in Orange Walk).

Sitting out on the end of the pier looking across Chetumal Bay which leads out behind Ambergris Caye and San Pedro into the Caribbean Sea I know that Belize is just across the water on the right, to the South. Corozal is tucked away in a sweep of land which reaches out to Sarteneja and the Shipstern Nature Reserve. The lights of Sarteneja can be seen at night as I noted last time. There is a haze and the Cayes cannot be seen at the moment, giving the impression that the view reaches right out to sea. The water close in is green and lazily choppy – with an onshore wind. Sea birds of many different kinds are everywhere. The sea further out is blue. Chetumal pollutes the water but nothing like as heavily as Belize City. Birds dive to catch fish from the water very skilfully; spotting far more than I do - although I am not looking as keenly and it isn't as urgent for me. The Frigate is a particularly graceful bird with long, slender, crescent wings, and there are many of them. They flap against the wind to hover as best they can over the water, looking downwards. When they spot a fish, they fold their wings and dive. Almost every time they rise with it caught in their long sharp beak and swallow it on the wing. The Frigate bird is more or less white with black round the eyes and a few black markings, black feet and a black strip along the back edge of the outer wing - the back of which is grey. They are able to use air currents very skilfully, to soar at the best of times but with the present wind many of them are maintaining an effectively stationary position with reference to the water.

I arrived back at the hotel for a beer drinking session with Tabo and Marco at 3:00pm. This was conducted from the back of somebody's truck in the hotel car park. This was also where I learned what Mr Leiva is called, which he doesn't like. He is Tabo to his friends! The session ended at 5:00pm after each of us had consumed six cans of strong beer and I hadn't eaten very much. We were all due to go to the Fair at 6:30pm so I settled down to overcome the effects of the beer, having set my watch for 6:15 to be properly awake by the time we left.

I drifted off into a deep sleep and was suddenly awakened at six o'clock to go immediately as their friend was waiting with a car. I was a bit wobbly but managed okay and arrived at the Fair.

A Mexican fair has to be experienced to be properly imagined. The lights, the activity, the people and their colourful clothes, the huge space, the sounds and the smells all have an excitement and a flavour of their own. I feel as I if I might be floating along as in a warm and balmy sea.

Practical needs in my new home demand that I first go round the area selling kitchen utensils. There are pans of every type and size, all bright and shiny; stacked high, reflecting the light; wooden, metal articles – enamelled, glazed. Every conceivable thing except what I wanted. No wooden cooking spoons - only the deep ones. No decent chopping boards. No trays. I bought a wooden mixer which I would never use but which would make a nice decorative item; two wooden spoons, a softwood chopping board, a ladle and right at the end on the way out, a japanned Chinese style tray in black and gold. From the kitchen area I went on down past the textiles which were being sold in the old fashioned way you still see in London of 'not one but two but three but four'. Then on to the Fairground which was attracting the children and where I left the family (with a mardy, grumpy Miguel) and went back and looked at the rest of the exhibition and sales areas. The three large hot dogs for which I waited ages didn't do me any good at all and so I went as we had arranged to meet back at the entrance at 10:00pm where I found that all the others were ready to go back to the hotel and we left by taxi.

Before returning to Belize next day I joined Kathryn and two other Peace Corps for breakfast which was most enjoyable: Fruit juice, Mexican egg, toast and coffee. Then I wandered around the market again and around the outside of the museum where there were extra displays of art and Mayan culture. Then it was back to the hotel for another shower at 11:00am, domestic shopping using Visa in San Francisco supermarket next to the bus station and away on the Premier bus with the family.

One way and another there was a great deal of writing to do; much more than I had anticipated. My journal, stories, letters, cards, the all-important promise I had made to stay in touch with children as they moved on to year seven and the endeavour to set up a schools' link for them took up huge chunks of time. Fortunately my work fitted very well with everything else and the whole effort took on integrity of its own; and letters from home had long since started to arrive. Letters received and sent and stories already counted in dozens. Even so, life became hectic especially in the first month. There was no way the marriage of so many strands of learning and activity could have been anticipated to develop as they did from early morning until late at night every day. Quite apart from all the newness of people, environment and task, planning, meetings, workshops and testing ideas, the first schools to work with were spread over nearly forty miles and meetings back at base in Belize City were a fifty four mile bus ride each way involving a very early start and late return; the 'Bluebird' relics from better days as US school transport being the only means of covering the ground and severely limited in comfort and more often than not, even seats; no relaxation whatsoever. Outside the windows, however, the view ignored by all others (those with seats would be asleep) never ceased to provide interest and distraction for me. Even at night there were always stars and fireflies; so many of them.

Field Testing of Outcomes for the New Curriculum (Division One) in Orange Walk and Corozal Districts started in earnest in Orange Walk with two hours of my going through a presentation of the mechanics of the new curriculum and emphasizing what participating schools were being asked to do. Essentially this meant, for each Outcome in the assigned Area: to brainstorm the content required to reach 'each pupil should...' by the end of Division One; to sequence that content into the three separate years as thought fit, bearing in mind that some outcomes may not be treated in this way; and to identify the activities which pupils might undertake to effect learning within the stated content. In other words: 'Outcomes' identified what children would be expected to be able to do and understand over time and what resources and activities would empower them; exciting stuff!

Six schools had been chosen for the field testing, three in each district. The first outing was to Corozal, meeting early with the District Education Officer, Pedro Cucul and Principals Orvin Rancheran of Calcutta School and Ismael Vallejos of San Antonio School in the morning and Valerie Rogers of St Paul's Anglican School in the afternoon.

After a rather fruitless visit to the District Office in Orange Walk next day, the Principal of Louisiana School Mr Cawich was found to be very enthusiastic and decided that he wished to involve all eleven of his Division One staff in the exercise. Sadly, it was necessary for me to be the one to inform him of a meeting to take place in the District Office in one week's time and that meant a second visit to the Orange Walk District Office for discussions with Urbano Uck whom I then discovered was the District Education Officer. People I found to be great; communications were not! That same afternoon I met again with the staff and principals of the three Corozal schools: San Antonio, Calcutta and St Paul's Anglican thirty miles away, travelling on the regular bus which needed getting used to. Two more hours were spent going through the same presentation. Mr Uck was busy with his budget the next morning and asked me to return at 1:00pm which I did. As he hadn't finished then either, I waited until we were able to visit San Pablo and Carmelita schools and repeat the process of introduction with Principals Estelita Rodriguez and Raguel Moreno and their staffs.

Plans were made and meetings arranged to bring together working groups, liaise with staff from Belize City and apportion responsibilities Needless to say, not all schools are the same and decisions would have to be made noted at the time...

'There must be some kind of feedback: also, an official recognition of the importance of the part which has been played in the process and the time given to it outside the staff's regular work.
Now that the participating schools know the process, there would be considerable value in their sharing the Outcomes with each other - preferably including a workshop across the two Districts.

New schools participating need to become familiar with the process but this need not take so long if current schools are able to help facilitate. If the increased pool of expertise so far gained is to be used fully, there will be implications for children's uninterrupted learning; travelling expenses, time and reward given to participating staff. As the net widens, so the implications for funding will increase. The biggest single difficulty in this exercise has been staff finding the time to give the Outcomes the attention they deserve. Lunchtime, before or after school are not good times to engage the whole attention of any staff at the best of times and these people are being asked to work in an entirely unfamiliar way. Eventually, it is to be hoped that all schools will have their programs and activities sequenced right across the Division One curriculum. When that happens they will know what resources they need!'

My new home was wonderful. I had plenty of space and furniture and it didn't take long to acquire the few utensils needed for easy relaxation after long and busy days. The large balcony high above the ground (as was the house) gave a great view across to the New River on what I considered to be the most interesting side of the town and a perfect place to watch the Caribbean sun sink gently away while enjoying a Belikin beer as the locals do straight from the bottle. While having great resource and independent security there was also great friendliness and interest shown by the Burns family next door, the owners of my house. The Alcoser family, met on first arriving in Orange Walk, took me with them to spend a most enjoyable day in Chetumal; the first of many. Negotiations for a second hand 486 computer had proved successful and this was quickly up and running, making it unnecessary to save typing for visits to Belize City.

My home in the UK was let through an agent and now having a permanent address in Belize, correspondence could be sent and received. FAX was also available through the Education Development Centre and now email. Bringing the agent up to date was a joy…
'I trust you are well - not too cold and wet. It has been much cooler here than usual today; a mere eighty five; a good ten degrees less than it often is. Also, it has been wet but not in the way you know it. Wet is a dry period with most rain concentrated in violent downpours lasting about ten minutes and which begin and end with almost no warning. It doesn't matter though, because you just stop and shelter - and if you can't, well, the water's warm! There are many times when I think about home of course, but it is terrific here in all respects. The people are great; very friendly and welcoming and I am able to get to know them easily because of the work, the way things have gone and because I am the only VSO and the only Englishman in

either Orange Walk District or Corozal District where I am based. As for the country: it is all I had hoped and much more…'

Experience of Orange Walk for this first month was almost completely restricted to food and utensil shopping and work. The first real town activity is recorded in a letter to one of the year 7 pupils back home…

'…The last film, on the 20th of November, is of a March for Jesus which was followed by a mass at La Immaculada Church - or at least, in the grounds behind it. I think it speaks for itself so I will leave it to do just that… Perhaps I should point out that Orange Walk Town is smaller than Barnstaple then that will give you some idea of how involved people are…'

The first real exploration out of town began on the last day of November with a walk of about five miles around Palmar and a back road leading to the Belize Sugar Industries factory. Many such outings were to follow with the added bonus of being well known and making many friends throughout the whole of the north of Belize.

Communications with the United Kingdom were not as expected in 1997. Airmail took three weeks and mostly still does. Email provision in Belize was very much in its infancy in terms of both access and speed even from the Education Development Centre (EDC) in Belize City. Having a laptop at that time was quite out of the question but I had at least anticipated the problem of paper storage and brought a modest second hand portable word processor. The volume of writing however, was not anticipated. Letters sent alone reached nearly eighty by the end of November, averaging ten a week and rendering my pre-planned technology quite useless along with the £100 it had cost. Thankfully, it did someone else some good and was given away after a couple of weeks. Fortunately, there was desktop access in the EDC office which I was able to use not only for work but also for my journal, story writing and the all-important letters, writing through breaks and lunch and after hours. This was also helped by work time being quite slow before moving to Orange Walk. Email was available but none of my contacts had email at the time and the secondary school with whom the year 7 linking was to take place was only just getting it up and running and it took a long time to make successful contact. The office facility was not to last of course and acquiring a desktop and telephone with email access was top priority for the move.

Add to all this that life back at home hadn't changed simply because I had chosen to volunteer. Individuals: friends, colleagues, pupils and scouters wrote and replied very quickly but schools have routine demands and can be ponderous vessels and maybe that was hardest to deal with. Anyway, some progress towards schools linking was made in November. A primary-secondary link might seem out of step but certainly not in age because primary schools in Belize go up to age thirteen and while our children might seem more sophisticated Belize children are more mature, confident and independent in other ways much as we were in the early fifties. I was getting to know primary schools in Belize and started 'sounding out' right from the start and even before that because my new neighbours had four children in the family attending La Immaculada, a Catholic School in Orange Walk and that seemed to be a good place to start. Their father, Landy (Orlando) was a major business man in the town, a supporter of the school and a very much committed Rotarian so introductions were easy despite the school not being one of the ones chosen for curriculum trials. The mail delays rather spoiled that option but the exercise was useful in establishing workable initial contact with staff and children.

Early beginnings are probably best illustrated through a small selection of mail starting with a letter from the Year Group Head at the Senior School where children from my junior school had gone into year 7. There were four classes in the year and these were to be linked with the oldest class in four primary schools in Belize, each sending a Buddy (a soft toy) to the other…

'Thanks very much for your letter and video – here is my reply at last! I apologise for the delay but I hope by now that you have received some letters from your past pupils to keep you going. A large number of them took your address and promised me they would write. I have now got through all the necessary early year seven geography and can concentrate on the 'Belize Link'. So far I have used your video, atlas work and some general research tasks to introduce Belize. This week, each of the four classes I teach will be voting to elect their 'travel buddy' to visit Belize. We have gone through the full democratic process, including

speeches and campaigning! I anticipate them buying their air tickets soon and arriving with you by the end of the month. It would be great if you could find suitable schools or individual children to host them. Ideally, I would like each 'buddy' to go to a different school. If not, then George the Snail will have his work cut out! All of the buddies have an important diplomatic conference to attend back here in England so will need to return to South Molton by the start of the New Near. If all goes well they will be able to return again soon after. Each Buddy will have the following items in his/her diplomatic luggage:

a) A letter of introduction

b) His own official passport

c) A travel diary (which will contain notes describing his departure and which can be added to during his stay)

d) Photographs of the school, town, local area and pupils

e) Pupil 'dossiers' (possibly to be used by pen friends)

f) A set of stamped, addressed envelopes (for use as you see fit)

g) Some small gifts for Christmas

h) Information and artefacts from our local area

i) A tape containing a message, song, National Anthem etc.

j) Possibly, a short video film

Each 'buddy' will also carry a disposable camera, which can be used to record trips, people etc. If he brings this home, I will arrange for the films to be developed. I hope that each 'buddy' will return safely, accompanied by a Belizean counterpart. My classes have already started to think about how they will look after their visitors and some of their ideas may be useful to you:

1) Each 'buddy' will stay for some time with every pupil in the class and the host pupils will help the visitor write and illustrate his diary.

2) The visitor will be taken on family outings, school trips and given a guided tour of the school.

3) Each 'buddy' will be provided with a camera on arrival.

4) Each 'buddy' will be helped to collect items to take home to Belize.

5) Pupils will make the visiting 'buddy' as comfortable as possible by building a special 'buddy house' for him to stay in.

6) A guest appearance will be arranged with the local newspaper – North Devon Journal.

I have enclosed your videotape – it was great! More please! I have kept a copy of the tape at school for you. I hope we can get this project moving now. The idea has been well received at this end, with special enthusiasm from your old pupils. In my experience, these projects take a lot of effort to begin with but soon gather momentum and become self-sustaining. I hope we can make it work… P.S. Thanks for the tee-shirt! I will announce the winner in the next letter!

Difficulties with communication were immediately apparent starting with first schools access at the end of November and the request that Buddies 'will need to return to South Molton by the start of the New Near'; anticipation versus reality as much the part of learning already!

Children did indeed write; many of them…

'…I hope you are well and have completed your move to Orange Walk Town. We have had rain, wind and sun. It is a very mixed up November. I have been very busy at school and I can now count to trente-neuf (39) in French. I have just had my interim report from school and I am very pleased with it. I am reading the new George the Snail story and when I have finished the illustrations I will send them to you. As you can see I have use of a computer. This letter was written on Microsoft Word. We have Encarta 97 Encyclopaedia, which helps a lot with homework for school. It helps with history the most because it gives information e.g. William I, at the click of a button. Football is also going well. We have played 6, won 2, drawn 0, and lost 4, which gives us a total of 6 points. I have scored 3 goals out of 19 goals (the second highest)…'

'…I just thought I would write since Mr Berry gave me your address. The video is lovely, especially the procession. It looked very hot and very loud. Mr Berry couldn't get the video to work. School is going brilliantly well. I am really enjoying it there. I was the first person to be picked to go to Lundy Island for one week's stay. There you can swim by the seals; snorkel and you do lots and lots of walking. I am also going to Beam House with the school as well as Lundy. It sounds a bit like Fairthorne but it is different really. I had an excellent first school report. I've also had lots of tests. In a science test I got 85%, in maths twenty out of twenty and we've just had a French test. We also had a big test called the cognitive test or something like that. If it is possible, could you find me a pen friend about the age of 11 or 12? …' and maintained their well-known priorities.

Scouters also wrote. I had long been County Commissioner for Devon Cub Scouts and was hoping to provide some linking for them also…

'…I hope by now that you have settled in and are finding your new job and environment to your liking. We thought about you on the 6th, departing on such a sad and emotional day. I was on my own as Mike was in Norfolk attending the wedding of his niece, and I spent most of the day in front of the television watching the funeral… Scouting wise, things are quiet at the moment. Tony rang at the beginning of the month to postpone the ADCs meeting to 1st November. He said he knew me (I thought that sounded ominous as it is usually the naughty Cubs you remember). I still can't picture him but several of my Leaders have met him on their training weekends…'

…and a typical reply…

'You are ahead of me with your letters and I have looked forward to them and enjoyed reading them very much. At last, I am settled in my permanent home whilst in Belize. It is a lovely place. I have been very lucky as it has everything I have been looking for… Moving in has not been easy in other ways. The house is let unfurnished as VSOs pass on essentials at the end of their term. Mine had been in store as well and its condition was disgusting. It took five hours to clean the cooker to a condition even approaching my satisfaction. I have managed to acquire a fridge, thank goodness (the daytime temperature has rarely dropped below 90) but that took a similar time to clean. Also, I thought I would try using boiled tap water for drinking and cooking. That was a mistake which will not be repeated. I use bottled water now which I buy in refillable plastic containers which hold about five gallons. You have to keep drinking all day, yet very little comes out the other end… Hurricane Pauline was further North and on the Pacific coast. Belize City is constantly on the alert because it could be so vulnerable but there is much less risk here as Orange Walk Town is well inland. The effects in Acapulco were awful and obviously of much concern here. Mrs Leiva has a sister there. The family were not hurt but life is very difficult for them because the entire social infrastructure has collapsed…'

…cut and paste was wonderful; people who were likely to talk to each other had different news but it saved a huge amount of rewrite for other groups and the division of news was also part of my hope to share the experience and more so by becoming 'shared' among people, especially children of course. And writing to Scout Leaders county-wide…

'…Enclosed is a contribution for Scoutlink. Would you please send me four copies as soon as it is printed? Time lapses are much greater at this distance and in this part of the world especially, and if I am to make any headway I need to find ways of cutting them down. There is a great deal more to report but I thought this would be the best way to start. The quicker I cease to be a link in the chain the more successful it is likely to be. Except that, for the time being, I will probably have to do some word processing for Scouts at this end if Devon Scouts want to use email… I will have to tell you what Belize is like bit by bit. It is a whole new experience in itself and like so many things in life, it has to be lived to be appreciated and understood. Certainly, anyone would be awestruck from the start by the flora and fauna. The trees are always green! New leaves must stay or grow so fast that the old ones dropping off go unnoticed. There are seasons, the same as ours, as Belize is (just) in the Northern Hemisphere, but they are very blurred… Anyway, that's it for now. Enough, I hope to enable you to arouse some active enthusiasm among Leaders. I will certainly 'facilitate' any reasonable venture as far as possible - and Scouts here are keen…

'…From Belize, Central America It is not yet twelve months since I decided to go on Voluntary Service Overseas and less than six months since I learned that I would be coming here - and I hadn't given Central America a single thought. In fact, I had first to go and check that I had the right idea about where Belize might be. I'm not saying whether I was right or not. Anyway, I decided before coming, that I would try to keep my Scouting alive and if possible, find ways of setting up links in Scouting or providing 'in country' information for any of you that wishes to take it up. There are plenty of opportunities in the Scouting programme. David Moate, your ACC (International) was very helpful in setting up the contacts for me and I am sure that he would give full support to any Group needing it. Now I am here, I am more convinced than ever about the value of links with the UK, both ways equally. Scouts' idea of hiking/camping here, to take perhaps a rather extreme example, is trekking through the rainforest. When I asked what sort of boots they wear - thinking the fabric ones I brought might not be adequate - I was told that many Scouts go barefoot. I hardly dared ask about leg protection, arms and body but you might guess the answer. I said I may have to be carried - horizontally, in a plastic bag! There are no assumptions to be made. I have found a great deal of talent and enthusiasm and when Scouts are in uniform they are very smart indeed and proud to proclaim their belonging to all who will see them. Of course, there is the usual problem of shortage of Leaders - except that it is much more acute in a country with such a high proportion of young people. Interestingly, what has happened is that there is a large Venture Scout population and they are very active in maintaining Scouts and Cub Scouts. That is not the ideal of course, particularly for the Venture Scouts who have their own training to attend to, but it does demonstrate the level of commitment. It is difficult to know where to start in promoting links of this sort and the links will be best when I am no longer needed to facilitate them so I asked for contributions from some Belizean Scouts which are as follows…'

Hilberto Riverol, National Scout Executive - A Brief History of the Scout Movement in Belize…
'The oldest records found to date in England indicate that Scouting in Belize started in 1911 with a census of two troops, twenty Scouts. The following year numbers were one troop, three Scouters and twenty-four Scouts, a total of twenty-seven. The Belize branch of The Scout Association was officially registered in 1917 with a census of eight Scouters, one hundred and thirteen Scouts and fifty-nine Cub Scouts, a total membership of one hundred and eighty.

However, according to a research undertaken by Mr Leopold Flowers former Executive Commissioner of the Belize Scout Association and Mr William Faux, presently Deputy Chief Commissioner, Scouting in Belize was started in 1910 when Henry Longworth of St. John's Cathedral established a troop there. In 1915 Robin O. Phillips, an American Scout of about 17 years of age is said to have invested 20 young men as Scouts. This took place at Robin's home, then situated at the corner of Wilson Street and Barrack Road. When these Scouts were considered well trained, Robin's father approached Governor William Hart Bennett to seek assistance and support for the Scout Movement. Governor Bennett then selected Mr George Graham, then manager of the Belize Estate and Produce Company Ltd. Mr Graham in turn appointed as Scout Masters to assist him, Mr Philip Ely, Mr Wexham and Mr Paul Shepherd Berry, then superintendent of the Belize Wireless Station. The Movement flourished for about three to four years then died when Mr Graham left Belize.

Scouting was revived again in 1934 in the Belize City area by Brother John Mark Jacoby. Hundreds of boys (including many leading citizens) were led by 'Bra Jake' as he was known. For many years Scouting revolved around activities held at the Holy Redeemer Scout Room (the home of troops 1,2 & 3) and at an annual summer camp at San Pedro, Ambergris Caye.

In 1936 Scouting was introduced to the Districts beginning with the Stann Creek District and eventually spreading to all the others. Since that time there has always been Scout activity in the country. The level of this activity has varied considerably over the years, depending largely on the Movement's ability to attract and maintain committed voluntary leadership.

In late 1950's the Association acquired from Government 100 acres of land in the Burrell Boom area. Later named Camp Oakley, this site has been the venue for many national camps, training seminars and other Scout programmes. In 1974 with the help of a grant from the Baron Bliss Trust, a concrete building was erected at the camp. Scouts from Belize have taken part in many international camps in the Caribbean, Mexico, Central America and the United States of America. In 1979, the Association embarked on a revitalization Programme which continues today. Existing to date are some twenty-seven Scout Groups located in the six Districts and having a combined membership of one thousand two hundred Scouts…

'A Brother Scout… 'My name is Ricardo Alcoser. I am a Belizean Venture Scout from the 1st. Orange Walk Scout Group. I am the secretary of the Venture Unit. I started as a Cub since 1987 and was invested in December 1987. As a Cub I attended many camps that the group organised which was the 1st Corozal Cub Pack in the northern district of Belize. From there I moved to Orange Walk where I joined the Scout Group. When I started, the Group had just formed so I tried to do my best. With the 1st Orange Walk I became one of their best. I moved up from a Member to an Assistant Patrol Leader to a Patrol Leader of the Wolf Patrol. As a Patrol Leader I was elected to be part of the elite patrol to attend the XVI Central American Camporee in Valle de Angeles, Honduras in 1992. When I came back I had enough knowledge to help our Scouters with their Scout Spirit which was low. In 1996, last year, I formed part of a delegation that represented our Country Belize, at XIII Rover Moot in Panama…'

Scout Leader, 7th Corozal San Joaquin… 'The Overnight Eggs! This was one of the greatest overnight hikes ever done by the 7th Corozal San Joaquin Cub Scouts. It was 3:30pm, all gathered on the main Plaza, ready to go when Akela blew the first whistle and said "Okay Cubs today is a special day for you all because today all of you will be called chicks and the Leaders will be roosters. You will be performing things chicks do. You will mine an egg. You have to take this egg everywhere you go!" Then Akela started giving each and every one a marked egg. After everyone got one Akela blew three whistles and the fun started. All the chicks were amazed with their egg but they were also singing, shouting their calls and releasing their inner motivation with the Scout Spirit. All are very happy. Five minutes later the first egg broke up, accidentally and the first chick has failed and had to go to the end of the line. While passing through the woods five eggs got broken inside trouser pockets. It was fun seeing these chicks worrying about their eggs. After walking and learning about nature and conservation the chicks reached the finishing line. They have reached San Pedro Village. Some chicks were happy. After three and a half hours we reached mother home, San Joaquin. The roosters started to look for the good eggs. Only three chicks were found with their whole egg. These chicks were given a special award for their carefulness and at the end all 15 chicks got their special badge for participation in this overnight hike. Close your eyes and see the chicks and their egg, the good and the broken ones. Try something like this and see the fun of it. Hope you enjoy it as I did…'

Finally, I must say that I have found such enthusiasm and spirit here. There is no way I can do justice to that by simply sending news. There must be a multitude of ideas for sharing and joint projects home there in Devon and I would be very pleased to make introductions and help things along until links are established. Akela Max…'

Turning back to the schools link…

'…The work I was doing in Belize City is finished and I am now where I should be co-ordinating the process of trialling and piloting the New Primary Curriculum. Primary here means up to thirteen/fourteen years of age (Infant 1-2, Standard 1-6). The present work is with Division One which comprises the first three years (Infant 1-2 & Standard 1). I hope the material I have sent so far has been (or will be) useful. There is a great deal more to send of course. Now that I am settled in my permanent home here, it is much easier to collect and send. This can be photos, film, sound cassette, local items and text. I have collected quite a lot more already and heavier items can go by surface mail. Most important is students communicating…

Of the six schools I am currently working with in the Orange Walk and Corozal Districts there are three of which I am certain of the full support, enthusiasm and commitment of the Principal to Linking. All the schools cover the year 7 age range plus two extra years. Also, the level at which children are educated is high by any standards and, interestingly, that education is conducted in English which, for most of the children here, is not their first language. Most families speak Spanish at home. At the time of writing, I have discussed ways of starting with the Principal and staff at a rural school in a village called Calcutta in Corozal District. Standards 5 & 6 will have some written material ready by next week. Perhaps you could make a start in a small way too. I expect to be having the same discussion with the Principal of a school of 800 pupils in Orange Walk Town on Friday. I see no reason why we should limit to one school and I have in mind another one in Corozal Town which looks out across the Caribbean towards Ambergris Caye! That way you will have a good cross section of the variety of schools in this part of Belize.

I have managed to purchase a second-hand 486 which has both Word for Windows and Word Perfect so I can put any written work produced in a school without that capability, on to disc. Two friends here have offered full use of their email so that material can be transmitted and received without delay. This will improve further when I can afford that facility myself. Also, of course, I can send discs to you - and receive them - which can be used direct (although that still depends on the post). Having got that far, I would like to get started right away. There is nothing like delay to dampen enthusiasm. Let's try to have something going before Christmas so that it can be built on with the new term. I need your email address!

The purpose of getting started quickly and in this way also has longer term implications. I need to be able to demonstrate some progress to attract material support and, most particularly, funding. Once we have started it will be relatively easy to produce a business plan to put before potential providers. My neighbour, who is a businessman in Orange Walk Town and the owner of the house I have rented, has four children who attend a town school of which he is a Governor. He is very interested in the linking and is particularly concerned to develop IT in the schools. The District Education Officers have given full support and, more importantly, so has the Chief Education Officer. He is prepared to sanction the project with the Ministry and internationally where necessary. I will then be able to act on his behalf. Officers from the ODA (Overseas Development Agency) and the World Bank have been in to the Curriculum Development Unit with whom I have discussed funding. There is a small project fund which might be tapped and which I am waiting to hear about. There is the business world of course. Local businesses respond well to well-prepared plans. VSO too will make small grants - every little helps! Since writing this I have received your letter - brilliant! Today is Friday, 28th November. Your letter reached me on Wednesday when I was in Belize City for the day at the Education Office - reporting back on field work.

I spent yesterday responding to the wonderful progress you have made… Four schools will take part: Louisiana is a Government School of 800 pupils in Orange Walk Town. (population 13,000); La Immaculada is a Roman Catholic School of 1500 pupils in Orange Walk Town. St. Paul's is an Anglican School of about 120 pupils in Corozal Town (population 3,500) - right on the edge of the Caribbean Sea; Calcutta is a rural, Government School in the village of Calcutta on the Northern Highway between Orange Walk Town and Corozal Town. The schools are spread over about 50 miles. All four schools have *an age range 5-13 in three divisions. The linking will be with the Upper Division - Standards 5&6, age 11/13 (your Year 7/8). There has been a great deal of excitement, especially when I outlined all the points in your letter. I have done this directly with pupils in Calcutta and had a wonderful time. They stayed until 5:30 after school so that I could meet with them and there are 35 letters enclosed, which they have written. Also enclosed is a map of Belize which I expect you will find useful. (These are coming by post).*

The second video is ready. I will send it to you when I have finished the commentary. Photos will be arriving in South Molton as Christmas Cards. I will provide more of those later by sending undeveloped film (very expensive here). VHS machines are US format so our tapes don't work. If you send any, they need converting (can't be done here). In the meantime could you please send a 21-pin Adaptor and Audio/Video Cable - Panasonic VFA0151 and VFA0028 as I didn't bring mine? Then I should be able to show my tapes here as well. I expect it will be expensive and I will pay for it when my ship comes home! Please hold on to the original video tapes until I come back. I have another tee shirt to send shortly and artefacts etc. which I collect will start to flow when my finances improve. Buying the computer has knocked seven bells out of local funds...'

Colleagues were very interested and supportive too. Only the delays were unhelpful...

'...Everything seems to be going very well for you and it is good to hear about progress with schools etc. Lorraine told me that some of the year 7 children who work with Paul have started work on a project about Belize. I gave her your District Education Centre address. I hope this was alright. I have lent them two books, which I had about Belize. He said the children were enthusiastic about the work and were planning what to find out and explain about South Molton in order to send it out to you...'

Progress seemed to be moving well even though the time scale of hopes and reality differed...

Herewith, your second tape and commentary: as before, would you please ask Alison if she will copy it for you to use and would you please keep the original safely until I return. I have a copy of the text. Anyone wishing to write from now on should use the above address. I know I have said this several times but it will save mail chasing me around. Before the commentary on the tape I have written something of a record of the progress I have made with 'linking' in story form which you might like to use. Also enclosed are 'Shopping in Chetumal' and the story of the part of the video which deals with the outing to Double Head Cabbage. This is called 'Dis is where de action is!' Lastly there is a piece called 'Circular walk round Yo Creek from Orange Walk Town' which is a few thoughts recorded whilst walking. You could get quite a lot of these...'

'Greetings to Year7 - Continuing the adventures of George the Snail in Belize, once again...

You are Welcome! I expect you will know that Mr Berry and I talked quite a lot about "Buddies" before I came out here and I thought that I would bring my own. George was the obvious choice for me so I asked my friend to design and make one for me. (Yes I know you are all doing your own but I didn't have anyone to make speeches and campaigning for. George was flying out on his diplomatic mission anyway!) Of course, George was travelling for his own adventures as well, but I didn't realise at the time, just what an important role he was going to play in organising the diplomatic link between the two countries - England and Belize, Belize and England. He soon put me right there!

There are four diplomatic centres here in Belize which will be visited simultaneously by one of the four "Buddies" coming over from England. Each of the four centres is to be located in a different school and a different kind of school, so this involved George in quite a lot of organising. I went along at his request to carry his bits and pieces. Also, as I had already visited the schools to do some work with them, he said that my contacts and experience might come in useful as long as I didn't get above myself and get in the way and took care to let him do the talking; and a fine diplomat he proved to be. I listened with quiet admiration and not a little pride! George and I discussed the choice of school at some length before it was decided which ones to approach. George didn't want anything to go wrong at this stage. Two large town schools in Orange Walk Town seemed to be rather the same but one is a Government School of 800 students and the other is a Roman Catholic School of 1600 students, each with its own particular identity. In Corozal District, one of the schools chosen has 200 students and is in a village called Calcutta on the Northern Highway and the other is an Anglican School in Corozal Town with 180 students, right on the shore of the Caribbean. The schools are called Louisiana, La Immaculada, Calcutta Government and St Paul's.

When the selection had been made George decided to start at the top, his being a diplomatic mission and all, so off he went to discuss his ideas with the Chief Education Officer and then with the District Education Officers of Orange Walk District and Corozal District where the schools are located. (That just happens to be where I am working - George thought that might be useful too!). He said to me afterwards that he thought all that went rather well. The CEO and the DEOs were very enthusiastic and quite happy that the schools should become involved so George set off next to meet - separately - the Principals of the four chosen schools. This is where George really came into his own. He was magnificent...

First he announced that he was expecting a large number of letters from students in England with up to date news of progress in the preparations being made for the forthcoming diplomatic mission. He said that I had sent some information about Belize to England and that the students had been familiarising themselves with Belize and Central America through general research. All of the Principals were most impressed. Then he said that 'Travel Buddies' were being elected to visit Belize; that the English students had gone through the full diplomatic process, including speeches and campaigning! At this point, though, George had expected a profound reaction but he was wrong. He was met with stunned silence. Without exception, on each of the four separate visits, a glazed expression spread across the face of the Principal; a slightly worried look; certainly a very puzzled look.

"Travel Buddies?" they said. "Visit Belize?" they said. "Won't that be expensive?"

I've never seen George lost for words before but he was now - for a time. In fact he was a little offended too, until he realised that he had been thinking about this mission for so long that there were parts of the idea that he had begun to take for granted. But he didn't quite **swallow** his pride. He drew himself up to his full, if rather diminutive, height (This is difficult from inside a shell but his neck was extended and his antennae stood up vertically, like tiny knitting needles.) and announced, dramatically "I'm a Travel Buddy!"

He sniffed and added... "I may be valuable (Extremely valuable)." "I may not come cheap...

...but I am not, repeat **not**, expensive."

After that it was plain sailing; or perhaps it might be said that George was flying... He explained that the "Buddies" were buying their air tickets soon and hopefully, arriving by the end of the month; one "Buddy" to go to each school - "After all, you can't expect me to do it all on my own!"

All of the "Buddies" have to attend an important Diplomatic Conference in South Molton, England, in the New Year, and would be able to return to Belize to report in full afterwards. The whole process would involve considerable dialogue involving many students in each of the two countries and because large numbers of students would be involved in Belize, the conferences there might affect the travel dates. George continued to explain that each "Buddy" will have the following items in his/her diplomatic baggage: a letter of introduction; his/her own official passport; a travel diary (which will contain notes describing his/her departure, and which can be added to during his/her stay); photographs of the school in England, the town, the local area and the students; student 'dossiers' (possibly to be used by pen friends); a set of stamped addressed envelopes which will be useful (George wonders how the English will put Belizean stamps on - which are much nicer anyway!); some small gifts for Christmas; information and artefacts from the local area in England; a tape containing a message, song, national anthem etc.; it was hoped to send a short video film but the frequency is different so there is a problem to be solved.

When George added that it was hoped that each "Buddy" would return safely with a Belizean colleague, each of the Principals could contain themselves no longer and thought that their "Buddies", too, would be very busy before making the journey to England with their new friend. They were especially pleased with the ideas coming from England about the ways in which the Belizean "Buddies" would be looked after and thought that the English visitors could expect the same sort of hospitality (George has often commented to me that Belizeans seem to be a very friendly lot, lively and much given to sport and music - especially Punta-Rock).

Well, that was not all. George was invited into the two Corozal schools straight away, to talk with the students, which he enjoyed very much. In fact it became more George listening to them. Now all they are waiting for is the arrival of the diplomats in each of the schools. You realize, of course, that I have to do George's writing for him because he makes such a mess on the paper. It looks as though he has crawled over it when he has finished, leaving an uncertain trail which bears little resemblance to writing. However, this shouldn't last long because he is learning to type which could prove very useful and a lot less work for me. Any way, he asked me to tell you that the ages and stages of the schools here are different. Primary schools start with five year old children as yours do but the classes are Infant One, Infant Two and Standard One in the First Division; Standard Two and Three in the Middle Division; and Standard Four, Five and Six in the Upper Division. Your Year Seven equates to Standard Five but students do not move on to 'High School' until they are thirteen. Two out of five do not go to High School at all.

Now, this second film records some of our own travels. It is by no means all of George's adventures to date - just the ones when he persuaded me to carry the camera. I expect you will hear about the other adventures eventually. George is very slow. Well, he is a snail remember... Also, he gets some of that from me!

Right at the beginning of the tape there are several shots of George. The first is George taking it easy in his chair on the balcony. You may not get this if you have not wound the tape back far enough. The second is of George looking out over the balcony rail at home, towards the North East. The third shot is taken South East but George is looking back the other way. After that the first sequence starts, taken on the 10th of October, 1997, when I visited Chetumal and stayed at the hotel Ucum. George was very comfortable there! This whole story is told in a piece called Shopping in Chetumal… The next sequence is of a visit to Double Head Cabbage with the Lions Club. The film shows some of the action which I will leave you to think about. Perhaps next time you go to the dentist or to have your eyes tested, you might think how lucky we are… George was amazed and wouldn't allow himself to be filmed at all in case he got involved in the proceedings… A walk around Orange Walk Town follows, beginning with a welcome. This was actually Garifuna Settlement Day when, I had been told, there was going to be a celebration in the town which was why I was out with my camera. The event didn't take place as it happened. In fact the town was unusually deserted, especially for a public holiday and so I was able to take some film quite peacefully… The last film, on the 20th of November, is of a March for Jesus followed by a mass at La Immaculada Church - or at least, in the grounds behind it…

We are certainly very lucky to be living here for a time - "Aren't we George?" …'

(On the 20th of November, I was also able to organise a workshop for Louisiana staff which would enable them to get their five Apple Mac computers going. I had been invited to attend, also. That would take place in January.)

Circular Walk around Yo Creek

I set off much later than I intended at 8:30am and set out along Guadalupe Street until I reached the San Antonio Road which starts by the Fire Station close to the park in the centre of Orange Walk Town and I am now walking straight out of the town in a westerly direction. I think it must be about six miles to Yo Creek and ten miles to San Antonio, once you have started on this road. I may not make it that far, even to Yo Creek. The longest walk I have done since coming to Belize three months ago is five or six miles in one go. It is not easy to get started: it is very hot, especially in the afternoons; it is difficult to determine which are the hazardous routes and places; and no-one I have met here seems to walk very much at all, except to and from work (although that could involve walking home to a village somewhere from the nearest bus route after a day's work). Also, I still attract a great deal of attention. My white legs, which you would call brown now, often the object of open inspection. But people are friendly in the main, and many will offer greeting or respond to mine.

It is a beautiful day; a clear blue sky; not a cloud in sight in any direction; just a hint of haze on the horizon, which is a slightly darker and duller blue. The horizon here being referred to as the imagined distance of the sky above the trees because the immediate solid horizon from my viewpoint just now, the land being so flat, is exclusively the tops of trees measured in distance from where I am walking, in mere hundreds of yards or less. The road has quickly given way from the tarmac of the town to something like that which I know as Murrum: a planed mixture of mud and stones which is raised from the ground around it and quite hard so that it resists the erosion of the rain. It is interesting to see here, the flowers at the side of the road. Even convolvulus is large flowered and deep purple, some being the more familiar white but with a magenta heart to it.

The road is paved again for a short length over a new bridge which was 'Constructed through the joint efforts of the Ministry of Works, The Government of Belize and USAID under the Rural Access Bridges Project, June, 1996'. The water under the bridge is very still here and there are many, many wading birds of the long-necked variety; huge white stork flying over and the smaller grey ones, the herons; other water birds that I don't recognise at all really. 'Must get a book' as they say. The large white water lilies with flowers not unlike a huge daisy having a brilliant yellow centre - prolific and in full bloom - in December! Enormous, brilliantly coloured butterflies flit to and fro and birds sing in the trees. Very long grasses grow beside the road. Heaven knows what is in them but there is certainly a lot of movement as I pass by. And one startled stork: huge, white and very close, rises sharply from a hitherto unseen position; it's neck making a graceful double curve of an 'S' in contrast to the hasty flight; a wonderful view. The other birds are beautiful too. One variety which looks distinctly like a woodpecker - and I believe there are lots of them - has a brilliant yellow breast against a grey back and black head and a cry which is just as startling. Everywhere is bright green as apparently it always is, but it seems to me to be even more amazing at this time of the year to see the brilliance of flowers in bloom, birds and butterflies in flight; some of the flowering trees having really exotic blooms with huge and intricate and extremely delicate shape and design.

An amazing peacefulness on what is considered to be the main road from the village of San Antonio into Orange Walk Town. Obviously quite heavily used at times. The drivers of vehicles, just as obviously, knowing exactly where the soft parts are after rain, which might prove hazardous, and establishing a firm alternative through constant use.

More of the woodpecker-like birds, closer to, reveal that there is a black stripe, arrow shaped, down each side of the head, with a black cap and snow white in between. A solitary vulture circles lazily overhead, no doubt alert for food. There are lots of them by the river in Orange Walk Town, gathering together from time to time, although the variety here looks nothing like as sinister as the vultures that are usually depicted in films. They do have the same shape in the air, with the same ragged end feathers to their wings and there is no doubt about their strutting walk, but their necks are shorter and almost completely feathered.

There are fields and plantations of sugar cane visible through the trees and many of the tall grasses beside the road as mentioned earlier are of the same variety. There are lots of hardwood trees here as well; there being a whole range in scale of cane farming interspersed, from the very small to the very large. Cane is a monoculture product and I am told, reliably, through the Belize Sugar Industries (Tate & Lyle) that there are no plans for this to change but the area of Belize under cultivation is really very small compared with that which is left to Nature and the Rainforest as well as that which is designated conservation area. I do believe that the only great ecological damage that has been done here, either on land or at sea, has been the massive use of mahogany - much of which either went to England or was shipped out by the English. Lots of mahogany trees are left though. There was one in the old cemetery just down the road from where I live which was cut down last week because it had some disease and was becoming dangerous. After it had been felled, the smell of raw mahogany was distinct and pungent. I have only ever smelled that smell that strongly before in an enclosed workshop when the wood was being worked heavily.

The road comes out of the trees for a bit after a while, where the ground opens out into scrubland covered in grasses and small bushes; some of which is used as pasture for grazing cattle, Two large fabricated buildings in open country to the left are constructed so that they look as though they are used for drying of some kind, or dry storage. There is still plenty of sugar cane visible. I think it may be Cuello in which case it could be where they make rum and sugar would be involved. It is also where one of the Mayan ruins is the subject of an archaeological dig and which is high on my list for a visit but that does require making some arrangement because it is on private land belonging to the Cuello family from which the site takes its name. The road becomes nicely paved again as it approaches Yo Creek; not that it makes it much different to walk on as the mud road has had time to dry sufficiently to make it comfortable since the heavy rain last night. There are a few little tiny balls of cloud floating about as the morning progresses and the sun continues to rise in the sky now, judging by the length of my shadow, at about forty five degrees already. The time is five past ten which means that I must be about four miles out. Shadows are as deep as the light is bright. The clouds looking like those little cotton wool things thinly scattered about, beautifully white and still. There is little breeze but that little is refreshing and pleasantly cooling. My own cooling system is working much better now. It certainly didn't to start with!

Just met Antonio Valencio who has pulled up in his pick-up truck and emerged with a machete in his hand - which is quite normal in these parts and he would be going to use it to control growth somewhere. Also he wears a cap with USDA on it - something to do with agriculture. So we exchanged greetings and names and shook hands as is the practice here, and I went on my way aware that Mr Max is a little better known and with the knowledge that there is a short cut to where I want to go, almost immediately to the left. But I decide to carry on into Yo Creek: partly because I want to go there; partly because I learn about the terrain best by walking in big circles before exploring in between; but mostly because the land which has gently risen from Orange Walk, dips quite markedly ahead (rising and dipping here is not very much!) and since this next village has such an interesting name, I want to know what it is all about - or at least begin to.

And so the walk continued. Unfortunately, the batteries in my cassette went flat just as I reached a beautiful little Mayan family clutch of homes nestling in a lovely group of trees and surrounded by a small and well-kept holding. The breeze wafted the smell of their cattle across where I was walking and I was strongly reminded of home in the high summer after very dry weather. Yo Creek was as attractive as the name implies. I found the right route but turned east too early after the village and ended up having to return, in part, the way I came. All that description will have to wait for another time. I must remember to carry spare batteries. I brought plenty of rechargeable batteries and it would be a pity to repeat the loss of use of the machine.

I returned home at 1:30pm after five hours solid walking with which I was mighty pleased, having covered some fifteen miles and having made a real start back into that important means of getting to know the country, tired but really quite pleased with myself as well as having thoroughly enjoyed the experience. It was eerie walking the narrow tracks through the cane field, aware of the huge number of snakes they harbour and hearing much movement in there. And the great hairy spider was very big but all that is another story…

In the midst of life I learned of the death of a young man I knew, serious boy-friend of a pupil of mine then at University and close friend of another also; and so another letter, most difficult, even though no words could help except to share a little through some of my thoughts even from Paradise and included here because with others his 'Being' impinged upon my life too, and now continues to do so.

Then a pleasant surprise though hardly less expected, also answered…

Dear Mr Mackie, Thank you for your letter dated 14th October which I have only just received. I thought the post to and from the UK was slow. Perhaps I should look upon that more benignly! To be fair, my mail has been rather following me around but now that I am in fixed residence for the remainder of my stay that should improve. That you are interested in offering me a teaching post at Ariel is very pleasing. I find the prospect of working in Zimbabwe very attractive. I should point out, however, that my present contract with the Belizean Government, through VSO, does not end until spring 1999. I trust that the summer of that year might be acceptable, should we go ahead. I would not wish to displace a Zimbabwean but I do have a few skills which would come at no cost in training so the Immigration Department there might look favourably on an application. I will make some enquiries. You may be interested too, in the work I am doing here which I will describe briefly. I came to co-ordinate the introduction of a new curriculum across two of the six Districts in Belize. This has provided the opportunity to become directly involved with this development along with staff and pupils in the schools. An exciting new perspective and challenge! In doing so and living here as the only VSO or Englishman, I find that I am able to get to know local families very quickly and have made many friends…

(Note that letters received are included as dated not as received and as such may appear out of step with the chronology of narrative.)

Children in the Junior School at home were just as eager to take part as those in year 7 at the Comprehensive School and quickly fell into the way of reporting news…
'…Is it a lot hotter in Belize than it was in South Molton? We have had a warm October with temperatures in the 15/16 degree in the day and no frost at night. November has been dry up to a few days ago but now it is raining. Dad was pleased with the different insect stamps you put on the letter. They have now gone in the family stamp collection. Are there a lot of insects where you are and if so, are they very different from our bugs? … I thought that to make my letter better I would write a little bit each day, telling you of events that happen each day…

That letter covered two weeks in detail; not bad for an eleven year old boy. I couldn't get children to write like that in school. Replies had to be just as enthusiastic of course; there were many and often additional to the linking progress in response to individual requests…

'Dear Budge, (That's how I used to say your name. Remember? - of course I do!) I am ever so pleased with your letter. It is the first of the ones coming from Mr Berry giving my address - note that I have a permanent address here now that I have found a house in Orange Walk Town where I am based for the rest of my stay in Belize. I'm glad you said you liked the video… I have another video ready to send which has some gory bits on it so watch out… I'm not at all surprised that school is going 'brilliantly well' or that you are enjoying it so much. I rather remember telling you exactly that before you went. There comes a time to move on in any case, as long as you don't forget where you came from… You have your pen friend and you should hear from him direct before very long… Lots of things are happening with the links with schools… George asks to be remembered to everyone. He finds the whole adventure rather overwhelming just now but he has asked me to write a few notes and the first story is finished and is in England. All will be revealed…'

December dawned as a new beginning in a way as more stability took hold over what in many ways had been lurching from one new experience to the next juxtaposed with the tranquillity of the periods of retreat. The various and so demanding areas of interest and activity were becoming melded into a whole; experience and sharing, sharing and experience; life and letters, letters and life. Of course, it was no less awesome, frantic almost, but life was no longer in separate boxes and the Journal became a much more cohesive record of what started as and always remained the unexpected: Who Can Tell? Stories and the journal of life became a constant flow in support of the 'links' and to friends at home, encouraged constantly by letters and interest in return although the letters are far too many to relate all but a few. There was something of a new beginning in my work too, the second one I suppose counting the move to Orange Walk, and this was marked on each of the two days 1st and 2nd December when I travelled to and from Belize City to assess outcomes with the whole team and make plans for the next stage; and happily catch up with Kathryn at lunchtimes for what became an enduring friendship. Kathryn was working in Cayo District to the West and Jayne was down south in Toledo. Jayne also became friends and remains so although she came home early.

I was advised by phone that a Fax had arrived at EDU, Belize City, from my home bank asking whether transfer of four hundred pounds should be made in sterling or $Bz. This was to cover the cost of the now essential desktop making it necessary to ask a colleague to send a Fax back asking for the latter. The story 'Dis is Where de Action is' was rewritten to replace lost text from an office computer and documents were finished to send to Paul. Money was tight so storage was limited to a pack of ten discs which I decided should be enough for all Belize documents - excepting any to be sent home. Money was tight, however, only because I had made it so by wishing to set up links and generally share the experience I was fortunate enough to have with those at home. The arrangement that VSO had with the Government of Belize (GoB) included the provision of a modest income based on local conditions to cover living expenses. This proved to be more than enough for my needs and together with other arrangements made during the total of three years placement enabled provision well beyond my expectations as will be seen later.

Two sugar cane Lorries (called trucks in Belize, as in US) parked outside next door for the night. I spent some time watching the antics of the local children helping themselves. The trucks are loaded to a height of about twenty feet and the cane held down tightly by heavy chains but this didn't deter children (as young as eight some of them I should think) from climbing on top and breaking pieces or pulling them out. One child of about eleven arrived with a machete! They would then drag off their spoil or strip it straight away and start eating the inside which appeared to break off easily. The message gets around very quickly so that a steady stream of youngsters came and went, making no effort to hide what they were doing and with no opposition even though my neighbours were in.

Every year in my old school, I had taken a group of children for a residential week of activities and visits to Fairthorne Manor in Hampshire and this had resulted in great friendship and my becoming an 'Honorary Staff Member' now adding to the communications…
   '…Here's a tee-shirt for you. I thought it very suitable - plenty of valuable images. This is a great conservation area - the whole of the Yucatan and especially Belize. Tell Peter and Tony and the 'gang' that they would have them too, if I could afford it. I will miss you all next year but it is great that SMUJS is coming again. One of the children wrote and told me. Look out for Jamie, James, Steven and Wayne (all friends together)… At this point, the proposed link I told you about with South Molton Community College is just taking off. (That is where the children go after SMUJS)…'
And writing to the college…
   '…Here is another tee-shirt emblazoned with Cancun to use as a prize. I hope you can use it. I believe it to be a more sensible size but I would welcome your comments for future reference. Cancun is a longish bus ride from here, in the north of the Yucatan in Mexico. It is a resort which Americans head for from all over the US, so probably out of my league but I understand it to be very conservation conscious (there's money in it!) and the street cred is good (excellent in America - just anybody who's anybody)…'

I tried sending that as an email as well but it came back again; also a letter typical of letters sent to many others…

'…What a super letter you sent! Well done! I enjoyed reading it very much. It is the next best thing to talking with you. I have been wondering about 'Sir' at the start of your letter and, well, it doesn't seem quite right written down. I'm sure you mean it as I always intended it to be - just the same as a Christian name - but people write 'Sir' in formal letters. In Belize, everyone calls me 'Mr Max' when they want to be formal because children are not taught to put their tongue between their teeth so they find my surname difficult to say (Something to do with Creole speech which I will tell you about sometime). I like that because it sounds friendly and it has helped me to become known with Belizeans very quickly. You could just use 'Max' if you wish (No-one can overhear writing!) but you must talk it over with your Mum and Dad first… Yes it is a lot hotter in Belize… It is also the rainy season but I find it very difficult to see it as such. When it rains it does so very heavily indeed - sometimes like being in an unlimited waterfall - but it doesn't usually last very long and then the sun comes right out again. It is very rarely dull and even then, not for long. Perhaps I will understand the difference more when I have lived through the dry season which I believe is your late spring/early summer… Even the trees, which are mostly deciduous hardwood, manage to hold on to their old green leaves while they are growing new ones. So the seasons are not distinct like they are in England. They are blurred; merged, one into the other, so that it will take some time for me to recognise them. Of course, that is not to say that it is better - only that it is different… I never leave pots unwashed, for example. Some insects are very tiny and some are huge but they all seem to run very fast. A lot of them are otherwise quite similar to English ones. I don't mind the spiders and I'm tolerant of most of the others - you don't see too many in the house, probably because I take care not to leave them anything to eat and I am in the apartment 'upstairs', off the ground. But I don't like cockroaches. They can be well over an inch long and they move like crazy - usually in an unexpected direction. It took me a while to be quick enough to dispatch the occasional one I see and I have no hesitation in doing it. I have seen one of those tarantula type spiders while out walking last Sunday. It was big but it was dead. The ants had got it and they were in the process of burying it. I reckon you would be very interested in all that…'

When I went in to Louisiana School one afternoon as arranged, there wasn't anything to do so I made arrangements to go in on a Tuesday afternoon in mid-December to talk with students about linking and to introduce George.

Mr Max heard a request played for him on a Belize local radio, Love FM, from staff and children of a school in Corozal. Two songs were played. The first was one which was currently very popular 'And when I die..... I keep on living'. The second was one of my favourites which I have sung with children so many times 'Make me a channel of your peace'. Then another letter came from Paul clearly showing by some repeat the frustration of what we eventually referred to as 'snail mail' and the lack of success with email…

'…Seven Drake have bagged the excellent letters from Calcutta School causing some excitement here! You will soon receive an envelope including their personal letters and other information. Your first package, however, will be from seven Grenville. They have addressed their letters to 'Dear Friend' so I will leave it up to you to choose their twin school. Seven Drake's package will arrive next (for Calcutta School), followed by similar packages from seven Hawkins and finally, seven Raleigh. They are all mixed ability groups but Raleigh is probably the most able, followed by seven Grenville. You may want to consider this when you choose your twin schools.

Each form package will contain the following items: a 'Travel Buddy' – 'Spike' from 7G, 'Uncle Albert' from 7D, 'Heffer' from 7H (not a mad cow though!) and 'Sunny' from 7R; a letter of introduction; a passport – I awarded Bobby the T shirt prize for his passport idea for 'Spike' (7G) along with his efforts with the photograph collection; a pupil profile for each member of the form; a collection of personal letters/Christmas cards from each individual; a diary. The first few days prior to departure of the Buddy have already been written. It would be a good idea if children in Belize could continue the diary during his stay; a collection of photographs of the school and town; miscellaneous small items to help paint a picture of the local area, e.g. tourist brochures etc.; a 36 exposure film for the 'Buddy' to use. I will get it developed on return to help with costs; and an audio taped message. In the first package there are a few Christmas cards for you (more to come!) and also some leads for your video camera. I have 'borrowed' these from school so please look after them! I hope they are suitable. I have also returned your first tape and await the sequel. I will make sure a copy is made of each tape for you and will save for your return. The video incompatibility problem was a real disappointment. Each form had planned and shot a short film to send to you. Never mind, I will arrange for a tape to be made on a mini-tape and perhaps you can make use of that. I'm not sure whether you want me to store the mini tapes for you rather than return them for re-cycling. If I have made a mistake I will make sure I hold onto *them next time. I have also enclosed the recent edition of the North Devon Journal. They ran a nice article for me and I think they might be interested in future coverage.*

One very important thing before I forget. I have been rushing to get work sent to you before Christmas and confess that a lot of it has not been corrected for spellings etc. If you have time, perhaps you could look over everything before it goes to the schools. Please explain this to the teachers – I wouldn't want them to think that I haven't bothered. I have been really pleased with the response from the children here and must tell you that they have completed all this work on their own initiative with only the occasional prompt and guidance from me.

Where do we go from here? Obviously our first priority is to establish a link between each form in South Molton and a school in Belize. Once we have achieved this it would be nice if four 'Buddies' from Belize could visit us. Perhaps they could escort the English 'Buddies' back home some time in the New Year. Once we have reached this stage the process should perpetuate itself. I have had a lot of interest from other departments and intend to get them involved in the future. I foresee packages of poetry, artwork, maths quizzes and so on. I am also very keen to develop the IT connection. I was very impressed with the contacts you have made – we must try to get the best out of this. It has inspired me to think about making use of the school governors and the local business community. In answer to one of your questions, the school email address is ***. I have not as yet received any email though! Remember that it will need to arrive here during school hours when our system is up and running! I will leave things there for now as 7G are pestering me to take them to the Post Office to get Spike on his way. I will try to write a more detailed letter for you in the next package (7D's work for Calcutta School). The one thing that I have yet to arrange is a group photograph of each form. I think this would be useful to allow children in Belize to relate to one individual…

It hadn't occurred to me that the school email system would only be active during school hours; yet another communication problem. Belize is six hours behind GMT and therefore seven hours behind in British Summer Time. To make matters worse I could only use email from the office in Belize City fifty-four slow miles away at that time and none of the Belize schools had computers, let alone email, so it would be necessary to soldier on with 'snail mail' – a difficult position to understand in the UK. The following day I caught the early bus to send a Fax to Paul telling him about the failure of the email, to do some printing and to check whether the money transfer had arrived in the bank - it hadn't.

A gift of food was sent round by Mrs Burns on Thanksgiving Day which is also celebrated in Belize - chicken with fried rice and beans and potato salad, which was delicious. I then walked about three miles round to the Alcosers' house but they were not in.

A Visit to Calcutta Government School

I went to Calcutta Government School for the day on Monday 15th December, leaving Orange Walk on the Chells bus at twenty past seven, having sat on it for half an hour without it moving. Part of the journey was quite unnerving because the bus seemed to be afflicted quite seriously with out of balance front wheels so that it shook from side to side at times. Also, like so many others, some considerable effort was made to compete with the Batty bus for fares along the way. When I got off, Chells was in front.

On arrival, I was greeted by a student shouting a welcome 'Mr Max'. It was a beautiful morning; birds singing and sun shining after a cold night. I was told that the temperature at dawn was 55 degrees - forty degrees less than the daytime temperature I have become accustomed to. The sky was absolutely clear and there was dew on the grass.

The day started outside with the flag ceremony and the singing of the National Anthem, as it does in all schools, at 8:30am. For some reason, numbers were down on this particular day although it is the start of the last week before Christmas. In Standard VI, where I was to spend the day, one child was missing out of a class of seventeen. (Such a small number is very unusual in Belize where classes up to fifty are not uncommon). Two interesting things happened which were dealt with by children without any prompting. First, the rope had to be run over the pulley at the top of the metal pole which is about twenty feet high. This job fell to Valmar who is thirteen. The pole was extremely slippery, being very smooth and covered with dew. It took some considerable effort. As the flag was raised, the rope became detached from the flag and Valmar had to go up again. At the end of the ceremony I was welcomed again and asked to speak to the children; an unusual event for the school.

It was a voluntary day in the oldest class to get to know the children and I had been asked to spend the time trying to enliven their composition skills. They have a tremendous amount of grammar and comprehension pumped in to them which is a sure killer of creativity to my mind, so I had decided on an easy approach designed to remove as many obstacles to free expression and sharing of thoughts as possible. Children are not used to such freedom or responsibility. The day in the classroom starts with prayers and singing. This was led by the Principal whose class it is, but each child is supposed to know when it is his or her turn to make a personal contribution. Billy, who is fifteen, mumbled in a way which could not be understood - after which, everyone said "Amen". This led to criticism before three recited prayers were said by the whole class (including 'Our Father') and two old Baptist hymns were sung to guitar accompaniment. This really gave me the lead in that I wanted to relax the class. We all sat down, close together as one group with no-one at any distance and all able to make easy eye contact. Billy's feelings were explored using my own outside when facing the school. It didn't take long! We were soon exchanging ideas about each other and I was able to use the few photos I had brought with me, reaching back over many years. After that I launched into 'Elephants Don't Sit on Cars' which has never failed and which was met with the usual enthusiasm given by children in England in such a different environment. I did give some explanation of details first, which might not have been understood and made sure the terms used were the same here (especially 'number twos'!). This was followed by 'Macavity the Mystery Cat' and a poem of my own called 'Doorway to Adventure'. Discussion of ideas for writing was centred on things that had happened to the children themselves that weekend, which they were able to tell everyone about. Ones that I remember were Solomon going to see his brother in Belize City and Valmar taking an engine out of a bus. Key words were then written on the board and the time up to break was taken up with making notes about their own weekend.

After break, children were asked to make similar notes for a composition called 'The Flag', which would be used to tell the story verbally, to the others. Without exception, the result was a description of the flag, its importance and its symbolism. No-one wrote any narrative even though the morning experience had been quite distinct and unique. The story of the morning flag break was explored and notes written before compositions proper were written after lunch. I did reward the class who had made a good effort at writing, with a reading of 'Dis is Where de Action Is' and after break in the afternoon we all had a go at an open ended maths challenge using quinqunx - familiar to children at home.

Next day six letters were posted and a letter and the second tape for year seven, to Paul; cards and most Christmas presents were bought including Mars Bars and marshmallows for Calcutta parties on Friday. Three youths came to wash the house which is painted timber, and renew some of the paintwork. A talk about linking and introducing George to the whole of Standard five in Louisiana School was successful although it was not easy standing in front of all 58 children while trying to engage with each one individually. Reaching a point of easy dialogue was pretty well impossible but the children visibly relaxed, were able to ask questions and talked in little groups or individually afterwards. I was invited to another Christmas party in Mrs Romero's Division 1 class on Thursday morning. A welcome phone call advised of an email that had arrived at the office in Belize City; Subject: 'Travel buddies, for attention of Max Grantham: First parcel posted last week - should reach you soon; another due to go today; third should be ready before Christmas, and the last one shortly after.'

Wednesday 17th December is the third day of the winter 'cool' period which came very suddenly and which is apparently quite a lot colder than usual and isn't expected to last long. The daytime temperature is down to 75 and Monday morning, which was probably the coldest, it was down to 55 at dawn. The night-times seem really quite cold because most homes, including mine, are rather open to the elements. The windows are closed only by ill-fitting, parallel boards forming slats about four inches wide. These are mounted on simple hinges in the centre of each end. There is also a bracket at right angles to each end of the boards which is linked with a wooden bar joined by a pivot made from a single, small nail driven through - into the bar. As I result I have been wearing what I would normally wear as walking kit in place of my pyjamas at night (I have no blankets or duvet). So it's a long sleeved sweatshirt, joggers and socks. There has been the first snow in Mexico for over a hundred years.

What has remained absolutely the same however, is the sunshine during the day. It is 7:00am and I am sitting out on the balcony having a cup of tea. Sunrise was beautiful. The sun is now slanting through, reaching under the balcony roof, through the open front doors and right across the inside of the house. It is not hot but, to me, pleasantly warm - certainly after another cold night. The dew is visible on the grass; the air is still; the sky is clear – a light blue; and the birds are singing. Coconut Palms and Hardwood Trees alike are stationary, as in a picture. A few people pass quietly by mostly on their own on their way to work, the occasional one riding a bicycle; children are on their way to the shop which opens very early; a mum with her daughter. Two children are using the water pump at the end of the street for their day's supply of water; the only disturbance of the peace being the grass cutting with a motorised strimmer which started early next door. It is only when water doesn't run fresh, clean and safe when you turn on a tap that you begin to realise how important it is and how much trouble it is for some people to have enough of it. This can happen at any time. I have found that drinking even very well boiled tap water results in almost instant and extremely unpleasant consequences. As a result of this, I only drink or cook with purified water bought in bottles. This isn't hugely expensive if you use the large five-gallon bottles because these can be reused. The first one costs eighteen dollars - including the deposit. Subsequent bottles are $3-75 (about £1) as long as you take back your empty one. Drinking purified water from small plastic bottles is almost as expensive as buying soft drinks. $1-00 for the water, $1-25 for a bottle of Coke if you drink it where you buy it and return the bottle and $1-50 for a bottle taken away.

I was expecting Chris to come up from the EDU in Belize City with copies of the work that the schools had done on their respective outcomes and to demonstrate the use of the computer for laying out tables so that all the work could be put on a common format. He did this but in the event Corinth, Geraldine and Vandley came too. We were able to spend a very pleasant morning and had lunch in a little Belizean restaurant that Vandley knows (and now I do) in Victoria Street in town. This was Chris' 'treat', a Christmas gift to each of us. He is leaving in February. While we worked on the computer, Corinth, Geraldine and Vandley went to Muffles College where Vandley had some business. They had to leave after lunch so that Vandley could attend a funeral but Geraldine phoned when they arrived and I had also been able to give them their Christmas cards and send one each to Daisy and Fidelis.

The Infant 1 party at Louisiana was very enjoyable and I was made welcome by teachers and children alike. Not knowing at all what to expect in the way of provision for children's food I took along a large pack of butter shortbread biscuits which were readily accepted. I needn't have been concerned that children would not have enough, however. I know that there are some very poor children in the school but there was no way one might tell. Children are always well turned out and as for the food - the generosity of parents who made the provision was wonderful. There were the usual biscuits and sweets but there was also a huge bowl of freshly cooked rice and beans, another of the wonderful potato (and heaven knows what else) salad they make here and another of fried chicken pieces; far too much really. So the party went on all day. Instead of break there was cake, coke and biscuits; at lunch time there was the feast and instead of the afternoon break there was a bag of fruit, biscuits and sweets for each child. And more drinks provided too! A distressing but very proper beginning to the day was the Principal calling the whole school together (this is always done outside as there is no hall) and telling the children of the absence of one of the staff who's very young daughter had lapsed suddenly, into a coma. The whole school joined in prayer. People here are very aware of the presence of God and children are no exception.

When we went in I was introduced and asked if I would 'do something'! I don't spend a lot of time with five year olds and I had intended observing before committing myself but it was obvious that delay would have caused disappointment so... thinking on my feet as happens so often in teaching we played the finger game which held the attention and concentration and was a lot of fun. You know the one I play - moving combinations of fingers, starting with the easy ones and getting harder and harder. It was just the same as being in front of 200 children in the Junior School. The reactions were just the same; the expressions were just the same; the gasps and the laughter were just the same; and some children used the other hand to put the fingers in place - just the same - until we used both hands together. 'Stop while you are having fun!' (You remember!) Which we did! After that we went straight into the story of Cecil the caterpillar. Cecil has never failed me - 'Cecil is my friend!' I did make sure that caterpillars are known (which they had to be because the butterflies are huge, brightly coloured and plentiful) also that they are known to eat leaves. The only other change made was to drop the lisp. There is enough difficulty with language without that. So it was Cecil not Thethil; leaves not leafths; trees not twees; and, clearly, sick not thick. It was one of the best performances yet - but a strange feeling, nonetheless. What a tremendous privilege and a surge of emotion deep inside, which is quite impossible to describe. They had games, of course. They danced to Punta rock music and had the 'jump-up' – 'Follow De Leeda'! They watched a video and competed for prizes. The only real differences from back home were the lack of resources and display in the classroom and that both the doors and the windows were completely open to the outside world. Behaviour too, was just the same. Some got it right, some didn't. They had their differences and sorted them out. And their voices are just as loud even though they are very well behaved in ordinary class lessons where they are not able to move about much; lovely children and a very friendly staff which makes such a difference for a guest, a foreigner, living as I do, closer to the school even, than I did in South Molton.

A Fax arrived from the UK bank advising that cost of transfer would be £15 and I asked Daisy to Fax back telling them to go ahead all by phone of course. A note came from the Post Office saying that a letter had arrived for me open and damaged. Would I go to Orange Walk Post Office to collect it? Proper identification would be required. And great joy via another phone call from EDU, another email… *received your letter with thanks. It seems we are now connected! Hopefully you will have by now received one package and there is one other in the post. The next two packages will be sent in the New Year. Don't forget the Christmas holiday runs from 19th December to 6th January so any email will not be read until the new term starts. I will send a longer message in the New Year.* (The Christmas delay in the UK would be nothing compared with the difficulty at my end.)

Friday was not quite the day I expected. To begin with I couldn't catch the 7:20am bus to Calcutta as I had intended because of going to the Post Office which doesn't open until 8:00am and didn't open until 8:15am. The letter was open. It was empty and it hadn't been sealed at all so there was no fault on the part of the Postal Service. Neither was there a sender's address so it couldn't be sent back. I checked when I got home because I knew the writing.

The bus left at about 8:30am and I arrived at Calcutta School about an hour later, to a chorus of greeting from children 'Mr Max!' a very pleasant way to arrive. However, it was all change since Monday. The children had their party yesterday and the staff one was to include the parents of the Parent/Teacher Association and wasn't due to start until 3:30pm. In the event, that didn't start until an hour later either but plenty happened in-between!

The change had been made to accommodate the distribution of reports and having interviews with parents in the morning and this was about to start when I arrived - to run from 10:00am to midday. My time was taken up with telling stories and singing songs with the children. Cecil found his mark again and everyone enjoyed 'Heads and Shoulders, Knees and Toes' which was also led by one of the older students after my performance and various ways were found to distribute the party goodies I had brought. I also had the opportunity to talk with parents which was nice. It all helps to feel part of it all.

At lunch time, I went with Orvin Rancheran and the Standard 2/3 teacher for lunch in Corozal. This involves dropping people off all over the place and finishing up in a pleasant eating place (restaurant) serving Belizean food. I'm afraid I went for the safe chicken, rice and beans and declined the cow's foot soup (which did look nice, except for the cow's foot!). We came out to find that the Chevy Van wouldn't start. That led to rushing around in a taxi and the arrival of a mechanic with a new battery and we were away - to A&R to buy a Christmas gift as part of the chain of gifts given at the party. (A Chevy Van is a bit like a VW Combi but very much bigger). We got back just after three. At the party, I was expected to perform - especially at the warm-up joke session - and told a couple of true stories including the one about the disappearing toilet roll which (literally) went down well. Then it was into the food (lots of it) and the party proper. I caught the six thirty bus after a very happy time in which I was treated as 'one of us' and left with invitations to visit families who live close by.

The weekend began with the buying of Christmas presents for the Alcoser family and the two Leiva families and Sunday turned out to be quite an unusual day. I walked over to deliver Christmas presents to the Alcoser family, to reach there for mid-day, and found Ricardo and his brother-in-law busy unloading a truck which Alberto, who lives in Corozal, had driven down from Chicago. I was able to chat and give them their Christmas presents; had a drink and talked to Marbella about computers. She told me that her brother-in-law might be able to help me to sort out my hard disc (a new problem) or would know someone that could. She phoned him right away and he was very helpful, saying that he would contact me later in the day - which he wasn't able to do, but that's the way it goes.

I was then asked if I would like to travel down with some of the Chicago goods which had to be delivered to Crooked Tree. Not an opportunity to be missed! So, off we went - and had a beer on the way down. We turned off the Northern Highway to go to Crooked Tree, a distance of about three miles and,

I would say, a very pleasant walk. A good part of the distance is a causeway across a great, shallow lagoon which is rich in birdlife and which forms part of the Wildlife Sanctuary. The drive across was a good way to see how the land lies. Apparently the birdlife has been much greater but was disturbed when the causeway was built without linking channels from one side to the other. The result was that one side dried up and channels had to be put in afterwards. The lagoon has recovered but the wildlife has not yet done so.

The village of Crooked Tree is populated by people whom Belizeans refer to as Redskins. This is because, although their appearance is very definitely Creole, their skin is white and their eyes blue. A direct result of mixing by the loggers who came from Scotland and lived in that area when timber was being felled for dye. A lady who cooks for Mrs Burns next door to me has a Scottish father and comes from Crooked Tree. She could well pass for a European at a glance. The name Crooked Tree apparently originates from a trio from the old days known as the Crooked Three (pronunciation?). This I found out after looking out for an arboreal twist.

The regular way of delivering goods - and these were great packages and boxes, heavy things - most packages being cardboard boxes about three feet by two feet square or perhaps a little bigger. The regular way is to drive up to the entrance to the grounds of the house, once you have found it, and shout the name of the person to whom the parcel is addressed. As it was afternoon and if the addressee happened to be male, he would be having his siesta and only a great deal of encouragement would move him in most cases; not the only way the village seemed very detached from the world. Several deliveries were made and quite a bit of argument ensued because one truck on a previous delivery had been impounded by the Mexicans about twelve months ago and had not been released. So Alberto, who is about forty thousand dollars light over the matter, was in the hot seat.

The trees are amazing. The breadfruit and particularly the almond trees for which Crooked Tree is well known are very beautiful and full of fruit even just before Christmas. There are mangos and coconuts of course, all sorts of fruits including the citrus varieties, and plums; no shortage of fresh supplies at all. Everywhere is wonderfully green; there is clean, clear air, bright sunshine, shimmering water, no litter and the people are friendly when they choose to speak. We returned, having first travelled a little further south to make a delivery on the main road and I was brought back home - although pressed to go back and have a meal with the family.

When I reached home, I found the children next door very keen to have a party in the grounds downstairs - which of course, I am very pleased for them to do but the scale and organisation of it was really quite unexpected and very remarkable. It was Alexander's tenth birthday which seemed to be combined with a get together of the whole of Standard Six from La Immaculada School who are Nelson's friends. There were a lot of them when they arrived. It took a long time to get started as most things do here. I had to take a few photographs to record the event.

My house overhangs the bit downstairs fairly considerably and they had used the whole of that space to house their party and had closed it off from casual observation with blankets and things. They had set up a table and chairs and made a bar around the corner where they served soft drinks. "We are children. We don't drink rum!" I was told. I countered by explaining what stroking the chin meant back home. The music came from that area too. The two lights underneath my part of the house were wrapped in coloured paper and turned on to make subdued lighting and the whole place was decorated with palms from the coconut trees. It was very attractive, very lively and went on until half past eleven but was no trouble at all. They were polite children and happy to include 'Mr Max' from time to time.

In the early evening I phoned Neria Leiva and found after some conversation that I was expected to go down and stay with them tomorrow and possibly not come back until the 29th or 30th. Tomorrow is Marco and Miriam's joint birthday and they would like me to be there. The idea is then to stay for Christmas and travel down to Punta Gorda on Boxing Day to stay with Mayan friends for a wedding. I finished getting together the Christmas presents and birthday presents, cleaned up around the house and got ready to go to Belize City, took a card down to the San Estevan bus for Chino to deliver to my friends there, visited next door and had a very pleasant chat with Landy Burns. I was given drink and as we sat I watched him preparing apple and a huge tangerine which turned out to be for me. This is quite the norm for hospitality round here. I asked if the box could be checked for mail before I leave. (Unfortunately Elizabeth was unable to do this although she offered to drive down with me as I left. I didn't think that would be right as she was so busy, so I declined).

Fidelis phoned this morning to ask me to contact Margarita who, in turn, told me that there had been a reply to my email so at least the contact is established 54 miles distant. There were several cards waiting for me in the District office when I called in before going for the bus: one from Louisiana Government School and three from home. I then went down to catch the Batty bus which left at 4:30pm and was able to sit on it right away and read my mail which was nice. The journey down was extremely pleasant except for those parts where I was thinking about the cost of riding on the Batty bus which is 50% higher than everybody else's when going in the opposite direction at the same time; all to do with Government franchise and political favour. I arrived at the Leivas to a warm welcome just before six and was shortly joined by their relatives from San Estevan and Orange Walk Town. These are Neria's younger sister Benito with her husband Pedro and daughter Daiami and the youngest of her family, her brother Raoul, his wife and their mother. The evening was spent with the usual barbecue with rum and coke to celebrate Marco's and Miriam's joint birthday. The barbecue was not chicken but kebabs which were very nice. I went to bed about half past twelve in the room next to the one which I occupied when I first came. The only bit of bad news was really upsetting for those involved. The couple whose marriage was to have been the object of our all going down to Punta Gorda on Boxing Day have postponed the ceremony because of the death of the Groom's father.

I didn't get up until seven o'clock, had a lazy breakfast and a lazy start to the day but then went out with Pedro. We went into Belize City and had a super look round all the stores which I haven't really been able to do before. It was very pleasant to be able to walk around without being accosted because I was with a Belizean although he told me afterwards that he had suffered some unpleasant remarks about being with a white man. Invariably, these remarks are made by Creoles of African descent although that is not to say that it is more than a significant minority of them. It is troublesome though, unpleasant and counter-productive for all. I managed to get a diary for next year and some E45 cream as well as three sets of stamps for James and his family which I know they will be very pleased with.

While we were out, in the market, I got talking to a Belizean who owns Paula's Gift Shop and who does an awful lot of crochet. We talked at great length about ways in which people could help with craft in schools, which she is doing. I wondered whether there might be ways in which I could help this along and join it in with the work that I am doing, linking with SMCC. Anyway, we exchanged telephone numbers and quite a lot of useful information. Also, her family make lovely carvings and sculptures out of zericote (a smooth, black hardwood which is very good for carving) and cow horn. They live in Ranchito, close to Corozal, where Orvin Rancheran lives so it shouldn't be too difficult to make sure I have got plenty of gifts and souvenirs to take back, of the sort of thing that I like. We returned home by about five o'clock, had a meal and went out to watch the lighting of the Christmas 'Tree' erected on the Belcan Roundabout. The ceremony was performed by Prime Minister Escavel and the proceedings were conducted by the presenter from Love FM. They do like to make speeches which are long and don't say very much. Also the sound system was giving quite a lot of problems so that most people couldn't hear the various choirs and groups and bands. At the times when you could hear, it was being swamped out by Love FM's normal programming which seemed to hit the speakers at the same time so that the wait for the lights to be switched on was rather tedious. But everybody is very patient. They just stand and wait and listen and keep quiet. The 'tree' looked very effective when it did light up. The lights came on in seven stages starting with a set of blue lights shooting up through the centre; some large baubles of the sort you would put on a Christmas Tree but lit from the inside; a tree outline in lights; two progressive stages of rings of lights going up the 'tree'; a drape of fine lights to represent Angel Hair; and finally, the crowning piece - a shooting star. Quite imaginative - especially in the dark - as there is no tree! The whole assembly was mounted on a huge telegraph-type pole set in the middle with the conical drape around it set on wire ropes. Afterwards we all came back and spent the evening in pleasant conversation oiled by the 'Caribbean' rum. A film was made for year 7 along with linked text…

Belize City - Christmas 1997

The first part of the film shows the Christmas tree in Belize City; a Christmas tree but not a Christmas tree; a tree with all the lights and the decorations but no tree; an interesting challenge for the person who designed it! The shape of the tree is created by the lights; the rings of lights; the 'angel hair' glistening - also in lights; and the star on top with its trail of lights. These were lit in seven stages on the previous night. Some of the stages are shown in the photographs taken at the time. The only other Christmas lights I could find for you, close to the family I was staying with, was Barclay's Santa Clause; very commercial. In fact a lot of private houses are lit in a more extravagant way than even the brightest ones in England; more so, even, than that little group of houses on the Exeter road, just past the old Kings Nympton Station.

In Orange Walk, many houses were lit with hundreds of flashing lights (if only I had filmed them). The people next door to me in common with many others had the Nativity figures about half life-size and made in plastic, brilliantly lit from the inside to show the bright, rather gaudy colours. It is a great celebration. Orange Walk also had a real tree in the town square, which was about the size of the one in South Molton. It was richly decorated and illuminated from all directions as well as having coloured lights.

Belize City had no tree. I understand that the City Engineer was given the task of 'coming up with something' at the last minute. I thought the result to be very imaginative! The coloured baubles were made from hundreds of plastic cups stapled together with the insides facing outwards so that the cone of the cups created a ball shape. Their colour is simply paint. The 'sticks of rock' were made from plastic water pipe with a bend fixed on the end and painted in a spiral to give the right effect. You might like to try it next year and send pictures to Belize!

Just a taste of Christmas with the younger half of the family I was staying with: Miguel and Mariami give their interpretation of what passes for music - which I may say, is neither better nor worse than yours! Upstairs, with the senior part of the family, the scene is rather quieter; another Christmas tree, more lights and their crib. It is interesting to hear the fireworks. Fireworks (or at least, bangers - firecrackers) are let off at all times from around the middle of November through to the New Year. This takes in Thanksgiving, Christmas and the New Year. (Back at home in Orange Walk the walls of Mr Max' house are covered with Christmas cards, some of which some of you would recognise. George certainly enjoyed a good read.) Next we are off to the zoo which needs no description here. George was rather thoughtful and finally decided that this was the best zoo he had ever seen and if all zoos were like this one he could grow to like them. Maybe the story will turn up later but for now…

"Well," thought George on yet another bright, clear, sunny morning with a pleasant cooling breeze coming off the Caribbean Sea, "This is a turn up for the books; a snail going to the Zoo; I'm not sure that's wise at all! It is much better to curl up in a nice shady wall and sleep a while." Now his new friend, Pedro, was anxious to show him the wonders of this particular Zoo and, to be fair, George had heard something about it and had become very curious. Really, the only thing that worried George was that he didn't think zoos were generally the sort of place any animal would want to go - least of all a snail. And in a way it was exactly that idea that made him want to go. He had heard that some very special animals actually **wanted** to be there.

Apparently, back in 1983, there were 17 animals left over from the filming of a natural history documentary and no-one quite knew what to do with them. They'd had too much to do with humans to be sent back to their proper home so somewhere safe had to be found.

To reach the bus stop, we went over the Belize River, across the Belcan Bridge, and along the American Boulevard - turning right - out on to the Western Highway. That would be the point at which to catch the bus but George and Pedro decided to walk out along the Highway across the Cemetery and on until eventually a bus came along. They did wait for the last ten or fifteen minutes as they were now clear of houses at mile 3. The bus was a Z line (bound for Dangriga) which was superior to the Batty bus they returned on yet their charges were $2 and $3 respectively, even for a snail. It happens here as well! They were dropped off nicely at the Zoo where they were able to go in for $15 each (free for George if he had stayed) and given a very clear map to follow so that they didn't miss anything. They came out when they had seen all but the birds, to have some lunch. Rice and beans for Pedro and a hot dog for George, each with a soft drink. They went back in again to complete the visit which finished in the new Gerald Durrell Visitor Centre where the snakes and tarantulas are housed. There is also a display of skeletons including the big crocodile and the skin of the small American Crocodile all arranged as a 'do you recognise this' quiz with answers in a folder. The skeleton of a Manatee hung from the ceiling and two photograph albums were on display, describing the origin of the Zoo and the development of the new site in pictures. They set off back at about 3:30pm and got back home at about 5:00pm. George was very quiet thinking – yes that is a story to be told in time.

I surfaced on Christmas Day just after Marco and Miriam and the children who didn't get up themselves until half past eight. I lay and listened to the present opening which I didn't like to interrupt and emerged at nine o'clock. Any alcohol this morning, I firmly rejected!

After a very happy family day I returned to Orange Walk on the ten o'clock bus, travelling with Pedro, Benito and Daiami who were going on to San Estevan. Tabo and Neria are going there tomorrow and wished me to go with them or for me to go on there today as well, but I decided it was time to come home. I collected my post and settled down.

Tuesday was another lovely sunny day after what passes for a cold night here. It wasn't warm and I slept under just one sheet (now having got one!) The street opposite the house leads down towards the river, down to Palmar Road on which I am now walking, having decided that the morning is far too good to waste indoors and walking is so pleasant today. It is rather like a typical summer's day in England; cooler than usual. A gentle breeze stirs the palm trees; the odd tree displays an autumn red in someone's garden but it may always be that colour. Most trees are green, some are in flower and only a few noticeably lose their leaves. I pass Javier's Little Place which is a small eating place (Belizean fast food) standing in front of Javier's Little World which is the last shop in Orange Walk in this direction. Next to come across is the Orange Walk Branch of the Belize Ex-Services League, marked by an arrow which points along a 'street' going off to the left towards the river. I must go down there some time. (The idea of a street mustn't be confused with ours - or even those further in town. Here it is hard packed mud and stone, narrow, yet seeming spacious and with the dwellings widely spaced along each side and standing well back). On the right is what looks like an orchard but instead of apples, they have some orange trees and four coconut palms - fringed along the edge of the road with a row of flamboyan trees which have leaves not unlike rowan leaves and hung all over with huge, black seed pods up to fifteen inches long. A notice says 'Welcome to San Hosea Nuevo Palmar' just where the road passes the hut used by the Rotaract Club and the first shop here, which is Dorita's Mini Super.

People are very friendly indeed. I was about to say that more people are offering greeting as I am getting to be known. It makes so much difference to be able to talk to people casually and I have had really good conversations on previous occasions when I have come through here.

There is a big sports field, quiet now except for the domestic sounds coming from the houses scattered widely around it. The dense rainforest is clearly visible close by on the other side of the river. It seems somehow, strange to see eight floodlights on very large telegraph-type poles, standing sentinel over the playing field. A full size soccer pitch occupies most of the field, not Wembley turf and only minimally marked out but no doubt used with just as much excitement and enthusiasm.

Coming out of Palmar, the thinly spaced houses of the village become even more spread out and more traditional in construction. Another small lane leads off to the left which I must explore sometime. A hawk circles lazily, overhead. The narrow road, paved with tarmac this far, gives way to packed, soft limestone which makes an effective surface, laid so that the water runs off, although it can be quite rough. I have no doubt that it floods in places at times too. The rain can be very heavy indeed even though it doesn't usually last very long.

The birds are singing; although the birdsong is not so melodious here as it is in England - not by a long way. I wonder why that is? I must also find out why so many trees on people's property have their trunks painted white to a height of about six feet. It must be something to do with insects but what sort and how it works I can't imagine. There are a lot of termites here, which build huge nests which can be seen in the trees from hundreds of yards away. I am told that they can destroy a house in a matter of weeks. I always thought that termites were rather like ants but they are not at all. They are very small and they are what the name implies - mites. I suppose you could say that any timber they choose has its existence terminated but perhaps that is carrying it too far. I must look it up along with all the other things.

The road leads out on to the Northern Highway, South of Orange Walk Town. I am just turning on to the highway to walk south with the idea of exploring a short circuit on the West side. That is the road on which I intended to return from Yo Creek a while ago, when I took a left turn too early and came back out on to the road where I had started out.

You have to be a bit careful to avoid lonely places which run through cane fields because there are muggings which are usually drug related. I listen to the locals and then have decisions to make because some are much more fearful than others, ranging from 'Stay in the town' to 'the routes to places like Yo Creek are okay'. Of course there are people about when the cane trucks are going back and forth and roads to the large villages do have some traffic on them. I don't like walking on the Highway - there is too much traffic - but I haven't got to go very far. Just now, there is very heavy traffic with a lot of trucks heavily laden with cane on their way to the factory, which I can see not far away, and returning empty for another load.

The Northern Highway, in common with the other two developed major roads in Belize, was built through the British Crown Agents in the Colonial days which ended in Belize, sixteen years ago. The road is only wide enough for a single line of traffic in each direction but it is built to a very high standard and is held as an example by the local people who are not too happy with some of the roads that have been built since.

The road west is soon reached. It is located directly opposite the entrance road to the sugar factory and according to the map, leads directly to the road from Yo Creek to Trinidad - not that I am going that far today. The first part of it is very wide because it is used as a sort of holding area for trucks loaded with cane, which are waiting to go into the processing plant. Some of these arrive directly along this road because there are a lot of cane fields here. But it is wide and there are a reasonable number of vehicles about. Five great egrets are lined up on a little bank here, between the roadside and the cane field to my left. As so many birds do, they wait until I am within about ten yards and then fly off a little way further ahead to settle again. It always amuses me that all they need to do is fly upwards until I pass and then drop back down again - proof, perhaps, of having no concept of the future. But, now, they have taken the next stage which is to perch about a quarter of a mile along the road. The whole of the road along here - which is straight, as most roads are in Belize - is strewn with remnants fallen from trucks loaded with cane; brown-dried by the sun and not looking at all out of place as litter might - rather the opposite, softening the glare of the soft grey-white stone of which the road is composed.

There is what appears to be a thin grey cloud in the distance but this is actually smoke - not an environmental threat with so much air space, but the result of burning off some of the dead material around the cane as it is harvested. This is done to reduce the snake population and make harvesting safer. There are a lot of snakes in Belize. I believe there are fifty-one varieties of which seven are poisonous, including the much feared Tommygoff. The Tommygoff is a pit-viper growing to an enormous size, capable of jumping in the air and from trees, and able to inflict a fatal bite almost from birth. I have become very conscious of snakes and look about the ground very much more than I ever have before.

Now I am at the crossroads on the Orange Walk to Chan Pine Ridge road, which is what I have been looking for. I turn north here, back in the direction of Orange Walk where I expect to re-join the Northern Highway just before the outskirts of the town. Dragonflies and butterflies flit about here, even at the end of December; and many of them.

The road runs clear of the cane fields for a short distance, crossing open scrub before disappearing into woodland. There are a few medium sized trees of surprising variety; more to the left than to the right. Maybe the space to the right has been used for growing cane. I know that new strains are under continuous development and this is still not far from the factory. Maybe the land is rested from time to time but it certainly isn't a case of growing and moving on. There are very strict conservation regulations in Belize which is still about 70% natural rainforest. There are a lot of brimstone coloured butterflies in this particular spot which is otherwise not very inspiring this side of the woodland; and now a huge, deep orange butterfly with a clear black outline all around the edges and pretty amber flowers growing by the roadside. There is no one else walking, of course but I'm used to that. A couple of bicycles have gone by, probably cane workers, and a few cane trucks.

Up ahead I can see the very distinct transmitter mast in Orange Walk Town. These masts are extremely thin but they are very high and painted orange and white so that, from my point of view, they make a useful landmark. It is always comforting to know that you are heading in the right direction! Now I'm back to the trees and a much more pleasing aspect although I have reached the Northern Highway sooner than I expected at the end of my walk and the last leg home.

Ricardo (Richard) Alcoser arrived at about 5:30pm driving the big Dodge and accompanied by a Venture Scout from the Mexican Yucatan who spoke no English but the Scouting handshake is universal. Richard had brought a Christmas gift from the Alcoser family which they had but not wrapped when I went to see them before Christmas; a very touching gesture in a new country which pleased me very much. It is a wooden key hanger cut in the shape of a key and made from mahogany which has been black-japanned and a map of Belize painted on it in red, yellow and blue. I put it up on the wall straight away.

A little later on, just after I had discovered that the computer had broken down completely, Geraldine called for a chat which was a very pleasant interlude and came at just the right time. Not long after, Susan called for the same reason and to ask about her friend who is coming on voluntary service from Canada - as the third VSO on our team. She also wanted to arrange a visit to Orange Walk when we can go out to lunch.

It was a cold night after New Year's Eve last night with the inland temperature down to 45 degrees F but I had made sure that the windows facing south in the bedroom had been open all day, picking up the heat from the sun so that I was able to manage with a sheet over which I put a large bath towel doubling as a thin blanket and another sheet (luxury!) doubled over on top - and slept in jogging kit rather than pyjamas. This was all warm enough but very necessary in the small hours. In this respect, sleeping in most of the houses here is no better than sleeping in a tent; worse perhaps, because a small tent will hold the body heat of the person sleeping in it. There is little to prevent heat loss from windows having only the ill-fitting wooden slats in them. The only heat present is the latent heat collected during the day and retained in the fabric of the building.

And so… here's to a new year…

More Beginnings
I had intended going to the midnight Mass to see in the New Year but I didn't have anyone to go with as it turned out, and the knowledge that the church would be packed and that all sorts of revelries would be taking place in the town late at night, parts of which are best avoided, I decided to stay in and listen to it on the radio. Unfortunately it was punctuated by the inevitable fireworks round here, which are really very tiresome, illegal and which no-one makes any attempt to stem; a situation in which I can hardly interfere. Most of the letting off of fireworks is done by children who are very much under age. But the arrival of the New Year was also punctuated and marked afterwards by huge bangs such as one might hear in quarry explosions and which must have taken considerable preparation. I've always thought making big bangs to be rather childish when there is no other purpose to be served.

   I got up just before seven; had a leisurely breakfast; cleaned around a bit; rescued a huge spider from the bath, about which I am a shade more timid than usual but I can't kill them. I did, however, destroy a wasps' nest which I found being built on the veranda rail which had reached about two inches in diameter and was not where I was prepared to let it stay. I did this with what is used as a sweeping brush but which is more like a yard brush here. This has very long, extremely stiff bristles arranged in a kind of fan and which I don't use about the house. I don't get on with them and use the regular type of brush that we use at home. When I phoned Marbella to thank the family for my Christmas present I was able to tell her the sad story of the breakdown of my computer. She will discuss it with her brother in the morning with the intention that he will contact me tomorrow afternoon. Today, they are all off to Belize to visit relatives. They offered to take me but I declined. I don't want to get in the way. Later I walked to a point about half a mile beyond Victor's Restaurant to which I had been with Chris, Corinth and Geraldine a few weeks ago. That was where I feasted on Gibnut, known as 'Royal Rat' because it was served to the Queen on her visit to Belize. Victor's Restaurant is on the fork from the San Estevan road. Then I walked on to the next fork, which was a total of about six miles. This road isn't marked on the map at all and I was surprised to find that it forked again. I decided to return and find out a bit more about it before going on any further. On passing Victor's again I asked someone standing by the side of the road who told me that the way I had found goes to 'the camp'.

   I returned back through the town where I met the Belizean from Palmar who told me about the Flamboyan Tree. He offered greeting and made to remind me who he was, which wasn't necessary, but his main purpose was to ask for a dollar. So far, I have resisted this completely but his story about having to visit his family in Crooked Tree did hang together. The fare was three dollars and he already had two. Also, he freely admitted that he was drunk (I had already noted that his left eye was bloodshot). So I broke my rule, gave him the dollar and went on my way; a little saddened now, that just maybe the whole episode could put up a barrier which I could do without.

Jan phoned to say that she would like to come over tomorrow and stay for a few days and bring her walking boots - so that looks like an interesting interlude just at the right time with the computer having broken down. It was odd that I should have gone the way I did this morning as it turned out. After lunch I went round to see Landy to give him this month's cheque for rent and also to say that Jan would be coming tomorrow - so as not to alarm anyone!

Landy and I went to Honey Camp Lagoon with the boys and three of their friends to his piece of land by the lake where he has a deer, two dogs, a pony and a keeper who lives on the site; also a building which has two bathrooms and a store with a thatched picnic area over the top. The route was across what is known as Doubloon Bank but which (certainly just now) is a shallow lake and where the track goes across it, there are three very large pipes allowing water to drain from one side to the other where it makes its way through Doubloon Bank Lagoon and Button Lagoon and on into Freshwater Creek - there being no surface water running in! Honey Camp Lagoon is a beautiful lake, also with no surface water running in. The boys went in swimming although it was cold and it rained while we were there. I was offered the use of it any time and also the use of a motorbike to get there. Landy treated us all to rice and beans with chicken and coke at Victor's on the way back. This was the same route as I was wondering about. Apparently the same track eventually reaches Sarteneja and passes through the Shipstern Nature Reserve alongside the Shipstern Lagoon. That must be quite a drive and certainly very rough country but Landy is determined to do that one day and has offered to take me with him - perhaps even camping overnight.

Letters to write – by hand…

'Thank you very much for your letter, Christmas card and present. The Toblerone is in the fridge, partly to keep it cool and partly to keep it out of sight so that it will last. Your Mum and Dad will understand that. I haven't quite used up Wallace and Grommit yet either. Tell your Mum it wasn't goodbye when I came away and I knew that. I couldn't possibly do what I am doing now without the support of my friends at home.

Yes, I am very well settled thank you. The house is fine; the neighbours are friendly (their four children are in and out sometimes and meals have been sent in on special occasions) and people are beginning to speak to me around the town much the same as in South Molton.

Of course, I am getting to know a lot of other children as well. I have six schools to go in to for work… George (my Buddy) went in with me to introduce the whole idea and he is very excited. I think you met George the Snail before I left. You certainly know of some of his adventures! He is having adventures all the time now and some of them are turning into stories… I watched an army of ants burying a dead tarantula for a later meal the other day…'

'Dear Max, It was great to read your news in Scoutlink. I had no idea of your address. Since resigning as ACC and not being involved at Group or District level, I am rather cut off!

Belize sounds very interesting but I'm sure things must be strange to you. Obviously Devon Scoutlink space does not allow for a full story of your activities but I hope your work is fulfilling and that you are keeping well… Have you come across anyone who knows Father Alec Tatnall? As far as I know he was in Belize for a number of years. I knew him while he was in Exeter as priest at Livery Dole Alms-houses in Heavytree. During this time he was involved with 2nd Exeter and Exeter District. The last time I met him was when I went to the Gilwell Reunion five or six years ago and he came across to see the Devon contingent…'

I phoned Marbella's brother, Armando about the computer on Friday and met Jan off the Batty Bus at about 1:00pm. She was an hour late as the bus had had a puncture. We walked around the town and then went to see the Alcosers and spent the evening with them chatting and drinking rum and Campari until 2:15am. The morning was wet and we lost quite a lot of time but finally went to Corozal, returning at about 4:00pm. We wandered around the town and the seafront, meeting quite a few interesting people including fishermen and two boys who wanted to know if Jan was my wife ("Well, your sister , then?") there were a lot of birds to see including Frigate Birds. After having lunch in a little cafe for $2:50 each (about 80pence) we went in to St. Francis Xavier Church which is quite remarkable in having an imaginative use of concrete and a wonderful, life-size carving of Jesus on the Cross. Armando came at about five o'clock and the computer was fixed late in the evening after which we continued the previous evening's activity until about 1:30am.

Jan went about midday on Sunday and Armando came round again to see if the computer was okay and to check if an elephant pendant was here as he has lost one (It wasn't). We had a long discussion about linking and the possible result and the ways in which he and Belize Sugar Industries could help; also about education in Belize.

Two meals were sent round from the Burns family at about 2:00pm together with my mail (A Christmas card from Fairthorne; a note from Barclays confirming the transfer of money from the UK; and a note from the Post Office advising the arrival of a parcel). I gave them the photos I took on the night of Alexander's Birthday.

The first working week began when I phoned the EDU from the Orange Walk District office. Ellajean, the Director, asked if she could phone back - at home (she didn't). I had wanted to leave a message for Margarita but she wasn't in so I had to phone from home later in the day to ask for floppy discs for Windows 3.11 and the password to get into the system. It was no greater success when I tried to collect two parcels from the Post Office. The official note sent asked for proper identification which means my ID card which I presented. I was then told that the parcels 'could not be released' because of 'Duty'. I explained that I do not pay duty - being VSO (also that the contents had no commercial value and were for Belizean schools but this made no difference) and was then asked for proof. There was nothing on the official note asking for such documents and nothing to say that a number would be required. Phone calls were made to the Head Postmaster in Belize City but to no avail. There was nothing for it but to return for my copy of the agreement between VSO and the Belizean Government. This was not accepted either. This because it doesn't have a number on it, despite having been signed by the appropriate minister and clearly stating that duty did not apply. I stood my ground and after three more calls to Belize City the parcels were released with the explanation that Belize City Post Office had my name on a list but had not sent it to Orange Walk. All that took two and a quarter hours and I was charged a $1.00 'handling fee' for which I insisted on a receipt. Small change but I intend to have that refunded and not to disappear into someone's pocket.

The parcels were exciting and I made immediate arrangements to take them for Mrs Elda Vega, principal of La Immaculada School to see. I hadn't actually been working with La Immaculada School and I wanted to bring the enthusiasm on to an equal footing in all four participating schools. To some extent this will have to be done with Louisiana and St Paul's as well because this parcel is for Calcutta School and I have spent most time with them as well as their having written letters to SMCC already. One parcel contains replies.

The rest of the day was taken up with a visit to the library and obtaining an application to join. There seems to be a good number of books I would read. Unfortunately, I didn't have my wallet with me this time and of course my ID card is needed. Also, I started catching up with letters already written and journal recorded while the computer was down before making a set of new discs for each of the groups of writing I anticipate doing - including curriculum. Work at the keyboard continued into the next day also including setting out the work my six schools had done on 'Outcomes' in chart form on disc, finishing 'Carmelita' and the format for the other five.

'Dear Max, Happy New Year! First of all thanks for all the letters – brilliant reading! You really ought to compile these into a book at the end of your stay. I hope by now that you have received two 'Buddies' – here is number three! The final package will take another week or so. As before, I have not corrected any of the work. Please explain this to the teachers concerned. Also, I have not listened to the audio tape – perhaps it would be wise to check this yourself. I was given two chocolate bar prizes to include but thought it best not to send them. Could you come up with some replacements please? Everything is rather rushed again! But I really want to speed things along and get things up and running. I have received your email letter – first class! I would like to know if you have received my messages. If this link can be confirmed it can be used regularly. Thanks again for the letters – can't wait for the Buddies!'

'Dear Friends in 7D, I have just received your two parcels for Calcutta Government School (posted 16th December. That is good for a variety of reasons which I will explain sometime. Allow two weeks each way, normally).

I can tell you that opening the parcels was quite an emotional experience as I know so many of you. Also, it is breaking new ground and I know the young people here pretty well too. I can't wait to see everyone when school starts again next week but there is a lot that I can do with all you have sent before then. It will be seen by the Chief Education Officer, the two District Education Officers and the Principals of the other three schools as well as yours. Calcutta Principal, Orvin Rancheran, is a particular friend. I need to do all this to gain as much support as possible and I have already 'launched' the idea with these people as well as others. One of the big problems is funding and providing resources for the schools, which you take for granted. I have been working hard on that (as well as the people mentioned). As soon as the link can be demonstrated and be seen to be working, Belizean friends I have made in the sugar industry and the Rotary and Lions Clubs tell me that funds can be made available. They have helped me a lot already. Primary Schools here go up to fourteen years old (Some students are older!) and only five of them in the entire country have computers which are old Apple-Macs and are not compatible with yours. Louisiana, one of your schools, has these. It is my dream (and intention) that, by the time I leave, you will be able to communicate with each other directly, by email. I have already found someone to help with the business plan. In the meantime I'm working on making email accessible myself.

Your Buddy Uncle Albert is rather tired. At the moment he is leaning against George who is comforting him in his slow kind of way. Uncle Albert won't take his pack off - especially as he has an appointment with one of the other Principals right away. George has just asked how long the pack has to rest on his shell because it is heavy. Well done for all you have sent. I listened to your tape outside in the sun as it is cool today (only just over 80 degrees F)…'

The computer locked out several times today at the same point while working on the St. Paul's document. I thought I had lost the whole disc and three day's work at one stage. I thought that the fault was overheating so I moved the computer to the coolest spot in the house and left a message for Ormando Sanchez at BSI but I now think that I had run out of memory. Charts use a lot but there was no warning. Reducing the document size - into a second one - seems to have solved the problem. While I was sat waiting for the computer to cool down, or forget, whichever it was, I managed to relieve the boredom by catching Nelson and using the time to help him with his letter to Leanne. He wrote a super letter and I am sure Budgie will be pleased with it.

'…7d's Parcel is an excellent start and well received. It is the first day back today so I went through it with the Principal of Calcutta School (we spent over three hours swopping ideas) last week and gave it to him to start sharing ideas with the students today. I also used it to keep the pot boiling with others but… The other three schools are crying out for their parcels… I am now working on ways to make as much of the communication direct from school to school as possible. There are lots of other things I can do to help it all along. Tomorrow I hope to see the Chief Education Officer with several points in mind, including a small operating budget for each of the schools (They haven't got much and I will enlarge on that when things have got going fully) and markers for publicity. I intend to send you a parcel of books as soon as I can afford it. I hope to beg the new Belizean school text books for environmental/social studies and several others. There are also some really good books (not all that many but good quality material on Belize that you certainly couldn't get in the UK. This should arrive before half term. I will probably send it surface mail which takes about four weeks but I haven't got the books yet. (My funds have improved fairly healthily).'
Then trying email again…
'This communication has to be email because the last one may have worried you. The second parcel from 7G containing 'Spike' has arrived. Both parcels will be in La Immaculada School by the time you read this. It is a lovely school but I won't tell you any more about it than I already have because you can find out for yourselves. As each school comes 'on stream' as it were, I am suggesting to the students that some communication, however small should come back to you right away (direct); I am suggesting to the Principals that it would be a good idea for them to write to their respective teachers right away as well; and that all communication should now be direct unless it is to be sent by email in which case I can help. You may like to think along the same lines (you probably have). I know from my own experience, that waiting for mail is very frustrating and the wait for a particular answer is much easier to cope with if there is a steady flow of mail keeping the lines of communication open (and feeding the enthusiasm). Your Principal is Mrs Elda Vega. She is Principal of Upper Division because the school is large enough to have three principals. The address would simply be La Immaculada School, Orange Walk Town, Belize, Central-America. The Principal for 7D is Mr Orvin Rancheran. He is the sole (teaching) Principal of Calcutta Government School, Calcutta, Corozal District, Belize, Central-America. It important to include 'Government' in the title as it may otherwise go to the wrong school.

This doesn't mean that I will sit back and have nothing more to do - quite the opposite. I have put in a considerable amount of groundwork and made friends with a huge number of people - teaching staff and students alike. I will be just as *involved in what they are doing but in a different role. It has been interesting already to share some of my experience with Calcutta. My expectations in coming to Belize were way off the mark! The job the students have to do in learning about each other, without living in each other's country, is endless; a classic case of the more you know the more you realise you don't know. It is a tremendous privilege for me and very exciting. I hope that is what it will be for all. And this is only a beginning as you say. The new Programme Director for VSO is coming to see me for the day at the end of this month. I intend to take him in to at least two of the schools because I'm angling after a VSO major project grant for them, which would be 1,000 pounds sterling (about $Bz3200). That is one of the sprats to catch some of the mackerel there are about. The newspaper cutting you sent will also help. The main move for funds will be made when the links are able to be seen to be flourishing strongly and it has become the talk of the community (which is growing already). I intend to donate the equipment I have accumulated when I leave. I have linked you with Elda Vega and La Immaculada School for lots of reasons. One of them is that she is trying to assemble a history of the development of Orange Walk Town which I thought you would have a particular interest in.*

It does say in your letter that there are some Christmas Cards in 7G package (which was overtaken by 7D!). There was one from Sophie and only seventeen letters (or cards?) for students. The number of letters will cause a problem and I think you will find yourself having to muster at least thirty. I know that La Immaculada could very well link with more. It is a big school - as is Louisiana, next in line. There should be no problem with St. Pauls although they are talking about including slightly younger children, also, to build in resource for the future.

Thank you for the leads. I think they will do the job. I will have to beg the use of a TV now! Also, the tape you sent back will be useful to try and there are things on it that some people would have liked to have seen. Perhaps you could send the second one back with the Lions outing to Double Head Cabbage on it because they could now have a copy of that but please don't send any more. I am not going to record over them and it is a (small) extra risk of loss. I think your idea of recording on to VHS C to send this way is brilliant (why didn't I think of that?); as soon as you can please. That will have to be sent to me of course, but there will be no delay in making a copy for the schools to run on their equipment because I have already arranged that in the town. All that is needed is my camera, the battery charged and the leads you sent.

I was a bit disappointed with the audio tape as there was less than half a side. The pop music is fine but I am certain that the students want to hear your student's voices. They are very different. It will be good to hear English-English and the Devon brogue. The first language here is Spanish. Children are taught in English and there is a great deal of Creole spoken among friends. Many people, especially further south, regard Creole as the language of Belize. Often I hear a mixture of all three. How many languages do our children speak? There are others here too - including some of the Mayan tongue.

Since you wrote your letter (11th December - received today, 15th January, you may have been a long time at the Post Office with 7G - joke)… You needn't worry about progress. It is all in hand. We have only been waiting the arrival of the Buddies. Be assured that you will be having returning envoys who will be bringing Belizean Buddies with them - or the other way round! But it is important to keep the flow going as well as the 'biggies' as I said above. As for visitors - I have some room and finding additional accommodation with a Belizean family, I am certain, would be no problem. Now a letter for your class:
'Dear Friends in 7G, I have just received your two parcels. I telephoned the Principal of the Upper Division of La Immaculada School, Orange Walk Town, at home this evening. All will be arranged with the students next week. I can tell you, as I told 7D, that opening the parcels was quite an emotional experience as I know so many of you. Also, it is breaking new ground and I know the young people here pretty well too.
One of the big problems is funding… Spike is very tired but his temper is improving. He says there were a lot of delays at airports, customs and all sorts of unexpected places as well. Apparently, it took long enough just to get to South Molton Post Office although I wasn't aware until now, that they dealt with international flights for diplomats. But there, I'm not a diplomat so how would I know? Also, he says that the seating space on the two flights (he went via Miami) was very cramped and the never ending overnight accommodation was even worse. It was a long time before he could sit up straight properly but he reckons he will be okay to meet the Belizean students and is looking forward to delivering all that you have sent and sharing your ideas with them. At the moment he is talking to George who was a bit doubtful about Spike to begin with but it was quite clear that Spike needed some comfort and George likes to do that so they were soon chatting away like old friends. As a matter of fact they are still at it and I think it is time they went to bed… Oh dear, now one of our wild storms has started and they have both gone out on to the balcony to watch. Perhaps it won't last long…'

I had a sleepless night thanks to the little dog 'Kiko' from next door who gets through the small gap under the gate to meet up with 'Brownie', my bitch, who is very much bigger and set up tremendous barking during the night. I did get up and caught 'Kiko' wonderfully with a well-aimed broom right in the middle of the back. That worked for some time but they were at it again before the morning. I caught him again when

I got up in the morning and fixed some short pieces of wire ends under the gate which 'Kiko' has inspected, as has Brownie, and so far, this seems to work. I also discovered 'Kiko' is deaf to my zapper.

The end of the week was marked with more telephone problems. I called into the District Office first and then descended on Belize Telecommunications Limited (BTL). I had to phone Ellajean from the District Office after waiting all week to find that she had called a meeting in Belize City for next Tuesday. BTL said that the phone would be attended to before 5:00pm. It wasn't. I reminded them just before 5:00pm and they came next morning to repair the telephone and replaced the instrument. Orvin Rancheran brought his whole family and we had a very pleasant afternoon going through the parcels from 7D and meeting 'Uncle Albert'.

Two rough days followed. After a dreadful night I came to with stomach cramps and a very sore throat; weak and wobbly with aching limbs, I alternated between re-writing lost journal for Oct/Nov and sleeping; staying in both days and missing the first day back at school when Calcutta would have met 'Uncle Albert'! Also the Prime Minister's visits started in Orange Walk; a pity to miss that too! But there were letters to write…

'…You may be rather cut off but the response to Scoutlink received here on 9th Jan, the day after my copy arrived, must be a record for the publication! One of the contributors received his copy the same day and the other two will receive theirs tomorrow when I go to Belize City; just what I needed to kick-start direct links… I will enquire about Fr. Alec Tatnall…'

'Thank you for your super letter and card… My copies of "Scoutlink" arrived by the same post (you will have read my article by now). Yesterday I went to see Hilberto Riverol (Chief) to give him his copy. This was done so that he might communicate directly with Roger A, which he is keen to do. The aim is to establish International Links which he is very enthusiastic about. I have your Cub Pack in mind - for one…'

'…You probably know that I write to quite a lot of scouting friends and I had a super letter from Helen on the 9th with all the latest Pack news. On the 10th a letter arrived from David in response to the Scoutlink article. I will take these along to Hilberto as well and suggest that he contacts you direct. I don't think they have email but here is his FAX. Please pass on my thanks and compliments to Stephen. Tell him that I also noted and appreciated the design inclusion. I think it is Aztec which is next door to Mayan Culture - very close…'

The prospect of the CDU meeting in Belize City didn't meet with the way I was feeling and it was long, given also the five hours bus travel and waiting for it. Days are short all the year round in Belize and much of the bus travel takes place during darkness. The meeting was necessary and fruitful however: dealing with planning for Goals in years 1-3; with projected and recorded diaries of activity and with budgets. I now had two Belizean assistants, Bertha and Onelia for the next phase in my two districts. Bertha would visit the Orange Walk Schools while Onelia would visit Corozal Schools and I would cover all of them. The budget was for the three of us covering both districts during February for travel only, since the schools chosen were located on the main bus route. The Diary of Activities was for Phase 2 of the development of the New Curriculum through January and February. The planning for Orange Walk and Corozal in Phase 1 had been carried out with four schools: Louisiana, San Pablo and Carmalita in Orange Walk and Calcutta in Corozal. Much appreciated was the weather in Belize City all day and especially the temperature.

The news from home was much more dramatic as a letter recorded…

'…The New Year has started with gales and yet more rain! On Sunday 4th January the weather was really awful – winds up to 80 miles per hour and sometimes 100mph with lashing rain and hail. It was quite frightening – I was waiting to hear crashes. I had to bring the dustbin in from the back yard as it kept blowing over and the lid was flying around. Some of the neighbours lost slates from their roofs and one roof, which had been 'felted and tarred' over the slates, lost pieces of the felt. There were several bits of debris blowing along the front gardens – flowerpots, pieces of slate and Perspex from someone's greenhouse. The scaffolding around the Church tower didn't seem to have suffered any damage. Several places in North Devon 'lost' their electricity and telephones. Some were without power up until last Wednesday and Thursday. I didn't have any power cuts. I have enclosed a cutting about the damage to Chittlehampton Church Tower. The pinnacles had been replaced after the 1990 storms. Loxhore Church lost several slates but they were replaced on the following Tuesday and the lead valley, which had been repaired temporarily, didn't leak. I think several houses and shops in South Street lost slates, as there were lots of pieces in the street. Last weekend was a complete contrast. It was quite sunny with temperatures up to 58°/59°F! It was supposed to have been the warmest January day in some places since weather records have been kept…'

There followed multi school visits in the remainder of the week involving much bus travel on Thursday (and excitement resulting therefrom): San Pablo and St Pauls Anglican to review phase 1 and give notice of phase 2; also to ask if they had copies of missing documents lost by CDU); Calcutta Government to review phase 1 and give notice of phase 2; also to talk to students about the Buddy arrival from England; Buena Vista, Calcutta SDA, St Francis Xavier, Corozal Methodist, Christian Assembly of God at Santa Rita and San Antonio to introduce Phase 2; and La Immaculada to discuss linking but Mrs Vega had gone home. On the Friday the visits were to Nuevo San Juan, Chapel, St. Peter's Anglican and Palmar in Orange Walk; with Mr Uck for Phase 2 introduction and to make new arrangements to introduce linking for La Immaculada Upper Division staff on Monday. The weekend was quiet other than a visit from Pedro and Daiami which was also an opportunity to give them the zoo photos and make tentative plans for visits with Pedro on his motorbike. Having a companion would make a big difference to the number of places that it would be safe to go and safe to use the camera - as well as him being Belizean. There were letters of course…

'…Would you believe I've had flu? There is a lot of it about and the Belizeans blame it on the nights being cooler! Nothing changes! It is cooler at night but only down to our daytime summer temperatures. Viruses must go in cycles like everything else I suppose but it is a bit much coming here to be laid low by one that might have done it in England. It hasn't stopped me but it has been quite unpleasant and I still have the cough… Finances are sorted out now so I will be able to send the book I have in mind. My next project is a printer as I don't often have access to one now. I'm hoping to be able to buy one through VSO but there is no such hurry for that. If you should happen to think about sending photographs it would be a nice thought but it is expensive and I have seen a lot of photographs sent by children to the linking schools – so save the pennies on that one. The linking is going absolutely brilliantly. Calcutta Government School are now in independent communication with 7D. Their parcels arrived with their Buddy, Uncle Albert, on 5/6th January. The Principal came to see me on Saturday 9th and Uncle Albert (+baggage) met with the students on the first day of term, 12th January. I went in to Calcutta School on the Wednesday to find that they were already working on their ideas and left them with the thought (from experience) that a flow of communication will be necessary as well as waiting for the 'big one' - for staff as well as students. Now I can step back and become a resource. The second two parcels arrived this week as the baggage of 7G Buddy, Spike. He is to be introduced to the staff and children of La Immaculada School on Tuesday 20th January. This is a school that I don't actually work with but I got to know the Principal through her Brother who is a District Education Officer and a member of the Leiva family. This gives a whole extra dimension to the venture which I will be able to explain better when things have moved on further. The parcels from the other two forms, and their Buddies, should be in place in about two weeks. Then the fund raising fun starts. Scouts are doing well too. I sent a long report which Devon Scouts have published in the monthly magazine… The first response from Devon arrived the day after I received the 'Scoutlink'…'

'…Everything else is going really well. The job has given me close contact with schools where I have made friends and got to know many of the students. There have even been times when I have been able to work with some classes and join in with their Christmas parties. Christmas was good too. I spent five days with the Belizean family which started with the celebration of the joint birthdays of the eldest son and his wife just before Christmas. People have been wonderful. I could have stayed with the family and joined the visit to their relatives, until the New Year and there were four other families who invited me to stay with them. The computer is working okay thanks to a friend who stayed late one night and had it all stripped down to find faults that developed. He looks after the computers used by Belize Sugar Industries which used to be Tate and Lyle in colonial days…'

The Prime Minister's visits started in Corozal on Monday 19th January which would have been of interest to experience the gatherings and emotions of people but only as a visitor in the country. I had in any case noted that politics divided people much more strongly than I had been used to – or understood. In any case I had a meeting with Elda Vega, Principal, and the whole of Upper Division staff of La Immaculada School at 4:00pm to discuss the parcels that had arrived from 7G and their next step and wished to remain in Orange Walk. That meeting proved to be hard work in terms of raising enthusiasm and was felt to be a first disappointment quite apart from the frustration of delays and difficult communications. I later gained the impression that there was a 'separateness' making Catholic Schools quite distinct from others, including other faith schools, not unconnected with the impression I had of politics. A parcel also arrived with 'Heffer' the Buddy from 7H to fully raise and restore the spirits however, and set the enthusiasm going again…

'…The parcel from 7H arrived today. I've got to the stage now, where it is placed on the Post Office counter as I walk through the door - presented with a smile and a "For you Mr Max!"

The value of what you have going for you here is endless. Do please keep the flow of correspondence going now that you are dealing direct. I will be giving you a lot of background information now that I shall be able to concentrate more on that end of things. I'm pleased you like the writing you have received so far. I intend to write a book or books but please feel free to use all the material I send as you see fit. You may like to ask Richard if he has finished illustrating the latest George the Snail Story. When he has, you can make a copy of that. (You will have to ask him for permission to use the illustrations). The arrangement that we have is that when it comes to publishing, he will be the illustrator! I do explain that the work sent is 'as written'. There is no need to worry about that. However, don't be surprised that the quality of many aspects of work sent from here will be high. I have been amazed at the capacity (and pride) of students when I see the little that they have to work with and the shortcomings in the system in which they learn. More than ever, every day, I am reminded that there is no limit to the amount we can learn from each other. I have been going through all that you have sent. Apart from anything else, it is a very strange and rewarding experience for me; so much so that I begin to see the difficulty of doing justice to explaining that even to you; another reminder that the culture and the environment is so near in so many ways and yet so far. All the more reason to 'try harder' - to use a well-worn phrase! The tapes need to have much more of the children on them. There is no shortage of pop music here. The children were not to know that of course, and there is value in finding out. Tell 7H that Barbie Girl, which was on their tape twice, is played on the radio here at least ten times a day (or so it seems). Also, it will be necessary to speak more clearly if that can be done without losing the natural sound. Mostly, though, the message is that there needs to be regular communication and those who have not sent letters or pupil dossiers should do so without delay. Each class is dealing with a school and that means the whole of their equivalent year: Calcutta 35, St. Paul's 30, Louisiana 100 and La Immaculada 150 - all 11/12 years old! The parcel from 7H contained only 13 letters and 16 pupil dossiers. Belizean children are working out how best to respond and they are very keen. One lot waited two hours after school just to see me - on an occasion when the bus broke down!

I have now written direct to 7D, 7G and 7H. They can expect more direct from me now, as well as more general things sent for you to distribute. It will be much more effective by being a two way effort of course. All letters will be answered one way or another.

7H will be linked with St. Paul's Anglican School in Corozal Town tomorrow. They are good friends of mine and their school is separated from the Caribbean by no more than a quiet little road and a narrow strip of grass. They often sit outside for their lessons; good note on which to end…'

Bertha and I spent a morning going through immediate plans at the District Office before I set off to Corozal to talk to Pedro Cucul, the District Education Officer there about the Curriculum plans and progress and to show him the parcel from 7H; also introducing 'Heffer' who made a great impression. The reception at St. Paul's Anglican to Heffer and the parcel from 7H was even more encouraging with a huge welcome and great excitement and interest from all the staff.

Mark Wright the VSO Programs Director made a welcome visit showing great interest, visiting the District Office in Orange Walk, Calcutta School, Corozal District Office and looking around both towns; also a visit was arranged for Mark to see Perfecto Victorin of the local Co-op. Management at the CDU was discussed; also Scouts' links and links with schools; plans for raising funds for schools' links including advertising, VSO and British High Commission grants; the purchase of a printer and modem through VSO and the offer from Zimbabwe as the New British High Commissioner for Belize was Deputy in Harare. Mark was and remained an enthusiastic supporter of both the work involved in my placement and the personal projects and links both in the UK and Belize. It was also a great joy to be driven around in a rather nice four wheel drive and air conditioned comfort!

The working week came to an end with a presentation of links to 150 students of Standard Six of La Immaculada School and introducing Mr Spike; later taking part in the Apple Mac computer workshop day at Louisiana School which continued into the weekend.

I had arranged for Stanley Bermudas the Ministry computer expert to come up from CDU to lead the work which was attended by twelve staff on each day. It will be interesting to watch the use of the computers growing in the school and it was a useful opportunity to discuss the hardware side of the Linking Project. It is particularly useful that Louisiana School is part of that; another one of the many strange, seemingly random events that kept occurring which add up and point the same way - not only in the job that I do but in the contacts made, the way they have occurred and the events leading up to coming to Belize as well.

I am beginning to feel better today, Sunday. The flue, bronchial cough and cold have been really quite a trial and I have had to cut down on the effort. As it happened there was a power cut which affected everything, including the radio, early yesterday evening so I went to bed. Before I did so I used the light of the bottled gas to make a cup of coffee and went out on to the balcony to drink it. It is not often that there is the opportunity to sit in the low level of natural evening light and I was able to watch the fireflies leaping and dancing among the trees opposite very clearly. The light is tiny but very intense and may last for a couple of seconds - covering a surprising distance as it shines out with little meaning beyond that understood by another firefly. I wonder what they would look like close-up.

The letters had to wait for 'me-time' just for once; well, except for computer failures…
    'Dear Friends in 7H, I have just received your parcel for St Paul's Anglican School…
    When she arrived, Heffer just sank! She was very tired and as she settled herself down, the upper part of her body seemed to sink down in between her hips and her head seemed to sink down between her shoulders. Nothing would move her - in any way! George thought it was highly amusing but that didn't please her at all and she made that quite clear to him so that he spent most of the evening trying to 'make up'. They are best friends now, I'm glad to say. It is rather nice for George too, because the other two are men Buddies and George has a bit of an eye for the ladies! Arrival day was Monday 19th. Today is Wednesday and Heffer was introduced to the students of St Paul's Anglican School yesterday. It was rather a job to drag her in actually. It is a very friendly school and she was very happy to meet everyone - that wasn't the problem. The problem was that the school is right on the shore of the Caribbean Sea and so far, she has only heard about it and it was much better even, than she imagined. I don't think it will be too long before there are rumours about a swimming cow. I hope the press don't get hold of the idea…'
    The computer had broken down already but three days in Belize City provided the opportunity to make arrangements to have it fixed and to haul the desktop cabinet to the bus, on the bus and from the bus down to EDC. My own recent experience of computers had been with the BBC micro and more recently the Archimedes. These used floppy discs as software for both programmes and working memory which, while somewhat pedestrian and lacking in power, were extremely user friendly otherwise and virtually incorruptible. The IBM I had bought, so Stanley at EDC advised me, was in a mess. For a start, I didn't know about defragmentation of the hard drive which was all over the place and in the end had to be cleaned thoroughly and reloaded. Nowadays by comparison only simple precautions need to be taken as the whole thing is managed by the software and antivirus manufacturers. The 'tower' was also extremely heavy and vulnerable to be carried on the bus which was a 'regular' which stops everywhere and indeed anywhere. It was always very crowded, even overloaded and would often stop more than once in a few yards as locals insisted on being dropped at their own place; a situation exacerbated among a small population where everyone knows everyone else and many (say around a half!) know those in government or business or both. All of this was well understood without comment by Belizean colleagues and the return journey, much later, was volunteered by my good friend Delia in her car. Otherwise, on Monday there was a presentation to new officers on the Philosophy and the Goals of the New Curriculum; the preparation of a programme for principals of new schools joining phase 2 of curriculum development on Tuesday and on Wednesday an Orientation day for principals of new schools joining phase 2.

Being in Belize City always meant contacts and I was able to talk to Ernest Raymond the CEO about supporting the linking schools. He asked for a summary of what is going on and agreed to write to the principals giving his support; also provide an open letter for me to use and allocate a small budget for postage etc. to the two Government Schools, Calcutta and Louisiana. I also told him of my discussions with Stanley in respect of appropriate IT equipment. A summary was given to him next day and his advice sought about the purchase of books. He gave me an introduction to Mrs Encolada at the Government Bookshop to purchase books at schools' rate. Ten books were purchased for $116.85.

Mrs Encolada then offered to arrange to have them delivered direct via the representative from Ginn and Co.

Letter to the Government Bookstore, Belize City…

'Herewith - brief notes on the linking project as promised today. Also a letter to include with the parcel of books being delivered to South Molton Community College by the good offices of the representative from Ginn and Co. The full address is at the head of the letter.'

'…I'm sure you will find this parcel of books useful! They have been purchased from the Government Bookstore in Belize City at Schools' rate and with a discount so they have cost much less than I anticipated. Also, the manager of the Bookstore, Mrs Encolada has kindly arranged to have them delivered to you through the good offices of the representative from Ginn and Co. That not only means a considerable saving in postage but also a saving in time! I think these are all the books you are likely to find useful from the store except an excellent 'Atlas' of Belize which is not available just now but I will send a copy when it is. If you would like any more copies please let me know. There are many more books published by Angelus Press and others in the regular book shop which will be useful to you and I intend to send these as funds become available but I thought a 'quick injection' of resource would be especially welcome at this stage.*

If we think of the whole project as a plant: the seeds are sown and have germinated; there is every sign of healthy growth; considerable interest is being shown in this new variety; and the weather is set fair! My attention now turns to feeding the plants with the intention of securing a perennial strain!

The Chief Education Officer (Mr E. Raymond) is writing to the participating schools giving them his support and I hope that there will be some small operating budget provided for the Government schools (Calcutta and Louisiana). He is also providing me with an open letter of his support. I have discussed computers with the manager and technician nationally, so that I know which way to go to be in tune with what is happening in the high schools. The next thing is to find the money. I am sure that can be done but it will be helped by generating as much activity as possible around which publicity can be gained and a business plan written. I have contacts for a substantial number of sources. So many things have happened at just the right time and so many people have shown an active interest - as well as the enthusiasm of the students - that the project has to be right. It would take a book to relate the whole story to you. The links are established (with just Louisiana to receive 'Sunny') and there will be a steady flow of correspondence as well as the visits of the four Buddies from Belize to take place shortly…'

Having funds in mind, I also managed to obtain a World Bank contact phone number in Washington DC and used this to obtain the address of their representative in our area.

It was almost a relief to travel thirty-odd miles in the opposite direction to meet with my new colleague Onelia, and Pedro the District Education Officer at 9:00am next day in the Corozal District Office where we went through the history of phase one and the process of phase two.

I wondered then 'what is the role of the new field officers' especially now that the outcomes for one area only, are to be worked on centrally by a team drawn from the participating schools in the Districts (Orange Walk and Corozal). Then checking dates with EDC I found, not for the first time that these have been changed. The 'training of Trainers' is to take place in the two weeks beginning 10th March and the teams' planning in the six weeks beginning 20th April. Hey, Ho, sufficient unto the day; let's progress with the immediate and practical; I decided to make the initial orientation with all participating schools together and then follow up in more depth with schools individually.

It was back to Belize City and the Curriculum Development Unit on Friday where I obtained copies of the basic presentations made by Ellajean and Corinth for Principals' use next Wednesday and with the intention of using them as the basis for my own presentations to be made for participating schools in Orange Walk on Monday and Corozal on Tuesday.

I was hoping to be able to collect the computer but it was still not finished. That was a pity especially as I had managed to arrange a car ride back rather than use the bus. It took some time for it to dawn on me that my lift was with Raul Alcoser, his wife and four year old son. Raul is Neria Leiva's brother and his wife teaches Standard Three children at Louisiana School; so many new beginnings and seemingly in so many new directions yet all sharing common purpose and belonging somehow together. Letters helped with the 'gluc'…

'Hi! How are you; enjoying missing the English weather no doubt? It is absolutely freezing here, so please send us some warmth. Many thanks for your Christmas card and lovely long newsy letter. You certainly seem to have settled in well and keeping busy. I was pleased to hear you had moved into your new flat. I am sure that must make a big difference. Jenny and I met up in Exeter one Saturday and went for a 'cuppa' in Dingles and had a long chat and swapped news from your letters… Our District Carol Service was small compared to last year's 80th birthday event but nonetheless enjoyable, held in the beautiful Parish Church at Silverton. Tony Lane came, which both pleased and surprised me and on introducing him to Frank, our District Commissioner, Frank was quick to seize the chance to say how supportive you had been to our District…'

'…I vowed to reply within a month and have just about made it. I was pleased to read about the friends you have made, the five days you spent over Christmas with a Belizean family and above all the letters the children continue to send. I too have experienced the warmth and friendship from children, so I can appreciate just how important it is to you, being so far away…'

'…I helped Ken with scanning the sheep last week. Rosie is expecting twins. We have five lambs already. They were born at Christmas, two sets of twins and a single. I call them Eeeny, Meeny, Miney, Mo and Fred. They were early because they came from a farm where they had been 'living'. The bulk will not arrive until April…'

It was a case of 'and now for something different' at the weekend as well if that isn't really 'more of the same'! Another visit to Belize Zoo started with leaving home at 6:20am and catching a bus straight away. There was a wait of about twenty minutes at the Western Highway and I arrived at the zoo at 8:30am – a journey which could have taken much longer, being a total of 84 miles. The intention was to meet with Kathryn at 9:00am. It should have been more likely that I would be later and we had arranged that Kathryn would wait until 9:30am and then go in if I had not arrived. In the event it was the other way round and I met up with her when she arrived in the zoo at about 10:00am. Sharing that day which was filmed enriched both the material and the resolve to be written into the George the Snail story 'Home is the Belizoo'. We left at 4:30pm and I arrived in Belize City to stay over with Neria and Tabo Leiva at about 5:30pm. The evening was a social one until about 11:30pm!

I went to the Mayan Site at Altun Ha with the Lions Club from Belize City; a social event through the family which was just as enjoyable as the outing to Double Head Cabbage and Bermudan Landings 'Dis is Where de Action Is'. A Belizean Garden Centre is located close by with an amazing variety of plants growing in an extraordinary location on good soil.

The outing was much more restrained than the one to Double Head Cabbage and there was no drinking on the bus although there was plenty with the picnic lunch (rice and beans and chicken with potato salad for the main course). This was probably because the previous outing was for the benefit of a team of Lions Club eye surgeons and specialists who had come down from the States to give a week's free attention to those who needed it – so I was honoured to be invited to attend.

Altun Ha was filmed for year 7 and I was lucky enough to find a guide who agreed to give some idea of what it is all about. He was quite a character and I found it quite difficult to say anything which would be helpful - so his request for questions met with none! Anyway, here it is… 'Altun Ha is one of the most important Mayan archaeological sites. It was a major ceremonial and trading centre and is thought to have had its first settlement there around AD 150. It was abandoned in mysterious circumstances around AD 1000. Many of the ceremonial tombs show unmistakeable signs of desecration which couldn't possibly be the action of looters in recent times. Modern interest in Altun Ha began when local quarry workers found a jade pendant at the site which led to an archaeological dig and some restoration. Altun Ha became the second site to be opened for tourists in the 1970s, after Xunantunich some of which was shown on the first film I sent to you. It was surprising to find that the tombs in the main temple were not those of warlords or dynastic rulers, but priests. Also, there were remains of a unique sacrificial offering at one of the temples: charred bits of jade and copal resin jewellery, which had been smashed to pieces, thrown into a fire, and then scattered ritually just before a new construction was built over the older altar. The most spectacular find lay deep within one of the tombs in the so-called Temple of the Masonry Altars, alongside the remains of a priest: a massive carved jade head of the Maya Sun God, Kinich Ahau. Standing 14.9cm high and weighing 4.42kg, it was the largest carved jade artefact ever uncovered in the Maya world. The jade and other materials could only have been brought from places like Guatemala and Mexico and over a distance of some 1,100km. Jade does not occur in Belize.

The site consists of 13 structures surrounding two main plazas. In one of them over 300 pieces of jade were found in a single tomb. Shells have also been found which have come from the Pacific Ocean which is evidence of Altun Ha's importance along the Maya trade routes. The Temple of the Masonry Altars (or Temple of the Sun God) is the largest of the pyramids at Altun Ha and rises 18m above ground.'

We returned for Belize City at about 4:30pm and I asked the driver to stop at Sandhill which is at the junction on the Northern Highway, so that I could wait there for the bus North to Orange Walk. He had other ideas and said he would stop a bus. We had only gone about two miles South of Sandhill when an Escalante bus appeared heading the opposite way. It was signalled, stopped and the transfer successfully made. I arrived home at about 5:45pm.

February was almost routine compared with the frenetic experience thus far, beginning with the preparation of an orientation programme to be given to teachers in the Lower Division of schools participating in phase 2 first in in Orange Walk and then in Corozal each lasting about an hour and which excites my own commitment to learning: a philosophy which sees education as the lifelong acquisition of knowledge, skills, attitude and values for full personal development and active participation in society; principles ensuring that the learner learns to learn, is respected as a unique individual, and given the opportunity to be productive and interact harmoniously in the social and physical environment; best represented by UNESCO's four pillars of learning (to live together, to be, to do, and to know). Principals were advised of the progress thus far and the plans and arrangements for Phase 2 involving fifteen schools in the North; the two Districts together, working on Language only at this stage, that is to say English and Spanish. The start date is 20th April and six weeks have been allocated to complete the work. One teacher is to be withdrawn from each of the participating schools to take part in planning for the Outcomes in English and Spanish. This planning will be carried out together, as one team. At the end of the exercise, it is expected that prototypical curriculum planning will have been completed for the three years of the Lower Division. This will provide a basis for planning the trialling of the curriculum in the Lower Division from September, in the participating schools. It is not intended to be prescriptive in any way.

There was so much promise throughout and neatly confirmed in that brief last sentence for curriculum to be developed with and for and by teachers and children.

Letter to 7R after the arrival of Sunny (copy and paste is great although it would be easier when my own machine is returned working)…

'Dear Friends in 7R, I received your parcel on Friday and I have seen the Principal of Louisiana School today. Arrangements have been made for me to talk with the students in Standard Five (who are the same age as you) again on Wednesday… Sunny was less fatigued by the journey than the other three Buddies. Perhaps it is his shining personality - or maybe it is easier when others have gone before you. Whatever it is, He has just spent a weekend with George and me, which was a lot of fun. We went to the Belize Zoo on Saturday and a Mayan Ruin called Altun Ha yesterday. I made a film of these two visits, which will be on its way to you this week. George wouldn't let Sunny be in that film because he said it wouldn't be fair. He said that was his job. Sunny wasn't bothered though. He says he is going to make his own film with the students of Louisiana School. (He has heard that Mr Spike, Uncle Albert and Heffer are making films too. We are all a bit jealous of Heffer because his school is right by the Caribbean Sea! A parcel of books is on its way to you. This should give you some useful information about Belize which you might find difficult to get in South Molton and it will give you some idea about the books that Belizean students use as well. I will be sending other things as I collect them to help you with your understanding. Don't assume anything! I thought I had a good idea what to expect here but I was wrong in lots of ways. Some of the descriptions and stories I plan to write will help too. Now that the four schools are linked, I can spend more time collecting things for you, taking photos and video, writing stories and writing descriptions (food is a good one!). Also, I am a resource for the schools here but you will do the most important learning for yourselves - by asking questions, explaining all you have to tell carefully, keeping the contact going and using your imaginations to find ways of making your new friendships even more exciting and interesting. You could also write to me. There are lots of things I can do to help things along while I am here but I can't think of everything - not even with the help of the Belizean students. Your letters will give more ideas and certainly, more encouragement… Also, it says on Sunny's passport 'Boy' - Perhaps it had better stay that way so as not to upset the Immigration Department…'

'…This is my record of letters and pupil dossiers that have been received: the names in bold are children for whom there was *no letter or card. I haven't checked the dossiers yet. Please don't see this as some kind of reporting. What I am interested in is leaving a healthy, enduring and developing link when I come back home. There isn't a great deal of time and relationships need to be worked at. Also, as I found in my first couple of months, the initial writing is difficult but once it has started it becomes easy…'*

Biographical details had to be collected for participating staff and schools. Happily Onelia and Bertha did that. They must have sensed that I would not be comfortable with that since I didn't yet know the teachers involved. That task wasn't even discussed and my role was merely to collate the information although I did visit all the schools, more especially those three schools taking part in the Link of course. Unfortunately, I hadn't anticipated that Immaculada would not be involved in phase two of the curriculum development programme and that made for more difficulty beyond the sheer size of the school in relation to the norm and the nature of the establishment and change was not possible at the time. The only other concern was at St Paul's School, nothing to do with the link although they were taking part. Two teachers would not be available after the end of phase 2 which, if they were chosen, would mean a lack of continuity and a loss of expertise from the school in respect of the new curriculum.

Arrangements were made with Pedro Cucul to make an appointment with Buena Vista for their orientation. So far there had been no contact from the school other than my original introductory visit when the Principal was not in school and his place had been taken by his father! More arrangements involved going to Belize City for discussions with David Price who was now running the project: dates, what to do now, the role of the Field Officers, the provision of teacher replacements and biographical forms; also with VSO for the purchase of a modem and a printer which would be bought and delivered to Belize City for me to collect. Such 'arrangements' would pass by almost without notice at home but there were 'ways' and 'circumstances' less obvious at home that I had quickly to learn in such a sparsely populated and highly political country (already noted). Distance was always a consideration too. The VSO office was in Belmopan over a hundred miles away and all communications were less than easy.

When I went to Louisiana one afternoon to present 'Sunny' et al to Standard Five students I was greeted by a six year old from Infant 1 who jumped in the air, flung his arms wide and upwards, bringing them down and inward just as fast until his two projecting forefingers were a mere inch apart. This is the last act in a favourite story of mine performed many times for hundreds of children over the years (though only ever once for each). The delight on his face when I acknowledged 'Cecil' for him was wonderful. I had performed that for his class at their Christmas party. In all the years that I have done it, no one has ever made such a demonstration - and here I am in Belize in communion with a Belizean infant!

In Corozal District some time was spent visiting Guadalupe Primary School which is an extension of St Francis Xavier (the Principal there proved to be the sister of Marbella Alcoser) before going on to Buena Vista for a meeting with the Principal and Division One teacher for their initial orientation which they had missed due to lack of communication, and to begin to know the 101 students of whom 30 were in the Lower Division.

Mail generally took about three weeks each way by air between Belize and the UK which made continuity very difficult especially for the linking schools even in the ordinary event and much more so when the project was being set in place over such a wide area in Belize and alongside similar difficulties and the demands of exercising curriculum development and coming to terms with so many new relationships and experience. But occasionally there was an exception…

'Thank you very much for the book about characters and caricatures in Belizean folklore, the copy of your writing about your walk to Yo Creek and the letter of 25th January. WOW! As George might say; two letters and all the other things in one week! It was a lovely surprise. I was interested to see that the book and letter took only three days to arrive. The postmark was 28th and it arrived on Friday 30th. I think that must be a record…'

Delays weren't always detraction either…

'I enjoyed reading the book and was especially interested to read about Anansi as I once did a Music and Movement tape about the character. I found it fascinating to see how the characters seemed to have evolved from the different cultures and peoples of Belize. The illustrations also helped to give greater detail to the characters. I intend to read it again so I can compare some of the characters with perhaps some of the versions of our folklore and legends. It is a book that I shall be able to go back to and study in more detail…'

But delays didn't fit with curricular demands at home…

'I showed your letter to Lorraine last night (the one which you wrote about the arrival of the buddies and their reception in the schools). She said she would pass on the information to Paul. She said the children were asking when they could do some more work about Belize. They had gone on to other work they have to cover in year 7…'

Kathryn and Rachael from Cayo and Belize Districts respectively also wanted to discuss the same issues with David Price which made it easier to make sure nothing was missed. As always, a visit to Belize City was an opportunity: this time to enquire about ink cartridges of Stanley Bermudas on behalf of the Orange Walk office; to collect packages to deliver from him to Louisiana School; and collect a supply of documents covering Goals, Specifications and Outcomes. The remainder of this month is to be used for extended orientation and it is intended that we should support schools' planning during August. There was even time to call in on the family with a thank you card and collect my computer again to bring it back on the bus with Alphonso Yah's help.

There are always days to spend cleaning, washing and cooking and now even enjoying the hammock! But now I've run out of gas! Why on a Sunday? It had seemed perfectly okay when I turned it off yesterday. I got ready to go to church thinking that the service started at nine and was there at 8:45am to find that it had already started. I will have to try 8:30am since the times are not in evidence. I went for a short walk for about an hour before meeting 'Pete' from the States, who is using the apartment downstairs for a holiday for six weeks. He is retired but his wife, still working, had to go back after two weeks. We were both invited to go out to Honey Camp Lagoon to join a family party which Landy Burns was giving. The idea was to follow them out sometime after they had left. "Max knows the way." says Landy. I was quite pleased with my navigating as I have only been there once and I wasn't paying much attention to the route. We didn't go wrong at all despite there being a substantial number of choices to make. The sun helps! As good as any compass! The party was given to celebrate the birthday of a family friend who, I believe is the Lady Chairman of the Rotary Club. As a result of meeting her, Landy began to explain the 'Links' and other connections and I was asked if I would talk with the club at their next meeting. Of course, I agreed.

A large tent/marquee had been put up without its sides where all the women were sat at tables and where the food was being prepared. The men were all over the place chatting, drinking either beer or rum and coke, or playing games. The girls were in the open cabana above the two bathrooms and store, in hammocks and with the very young children. The boys were in the lagoon splashing and fishing. I think the fish were caught more out of fright than anything else. There were bicycles all over that had been brought out in the small fleet of vehicles, and a small motorbike which anyone seemed to zip around on from time-to-time. The whole lagoon, which can be measured in miles, was otherwise empty of humans but well-populated by birds. A pair of binoculars was available for anyone who wanted to use them.

It was a very pleasant afternoon which continued right until sundown when we thought it prudent and polite to leave. On the return journey, the short afterglow before complete darkness seemed to hang between the water and the sky; the one an image of the other; clouds in the water, ripples in the sky stirred only, by the gentlest of breeze.

Meeting with Onelia and Bertha to give them an update of all that had happened on Friday at EDU we agreed to continue the next stage of orientation on the basis that I would visit all schools with one or the other in the appropriate District and they would make arrangements so as not to clash. Mark phoned next day from VSO to say that my printer and modem are in Belize City where he has left them with Jack. I phoned Jack to arrange to collect them tomorrow and, hopefully, to learn how to install the modem and the printer driver.

I was approached by a young man in his twenties as I was returning from another fruitless visit to the post office (closed early). He made the usual sort of introductions which generally lead up to asking for money but his story did hang together. He claimed to have rushed from Punta Gorda to his father in hospital in Orange Walk and to have nothing. He didn't want money. Could I buy for him, some toothpaste, toothbrush, toilet paper and some soap? This I agreed to do but I am sure I was taken for a ride for two reasons. Firstly, he was shouted to by someone in the back of a lorry. When I commented that someone seems to know him his quick response was that they were shouting at him and he didn't know them - but he had given a slight response which I had noted. Second, in the shop he picked a pack of four toilet rolls and tried to add some shampoo and asked the shopkeeper if it had conditioner! I told him to put that back and use the soap. I suppose the most telling point was that if he was feeling as bad about asking for help as he had claimed to be, his position would not have been overtaken by greed. It cost me about nine dollars but what is most upsetting is that it says little for Belizeans and I do not wish to find myself trusting no-one. The plus side is that at least the action I took was honestly given! There still remains, of course, the possibility that he was genuine.

Nelson Burns posted his letter to Leanne at last - well. I put it in the box for him!
I met with Bertha again at the Orange Walk District Office to complete arrangements for visits to school in the Orange Walk District. Louisiana is changed to Tuesday 24th at 3:30, after the session at Palmar. There is clearly some reluctance to give the time on the part of staff. The necessity for all the staff to know what is happening needs to be further reinforced.

The modem and printer looked very good. Unfortunately there were no instructions with the printer and no mains connector. Mark made arrangements for these to be sent to Angelus Press in Belize City. Kathryn phoned to make arrangements for the weekend so I will meet her at the end of the Western Highway at 9:00am on Friday morning and we can go down to Angelus Press from there.

There were many letters, too, from individual children which needed to be answered…

'…Thank you for your letter which came with your form parcel sent for La Immaculada School here in Belize. Actually, the school is not far from where I live and I know a lot of the children there - of your age. What a lot of animals you have. Most people have dogs here to let them know if anyone is around at night. There are a lot of different wild animals too: monkeys, pumas and jaguars (big cats), anteaters, wild pigs, storks, pelicans, toucans, hawk eagles, vultures, crocodiles and lots of snakes and huge spiders (tarantulas). You might like to look some of them up. The weather is different here too. The sun is shining as it does nearly all of the time. Even now, in the 'cool' season, it is as hot as it gets in England in the summer. Today it is about 85 degrees. It can go as high as 115 or even 120 in July/August. I like it…'

'…I was ever so pleased to receive your letter and Mum's one. Knowing you as well as I do, I know that it will have taken a lot of effort to write. That is appreciated – thank you. Also, I miss all of you loads but I have kept in touch and the schools' linking with year 7 is going very well and I have never felt homesick. You must have felt awful when your letter came back and it has only just reached me now. I'm sorry you had that happen - I know what it is like when mail goes astray this far away. The address you used was correct too. The family there are good friends so I don't know what can have happened. However, if you use my permanent address on the back of this letter, yours will arrive in two or three weeks…'

'…Your Christmas card has arrived (12thFebruary!) together with your letter dated 28:10:97 and at the same time as the 15th January 98 one. Goodness knows where the first two have been. I know I thanked you for your card. I did that because I reckoned you would have sent one - so thanks again…'

'…I have often thought about the decision to come to Belize but perhaps not in the way you might imagine. Mainly, I suppose, I have learned a lot about myself, about other people and what matters to me. One of the more obvious things is the knowledge that people don't have to be close by to be still there. I have already said that I couldn't have managed without proof of that. Another is that it is possible to swim far out into the deep water of another culture (and it is very different) and still relate to new friends. My life here is just about as Belizean as I can have any right to expect. There are many other things but one of the most moving is that so much has dropped into place to support what I have chosen to do with children. It seems, almost, that the decision was not a decision at all but inevitability. Meeting children in the street brings that home every day…'

'…I asked VSO to find a printer for me as it is cheaper with their suppliers and I have bought a modem by the same means. This will enable email to be used which will considerably improve the links with SMCC. I will use the equipment until I leave and then I intend to present the whole set to one of the schools. While on that subject, I have been asked to talk to the Rotary Club in Orange Walk - aimed at fundraising…'

'…The process of introducing the new curriculum is a long one which I will write about more fully presently. So far, the elements of the curriculum itself have been tested to see if they are understood, and revised slightly. The present stage is to find out what support trial schools will need towards its use with children, starting in September. I will be long gone before it completes a cycle and hopefully, 100% Belizeans will have taken over…'

After preparing a presentation for further orientation of schools I went to Belize City to meet Kathryn; also to pick up the mains adaptor and the instruction book for the printer. I checked my postal address with the bank and did some shopping, visited the bookshop opposite Belize Telecommunications Ltd (BTL) and posted some letters before setting off for Orange Walk with Kathryn from the Batty Bus Terminus. Back in Orange Walk we went for a walk along the river bank, around the town and to do some shopping. We decided that it would be nice to do some canoeing so I went along to talk to Chino, a family relative who drives the bus from San Estevan. He was very helpful and said he could arrange it for tomorrow.

Back at home we were invited downstairs at the end of the afternoon by Pete. Three of his local 'friends' were there (money no object), including one of the Novelo brothers from Jungle River Tours (which was useful). All of them were drunk in various stages, Pete being by far the worst. We excused ourselves as soon as a polite opportunity presented itself. Not long after they went out in Pete's vehicle but soon returned as he had to be put to bed, which meant my seeing to the lock on the gate for the night. As well as having the bull terrier provided for security, the ample grounds around my house are enclosed by an eight foot high wall with a very substantial rolling gate of the same height.

On Saturday we set off on the bus to San Estevan with Chino at 10:00am. San Estevan is about eight miles further down the wide and slow-flowing New River which also passes close by my house in Orange Walk. As well as Chino and his wife and family a large branch of the Belize family live in San Estevan. We were then taken to a friend's house to pick up a pair of paddles and on to another one to borrow the canoe. The owner had just returned from the rainforest where he had caught and killed an armadillo which he said was very good to eat. The canoe was a dug out from a mahogany log which was quite stable and easy to control. The time on the river was beautiful; very quiet and peaceful with little wind or current. The forest was quiet although we saw quite a few birds: plenty of kikadee as they are called here, colourful and lively, and kingfishers. The water was very deep and brown with the sediment it carries at this mature stage of its journey to the sea, so we didn't see many fish and no crocodiles. We did have an argument with the ferry cable which was very greasy and low over the water. Kathryn got knocked flat on her back in the canoe. It was just as well she was in the front of the boat but then, if she had been sitting where I was with the paddle and steering she wouldn't have been knocked flat (or covered in oil) as she pointed out. We were rather better prepared on the way back and picked a spot even closer to the bank where there was no grease on the cable just in case.

Back home in the late evening we were invited and joined a family barbecue next door with the Burns family and a few of their friends.

Many photos together with descriptive captions were sent to South Molton Community College as well as film, stories and descriptions of places and events.

We spent Sunday morning walking to and around San Juan Nuevo Palmar and found a way down to the river there. The whole area is quite accessible and useable during the dry season which it now is, but it is quite clear that there would be a great deal of water everywhere during the wet season. This was confirmed when we met a local man (whom I believe would have seen us much earlier than we saw him). He also said that there would be a lot of mosquitoes in the wet season and that the river was very dangerous with many crocodiles at all times. He was carrying home some long poles for his washing line at the same time as we returned so he showed us a short route back into the village. The river is very beautiful there: wide with huge meanders; many broad extensions especially on the curves; and a wonderful variety of trees and vegetation. The epiphytes are amazing. They look as though it is approaching their flowering season - a sight to look forward to and to photograph. It is wonderful to see such a huge number of the plants such as I have nursed at home since 1962 when we were first married.

San Ignacio where Kathryn lives is beyond Belmopan some hundred and forty miles away so she caught the one o' clock bus to go home and I spent the rest of the day quietly.

The new week started with a visit to the Orange Walk District Office for the morning where I sorted out a few papers after which I phoned VSO to check on the printer cable supplied and to find out about an eye specialist as I have started seeing flashes across the right eye. These occur (or are noticed) mostly in bright light as dark lines shooting across the periphery of vision around the outer side, and in darkness as flashes of light following the same path. I had begun to seem to see things flash by occasionally around the time of the illness in the New Year and wonder if the two are connected.

I left for Corozal at 12:30pm to attend an Orientation meeting for Corozal Methodist and St Paul's

Anglican at the Methodist school. Apart from being there it was my role to support Onelia's presentation and mini workshop as we had arranged last week, with an introduction, comments and conclusion. Afterwards, I went on to St Paul's to talk with the Principal as she had not been able to attend because of the pressure of the forthcoming Belize National Selection Exams (BNSE) for her class. It was 7:00pm and dark by the time I was able to catch a bus back home but that is never a chore as the sky is usually clear and full of stars with enough light to add new mystery to the countryside, here mostly scrub or cane fields and the occasional village once you leave the sea. My itinerary for the two weeks of February remaining was straightforward enough: schools visits, liaison with Orange Walk and Corozal District Officers, eye appointment at the hospital and an event at Orange Walk Crystal Palace. The two weeks from Monday 3rd to Friday 20th March would be at EDU in Belize City. I had elected and indeed insisted from very early on to work from home on my own computer for all planning, preparation and record keeping, using district offices only to learn and keep in touch.

The day of the Orientation meeting for St Francis Xavier at the school in Corozal was pretty much a repeat of that at Methodist School although I was maybe an hour earlier getting home and so watched the rapid decline of day into darkness from the bus as it occurs in the tropics.

I went to see the Ophthalmic Specialist at the hospital this next morning. The appointment had been kindly organised by Mr Uck yesterday (everybody knows everybody remember). I had an eye test which showed that I need new glasses for distance as well as close up. The eye examination revealed no problems and both eyes to be normal. It was explained that the condition is one that does occur from time to time and I was given a prescription for tablets to cure it. The chemist did not have the first ones (Fluziva or Fluxariziva) and after going back to the hospital, I was supplied the alternative Cinarizina.

The afternoon was another orientation meeting, this time for Christian Assembly of God (Santa Rita), San Antonio and Buena Vista at the District Education Office in Corozal the same as before except that Bertha attended as part of the liaison we are undertaking.

There was a phone call from Ellajean, early this morning, asking why I wasn't at EDU. A message had been left at the District Office yesterday morning when they said they didn't know where I was. Nonsense of course; I always made sure they knew my itinerary and in any case I was at that time in the hospital as arranged by Mr Uck the District Education Officer. They had also been told by Bertha and by me, that we would be in Corozal in the afternoon. I immediately copied out the itinerary that I had not been able to print and asked for it to be typed. I went to the 'Crystal Palace' at 1:00am where I had agreed to officiate as scorer in the Spelling Bee. This was rather spoiled by the hundreds of students having to wait for an hour beyond start time for the contest and continually getting up to buy refreshments at the door. The Spelling Bee is sponsored by Coca Cola across the whole of Belize!

'…I told Lorraine about your letter. The class she works with have been told that a parcel is on its way from Belize and they were thinking about the different things they would be able to show the buddy…'

'…Time seems to fly by. My first six months is almost up - and I haven't had even the vaguest feeling of homesickness. I suppose both conditions are a measure of how well I have been able to settle into life here and life with the Belizeans. I will certainly come home for two or three months when the time comes but, whether I will stay home, return here or take up the post in Zimbabwe - I haven't decided…'

'…People in Mexico have suffered from the cold this year too, and the houses throughout Central America are generally without heating or insulation (ill-fitting hinged slats in the windows). Some of the traditional Mayan huts are much more open, even, but they have cooking fires (the smoke 'cures' the thatch). Here, the 'cool' season is over; the lowest night-time temperature about 55 degrees; the lowest daytime temperature about 80. It is now in the mid-nineties during the day and climbing. I sleep with no bedclothes…'

'…I have had something which I passed off as 'flu but I suspect it wasn't. It took its toll and lasted three weeks although I didn't give in to it and am better now…'

'…All four schools are 'linked with South Molton successfully and I am moving on to the next step of funding for the schools' computers and email as well as being a resource for them and sending my own material home…'

'…The curriculum is moving forward. The implementation could be (much) better planned but working with the schools, staff and children is great. Food is good; the house is great; and my funds have recovered from buying the computer…'

The end of the week was the turn of Calcutta Government School and SDA Church School, both inCalcutta, Corozal District for their orientation. I also elected to do some language work with Standard One while their teacher arranged a barbecue and the Principal took a team to play soccer at San Juan. I like to do this whenever I can to better know the children, their environment and their culture; certainly not merely to support my work although clearly it does. More than that, it is fun learning together and often almost feeling cognition taking place. I stayed for lunch and went with the Principal to the schools' soccer tournament in Corozal in the afternoon, returning once more on the 6:00pm bus.

The weekend involved travelling as most things do although Saturday's travel was in the huge 'Chevy' as I went to Chetumal with the Alcoser family. We made several family calls in Corozal and shopping stops in Chetumal which were very happy times as it is so easy to feel included even though so much is so new. By that measure we had a wonderful lunch which for me was fried red snapper and plenty of beer of course. The Mexicans really know how to present meals as well as make them. Even having beer is attended with a whole table of snack goodies and there are usually musicians and often dancers adding to the atmosphere – almost outdoors in warm, balmy air. I even entered mildly into the Belizean buying frenzy when in Chetumal (so much more availability and much cheaper) and bought two CDs: 1812 Overture, William Tell Overture, Pictures at an Exhibition, first movement of Beethoven's 5th Symphony, Egmont Overture, op.92 and a Rimsky Korsakov, some beer and a large bottle of Bacardi which I like with Pepsi.

Tabo phoned on Sunday to say that they were on their way to San Estevan and I arranged to meet them off the seven o'clock bus but missed them somehow. The double whammy was that I was then to have gone to Caledonia with Alcoser family in the afternoon but we were unable to go. I began to feel it rather a fruitless day except that Marbella got the printer going - albeit slowly. I suspect a computer problem round the driver rather than the printer and hope that I will not have to drag the cabinet down to Belize City yet again. So, all that aside, an opportunity to prepare notes for my talk to the Rotary Club…

Trust the Future
<u>Trust the Children</u>

Will you help them to use modern technology to widen their horizons?
… My talk was to tell the story and raise interest and support in the community in the North.

Being now fired up the evening's effort also includes a first letter with news to date to go to Fairthorne Manor remembering also the years of residential visits full of activity and enjoyed with the children from school. No great creativity is required, just a lot of cut and paste where news is unlikely to be shared but important too, since much of the comfortable clothing I now wear was a gift from the staff there and soon the next group of excited children would arrive.

An orientation meeting for San Pablo and San Juan went well to start the new week in Orange Walk. This was Bertha's presentation and mini workshop, arranged the week before last, with an introduction, comments and conclusion from me and an earlier return home, being finished at 5:00pm and already in town. Lunch time, however was spent with a second visit to 'Optica Professional' in San Antonio Road after having arranged for new glasses earlier using the prescription from the hospital. I was surprised and most pleased to find that there was a full technician's workshop at the back and that they could make up my glasses that day; surprised also that the workshop was little more than a shed really, filled with grinding machines and stock lenses ready to be worked on. I supplied my original frames and had bifocals made and fitted using 'React-a-light' glass at a cost of BZ$150 which I thought was very reasonable. I was wearing the glasses by 1:30pm and found that they were all that I need for all purposes. I phoned Roberto Gongora in the evening about fitting the modem - which he will do on Thursday at 5:30pm. Being home in time shouldn't be too difficult as it is a working week only in Orange Walk.

'…Enclosed is tape 3 and some notes to go with it. There are lots more to come but I am collecting most of them to send as a single parcel by surface mail with the intention of you having quite a substantial resource by next term. I hope you have received the books I sent. If not, you will need to contact GINN as they were sent with their representative who happened to be visiting Belize at just the right time.

I now have a printer and a modem. The printer is working but the modem is waiting to be fitted. As it is an internal job and I have identified two places where it will plug in, I am leaving it to the expert - fortunately another Belizean friend. After that I have to get hooked up but you should receive an email shortly after this letter and then you will be able to communicate with me directly, at home. Once this happens, that is a route we can use to speed things up for some of the students' mail.

At the end of my stay here, it is my intention to donate this equipment to one of the schools. I'm not sure when that will be. I am here on this contract until March/April next year and will then return for 3/4 months holiday. (No point in pussy footing about with weeks!) During that time I will be sixty and I intend to have a grand beano for as many past pupils and friends that can make it. You will have a role to play there, if you will. After that, my current thinking is to a) take a teaching job I have been offered in Zimbabwe (Harare) b) keep on this house and come back here c) buzz off in a camper van or d) stay at home. Those are in order of preference but there is not a lot to choose between the first two given the amazing way in which I have been able to settle in to Belizean life. (I can tell you a lot about the realities of life here, now, and will do so. On the subject of equipment, it is looking increasingly likely that it will be possible to find sponsors so that each of the four schools would be able to have a computer, printer and a modem. Belize Telecom Ltd will provide the link. I'm not quite ready yet though, to start approaches. There needs to be a lot more visible action and up-front thinking in the minds of students first. Even so, I have been asked to talk to the Rotary Club.

The four schools are each responding in a different way and should give you an interesting picture but it will be very useful if I could form a picture of how your children see it all. It would be best to hear that from them direct, of course; also some thoughts from you. If there is anything you think I have missed or you would like to add to (or take away from) please ask. I know that Calcutta Government School and St Paul's Anglican have sent parcels already. Louisiana and La Immaculada will take a little longer but we are already close to the point where I can enable the schools to share ideas and responses etc. I am in regular contact with all of them and even teach/work in three of the schools when I have time. There will be a video coming from each of the schools as well. Students are planning it. All I intend to do is act as cameraman - and when it comes to it, I may even give that over to the right person.

Work is going well and I do have time to get about too - with the locals. Last weekend I went canoeing in a mahogany dug-out with a mahogany paddle! That was wonderful. So peaceful; no-one else on the river at all (you wouldn't know that it is full of crocodiles); the birds silent in the heat of the day but still in evidence; the incredible variety of plants; the wide, deep, slow river, brown and mysterious; the depth of the rainforest. It is the tourist season but there has been little evidence of that where I have been. The week before was when I went to Altun Ha with the Lions Club from Belize City; also, to the Zoo.

I don't spend any time on the tourist trail even though it is now that season. I have found that simply settling in to Belizean life opens more than enough doors to provide a very rich experience…'

The day's mail necessitated a letter to my bank in the UK…

'…I have received two Coding Notices from the Inland Revenue! I find that I am not only paying tax on my pension but also that they are claiming and deducting tax underpaid. As I am away from the UK for the requisite period, I believe I should not pay tax at all. Also, my tax affairs are being dealt with by NatWest (Bristol). I cannot be any more specific than that - I didn't expect to be involved and didn't bring any papers with me; Bristol have them all anyway. Could you please alert/arouse the right person for me? I would prefer not to be writing to the Inland Revenue from here (or at all, actually!) I enclose the offending documents in the hope that they might be useful…'

Orientation meetings in Orange Walk continued over the next three days at San Juan Nuevo Palmar, Louisiana, Carmelita, St Peter's Anglican School and Chapel School over by the hospital and the road out to Corozal. Considerable concern was shown - as it has been in other schools - for the commitments of staff from September, other than and in addition to the trialling of the New Curriculum. A duplicate request was received at the Orange Walk District Office for principals' biographical information - after having met with most of them twice already and starting each day at the office! Onelia kindly elected to collect Corozal information and produced a new form for use in Orange Walk.

It was easy to find time to go to the BTL office in town and arrange to be connected for email. Roberto also came in the evening on Tuesday when he fitted the modem and loaded the software. There was a charge of $30 for which I had to give him a cheque due to my being almost out of money after having been to Chetumal and having to pay for my glasses.

Gaps making unusual free time during the week provided an opportunity to write to people back home that were not among the long list of regulars, fourteen of them including the past Scout County Commissioner who appointed me with this typical extract…

'…Here is a letter at last. I have tried to write regularly to at least one among people who talk to each other. The letter writing load has been heavy, especially setting up the linking of schools which is going well. My work times are unusual when I am going into schools in my two Districts as I am just now. Today, I start at 2:00pm. This is because it is difficult to work with teachers when they are trying to teach. In the Lower Division with which I am concerned, primary children go home at 2:30 having started at 8:30 and having had only an hour at lunch. (That is interesting as most schools do not accommodate children in any way at lunchtime.) Consequently, I am sitting here at 9:00am on a Wednesday morning, writing to you! This is the second letter and I have done the washing (by hand of course). The sun is shining brightly as it almost always does, slanting across the balcony, through the wide open double front doors and clear across the inside of the house to the other side. The window slats all round, are adjusted to let in the light but not the direct sun where I am sitting. Belize radio is giving news of the day or thumping out its music (at modest volume) behind me. I have found a way of amplifying my tiny World Bands radio. It looks and feels very comfortable and completely home. Some things, carefully selected before I left, add to that feeling. One of these is hanging on the wall to my right. It is a cross-stitch with the Torridge badge on it - one of the things which prompt Belizeans to ask about. You will remember asking me to go into Torridge 'for about three weeks'! On the table where I am writing is a 486 computer which I have managed to acquire by some considerable effort, and a Canon BJC250. My phone was 'activated' for email yesterday and an internal modem will be fitted tomorrow. This is a great boon as I do a lot of writing for children including stories, and keep up a detailed journal. When I leave, I intend to give the lot to a linking school as they don't have much. We are well into the dry season. The 'cool' time is over when we reached the lowest night-time temperature of just over 50 degrees. Making the bed isn't much of a job! The 'wet season' as a descriptor, is somewhat misleading. Generally, when it rains, it is very heavy and everyone takes shelter for ten minutes until it is all over. As I explained to a group of 150 twelve year olds (amid howls of laughter) "If you do that in England, you could still be there three weeks later" …'

It wasn't as great a chore to write them as it might have been since much of it other than above was copy and paste since all recipients were well separated.

I left for Belize City at 6:30am on Friday to talk with David Price and to obtain stationery for Onelia and Bertha. There were a number of issues which needed to be reported covering concerns raised by schools. In the event, there was a meeting at 2:00pm which addressed most of these issues. It was a pity that all the Curriculum Co-ordinators hadn't been asked to attend. A memo was given from Ellajean on the subject 'Plan of Activity March to August, 1998'; also a paper with the title 'Planning the School Curriculum: Yearly Plans and Units of Work in Primary Schools, Plan of Action: March - August, 1998' (that was the title!). Copies of these were supplied for Onelia and Bertha. I phoned Onelia and Bertha later in the day to arrange to meet in the Orange Walk Office to re-visit the Division 1 outcomes in the light of the plan of action. It was good to meet with Ernest Raymond in the morning, who advised that he had prepared the two letters promised although he had not yet sent them; also going to see Cynthia Thompson and Olga Manzanero to establish my interest in a two day field trip arranged for teachers to Rio Bravo, Lamanai and Yo Creek arranged for Thursday and Friday 7/8th May. Margarita also suggested a Science Fair at the Belize Zoo which she will let me know about (this may be on Friday 13th which may not be possible because of the planning for the workshop but in my mind that is an obstacle to be overcome). She located a screen for my display unit (for schools' link) which she will send on Wednesday, with Stanley Bermudas who is coming to Louisiana to work with their Apple-Macs and to help with my 486 and email at home. Nora Bradley offered some RAM chips which would help boost the computer memory. Stanley will also bring and fit these. In the evening I went to see Neria and Tabo to stay for a barbecue and stay the night. I went to bed at 3:00am and got up at 6:00am to go back to Orange Walk, normal for a Friday.

I returned to Orange Walk on the bus at 8:00am and went straight to the Library to meet with 14 children at 10:00am for a reading session which I had agreed to do some time ago; now on a regular basis. I read three stories, did some acting and illustration for them and finished at 11:30. I was to have gone back with eldest son Marco and his friend but there was no sign of them when it was time for the bus so I left. They arrived with the two girls and Tabo and Neria later. I saw them as I came back up Main Street, past the Leiva house. All came home for part of the afternoon. I shall have to try to keep in some sort of food for unexpected visitors. Anything can happen here.

Writing a journal provides an extra focus on dates as does the first of the month and being away from home, although the latter doesn't apply since this is very much my home. March the first was my Dad's Birthday. He would have been 83 had he made it that far. Maybe that is why I have had a quiet day pottering about catching up with my Journal and Work Diary, doing some reading and writing letters. That in turn may well have something to do with phoning Kathryn and arranging to go to Caye Caulker on Thursday. This would be a first relatively distant adventure to visit and explore the island (caye) reached by water taxi from Belize City and very popular with tourists and locals alike.

Next morning, to start the week, there was a meeting arranged with Bertha and Onelia to discuss Outcomes in the light of the latest proposed mode of introduction with reference to the Orientation and Training Workshop. This was so that we would go to the three planning days with some ideas. Ellajean was advised of this arrangement as the rest of the time until we meet in Belize City on Wednesday 11th would be leave; eight free days from now, including the weekend. In the event, Bertha rang in sick so we were finished by lunchtime. I suggested to Bertha that she phone me one evening to make some arrangement for her and the afternoon was spent writing letters, finding the printer a great help rather than having to wait to print saved writings in Belize City.

When I decided to have a go at loading BTL 'Kwickmail' myself I ran into a problem with 'User1' which I couldn't resolve and spent most of the rest of the next day writing letters and reading (having made friends at the library and found quite a lot of donated books of interest that I hadn't read. Needing to get out later, I looked round town for a bicycle but could only find ones with very small wheels and frame.

Almost a whole day was next spent trying to resolve the problems with Kwickmail including phoning BTL repeatedly on what I was given to understand was a helpline. I suspect that may not be the case so I will probably have to question the bill when it comes. Eventually, I got over the problem with 'User1' and got 'logged on' only to find that I couldn't send because I was getting the prompt 'DLL not found'. More phone calls until I was asked to FAX information from 'editscripts' (LOGIN.CMD from Dialler in Trumpet Windsock). Eventually I found out how to use FAX on Cheyenne Bitware but it was just gone five by then and BTL were closed; all gobbledygook to me so it was back to the reading and listening to CDs for the rest of the evening.

Stanley Bermudas was to have come to Louisiana today but he is not now coming until tomorrow. Kathryn phoned and we agreed to postpone the proposed trip to Caye Caulker which was to have been tomorrow. This was because the weather is not expected to be good but it gives me chance to liaise with Stanley over the mailer problems and keep up to date with progress at Louisiana. In the event I managed to send a FAX to BTL and received a reply almost straight away to make some changes in 'editscripts'. This I did but it didn't work resulting in the same prompt and a new FAX to BTL. No reply up to lunchtime would cause difficulty in going to Louisiana for their 'Children's Week' celebrations and meeting with Stanley so another FAX was sent to BTL advising them when I would be at home.

'…The fun afternoon at Louisiana was excellent. Instead of the students taking part in the events, they watched while the staff wore themselves out and supported them with excellent behaviour on the whole and a great deal of sporting enthusiasm. The Principal was Leader of the Clowns. The other two teams were: Logos and TTT. Many of the actual events are on video 4 for SMCC and some photos. The events I can remember were walking race round the perimeter of the field; a version of the Cub Scout activity 'late for pack' with walking, sack race, skipping and running on respective legs of the track; running; tug of war; controlling the football with the feet; controlling the football with a stick; and a cheer-leading demonstration; a good fun afternoon - Look out SMCC. The film was introduced by two girls who are taking part in the linking and there is a shot of a boy with Sunny asking "What do you think of it so far?" Also, some stills of all the buddies and some of the linking group…'

'…It was great to go to St. Paul's Anglican School in Corozal to spend their Children's Day with them. All the classes were going on outings in the morning so I chose to go with Standard 6 to Consejo from where there is a clear view across the Hondo River, which divides Belize from Mexico, to Chetumal. Twenty-one children piled into the back of Valerie Rogers' covered Ford Pick-up with Valerie, Einstein, one other and me in the cab. Einstein is seriously disabled, being completely without the use of his legs. As there was no room for his chair I carried him when we got out. The journey was about eight miles along a road that goes no further than the village where the customs post is and small boats ply their trade to Chetumal. We didn't stay there long but turned back a little way to pick up another track which goes a little further along the coast to a restaurant and visitor facility which is beautifully situated on a remote part of the Caribbean shore. There was plenty of space among the palm trees for games and to dream of staying in one of the cabanas there.

Needless to say, the children soon found plenty to do. The boys especially, once they had found the volleyball net. Others spent their time fishing. The afternoon was spent back at school, starting with a picnic for everyone and the games and dancing - 'Jump-Up' and mostly 'follow De Leada'…'

I got back in time to contact BTL again but attempts to make Trumpet Winsock work failed and they promised to send me 'Spry Dialler' on Tuesday, to pick up at the local office. This will apparently explore the Internet as well. If it does, then the machine will have everything in it. I don't think I will be using it even so, as I have no need of more than email and the rest is expensive. Some letters were from primary school children…

'…I hope you enjoyed Christmas, I know I did. I had a radio controlled car and went out with it on Boxing Day, no one was out: it goes faster than me running. I will be going to Fairthorne in April and will be visiting HMS Victory and the Mary Rose. I wasn't too sure about going, but after having a chat about it I think it will be fun…'

'…One weekend my aunty had her 70th birthday party at the Coaching Inn. Our cousins came down from near York; we had a second Christmas with them. They gave me a Lego Technic set. I am now a collector of Corgi Classics Models and have joined their club. This gives me a discount off some models. I had a Corgi Eddie Stobart lorry from my grandma. I also have a police car, a bus and two lorries…'

'…As you can see I have got a new typewriter, it has taken me quite a lot of time to get it to work. Mum has helped me type this as it is manual with no corrective ribbon…'

'…At school we are doing about the Rain Forest and the problems we face because of its destruction. Did you know that 50% of our oxygen comes from the Rain Forest? …'

'…I bought a new computer, it is a N64. The game I had MRC (multi racing championship) as a game. I swopped Diddy Kong Racing with James…'

'…Philip, Luke, Elliot and Michelle helped Mrs Hare build a 3d model of South Molton and it was displayed in the market place. The town people were asked to give their opinions of what they would like to alter or improve…'

A reply arrived from Fairthorne…

'…Thank you for your letter and story, everyone has been most interested. The season is just starting here at Fairthorne Manor with seven new staff already training and twenty four more due to arrive at Heathrow on the 9th. You may have heard that things have changed here. I am now solely in charge (not bad for a community programme boy), Tony has left but Marian, Pete, Chris, Don, Robin, Sue, Cheryl et al are all still here. We are expanding our operation to include weekends and most exciting of all, we are about to take over the nursery school and set up a sixty place childcare scheme. This will mean new staff, lots of them, so we have spent all winter converting new bedrooms and building a new set of offices.

The old place is not looking so bad. We have completely carpeted Pembroke House and decorated Heald House. We have a brand new awning in the rose garden on the front of the old coffee bar, which has been converted into the new tuck shop. This will be the venue for the weekly disco as well as providing a new place to take morning coffee.

The programme is having a bit of a facelift too! We are expecting a fleet of Zephyr sailing dinghies, which will allow us to provide a short 'messing about in boats' session. The aerial runway has a re-built platform and is about to become part of a larger ropes course.

I went to Romania during the autumn to look at some of the work carried out by the YMCA with a view to setting up an international project for Fairthorne Manor. It seems likely that we support the development of a summer camp by providing and training a staff team. I hope it goes ahead, as everyone seems very excited about their part and their trip abroad…'

And a thank you sent to VSO…

'…This seemed to be about the best way of saying thank you for your help. At least, it will be if it works. Perhaps you could send a reply to confirm. I don't know whether I can receive FAX on my telephone number, I don't see why not. The computer will be on until 12:00. If not, perhaps you could phone. (If this finishes up with Angelique, please smile and give my apologies.) The modem was fitted by a Belizean friend here and the 'Cheyenne Bitware' software is fitted also. That is what I am using. I don't expect to be using the other facilities but it will be good for a school to be using the internet, FAX and perhaps voicemail later on.

Yesterday I had a shot at installing BTL Kwickmail for email. Oh dear, what a job that turned out to be. Long phone calls to Belize City on what I was led to believe was a help line but which I now doubt so I expect there will be further discourse about the cost. It still doesn't work and I now have to send them a copy of 'edit scripts'. Woe and Thrice Woe! The printer is fine. The problem was that I wasn't waiting long enough for the computer to talk to it. It takes ages so that is something else to sort out. I think these things wait for me. Anyway, once again, THANKS for your help…'

It is time for a first report to VSO who brought me here…

'…Having in mind the relevance of the UNESCO Four Pillars of Learning - to **live together**, to **be**, to **know** and to **do** - the job couldn't have been better. It has been made easy to learn to live together with Belizeans, both because of their welcome and the location in which I live; the sense of being is heightened by that relationship; the knowing which comes from my past experience is valued in a way which enables it to grow and there is no shortage of useful and rewarding things to do. With respect to the defined purpose of our being here - mainly to *Assist in the delivery of the Teachers' Handbook and resource materials at District level*' the picture is somewhat different. A more telling paragraph under significant assumptions or constraints is *'This project is still in its infancy and as such has not yet attained a coherent and co-ordinated structure'*. Although the delivery of the New Curriculum is much closer to the classroom now than it was the last quote holds as good to date as it did at the beginning. When we arrived at the beginning of September there was little prospect of our being stationed in our Districts as expected, before January and not much urgency. There was in any case, no Teachers' Handbook being planned - rather a set of 'Outcomes': statements of what a child should know, understand or be able to do on reaching the end of the Lower Division of Primary Education, much along the lines of the English National Curriculum but uniquely Belizean and firmly rooted in a philosophy derived from the Four Pillars referred to above. This new 'Curriculum' rather than a handbook, in my view, is excellent and very exciting indeed; puts the ownership of learning with children, the ownership of teaching with the staff and accountability with the school where it belongs; and offers the benefit of being pro-active rather than re-active. We felt able to take part in an acceleration of activity and found ourselves in the Districts at the beginning of November, ready to take part in phase-one of testing which was to determine the clarity of the outcomes. Changes in the work pace are to be expected as evaluation takes place but there has been a disappointing regularity in change of plan, sometimes overnight, which has involved leading schools in one direction only to be faced with the task of leading them off in another - again and with an immediacy which is difficult to justify. The worth of the project is beyond question, the planning is at best without sufficient account of its effect and the delivery is challenging (none the worse for that to my taste!). It remains for me, very exciting and offers many almost random opportunities to work in schools in other ways. It simply has to work.

Learning in another culture has been more exciting and revealing than I had imagined. In many respects my expectations were wrong. I had an image for example, of the position a developing country might be in, which was quite different in technical expertise yet as expected in living conditions - but by no means universally so. On the other hand, it has been very easy to settle into the Belizean life almost exclusively among Belizeans. An open mind is essential - there are many ways of living, loving (in the widest sense) and learning which are just as valid and often better than ones we are used to - and a sense of awe and wonder.

I managed to acquire a computer (certainly didn't expect that!) which has helped enormously in all forms of writing. Experiences have been recorded in detail as a 'Writer's Journal' which has proved invaluable in writing stories for children and letter writing too. The stories have been easy. There has been no shortage of material. Photographs make description easy but all you have to do is to sit outside with your eyes open.

Communications with Primary Children, Scouts and a Secondary School have been very successful. The first depends largely on my own writing and journal but the latter two have been made easy by the enthusiasm of Belizean Scouts and the four Primary Schools who are taking part. I think I have learnt as much from sharing the children's understanding of each other's culture than in any other way - not that there is anything new in that. It looks as though the links will strengthen, as I had hoped, to make me redundant to their growth, not by the time I return home but long before. Already I have become more a resource than catalyst.

The interactive Schools' Project is under way as explained. The next step is to find sponsors to provide email for participating schools. Working with Belizeans and having Belizean friends in business I have found a great deal of enthusiasm for that too. Many things have just found their own place to interlock.

Belizeans are so polite that the cues and mannerisms which usually indicate understanding in the UK can often confuse. Even after six months, I have left teachers thinking that what has been said has been understood when it hasn't at all. In school and in the classroom teachers are very caring as one would expect but there is a large gap in accounting for the child's point of view. Indeed, there is little expectation of such in children too. Most teaching is at present, a matter of rote; very much telling, listening and remembering with lots of repetition in between. In the face of the rate of change of plans it would be all too easy to 'react to the last command' but, happily, initiative is appreciated, generally accommodated and always acknowledged with thanks by recipients.

There is an amazing level of bureaucracy and duplication. As an example, expense forms are filed and kept with all receipts even after being checked four times and have to be written with a ball point for durability. Fountain pen ink is not enough. This I discovered after a meeting had been told by a high ranking official that the British always write everything down. Perhaps that is from where the practice grew. Time often has little significance. 'Right now' has no more immediacy about it than 'In a minute' would have. It could be anything from soon to never. Start times are similarly flexible and it is difficult to have meetings start on time although the politeness of Belizeans will often find a response if you persist in being on time. An indulgence perhaps but appreciated nonetheless.

The means for promoting understanding are very much in place through the efforts of young people and the adults who work with them on both sides of the Atlantic. The story of that process and the opportunity to tell it when I return should attract an interest and enquiring minds. There is no intention of telling what I have done; rather what others have done and are doing and a record of what life is like. One vehicle for this is the children's stories which are all set in Belize and based on true experience. There is the journal to use as a written record, photos, audio and video tape. The initial 'audience' would be those with whom contact is already established and has been maintained. Beyond that, promotion would be reactive (hopefully). It would be useful to work from a base of people who are trying to promote international understanding themselves but talking to each other about it is to be avoided except to reinforce interest and resolve. Just as there have been groups of young people who expressed an interest and a willingness to establish links before I left, there are bound to be others who will wish to do so when I return - especially now that there is an established programme - in just the same way as more are showing interest here. Again, I see this as being largely self-generating; needing only a small input and awareness of potential to maintain momentum. When I left and while I have been here, considerable interest has been shown by Lions International and Rotary Clubs. Both would provide a base from which to move forward. There are in any case, many aspects of life here which are very different from my expectations and which I would wish to explore further through exposition and dialogue with other people. Also, South Molton Town Charity has a staked interest in my coming here and has their own way of looking at both need and privilege.

I have felt very much at home in Belize and most especially here in Orange Walk. I am sure that feeling has its absolute root in a determination to 'live Belizean' but that was helped considerably through the family placement on moving into Belize City at the end of the Orientation Week. I stayed with them for the whole two months that I spent in Belize City. Belizeans undoubtedly appreciate their guests becoming 'as of family' which means that the original intention is well supported but also that the family welcome is an enduring one. It didn't stop there because the same family come from Orange Walk and a neighbouring village called San Estevan. We (there were four of us to start with) were taken to spend a weekend with the extended family in San Estevan at the end of the first week with them. Also, I came here to Orange Walk knowing a number of families already as a result of their many connections freely shared. This provided a very good start and was added to by the many opportunities I had through the 'Linking Programme' and my work of talking with (often large) groups of children and working with their teachers. I have just about got used to being called 'Mr Max' and have to confess I like it!

It has helped that I have no particular wish to travel great distances sightseeing. Instead, I have found myself mostly being taken on family outings and sharing the 'sights' with them. Rarely a weekend goes by without something of the sort. One drawback is that many country areas are not safe for walking because of muggings which occasionally take place. This would be okay for many people, probably, but I like all day walking and this has been a disappointment. However, I have a bicycle and that increases both scope and range. What might be not too good for a walker might be less hazardous for a cyclist?

Many people have said to me before I came here, that there is nothing much in Orange Walk. I suppose that would seem to be the case if you judge an area by the number of tourist attractions there are and here there are few. However, I have found many beautiful places unspoiled by hordes of people and visited only by a few locals. The cycling is easy as the land is flat and the industry, mostly sugar, is interesting. Also the flatness does not mean that the countryside is featureless. On the contrary, the flora, especially, varies considerably because of the location of rivers (the New River is magnificent), the lagoons and the sea…'

I've bought my bicycle. It is an American 'Murray Ultra Terrain Sport' with eighteen gears. The gears work beautifully. It is very sturdy, comfortable and has very chunky tyres which are ideal for the rough roads. I hadn't intended going far in trying it out but ended up taking two hours to cover the twenty five miles I didn't do when I did my sixteen mile walk round Yo Creek. It was hot but with plenty of breeze and not full sun most of the time. Even so, I looked as though I had been lying in the sun for two weeks rather than cycling for two hours. The bike cost rather more than I intended to pay but I did well at $400 against the marked price of $450. Mind, I did buy it at Landy's hardware store after much looking around for weeks. Also VSO had given me $300 to buy a bicycle which at the time, I chose to put towards the computer.

I returned to find a very quick reply from the past Scout County Commissioner…

'…Thank you for your long and 'newsy' letter. As I read it I could almost picture you sitting there and writing. The least that I can do is answer it quickly before you set off on explorations new. It seems to me that you have thoroughly enjoyed the change in interest and that you do not have any regrets…'
A much slower reply from an eleven-year-old due to the regular mail problems and reproduced in full shows admirable self-confidence…

'…I'm sorry that the letters didn't get through, so I'll have to write again. I haven't done much to the story because I have been busy with schoolwork and I have also started a paper round, which means I have got to be up at 6:00am every morning except Sundays but I get paid £8 a week, so it's worth it. We had a good Christmas in our house this year. How do you celebrate Christmas in Belize? I got a personal Compact Disc Player (CD player) and mainly clothes. I also got a bit of money and added with what I had left from my birthday money I went shopping and bought myself a brand new pair of red football boots and a rugby ball. Thanks a lot for the present you gave me; it was great. School has been going all right, except in some subjects. Sport though, is what I normally have to talk about, so here I go.
FOOTBALL Since I last wrote I have been selected to represent North Devon U/13s in a squad of 20. Our team isn't, unfortunately, going so well. After starting so well our season has crumbled, mainly through players being ill and not performing well when they are playing. Luckily for me I am not one of the ones who have been ill but not so good I am one of the ones that haven't performed regularly. We have now had a good rest over the winter and only played two games this year so far, due to bad weather. School-wise is not so good either. We were knocked out of the cup in the first round after a close battle with Pilton. We lost another game too but again the rest have been called off.
RUGBY Last term in school was the rugby term. Our rugby team isn't as bad as the football team. We lost our first game of the season 30-10 but that was with a misfit team. But from then on we never looked back, winning our next game away to Ilfracombe, 44-0 (a couple of conversions and a try from me). We then played five more games during the season, winning them all comfortably. In the end I finished the season with 47 points (17 conversions, 2 tries and a penalty). Next season I'm looking for at least double that, as my kicking is impeccable and can kick between the posts anywhere inside the opposition's half. Last season I played scrum-half but next season I want to play as one of the centres, as you get more of the ball and it would make our backs stronger, as they can't tackle. I hope you are well…'

There was another step in independent travel next day as I cycled to San Estevan, about fourteen miles round trip and called in on some of Neria's relatives and where I was invited to dinner but for once didn't stay; confirming the independent travel maybe.

The 9th March is 'Baron Bliss Day' in Belize. The British Baron Bliss was a significant benefactor to Belize who meeting with Belizean hospitality after disappointment in other parts of the Caribbean at the end of his life decided that was where to leave most of his fortune of which only the interest was to be used and for closely specified purposes for the benefit of the citizens. I had hoped that the 'Fair' down by the riverside would have been more than it was and it turned out to be of little interest to me.

The last day of leave, as I supposed, seemed to provide a good time to go to La Immaculada School for the afternoon to discuss progress with the linking group from Standard Six. The school is close by, almost overlooked from my balcony and the District Office is only five minutes further where I called to see if there were any messages. Daisy rang through while I was there to say that we were not required to go in to the Belize City Office until Monday - again! I consider this kind of abrupt directive without consultation or explanation, to be both rude and unprofessional but a sneaking doubt of a prejudicial way of seeing things has been rising in my mind in living among people here and I quickly see that offence is far from the thinking and I look forward to another five days to enjoy other things.

Unexpected extra time always presents its own challenge and so next is mostly a domestic and letter writing day although I did go for a ride out to Chan Pine Ridge, crossed to the Guinea Grass road, almost into the village and returned passing the toll bridge and coming through San Juan Nuevo Palmar - a distance of about eighteen miles. I had arranged after knowing the time was available, to go to Louisiana School for the afternoon but one of their pupils from Standard Three was drowned at the weekend and his year went to the funeral while the rest of the school was dismissed. I saw a lot of the children go past the house from the cemetery afterwards. George Cawich, the Principal and two members of staff called in at my house afterwards – an important time. We are all very close.

The morning of a day at Calcutta Government School with Standard Five and Six was spent discussing the linking progress and leading them in some creative writing for which I used part of the story 'Home is The Belizoo' and this was appropriately followed with a day at the Children's Science Conservation Fair at the Belize Zoo. I left as usual on the 6:30 am bus to meet David Eck and Margarita Gomez at the EDU at 8:00am and from there we went by car to the Zoo. David was one of the organisers of the event and Margarita was a judge. The computer first prize was won by Belmopan Primary Upper School. The event was recorded in photographs for SMCC and provided a most enjoyable and interesting day as well as underlining the current interest in computers in Belizean schools. I arrived back just in time to pick up the software for Internet Explorer from BTL - which turned out to be the wrong discs!

At last I managed to find the right time to go to St Peter's Anglican Church. The communion service starts at eight thirty although the time seems rather flexible as it often is in Belize. I arrived at about ten to eight just to be sure and spent some time talking with the minister who is retiring at the end of the month. There is to be a big farewell service for him on the 29th with Anglicans coming from all over Belize. I think I would like to go to that although I had thought to go up to Cayo to stay with Kathryn that weekend. I went for a bit of a bike ride around but spent much of the rest of the day writing letters, enjoying letters received and getting ready for a week in Belize City…

'…Thank you very much for the parcel of four books and the birthday card and for the letter and two pieces of writing. The parcel arrived last Saturday (7th March) and the letter came on Tuesday (10th March). The parcels seem to come quicker than the letters! I received the parcel containing the book called 'Characters and Caricatures in Belizean Folklore', a copy of the account of the walk to Yo Creek and a letter. I wrote a letter in reply dated 5th February and enclosed it with some newspaper cuttings, a card and a CD called 'Piano Favourites'. I put them all in a padded envelope and posted it from South Molton on 6th February. Perhaps that is the parcel that was mentioned in the note you mentioned in your last letter. I hope it is and that you have been able to enjoy listening to the CD…'

'…Thank you for the copies of your writing. I'm surprised you could do any filming after the cups of rum and coke! Double Head Cabbage does sound an unusual name for a place. The Lions Club seems to help other people in several practical ways. It must have been quite a day! Did the filming of the baboons turn out to be successful? Have the Lions Club been able to use your film for fund-raising? …'

'…How lovely to hear from you and I am glad that you are well and happy and enjoying your life in Belize. I was very interested to hear all your news. I envy you with all that sunshine, as I feel better when I am in hot, sunny countries but I suppose even the sun gets a little wearing at times. I shall think of you sitting in the cool of your veranda… You did well to acquire a computer and printer, which will be very useful I would imagine and also on the email…'

'…pleased to hear you have your memories with you. Isn't it lovely to know people really thought of you? Do you write children's stories just for the school or for publication? …

'…The story 'Home is The Belizoo' is now finished and I'm quite pleased with it. I expect I will send you a copy some time but, for now, I am taking it to Belize City to a Belizean friend who is a member of the curriculum team in the office. She writes stories as well and we have shared quite a few ideas. I went to the Zoo again on Friday in company with one of the organisers of the Science and Conservation Fair for Primary Children there. Also, with one of the judges as it was a competitive event with a computer as prize. That went to Belmopan Upper School. One of the Corozal Schools got second. I forget what that prize was but all teams got a prize and they were all useful ones - and imaginative. It was a brilliant day again. There were about 600 children with some excellent projects which I have recorded with photos this time. I'm not sure whether another story will emerge. I will have to see after I have had the photos printed. That shouldn't take too long because the film is finished…'

'…Funds are going pretty well now, especially as I don't have any great expenditure rushing about as seems to be the norm. In fact, now that the initial high expenses have been met and having moved some funds from home early on, things are pretty comfortable. I intend to spend the Easter holiday around and about on the bicycle and staying here and there as seems most convenient, although it will be planned and some places booked beforehand…'

'…Today is the end of an unexpected leave. We were all given a 'thank you' for work done based on St Paul's reference to the parts of the body, each serving the whole and working together. While that is to be appreciated in its way, unfortunately the reality is that forward planning and good management are often absent from the equation! Anyway, we have had ten days off and that has been very useful for keeping my other school contacts going and becoming even more a part of life round here. (I can claim little credit for that. Children and adults alike are wonderful in their welcome into their circle of life.) We were supposed to have started again with a three day planning session in Belize City from last Wednesday but that too, was postponed at the last minute and doesn't start until tomorrow. (It is too late to change that because I will be on the 6:30am bus tomorrow morning!)…'

'…I'm still having computer problems but most things are working. I suppose things are more worthwhile if they come with a few problems. That's what I tell myself anyway. I do have a filter screen now which helps my eyes. The latest is that the BTL (Belize Telecommunications Limited) software for email doesn't work despite much telephone communication with their experts. Now they have 'sent (?)' me the full Internet Explorer free of charge. Unfortunately the package contained the wrong discs so I'm no further forward at the time of writing! Hey ho! ...'

'…The new glasses are fine. So good in fact, that I don't have to close them up because I can wear them all the time and I don't need the cord thing I used to hang them round my neck. The react-a-light is excellent for the very bright light too…'

'…I am particularly fond of the Anansi stories I think, because of my familiarity with Brer Rabbit as a child. The nature of the two characters is much the same as that of a lovable rogue. I have met a few such people in my time and remember them too, with fondness. There are tapes of storytellers telling their tales in Creole - some of them being of Anansi. I have borrowed one but what I really want to do is record the reading of people I know. I'm working on that…'

'…One of the things that have been of most value in coming here is to make some more progress in identifying what really matters in life. It has been very pleasing too, that the values I came with are not changed but developed. What has changed is the knowledge and understanding. The 'sameness' I have found in a very different culture and environment has been very enlightening indeed. I came here with my material life in two suitcases. I realise now that I could have managed just as well with one. That is not to say that I don't have things with me that are precious; I do, but they are not tucked away; they are used. Your making of 'buddy' George has had a worth far greater than either you or I could have imagined. He has been admired and fondled by so many children here as they have heard his story that I couldn't hope to count…'

'…I have only seen two snakes out and about. Both of these were water snakes of about two feet in length. More interesting was the tarantula I met in the bathroom when I first came here. He used to come out at night and stay out after the light was switched on. I sat and watched him for a long time, night after night until I tired of it and tapped on the wall when he would run and hide. He gave up after about two weeks and I haven't seen him since. I must say that I am careful not to disturb any inhabitants that I cannot see but that is no more than I used to do when out walking in England. The flowers really are amazing, and the butterflies. The colours are so brilliant and so many of them are huge. A lot of the trees also have very striking flowers which seem to last for a very long time. Also there are the epiphytes and others parasitic plants which live in the canopy of the trees, in town just as much as in the rainforests which are in sight of my veranda, barely a mile away…'

Home is.......
The Belizoo!!

George hadn't thought much about his shell. You could hardly expect him to. Certainly, he was attached to it. He liked it of course. It was his home and very much part of his life and even part of himself. That is how it was for a snail. You couldn't get away from it and anything that was as familiar as that - well, you just don't think about it very often at all.

Today was different. George was thinking about his shell. He was very much aware of it as his home. He loved its close fit. Some people might feel a bit closed in by such a small space but it made George feel safe and comfortable. More than that, it was his and that was where he belonged.

So, how was it that George was thinking so much about his shell? Well, it might sound odd but it was because he was going to the zoo! George was fascinated by zoos. He loved to see the great variety of fellow creatures that he would not normally see unless he was very, very patient and looked in all the right places at just the right time. Even then he might only see one exciting and secretive animal in quite a long time and after much waiting. In a zoo he could see them all - easily. But, fascinated as he was, George was uncomfortable about the idea of zoos. He had tried to think about them from the animals' point of view. You could hardly call a zoo home with all those cages, concrete, steel and timber and bits of dying plants thrown in as a pretence of the real thing. And mostly, the animals didn't belong there at all. They were condemned to pace about in an unfamiliar space. Worse than that, they were often far across the sea, a long way from the land where they were born, and the weather they were used to.

Yes, today was different. George was thinking about his shell. George was very happy about his home. He loved its close fit which made him feel safe and comfortable. More than that, it was his and that was where he belonged. Today was also different (George hoped) because the zoo was different (or so he had been told). This zoo had only animals in it that belonged in the country where it was. More important than that, someone had had a brilliant idea (George thought). Instead of taking the animals to the zoo, they brought the zoo to the animals. This was where they lived. This was Belize; a tiny country on the Western shore of the Caribbean Sea, protected from flooding by a great Barrier Reef and still having a wonderfully preserved habitat for its rich variety of wild animals.

So George thought - as he was sitting on the rucksack of his companion waiting to go in to the Belize Zoo early in the morning on a beautiful sunny day; 8:30am on Christmas Eve, 24th December 1997; 'All the days seem to be beautifully sunny here,' George reflected, and he looked around.

They were at the entrance to the long drive from the road which passes through the rich variety of forest trees and plants; still at the bus shelter where they had got off the bus from Belize City thirty miles away. Their morning had started with the 6:30am bus from Orange Walk Town, sixty miles north of Belize City. 'A journey of ninety miles to go to the zoo, I hope it will be worth it,' he thought.
Looking round the shelter, George's eye fell on a small poster stuck to the seat:

'De bird in de hand wort two in de bush.'

George smiled to himself. 'That's a good start,' he thought. 'I'm here. No point in thinking twice about it. Let's go, man, let's go!' Looking up, he signalled his intention to his companion but paused as Mr Max was talking into that recorder thing that he always seemed to be carrying with him. 'Still, that might be useful,' George allowed, 'In case I forget anything.'

"This is the Western Highway. It's a long way from anywhere in particular. You can just see the hills of Cayo in the distance. It's not a busy road. The traffic that does come along it moves quite quickly. And this is the site of... The Belize Zoo.... ...'the animals of Belize in their natural habitat'.... open daily from 9:00am to 4:30pm.... Where George and I are going to spend the day."

At the entrance to the zoo there was the usual information for tourists and visitors:
'The Belize Zoo - a haven for wildlife.

The Belize Zoo was started in 1983 when 17 animals were left from the filming of a natural history documentary. Since then the zoo has grown and now features over 100 animals, all indigenous to Belize; many endangered. The new zoo opened on 7th December 1991 and features animals in spacious exhibits. Entrance; Gerald Durrell Visitor Centre. Welcome.'

"Yes! I've heard of him," George remembered. "He's that chap who said that zoos should be for the animals more than the people - or something like that. Yes! This could be good!"

Oddly enough, it was the Visitors' Centre that was the only place that made George uncomfortable and he didn't understand why. Perhaps it was the snakes: 'the largest venomous snake; found throughout Belize as well as the Caribbean and South America - commonly called the Yellow Jaw Tommygoff or Barbar Amarilla - the Fer de Lance; feeds mostly on birds and rodents.' Or the tarantula: one of the largest of the spiders; or the skeleton of the Manatee. Not the Boa Constrictor, even though it could be thirty feet long: 'Boas are harmless snakes that like to hang around places where rodents are plentiful as this is their favourite food item'. Possibly the skeleton of a tapir; 'I've heard about tapirs,' thought George, 'I hope I shall see one.'

The first resident outside (just like any home - having residents) after the 'Welcome to the Belize Zoo map', being a bird, was one that George wasn't too comfortable about either but he didn't think this one would bother with snails.

'Yes mon! We are King Vultures. The biggest Vulture that Lives in Belize. And the very prettiest! And the most rare! Don't you think we look kingly? Betcha don't think we dine very kingly (unless you know of any kings who eat road kills). Hey! We are important birds! We help to keep your countryside clean of dead animals. We help to prevent the spread of disease!'

The sign reminded him of the poster in the bus shelter.

"Hey! I like that!" He said out loud.

"What do you expect?" came the reply.

George jumped and looked around but the sound had come from above and there, sitting on the branch, wings partly open, catching the air was a huge vulture with ugly features and a hooked beak ideal for tearing flesh from bones. George hurried on - or he tried to but Mr Max was recording again:

"Two unique things about this zoo are that it contains only Belizean animals and also that it is part of the rainforest...."

And then....

This Way. Yes Mon! De White Tailed Deer and De Spider Monkeys.'

None too soon for George, they moved on to see the White Tailed Deer looking up at them with their big, brown, liquid eyes and their tongues licking them in welcome; ears alert; friendly, and liking to be stroked.

"Do you like it here?" asked George, for the thoughts he came with were still at the front of his mind.

"Of course!" said the first deer, "Why?"

"Oh well," replied George, embarrassed by an answer he didn't expect, "I thought......... Well, you are shut in by a fence aren't you?"

"No! You could come in because I like you. But mostly, that's for keeping out animals that I'm afraid of. This is my home you know. I live in the forest and this is the forest. In fact this is my forest. It is home. The trees are right, the plants are right, the weather is right and I get extra food and water just for being nice to visitors. And we all like to be nice to visitors don't we?"

"I hadn't thought of it like that. I'll come back to see you before I go." And George wandered off.

'If you're in the mood for something kinda funky, then look up here at we Spider Monkey. We swing through the trees with greatest of ease. When you're minus a thumb brachiation is a breeze!'
'We spider Monkeys once lived plenty in your Nation 'til yellow fever came and reduced our population. So whatever you do, don't ever forget we Spider Monkeys make very bad pets.'
'So if you are proud of your country and you really should be, then keep us for ever in the jungle can-opy.'

"I do like these signs. They're kinda groovy too" George muttered to himself, distracted until he saw a mother and a baby spider monkey playing in the trees. "Hi," he called.

"Hi, yo down there, come da up a play." Mother called back as she went to fetch her baby so that both sat and faced George below.

It was not difficult for him to get through the fence and under what he recognised as electric wires inside and soon he was sitting alongside them. "Great view," he said, "But I see none of you climbing the fence. You could do that without even thinking about it!"

"That's the point," she laughed, "And then where would we be? No, we lost enough of our number through Yellow Fever without losing more through carelessness. That's what the electric wire is for - to remind us that the fence is close by. Our cousins, the Howler Monkeys had the same problem but the Spider Monkey has a much longer gestation period - it takes much longer for us to make babies so our protection is even more important."

George was impressed, thinking that he could happily live here too. He idly watched two other spider monkeys. One was sitting comfortably below the other while the one above hung from a branch only by his tail as he attended to the removal of ticks or other parasites from the one underneath.

And George remembered being told that the Howler Monkey recovered well from the Yellow Fever epidemic - especially with the preservation in the 'Baboon' Sanctuary. He remembered too, reading a story somewhere, called 'Dis is where de Action is!' which was about a visit to the Community Baboon Sanctuary along the banks of the Belize River from Bermudan Landing to Scotland Halfmoon and including several other villages with equally strange names like Big Falls, Double Head Cabbage, Isabella Bank, St. Paul's and Willows Bank.

Yes, George could live happily here. Parts of the forest have to be fenced off of course, but if they weren't no-one would be quite so comfortable. And the birds are kept in enclosures which are simply nets thrown over their native forest trees.

Over the forest trees! That was it! This is their home as well. The spider monkeys here are even given some ropes to play on too.

Spider monkeys don't jump from branch to branch - hence the name 'spider'. They climb or run, swinging from branch to branch using any combination of the four limbs, often only one, or the prehensile tail.

"Better not stay though, must move on," and as he made to go the mother smiled and the baby jumped up and down.

A small crowd of monkeys gathered. The clown amongst them hung from a single branch by the arm and leg on one side. He scratched himself with the hand on the other arm and reached out with his tail to another branch, letting go with the hand and foot. Then, hanging completely upside down, only by his tail, he crooned softly "You won't mind if we don't join you?"

The next home from home was that of the Central American Tapir - the Mountain Cow. The approach was heralded by a series of boards, yellow on black, which read:

'I am a handsome Mountain Cow. You can call me Tapir too. I only eat plants and I am related to the horse and the rhino. And.... we Mountain Cows are proud to be named your National Animal.'

'I am so special; they made me the National Animal. I am a Mountain Cow. Okay, you can call me a Tapir but I do get vexed when people say that I look like an anteater. I am related to the horse and the rhino and I am the largest land mammal in the neo-tropics and one of the rarest animals in the world.'

'It's me! The very famous April! The Tapir! Me and my he-tapir are part of a regional breeding programme - Hey! Our species are endangered and we want to be your National Animal forever.'

"So where's April?" asked George. "You're definitely not an April!" He said to the huge male Tapir pacing back and forth inside, "And you don't look very happy! Don't you like it here?"

"Of course I do! It's certainly not that... The cow's gone inside (don't take that the wrong way... naughty!). She won't speak to me and I don't know what I've done to upset her. She won't even let me come near."

'Snails don't have that problem but it won't help to mention it,' thought George. Instead he said that he thought it was always like that with the females and the Tapir ought to try to get on with his own job. Actually George didn't realise quite what he had said but he soon found out.

"I can't hang around here, pacing about and talking to you. I have to get on with my own job." grumbled the Tapir as though he had thought of it for himself, and George watched to see what would happen.

First, the Tapir went to his water hole and **drank... and drank... and drank...**

until George thought that even such a big animal should burst.

It was hot but this seemed ridiculous. Then the great beast resumed his pacing up and down, back and forth, until George was quite giddy with it all. He had almost made up his mind to go when the pacing

stopped and caught his attention once more. A huge body sort of...... poised. The back end gave a little wiggle. There was a slight straining of muscle and ~~squirt....~~ **big squirt....**
very big squirt!

"Wow," exclaimed George, as he always did when there was something to wonder at. "I wondered why he drank all that water - and why he had to pace about (think about it!). And what a lot - and what a shot too!" The base of a small bush was more exposed than before, thoroughly washed and beginning to wither.

The soil around its base had formed into a distinct hollow, freshly carved. And that was not all. The performance was repeated time after time, each in a different place - all around the Tapir's home.

"I know what you are doing!" George couldn't even catch the attention of the beast let alone boast to him. "You're marking your territory!" he shouted. 'But wait a minute.' A thought had occurred now. 'Just how does he do that?' For the hot, steaming stream always shot out one way - backwards! 'How does he do that?' Male animals don't have anything that... Oh dear... Male animals point... If these are Mountain Cows then this is a bull - and bulls... Well, you know! It can't be done!

"Must go and have a look; must find out!" And before anyone could stop him George had positioned himself just right to watch. All seemed perfectly normal. George was even more puzzled... until... The back end gave a little wiggle.

There was a slight straining of muscle and **squirt...big squirt...**
very big squirt!

George had seen it. The slight straining of muscle was the clue. It seemed the Tapir had an extra talent in that department, and if he chose he could fire backwards... and fast... much too fast for George who had learned a lesson the hard way as usual and moved on, drawn by water, to the lake.

That was enough excitement for now. George gazed as in a dream, at the lake; forgotten was his short embarrassment. Glassy water was shining as a mirror. Turtles were resting on a log floating in the water. Fish were disturbing the otherwise still surface which was reflecting the trees. There was movement of the turtles beneath the deep green: water lilies, more turtles, floating logs; reflection of clouds as well as trees. In the midst of all there was a glimpse of a turtle coming to the surface. It takes air, leaving tiny rings spreading rapidly out across the glassy surface, and dips down again to disappear out of sight.

Reflection... Reflection of light... Reflection on the beauty of it all... Reflection on what we are doing. George thought 'Throughout the world, tropical forests are being destroyed and animals dependent on these forests are threatened with extinction. Much of Belize still has a healthy population of wildlife. Thank goodness for that. You'd better Belize it!' And he smiled.

'Belize, stand proud as a Nation. The richness of your flora and fauna will be an everlasting enhancement to your natural heritage.'
'Colour! You want colour? Character! You want character? Then you want me! I'm your National Bird, the Keel Billed Toucan. Aren't you proud that I am a Belizean too?'

The Keel Billed Toucan is the National Bird. Their beak is like our finger nail but huge. George wondered at it. "How does it manage to balance let alone fly?" This one sat, unconcerned, moving its head slowly from side to side; tilting it, watching through one eye then turning to use the other; blinking slowly, sometimes with both eyes together and sometimes with one; deep, black, liquid, expressionless eyes; eyes that swivel independently like great orbs controlled by an unfathomable, watching brain. Yet beautiful: the most brilliantly coloured bird of Belize; shimmering blue/black on its back and the top of its head; beak and chest feathers, all the colours of yellow, green and blue and patches of brilliant red blending where they will, and quite unmoved by the number of Toucans that fly in and out of the zoo, skimming the canopy of the rainforest with their mates.

The anteater lived close by:

'Gwon! Of course I am sleeping! I am an anteater! (We are very nocturnal). I can eat over 1,000 termites each and every day!'

proudly displayed under the name of his home.

George thought this an excellent idea. The very thought of termites made him itch most uncomfortably under his shell where he couldn't scratch it (it wouldn't be polite anyway!). But even termites had their place in the scheme of things and it was interesting how many huge termites nests there were in just the right places in the zoo. 'Somebody must have given the matter some thought.' George jumped as a voice commented "Just as well, says I" and the anteater turned away from him and resumed his feast.

'It was lucky to see him active during the day,' George thought, and was pleased. 'Now he is taking absolutely no notice of anyone outside his space; hunting with his great, long snout curving slightly downwards as if designed to enable him to see at the same time; powerful arms; able to hold very still and balance on the back legs; finding ants or termites easily with his long tongue flicking rapidly to search them out.'

Then he came across a succession of homes all as comfortable and natural as the last. The ocelot, tiger cat, so well camouflaged, spattered, dark and white, asleep in the undergrowth under the native trees of its home habitat.

We like the way we smell! We are Warrees and we rub that smell on each other and on things in our territory. That is how we Warrees communicate. Our species is threatened in Central America due to hunting and habitat loss but here in Belize we live and smell on. Warrees are a unique part of your natural heritage.
Please let us have a future in the wild.'

Another of the notices painted on slices of big logs cut at a sharp angle, announced the Warrees or perhaps more properly, the White Lipped Peccaries. The Keeper had brought food - Grunt, grunt. The peccaries' snouts were mobile making up for their poor eyesight. They were sniffing; searching back and forth and eating greedily. They rustled as their backs, covered in the thick bristles they had for hair (almost like spines), rubbed one against the other. George was not sure whether some of the noises were grunts or belches. He decided that it was probably both and watched in wonder, knowing that peccaries are easily spooked but "Not just now because we are busy eating, thank you!"

The Collared Peccary is smaller than the Warrees. It is not so coarse. It makes less of a mess of the ground and likes to run among the trees and bushes rather than out in the open; two of them nearby chased each other in some game in which there was no time for chatter; not at all spooked as their cousins might have been but just as little time for talking to George. He stayed a while, watching, and then wandered on.

'If you say Puma and I say Cougar
You say Mountain Lion and I say Red Tiger
Puma, Cougar, Mountain Lion, Red Tiger
Let's call the whole thing off.'

The Puma (or Cougar, or Mountain Lion or Red Tiger) was lying, long, with his tail twitching towards George at its very tip. Bright yellow, unblinking, fathomless eyes stared back over the right shoulder at George who was looking on from a safe distance. The eyes, the whole posture seemed to be challenging George to say something. It was only then that George realized that the cat was at home but not 'at home' to visitors. Once more he slipped quietly away. No threat? No sweat!

Yes, George could happily live here because this zoo was different. This zoo had only animals in it that belonged in the country where it was. What was more important than that, someone had had that brilliant idea, instead of taking the animals to the zoo, bringing the zoo to the animals. This **was** where they lived. This **was** Belize; a tiny country on the Western shore of the Caribbean Sea, protected from flooding by a great Barrier Reef and still having a wonderfully preserved habitat for its rich variety of wild animals.

The Black Howler Monkey, the 'Baboon' as it is called in Belize, is quite different from the ugly brown, African variety that has the big red bottom. It is not as heavy but just as powerful looking as an African Baboon - and handsome - and utterly black. One of them lay straddled on a branch with his arms and legs hanging down either side in perfect balance. Another preferred to sleep on the ground by the fence; a permanent smile on the smooth round, mouth-part of his face which covers the great sharp teeth and which is surrounded by rich dark hair covering the rest of the face and body - parting only to allow the deep and penetrating, dark brown eyes to open.

Then came the howl! George jumped! George very nearly jumped out of his shell! It came again, and again, and again. George had never heard anything quite like it but with each new piercing burst of sound George relaxed to really listen. First he realized that it wasn't really threatening, it was some form of communication. The Baboons were sharing; telling each other something important. They were **talking** to each other. And what talking it was. You could hear it all over the forest. There would be no doubt about what they were saying - if you could only understand the language.

Then George realized that one of the howls was slightly different: softer, weaker, questioning. It was the man who fed them. They were talking to each other! "I wish I could do that," George said, softly, to himself. "Perhaps you could if you feed them," muttered an unmarked voice nearby.

George looked round expectantly but all he could see was another lake with a storyboard displayed in a covered walkway alongside. It told of 'Bert, the famous Jabiru, who was found in a sorry state and nursed to health at the zoo'. This was a bit worrying for George because he hadn't heard of Bert and if Bert was famous then he ought to have heard of him and well... one didn't like to... you know?

The next sign helped...

'I am you rare Jabiru! How about that? Belizean wetlands are my habitat. One thing I know, this is for true: save that habitat for all we Jabiru.'

And there he was: Bert, the famous Jabiru Stork.

At that moment Bert had his head turned right round. He was preening feathers in the middle of his back with his long beak shaped like a slender dart. The fat black neck showed no sign of the twisting necessary to reach so far round. Bright, beady eyes shone, alert from a black head which had just a little white on the top. The huge white body stood erect on long, straight legs.

"Hey kids! How do you measure up to the Jabiru Stork?"

The silhouette of Bert painted on a board by the path, stood over five feet high. The words were painted alongside but the sound came from Bert who was still preening himself, seemingly without pause. "How did you do that?" George asked, looking straight up along the line of the beak into the bird's eyes. "All in the throat," came the reply, and the nearest eye gave away the merest twinkle of amusement as it fixed the thought in the mind of George. "It's not difficult really. It's all a matter of keeping your mind on the job and talking as best you can. This is an important job you know." "I'm sure it is," murmured George.

All was peaceful. Whistling ducks were twittering away, keeping together out of the water, following each other in their fussy way. The pretty, pink and white Roseate Spoonbill was darting fitfully over the smooth surface of the water. A Great Egret sitting hunch shouldered, was watching for any movement that might be a fish. There are many Great Egrets all over Belize and they are easy to see; their smaller cousins following cattle for reasons that George didn't like to think about - especially of such a pure white bird. This one was sitting on a branch out over the water, moving only his neck to get the right angle to be able to see - and otherwise still.

'If you value your paws, keep them out of the exhibits!'

A great crocodile rests perfectly still, seemingly asleep on the mud at the edge of the water and enjoying the sun. Morelets Crocodile his house name says. George wondered how crocodiles got so big. This one was about twelve feet long. Then he stopped thinking about it because he had thought of a reason and he didn't like it much. There were smaller ones laid out in the sun on a log but they looked just as dangerous. You probably wouldn't see them at all if they were in the water. Then he remembered all the crocodiles in the New River at home in Orange Walk - and shivered.

Looking up and around at the rainforest, George noted the sun shining through the trees above and a suggestion of haze in the space below the canopy. Below were two jaguars - one black, one spotted, the black one and the male, lying in the trees, watching. He was utterly black; enjoying the day; laying on his back, stretching out; looking. His great cat's eyes were glowing, wide; the black pupils, pools of mystery, staring.

'I'm a Black Jaguar. This ebony sheen comes from my genes. Spotted or black, we are still the same cat. All cats alive want

A woodpecker pecks: Tap; tap, tap, tap. Tap; tap, tap, tap - high in the canopy - stretching back to look at his handiwork! The spotted jaguar, bigger than the male, was also stretched out asleep on the ground. She had found a comfortable spot within the trees - partially sunny, partially in shade and surrounded by lush plants.

A pair of Yellow Head Parrots were sitting side by side; one preening; the other watching, carefully, slowly exploring the chest of the first with his beak only to find that his mate immediately turned round and did the job for himself. Further tentative interference led to a loud and violent attack until both were distracted by George.

Then while watching, came the boastful - "Hello!"... "Hello!"... The feathers going up on the back of the head in the same way as they do on a budgerigar - but much bigger of course, and much slower and more deliberate in the movements.

Now they show how they like to play: one hanging from the roof of the enclosure by its beak, transferring its hold to one foot; the other facing upwards as they explore, beak to beak, until they tire of the activity. George gave up on the speech as the parrots had done. You can't really talk to parrots he decided, they just copy what you say. There wasn't a single idea in their pretty little heads. George looked again. 'Big heads,' he corrected himself.

'We are Great Curassows. What's so great about us? Well we are great-looking! But did you know that we Great Curassows mate for life and raise our young together? (She's the brown beauty and I'm the handsome black fellow). If you hear me making strange noises this means "Back off!" You are too close to my woman and my territory. Some of you point to us and say that you hunt us for food. Well... We may be related to chickens but chickens are far more common than Great Curassows. And Chickens taste better too (Honest!). So Listen... Please give us a break. Great Curassows are a great part of your natural heritage."

A Crested Guan sitting in shade well away from the path used by visitors. Totally unconcerned and unconnected with any others' activity but interested in its immediate surroundings and fascinating to watch, giving out just a little cry.

George found the owls difficult to spot but once he did he could see that they were very beautiful. There were two kinds: the Mottled Owls and the Barn Owls. Their beaks curved inwards, sharp down, below and between the eyes.

'We are mottled Owls. A dinner of mice and bugs makes us hoot happy.'
'We are Owls from the city and what we eat isn't pretty. You may like beans and rice but Barn Owls dine on Charlie Price. We soar around and work to see that city streets are rodent free.'

Great eyes surrounded as they are, with feathers arranged in such a way as to make the eyes seem huge. Looking back at them as they stared at him in that rather superior way, George was reminded of the story of 'The Most Beautiful Creature of the forest'.
All the creatures of the forest had met to discuss who was the most beautiful of them all. As they could not agree, they turned to the owl (for he was wise) and asked for his opinion. The Wise Old Owl went through all the animals and pointed out that each was beautiful in his own way. All the animals were pleased with this until the owl went on... "Of course, the most striking feature of all is the eyes... The animals all left in disgust! It was a mistake for George to tell this story. The eyes of the owls simply closed, slowly, and not a sound was made.

The Coatamundi hurried hither and thither. A beautiful animal with dark, soft shining fur; its long tail held vertically for much of the time, exploring the ground, digging with powerful front claws. He wasn't going to talk much either. A bird whistles in the trees.

Then the Kinkajou was scratching, curious. George had been seen. "Are you busy?" he said, for want of something better to say.

"Why?" replied the busy creature, "Should I be?"

"You look as though you are!" George was somewhat taken aback by the question.

"So why ask? As a matter of fact I'm not!" The kinkajou had stopped scratching or even moving any part of his body but remained motionless (other than speech - for any clever clogs reading this). He had his head down, twisted through the branches of a tree, staring at George with big, round eyes, glistening with reflected light.

The two remained like this for several minutes until the kinkajou, feeling that he had the upper hand, decided all was well, lifted up his front, right paw and continued scratching underneath his belly with the back one - all the time remaining in position on his two left limbs - and having another look before turning away, unconcerned, to find another attraction.

"I think you're rude," George complained, "And I was hoping to have a conversation with you."

"I think you're a snail!"

"What do you mean?"

"You are a bit slow," came the reply; "Not deliberate in action like me; slow in the head. I know you want to ask if I'm happy here and is it my home and are there people to talk to? - and you haven't yet!"

"You look as though you are!" George was somewhat taken aback again.

"So why ask? As a matter of fact I am and it is and there are! So there!"

George wandered on, a little hurt but wiser, and captivated by the way in which all the animals were settled, still in their own homes, but safe; able to survive in an uncertain world.

The Jaguarondi was a beautiful little animal but restless today and grumbling. George wondered if it was near feeding time and it was hungry. Perhaps it is a pity that more of the animals can't find food for themselves as the anteater can.

Passing by the Red Brocket Deer George thought how much he was like some of the deer at home in England - except that the horns were short, almost straight, with just a slight curve upwards and out. The Fox, too, was quite distinctly a fox but so much smaller than British ones. It was very attractive. Its sleek fur was beautifully marked and ending in a long, bushy tail. The features were very sharp as you might expect. Its eyes and ears were alert but otherwise the animal was lazy in the heat of the day. The second of the pair came to be friendly but the first one was having none of it. He wanted to be left alone and made that very clear. Both took absolutely no notice of George watching from beyond the enclosure.

'I am a Great Black Hawk but guys who take shots at me are great big turkeys! Yes mon! We get shot at because some people think we raid their chicken coop for our dinner. Chicken?- I tell you, we Great Black Hawks would much rather eat a frog or a snake any day. (Psst!!! - Tell your friends!).'

'I am an Ornate Hawk Eagle and someone shot me! Yes mon! Shot me! And look Ya... Not many countries have birds as big - and as pretty - as we Ornate Black Eagles. Listen... My species loves to eat snakes... Not like you! And my species loves Belize... Just like you!'

'Surprise! Betcha didn't think we're both Ornate Hawk Eagles! Yes mon! Me, I'm big and beautiful and female. He's my mate. Someday I'll have darker feathers too... But right now, I'm just a young t'ing!' Look Ya!'

The Hawk Eagles were perched in the dark of the canopy. They were watching and George felt that same fear as he felt under the eye of the King Vulture even though he knew that he was probably in greater danger from the average crow.

All too soon was the time to go. George wondered no more that the Scarlet Macaw, a favourite of the visitors, should be playing up to all the attention he was getting. Slow, deliberate movements, showing off his best side, his extravagant plumage, his vivid colours; hanging, crooning and sticking out his round, rod-like tongue through a slowly opening beak as he watched for every sign of praise. But George had spotted the Tapir again. Why was he in a different place? The male was much more disposed to speak now. In fact he was quite unhappy and seemed to want to get something 'off his chest'. He must have upset April quite a lot because he had been moved to a new home on his own while George had been somewhere else in the zoo. The transport had been a large wooden crate which was open on the ground as he had just emerged from it. He looked as though he had lost his job too.

'Poor fellow,' thought George, 'He's completely drained - but at least he's at home.'

"Yes," replied the Tapir, reading George's thoughts, "It's April that's upset and I have to move away. It isn't fair you know. I'm in love with her and she just isn't interested."

"That's the way it is though." George had been surprised by the outburst but pleased to be someone to talk to. And he repeated, rather unnecessarily, "Snails don't have that problem."

The Tapir ignored the comment however, and went on... "It's not as if I'm in the wrong. They **want** me to be in love with her. They **want** me to. But she doesn't. Oh dear, what else can I do? She went off in a huff behind the bushes... That's why you couldn't see her."

The Tapir looked dolefully at George who dropped his eyes in silent respect. "Oh dear," he went on, "I just kept myself busy, like you do. I was marking the territory just to be sure, like you do. That's my job. Then she goes and has a fit. Chasing me all over she was and I get moved. It isn't fair you know," he repeated, "I'm in love with her and she just isn't interested. There isn't even any point in marking my territory here!"

The Tapir brightened. "Mind you, it was fun to see your face!"

"Happy to have been of service." replied George, doubtfully.

"You were right!" George remarked to the White Tailed Deer when he called by as promised, on his way out. "This is your home. I know that now. You live in the forest and this is the forest. In fact this is your forest. It is your home. The trees are right, the plants are right, the weather is right and you get extra food and water just for being nice to visitors. And we all like to be nice to visitors don't we?"

Yes, today was different. George had learned much of these animals and from them. This was their home. They belonged here. They were safe.

So George was thinking about his shell. He was very much aware of it as his home.

He loved its close fit. Some people might feel a bit closed in by such a small space but it made George feel safe and comfortable. More than that, it was his and that was where he belonged.

Always setting off for the office in Belize City on the 6:30am bus but for once going straight there; usually I would join with the family for breakfast fellowship and relief from the journey. Today the bus was late as we had to go round Burrell Boom and on to the Western Highway; the Northern Highway was blocked as I discovered later by an overturned tanker. The day was spent looking at some of the issues that would be likely to be covered when the 'Training the Trainers' week starts next week. We arrived at a possible shape for what was to be called a Lower Division Plan. There was some considerable debate whether or not to use the word 'annual' in the title but that was felt to give the wrong idea (thank goodness) as the plan was intended to be applied over the three years and would possibly be broken down into three if that was the way that a particular school would wish to work. It wasn't a good start because the present planning was only scheduled for three days. The contrast continued into lunchtime at Raoul's Rapido with Kathryn and Pamela who is the new VSO – and can't she talk – pleasant and friendly but another reason to be thankful for Kathryn!

I phoned BTL during the morning and arranged to visit their workshop in the headquarters after work and it really is a workshop, giving the feeling that all technology in progress is housed in the one place. I took the discs with me and was advised that I should have been installing from windows instead of trying to install from DOS. The only instructions I had were for Kwickmail which were to use DOS!

At home in the evening and trying again I find that everything is fine until disc 3 is used. This could not be read.

Heading for the EDC office and breakfast next included a visit to the bank and the post office on the way in. The day continued with the Division 1 Plan and some curriculum content in mind punctuated by lunch with Kathryn by the Belize Teachers College and a walk down to sit at the landing stage at Moho Caye which had been the original setting for 'A Lesson for the Day'. BTL was again contacted during the morning to arrange a visit after work. I took the discs with me and was given a replacement disc the result of which was that I managed to install Internet Explorer in the evening but couldn't log on.

The pattern for 'Training the Trainers' was finally established on Wednesday as 'getting to know you' and forming the working groups as districts; an overview; discussion of the four pillars; mission statement; allocation of time; the what, the how, and units of work. Rather optimistic I thought but who can tell; not too much telling hopefully; challenge and some listening at least. A Chinese lunch with Kathryn and Rachael was very pleasant, if rushed, and after yet another visit to BTL and an explanation of what was happening resulted in being given what I thought was the information I had been using. In the evening I found that at least my thought was right for I was no further forward.

Back in Orange Walk, after delivering a letter to Urbano Uck and having a discussion with him about the plans for the work to be done and what might be a suitable venue and after a visit to BTL local office where I was only able to pay my bill there being no technical element; also having a haircut, going to the Treasury to receive expenses, taking two films in to be developed and printed which wouldn't be ready to collect until a week on Saturday, most of the day has been spent waiting for BTL and trying to sort out Internet Explorer by following their instructions on the telephone, some progress has been made but I'm still unable to log on; phew!

'Dear Chris, Thank you for your letter and the copy of the Fairthorner magazine. It was a good read, particularly so as a record of the 50 years which of course, I often display proudly in Belize when I am out and about and not at work, wearing the kit presented by my friends there (Belizean working attire is very formal). I look forward to the next issue.

It would be nice to make some regular correspondence with Fairthorne for the remainder of the time here, especially now that it is easier for me to write and include some of the things I have already written.

I know it is a busy time for you but there may be ways in which I can be of use and there are enough of you to share the 'burden'. I don't know what you would be particularly interested in: education, perhaps, or the wonderful conservation work that is going on here. In many ways little Belize (pop 200,000 and the size of Wales) is leading the World in this field. It helps to have questions! Also, I don't really know what sort of contribution you would like for Fairthorner. Is the story I sent suitable and what about the length? Previous issues suggest that the subject and style would be appropriate but the current issue doesn't. I am quite prepared to write specially if I know what you want and the approximate number of words. I have just finished a George the Snail story about a visit to the Belize Zoo but that is rather longer than the account you have had. There are also pieces written on some of the Mayan ruins which are dotted all over Belize…'

Other than Kathryn who was a Peace Corps volunteer from the US, people I met were almost exclusively Belizean and rarely VSO but the weekend was different both for meeting with VSOs and starting on Friday. I set off for Belize City on the 6:30am bus as I would normally do to go to the office but stayed on right to the terminus and then walked down past the Swing Bridge, the Market, the Battlefield Park and the Bliss Institute to meet with the other VSOs at the Belle Vue Hotel. We were due to meet at 8:15 and I arrived just before eight to find only Bernie there. We had coffee and a fine old chat after so long and waited until the others arrived. The speedboat left for St George's Caye, a small island in the Caribbean, at about 8:40 for about a half hour journey over smooth water but with not a particularly promising sky - rarely so! We quickly settled into our rooms at the Cottage Colony. Tony and I shared room eight. The last time we shared was in Miami and we were both with Mr and Mrs Sosa in Belmopan for the first week in Belize. We had not met since as Tony went straight to Punta Gorda from there to teach woodwork to technical students.

The Welcome and Introduction was given by Mark Wright, the Country Director for VSO, from 10:00-10:30 followed by a review of VSO's future in Belize and what was called the Compass report. The economic indicators used to determine need were rather against a continued presence in Belize but it is not unusual for offices to close and open elsewhere. Having spent a month in Kenya in 1957 and seen the squalor in a large part of Nairobi (compared also with what was then known as the 'White Highlands') it had already occurred to me to wonder at continued need in Belize. On the other hand not all parts of Belize City were wonderful and primary schools certainly needed to better serve their pupils which suited me. As things turned out with several ever-more-demanding placements which followed for me in other parts of the world Belize was a relatively gentle introduction that I could not possibly have anticipated; always 'who can tell', both statement and question.

There had been some disquiet over what appeared to be inconsistencies in 'Sectorial Priorities' and 'VSO material support (phones, bikes, etc.)' giving rise to working groups but I can't say I had any cause for complaint and tended to think that we were given too much rather than too little. Discretion was reinforced in anticipation of approaching lunch.

12:00   Lunch was a rather nice salad but disappointing in quantity.

Said Flores (General Manager, Banana Growers Association) gave what I thought was a rather one sided presentation on the banana industry: its workforce, preferential markets, international agreements etc. and felt it would have been interesting to hear views of other interested parties. It was nice to have the time to think about it though.

Osmani Salas (Director, Belize Audubon Society) gave an interesting talk entitled 'Wildlife Management in Belize' although it was rather more about reserves than wildlife.

Both talks were given out on one of the landing stages, which was a very pleasant location but neither talk had anything in the way of visual aids and both were delivered in a rather low key manner (telling!) One of the reasons for being outside was that the generator had broken down and up to this time there was neither electricity nor running water (in the taps!).

During discussion on setting up a debate for the next day I rashly agreed to propose the motion that 'This house believes that there is no longer a role for VSO in Belize'; not one that I relished in any way.

The evening was spent swimming and lounging about drinking and chatting. There was not much of a walk as there is not far to go and the mosquitoes were biting. Late in the day, a generator was shipped over from the mainland but not much thought was given to the unloading which resulted in the partial collapse of the jetty and still no water or electricity until late into the night. Mark was going to sleep us on the mainland but we all refused to go and he decided to stay put. The generator was running by morning.

After an overview of the five year plan for VSO in Belize currently in its second year, we had time to prepare for the debate which was to take place before dinner in this evening. I was working with Maria and the motion was to be opposed by Caroline and Bernadette. We decided to present our case with some humour as neither of us would like to see VSO leave Belize. I was to present the serious points and Maria the send-up skits.

A presentation by Moses Cal (Programme Officer, UNDP) on 'Economic trends and the changing role of the donor community in Belize' was dreadfully dull although the content was interesting. It was with some trepidation with which we entered into the next session, after break, to be presented in the same way, but that turned out to be more interesting: 'Refugees - current status and future implications for Belize' by Carlos Moreno (Programme Officer, UNHCR).

For the debate 'This house believes that there is no future role for VSO in Belize' we centred on the need for Belize to: abandon the 'gi a mi a dolla mentality', find some real work and separate politics from profession and employment. The evening was much the same as last night except that we had a barbecue which was absolutely wonderful. The generous chicken was served with salad and potato salad and followed by a large number of huge prawns, perfectly cooked.

Diana Haylock (Programme Officer SPEAR) was supposed to give a presentation on 'Political Reform and the Electoral Process' but she phoned in sick next morning leaving us with free time until the arrival after lunch of the boat arranged for the return journey which was fun as the weather had not improved. It was windy and consequently rough! Worse for me was having to wait until 4:30 for a bus back home so I didn't get in until gone six with a six thirty start (five am rise) next morning.

A whole week of travelling back and forth between Orange Walk and Belize City could have been avoided by staying with the family but there were things to do at home and writing to keep up which would otherwise have been left and some forgotten for certain, so a busy week became 'sandwiched' beginning with the usual 6:30am bus for Belize City to take part in day one of the training workshop for Principals: schedule, philosophy and processes, areas of study, basis of Language Arts, Mission Statements, time allocation, school curriculum: the 'what' and 'how' of planning, Units of Work, new curricular areas, assessment strategies, support material and resources.

The 5:00pm bus to Orange Walk each day meant arriving home at about 6:30pm followed by a much looked for quiet Saturday shopping going to the library, cooking and reading.

The 3:00pm Eucharist at St Peter's in Orange Walk Town celebrated the work and retirement of the minister Hardy Gordon, led by the Bishop of Belize whom I had met so early on in Belize City. People and clergy travelled from all over Belize to attend yet the congregation felt as one big family. What better inspiration could there be to attend to applications for funding to support schools taking part in the link with children in the UK…

'…Now that my first six months in post are accomplished I wish to apply for a VSO major grant in support of a personal project in which I have been engaged since my post in Belize was confirmed. I am happy to say that it is progressing well. Primary schools in Belize generally do not have computers and this project would be much more effective if email could be used. I understand that VSO will support small enterprise and request that you consider this one. Now that there is visible evidence of progress here, I am about to embark on local fundraising. Belizean friends in business have already shown their interest and this computer will also be donated when I leave. I have also written to a contact at the World Bank, suggested to me when their representative visited the Education Development Centre recently.
I will, of course, provide you with all the information you require but for the time being, offer the following as a brief description of the project…

…The grant would be spent on an IBM computer as itemized above and purchased through the Ministry of Education without the addition of VAT. This would ensure that maintenance would be at no cost to the school. The cost of ink cartridges, paper, email connection and line rental ($20 per month) would be met from School and District funds. The intention is to support a direct link between Calcutta Government School and South Molton Community College in the United Kingdom. The link already exists, having been set in place from September 1997 as described in more detail on the sheets attached. Electronic mail, word processing and printing facilities would considerably improve on the 'snail mail' which rather dampens the enthusiasm of 11/12 year old children. The equipment would incidentally provide a much needed resource for the school. There are thirty children directly involved in the Belize School and in the UK school. The indirect benefit would be enjoyed by 125 and 600 children respectively. The Link is ongoing and likely to grow rapidly with improved communication. Belize has been adopted as part of the Geography curriculum by year 7 in South Molton and their school environment is part of general study in Standard 5/6 in Calcutta which is a Primary School. Other departments in the UK school are intending to integrate study for the students as all four classes in the year group are involved, each with a different school in Belize. Funds are being sought to support the activities of the other three schools. With the enthusiasm of youngsters learning from each other, the long term benefit can only be guessed…'

'Dear Mr Carlson, Carolyn Winter of the Human Development Department suggested that I write to you when she visited the Educational Development Unit in Belize City on behalf of the World Bank. I am a VSO from South Molton in the UK working as a Curriculum Co-ordinator in Orange Walk and Corozal Districts in the North of Belize. I also came here with personal objectives as described below which I am happy to say are progressing well.

Primary schools in Belize generally do not have computers and this project would be much more effective if email could be used. I understand that your department will support small enterprise and request that you consider this one. Now that there is visible evidence of progress here, I am about to embark on local fundraising. Belizean friends in business have already shown their interest and this computer will also be donated when I leave. I will, of course, provide you with all the information you require but for the time being, offer the following as a brief description of the project…

…These have obviously provided some ideas for Belizean students but they are using their own imaginations to take the whole venture much further. Also, as friendships grow and with so many involved, there should be a continuous flow of 'news' as well as communal contributions and packages. The first packages have been sent in return to England in the care of the original 'Buddy' and a Belizean 'Friend'. Many children have returned their own personal letters and gifts. I have sent a considerable amount of my own written material - including stories I have written for children about Belize, film and photographs, and as much published material as I could. Belizean schools are using my being here as a direct resource and as I already work with them this is not difficult to organise.

The Belize Schools mentioned above, are Calcutta Government in Corozal District, La Immaculada Roman Catholic in Orange Walk Town, St. Paul's Anglican in Corozal Town and Louisiana Government in Orange Walk Town. These are primary schools as education in Belize provides for children at this stage up to 13 years (Standard 6). Children who do not pass the Belize National Selection Exam (BNSE) do not progress into secondary education. The total number of students in the five schools is well over 3,000. The project has the full support of the Chief Education Officer, Mr Ernest Raymond and VSO as well as the two District Education Officers and their Principals.'

The dialogue by snail mail continues unabated and represented by one such to a pupil still in the primary school…

'…Typewriters are difficult to manage and I think you made a really good job. Apart from the typing though, you are learning all sorts of organisational skills without realising it. It is also useful to learn to do the job without making mistakes! Even with word processing it is a nuisance to have to make corrections so I learnt to type without making them. I don't use a spell check either. They are a special nuisance here because they are programmed to American spelling which I don't like (because it loses the root - or history - of the word).

Yes I did enjoy Christmas. It was one of the things I wondered about when I came here. I came to a very different country completely on my own and Christmas is one of those times when it is most likely to tell but there are two reasons why I felt very much at home. First - I haven't felt apart from my friends as I feel that they are just as close, at least in spirit. The letter writing has been very important of course and it is all helped by the schools' linking and story writing for children. Second - I have made a lot of Belizean friends and I went to stay with a family for Christmas… …Anyway, you may imagine that I didn't have a radio controlled car (although I would have loved to share yours) and there was a distinct shortage of 'pressies' but there were plenty of toys and children to play with. I would be very interested in your Lego Technic and your Corgi Classics as well. I expect you remember my collection of Lledo vehicles (which took a long time to collect!) and I have a set of Corgi tramcars. I was very fond of trams as a boy.

I like Paignton Zoo because it is one of the better ones from the animals' point of view. I have taken many children there - including 2000 Cub Scouts on one occasion. Now I have found a new one and I will let George tell you the story so I have enclosed his account. The story isn't quite finished as there are one or two incidents that I want to include. Also, you may find one or two mistakes as I haven't checked it. When it is finished I will send it to Richard to be illustrated along with the others. George gets around quite a lot for a snail and he has met around 300 Belizean children and some of their Buddies as well as Uncle Albert, Spike, Heffer and Sunny from England (from year 7 in a school in somewhere called South Molton). I have been to the Belize Zoo four times now. The second time was with Pedro Sanches, Daiami's Dad, at Christmas. The fourth time was a couple of weeks ago when I was invited to attend the Primary Schools' Science/Conservation Fair. The zoo is **in the rainforest** but George can tell you about that. Your comment about oxygen made me think! Belize is a huge net producer of oxygen. Much of the country is designated conservation area and most of that is rainforest. There is very little industry and not much traffic so the balance in respect of the atmosphere must be to the benefit of others. Quite a thought!

I hope you have a lot of fun with your new computer and learn a lot from it. This one that I have been able to buy is part of my hopes for the schools' linking… …I was sent a cutting of the newspaper report on the model of South Molton and I was very proud to see it. Well done to all of you. I also had cuttings of the progress of the church tower and yes it is sad that parts that might have been saved were vandalised. Unfortunately, that is how many people are. The good thing that comes out of it is that it is a reminder of the things we need to put right ourselves - something that I wouldn't ordinarily say except that I am sure you will have thought about it. I hope the new entrance to the school will be good. It has been a long time coming. Most things of that sort are worth waiting for.

I had to stop and think when you asked if I have any gadgets. I suppose this computer is one. I was very lucky to get it and I didn't dream that it would be possible when I came. It is so useful for all the writing that I do and to organise my ideas as well as print them out. A side effect is that it has an amplified sound system and a CD drive. I had a couple of CDs for Christmas so I can play those. Also, I can use my tiny World Band Radio and the Micro-Cassette recorder I brought for making notes for stories with the amplifier so I can get really good sound. I also brought my camera and camcorder with me. I don't hanker after much but I would like a pair of binoculars because of all the wildlife… I will probably go across to Mexico before Easter to see what I can find. They would be much cheaper there. Then I am hoping to stay in a couple of rainforest villages during the holiday. Oh - I have recently bought a bicycle to get about on. At the end of your letter, your writing is big, big, big, and big! I haven't forgotten and it is good to see, just as it is good to hear about all the things you are doing at school. I am especially pleased that you are going to Fairthorne and that the school is going again. I have written to my friends there and had letters back and I wear the Fairthorne tee-shirts etc. regularly. I went to Altun Ha at the beginning of February…'

Much of the next week was spent sharing the outcome and content of the workshop with affected and interested parties across the two districts who had not been invited to attend and to acquaint them with the programme so far for planning at the end of next term; also the proposed preliminary meeting of Principals from the North involved in Phase 2 to be held at Corozal Methodist School on Thursday of this week at 2:30pm. Margarita Gomez phoned from EDC asking for information on Technology which I could gather from the northern Principals and could do at the same time. She went on to ask if Corinth would be attending so that she could bring the forms and was told by Ellajean that the meeting should be postponed but was given no reason. Later David phoned to ask if there was any cost implications because EDC wouldn't be able to meet them. I didn't think there were and hadn't really thought about it but talking later to Mr Uck about the lack of reimbursement resulted in phone calls to the Chief and Ellajean and the decision that expenses would be paid in the new financial year. It should be noted that the meeting is to be held two days into the new financial year so I can't see what the fuss is about. The request was also made that the Principals should be contacted to ensure that they would clear their absence with their managers. I had thought that the Principals would be sufficiently responsible to do that for themselves but Mr Uck nevertheless agreed to contact them. These problems do not apply to Corozal, being the home District.

The Circus has been in town all week. It is an old Mexican family circus and it looks exciting but I haven't been nor do I intend to go because the main attraction is seven full grown polar bears and I think keeping them in temperatures well into the nineties is ridiculous. Also the cost is 20 pesos in Mexico, just across the border and 20 dollars in Belize which is four times as much!

The first of April is the anniversary of my assessment for VSO. That may have only been a year in time but the direction of travel was profoundly changed and now seems to belong in a different world. I contacted EDC to ask Stanley Bermudas to produce costing for a full set of appropriate and compatible computer equipment for each of the 'linking' schools to be able to use email. He was unavailable as usual, being the sole technician in much demand with new equipment, but I was able to leave the message with Nora Bradley.

Rudi Novelo, Bertha Campos, Raquel Moreno from Carmelita and I left at midday so that we could travel up to Corozal together for the first of the Northern Principals' meetings. Corinth and Pamela came up from Belize City which was very useful as Corinth was able to give us an update on the current position. She also brought up some letters to go out to the staff of each school seeking their co-operation in the summer planning (also my pullover and four 1mb RAM chips which I had left in the office). Bertha took minutes in shorthand which she is converting for me to word process. We left Orange Walk at 12:00 and returned at 5:30. Rudi was planning to go on to Chetumal after the meeting but he hadn't reckoned on it lasting until 4:30 as it did. The next meeting is to be held at 2:30pm on Thursday 21st May at St Peter's Anglican School in Orange Walk.

Being now into the school holiday, I went to Chetumal on the 7:20am bus on Friday to buy birthday presents and got back to Orange Walk at about 7:00pm…

Chetumal

It is 9:00am and I am walking away from the new market where the bus had stopped, headed East but I think I may have come the wrong way so I am now heading back again to where the bus stopped to find my way into town. Thinking back to dashing about with the Leiva family and which way the many taxis went, I think by walking this way I have got my bearings and I know which way to go. Maybe the direction I had first taken from here was the one I should use from the other bus station. There is no rush. I can either catch the bus I came on which leaves at 12:15 or the Batty bus from there or the other bus station, much later on. I know my way to find that from the centre, having insisted on walking it a couple of times when the family took their taxis.

The idea of the English as a nation of shopkeepers is beaten hands down by this part of the world. Everywhere there are rows and rows and rows of shops, both here and in Belize Many of the shops here have open fronts and many of them are empty of people other than the owners or assistants. I often wonder how many of them make a living let alone a profit. Selling seems to be one of the easy things to do. I think that there is a connection between taking the easy way to a living by selling everyday goods and the same idea taken further in selling less social items such as drugs. There seems to be the idea that there is little other hope in life but selling and one thing leads to another. Once trapped, there follows the exploitation by others who are even less scrupulous. The huge range from 'haves' to 'have-nots' is evident everywhere - both among people and things. Things of course, represent a degree of 'have' but when you look at some of the vehicles, even the taxis, you begin to wonder about the benefit of that and questioning the safety seems pointless. On the other hand there are vehicles that are extremely expensive and driven about in style with full air conditioning and tinted windows; all the accoutrements of privilege and prosperity.

The road, which has been straight for some ten minutes, now swings round to the left which is unexpected and a little disconcerting but I believe I am heading in the right direction if not the right way. Galle San Salvador - must look that up! Decided to turn right and away from the bend, for one block and then left because that street is going in the direction in which I started, keeping the sun to my left and therefore heading South. Avenida Des Los Heroes: I think this is the one I want. It is indeed! So my first inclination to go over two blocks from the bus station was evidently right, having now arrived at the Maya Museum.

The walk into town didn't produce anything. I found some shirts which I thought were expensive but no binoculars and nothing for Antonio or Miguel except, perhaps that a model motorbike mounted on a plinth might be a good idea. So here I am having changed $Bz250 for 1,000 pesos, still with 1,000 pesos in my pocket and heading back to the new market where I started. It is very hot and my shadow is about a foot long with the sun almost directly overhead. By midday I managed to get a shirt for Richard's birthday; bought that in the new market by the bus station. The big shop, Super San Francisco, which is just a supermarket, is somewhat further out so I am now headed back to the centre where the action is which is the area of the old market and the Mayan Museum. I have just been stung for a Sprite as I realise counting my change which is 16 pesos from 20 so I was charged 4 pesos and I noted that the till rang up 3-50. I don't believe the regular price is even that high anyway. Not that it is expensive in Belize terms at $1 and I suppose the vendor stings the tourist (which I'm not) but I call it stealing. It also happens in England of course but here, almost nothing is priced which makes it very difficult to know the value.

Sitting on a seat for ten minutes now, in the shade of a tree, watching the world go by, I find the breeze is very pleasant and the trees are dense with leaves even though it is only the beginning of April. It has been like this every time I have come here - or anywhere else in this part of the world. Palm trees and Flamboyan Trees and many other varieties that I don't recognise grow in the dividing space up the middle of the road. Just in sight in the way I am looking is the market; opposite is the hotel El Cedro and immediately to my left is a wooden house set among the shops, which I have admired several times. A fine veranda overlooking the street, all the windows shuttered now, but under the veranda is a front portico made of medium brown stained wood with nicely panelled doors overtopped with frosted window panels. A latticed fence set into the pillars completes the facade. A Volkswagen Beetle goes past with speakers loudly announcing some concert or other. Beetles are made in Mexico in large numbers. I can see four right-now, from where I am sitting and without turning any way. They are quite incongruous among some of the huge American varieties: the Chevvy and the Dodge, the Chryslers and the Fords.

Two o'clock and the people that are about are seeking the shade. Most shops are closed and it is beginning to look as though I have picked early closing day although I remember something about long siesta before opening again for the evening. It is beautiful even so; clear blue sky; a cooling breeze lessening the effect of a fierce sun; tremendously bright light and hard shadows; the streets more deserted than I have seen before; the Caribbean sea light green and choppy. Not a time to hurry.

Lunch was nice - in a snazzier restaurant than I would normally use. A local dish made with strips of pork, lightly fried, with green and red peppers, onions, fried stew beans and peas, tortilla chips and peppers. But it doesn't look as though there is going to be any binoculars and now that the shops are closed, the chances of finding something for Antonio or Miguel have slimmed also. I might well be taking the money I changed back with me. Cross to the shady side of Avenida Des Los Heroes and plod on!

I found a stationers in the end and did quite well - with a nice Sheaffer ball pen for Antonio; a set of four pens, ten coloured pencils, sketch pad and sharpener for Miguel; and some wrapping paper. These cost 113-50 pesos which is about 28 dollars. So, apart from the binoculars which are only for me and can wait, the day has turned out a success. I had originally wanted to buy a pair so that I could visit two special wildlife areas at Bermudan Landings (Howlers) and Crooked Tree (Birds and Wildfowl) at Easter but that plan is now deferred, first by my visit to Belize City and second by the doubt expressed about the route on my bicycle by Elizabeth Burns next door. The journey home was very tedious, especially as the bus took half an hour to start after the appointed time when I had already been sitting on it for fifteen minutes and bought my ticket half an hour before that. I got home at 7:00pm, hot, tired and quite burnt despite the tan I already have.

My own focus was on Belizean friends and living and working in the community but other volunteers would often come and stay. Orange Walk and later, Corozal are well placed and attractive for interest to non-tourists and in both places I was very fortunate with my house. I had met Jack, a Canadian volunteer who decided to remain in Belize after his placement ended and he was staying for the weekend. He worked with computers as a volunteer and later at the Government Computer Centre in Belmopan which proved most useful as he spent most of the afternoon setting my computer right and finally got my email working. A pleasant evening of rum and coke and conversation followed until about 1:30am.

Next day, Palm Sunday, we walked out to San Jose Nuevo Palmar and on to the river there. We found that Wifrido Novello's (of Jungle River Tours to Lamanai) cousin owns that piece of riverside and is busy clearing a site to put some cabanas and a restaurant. I have mixed feeling about that but it will still be a very nice place to go. One thing that the clearing has done is to expose the remains of a stone paved ramp running down the bank in one place into the river. As there are no such stones about otherwise it must have been made for a purpose. Also there is no known activity in the area in trading resulting from the influx of Europeans so it seems reasonable that the ramp is an ancient Mayan one. Not many people will have seen that! Apparently the crocodiles which I have mentioned before but not seen are both plentiful and large. It has been known for them to move down further towards Orange Walk (which has its own) on a couple of occasions when there has been accidental chemical spillage from the sugar factory a mile or so upstream from here. Jack left on the 5:00pm bus and was home in Belize City in just over the hour. Emails were sent to Paul, Jack and Pamela next day and I had a reply from Jack within fifteen minutes.

Communications were a huge problem for the schools' link at this stage. One letter sent from South Molton Community College on 21st March and not received until 6th April (quicker than some) and after a long gap before that tells the story…

'First of all – thanks for the recent video and yes, my package of books did arrive safely. Well done!
I'm sorry I have to resort to 'snail mail' but we have been off-line in school for a few weeks now, awaiting an update to an ISDN telephone line. I did receive some email from you but did you get any of my messages? I hope to be able to build on this link as soon as school is back on line.

I have received one package but was disappointed not to find a Belize 'Buddy' inside! The other groups are constantly pestering me for their package and I really need to keep their interest going before the idea slips from their mind. I can't really organise another box to send until they receive some direct feedback. Perhaps you could investigate to see if there are any problems at your end. I'm encouraging pupils to write on their own initiative but I feel that the project is in danger of losing some momentum.

I'm trying to get other departments involved and intend to base my next offering around taped messages as you suggested in a previous letter. I am trying to plug the 'pupil profile' gaps on your list so that no-one has 'slipped the net'.
A couple of questions – Firstly, is it possible for schools to send a 'Buddy' with their parcel? Second, will we be receiving any photographs? It would not be a problem to get the film developed in England.

I think we are at a bit of a crossroads now. Unless we can establish a regular flow of information in the very near future then the project will fade away. It has been a real disappointment to me that the school chose this moment to fiddle around with the internet. It would have been a great way to keep things going. I rather hoped to find more in the first parcel although the letters were really nice. I tried to forge a link with schools in Guyana a number of years ago but after a lot of effort it dwindled away. I really hope this doesn't happen again so perhaps we can take stock of things and think through the future.
Anyway, what about you? I was quite jealous to read of the opportunities that have been opened up for you. I wonder where you will end up next. Travel is such a rare pleasure. Enjoy it while you can!

I can't remember if I have told you in an earlier letter that Bobby was the prize winner of the first T shirt competition. He came up with the passport idea for 'Mr Spike'. I gather he has to guard it carefully as his sister has taken a liking to it! I am working with Richard at the moment to illustrate a 'George' story. This should be with you soon. I'm really pleased to hear how much you are enjoying your time in Belize and really appreciate the letters and videos. Keep in touch and let's see if we can give the project a big booster injection. Let me know your feelings/ideas.'
And in reply coinciding with some email progress…

'After a great deal of difficulty which I won't go into just now, I now have email which is hooked up and working. This is really by way of a test so I would appreciate a quick (and short) reply. Our schools are on term but it is just possible that you are still there for part of this week. If not, I suppose this will hang about somewhere. My email address is mrmax@btl.net. What I don't know yet, is whether there is any additional bit for incoming international mail but I expect that your 'reply to sender' will find me. We do have a lot to discuss with respect to the linking which is going well at this end except for the delay in the mail and that quite a lot of SMCC pupils do not seem to be responding (There hasn't been a lot from the 'boss' either but the email should solve that). I will send and receive for children wishing to do that. Also, I have started the moves towards raising sponsorship to provide schools with the means to use email themselves. I have done a lot of work on that and it looks promising. In any event I will be giving all of this equipment to one of the schools when I leave. Just a taster of what there is to talk about!'

Also, still having to attend to domestic issues in the UK that I hadn't anticipated was not exactly a welcome chore…

'Thank you for your very helpful letter dated 5th March. I will be pleased to forward any further communications from the Inland Revenue to you without delay! The action taken with respect to the married couples allowance seems very proper as it dates from my first becoming aware of the position and drawing attention to it. I had had no tax forms in the intervening period and I was under the impression that the adjustment had been made as I remember a tax change at the time of my wife leaving. Not that I was functioning particularly well in anything but work at the time! I do not receive pay in the ordinary way from the Belizean Government. As a VSO volunteer I receive a bursary for living expenses from the Government here and this is not taxed. I therefore have no business with the tax authorities.

The eighteen month contract theoretically comes to an end early in March 1999 although I would not expect to be coming home until at least the following month. In any case, I will have spent no time in the UK since 5th September 1997 so I suppose that the 91 days would apply on return as well? It is not my intention to remain in the UK for any time other than a holiday. I have been offered a post in Zimbabwe if that is allowed by the Immigration Authorities there. Otherwise I will be looking elsewhere or returning here for several years yet. My finances are being managed by NatWest. I trust that the proceeds from the Halifax savings account are suitably invested. I will need some funds on return but that doesn't seem to be of concern as there is a gently growing sum in my current account. Perhaps the interest earned could be added to the current account and the capital reinvested but that is only a suggestion. I would rather the affairs be conducted as arranged.'

Others hadn't caught up with my departure…

1998 St. Michael's Cub Scout Six-a-Side Football Competition

'Thank you for your invitation once again. I am assuming that you are aware of the change of ACC Cub Scouts but you must not have caught up with the reason for it. I retired from teaching in England in order to come here on voluntary service with VSO at the beginning of last September. I remained in post until I left.' Letters received had often focussed attention on things I hadn't really thought about…

'…There is television here but I don't have it and what I have seen of it is largely American and less than stimulating. Being able to read and write is much more important to me anyway. I hope you enjoyed the video. I have just read Lorna Doone again, which I was surprised to find in the town library. Most of the books I have borrowed have hardly been off the shelf and I can't imagine many Belizeans making much sense of Lorna Doone although it was wonderful for me. I know all the country, towns and villages intimately and most of the family names too. North Devon is that sort of place. I read To Serve Them all my Days again recently too…'

'…The unbelievable humidity here can be wearing if you don't make allowance for it. We are in the dry season but that doesn't seem to affect the humidity at all. The ground doesn't have surface water, the swampy areas have receded and we don't get the short, sharp periods of rain. Otherwise, the environment remains largely unchanged. There is no shortage of water in the ground; plants flower in their season but what leaves are lost seem to be replaced before they drop off so it is always green (with brilliantly coloured and huge flowers on practically everything)…'

'…I do miss my Church. It shouldn't be like that should it? But I suppose that it is a matter of beauty rather than spirituality. The churches here are concrete and timber with corrugated iron roofs. There is rarely any musical instrument and singing can really only be described as enthusiastic. On the other hand, the spirit is strong and the welcome genuine. I do not feel at all out of place as the only white person present (That is true too, of life in Orange Walk - I have made a lot of friends)…'

Others of my letters had to have an eye to the future…

'I wrote to you on 1st December last concerning your interest in offering me a teaching post at Ariel School. I would like to pursue the matter further and wish to learn more of the situation. I would be able to offer say, five years' service from June of 1999. I am English of course and understand that there may be difficulties in obtaining a Temporary Employment Permit. I have made some enquiries from here but this is difficult. There is no way in which a request could be made to VSO for a named individual but it is possible that the VSO Field Office in Zimbabwe may be able to assist. The only other avenue I have here is to meet with the newly appointed British High Commissioner for Belize who is arriving from Zimbabwe.'

Belize schools have four terms but Christmas and Easter holidays approximate to those in the UK as a letter sent from a pupil on 7th April and received weeks later gave news…

'…We have just broken up for our Easter Term but when we go back we have only two weeks before 'Exam Week!' School is very different and it is a lot longer walk! I have a pen pal in Calcutta School called William Parada, who is 12…'

On Tuesday I left Orange Walk at 7:30am and spent the morning at Calcutta Government School helping students with their preparation for the BNSE. They are doing this with their teacher who is also the Principal, every morning throughout the two week Easter break. After that he and I went together to Corozal where we had a late lunch. I had conch soup which was very generous and extremely filling, and a fruit juice which I have forgotten the name of but they will remember serving it when next I go. They always do. I can't imagine what such soup would cost in England or where one might find it but the local conch is fished with as much as a pound of meat inside it. And very good it is too! I returned to Orange Walk for about 5:00pm. Next day I went to the District Office (after doing the washing - I usually do that early in the morning) and phoned Stanley Bermudas to see if he had produced the costs for me for computer equipment for the linking schools. We arranged for me to pick these up tomorrow when I go to Belize City for the weekend.

I then went off for a bike ride which I didn't intend to be very far but finished up doing over twenty miles by going down the Old Northern Highway towards Maskall which is the road that I was led to believe is hazardous as the area is known to have a lot of drug addicts. It seemed OK as far as I went so I will try some more another day. I returned three hours later, just after one o'clock. There were three email letters in: two in reply to my local ones and a failed contact with SMCC stating that it was not a valid email address. A helpful note was added that I could check with the operator of the UK system they use.

Jayne phoned from Punta Gorda to say that she was back from England and feeling much better having attended her grandfather's funeral and met up with her friends at home. I am pleased for her sake that she is now disposed towards completing her time here. I started the Thursday by checking email and sending yet another letter to Paul to ask him to check the email address at SMCC although I couldn't see how it could be wrong.

It is 9:50am and I am now setting off to catch the bus for Belize City and with the intention of posting the letter as soon as I get there rather than miss the bus. In fact the bus is just coming up the road as I get to the end of Mahogany Street. It is a Venus Bus about which I have bad memories from my last journey with them on this route. The driver at that time was behaving like a complete maniac, travelling with his foot hard down all the way and not seeming to know how to use the brake. Now, as we approached the junction coming in from the right from Burrel Boom which joins the Northern Highway on a left hand bend at about mile fourteen, a heavy truck loaded with a great weight of stone pulled out on to the main road in front of us and it was clear that it was not going to stop. The reaction of the bus driver, rather than slowdown from the 65-70mph, at which we were travelling, was to sound his wind horn which had no effect other than to heighten the tension among the passengers. The conductor took over the wind horn as the driver applied greater concentration to the aiming of his vehicle; still no change in the forward motion of the truck which was now blocking our side of the road completely. Remember that we drive on the right hand side of the road and, as I was sitting over the right hand front wheel arch, I was on the nearside, alongside the truck, as the bus swung left to avoid hitting it and the two vehicles rounded the corner together - the truck blocking the right side of the road and the bus blocking the wrong side. Also the truck was moving fairly quickly by this time. Coming in the opposite direction was a big Chevvy Pick-Up..........

I have to say that the tension now erupted into panic. Passengers were screaming. The driver clearly didn't know what to do and sat hunched over the wheel... aiming - or, rather, veering about trying to make up his mind. I was sitting with my knees drawn up over the wheel arch having been reading and resting a book on them, and decided that the risk of hitting the stone truck was less than head-on with the pick-up and it was as well to stay as I was. The conductor continued to hang on to the horn chain for want of something better to do and probably to keep him from collapsing on the floor. It seemed to me that the lunatic at the wheel was locked into a course of action that would be terminal; certainly for him as he was right in line....
Fortunately the Chevvy got right off the road!!!!!!!!

11:25 Well, it wasn't a bad journey then. The bus was pretty rickety and didn't seem to have any springs but now he was a careful driver which accounts for the extra time taken rather more than the number of stops made which were very few. Now I post the letter and carry on down to the Leiva family to have a chat with Neria; unload; and after lunch, carry on to the office to print some minutes and pick up the computer costs for the linking schools. My goodness it is hot today (96 in Orange Walk). Passing between the Fire Station and the Atlantic Bank nothing much seems to have changed and it is a while since I last came. Five children are playing in a plastic paddling pool outside one of the houses. The large building painted in various shades of purple just beyond the Leiva's is still painted in various shades of purple and the fence round the house on the corner is finished.

Neria isn't in which is a bit of a blow and the girl she has in for cleaning speaks almost no English but it seems as though Neria will be back for three o'clock which should give me time to walk down and catch

Jack before he leaves work at twelve, have some lunch and go on to the office before coming back. So it is out on to Freetown Road and head for Jack's office over Benny's Home Centre. He can also give me the latest advice that I need for email.

At 1:15 I had lunch at Jack's which was very pleasant. Both he and Karen are off for the weekend from this afternoon, to spend Easter on one of the Cayes; sun, sea and sand! I am now on my way to the office, heading up Freetown Road, back to the Belcan Roundabout to turn right along Princess Margaret Avenue. The sun is still fierce but there is a nice breeze.

3:15 and I am just leaving the office. Missed Stanley who I saw rushing away as I arrived so I suspect that he hasn't yet done what I asked for in finding computer costs and that means having to come back into the office before I go back to Orange Walk on Tuesday. The lizards are enjoying the heat. I have seen two very prettily marked iguanas, each about two feet-six long, in the grounds of the EDC and scuttling into their hidey holes; one under a concrete path and the other in a rarely used storehouse which has a hole in one of the wooden panels. Some of the wading birds are still evident in the swampland across the road by the extensive grounds of St John's Secondary School but being the dry season there is not such a great variety or such a great number and no immediate evidence of any frogs or crabs.

5:00 and I'm settled in; bought the rum! Ready for the action! Had chats with the family; met their friends again from Chetumal that I have met when we have gone up there together and who are staying for the weekend also. Had a shower, so all I have to do now is to go and find some Easter eggs for the children which so far, has been unsuccessful even in the local supermarket (SAVU) and I was banking on that; changed from long trousers into shorts and flip-flops. So here we go!

There will be plenty of Spanish this weekend - not that I ever learn very much! After tea we went down town together to the shops that are open in the evening but I was unable to get any Easter eggs and gave up that idea. Neria wasn't keen on the white chocolate Easter Bunnies. Pity! I would have liked those - still do!

Two more friends arrived from Cancun with their children for the evening and I lost track of all the ones that passed through. I can understand some of the talk in Spanish because of the combined similarity of some of the words, the expression used and the gestures and body language which are both expressive. I wish I could remember the words but I'm afraid I am just as hopeless as ever. Anyway the conversation was good and it made for a very pleasant evening in which a lot of concession was also made to English for my benefit. The remnants into the night were Tabo, Marco and I. We went to bed just after three.

Good Friday was Miguel's and Antonio's birthday. They were pleased with their presents - Miguel especially. I managed to remember to go and feed Jack's cat fairly early in the morning, which I had promised to do while he was away as I was staying nearby. I missed going to church but it was a very long Catholic service followed by the Stations of the Cross so it would have been a great penance for me.

The friends from Chetumal and also the ones who came down from Cancun went at about 1:00pm without staying for lunch which left Neria with huge amounts of fish soup made with the fried snapper that I like so much. The rest of us fed even more than usual. It has been a quiet day so far and I am now on my way down to see the opening of the swing bridge which takes place at 5:30 every morning and evening. That is if I get there in time. It has been very hot again today but it has gone sultry now and is much cooler. The temperature inland yesterday was 104 degrees! Walking down North Front Street it is almost deserted; no traffic; I have never seen it like this. There are only two people around the Belchina Bridge (funded by the Chinese) and a car or two at the crossing on this side of it. What I really want to do is to watch the swing bridge opening, see what it looks like and how long it takes so that I can film it tomorrow. I arrive in time to see one of the Easter processions coming over the bridge so it can't have been closed yet. Perhaps three or four hundred people of one church are following the cross and singing in between readings from the Bible and prayers. It wasn't very successful so far as the bridge was concerned because it isn't opening today and as this isn't a place to hang around on your own I am now making my way back by another route using Barrack Road and Freetown Road and looking forward to a shower when I get in. It seems quite bizarre to have a religious procession at the same time and in the same place when and where you are being 'eyed over' as a target, which happens as soon as you stop and sometimes as you are walking along as happened on the way down. (I was approached by a tall Creole who stuck his hand out to shake and told me his name, asking for mine. Having been caught before, I didn't stop, looked at his hand then at him and said "That's nice for you!" I was followed down the road by a hail of abuse and heard the iron bar he had been carrying strike something hard behind me. I have learned not to flinch. Apparent weakness attracts more intimidation.)

Saturday morning, 10:45 Just walking up now to watch the cyclists come in at the end of their race which went from the National Stadium here in Belize City at 5:30am, out through Belmopan to San Ignacio to return by the same route. I have just had a look at the trophies which they are finishing off across the road; work which I have been watching from time to time from the balcony. That is as near as I shall get to one of those. The morning so far has been spent in pleasant conversation aided with Black Label Scotch whisky. At the roundabout, a fleet of vehicles has just gone through on their way back to the Stadium. Not a large but quite a significant crowd gathered mainly at the Belcan Bridge to watch the cyclists as they come over the rise in its middle. I am making my way to the pedestrian bridge to gain some elevation just as the first cyclists come in; a large crowd coming through. It didn't last very long but it was good to watch them. Now I am wandering down Freetown Road to buy another bottle of rum and go and feed Jack's cat. A litre of Caribbean Rum is $15 at Li Chee whereas at SAVU where I have been buying it, it is nearly $18. It is actually 50c cheaper at Li Chee than in Orange Walk where it is made. Neria's Mum and Stepfather arrived about mid-morning, from San Estevan with Tabo's aunt, also from the village.

The socialising went on throughout the day and the late afternoon was time for children's breaking of the Piñata which I filmed. The Piñata was made of paper maché and had been filled with sweets earlier. It was designed to be beaten with sticks to release the sweets but Marco had intended to have the one which has a cord to pull to release the contents. Miguel was to have pulled it as it was his birthday yesterday; in the event the children beat it with their fists as they were not allowed to use sticks. This seemed to be rather like closing the stable door to me as they use sticks on each other whenever they get the chance but I must admit that I don't like the idea of 'beating' the Piñata either.

Walking down to Jack's to feed the cat on Sunday morning. The children have had their Easter Baskets each containing sweets, small Easter eggs and an Easter Bunny. We have all had breakfast and preparations are under way for a barbecue. It is another very bright, hot, sunny day. The streets are quiet again. I have just heard one car in the distance and the sounds of radios (muted for Belize!) coming from the open, slatted windows; muted perhaps, because the current programmes are almost all services being broadcast.

As the preparations proceeded I could see that the rum supply was getting short again and as this is one of the few contributions I can make I have set off to buy another bottle although I don't expect that there will be much drinking today. The little shop I referred to as Li Chee is run by Chinese and serves take away food. The $1, $2 and $3 chicken (with chips) is of very generous proportions and extremely good value as I have confirmed several times. I have never seen it closed. There are always people asking for money around it but most don't seem to be in any particular need. Today, there was a boy of about fourteen asking for money to buy food. I said no all along the pavement outside the shop but there was something about his pleading that was unusual and he was clearly hungry. Round the corner, out of sight, I got out some money and started to walk back to give it to him but I didn't get far as he appeared again. What made him come round the corner after such a delay? There would have been no prospects in that street. Anyway, there was no need for him to go hungry that day and I could see to that without being seen. Poverty and need are very difficult problems here, which are made much worse by many who take advantage of it – "Gimme a dolla!"

The day was very much confined to family. That is to say: Tabo, Neria and Antonio; Marco, Miriam, Miguel, Mariami and Martin; the grandparents (or great grandparents in the case of the three young children) and aunt; and me. I spent much of the afternoon reading 'George beneath a Paper Moon' (Nina Bawden) having finished a re-read of 'The Big Fisherman' (Lloyd C. Douglas). In the evening the three ladies, Miguel and I went to church at St Josephs.

Monday was a quiet day. Fed the cat and did quite a lot of reading. Went for a walk down to Ramada Park by the sea with Tabo, Neria and the children in the late afternoon when it was cooler. Even so there were only a few frigate birds about and not all that many people.

I went in to the office for eight o'clock on Tuesday to discuss progress and to talk to Stanley. On the way back I called in at the bank. The weekend after next is the Lions Club Convention to which I have been invited. Also the Anniversary dinner is on May 8th. I managed to persuade Neria to let me pay for her ticket as well as that is her birthday. I stayed for lunch and caught the 12:15 Urbina bus back to Orange Walk where I arrived in time to do a small amount of shopping and change my library books for 'Wycliffe and the Windsor Blue' (W.J. Burley) and 'The Legate's Daughter' (Wallace Breem). Mail arrived in a bundle.

Next day, after collecting a parcel from the Post Office at 8:30am I went on to the 'Crystal Palace' to see what the Annual Convention of the Belize National Teachers' Union was all about. What a waste of time this first morning of their assembly was! I stayed until lunchtime because the licencing of teachers was on the agenda but I left in dismay at 12:15. The behaviour of teachers at the back was the same as I had witnessed from students at the Spelling Bee. The noise was horrendous. There was no heckling - it was just chatter and eating exactly as described for children. At one point the proceedings were running over an hour and a half late which is not bad on the first morning apparently. Two causes for this were the late start (30 minutes) and the amazing number of speeches which amounted to nothing more than a repeated list of credits, by way of introduction. It was a relief to come home and enjoy the contents of my parcel!

Following that there was no reason to go into the office and I had a domestic day, writing letters, reading and generally being ready to go to San Ignacio for the weekend tomorrow. Having had no further news one of the letters (email also) was sent in further reply to the last mail from Paul…

I wrote to you on the 9th. April giving details of my email but here is my address again: mrmax@btl.net I haven't received messages from you so I have no idea what you have sent. Perhaps you could recap. I have a full record of everything sent from here which I will put together for you to check shortly.

You should have received packages from Calcutta Government School and from St Paul's Anglican School. They were the first two who had packages from you. The other two haven't been sent yet. I'm afraid they have been caught up with the Belize National Selection Exam (BNSE) which is a particularly nasty idea which determines whether a 12/13 year old will be able to continue schooling so it takes up (and wastes) a great deal of time. There was a Buddy with the parcel from Calcutta but I found out too late that St Pauls hadn't sent one. I have lots of ideas for increasing the pace which I will enlarge on later but there are two essential factors for success bearing in mind that much too much time is spent waiting for something to happen.

1) You and I must keep up a constant dialogue. I have made sure that it is understood that the link is school to school but I have had to keep behind it very closely as well as being a resource in these early days (This is mainly to keep the interest as mail is so slow and there seems to be much less coming than was expected). 2) Email is essential. If you want a couple of levers I will tell you now that I have spent the whole of over two months income on equipment to secure email and to support links. Finance was tight right up to this last month. All of this will be given to one of the schools when I leave. Also, VSO have agreed to one of the schools making an application for funds and I am waiting a reply from the 'schools tutage' section of the World Bank in Washington. I will be giving a presentation to Orange Walk Rotary Club for the same purpose next week. I will write more often to you to keep you up to date but I need feedback and the sharing of ideas and circumstances as well. I think there is a lot that I can tell you about schools here which will increase understanding and give rise to more ideas. I think, too, that it would be a good idea for me to send a weekly letter for Year 7. That will not be difficult to do but it will be much easier if it is two way. I write the occasional letter to some children already as you know.

Perhaps it would be a good idea to keep a 'movement's log'. I did suggest to the Principals that it would be a good idea to write to you but I guess this has not happened. Perhaps you could send letters to them. I will send you all the background you need shortly. I have also been encouraging pupils to write directly and I know that a lot of the children in the above schools have done so - and most have sent their letters to your pupils' homes (another reason for a log?).

I have just finished another tape (fourth one) which features Louisiana School and St. Pauls which I will send next week. I am trying to get it copied on to local cassette first. There are also some photographs which I have taken. I will make sure that you have more photographs one way or another. The most important thing you can do just now is to provide me with an email address through which we can communicate. This can be extended to pupils. For me it will mean typing out children's letters for them for the time being but it would not be difficult for you to load yours from floppy which could be made by the children at school. Do not be downhearted! From my point of view it not only has to work but it will work. It represents a large part of my being here. I have made friends with children here just the same as at home. It is wonderful for them to get to know each other and take it all from there. You told me about Guyana and I think there are lots of differences this time, working in favour.

I too, wonder where I will end up next. There doesn't seem to be any shortage of choice (subject for another letter) and it seems they would like me to stay on here. Certainly that is the sentiment expressed by the many Belizean friends I have been lucky enough to make. What is for certain is that I will be at home for my 60th birthday on May 28th next year when I intend to have a party for all friends and especially past pupils. You did tell me about Bobby. I have some more bits and pieces to send and I will send some more tee shirts but such parcels have to be occasional and come by sea. The mail is very expensive for us, especially in relation to income. Very pleased to see that you are working with Richard. He is illustrator for George. Tell him I am about to write again and there is another one for him to do. I have lots of George stories lined up. Perhaps there will one day be a book 'George in Belize'.

I will write to year 7 next week. They really are involved in the seed of something big and when it flowers they will be able to say "We did it ourselves and it is enduring". We can't let that slip away…'

I set off for San Ignacio to stay with Kathryn, leaving the house at 10:50 and looking forward to a very relaxed weekend - not even requiring much kit as I will be wearing sports tops, shorts and flip flops. My day sack is only half full. Also I decided only to take the video camera, a book to read and some recent photos to show Kathryn together with the book of pictures of North Devon which had been sent for me this week. There is enough power in the camera battery to power the one half hour video tape so I haven't even got the charger!

11:20am Venus bus in sight, entering the main street to stop by the taxi rank. All the buses stop in different places. I hadn't noted the driver of the near fated bus and wondered whether he might have been the same one on a learning curve! It finally left Orange Walk at 11:50 and dawdled all the way to Belize City. A crowded bus but an uneventful journey except that the conductor looked hard at the three dollars I gave him for my fare before deciding to accept it at that and issued a ticket. We made erratic progress to arrive at the bridge over the canal by Novello's Bus Station at 1:30pm having taken two and a quarter hours for a one and a quarter hour journey and arrived half an hour late for the bus I had arranged to catch. Parked by the canal are a bus for Placentia, one for Dangriga and a Tillett's bus in from Orange Walk. No sign of anything else. The next bus leaves at 2:00pm but how long will it take? Well, there is nothing I can do about that so I pay my five dollars at the ticket desk, have a coke and settle down on the bus going to Benque to wait. A visit to the bathroom is 50 cents as usual but I had been and gone before there was chance to have to pay for it. Fifty cents for a pee is a racket, especially when you are already a customer. The seat I chose was at the front over the nearside wheel arch but as the bus filled up a girl stopped to say that she thought I had her seat. I didn't realize that the seats were allocated with a number on the ticket but waited for the assistance of the conductor before moving to the place marked as seat 19 near the back of the bus. By now I had to sit on the offside isle end of a seat made for three children and after the journey I had already had, that was not very comfortable. The other two people in the seat were together, a young man and woman with the man sat in the middle. He sprawled backwards with his legs apart also taking up a disproportionate amount of room so it was some little time before that was resolved with the aid of every right hand bend! Even so, he was continually falling asleep with his head dropping on my shoulder. I am always amazed at the insensitivity of many Belizeans and that view was not helped by the large number of times I found myself having to move his head before the penny dropped. About halfway through the journey a well-dressed woman got on the bus and was immediately loudly abusive with someone who was sitting in a seat with only two occupants where she expected to make a third. There was no question of asking or indicating politely that she would like to sit down. I thought this was a bit much even in terms of bad manners but also, if the people sitting had been doing so as long as I had, the woman who had just got on would have been feeling a good deal more comfortable at that point than they were! Anyway, she sat down and the tedium of the journey resumed. A little later, the couple sitting in my seat got off the bus and this same woman moved from the seat behind and came and sat next to me. It turned out that she was not only a secondary school teacher but also someone who was distributing leaflets for the Jehovah's Witnesses! Kathryn was still waiting when I arrived. She signalled to stay on the bus which took us closer to where she lives and enabled us to do a little shopping in the local supermarket before going in.

Kathryn has the middle apartment of a concrete block with three apartments in it, one above the other, and standing next to a similar one. The view from the balcony stretches round from the twin block to the left with trees behind and the hill rising to the Mayan ruin at Cahal Petch; single storey concrete houses in a short row at Apollo Street, one of which has a caravan parked outside - the first such caravan I have seen in Belize; stretching round with houses well-spaced; one or two almond trees as well as the palm trees and a variety of others that I don't know; a whole village atmosphere with lots of little shacks - some of which will be bathrooms and others contain livestock. We are on a hill but the track coming in immediately opposite is fairly level and the view to the extreme right reaches out again to hills. The house has all the accoutrements: double-sink, new cooker, large fridge, washing machine, television etc. a veranda front and back, two bedrooms, full screens, burglar bars and slatted glass windows operated with a thumbscrew; and a well fitted bathroom where Kathryn has installed a shower heater; luxury!

In the evening we walked around the back of San Ignacio Town along a track away from houses which passes close by Cahal Petch, another Mayan site which is currently being excavated. There are a lot of trees around the site now but without them it would have commanded a dominant position and extensive views all around. The name Cahal Petch means 'Place of the Ticks' which was given in the 1950's when there was a lot of cattle pasture in the area. There are 34 structures of which the tallest is 23m (75ft) high. The Belizean archaeologist Jaime Awe who has been working there has dated Cahal Petch as having been founded around 1000BC and abandoned during the Late Classic period (800AD).

In the woods there was a considerable cacophony of very loud and high pitched sound coming from the trees. Whether this is some sort of insect like a cricket I have yet to find out but the pitch of the sound is so high that any mechanical movement would have to be very rapid indeed to produce it. At one stage the sound sort of 'wound up' from one quarter, starting low and slow, a heavy clicking, and rising to the crescendo described. That was a sound of some power at both ends of the scale.

There was unexpected decision to be made on Saturday. Kathryn had suggested a much longer canoe trip than the previous one; this time from a point high up the Macal river back down into the centre of town in San Ignacio. This time our roles were reversed although I can never be sure whether it had to do with my then being able to take both film and photos as we passed along or for Kathryn to take control; I certainly wasn't going to ask. The river is in any case very different from the New River which is slow and deep. The Macal comes down from the highlands and flows quite swiftly at times; no ferry but with some very shallow parts to be avoided today and remembered on a visit much later where the Raspaculo ('scratchy bottom') joins the Macal much further up at Chalillo.

Our day began at the Hawkesworth Bridge over the Macal River in the centre of San Ignacio Town with an extremely bumpy journey along a hair-raising track in a large pick-up truck also carrying the canoes and adapted for the purpose; canoes similar to the Canadian open canoe but smaller and disappointingly made of plastic. We set off down river with about eight miles to go some time after 9:30am and didn't arrive back in San Ignacio until about 4:30pm although we did stop along the way and there were many other places where we risked capsize (even without thick, greasy wire rope) and paused to wonder at the rich variety of forest trees and flowers, birds and lizards, sounds and signs of movement unresolved; peaceful, yet exhilarating. I managed to get some shots of birds but it is difficult to catch them with the camera and there are few places along this stretch of the river where it would be easy to see the animals; only the tell-tale sound and movement. The Howler Monkeys which are easiest to see inhabit the forest along the river further up and also much further down from Double Head Cabbage to Burrell Boom. There is a programme taking place to reintroduce Howlers along here, following an outbreak of yellow fever which reduced their number, but so far they have persisted in moving further upriver. Nests hanging in the trees, I can only guess, would be of some kind of ant rather than termites. Termites' nests surround trunks and branches and sometimes wooden posts that have been set in the ground or are even on the ground; they do not hang.

The clue for our long stop was not so much a clear landing stage as a group of canoes tied up by the forest trees at the left river bank; no commercial display or fanfare here; the gap in the trees only becoming obvious after focussing on the deserted crafts and only then the tiny wooden platform and insubstantial natural steps reinforced with wooden risers; the whole seeming, delightfully, to belong. This is Ix Chell Farm from which plants are being tested on two AIDS viruses and 300 types of tumour as well as being used to treat many other ailments. A small factory is tucked away in the trees and paths which, while easy to use, are just wide enough and do not present as an intrusion in the forest; rather, the visitor is transported as into another world. There are simple boards close by or attached to trees giving their name and medical usefulness with many spelling mistakes or what one may imagine to be spelling mistakes but this is not unusual in Belize where notices are usually a DIY job!

The best guide to the range of wildlife active at this time of day is the sounds that are as varied and distinct as the different layers of the forest yet merging as a whole. The forest is not particularly dense here although there is still a good impression of some of the tall trees which form the emergent layer. Most of the forest of course, is not conveniently laid out with a path and you certainly wouldn't be wandering there in shorts and flip-flops as I was on this occasion for as well as the important scientific and medicinal purpose of this small area, it is also very much a tourist attraction for those that make the effort to canoe down the river.

I am told that a screaming sound like that heard last night is some kind of cricket-like insect. I have only heard this noise up here in Cayo although the more regular crickets can be heard all over, especially at night. Sometimes they sort of wind up, starting with a heavy, slow clicking which develops rapidly into a scream. It really is quite deafening after dark. A termites' nest succeeds a Custard Apple Tree - which compares with the hanging ants' nest I had already seen. I didn't touch the Black Poisonwood Tree; not a good idea according to the discreet sign although I don't think that you would want to really, even if you didn't know anything about it. The Breadnut Tree reminds me of one in the grounds of Corozal Methodist School which has been there as long as generations can remember and has survived the attentions of a strangler vine which is living off it. Apparently, the Breadnut was used to make very coarse flour which provided the Mayan people with a reserve supply of food when times were hard.

I rather liked the Mayan mask which I found at the outward end of the trail. It clearly meant 'Don't go any further' for there was nothing inviting about the dense undergrowth beyond. The remainder of the trees marked were on a different route back, leading to 'Granny's Garden'. The hut there is where the medicines were originally prepared. The hut is a typical Mayan one although it does have rather more gaps in the walls than their huts usually do. The ones built more recently sometimes have even the narrowest gaps filled in and some are plastered. A Quamwood Tree is covered with masses of brilliant yellow flowers. Many of the trees here are similarly covered and provide an amazing variety of colour in season. Another of the great joys is that you can go and collect many of the fruits of the land for yourself and children do. Coconuts, bananas and oranges, mangoes, grapefruits and pineapples are all readily available together with a huge variety of nuts (my favourite is the almond which grows everywhere on a most beautiful tree with broad, bright green leaves which also give wonderful shade), other fruits and vegetables. Back on the river I managed to get a good shot of one of the many waders and another termites' nest. It is surprisingly difficult filming from a canoe especially when it is so windy. Needless to say the wind was against us and the slow flow of the river at this time, not much help.

What a joy are the rivers for children and this no exception. The river passes close to a village called Cristo Rey and children here go to a school which is involved in the new curriculum programme. They are using Belizean Creole. "Deah flip boy, deah flip!" Overhanging trees, vines, rapids, shallows and pools; what better for challenge, skills and showing off. The forest rings with shouts and squeals of delight and approval and mock scorn. Then we reach a calm spot in the river. The water is very low as we are well into the dry season. Trees are leaning over, high above the surface. There are times in the wet season when this water can be thirty feet deeper and extremely dangerous.

We come back in sight of the bridge which is a good indicator of the floodwaters which reach to just below the under structure. It is single file, one lane traffic; one direction only, controlled by the only set of traffic lights outside Belize City (There are only two more there!) and the surface of the 'road' across the bridge is quite simply an open steel mesh which accounts for, at times, quite deafening noise. Back up on the bridge the mesh is almost intimidating as is the swaying of the suspension wires when the traffic goes across. More swimmers are in the river beyond, where the waters make their way towards the confluence with the Mopan River to become the Belize River about another mile downstream.

On Sunday we walked down into San Ignacio Town and out to the North, in the same direction as the Macal River downstream, along Savannah Street and past the sports field. The town is quickly left behind at this point and a quiet country walk of about half an hour brings you to Branch Mouth where the Macal River meets with the Mopan River to become the Belize River. The walk is close to the river but it is out of sight until you get quite close to Branch Mouth where there is a wire rope bridge laid with planks to walk across to the village of Santa Familia. The trees are of great variety and there is farmland along the way. Many iguanas can be seen almost anywhere but especially in and around the bamboo down by the river - a place to look into but you need to be wearing boots and long trousers to go in and even then it may well be unwise because of the snakes. I bought a ticket for the Batty bus on the way back through town and caught the three o'clock Premier back to Belize City to connect with the 5:30 for Orange Walk, arriving home just before seven.

The ever present communication problem via snail mail – part of a letter dated this day, 19th April and received much later on 4th July 1998…

'Hi, thanks for your letter telling me about your work and where you are living. It sounds great. School is going well and we have set up a tuck shop in Chatterbox. We have been selling cakes (made on Thursday) for 15p each on Friday and so far have made £60. I wrote to the Prime Minister after seeing an article about tuck shops in the newspaper and had a letter back from him with a signed photo…'

Chatterbox is a workshop created from a redundant toilet block at the Junior School through the good offices of friends on my retirement from teaching in the UK.

The time taken for the letter to arrive was by no means unusual and was no doubt experienced even by children writing direct to each other individually. Email had to be essential. The address problem had to be solved and the participating schools in Belize would have to have a computer and access to email as soon as possible; the latter being the most difficult to achieve. In the meantime it would be down to my own writings and maybe some transcription.

I have always viewed management as a rather poor substitute for leadership which it has to be admitted we can't do without, societies being populous as most now are. Many corporate activities would fail and needs cease to be met. I tend to regard shortcomings of management with quiet amusement rather than irritation however, especially when I have made at least some effort to overcome them. One such, of many over time, came on 20th April in the form of a request from Ellajean for immediate despatch of teachers' consent forms. These only went out to teachers on the day before the end of term (there were not enough) and today is the first day of the new term so the timing is rather unreasonable. Also, teachers had been asked to mail their response. The rest of the day was spent tracking them down and arranging to deliver extra copies where they were needed. I had been to Belize City on Thursday 9th partly to collect a new supply and distributed them in Orange Walk.

I went to Corozal on the 7:15am bus, leaving home at 7:00, to meet with Onelia and we distributed teachers consent forms that had been short before the holidays and arranged for them to be completed and returned. I delivered minutes of the last Principals' Meeting held at Corozal Methodist School, visited Methodist and St Paul's Anglican School in respect of the forms while Onelia undertook to collect the others or have them sent to the office and took the opportunity to discuss fundraising of email and progress for the 'Links' at St Paul's. With four schools involved and widely separated this approach was very useful.

Back in Orange Walk I went to Louisiana School for 10:30 to discuss the current position with the Primary Curriculum Programme with Jose Cawich; also to advise him of progress with fundraising for the 'Links' in respect of email and to encourage a speedy despatch of the Standard 5 parcel to England. Then on to St. Peter's School for 1:00pm to discuss the current position with the Primary Curriculum Programme with Barbara Blades and to give her a complete overview of the history and process of development from philosophy to the planning for Divisional Schemes and Unit Plans; also to outline the procedure to be followed from the prototypical plan through to delivery in the classroom. The view in the North is that it would be a good idea to trim the prototypical plan to suit the Districts before attempting to adapt for individual schools (if desired at that stage) and making weekly plans. Some time was spent in the DEO afterwards chasing teachers consent forms that have not yet come in.

I went in to the office on Thursday morning in the hope of catching Principals who had not sent in their forms but had to leave the request with Mr Novelo. Returning in the afternoon always careful to check, there was no sign of either the forms or Mr Novelo.

Louisiana School being within sight of my house I was able to meet with the Principal Jose Cawitch at home during lunchtime. Many friends often turned up there anyway.

At 3:30 I met with the 'Linking' students and their teachers again at La Immaculada. They will send a letter immediately. Some students have written independently and plans are going ahead for their parcel and Buddy. We discussed a whole range of ideas to build on, including a video film for which I will be cameraman or give loan of my camera if I am not available.

A package sent for Paul…

'…Enclosed are video cassettes number four and five with notes. Cassette four should be especially useful to you just now as it features two of the 'Linking' schools, Louisiana and St Pauls. There are also some more photos which have details written on the back. A list of the photos and their details is included which might be useful for display purposes. In some cases the list is more explicit than the handwritten details on the back of the photo. You have had the photos from film 2 which were Calcutta Government School and the Belize Zoo. If you would like more copies of anything I will be pleased to send you the negatives but I would send them all to keep them together. Everything is numbered so it would be easy to identify particular pictures. Also enclosed is another tee shirt. I suggest you use it as a 'carrot' for the best ideas on ways forward - or whatever you think might be beneficial. I intend sending some more by surface mail when I send that parcel but it may not get there until the end of term. I* am sorting through all the mail and other items I have sent so that you will be able to check that you have had everything. The next step is to put in place a regular letter to year 7. I dare say this will include quite a lot of news about the schools which they haven't thought to send themselves. In any case, I will give you an update of exactly what point they are at. I can't emphasize enough that we must have email and there needs to be regular information and ideas coming to me in return (There are many who could share this task! Everything sent will be put to good use). Then there needs to be communication between staff of SMCC and the Linking Schools here. I see these as the stepping stones to leaving the whole thing as an enduring and growing enterprise.

And a letter sent to year 7…

'…I have not written to you regularly because what you really want to do is to work directly with your Linking Schools to make friends, share an adventure together and learn about each other. This is still the aim but things have moved so slowly that I think I should help out directly. One of the things I have decided to do is to write to you every week. Each letter will contain some news, answers to your writing to me (!!!!) and some writing on one subject (for example - travel on the bus which is very different). One of the problems is what Mr Berry calls 'snail mail'. George is not at all happy about this term because he says that snails get along pretty well when they know where they are going because they don't keep stopping. You must expect an airmail letter to take two weeks however, so a reply will take four weeks. Of course, that assumes that people write straight back which they usually don't. So what do we do about that? I have managed to acquire enough computer equipment here at home to run email. My email address is mrmax@btl.net. Any of you can use that address if you have your own access to email. You can also use my postal address above. I will forward any messages to your link schools or to individual students and I always answer letters sent to me. I have been very busy trying to organise funds to enable the four schools to be able to use email. This looks promising and in any case, I will be donating this equipment to one of them when I leave. A big setback has been that your school is not able to use email at the moment. If you could it would make a huge difference, even now, because you would be able to use this address directly from school and with no delay. What are you going to do about that?

The linking project you are involved in with the four schools here in Belize is probably much more important than you imagine. I have found that there is not only a lack of understanding of one culture for the other, there is also misunderstanding. I came here with ideas that were quite wrong and I had done a lot of homework before coming - including talking to people who had been here. Significantly, perhaps, none of them had 'lived Belizean' as I am trying to do. Also, I have often formed the impression that some things that I had said about England were understood by people here only to find later that they weren't! This happens the other way round too! By sharing in an adventure using the 'Buddy' ambassador, understanding will develop naturally. It is the next best thing to one of you or one of the Belizean students making the trip yourselves. But to make it work there has to be a lot of commitment and contributing ideas. Don't leave it to other people and don't be put off by delay. Those problems are there to be solved. I can help but, in the end, I can't do it for you. Perhaps the biggest responsibility you face is the point you leave for other students (and their families) to follow. There is no reason why the link shouldn't grow even within your own school but also beyond. Once you have email the internet is the next step and your 'Buddies' will make sure that the link is 'real'. It would be very useful if you could think about ways that you could remain involved next year too. That is enough for now I will use the rest of this letter to tell you something of the four schools. Some things you will know but it doesn't hurt to repeat them. I will put a set of photographs together too, which will reach you before the end of term.

All the schools are Primary. This is because students do not transfer to Secondary until they are 13, two years after you. The students you are linking with are generally your own age although some are up to a year older and a very few are a little younger. At age 13 students take the Belize National Selection Exam. This exam determines whether they will be able to continue schooling as there are only places for about half of them in the Secondary Schools. Some students stay on in the Primary School for as much as two more years in the hope of making it into the Secondary School. This exam will be on 4th May, a week on Monday, and it is one of the many delays which have affected schools' ability to give enough time to their parcels. I expect that students will give their own view of BNSE and that will be more meaningful for you. My view is not printable!

It was unfortunate that your parcels could not arrive until well into the spring term. It will be much better when things can happen in the autumn term which is much less stressed. Lots of interesting things can be easily shared in the run up to Christmas. Schools here are only just finishing the National Spelling

Bee, sponsored by Coca Cola, which can be of considerable advantage both to the winning school and winning students. There are a lot of public events which schools are involved in and, just like you, many other things they are expected to do. None of this is to give excuse. It is simply how it is. We must learn from it and find ways for the Link to become a more regular part of school life and I am certain this can be done.

School buildings are in a completely different environment from yours. I could describe them in detail for you but it is better that you should find out for yourselves. Think about the difference it would make to the design and facilities of your school if the weather was as it is here. The daytime temperature is in upper eighties or well into the nineties most of the time. It hit one hundred and four degrees in Orange Walk last week. There are no seasons as you know them. There is a wet season and a dry season but for practical purposes this doesn't make much difference. If you think about tape 5 which I have just sent, you will note that there is a huge difference in amount of water between the two but there is never a shortage of it; this land is part of the Tropical Rainforest after all. In this part of Belize there is very little dull weather. When it rains it doesn't last very long; there is a lot of it and it usually comes straight down. The ground surface quickly dries off and life is back to normal with very little interruption. Although the humidity is very high, evaporation takes place so quickly because of the high temperature. School buildings and schools themselves also lack many of the facilities which you take for granted although you must make comparison with your Primary School in that respect. There are no cleaners or caretakers. The premises are kept clean by children and looked after by staff and parents. There is a lot of dust, no corridors and no glass in the windows so this is no easy task. Floors are concrete. Water is splashed around first to hold down the dust while they are being swept.

Calcutta Government School was the first school to receive a parcel from you in the care of Uncle Albert from 7D. They responded quickly. It was a good time for them although they had been 'geared up' to receive it well before Christmas. They sent a Buddy which I haven't seen and I know that many of the students have sent mail: letters, photos and Belizean artefacts independently as well. I know too, that some of them are disappointed at not having had a reply. It is very much a family atmosphere in the school. The oldest pupils look out for the youngest and all are friendly towards each other. A lot of sharing goes on so that most of the students benefit when one receives some mail. There must be about 150 children ranging from five to fifteen years old. Mr Rancheran's class (the Principal) is small, being about 22, because they are the children affected by BNSE this year. The rest of your linking students are in the next class. I have spent quite a lot of spare time working directly with the students - usually taking the class. That was fun! The village is on the Northern Highway between Orange Walk Town and Corozal Town which are thirty miles apart. There are a lot of cane fields between the two and twelve villages strung out along the route, some bigger than others, some very small: these are San Jose/San Pablo, Buena Vista, Santa Clara/San Roman, Louisville, Concepcion, San Francisco/Aventura, San Joaquin/Calcutta and Ranchito. Trial Farm has become part of Orange Walk Town and San Pablo is the last village in Orange Walk District. The rest are in Corozal. Outside the school is a very nice sports field which has just been equipped with floodlighting by the efforts of the Village Council (a voluntary body) and which is used by all the children all the time. They are very keen on soccer - with excellent ball skills!

La Immaculada School was the second school to receive a parcel from you in the care of Spike from 7G. Immaculada is the only 'linking' school which is not in the curriculum programme in which I am involved so I don't go in there in any official capacity. There are 1500 pupils in the school of whom 150 are in your age group. For these two reasons and because the school was heavily involved in fundraising to overcome a serious roof problem at the time, it was a lengthy process to get going. It is reckoned to be the oldest school in Belize although much of it is quite striking in appearance - and certainly in achievement. I wanted to include La Immaculada for a lot of reasons which I won't go into now but which I think will bear much fruit in the long run. After some deliberation, the staff and students decided to include only those who especially wanted to link with you and followed this with some form of selection to reduce their number to be the same as yours. You will see that this gives each one of you a special responsibility too. They also decided to make that group into a club which is essentially a writers club although they are aware that the whole project is much more than just writing. Their parcel isn't ready yet but you should be having a letter sent at the beginning of next week for you all, and some students have already written independently. The school is Roman Catholic and situated here in Orange Walk Town. Although I am an Anglican I have been to Mass in their church which was conducted in Spanish. One outside Mass is on one of the videos

I have sent. The school and the church are really on the same site - but for a road which divides off part of it.

St. Paul's Anglican School was the third school to receive a parcel from you in the care of Heffer from 7H. They too, responded quickly, having been similarly prepared. Unfortunately they didn't send a Buddy although we had talked about the project in considerable detail. When something hasn't started off as your own idea things sometimes don't sink in. Also, although we all speak English there is a considerable difference in the use of it. I should speak much more slowly but I find this very difficult to do and people here are much too polite to tell you when they haven't heard or understood. That is something you can put right for yourselves. There is no reason why you shouldn't make suggestions or requests of each other. They too, are waiting for replies. The school is in Corozal Town and I have told you something about it already, especially as it is right on the shore of the Caribbean Sea. Some of the scenes of a Children's Day there are contained in video tape 4 which I have just sent. You will have discovered that the post is expensive. It is a great deal more so coming your way because incomes are that much lower here. The town is much quieter than Orange Walk Town. It used to be the other way round but there has been a sugar factory closed at Libertad not far away and this has resulted in a steady decline in employment. The refining of sugar is at present concentrated at the factory at Tower Hill just South of Orange Walk Town. Employment affects the school of course. As families move away to find work the school population goes down. There are about 180 children at St Pauls and I have spent a considerable amount of time there too. There is very much a family atmosphere here as well, surprisingly so for a town, but it is not as close as Calcutta.

Louisiana School was the last school to receive a parcel from you in the care of Sunny from 7R. This one didn't arrive until the beginning of February and the school has had many extra commitments and interruptions over the other three. However, I am assured that their parcel is on its way to you this week. There are over 800 pupils in the school. I have spent some time with the older ones but not really enough as it is more difficult to do in a large school. I have, however, spent quite a lot of time with their infants who have heard a few stories as well! Theirs was one of the Christmas parties I went to. Video tape 4 and some photos show their Children's Day event. Many of the children of Louisiana School and La Immaculada School pass my house on their way to and from their homes. If I happen to be around which is quite often, I sit outside on the veranda and we exchange greeting. Then, and at times around the town, there are often shouts of "Hi Mr Max!" even if I haven't seen them. There is a huge range of children at the school which is very caring of them. Grace Tillett is representing Orange Walk District in the finals of the National Spelling Bee in Belize City tomorrow. I was in school today talking about the linking as she was learning her words over and over. She did ask me for some pronunciation but I am a bit reluctant to give it because it is unlikely that the Question Master will use the same pronunciation if the area finals I have been to are anything to go by. In any case, English and American spellings are acceptable making a further complication. Perhaps you will ask for the result when you write to them. I found when I first came to Belize, by the way, that some people didn't answer my first letter so I wrote another. Don't give up! If a job's worth doing...!'

Calling in to the office to check on the remaining acceptance forms revealed that San Pablo and Carmelita are still outstanding which I left with Bertha to collect.

After doing all the washing to date and washing the floors I spent most of the rest of the day writing to year 7 and getting ready to go to Belize City for the Lions' Convention.

Set off from home, for Belize City at ten past three. It is a lovely sunny day as always and there is a nice breeze blowing as I skirt around the Old Cemetery, on the East side, on a little road which lines up with La Immaculada School which is nicely on the way to the Post Office. Cockerels are crowing nearby but there is nothing unusual about that. There is very little traffic this way, which is a route that I don't normally take. La Immaculada Church emerges from behind two tall trees as all the school buildings also come into view alongside and just beyond it. At this point it is best to turn west for a short distance, back into Main Street. Then continue north along the street past various bus stopping points; the Scotia Bank and the People's Store on the left; Happy Valley Chinese Restaurant, Mike's Spare Parts and Service Centre, China Store, Attitudes, Pharmacia De La Fuente and bright orange painted St Christopher's Hotel on the right before reaching the market where you fork left just short of the bridge over the New River at the start of the San Estevan Road. Zeta Water, Cuello and L & R Imports are on the left now, to mention just a few. Sing Wong Chinese Restaurant is the last business on the left before the fork but there are a couple of houses as well, alongside the short rise; then the Magistrates' Court, the Statistical Office, the Treasury and the Post Office on the right, opposite the very nice Library which I use regularly. The Police Station completes the group, tucked in beyond the Post Office and bordering the main road through town.

I arrived at the Batty Bus Station at three twenty but at three fifty I found out that the bus I had seen disappearing up the road was the three thirty which went early. That means going on the Premier at $6 instead of $4-50 on the regular bus. Other companies charge $3 and often make the journey in almost the same time, but none of their buses have the franchise for this direction and time of day. At least the Premier that I'm now sitting on is one of their better buses and I have got a window seat so that gets over the curtain problem as I can choose to have it open - that is unless seat number 29 turns up and finds that my allotted seat is 30! A basketball game, as part of a film, is generating a great noise on the video which is provided with these buses, along with the air conditioning. It is a good picture so that could turn out to be interesting although the story line is somewhat lost by now, since it started just the other side of Chetumal, probably at the Mexican border about an hour ago. Even so, I prefer to travel on the regular bus as it is more human and there is more happening. I quite like the stops too, as they break up the journey and provide extra interest. The bus which is scheduled for four o'clock, left at nine minutes past. Why does it always happen like that? Early when you are not there and late when you are? I forgot about the food though! That was good: salted, lemon flavour peanuts and Jumex Apple Juice! We arrived at the Belcan Bridge in Belize City at ten past five. This bridge was funded by the Canadians.

I completely lost track of the number of people who arrived to stay with the family. Chino brought his bus down from San Estevan, filled with Lions Club members and family.

There were four presentations at the Convention. The one from Belmopan was an excellent recitation about the life and experience of a 'Logger', brilliantly performed in Creole. San Estevan performed a sketch about a baby's distress during illness and the confusion and hasty attention that went with it. This was conducted in Spanish which even for me, contributed admirably to the melodrama, and the humour resulting in gales of laughter. The one from San Pedro won the prize. Their contribution, in music, prose, verse and dance, covered the history of Belize, particularly in San Pedro on Ambergris Caye: The ancient Mayan culture, the Spanish invaders; the fishermen; and the tourists. Belize City depicted Belizean men and Belizean women in their separate groups, trying to enjoy a night out at the same venue; the men playing dominoes and drinking; the women socializing. The effect of one group impinging on the other was very well observed, hugely exaggerated and portrayed and was extremely funny. At the end of the evening everyone was invited to tour the hospitality booths which had been set up by each of the five Districts, including Stann Creek, and at which there is a surfeit of every imaginable food and drink, fruit and produce of the land. Strong plastic bags were provided which were filled with huge numbers of give-aways: gifts ranging from bottles of rum from the North and fruits from the South to jars of hot peppers and jams produced in the West - and all sorts of other goodies in between.

The family house absorbed everybody and yet I was given my usual room which must have been at some cost to other people as there are three beds in it. I am even more confused by the coming and going at breakfast. I had to say to Neria that I had forgotten to put my name down for the trip to Belize Zoo which I must do this morning. It didn't turn out to be a problem however. It was a good visit and I managed to make a more complete record of the rather colourful language used on the notices there, guiding visitors round the grounds.

Church next morning was followed by the Parade with the San Estevan Lions float and a 'Welcome to San Estevan Lions' Den - an open thatched affair with 1985 on it. A large birthday cake over the cab of the float celebrates 20 years. It is a pity I have no film left as Tony used it all up last night - still! San Pedro has a huge parrot fish mounted on an electric vehicle. They use electric vehicles in San Pedro and Ambergris Caye and this one was shipped over for the purpose and will be taken back again by the same means. The Belize City float has a party on board and, of course, the new Lions' Queen for Belize who comes from Belize City. She is the daughter of one of the headquarters Scouters whose name is Duran. The Belize City Tour Bus goes through, giving the passengers an extra spectacle to see as the parade starts to come together. The dancers took the lead followed by the percussion band, the floats and the members of the five clubs walking; the queen throwing sweets to the kids who clearly expect it and fishing for new members to preserve District 59 for the year 2000. It was a lively spectacle on arrival at the Belize Technical College grounds.

There was a workshop for the support team at EDC in Belize City over the next four days up to Labour Day public holiday on Friday, May 1st. At last I was able to collect estimates for computer costs for 'Link' schools from Stanley. Ernest Raymond produced an open letter of support for 'Linking' and apologised for it having taken so long. And I gave my talk as guest speaker to Orange Walk Rotary Club. This was very successful. It appears that they are considering seeking the support of other clubs to go country-wide with a view to having at least one computer in every Primary School in Belize. That would be good if it happens!

Having had so much difficulty with email and telephone, BTL was not my favourite…

'…Please find herewith, my cheque for $98.27 in settlement of my account ending March 31st 1998. The numbers 02-32868 and 02-45931 are your technical support lines at BTL head office in Belize City. They were used in connection with your supply of Kwick Mail software which did not work! I was eventually supplied with Internet Explorer (although disc 3 of Internet Explorer had to be replaced also). I was given the numbers as Help Lines by you.

Please note that I have had to collect this account today. This is a regular occurrence and I would appreciate the bill being delivered. You could always send it to the box number above or leave it with my neighbour Mr Burns. Neither WASA nor BEL has a problem with this…'

Not being particularly interested in Labour Day most of it was spent just pottering about and reading, finishing The Nipper by Catherine Cookson and The Ipcress File by Len Deighton ready to take back to the library tomorrow. After domestic chores, shopping for food and going to the library on Saturday, by mid-morning I am ready to set off on a visit to the Cashew Festival at Crooked Tree and I have left home at 11:40. If I get there I expect to see Jack, the VSO from Canada, who intends to travel up with other VSOs from Belize City. That information was sitting on email but I had got it late as I couldn't operate the system for two days. That often happens here on top of the other problems. The VSOs have a vehicle but it is unlikely that our times will coincide so that I could get a lift from them for the three miles in from the Northern Highway. I believe that the opening ceremony is intended to take place just after midday but that could be anytime in the afternoon!

It is very hot! There is no sign of a bus so I turn off the end of Mahogany Street, North along the Belize - Corozal Road and down to the centre of town. There is a bus parked beyond the Clock Tower and the taxi rank but it is not one that I recognise by its shape, as being on the route to Belize City. Most buses have a flat front and this one has its engine in front of the cab. As I get closer, however, passing the Clock Tower, I see that it is a Venus bus and it is marked Belize. The bus is a Ford of the kind that is usually used on the rough shorter journeys to the villages. They travel more slowly, which I prefer because I can see more, and there is generally more movement on and off the bus as well. Even so, there was no loss of time as we left at 11:51 and arrived at the junction of Crooked Tree Road with the highway twenty five miles away, at 12:31. There are people waiting in the shelter at this point, including two Americans who are also going to Crooked Tree. The bus from Belize City has just gone past on its way to the festival so I set off to walk; a long, hot, dusty, three mile walk in blazing sun; not entirely alone because three youngsters are walking ahead. Three boys aged about fourteen, eleven and ten, who got off first from the same bus. I catch them up.

"Hi! Are you going to the festival?" The affirmative is chorused in their different ways and followed by a conversation of greeting which is not uncommon out of the town and since I have got to know so many youngsters, in the town as well. "Oh well," I remark, "Three miles. That will be about an hour's walk as long as we keep up this pace!" There is no indication that the boys intend to drop behind or separate in any way.

"You don't remember me do you?" This is the eleven year old speaking.

"Yes, of course," I say. "Louisiana School but I'm not sure whether you are Standard Five or Six?" The look on his face tells me all. He is delighted. In fact it turns out that all three live close-by where I live and we are soon old friends. That is when the whole situation really hits me for we are twenty five miles from Orange Walk Town with nowhere in between and nothing in sight but savannah, bush and light forest, walking along a remote, narrow, dusty mud road which stretches straight for over two miles.

A couple of vehicles pass on their way to the festival and a third seems to hesitate as it approaches. "Don't look round," I say, "He will stop if he wants to." And the pick-up slides past and stops just ahead.

"Would you like a lift to Crooked Tree?" (Or something that has that meaning) addressed to me by the driver who is on his own. "Yes please. That would be great." I reply - and stand back for the boys to climb up over the back before I do so and the conversation continues.

As we reach the lagoon and cross the long causeway, I can see that the dry season has had a great effect on the amount of water since I last came along here with Ricardo Alcoser and his brother delivering goods sent from Chicago by relatives who have left the village and travelled far to the north to live in the States. There is a vast expanse of rich wet mud and shallow water. Thousands of waders of an amazing variety are feeding; almost too much to take in as my mind is somewhat occupied with staying in the truck - a matter which didn't seem to bother the boys any and which is proved by their spotting a Jabiru Stork which I have to have pointed out. The Jabiru is very much an endangered species and a most impressive bird standing about five feet tall.

I am brought back to earth in more ways than one as the journey ends and we tumble out amid the huge number of cashew trees laden with their deep yellow ochre fruits waiting to be gathered. The boys are off at once to do just that. In fact, as I had noted before, there is just about every tropical fruit bearing tree imaginable just round here, in rich profusion; all ripe for the picking and generally easy to get at. The village is a very beautiful place. Not a great number of vehicles about, most of which will have come for the Festival. Crooked Tree is in many ways quite separate from the world. The track only comes here if you discount the even less used way to Backlanding and the seasonal passage which wends its way back to the Northern Highway sixteen miles or so back towards Orange Walk. And the history of Crooked Tree has given it a distinct character too, occupied as it was by loggers mainly from Scotland, who mixed with the local population and produced people who are affectionately known as redskins on account of their Creole appearance mixed with Western colouring and most surprisingly blue or green eyes. The time is 12:39, barely an hour from home!

A rope is stretched across the entrance to the village sports field in order to collect the $3.00 entrance fee. I have only a ten dollar bill, a fifty dollar bill and a few cents - a position I usually try to avoid. However, change for $50 is no problem and I am in. The boys have disappeared! There is one large field; a large open sided marquee with stage set up and chairs and the inevitable refreshments bar at one end which serves mostly rum and coke, Belikin beer (which is all you can get in Belize) and soft drinks; a food marquee serving and selling local produce; and a number of stalls such as you would find at an ordinary fair.

In the middle of the field is a huge metal frame which will hold a big screen later on so that a film can be shown after dark. Not content with that, the villagers have arranged to show Star Wars! Apparently this will be the first time any film has been shown on the big screen in Belize and while it might seem unusual to the British to show it outside, there must be very few buildings of any kind in the country that could accommodate a structure of such a size! The whole idea that such an event should take place in a remote village in the middle of an important conservation area located in the tropical rainforest seems quite amazing but people here are very resourceful. You can be sure that it won't rain at this season and there's unlikely to be enough wind to cause problems. Most community activities take place outside.

Around the field there are a large number of 'cubicles' of the shape that you might find used for separate stalls in any market. These are made with rough poles as cut from trees at each corner and at each side of the opening which makes a doorway. More poles are laid across to support the roof and at waist level to form an opening above that height at the front and sides. Each of the sides of each 'cubicle' forms one side of the next one so that they stretch out in a line. The real difference from anything I have seen before coming here is the space given to protection, not from the rain but from the sun. The 'walls' and 'roof' are just a thin layer of palm leaves fastened in place to make a comfortable and airy space inside.

The stalls are steadily being occupied by a variety of organisations' displays and local producers selling their wares. A first rate barbecue is busy producing very cheap meals with very generous portions of meat if you want it as well as the regular rice and beans. Most of the activity is scheduled to take place in the marquee and on the field. Apart from the film the main events include cultural displays, music, dancing (Punta is amazing to watch) and sports.

The boys have appeared again with big beaming smiles and a large bag of cashews of which they are busy eating the fruit and saving the nuts. They are altogether too squishy for me.

"You picked your cashews then?" Big smiles become bigger ones with a trace of giggles and a few nudges.

"Were they round about where you came in?"

I hit right on the button as the smiles spread into outright laughter and I recognise a flash of the unspoken question in facial expression, of that thought I have seen so many times: 'How did he know that?'

"I was a boy once myself," I say, "Long ago". Boys the same the world over - and yet, how different it is here from the world I have mostly known.

A traditional Belizean band begins to play as the preparations for the festival continue. There is no such thing as fixed times for these events here. There is one stated (one o'clock) but I know enough to know that it will start when it is ready and in the meantime people are more than content to sit around enjoying each other's company while children go off and make the most of any attractions or distractions that cost nothing or very little. I spend some time sitting listening to the band, wandering around and taking in the drinks made necessary by the heat of the day as well as for pleasure. In an interval, I manage to make conversation with a tall, thin Garifuna who seems well placed in the band and find that he is Lennox Blades whom I have watched play and sing before but now find that he also writes music and Anansi stories in the traditional style. More than that; he tells the stories as well so I buy a tape from him to send home to Year 7.

In one of my perambulations around the field, I find myself sitting in a convenient spot watching more preparations as the oldest of the three boys comes and sits next to me. We chat until "Will you lend me a dollar to buy some food?" Pause... "You shouldn't really be asking for dollars." He looks sheepish but still smiling. "Have you no money?" "Not now!" "What about your friends?" "They're okay." I give him a dollar which is what he asked for. "Have you got money for your bus fare?" "No!" It occurs to me that as his bus fare is a dollar he would now have it but that thought doesn't register on his face so I let it go. "Have your friends got their bus fare?" "Yes." Come and see me when you are ready to go home. I expect to go about 4:30." This greeted with an even bigger smile, showing a perfect set of even teeth in a clear natural tan face which Europeans would love to have and can never achieve! I have to admire too, a spirit which takes him this far from home across hostile country with slender security; however I might view the risk. I was just the same at his age so no more is said.

Now the Youth Connection Band from Sugar City (Orange Walk Town) are setting up their equipment and mountains of high powered speakers in the marquee and the traditional band give way to their test pieces. It is every bit as loud as anything in the UK might be and it looks as though there might be some action soon. It is just after 2:00pm.

The other VSOs arrive and we spend some time catching up with the news over a few beers. Nearly 3:00pm and the first announcements are made, prayers are said, the National Anthem is sung and I settle to a mixture of heavy Punta Rock and the wonderful spectacle of people of unexpected shapes and sizes and all ages dancing their extraordinary movements and rhythm. Children's cultural presentations are made, mostly by girls in company with the festival queen. I see that the pace will quicken as the night draws on and settle into a more relaxed state, at least for the spectators when the sports take place tomorrow.

At 4:30 I decide that it is time to make my way homeward as transport and times are indeterminate to say the least and it is a long way. My walk to the main road is cut short by the welcome vision of the buses which came from Belize City in the opposite direction from Orange Walk. 'Yes there is room for me as far as the Northern Highway.' Brilliant! Better still, as I have a great view of the thousands of birds while travelling back across the causeway and mixed feelings as the driver uses his wind horn to stir them into action. 'Great' I think to myself, when the birds take not the slightest notice. The boys are already back at the bus shelter so I fix the bus fare and we chat for a short while as the bus isn't long in coming. They saw one of the big crocodiles on the way out too. I missed that!

On Sunday Pedro Sanchez brought his wife Benito and daughter Daiami over from San Estevan for the afternoon at about midday. They arrived on Pedro's motorbike. Benito rode pillion and Daiami was perched on the tank. Benito had prepared dinner of Escabeche which she brought with her ready to be served and eaten. This was wonderful. Benito took over completely, setting everything out for four round the kitchen table as had never happened before and we all sat down to a delicious meal after which she insisted on clearing up completely. Needless to say, the visit was a very pleasant one with good friends.

Escabeche is basically an onion soup with chicken which is served with warm tortillas. It is traditionally served at festivals and special occasions so it had a particular poignancy on this occasion which is very much appreciated and which is intended as the beginning of Sundays out visiting places of interest with Pedro on his motorbike.

Monday 4th May… The working week began with the 7:15 bus to Corozal to bring Pedro Cucul up to date with the current position with the planning of the curriculum (planning, trialling, staff, venue, local managers, support, co-ordinators and gathering of information) and to discuss the application for a VSO grant for a computer for Calcutta Government School. A letter was produced to go to Local Managers of schools to invite them to a presentation on the curriculum on Thursday, 14th May in Orange Walk office at 3:30pm. Bertha and Onelia obtained names and addresses. Corozal Methodist School was visited to confirm that as the venue for the Corozal District planning with Henry Neal. All the facilities can be provided and the details will be discussed at the Principals meeting at 2:30pm on Thursday, 21st May at St Peter's School, Orange Walk.

At 1:00pm Onelia and Bertha and I met to discuss further action which can be taken. The first priority is to deliver the invitations to Local Managers but we also discussed looking for resources for Spanish in Chetumal schools with the help of the Mexican Consulate and made arrangements for a series of discussions timed to coincide with the meetings arranged.

Similar discussions with Urbano Uck had to be cut short because of a serious incident that he had to go and deal with. The time was rearranged for 2:00pm but he had not returned so that was deferred to Wednesday. David was contacted at EDC for copies of conference notes and latest Curriculum document for Managers and DEOs; also to advise of meeting dates for the benefit of Corinth, Ariola and Alphonso.

And still there were issues to deal with in the UK…

'…Thank you for your letter dated 6th. April. I have not received a tax return from the Inland Revenue (thankfully) nor any other communication since the notices of coding which I sent via my local branch of NatWest. I have no new source of income and I wouldn't expect that situation to change in the present tax year. Please find enclosed your form (ref 8 SW/SRT) duly completed - although there isn't much on it. Most of the information you have and I don't. You have details of my pension and I believe you may have the form P60. I do not have it here. I cannot provide you with details of the letting of my house in the UK but these can be supplied by the agent. Judging by what appears on my bank statement, there have been very substantial outgoings from the rent…'

More creatively, the story of the festival at Crooked Tree was sent to Year 7 as were all stories especially from now on and including the Belize Teachers' Training College·Field Trip I was fortunate enough to join on Friday.

I was up at 4:00am ready by twenty to five to try (again) to send an email to Paul. Even by half past five the email to Paul still wouldn't go for some reason but it wasn't for want of trying so I felt free to set off along South Main Street, around the corner into Mahogany Street…

It is relatively cool with just a slight haze. I'd say it is going to be extremely hot again today. I have plenty of time now, to walk down to the Batty Bus Station. I have reached the Belize - Corozal Road. The bus has to pass me to meet me there in any case. It occurs to me that the bus will probably stop by the square which everyone calls the park. It would have to pass there anyway so I decide to wait. 6:15am the sun is shining brightly. No sign of the bus yet. The town, which was quiet to start with, is now getting busy for the day; buses are everywhere and trucks loaded with cane are pounding through. At 6:20 the bus arrived and a whole group of teachers appeared as if from nowhere and prepared to get on. Among them is a Peace Corps, Amy Scanlon, who was fellow scorer at the area final of the Spelling Bee. It hadn't occurred to me that some of the teachers must live in Orange Walk. Olga Manzanero, who organised the trip, is smiling and saying Hi at me through the window so there is no need to check. Those are the only two I know in two bus-loads. We didn't go far as the bus stopped a hundred yards further on at the bus station for a refreshment break! We finally set off for Blue Creek at 6:45am. Four o'clock seems ages ago. The other bus set off for Chetumal for a reverse tour. They are playing Volley-Ball at the University.

7:50am Arrived at Blue Creek which is perched on a beautiful and surprising escarpment which I had watched grow on the horizon as we approached. To find such hills after a vast expanse of flat land is very welcome. Disappointment followed for a while as we turned and came back down again. It was to be a day of surprises in any case as I had only the vaguest idea of the agenda. Turning off some way back along the track we had come, we stopped at a lovely stretch of water which turned out to be the Rio Bravo just upstream of the Rio Hondo, two important rivers in the North of Belize. Also, the Rio Hondo forms the border with Mexico. A small dam reaches across the river at this point which has a regular flume for overflow and sluice gates which would empty the water back to natural river level. A guide appears from what turns out to be a small hydro-electric power station a little way off and the theme of the day begins:

conservation and sustainable use of land and resources.

There is a natural fall of three feet from the Rio Bravo to the Rio Hondo at this point which is of little engineering advantage but the dam raises this difference to ten feet enabling a simple horizontal gravity wheel to be installed which, in turn, drives a generator capable of producing 150 kilowatts of electricity and supplying 70 homes. The water supply enters through a four foot diameter pipe. A hydraulic governing set controls a set of shutters which regulate the water supply to give a constant output. Not very great but sustainable and demonstrating the effectiveness of private enterprise even in difficult circumstances. How much better it could be if the Government of Belize were to make controlled concessions to take place in areas where the fall of water is great as, for example, the 1,000ft fall in the Western mountains which is actually 1,300ft. Even here, there is enough flow to double the output with a second generator set alongside the first. The extra head of water also enables the adjacent field to be flooded to support the rice crop. Belize grows all its own rice here and has a surplus for export. The water behind the dam is continually moving so there is no silting and the animal population has increased including the crocodiles!

From the power station we set off again towards Blue Creek which was lovely. The view across the vast flat land below is amazing and the whole space shimmered and throbbed with the heat although it was still not long after nine in the morning. About six miles East outside the village, we turned South at tiny Rosita having already passed through the hamlet of Neuendorf which I guess must have Mennonite connections. Then we continued perhaps another twenty miles deep into the Rio Bravo Conservation Area to the headquarters and field station of Programme for Belize. And what a beautiful place it is; a lovely setting of cabanas in a clearing in the forest. Electricity produced by solar panels; all waste, including human waste, recycled for fertilizer; natural materials in use everywhere but the power to exploit modern technology to the full; a wonderful setting to study a balance for flora and fauna and especially the trees of the forest.

We were given a history of the project and an indication of some of its work which owes its origin to the Audubon Society and a concern for the habitat of birds: also a very informative walk through the forest - on the chiclé trail - looking at the special adaptations of trees and in some cases their paired animals; the evidence of Mayan habitation and land use; some of the variety of forest types and the reasons for them; the forest layers; the emergent species; the epiphytes which, including vines and creepers, form 20% of the vegetation; and the adventitious and buttress root systems. The whole of Belize is secondary forest, having been used by the Maya for centuries but in a way which has allowed regeneration to take place. All the forest is tropical of course, and that which is to the South and West where there is higher rainfall is classified as rainforest. The dry season has a much greater effect elsewhere and the forests in those areas are much denser along great meandering rivers that never run short of water. The original chewing gum was made from chiclé but I believe it is now made from oil!

We had to come back through Orange Walk to go on to Chetumal so I excused myself as there was no great benefit in my going to the University and I could usefully write to Paul and year 7 again next day, a short email (again and at last?) and a letter…

'…Thank you for your email sent on 2nd May. I have been trying ever since to 'Reply to sender' but that will not work for some reason. Please send me the email address in your next communication. At least we can save time with mail coming from you now and if I have the email address you have used that should work for me to send. It has with others. The obstacles to progress have been very frustrating. The letters and parcels you have had from me are only a small part of the personal effort. However, obstacles and frustrations are there to be overcome and the final (and on-going) result will be the stronger for it. Two schools have sent packages (at the same time) ages ago. One was St Paul's who didn't send a Buddy so I assume that is the one you have had. The other is Calcutta. Also, many children have sent personal mail to their counterparts. The other two schools are just sending or have just sent theirs for a variety of reasons. The two schools that are only just sending their parcels have been a disappointment but I am sure that the wait will be worthwhile. The parcel from Louisiana was posted yesterday along with a letter from the Principal to you (Sent registered post, I gather). I really do think it would be a good idea for staff to write to each other. I had expected that you would have had addresses long ago and kept hoping! Anyway, the names of the Principals and the addresses of the schools are listed below for completeness. Perhaps you would like to write to them. One of the pupils at La Immaculada has written to 7G in the interim. It seems that mail is going astray. I have a record of what was in the parcels you sent but it would be useful to know what else has been sent, to whom, at which school and who from. Armed with that information, I can check much more effectively.

The school that has put in most effort and enthusiasm - both with their parcel (and Buddy) and individual letters is

118

Calcutta and I am getting the impression that you have had nothing from them. This is dreadful if it is the case. They are linked with 7D and Uncle Albert. That was the first parcel to arrive. It was placed right away (as were the others) and I had introduced and developed the whole project with all the schools long before that. Also I know the staff and the students very well indeed at Calcutta. We are all good friends at all the schools but Calcutta is really special. There is no lack of commitment there but a good deal of disappointment. You will remember that they wrote letters to you even before the parcel had arrived. If you will put together a list of children who have sent letters but not had replies, I will see to it that they get them as quickly as possible. I will need to know to whom they have written and in which school. Better still - if they send letters through me I will gladly act as postman. Perhaps some children might like to write via my email if you can arrange it. I will deliver the mail and transcribe replies. Until the return email is working I will use the post.

I will be going in to all four schools again next week to find out exactly what has been sent and received and discuss what is being done now and what might be done next. I have talked with all of them with a view to making a film as I have said in an earlier letter and now that BNSE is over it is a good time to concentrate on that. The planning and work will come from them of course. I am just a camera man. I have also said they can use my camera if they wish. I have it in mind to encourage a fresh batch of letters as well. They all know who their pupil buddy is and it never hurts to send an extra letter. I have suggested this many times but I intend, temporarily, to take a more directive role. Have you had the parcel sent on 22nd April? It contained video tapes 4 & 5, a lot of photos from films 1, 3 and 4, and another tee-shirt. Your recent letters will have been dated 23rd February, 6th, 9th 16th and 22nd April. You didn't get anything through March because it was the Easter holiday. I also wrote to year 7 (via you) on 23rd April and 5th May which I will continue as a weekly epistle.

The best news I have to give you is that I have been given leave to apply to VSO for funds to equip Calcutta School with a computer and that application is now only waiting for signatures and will be sent off next week. The amount of work necessary to clear the path and ensure that the school will be able to have the equipment maintained, put in a secure place and be acceptable in terms of compatibility with the secondary sector and with future plans is considerable. This has involved all levels: Chief Education Officer, the Education Development Centre, District Education Officer, Managers and Principal as well as suppliers for costs etc. That looks pretty hopeful. My equipment will be donated to St. Pauls when I leave in any case. And that is not all. I gave my talk to the local Rotary Club last Wednesday to a very attentive group of influential people who asked a lot of lively questions. It seems that they are very enthusiastic about the project and I gather that they are looking into going beyond what is being asked for. Enclosed is a copy of my notes. Obviously, they are prompts for me but they will help give you a fuller picture of what is going on.

Do please keep up a dialogue with me - at least until the whole thing is running strongly. It doesn't matter who actually writes from yourself or any of year 7. It will all help me to take the appropriate and timely action. I know only too well the difficulties imposed by distance and fully sympathise with anyone waiting for mail. Much harder it must be for youngsters to understand, who haven't had the experience we have had. All mail coming to me will have a prompt reply and I will convey any messages requested.

I hope all that helps. The youngsters here are great and once bonds have been made the links will grow. I have to say, though, that time does not have the same significance in Central America. One of the things I have had to learn!!! Perhaps I will produce a piece of writing on that - sometime!

I bought 60 air letter forms, rather more than usual, for a blitz on letter writing next week. Onelia, Bertha and I met to plan their visit to the Mexican Consulate to identify resources for teaching Spanish and afterwards I went to the Belize City Lions Club 25th Anniversary Dinner at the Radisson Fort George. The Prime Minister was there although he hadn't been invited to speak. Dinner was excellent but a great deal could be learned by such a prestigious establishment about etiquette, service and presentation. I stayed overnight with the family after treating Neria to the outing as today is her birthday.

Unusually, I returned to Orange Walk from Belize City for the weekend on the ten o'clock bus. Bertha called round in the afternoon as arranged on Saturday so that I could type out and print the letter to the Mexican Consulate. It hadn't dawned on me that it was to have been in Spanish! I only made one mistake - o instead of a so that wasn't bad…

'…Srta. Cervantez,

Esperando que tenga un buen dia, me dirojo a usted por medio de esta carta para solicitar informacion que seria benefica para nosotros. Nosotros estamos trabajando en co-ordinacion con un nuevo programa del ministerio de educacion para implementar la ensenanza del espanol como segunda lengua, en las escuelas primerias por primera vez en Belice.

Estariamos muy agradecios si les es posible ayudamos con lo siguiente:

A) Informacion: (i)   estrategias de como ensenar espanol como segunda lengua

(ii) referencias de citiones hechos por varios psicologos y educadores referentes a "ciertos ninos" particularmente a ninos en los primeros anos de primaria.

(iii) estructura y organizacion del sistema educacional de Mexico.

B) Recursos: material: libros   videos
                        audio - cassettes   planillas
                        juegos educacionales

C) Permiso para visitar algunas escuelos para observar/visitar

Esperando su mas rapida contestacion a nuestra solicitud si fuera posible antes del fin del mes de mayo 98 y agradeciendo enormemente su amable co-operacion y su contribucion al nuevo sistema educacional de nuestro pais.

Atentamente…'

A great deal is made of the Mothers' Day aspect of Mothering Sunday here as this is Central America and many such things are dominated by the States and extreme commercialism. Worse than that, the ugly face of politics gets in on the act also. Delivered to my house on Friday was a roll of glossy white paper, printed in shining colour and held by a rubber band. Inside was a sort of scroll and a folded invitation. The scroll was: 'Mother Dearest

Dear Mother:
You are the Best Gift
That God has given to us
You are our Guardian Angel
You are our Strength
You are our Hope
You are our Love
Without you, we are Helpless
Thank you for always caring
Today, your' very special Day,
May God always protect and Guide you.
With Love Always

From: Hon. Ruben R. Campos
Minister of Mobilization & Coordination'

The invitation has 'Special Tribute to Mother' with a red rose on the front and underneath: 'By UDP Orange Walk Central Committee to Elect Hon. Ruben Campos. Inside it says 'Hon. Ruben Campos and Family together with the UDP Orange Walk Central extend a warm invitation to you Dear Mother, on your special day to be a part of our special 'Tribute to Mother': The Peoples' Stadium at 7pm - 12 midnight; Delicious food, Refreshments, grand raffle prizes. 'Youth Connection' and 'Los Cometos' will supply the music; for Mothers only on Your Special Day.' On the back are the words: Ruben Campos The new hope for Orange Walk Central. Together we shall create a better Orange Walk Central for you and our children. Venceremos!! (I assume venceremos comes from the verb vencer - to defeat).

This is altogether too much for me. I think that politics and politicians often degrade what should be an order of high service but this just about takes the biscuit. Mothers' Day has already become sickeningly commercial and this act of folly seems to me, only to compound an already distorted image of love into sentiment. What does this make it?

What was I going to meet when I went to church this morning? To make matters more uncertain, the last time I was in Orange Walk for church, three weeks ago, it was the minister's last service and I know there isn't an immediate replacement and that it hasn't been possible to hold communion in that time. I needn't have had any concern. All I can say is that any doubt I might have had was quickly turned to joy and fellowship. Oddly enough, the thoughts didn't match my feelings anyway when I left home as there was a sort of eagerness that I couldn't quite identify and certainly couldn't explain.

Time is not given a great deal of concern here in Belize and when I arrived at 8:25am for an 8:30 service there were only three people in church! However, it filled up soon after time and the service started just before 8:45 with singing which became enthusiastic by the middle of the second verse of the first hymn. There was a large wooden cross with a lot of small holes in it in front of the altar and a much smaller number of single red roses wrapped in clear cellophane laid out neatly on the top of the table. It was also, clearly going to be a communion service. Otherwise there was no clue as to the length and breadth and depth of what was to follow - that is until three clergy appeared together with the four boys who serve as stewards! The structure of the service was regular communion of course but woven into it were a number of other important elements. The baptism took place of a young man of about eleven who sat in the pew just in front of the one I occupied with three others, in the third row from the front. The sermon was for Ascension Day which is a week on Thursday, 21st May and centred on 'glory', the only word we have which is adequate to glimpse the life to come. This approached from the way we hang on to the present life with all its trials, pain and frustration because it is the only life we know. There was a blessing of rings for a couple sitting next to me. This was a very joyful experience greeted with great enthusiasm and which I haven't seen done before. A statement and symbol of commitment made in public - and shared. The announcement was made of the confirmation of a significant number for the size of the church, which is to take place next week at 3:00pm at a service conducted by the Bishop whom I have met twice before. All the candidates stood up and were applauded. Also standing for applause at another time, were all mothers who came forward to receive their roses and return with them, smiling, to their seats. So what of the wooden cross with the many small holes? Well, I'm coming to that. For me, that made a special communion very special if that can ever be a matter of degree. Everyone collected a rose for their mother to place on the cross; a red rose for those who are living and a white one for those departed. Mine was a white one. Somehow the sermon took on a meaning beyond the words at this, the first time I have been able to express my love and thanks for my Mum in public since her passing. A white rose at the heart of the cross and the closing hymn 'the day thou gavest, Lord, is ended'.

The first meeting of the week was with Pedro Cucul to discuss the application for grant from VSO for a computer for Calcutta Government School to help them with their 'Linking' and to obtain his signature on the application form which is now almost ready.

9:30am St. Paul's Anglican School to discuss present position of 'Linking' with the students involved. They agreed to send a Buddy separately as they hadn't sent one with their parcel and the Buddy is an important actor in the adventure taking place. Also, each student undertook to write and send another letter separately to their partner. This was addressed to Mr Berry for the recipient so that he sees that a letter has arrived in each case and will be receiving some 120 letters by the time all students have written their extra letter from the four schools. I provided the aerogrammes and demonstrated how they work. Surprisingly, the children had not seen them before nor, in most cases, had the staff. Teachers are writing letters to Mr Berry as well. 12:00 Set off for Calcutta Government School to perform the same exercise and 8:30 next morning at Louisiana Government School after obtaining a new supply of aerogrammes from the Post Office. It was necessary first to identify those who had contributed to the parcel sent last week and add a few more to the number. Some of the students were at confirmation classes but Mike Cawich undertook to see that their letters would be written. Jorge Cawich had written to Mr Berry when the parcel went last week and the parcel was registered. I took some photographs in the afternoon at an art and craft display at Louisiana to add to the many already sent to year 7.

In the corner of the garden outside my house, there is the trunk and the remains of the long leaf fronds of a coconut palm which is dead. Something is happening to the coconut palms. They are being attacked in a way which is causing some of them to die prematurely. This is not a great problem however, as most survive happily and the ones that have died make a curiously attractive shape and act as host to a wide variety of wildlife. I have watched several different kinds of lizard going up and down this tree, or what remains of it - grey and brown and dry. The great attraction is that it is only about eight feet away from the corner of the veranda and I can see straight into what remains of the leaves (If the coconut palm can be said to have leaves as we recognise them). Anyway, directly opposite where I am sitting now I can see a gap between the trunk and some of the dead leaves which are hanging down. In that gap there is a bird's nest with some youngsters in it which are currently being fed. It is fascinating to watch so openly. The mother bird - I assume to be the mother bird because she is the smaller of the two - flies back and forth about every two minutes or so to be greeted by the youngsters as she feeds them. Looking through the gap, I can see their open beaks silhouetted against the sky showing through on the other side. I can see too, the beak of the mother bird as she thrusts inside and regurgitates whatever it is that she has caught for food. Interestingly, high on a tree across the road, perched on a wonderful vantage point surveying all there is to see is what I believe to be the male parent who, from time to time, signals whatever warning he has in mind to the female. I have noticed that when he is quiet she comes to the nest and when he isn't, she doesn't. All this is going on at the end of what has been an extremely busy day. It has been very hot. As I said, the temperature has been over a hundred degrees at times for two weeks and I am relaxing with a book - or at least, I was. Life goes on. The children next door have been playing volleyball and are now playing billiards. The Burns family have most things and that attracts a lot of children to come and play. You might wonder what the birds look like. In fact these are not the brightly coloured birds you might expect even though there are many such hereabouts as well as elsewhere. We have a large number of wonderfully coloured woodpeckers with a bright crimson patch on their head which can be seen frequently. Many of these use the dead trunks of coconut palms although I haven't got one. Not far away, by the river, are flocks of yellow head parrots. The brilliant yellow kikadee flits through the trees and occasionally lands in the garden. Tiny hummingbirds hover at exotic flowers on some of the bushes. And heaven knows how many species I see from time to time that I can neither recognise nor have found time to research. No, these birds are ordinary; they're black; they look as though they ought to belong to the crow family, being almost the same length as a rook but much more slender and light; active and much more solitary. They have long pointed beaks which look very sharp and a raucous cry which, along with the numerous cockerels people keep, can be one of the first things you hear when woken from sleep just before dawn. And yet, in their way, they have a sort of ordinariness about them which itself is fascinating if you take the trouble to look.

The next visit to Louisiana School was for 8:30 to act as a judge for their Drug Elimination Quiz. Bertha Campos was also judging. Returned at 11:45 and continued with Bertha, direct to Corozal to meet with Onelia to finalise preparations for the meeting with local managers and posted the grant application to VSO. Among letters to primary children at home…

'…Last week was Education Week. I can't remember whether that takes place at the same time for you. On Monday I managed to spend almost the whole morning with the students at St Paul's Anglican School in Corozal Town and all afternoon at Calcutta Government School in Corozal District. It was quite a day - especially as I had to see the District Education Officer first thing - to obtain his signature as the person responsible for any equipment that might result from a grant application to VSO on behalf of Calcutta School. That would improve communications enormously - I wish…'

The meeting for Local Managers at Orange Walk Office outlined the Philosophy and Development of the National Curriculum together with progress and plans for the implementation of Phase 2…

'…The Task Force has produced the Goals and Specifications for the National Curriculum. The Curriculum Team have produced, tested and revised the Outcomes for the Lower Division. For Orange Walk this involved Louisiana, Carmelita and San Pablo Roman Catholic schools. In Corozal, Calcutta Government, San Antonio and St Paul's Anglican took part. These six schools worked on almost the entire curriculum between them. Work is in progress on the Outcomes for the Middle and Upper Divisions. Phase Two of the implementation has begun. Fifteen schools are participating in the North. These include the original six plus St. Peter's Anglican, Chapel, Nuevo San Juan, San Juan Nuevo Palmar in Orange Walk, and St. Francis Xavier, Corozal Methodist, Christian Assembly of God (Santa Rita), Calcutta SDA and Buena Vista in Corozal. The two Districts will be working on Language Arts only at this stage; that is to say – English and Spanish. The start date is 22nd June and four weeks have been allocated to complete the work. As far as possible, the whole staff of the Lower Division and the Principals from each of the participating schools will take part in planning for the Outcomes in English and Spanish. This planning will be carried out as two coordinated teams, at venues accessible to all concerned. Toledo District is also working on Language Arts. Belize, Cayo and Stann Creek are concerned with the other three Areas of the curriculum. At the end of the exercise, it is expected that prototypical curriculum planning will have been completed for the three years of the Lower Division. This will provide a basis for planning the trialling of the curriculum in the Lower Division from September in the participating schools. It is not intended to be prescriptive in any way…'

Only local managers from Corozal Methodist, Christian Assembly of God from Corozal and the acting assistant DEO for Orange Walk came. Corinth, Alphonso and Ariola came up from Belize City. Clearly there would be much more to do and the last sentence at risk!

I went to the Teachers' Day on Friday held at the MCC ground (yes it is the same - a relic of colonial days) in Belize City. There is not really much to tell about that except that we had a stand there 'The Belize National Comprehensive Curriculum - Helping Children to live in a World of Change'. I say a stand but that could be misleading too; four rough poles with an opaque plastic sheet stretched overhead from a high wall. This kept some of the sun off the underneath where we attempted to answer some of the many questions which, perhaps, might have been better answered before now. But it was a useful day, the display was good, and it was good to talk to so many teachers that I know already - and I had travelled on a chartered bus with teachers and principals from Corozal.

One of the birds is in and out of the nest. I think that one or two must have flown yesterday; next day all the birds have flown. The confirmation service at St Peters at 3:00pm was well attended as there were visitors from Belize City as well as the Bishop being there for the Confirmation. We also had a keyboard so the singing was better. One of the visitors was Neria's neighbour with whom I went to St Mary's in Belize City all that time ago. She came and sat next to me and greeted me straight away which was nice. The new candidates for confirmation were mostly boys and girls around twelve. The boys were dressed in black trousers and white shirts and the girls in white dresses which seem to be the norm here. After writing letters to all the Primary Children and cards for birthdays, in the evening until late at night Landy had a party to which I was eventually invited after the boys had violated my space and I sent them packing. I declined of course, as it was a family party (probably to celebrate confirmation also) but it was thoughtful of him to make the apology for the boys' rudeness. They had been using the space downstairs and overdone it. He also brought round a plate of food which I enjoyed (another cue for not accepting to join them) but I had already eaten well so I was overdoing it a bit.

The letters and cards were posted before calling in at the office but I didn't stay as there were no messages and I used the time to explore the potential of (hopefully) sending successful emails. Letters included news for Year 7…

'…There was good intent in my saying that I would write every week. As my last letter was dated 5th May I haven't succeeded again! However, the intention remains the same and the reason for the delay has to do with you as well. I have been very busy indeed lately. The curriculum work has taken up a great deal of effort and there have been a large number of visits to make both in and out of working time but a lot more effort than usual has also gone into ensuring that your links with Belize grow. You will see the results for yourselves presently or you may well have seen some of them already. Two things are outstanding. First, I haven't heard that you have received the parcel from Calcutta Government School which was sent with their Buddy months ago. As Mr Berry was telling me that you had had only one parcel and there was no Buddy in it, I assume that was from St. Paul's Anglican School in Corozal. I found that they hadn't sent a Buddy after their parcel had gone. If the parcel from Calcutta is lost that would be a very great shame. You will remember that they were the first to write to you even before your first parcel had left for Belize and they are very keen indeed to get to know you better. They have just sent another batch of letters to you in the interim. Now is the time for you to give them maximum encouragement - not just from 7D, perhaps, if their parcel to you is lost. The second thing is to question whether any of you have not replied to letters received or perhaps not sent a letter in your parcel - or had that happen to you. One of the things I have been doing over the last three weeks is making a log of which I will send you a copy. All of you in each form have a partner here in Belize and some of you have more than one. It would be a shame if anyone, on either side of the Atlantic, is missing out on personal contact. I am here to smooth the path so please let me know where I can help. It would help greatly if I received individual letters from you too. I will always answer them.

Have you had the parcel sent on 22nd April? It contained video tapes 4 & 5, a lot of photos from films 1, 3 and 4, and another tee-shirt. I asked that in my letter to Mr Berry, dated 7th May and I apologise for asking again but the loss of those tapes would be almost as bad as losing the parcel from Calcutta. I received an email from Mr Berry this week telling me that the parcel from Louisiana School has arrived. That is very pleasing. You will also be receiving some extra letters from them and their Principal has written to Mr Berry. There is a lot of video of their sports and some photographs in the last parcel I sent - referred to above.

It will be good when your school is back on line again for email. Some of you will have a good excuse to use it of course. That will speed things up considerably. As I have said already, I will forward any messages to your link schools or to individual students and I always answer letters sent to me… Getting on to email has been quite an experience. I thought it would be easy once I had acquired the computer but not so. Belize Telecommunications Limited (BTL) has some very advanced equipment but it still suffers some fairly basic problems for all that. I can't afford to go on to the Internet so I was given software for what is called 'Kwickmail' (using Eudora) in return for my $20 connection fee and $20 per month for a maximum of five hours use - most of which I am never likely to need. Kwickmail simply didn't work despite the efforts of BTL and lots of long distance phone calls. I was then given Internet Explorer which has email on it of course and which would enable Internet use in the unlikely event of my being able to use it (Maybe the school that has my computer will if BTL eventually give them some concession). Disc three (of four) wouldn't load. More phone calls. I then found myself having three visits altogether, to BTL Headquarters in Belize City and their having my computer overnight. More phone calls. It still didn't work and it was finally fixed by a friend of mine who is a software expert. When the bill came in there was $90 on it for the phone calls. I didn't pay that! I had trouble fitting the modem as well but that's another story. Most things take a great deal of patience and perseverance to achieve. One thing more about BTL - in common with all the banks and many other similar establishments, you have to pass a man with a shotgun in order to get in!

Although their enthusiasm for the linking is great it has been difficult for Louisiana to attend to their parcel so it has been sent much later than they would have wished. The school has had many events and happenings (apart from BNSE) through from the middle of last term and a lot of building is going on as well. You can find out about some of those things for yourselves of course. I will be going in to La Immaculada School next week. I believe that their parcel has been sent to you too, but I will catch up with their news shortly.

Last week was Education Week… Anyway, it was up at 5:30am to catch the 7:00am bus to arrive for an 8:00am start at the District Office; a lovely morning, cool as I remember. The temperature couldn't have been much more than seventy early on. It has been nudging a hundred degrees for nearly three weeks in Orange Walk Town and that is **HOT**. One Friday it reached 108 in the shade in the town. I know 'cos I was there! When you think that the body temperature is maintained at 98.4 you realise that you have to sweat just to get rid of the energy released through breathing, pumping blood and digesting food. I can drink three litres of water and soft drinks during the day and still not have to 'go' until the evening. You tend to find as much shade as you can and as much breeze as you can to evaporate the sweat. A good practical science lesson that! The rest of the day was spent working with the students you are linking with. Valmar Rivero at Calcutta seems to have done rather well in contact with David. I don't know you, David, but I do know Valmar who is very active and full of fun. I have never seen him without a smile on his face - even now when he says he can't play soccer because he has hurt his leg. (I don't know what else that was when I looked out at break time!) There will be others too, of course but I haven't really studied my lists yet. I know Billy had several letters early on but he wasn't at school that day…

I spend days like that as often as I can in different schools. There isn't a better way of getting to know each other. It makes a change for the students and staff and I enjoy the days very much. If you have had any tapes of Belizeans' voices you will know that their pronunciation (and use) of English is very different even when they are not using Creole, so hearing my voice is quite a change. They do hear American voices from time to time but that too, is different. I am the only VSO in the North. There is one other Englishman in Corozal and one in Orange Walk. Two English girls have also worked through last half term at Guadalupe Roman Catholic School in Corozal Town before they start their course at University. The Principal there is the sister of a friend of mine. It is amazing how many people I have got to know through the original four families I made friends with when I came here. In a country with such a small population many people are related to each other. Put that together with the people that become friends through going in to schools and it makes life very pleasant indeed.

That day was **HOT** as well. I have told you that classrooms are open to the outside world - there being no corridors, halls or even window glass, as you can see from photos you have had. Well, one thing every school has is a freezer and almost everything that is sold for refreshment is cold; every kind of cold item you can think of which sells at a low price, but children are just as serious about drinking (cold) water as about drinking anything else. Water comes in five gallon plastic containers; some schools have coolers which dispense the water from the upturned container. Water comes in litre and half litre bottles with a pull out valve on the top like you get on a washing up liquid bottle; those are kept cold in a refrigerator. Water comes in polythene bags which you just puncture in the corner with your teeth and squeeze the content into your mouth; they are a quarter of a litre. Water comes from wells which is the supply in most villages although many of the villages pump it up into holding tanks from where it comes through pipes. In the towns many people have piped water but mostly, you don't drink that! The sewage goes down into the same ground as the water comes up from and the treatment is often not sufficient without the water being boiled. The bottled water is purified through reverse osmosis and exposed to ultra violet light. I expect you remember about osmosis (hope so!). I assume reverse osmosis to be a matter of exceeding osmotic pressure to reverse flow across a semi-permeable membrane. So instead of water to solution you get solution to water; literally against Nature. Mr Berry will explain all that.

You will notice that this letter is rambling somewhat. This is quite deliberate. I hope you can see that in telling of what seem to be very ordinary things about which you will have a mental picture, there are aspects which to us are not ordinary at all. This is part of the extent to which we learn about each other. It begins to explain why some things which we might consider to be important are not really important at all. Rather than give you examples of that which may not make sense to you however, perhaps you could bear that in mind and discuss differences as you come across them. On Tuesday morning I did the same thing at Louisiana School. (I did complete all my curriculum work for this week as well.) All the children went home as usual at lunchtime but had the afternoon off because there was an exhibition of art and craft work for parents as part of Education Week in the afternoon. There simply isn't room for such an exhibition to take place at the same time as school operates. Many of the older students remained of course, because the event couldn't run without them. They busied themselves, along with the staff, in transforming the school in what seemed no time at all. There are some photos on the next film that I will be sending shortly.

On Wednesday morning I was back at Louisiana as judge for a Drugs Elimination quiz. The questions were very searching indeed but the girl who came first got full marks and deservedly so. She and two others go forward to the District Finals. The drugs threat is very serious here. I know it is serious for you too, but this is Central America and Belize has to work hard to avoid the worst effects of the trafficking which goes on. In Orange Walk Town the place to avoid at night is the Old Cemetery which is only a couple of hundred yards from where I live. Walking through there in daylight is perfectly safe and everyone does; but not at night. Then that is the place to avoid. It reminds me of a sort of small wood except that most of the 'trees' are graves that are made of concrete. I imagine that hiding at night would be very easy indeed. As well as the headstones you are familiar with, there are a lot of family tombs almost like small concrete houses which you can see into through bars. These have all sorts of memorial tables, tablets and figures as well as what I can only describe as casket containers inside, also made of concrete. Most people here are Catholic of course. They tend to regard such shrines and painted effigies as being very important. There are also some very big trees there. I think I told you about the mahogany tree that was cut down. Also, there are no formal paths; just winding track made by feet taking the same route to avoid the many obstacles. Yes there are many places to hide and the whole place is one to avoid at night.
On Friday I went to the Teachers' Day held at the MCC ground…'
An extract from another of the individual letters…

'…Thank you for your card. I was talking to William Parada just last week. That must seem quite strange to you and it will give you an idea of how remarkable it all seems to me knowing so many of you there and here as well. I regard the whole thing as a huge privilege. I have just written to Richard, now to you and then to Leanne with a special request. It would be useful to learn of your experiences with the linking with Belize Schools direct from the three of you - and from others too. If you have had pleasing experience say so and tell me about it. If you have had disappointments tell me that also. If you have had disappointment it would help if you tell me the things you might have done better as well as those which you expected and didn't happen…'
More of the picture in letters to Junior School children…

'…In Orange Walk Town the place to avoid at night is the Old Cemetery… I have just eaten a huge, ripe and juicy mango! Tropical fruits are wonderful and there is fresh fruit of one sort or another all the year round but now is mango time and I think that mango is the most delicious fruit of all - even better than pineapple. If you think of the most wonderful peach you have ever eaten, then imagine it much bigger, more full of flavour and sweeter with juice that is **thick** you would be getting somewhere near the pleasure of eating a fresh mango................ Mega, **mega**, *yummy*… Next door they are working up to having a party so it will be noisy this evening… My neighbours are well off. They own this house as well and I rent it from them. I was very lucky to get it. They also have two businesses and properties which are let in the centre of town. Many people are not well off at all but they still manage to have parties where all their friends and relations come together as one big family. In that case much more of the food and drink is brought with them. There are also a lot of more public celebrations. Hardly a week goes by without something of the sort going on. Eating is generally a much more communal affair here than we are used to. The Belizean equivalent of fast food is everywhere. There are a lot of cafes and some restaurants but by far the most common is the stall by the road all over town and in places where people pass in the country as well. These will sell fruit and chips (which are the equivalent of our crisps - but not crisp shaped - made from corn or banana). They also sell a whole range of hot foods made from corn or flour tortillas filled in a whole variety of ways. Then there are the fried tortillas which are crisp and covered again in a variety of ways to make such things as garnaches and tostadas…'

One of the problems for snail mail…

'…While I have been catching up with my mail the power has gone off three times. The last time it happened the computer was busy saving on to floppy disc. It was your file and it was wiped completely! As the power had gone and because it was doing that it was also wiped from the temporary memory on the hard disc so there is no way to recover. An unusual combination but there it is. So if I repeat myself it is because my system for not doing so has failed - and before you think of it, no it doesn't happen with a typewriter…'

Two of the problems for email…

'…As you will see I have email at last. It has been a long hard struggle: partly because of equipment and the fitting of an internal modem; partly because of problems with the software provided by Belize Telecommunications Limited (BTL); and partly because BTL are upgrading their system. Then according to Murphy's Law, as soon as I got on to email, South Molton Community College went off line so I am only halfway further forward. They are upgrading their system as well, which should become operable this week…'

A reply came very much later because email was down at the other end! An update was also sent to the World Bank both as a prompt, having had no reply and an update to show the efforts that have been made to raise funds elsewhere for computers and email.

Outstanding letters were finished, printed papers requested for the Principals' Workshop and arrangements finalised with Onelia and Bertha and teachers and pupils at La Immaculada were asked for individual letters to be sent to 7G with aerogrammes provided as with other schools. Just for fun (I'm coming to think) the computer hung up on receiving mail!

Considerable concern was expressed at a meeting of Principals about the two Districts working separately. It was agreed that working together in the same place was much to be preferred. Miss Pasos advised that $5 per day per person was to be allowed for lunch. It was agreed that lunch could be provided at the venue. Principals were to come to the next meeting having discussed this with staff to enable final arrangements to be made. Mr Neal and Mrs Blades will also bring their proposals with them. The merits of everyone taking their meal on the premises were widely approved and caretaker services would be met by EDC.

A stipend of $25 per person per day will be paid. Travel information is required for all persons attending (including those not residing at term time address) and the need for punctuality was emphasised. Registration is an important part of this and would be a requirement in respect of the stipend. Material, reference, language (learning labs?) resources have to be available and everyone was asked to be ready to contribute at the next meeting.

Onelia and Bertha reported on their letter to the Mexican Consulate and the suggestions being made. Mr Yah and Miss Pasos would accompany them on any visits. Mr Yah suggested that it would be most appropriate to visit classrooms when the first teaching of Spanish is taking place where it is not the first language. Miss Pasos noted that education in Chetumal is different although it is closer for observation.

The format for the Division Scheme and the proposed format for the Units of Work were shown, discussed and circulated, together with the Monitoring Instrument. The Principals' Workshop would take place on Thursday, 4th June at Corozal Methodist School and be concerned with domestic arrangements: teamwork and timing; the purpose of the four week Planning Workshop; the programme for the four weeks; a programme for the orientation of teachers; groupings of teachers and principals; educational and clerical resources; and a review of the planning process. Principals are asked to be involved fully in the decisions made. Miss Pasos pointed out that each principal is a facilitator for a group of teachers. Individual schools may wish to have some orientation and/or discussion for themselves in which team leaders/coordinator might assist.

Friday 22nd May 5:15am Turning the corner into Mahogany Street to walk down the main road as far as the taxi rank where I will be meeting a Batty Bus carrying children from St Paul's Anglican School, Corozal for a long journey. It will be a longer journey for them, down through Belize City, out on the Western Highway almost to Belmopan and left down the Hummingbird Highway which I have never travelled before, to go to Stann Creek where they are going to have a guided tour of the citrus factory and a visit to Dangriga Town. There is a fair bit of traffic already. People are on their way to work and already the cane lorries are pounding their way through the town on their way to the factory. I wonder from what time the cane trucks do start especially as they have to wait so long in the queue for the factory when they arrive. One of the two bendy-buses belonging to Batty Bros. has passed on its way to Chetumal. I went on one of them to Corozal once. It wasn't very comfortable. The mini-buses are dashing about as usual, picking up their passengers from every which way. They operate as little shuttles around the town collecting passengers who might otherwise escape and get on the opposition's bus. This competition is chiefly operated by Escalante and Urbina buses destined for Belize City with the large number of people from Orange Walk who work there. At 5:30am I thought that my Batty bus had arrived but it was going to Belize. The general arrangement is that Batty travels to Belize in the afternoon and evening. The morning is Venus time - and Urbina/Escalante of course.

A little boy who was confirmed on Sunday stopped concerned as to what bus I should be catching: Belize? No! Express? No a charter bus. Oh! Charter bus you going to Belize? No I'm going a bit further today; Dangriga, Stann Creek, with a school from Corozal. He seemed happy at that, said goodbye and went on his way. I wonder what he is doing out and about at five thirty in the morning although there are lots of people about and he is by no means the only child. The day starts early here.

The bus arrived at ten to six and the children were amazingly quiet all the way down. It was a long journey for them. Four and a half hours to the factory and then another eighteen miles into Dangriga Town before coming back again! They must have got home at about 6:30pm. We stopped briefly in Belize City at 7:15am.

The route from Belmopan to Dangriga follows the Hummingbird highway which passes through hills and mountains. This was the 'high point' of the day in more ways than one because many of the children have never seen hills in their lives (other than the man made one at Santa Rita, just by Corozal Town, which is a Mayan ruin). Imagine the excitement as the bus plunged down each successive sharp drop into a little valley. There were screams like on a roller coaster and children could be forgiven for wanting to be standing up.

There was a wait before we were able to go in. The journey down had taken four and a half hours for the children from Corozal and about fifty minutes less for me, joining them at Orange Walk. The children set off at 5:00am! I wondered about English children doing the same thing - and with the journey back to come. Anyway, there was a wait because it is difficult to be too precise about timing over that distance but we finally trooped into the factory in time to see one of the trucks full of oranges going in and on to the weighbridge. The loaded truck is weighed on the way in and the empty one weighed on the way out. The difference is the net weight of citrus fruits - that is, oranges or grapefruit.

Beyond the weighbridge the truck goes up a ramp which is set at about fifteen degrees and opens up the back to let out the fruit. At the bottom of the ramp is a large hydraulic flap which opens up to deflectthe oranges down into a trap underneath which has a conveyor at the bottom so that the oranges are automatically removed into the plant. There is space for about six trucks to unload simultaneously.

The fruit passes a number of operators who remove any obvious over ripe or bad ones and are lifted vertically by a bucket chain. Then they pass along another conveyor into the huge storage hoppers which are constructed of wooden slats so that air is free to circulate. From the storage hoppers the oranges are fed out as required on to another conveyor for the first stage of processing. More sorting takes place here. Next is a set of stainless steel machines for which I was not able to determine the purpose. Looking closely juice can be seen travelling along the pipe. It reminded me of Augustus Gloop in Charlie and the Chocolate Factory. The oranges are then taken up another bucket lift, eventually to arrive in a machine which washes them. This is another stage where bad ones are taken out. From there a mass of oranges is passed along a bank of machines which cuts and crushes them. A rather ingenious system ensures that only the right rate of feed goes into each machine. The surplus moves on to the next and then the next and then the next until exhausted. This is achieved through a series of gates which will only accept a predetermined maximum number. There are thirteen crushers in the row which certainly is an odd number to choose for such dangerous machines.

The factory is not very busy as it is at the end of the season. It has in any case, been rather a poor harvest this year - unlike the cane harvest which is extremely good. There have been problems with a fruit fly and some industrial problems.

One of the crushing machines is being cleaned and cleared. The orange drops into female tines and male tines come crushing down to fit in the space so that the orange is completely crushed, juiced and pulped. It all happens so quickly that you can only see the orange drop in and it is done! I didn't quite hear how the juice is separated from the pulp. The guide who took us round seemed only to be talking to those closest to him and as I was trying to film he rather left me behind. I asked about the pulp itself and was told that it is not used but simply thrown away. It is Creole that is spoken. A lady doing most of the talking with the guide in Creole is the Principal of the school, Mrs Valerie Rogers who can speak English perfectly well. Creole is very much the language of Belize and an important part of national identity.

Then we were given a demonstration of the drums being made up in which the concentrate is stored and delivered. One machine hydraulically puts ridges in the can to stiffen it and the other another turns the ends on. The inside of the can is coated with some sort of plastic material and a plastic liner is put inside which contains the concentrate. These used to be bought in as finished drums which were much more expensive and you can imagine how much empty space that would represent in transport. Also, one of the things Belize has to do is increase the 'value added' of its industries. Exporting unworked resources does not produce wealth. The filled cans are then stored in a large cold store. It really did seem cold inside. There was ice on the floor in the entrance where the moist air outside meets the cold, and the temperature outside was well into the nineties. Some new plant has been installed but again, I didn't manage to get the story of that. The whole operation is monitored on computer and we were able to see the oranges being delivered, caught rolling off the truck and fed on to the conveyor belt. Large furnace-like machines are actually steam generators. The steam is used in the sterilisation process. It may also be used in producing the concentrate but I didn't hear all that either - even if it was explained.

We continued from the factory for another eighteen miles or so into Dangriga Town, mainly to visit the Anglican School there and for the children to get to know each other; also for them to have lunch. We were only planning to be there for an hour so I took the opportunity to take a look around. It is not, in my view, one of the more attractive towns but I took a few shots to give some idea of what it is like in what is really the centre of Dangriga Town. Everything originated and was built up around the river so it is hardly surprising to find the more important parts close to the bridge. The market is a typical one. Wooden structures are used principally to provide shade but do give protection against the rain as well. When it does rain, it usually comes straight down so anything underneath would be quite well protected. It is not a very busy market day. There are very few customers and only about a quarter of the full complement of stalls. There are some more shelters by the sea which are intended solely for shade. They are looking rather sad now as it is coming to the end of the dry season and most of the beach parties will have taken place.

I had hoped that we would travel the same route back as we came as it was my intention to take some film of the hills and mountains but we travelled the coastal road instead. It was quite a lot of fun though and there are hills in the distance but not mountains. Mostly, the journey was hard mud for the first forty miles or so. This is not the worst of roads by any means. Also I believe that it was a lot less bumpy than it often is because it has been dry for so long and the ruts caused by water have been smoothed out. There is a huge amount of dust and I didn't film close to any time when a vehicle passed the other way because you simply wouldn't be able to see anything; the driving is blind for a few seconds after passing; and all the windows are hurriedly closed as the dust cloud, which is a vehicle, approaches. Many of the bridges over small rivers and streams are quite simply planks laid across from one side to the other. The bus driver lines up his bus very carefully on to these, so as to remain on the planks. I didn't film those. I have to admit that in the excitement I forgot and then the time had passed. A few of the orange groves are alongside the road. There are miles of these and strangely shaped hills. I believe that at one time in its geological past this whole area (and much of Belize) was under water, with the exception of the hills. It has also been found that many of what were thought to be hills were actually the site of Mayan ruins and had been built by them. Archaeologists are only beginning to form a picture of the extent of that great civilisation. Part of this revelation came about through the 1961 hurricane which stripped the hills of trees. Quite a thought!

A few pictures were taken of George back at home: first in seafaring mood with a sailing ship made from Zericote; then with a sailfish made from the same hard wood; and lastly trying to make some sense of the computer. Actually, he is quite good on the computer and even writes stories as long as I tap the keys for him. It is raining. A waterspout gushes from the end of a gutter. Lots of houses don't have gutters and mine doesn't. In the background is Louisiana playing field although you can't see much of it through the rain. This is not the heaviest rain by any means but it almost always comes down in quite an impressive way. It didn't last very long. Potholes in the road almost instantly fill up with water. This is one of the better roads. Even the Northern Highway isn't without shallow potholes in places and most of the minor roads are actually compacted mud or stone dust. Opposite the balcony is the bit of green where the children play football. In finer weather later on there is a clear view of Louisiana School with the 'No Loitering' sign on the end of it which was painted by one of the students aged thirteen. The flags are out because there is an election forthcoming.

Very friendly people live where a pickup truck is parked. They haven't finished building their house yet. They live in the bit underneath. Most of their income depends on the tractor parked alongside. Then there's my dead coconut tree. I'm waiting for it to fall and demolish the fence and the wall and take the electricity wires with it. The little house opposite has been empty for some time and just beyond it is the wide New River; and then the forest on the horizon, always near because of the flatness of the land and the height of the trees. There is a two storey house opposite and the road alongside which runs at ninety degrees to mine. Then there is a little house on the opposite corner. A cyclist comes up the road and children from the little house are at play at the back. One of them goes off to the toilet. I watched them build the new site for that - or dig it. You simply dig a new hole, fill in the old one and shift the shack from one place to the next. Best for the community is the piece of grass where so much soccer is played and the house where Elijah lives - one of the children 'Linking' from La Immaculada School.

Not a good start to the weekend, the computer is still hung up on receiving mail. The bicycle has a flat tyre, the pump connector is missing and I have difficulty getting a new one. All my library books are finished and the Library is closed when it should be open so no books for the long weekend! I cycled round to the Alcosers after the tyre was fixed but Ricardo and Marbella were out. Only Richard was in. Breakfast was good anyway!

I had hoped to be joining the San Estevan Lions on an outing to Honey Camp on Sunday but Pedro forgot. He phoned just as I was going to church and had just put washing in to soak. It would have meant trying to get a lift from the bridge had I gone so I declined. There were three Baptisms in church and I was asked (through Mrs Coleman coming up from Belize City last week) if I would read the lesson occasionally. I took the front tyre off my bicycle and discovered a tiny leak which let the tyre down overnight. The adhesive has evaporated away in the puncture repair outfit left by the previous VSO so I replaced the tyre, pumped it up and went out for an hour along the San Antonio Road. I later went part way along the San Roman road on my bike covering about 15 miles. Riding along the Northern Highway requires good concentration to get out of the way of vehicles coming up behind. It is as well to go off the road when vehicles are coming towards you because you might not hear something behind. I found out afterwards that the San Roman road is not a place to go as there have been a lot of hold-ups along there.

'Dear Friends in Year 7, I think maybe the rainy season has started. There is certainly a sharp change in the weather. It was dull for short periods yesterday, rained briefly during the evening and rained heavily during the night. Certainly, the rains are due and it will be interesting to find out what that means. My experience of rain so far is of short, heavy downpours and longer periods of rain at night. That is the pattern which seems now to be repeated. We shall see. It will make quite a change after such a long dry spell when it has been very hot indeed as I said in my last letter. Today has dawned cloudy. Not that that means that it is cold at all; it isn't. It is comfortable wearing the same sort of minimal clothes as I have been wearing. Nor does it mean that it is dull; it isn't. The light and the strength of the sun are so great that even a cloudy day seems bright. It has to be really raining to be described as dull and even then it doesn't seem to be because of all the action taking place.

Today is another Public Holiday. There are a lot more holidays here than you have. Here is a list of them for this year. The schools also have eight weeks in the summer as I seem to remember we used to have. 1st January New Year's Day, 9th March Baron Bliss Day, 10th April Good Friday, 11th April Holy Saturday, 12th April Easter Sunday, 13th April Easter Monday, 1st May Labour Day, 24th May Commonwealth Day, 10th September Battle of St. George's Caye Day, 21st September Independence Day, 12th October Pan American Day, 19th November Garifuna Day, 25th December Christmas Day, 26th December Boxing Day. Only the Garifuna celebrate Garifuna Day as you might expect but there are other days which take you by surprise. Children have been given the day off school by the visiting Prime Minister during this year which is election year! Children are often confirmed through their school and will be given a day off for that. Many children attend only a service (and no school) on Ascension Day (Last Thursday, 21st May). There are others! The best one I have come across is that most schoolchildren have the last Friday afternoon off in each month. This is so that their teachers can go and collect their pay from the local Treasury where they all queue up. It really does take all afternoon! I suspect that this persists more in respect of the Friday afternoon than the collecting of pay. My living allowance is paid into the bank so it wouldn't be difficult for teachers to do the same. On the other hand, there seems to be a great mistrust of banks but I haven't found a reason for that.

I did say that I would send you a copy of a log I have been making of mail sent and received. Well, I have gathered the information and found that some mail seems to have gone astray. However, we mustn't blame that. It also seems that lots of people on both sides of the Atlantic could have done better or are leaving it all to others. 'Could have done better' is covered in 'good intentions' but good intentions do not make for good communication. While I was doing this, I decided from my own experience of letter writing (which is now considerable) that sending a copy of the log isn't likely to do any good. Instead, I went and bought 120 aerogrammes and went into each of the four schools and asked all the students who are linking with you to write a letter to their partner in addition to anything else they may be doing, and to do it NOW. I was quite pleased with this idea. In many cases I stayed while the letters were written and even posted some of them myself. The most important thing is that it was the best way of ensuring that you all received a letter - so I now need to know of anyone who hasn't. Next, the teachers here know that the letters have been sent and as they were all addressed to Mr Berry, he knows that they have arrived and will be able to encourage a reply where necessary. Neat isn't it? Those of you who know me well will recognise that I haven't changed (although coming here has further improved both patience and tolerance). In the meantime of course, Louisiana Government School sent off their parcel and Buddy and I heard from Mr Berry that it had arrived. Also, St Paul's Anglican decided to send their Buddy, having omitted to do so before. (I need to know when she or he arrives safely.) Most of the teachers involved have written to Mr Berry.

I went on a field trip with St. Paul's Anglican School on Friday. They left Corozal Town at 5:00am and stopped for me in Orange Walk where I was dropped off again on the way back. The outing was to visit a citrus factory in Stann Creek and the Anglican School in Dangriga… I have made a film of the outing for you so I will leave out the details of the tour of the factory and a description of the town. There is not much space left on the tape so you should receive it shortly. I was a little bit disappointed as we set off for home because I had planned to film the mountains and the children's reaction to them on the way back but the driver turned off on to the coast road from which little of the hills and none of the mountains can be seen. However, that turned out to be exciting too, as the road was more of a challenge. So I filmed some of that instead. Wait for it!

I have put together a few thoughts on linking which might be useful: 1) Keep a movements Log. 2) Answer each point in letters you receive. 3) Find a way of sharing the arrival of a letter etc. from your partner with your form. The strength of the relationship you form will be helped by linking it fully with that of others. Things we do on our own are always strengthened by the knowledge that others do also. 4) Keep the flow going as well as sending the Buddies back and forth on their travels. This is helped enormously by the personal letters but it would be a good idea for the Buddy to send regular letters as well; after all, any traveller will send letters home. The more the Buddy becomes the ambassador - and is made to behave in as human a way as possible - the more successful the relationships will be. 5) Set up a teacher to teacher, teacher to children and children to teacher correspondence. Perhaps there may be some parents who would like to take part in this. The coordination of the link, especially in the early stages can involve one person in a great deal of work and this could lead to delay. 6) Have the school you are linking with and your own partner in mind as you go through your daily experience. Find a way of making notes of your thoughts as they occur to you. This kind of thinking helps us to really appreciate the lives of others and have some understanding of that which is different from our own - and just as valid. It also gets over the problem of what shall I do or what shall I write? 7) Try to form a picture of life in the other country in a concrete way. This can be done both individually and in groups. There are many ways of doing this. You could make a collection or a scrapbook, make a display, write a story or keep written records. These are standard ways but have you thought of trying to share your experiences with someone else (personally or as a group presentation); making drawings or plans; making practical products such as are traditional in the other country; trying out the others' traditional games; making competitions or role play; or telling your link school of these activities? The list of learning possibilities is endless but it works much better if it is active and practical and it will all help to cement the relationship. 8) It might help to put your ideas under four headings so that you can compare expectations and experience of life in each of the two countries. This could help to discover their difference and to try to identify what is really important and what is not. There are others but these are key: Health, Education, Technology and Environment. Where would you put Spirituality and Religion?

I always thought that my patience and tolerance were pretty fair. Certainly many people have made reference to the patience but living in a different culture has meant that I have had to revise that idea and really examine what I consider to be important and when I am likely to react. The first thing that I found was to question more, why people do what they do and why it doesn't necessarily fit with what I expect. The behaviour of people in simple things is an interesting way of looking at this. The English have mastered the art of forming a queue. People here queue too but it is a mistake to leave an empty space at a counter however many people may be waiting. The person that goes to that space will almost always be served first. This is not rudeness it is simple expedience. As far as I have been able to understand the queue is not ignored it simply isn't seen but the space is! The same applies when getting on a bus. While everyone is waiting there is quite a clear queue formed but when the bus comes, if there is even the smallest gap at the entrance, created perhaps to give way to someone else, it will be filled instantly! Most of you will know that I like things to run on time. Not so here. The actual start time for anything seems to be the earliest time that anyone could possibly be first to arrive. Events are often being prepared after the appointed time has passed. I have often witnessed the arrival of a band during the speeches (which started late anyway).

Talking of speeches, I thought the English were bad enough but... I went to the first morning of a two day convention of the Belize National Union of Teachers because I wanted to hear what was being said about the new 'Board Rules'. It was supposed to start at nine o'clock and by eleven it was running an hour and a half late. This is normal and there were an awful lot of people there. Needless to say, given that this is the way of things, not a lot of attention is paid to what is going on. Most speeches consist mostly of mention of this or that person who happens to be present and how we must all stand together. It doesn't help that nothing is suggested as to what might be done when we are standing together! I had planned to attend the whole two days but left at lunchtime on the first one. My meetings start and finish on time. I have a set agenda and minutes are circulated before the next agenda so that there are three reminders of each meeting. It is interesting how well this has worked and I haven't said anything - just done it. These are just little examples of what it must mean to be a developing country and be only sixteen years into independence. What is more difficult is the widely held idea that all foreigners, especially white ones, are rich. Some are of course, but it is also true that there are many Belizeans who are well fixed too. That makes the poverty there is among so many much harder to understand. 40% of the population lives below the accepted poverty line. On the other hand, people who have become friends are incredibly generous. I can go and stay with them at any time and it is expected that I can join in with any family activity if I am able or wish to. When I cross the road - if I have made an error of judgement, as it is easy so to do - any oncoming vehicle will stop until I have sorted myself out; in the town that is. On the highway it is every man for himself. That is all for now. I hope that some of you will write. If you do it will help me to help you and children in the linking schools…'

Back to the things I can do without…

'…Further to my letter dated 6th May, I have now received the Tax Return you mentioned. It arrived having been wet as some stage of its journey. I regret that I do not have the necessary information to fill it in. You have details of all my income so I would be obliged if you will take the appropriate action…'

I discovered from Jack that the hang-up on email could well be caused by an attachment sent by VSO. I phoned BTL and asked them to remove it. This cleared the system so that when I came home it worked. Could this be the beginning of better communication? Having also learned that the system has ability to handle very limited attachment size, care needs to be taken but how much?

Onelia and Bertha and I met to discuss results of the Principals' Meeting, forecast, resources and work plan; Ellajean was advised that principals all wanted to work together across the two districts. The venue was arranged with Corozal Methodist but I was unable to discuss this with Barbara Blades because she was ill. After doing some shopping and going to the library I came home and found the computer jammed again on email. Later in the evening I realised that it had sent waiting mail in the out box which couldn't be sent over the weekend. One of those was to VSO asking where the attachment was, as at that time I didn't know what it meant. VSO must have replied by sending another one! Then, of course, I had to phone BTL and have the attachment removed again and VSO to ask them not to send it again. Email sent to friends was returned as undelivered.

After meeting with Bertha at the District Office to discuss the venue for planning with Barbara Blades, I collected an EDC package from Batty Bus (regular means of delivery), completed minutes from the Principals' Meeting and the work plan for June. The work plan was sent by FAX so it will be there in the morning. My FAX works!

Thursday, 28th May is my birthday and it looks as though the email to friends has worked which bodes well for communications when South Molton Community College comes on line. That would be present enough but there was more to come; fun and better.

I went to Belize City early this morning to pay in the cheque from VSO for my glasses and to draw out some cash. This was quite exciting as the machine swallowed my card. It turned out to be a fault in the machine and I was given my money via counter cheque - with a smile. I nevertheless asked for a statement just to make sure. The second purpose was to purchase items for the parcel to go to Year 7. The first port of call for that was the Belize Tourist Board office where I managed to get four nice posters, a booklet and the Official Tourist Brochure as well as a little Belize pin. Next was the Philatelic Bureau where I got a set of Howler Monkey stamps and all the definitive stamps up to 75c. Last port of call was Paula's Gift Shop as I have got to know Paula quite well and she gave me a very good deal on a lovely variety of items. Some local produce and another tee shirt and the parcel should be able to go off next week. Met up with Bertha and Onelia in the afternoon when we discussed the work plan for June and I offered to do theirs; the minutes of the principals' meeting; and the planning process which we need to go through. It turns out that Onelia and Bertha are planning to take me out for a meal in Chetumal for my birthday and this is arranged for Monday; a lovely surprise. It didn't end there because a family barbecue is being planned for Saturday night, also to celebrate my birthday. Pedro, Benito and Daiami are travelling down to Belize City especially for the occasion! Mail and cards and presents arrived and even email. I can't remember the last time it was so good.

The parcel for year 7 was part packed on Friday and taken down to the Post Office to find out the cost. The weight at the moment is twelve pounds and the cost will be $66 plus packaging. Extra weight would be $2 per pound so I should be able to include some more items. Pedro Sanchez was doing the barbecue with the Principals' Association in the square.

The journey up on the bus to Corozal to work with Onelia and Bertha on the preparations for the Principals' Workshop was really beautiful. So many trees are in fruit. There are mangoes everywhere and the flamboyan trees are aglow with brilliant scarlet as the great unknown today is the day when Principals collected their students' BNSE results. I had to wait until the morning when I phoned Orvin to give thought to his brother who died this week. The BNSE was rather disappointing for Calcutta but the ones who should did get through. I have found the students there to be among the brightest and most responsive that I have worked with. That doesn't say much for the system. Anyway I was invited to go with the school to Cayo next Friday as Robert is one of the two Finalists from Corozal to go into the next round of the National Drug Elimination Quiz.

On the 25th, I said that I thought the rainy season might have begun. The weather during the week caused me to seriously doubt that as it has been very hot indeed. You could hardly move without breaking out into a running sweat (you are actually sweating almost all the time, especially during the day but you don't notice that). However, it has also felt different and there has been quite a bit of cloud; strange that the clouds hardly ever seem to affect the amount of bright sunshine which lasts from dawn until dusk. Also, the light on the clouds is so strong that they appear exaggerated - sharply defined against the most amazing fathomless blue of the sky, infinite, behind. However, it looks as though it was right to suppose that we are at the beginning of the rainy season because it rained with a vengeance last night and the ground has stayed wet all morning. A rare day when the sun is not in evidence although the light is bright; a day which is not hot; a day which is pleasantly warm - say around seventy five to eighty degrees. I suppose you would call that hot in England.

On the balcony, there is a moth which appears to be resting, perhaps from a battering that it may have taken last night; perhaps it is not hot enough for it to move (all things are relative and I suppose today might be cold to the indigenous species); perhaps it does that during the day anyway and hasn't found a more suitable spot; perhaps it is 'on its last legs'. Whatever it is, it is resting on the balcony so that I could have an opportunity to have a good look at it. A beautiful creature which responds to a gentle touch but shows no inclination to either fly away or even move but it did slowly open its wings so that I had an even better view! The span of the main wings must be nearly four inches (I've given up 'nearly' centimetres here, no-one else uses them) and they are striated with shades of delicate light greys with a few very narrow black steaks and tiny black spots. The secondary wings (I'm not familiar with entomological terms) are striated orange with black edging. The body is fat, even for a moth, and has black bars reaching out from a central grey bar rather like a skeleton set against the same greys as on the outer wings. It seems happy enough to be left there and not likely to come to any harm so far from the ground.

The 3:30pm bus for Belize City left at ten to four and didn't arrive until half past five. Pedro and Benito didn't come to my birthday barbecue because Benito didn't get back from Chetumal in time but it went ahead anyway with a very pleasant evening with the family until about 12:30. I had intended leaving on the eleven o'clock bus on Sunday but stayed for lunch which was barbecued fish and finally left after a really good day, on the Escalante bus which left the Belcan Roundabout at ten to four. I will have to remember that one next week after Tony's graduation weekend. Got home tired but after a birthday such as I haven't celebrated for years and there is still the meal in Chetumal to come tomorrow.

Monday 1st June Met with Bertha and Onelia from 8:00am in Corozal to go through plans for the Principals' Workshop, explore alternative groupings of Outcomes and try to put together some ideas for collecting resources. At 1:00pm Ariel Botes joined us with his big Chevvy and we all went off to Chetumal for my birthday celebration for which I was not allowed to pay for anything except the Nike sports shirt I bought from the market for Antonio's Graduation next Saturday. Unfortunately, I think that is going to be too small.

We crossed the border into Mexico and on to Chetumal where we went to a drinking place. These are set out like restaurants and all drinks are served. I like Mexican beer! The building is typical of the Yucatan (which includes Belize) being built of rough cut timber and logs and roofed with a palm thatch. There is seating for about 300 and non-stop live entertainment. From there it was on to a restaurant for my favourite pescado - grilled snapper. Then back again for more Mexican beer. As Mexican time is two hours ahead of Belize it was possible to be quite late there, with the entire atmosphere that provides, and yet return at a fairly reasonable hour. I have to admit to being somewhat worse for wear!

Tuesday morning was spent catching up with records of meetings etc. and setting out the agenda for the Principals' Workshop on Thursday. The finished agenda was faxed to EDC together with the minutes of the last meeting. I went to the library in the afternoon (in the vain hope of finding resources) and finished packing the parcel ready for posting tomorrow. Bertha called to say that she had heard from Ellajean who wanted a copy of work done on outcomes - some hopes. I resolved to phone Ellajean and managed to sort out her strange request, coming to the conclusion that she is at best, in a state of panic. Made final arrangements for the Principals' Workshop with Corinth and asked Margarita to come up with some material resources. Posted the parcel for year seven with which I was very pleased at a cost of $79; also a weekly letter telling the stories of the last week and

'… Last weekend I discovered something which may be important as there was a short period when I was unable to receive email. To cut a long story short (and it was a long one) I discovered that it was due to an incoming attachment. Mr Berry can explain those. The problem is that I only have Windows 3.1 at the moment so there is quite severely limited handling capacity. And the reason why I mention it is to ensure that you send only straight email and no attachments. I hope to get over this soon by increasing memory in the computer. (It is a 486 with eight megabytes. I have four one megabyte chips which I am told can be fitted but it means taking the machine to Belize City again!) I have two-way communication with Scouts in Devon so there shouldn't be any problems **when** you come on line…'

The afternoon was spent revising the agenda for the Principals' Workshop a copy of which was sent to EDC and also a copy to Jayne in response to her phone calls.

By Thursday email communication with Paul was established…

'…At last I'm on-line! Just to check that things are working correctly, I will keep this first message short and to the point. Please confirm my success, and I will start writing properly…'

'…I have made a note of your email number but I am first trying a reply to sender. It is good to hear from you. I have sent off another of the weekly epistles to year 7 by post today and a large parcel which should give you some ideas. Expect that in two to three weeks (less has been known)…'

'… Got your reply! We're now in business! I look forward to receiving my next package. In the meantime I will continue to encourage the letter writers. I'm off to bed now, but will write in detail soon now that I know we have made contact…'

'… Got your reply to my reply; just for fun here is a copy of the letter I mentioned that I have just posted. It may even overtake the one before it but you may as well have it now and it will tell you what to expect in the parcel. It will also determine whether I can handle a fair amount of text. While I remember, DO NOT send attachments to me as they are too much for Windows 3.1…'

Set off at 5:30am with Calcutta School to go to the finals of the National Drug Elimination Quiz. As I sat waiting for the bus on the wall of the Shell Gas Station on the main road, which is the most convenient place to meet from where I live, a charter bus drew up close by, which had Corozal Methodist School on board. Two local members of the National Drug Elimination Team were waiting there and got on that bus. It didn't move and the conductor got off to tell me that a gentleman on the bus wished to speak with me. This was Henry Neal, the Principal, wanting me to go with them. I didn't of course but I was able to wave to all the children and wait for Calcutta to come along. In fact the Calcutta bus was packed to the extent that about fifteen were standing so I was transferred to the Corozal bus when we got to Belize City anyway! I was quite pleased to sit for the long haul to Santa Elena which is the twin town of San Ignacio where the Novello Centre is situated. That wasn't the end of the bus saga because two of my other schools, Louisiana and La Immaculada were also taking part and wanted me to go with them. In the event I stayed with the Corozal bus and went on several little sightseeing detours on the way home. Four of my schools, therefore, were among the twelve schools taking part. Francis Sanchez of Louisiana came second on a tie break with a girl from Belize Elementary School and Robert Guy from Calcutta came fourth. I was disappointed with the result because Francis was completely floored by a 'life skills' question asking him to choose two activities for which he could be responsible in school. Children in Primary schools do not have that idea in their experience at all. By contrast, the winner's question was within her experience. What was worse was that Robert, who had been in the lead all the way, fell on another dubious life skills question where he gave the answer it seemed was being asked for instead of the one he knew was right and (knowing him) would have done. I was very sorry for Robert because the prize for each of the first three students was a high school scholarship which would have secured his future as it was conditional on him meeting the requirements for study. When I first met Robert (who is fifteen) at the beginning of this academic year, he had just been sent down from secondary school and was back in Primary. Not surprisingly, he had a pretty big chip on his shoulders and his parents were very worried about him. Through the year he has settled down, worked - and played - hard and obtained a good BNSE score. The scholarship would have given a tremendous psychological boost which would have been very much within the spirit of the National Drug Abuse Control Council. The school prizes which started with a computer for first place seemed much less important to me even though Calcutta and Louisiana are 'Linking' schools and I have self-interest there.

134

Sometimes the whole 'otherworldliness' has shadows of existence elsewhere. This can be a harsh intrusion that brings you up sharp like tax or preparations that have been missed or a pause for serious reflection as happened on Saturday 6th June, not quite out of the blue because it was a second phone call which I believe was from my wife who had left. It was 8:00am which would make it 4:00pm British Summer Time. I said hello more than once and wasn't able to hear the response properly so I asked "Who's speaking please?" The reply sounded like "Sara!" and seemed to be confirmed when I asked again. When I said "I'm sorry, I think you have the wrong number, this is Mr Max!" the reply was "Sorry, sorry". It wasn't said once it was repeated twice more as a sorry for trying rather than a sorry for wrong number. Also the voice was husky and sounded worried. This is the second call that I have wondered about in this way. The first was a few days ago when the caller listened to me speak until it was clear I couldn't have any more to say until I heard something and there was no sound as though the phone was dead. However, I sensed that it wasn't and waited long enough to hear the receiver put down very softly at the other end. It sounded exactly like that which had been done before at home. I thought that I had sent my phone number to someone who could have made contact with her but I hadn't been told. I couldn't be sure and I had no means of finding out. It was very disturbing far away where I had become so settled.

Set off for Belize City at about 9:45am and arrived at about 11:20 to buy a bottle of Caribbean Rum and call in at Jack's before going round to the family. In fact Jack had already been there all morning making a bridge for the newly arrived vehicle Marco has bought, leading across the drainage ditch to the little used space on the East side of the house. When I arrived, the men were all drinking beer as the job was finished. I declined because of the Graduation Ceremony including Antonio which was to come in the afternoon.

The welcome was as always and people were arriving all the time, mostly from San Estevan for the family part of the day. The rather nice Nike sports shirt I had bought for Antonio was too small as I had feared so I decided to give him $50 as well. This is quite a huge sum on my income but it is probably the only opportunity I shall have to really mark an event for him.

The ceremony was really good. The Graduates looked great in their white gowns and brown mortars doing a slow, slow, quick, quick march on the way in and out to the strains of 'Pomp and Circumstance'. The slow step was a slide of the back foot up to the heel of the lead one which I would find extremely difficult with the different steps in between and the rhythmic variation of pace. And I'm not sure that I have described it right now, even though I watched the movement carefully, over and over. The programme told the story and the students' presentations were very polished - with the clearest English I have heard spoken in Belize.

Afterwards we returned to a huge celebration back at the house as more and more guests arrived to add their congratulations and join in the hospitality offered. For those of us in the family, this continued until about two in the morning. I had been asked to take some photos but my battery chose to fail the moment of switching on for the first picture at the entry processional and of course with my camera, nothing will induce it to take any picture with suspect power. I hadn't noticed any warning. There must have been warning each time I switched on but I tend not to have my glasses on when using the camera so I guess I have missed the warnings as the display doesn't last very long. I managed to arrange with a photographer there who took pictures of everyone, to print some for me from the ceremony and went round to see a group of four VSOs living together in Belize City to see if they could help for pictures in the evening. Lisa Krolac lent me her camera so now I do have a finished film to develop and print. The house was heaving with sleeping bodies for the night - and still I was given my old room! I gave Antonio the $50 as I said goodbye to everyone just as I left; also saying that I expect that the Nike shirt would probably fit one of his friends; much too far into young people's fashion for me, even if I had wanted to take it back - which I didn't. I left to catch the 10:00am bus with Pedro, Benito, Nellie and Daiami. I had been invited to go to Corozal with Landy and the Rotary Club to film some American surgeons doing cosmetic operations on children. We were to leave at 1:00pm so I was anxious to be in good time. I needn't have hurried. When I eventually saw Landy at 1:30pm he said that he would be going between four and five. At the time of writing it is six o'clock and nothing has happened yet. I find it difficult to reconcile what are friendly and hospitable people with an attitude to time which is at best an absence of concern for people who are hanging around waiting. It would have been much nicer to come back from Belize on the 3:45pm as I did last week and that is especially what the family wanted me to do.

Good news from South Molton…

'…Thanks very much for your recent correspondence! Combined with the super photographs, excellent videos and an influx of personal letters for the pupils, my spirits have been lifted and I feel that our 'Link' is beginning to bear fruit. This will probably be the last time I will write to you via 'snail Mail' (Sorry George!) as I intend to go 'on line' myself during half-term (next week). That will allow us to keep in regular contact and speed up the movement of certain issues. There have been all sorts of frustrating problems with the school Internet connections – it is a pity they did not leave things as they were. The desire to upgrade and improve effectively held back a number of projects and activities – the link with Belize being one. However it seems to be sorting itself out and my plan to get year seven pupils sending email to you by the end of term is still a realistic possibility. As soon as I have my email address sorted out I will call you up. The photographs were first class. They now form the centre focus of a giant display, which covers the entire wall space in my classroom. Wall to wall Belize! I intend to make it available to the new intake pupils (Yes, it's that time of the year again!) and their parents on forthcoming days to give them a taste of what is ahead. I talk to new pupils and parents with confidence about an established link with Belize schools. The videos were equally well received. The zoo video was the most popular and it included some excellent footage of local wildlife. The toucan and the ant bear particularly impressed the pupils here. My personal favourite was the jaguar as I remember them from my time in Guyana. I brought into school, some plaster-cast footprints I made (Some from the middle of an overnight camp as evidence of a nocturnal visitor!) and a pelt that I was given by a local ex-colonial doctor to show the pupils. One of your clearly angled shots of George really confused us and it took a while before we identified him! It caused quite a bit of laughter when we realised that we were looking at George and not some strange new creature! The scenes from the schools were fascinating and the Louisiana sports day was certainly something a bit different! The atmosphere came across well. I'm sure that some video footage from here would be useful – it's still on the list of things to do. Perhaps the most pleasing development has been the increase in mail received by South Molton pupils. I am encouraging them to return the compliment, and am sure you will see a similar increase at your end from now on. I have also received letters from staff at the 'Link' schools and will write back in detail over the half-term break. To keep the momentum going I have enclosed some diaries written by year seven pupils. This was completed as a homework task to give each 'Link' school some feedback. As you deliver them please encourage the letter writers and inform them that they will be getting a fatter postbag themselves from now on. As mentioned earlier, staff will be contacted in the very near future.

I have been trying to summarise the amount of contact between schools and can conclude the following: 1) 7R were so pleased to see Sunny again and welcome Jose Luis from Louisiana Government School! They are taking it in turns to look after him and write up his diary and begged me to arrange for his stay to be extended over the half-term holiday. I have agreed to this and he will be 'posted' on Monday June 1st. The impact of this soft toy as a focus cannot be overstated. To the class it is something 'real' and emphasises the importance of this part of the exchange. Please encourage the other schools to return the South Molton 'Buddies' as well as send one of their own. 2) Jose Luis brought with him a number of letters from Louisiana Government School and others are arriving each day. Hopefully, they will receive individual replies soon (in addition to the package I will send to you). 3) A large number of letters have arrived from St Paul's school and another batch has just started to arrive but I know they would be more motivated if their 'Buddy' Heffer had returned along with her partner from Belize. 4) 7D have received a number of letters from Calcutta School and many pupils have replied. However, again a 'Buddy' has not been sent on with Uncle Albert. 5) La Immaculada School has been the biggest disappointment. A few pupils have written second letters after the initial package, but only three 7G pupils have received one of their own. They are also asking me about the welfare of Spike! This is a big pity because this is one of my more able classes and there has been a great deal of interest. With a speedy response, I am sure I can rekindle their fires…

…I'm not sure whether it is a realistic aim to 'pair off' pupils from linked schools rather than maintain a more 'open' connection. I am aware that some pupils have received letters and are not motivated to reply while others have not received a letter but are really keen to be involved. What do you think? What are the next steps? I brainstorm the following: 1) Consolidating contact between schools must be a priority – whether it is on a 'paired pupil' arrangement or not. I can contribute a lot here by writing to the staff – that's in hand. 2) Return of 'Buddies' is very important. 3) Visual exchange is valuable. I will explore video film from this end. I have to say again, the photos and videos you sent recently were top notch. 4) The diary exercise was designed to give a snapshot of everyday life in England – both at home and at school. My pupils have requested that a similar exercise be carried out for them. 5) I know you have worked with the Lions Club in Belize. I have approached the local branch and await a reply. This could be a really useful link for them too. 6) I have also been in contact with the Rotary Club in South Molton and received a good response. I think they will offer some help although I'm not yet sure what form this will take. 7) I think the email link is a really exciting possibility. I understand the problems you must face and congratulate you on the contacts and progress you have made so far. Perhaps this is where I can beg help from local charity groups. There would be so many educational benefits here for both ends of the link. 8) I have many ideas on how to involve other departments in the school but I have left these on hold for the time being…'

Nothing did happen with the Rotary Club and I had an apology this morning. I wonder if I should point out that not only was I kept waiting fruitlessly, I had also returned from a Graduation celebration early in order to be in time for the arranged time of 1:00pm. I haven't yet but I may well if a suitable time presents itself.

We were not able to meet at the office at 8:30am because Onelia had missed the early bus and there are not many of them running south from Corozal in the morning. We met at 10:00am and went as far as we could with the remaining planning that needs to be done. We can't go any further because everyone at EDC has gone on holiday and Margarita has not provided the minutes from the Principals' Workshop which she had promised to do. As a result, we have called a halt until the meeting at EDC next Monday. I spent the rest of the day cleaning and cooking but, as it turned out there was plenty to sing about.

All days are good days; but today is a brilliant day as Mark Wright, the Programme Director for VSO Belize phoned to say that my application for grant to buy a computer for Calcutta Government School has been approved. I phoned the Principal right away and he was delighted. He just kept talking!! It is an especially good time of course after the disappointment over the quiz and I particularly asked that Robert be given the good news right away. Not that that will give him the scholarship but it is what the school wanted; it shows the worth of effort and it could provide the much needed link with SMCC if we can get things moving quickly enough. It is only three weeks to the end of term.

I phoned the Chief Education Officer right away to find out who best to have the cheque made out to. This turned out to be the Ministry of Education, Belize for the attention of Ernest Raymond CEO and with a covering letter stating the purpose and providing a list of the equipment. He said that he could find a way of picking up the shortfall of about 160 dollars (about forty five pounds) as the maximum grant of one thousand pounds has been awarded and the equipment will cost that bit more. I then phoned VSO and Mark agreed to send the cheque direct and the covering letter as he has all the information to hand from my application. Both VSO and the Ministry are in Belmopan and this course will ensure that Mr Raymond will receive the letter and cheque in time to take action before he has to go off down to Punta Gorda. So now it is keep your fingers crossed time. Tomorrow I must tell Orvin Rancheran, the Principal what is happening and also the District Education Officer. I will pave the way further with the Technician at EDC as well while I am at it, to secure any maintenance and installation required. I am invited to the Graduation and reception at Calcutta on Wednesday week and Orvin has asked me to give the news to parents there. It feels really good to know now, that at least two schools will have email link with SMCC, one very shortly and the other when I leave. Yes, all days are good days but this day is brilliant!

I got up feeling pretty rough. Stomach gripes are not uncommon since coming to Belize despite my being very careful about water and hygiene generally. I suppose my diet isn't as good as it might be because of the difficulty of cooking for only one and having either to keep everything in the fridge or resorting to a covered container which is boiled up daily. I am sure I let things of that sort run on too long for the sake of cooking reasonable quantities at a time and for economy. I haven't got out of the habit of saving money and the cost of the 'linking' has been high. I went down to the office this morning to let Pedro Cucul know what was happening with the VSO computer for Calcutta; also Stanley Bermudas for the joint reasons of keeping him up to date and to ask him to discuss purchase with the Chief in the hope that it will help to reduce the time taken. The email still isn't working but I find that the server is down at BTL so I will have to wait to see what happens. It does seem to be about time I had some mail but I'm going to have to wait until tomorrow to find that out too.

Margarita phoned to say that the minutes were done and she would send them by FAX to BTL. Of course, I forgot that they closed at 4:00pm and arrived five minutes too late after having spent the afternoon on the bed trying to get over the stomach pains (which are not gone but better than they were by evening). I phoned Raoul this evening to see if he had managed to arrange a visit to BSI for Friday but he has gone fishing on the Cayes until Thursday night so I will have to wait to find that out too. There is a lot of waiting.

This evening has been very beautiful. There is a full moon in an almost cloudless sky. It is hot but a light breeze across the balcony made being out there very pleasant. It is really quite difficult to imagine that we have had two really heavy downpours; each heralded by violent winds only to die away fifteen to twenty minutes later and immediately followed by bright sunshine. I'm told that rain can last for a whole day in Orange Walk but I haven't seen it yet!

Mail on Wednesday…

'…Thanks for the last email - the snail mail version has now arrived as well. I look forward to the package that is following - full of goodies! Before I go any further, happy birthday! I can think of worse places in the world to celebrate another passing year! I have just sent off another two parcels, one containing amongst other things, letters to each school from myself. I hope you don't mind being treated as the Caribbean postman! There is also a nice little package within that was put together by Ben - all on his own initiative. I hope his personal buddy enjoys the gifts. The other package contains odd pupil profiles and diaries that came in late from absent pupils, as well as some personal letters. This envelope also contains the returning buddy Jose Luis, along with the well-travelled Sunny. You will notice that he suffered a minor accident while in England, but the good old Health Service managed to patch him up! Still no sign of other Belizean buddies - this remains a disappointment. I have received a good response from the local Rotary Club, and I think they will be able to contribute something to our project. I will suggest that they concentrate on providing something at your end, although I'm really not sure quite what; advice and suggestions please. I think I will also try the local Lions Club, and get them to try to match the support you have received. I am currently compiling a list of year 7 pupils to record the number of letters they have both sent and received. I will send you a copy as soon as it has been completed. What do I do with year six? I would like the project to evolve to include them, and keep the link rolling on. However, many of the year 7 pupils are jealously claiming their ownership of the link - and quite right too - so some sort of balance will need to be found. I intend to compile another large package for Belize before we break up for the summer. Do your pupils fully understand the concept of the changing English seasons? I know your year has its contrasts, but are they as marked as in our temperate climate? How many have seen snow, or woken up to a thick, hard frost? …
P.S. Have you heard of BRAIN (Belize Regional Alliance for Information Networking)? Email address is Manolo Romero at mrromero@btl.net. I came across them on the internet.

'…Mail arrived safely! I thought that I had better write straight away as I had told you of the server breakdown (it happens quite often - just one more of the frustrations I've had which are, hopefully, in the past!). Also, I haven't sent an epistle to year 7 this week yet (although one is on the way by snail mail). This is intended to serve for both. Thanks for the birthday wishes. The venue is brilliant of course, but what really made it was that it was entirely Belizean and doubly so. I have to pause and pinch myself occasionally and wonder what I have done to deserve so much. Then I stop and think what it is really all about. And it is all about people, especially kids (I used not to like that word but it has become an expression of affection). Then I begin to understand… By way of news here is a couple of extracts from my journal… I don't mind being Caribbean Postman at all and I look forward to collecting your parcels and taking them into the schools. If you send parcels addressed to the schools they will get a note in their pigeon hole at the District Education Office asking them to call at the Post Office. Some schools have the notes delivered direct and I think some may have parcels delivered. The best thing is for you to come to an enduring arrangement with the Principal or the Teacher concerned. I think your letters direct will be a very good thing. But that is not to detract from my being delighted to act as Postman. According to my records, Ben is linked with William Parada at Calcutta. He will be pleased. If the parcel arrives in time, I will be able to take it with me for the Graduation Ceremony next Wednesday. What with the news of the computer as well, that would be quite something. I will go down and see the Postmistress (also a friend now) and make sure I am advised direct and that no time is lost with a note sitting in Landy's P.O. Box; I can call in there daily. Incidentally, you will probably pick up as good a picture of life here through these little 'arrangements' as in any other way.

The balance of pupil profiles and diaries will be well received too. And Louisiana will be amazed at the rapid return of Jose Luis and Sunny. Trust Leanne to be the owner of the most travelled Buddy. She's sunny herself! You should have had a Buddy from Saint Pauls and I need to know whether the parcel finally arrived from Calcutta. More recently you should have had anything up to 120 aerogrammes sent through you (I was quite pleased with that brainwave!) The school term ends on 26th June so if you want anything else to go into schools it would be safer to use email. I will deliver anything sent but please remember that the two Corozal schools are thirty miles away. It would be helpful too if some of the children could write to me by the same means. I already write to Richard, Ben and Leanne. In year six I write to James, Steven, Wayne, Jamie and Philip. Any of the children could use this address to gain real practice at writing - using email which should be exciting, addressed either to me or to their partner although time for the latter before the end of term, is short. My neighbour, who owns this house, is a member of the Rotary Club here as I have already said. I spoke to him as soon as your mail arrived and he says that Rotary International will match anything your club does for Belize pound for pound! He will be writing to that effect so expect to hear more of that. I also suggested to him that he asks how the project is going at La Immaculada as they are being so slow. All four of his children go there and Nelson, the eldest, is one of those linking. I'm not sure who his school partner is but he has written to Leanne. Anyway, Landy says that he would pay the postage himself if that is what it is holding them up. (I would too, but I don't think that is the problem - just a matter of the need to get on with it. I have been in there many times. Nothing ever takes off until you let it go - there doesn't seem to be an absence of enthusiasm). Landy Burns has just bought a computer for his children and himself, which will be able to access the internet and therefore email. That will be another address

138

which can be used for access to *La Immaculada*. The best thing to help the project is computers. The other material need is for security. Rooms with expensive equipment in them have to have security bars. My house has security bars at the windows, a high wall with a security fence on top and a front gate which is high and kept locked. That should give you the picture. Not an attractive aspect but there it is. Other costs are things like postage and email charges (BTL only give concession to High Schools and there are only enough of those to serve forty per cent or so of the children who ought to attend them so that is no great cost to BTL. I'm biding my time there, waiting until there seems to be enough potential for publicity to have some influence). I don't imagine Rotary would wish to pick up any on-going costs but they might make a grant for the purpose. I'm sure that one off things like computers or security would be the best bet - or funding a room! The Lions Club here are mostly concerned with health so I don't know how you would get on there. Making contact with the Belize Club would be no problem as you will know from some of the writings I have sent.

Talking of writings - have all the ones for year 7 arrived? The most recent are numbered from page one to twenty. Most now will come by email of course. Is the email address you have the one at school or is it your own? I have assumed it is at school but I can't be sure from the code used. I wouldn't have suggested children using it otherwise. I can do it - I'm retired (allegedly) and don't have lessons to prepare!!! Will I be able to contact you during the holiday?

Of course year seven must continue the link. Of course year six and subsequent must enable the project to evolve. There is so much to be gained by so many that it is impossible to estimate the value. I suggest that each of the year seven forms send an immediate email to their respective schools (which I will print and deliver - and no doubt, present) outlining their wishes and suggestions after brainstorming the whole thing together. Obviously, personal correspondence could be maintained but that would be strengthened by keeping as much of the group together as possible. I'm sure that the schools could set that up. Wherever the students move on to, Belize has a small population. It is a pity in some ways that the equivalent year is in the Primary School although there are advantages as well. It will be quite easy at Louisiana and St. Pauls because they have used Standard Five who are the direct equivalent to Year Seven and they have another year to go before moving on. There should be no difficulty with Calcutta because it is a village and the community is very strong and very much centred on the school. The best route with *La Immaculada* is probably through the families as they almost all have lots of children and there would be younger members still attending the school. The project there has been restricted to the keenest ones as there are 150 in the age group. I don't know whether that will help. Go for it year seven. The continuity for year six will not be a problem. There are also other schools wanting to join in!

The concept of the changing English seasons will be known but not understood and experienced (in the States which is hardly the same thing) by the fewest of the few who have relatives living there. If you remember from the account of the visit with St. Pauls to Stann Creek and the Citrus Factory, few children understand or have experienced hills. If you think of many South Molton children's concept of snow and multiply many times you might come somewhere near the position. The main contrast here is between wet and dry and, frankly, in Orange Walk or Corozal that is not great as we might imagine. It will be very enlightening to open those ideas up in both directions. I have started with references made in various writings to you and will be very pleased to expand my own thinking in that way… I will follow up BRAIN. It sounds as though it could be useful. Also, I must mention that the Principals of Louisiana, St. Pauls and Calcutta (and their Division One teachers) will be attending a Planning Workshop I am running from 22nd June to 17th July so communication in that time will be easy with them. Don't forget the schools finish on 26th June.

A message came from Ellajean to say that she will not provide photocopies of the minutes of the Principals' Workshop for Principals. How crazy can you get? Not to worry, I'll print them myself; email to go to South Molton Community College won't need paper or stamps…

'…You will have received two letters in quick succession, one concerned that the server had been down and the other a sort of sigh of relief! I am only just beginning to get the better of both this equipment and BTL. The sun is low in the sky now and slanting right across the house from the open back windows. I haven't had much work to do this week so it has been a day of pushing forward on writing, reading and 'Links'. I went in to Louisiana School right away and told the children that Jose Luis and Sunny are on their way back. It is quite something that. Well done to everyone. I have also been in to La Immaculada (again). That is the only school that I'm really concerned about and it should be the best one. I'm going to talk to the Principal out of school (literally!) to see what can be done. Whatever happens we will find a way of making it right for 7G. Please tell them that they are not forgotten. It would help, though, if they could tell me what they have received. I know the children at Immaculada have made some individual contact. It may be better than I think…'

And on into next day…

'…It is Friday and another free day. The Director of the Education Development Centre to whom I am responsible along with the rest of the team has decided that we should all have a week off, quite arbitrarily! We were told last Friday. As you *might imagine, all sorts of work was planned for this week which has come to a grinding halt - not because I have been given a week off but because everyone else has and we are a team. I won't go into it in great detail in a letter because it would have to be viewed from experience in the English system. Perhaps I might write a story about it which would be more meaningful. What we would regard as strange acts happen all the time. It is something to do with the stage of development of a young country with a tiny population and I am only just coming to grips with it. Two things that are very clear are that the country is run much more politically than we are used to and the greatest concern of the people who are running it is not progress but control!!! As well as the election of politicians into government (supposed to be on the English model), the role of what would be our civil service and the top levels of professional service in all government departments are all political appointments. This effectively means that there is no civil service and no professionals, except in Non-Government Organisations. You can imagine what happens when there is a change of government. A whole heap of new people replace those who have at least learnt a little bit during the time of the last one. Also, the entire population has to be either red or blue! That bit reminds me of what it was like growing up in Sheffield during and immediately following the war (the second one!!)*

In order to try to understand this I have embarked on a distance learning package on Development Education run by VSO. You may therefore wonder how I find time to write as I do. The answer to that is that it all hangs together. One thing helps another and I came here with firm objectives in mind (although I found it very difficult indeed to formulate them when I went for VSO assessment. These thoughts seem to cover a wide range but they are actually only a small part of the learning. A whole range of attitudes, expectations, relationships, hopes and fears are held in question. One of the things I said at interview was that I wanted to test the values I have and it certainly does that. At the simplest level, for example, 'Does this person's behaviour mean what I think it does?' What has been confirmed very much is my belief that the two most important things in life are our loving and learning. That brings me to children. I share with them here in a most privileged way because I seem to have been adopted by them in much the same way as the family I stayed with in Belize City when I arrived and continue to do so from time to time and for all family celebrations (of which there are many). The children are just the same as ours. That is not surprising and yet it is at the same time. In some ways their experience might be compared directly. This country is about halfway up on the Human Development Index. It is not a Third World Country but it is in the middle of the middle band. I can give you the figures if you would like them. But if you start to look more closely the differences in experience are profound; they invade every aspect of their lives. Almost all children (it seems) have access to television (fifty-odd channels received free). Many children are undernourished and wear only sufficient clothes to preserve the most basic of dignity. I find the begging of children very difficult to deal with. I will expand on some of these things as time goes on. It helps if you all ask questions. That helps to focus my mind and it gives me some idea of where your thoughts are (typical teacher!). Of course, when I come back my time is yours so that will need some thinking about. So these are the children you are linking with. It is a mind blowing opportunity for young people to learn from each other. I have always believed that children learn best in company with and from other children. Teaching is at its best when we manage to tap into that. Attached to that is the notion that adults can become 'child-like' in order to bring their greater knowledge and experience to bear. (None of that is meant to be didactic.)

I will send you a copy of the notes I made for my address to the Rotary Club. So that you will recognise it - the title is 'Trust the Future, Trust the Children'. You may have to rearrange it after it has gone through email. The cutting you sent about the 'Linking' from the North Devon Journal 11th Dec. 1997, by the way, has been everywhere. One photocopy is on the wall of the Education Development Centre at the request of the Chief. Another one has gone to the World Bank Schools' Linkage Programme but they are the only ones who haven't replied - They will!

You said that the email is your own. I thought that might be the case. You may have some contact from teachers or principals. I will certainly try. Of course distance is something of a problem here as well as getting the writing on to disc. When will the school be on-line? I hope the school will be ready in time to receive from Calcutta. If not, at least it would be the right way round because your children could easily give you a disc if you don't mind that…'

I phoned Elda Vega at Immaculada this morning and met with her and Mrs Carballo to hurry things up for year 7. Nelson brought home fifteen letters to be transcribed for sending by email so I can get on with those. Their parcel is due to go on Tuesday…

'Dear friends in 7G, Here are some letters for you from La Immaculada School. I suggest you ask Mr Berry if you can write back the same way - immediately!! I will deliver your mail for you. Then you will get a reply before the end of term. Sorry I have had to type them out for you. They look much better hand written. I will send the originals on by post when I have got enough of them. For now, the important thing is to write back…'

It was a great visit to BSI on Sunday with Raoul which I recorded on video and later made text to go with it for SMCC. We returned for a couple of Belikin and Raoul phoned home as I was expected for a meal and went on to the BSI club for more beers in good company before being taken back to eat. Aidan and Eldan, lively boys aged six and four were great company and after being brought back home, unusually for me, I fell asleep!

Visit to Belize Sugar Industry's Factory at Tower Hill, Orange Walk. 14th. June, 1998.

The entrance to the Belize sugar factory is always jammed with trucks loaded with cane throughout the eight month long 'season'. Sometimes they are backed up, six deep in places, right in to Orange Walk some three miles away. The line into the factory appears much more organised. Trucks come in in single file and to order. They pass over the weighbridge and then wait to be unloaded by one of the two gantry cranes. A gentleman in a hard hat is Raoul Alcoser who is a production engineer and a member one of the families with whom I have become friends. I am wearing a hard hat as well! In front of us is the weighbridge. The trucks are weighed on the way in and the same truck weighed again on the way out. The net weight is credited to the supplier so that each farmer is paid in due course. Most of the growers are small farmers. The rate which is paid per ton may be adjusted if the cane is of poor quality or there are other plants included in the load. The cane looks black because the dead material in the fields of standing cane is burned off before cutting, mainly to get rid of the many snakes that like to live there. There are two gantry cranes. One picks up a maximum of seven tons and I think that the other one can pick up fifteen tons. A huge pile of sugar cane is collected and is moved as the gantry crane becomes available and as factory capacity is calculated so that the cane is transferred to a conveyor belt which delivers the raw material at a controlled pace into the plant. We pass a machine which chops the cane up. It doesn't half chop it up!

A system of conveyor belts and lifts transfers the chopped material which is then mixed with water before crushing. The sugar solution is thus washed and squeezed out of the cane. The remaining fibre is taken away. This process takes place between what can only be described as vicious, cutting rollers - some of which are ready to be fitted into the machines or are waiting for maintenance. Sugar cane is quite a tough material and tough measures have to be employed to extract all the sugar. The cane is a variety of grass. It is the tallest grass in the World. Just as you might chew ordinary grass when it is sweet in the summer, so you can chew sugar cane which might be an inch to an inch and a half in diameter. The resulting liquid is delicious to drink; not as sweet as you might imagine but sweet nonetheless. A great deal of equipment is necessary to process the cane which is not easy to follow without using diagrams, and much of the process cannot be seen, so I will concentrate on the main stages.

The juice which is extracted still has to be filtered. Material which has been filtered out is being scraped off a large rotating drum. The whole factory is becoming increasingly computer controlled. Much of the later stages of separation are achieved with a centrifuge before the water is evaporated off. Raw sugar is then transported using an Archimedean screw and the inevitable conveyor belts. Outside, the scale of the operation is enormous.

Sugar bags being filled are for local consumption. The sugar you buy in England (from Tate and Lyle) will be further refined. I think that the local sugar is much nicer in its less refined state. There is quite a lot supplied for local use and for others who use the bagged sugar at this stage of the process. A huge warehouse is often actually full of bags of sugar!

Curiously enough, I haven't seen any ants. There only has to be a grain of sugar accidentally dropped at home and the ants are there straight away but here, I saw none. A rotating, stick-like wheel is gathering samples to ensure that effluent is within environmental limits. After that I was taken to see the sugar-mountains; again, a huge warehouse and a lot of sugar. Imagine how much cane and how many cane fields are necessary to fill a warehouse with a mountain! Bags being emptied had sugar which got damp, returned for reprocessing.

Outside of the storage unit the sugar is further transported by conveyor to be eventually loaded on to barges which carry the product down the New River, out to Corozal, around Sarteneja Point and on to an unloading point offshore, where the sugar is transferred to larger ships and exported. This particular stretch of water is not part of the New River but a loop which has been made from it to form a dock for the sugar factory. It seems strange to find industry in such a beautiful place. A small building covered with corrugated sheets houses pumps supplying the factory with water. The barges can be seen occasionally passing by on the river at Orange Walk. They do not seem to disrupt the life on the river in any way where there are many crocodiles in the water, and plenty of fish.

The site is extensive with the bulk of the factory hidden behind the sugar mountain warehouse and the one with the bags of sugar in it. There is a large collection area for waste water and a treatment plant not unlike a sewage farm but without the smell! The main purpose of that is to vigorously aerate the water before returning it to the river. Many environmental groups have assessed this process and use it as a model for others.

The sudden decision that all staff should have a week off was followed by an equally sudden decision to change an order of events and call a meeting for all at EDC starting at 8:30am on Monday morning, 15th June. For me, this meant the usual 6:30am bus but for those in the Deep South it was a bus ride of five or six hours and heralded much rearrangement. I spent a day at the Orange Walk office sorting out details for their workshop and another at Corozal to make final arrangements for their Planning Workshop at the Methodist School; gave a presentation on the forthcoming planning to Chapel and St Peter's staff as their Principals had missed the Workshop; further consolidation in Orange Walk and most of Saturday preparing for the first two days of the Planning Workshop next week. I had been invited to the Graduation for Chapel School but by the time I finished at 3:00pm it was too late.

Seize the moment, however; I was able to deliver mail from Year 7 to St Paul's School, La Immaculada, Louisiana and Calcutta and attend the Calcutta Graduation ceremony, capturing another set of photos for their linking class. Unfortunately, I had to catch the last bus when the ceremony ended which meant missing out on the social afterwards. I made up for that by spending the morning at Calcutta School and had lunch with the Rancheran family before returning to Orange Walk to meet with Bertha and Onelia.

Email up and running was very exciting both for the links…

'…Your idea of sending the email messages to 7G was a good one. They were very pleased, and I will try to return the compliment. By the way, the school is now on line. Please let me know when Jose Luis arrives back. We are still waiting for more buddies - this really is the most important part of the link for the children...'

'…I'm pleased about the messages for 7G. Time is short for replies. Perhaps some children will be able to send straight from school. What is the email address and how would you like me to use it. I will continue to send yours to you but you may want to have some system which ensures that mail is shared as widely as possible whenever it can be. I know that there is more mail going back and forth already that is not widely known. I can see the need for children wanting to keep some of it for themselves but it would serve them as well as everyone else best if there is a balance and everyone knows that communication is taking place. That is one thing that is probably easier to do at this end as the schools are primary. Of course, it will help when more staff is involved…'

'…This regular communication link is really fun! I promised to tell you more about "BRAIN", so here goes: BRAIN = Belize Regional Alliance for Information Networking Non-government organisation, not aimed to make profit…'

'… Good news, thank you. Sorry for your report writing! I do not escape, however. I'm sure I told you that the schools' planning to produce a Divisional Scheme and three years-worth of Units of Work runs from 22nd .June to 17th July. I am responsible for the contribution from the North which is for the Language Arts (English and Spanish i.e. 25% of the curriculum) and a team of 15 Principals, 54 teachers and four specialists. After that I'm part of the core team that puts it all together. Then there is a week off before working with the same group for a week coming to terms with the planning others have done before launching the results for a year's trial in schools. I imagine, by the way, that your term ends on the 17th July. Remember that it ends here on 26th June. I will follow up BRAIN at the weekend thank you. It looks as though it could be useful even if only to cut some corners. Bureaucracy (a kind way of putting it) is madness here. I spend a lot of time cutting paths through the woods which might otherwise remain the secret province of binding growth you could put names to, in the analogy, better than I.

Of course, as you wrote, you couldn't possibly know that I would pick up the parcel of diaries for the four schools from the post office, together with your letter, on the same day. George commented with a degree of glee as he balanced on one foot better than any human "Snail mail still has its uses!" and reminded me that I have to send the 'proper' copies of mail you received in text from La Immaculada.

I am very pleased that the photos, videos and writings have helped. It has not been easy to keep up the impetus and my way of doing that has been to increase the pressure, not only in those things but here also. You said that you received the books some time ago and you still have the parcel of Belizean products, artefacts, publications and items of interest to come (posted as advised). In that parcel is the Atlas of Belize which was out of print at the time of sending the other school books. The atlas is absolutely super. In the coming months you may like to think of what extra copies of things you would like. I pay for them (nothing comes free!) but I only pay the price the schools pay, with some concession as well, and I will be able to do that okay. There is a total of $700 extra to come on the strength of all the work attached to the planning and I intend to spend that on the 'Linking'. Just for interest, there are $Bz2 for $US1 and $Bz3.4 approx. to the pound. The email is a great boon. I was determined right from the start that this was something the children should have. The difference it has made already has more than justified that stand in just a few short days. Not that I have ever been in any doubt. So many things have dropped into place despite the setbacks that I often find I can hardly believe it. A lot of High Schools (Secondary Schools) do have computers and some can use the internet but there is no Primary School that can do that YET! Calcutta will be the first.

It is interesting that the zoo video is the most popular. It is a wonderful place of course but that was the one which took the most planning. I'm sorry that there is no voice-over in a way but I prefer to concentrate on the filming. Nothing is edited in any way. In the parcel is the story 'Home is the Belizoo'. It matches the film so you may like to show it again when children have had the chance to read it. I would like to know what they think of that anyway. It was an extremely difficult piece of writing. I keep meaning to say that you could take video film on any camera, VHS or 8mm. All you need to do then is put a VHS compact (which my camera uses as you know) into the adapter, load into a video recorder and record from the camera in the usual way. I can then play that tape from the camera into a local format recorder without any difficulty. They will do that at a shop in town. It would be worth sending perhaps as many as four 45 minute tapes and I could have four copies made, one for each school.

The diaries are great. I have delivered Louisiana's already. St. Pauls and Calcutta will be delivered tomorrow and La Immaculada on Friday. I am sure that you will get a good response. Also, La Immaculada's parcel is to be posted tomorrow together with a Buddy! I was assured that a Buddy was sent from Calcutta. At least Uncle Albert is safe and I suppose from that, you must have had their parcel which is also a relief. The students involved at La Immaculada are also, probably, the most able because they are mostly the brightest of their Standard Six who are a year older than Year Seven and also a year older than most of the students linking in the other three schools. I think that will come right.

There are several other schools who would like to take part and perhaps we can talk about that at some time. You should have had diaries. I pushed the idea hard but much of the approach is new thinking here. Teaching has long been a process of telling and it will take time for the best of the points of contact to develop. I am sure this will happen at a much greater rate when regular communication with staff takes off and when replies happen quickly. Obviously, a lot of things will be sent by post but what I am talking about is establishing the dialogue.

I haven't been sure about the pairing of pupils from the start but there is no doubt that some aspects of pairing are important to the individuals. The trouble is that it is too much like 'pen pals' and that locks the children into a narrow idea. Perhaps it is something that children should debate for themselves on each side - and across - the Atlantic? We do also need to think more about the ways that we might turn the Belize Primary/UK Secondary link to advantage. I think that will happen when you start to involve other departments but I can see that is best done when it is all well and truly up and running. Speaking of which, it is really great to know that you are able to put the whole project before your new parents already. There is much more to talk about. This was only supposed to be a quickie…'

'Dear Friends in Year Seven, Jose Luis and Sunny have arrived safely this morning. It is just as well that I am friends with the appropriate authorities here because there was some trouble at Immigration. It was also fortunate that they remembered Sunny's first visit and their return together to the UK. Even so, there was a lot of excitement. BOTH OF THE FRIENDS TRAVELLED WITHOUT THEIR PASSPORT!!! I was summoned to the embassy early this morning to vouch for them as they had given my name. George answered the phone and was strangely quiet as he did so. My attention was drawn to the respectful way in which he was saying "Yes Sir, No Sir and Three Bags Full Sir!" and then he said "Yes Sir, I'll tell him right now," (George has learnt some Belizean). Then he put the phone down thoughtfully, turned to me and said "You are required to attend... ...and stand surety for two persons attempting to enter the country without passports!" Then he added with some feeling. "That is not something I have ever done!" Well, you can imagine, it was really quite embarrassing. George saved the day really because he calmed down Jose Luis and Sunny who were tired and cross. Sunny was quite behind the clouds. George can be quite patronising at times but I have to say that he was a master of diplomacy on this occasion. Anyway, Jose Luis and Sunny have arrived safely this morning. I had already arranged to talk with the students this morning and they went in with me. They had already had the diaries of course and despite the fact that it is the end of term next week (26th June, we don't have half term), you should be having some replies before you break for the summer.

All the schools have had their diaries and the staff their letters from Mr Berry. I just have a few remaining pieces that arrived this morning to deliver in Corozal next Monday. You should have replies from all the schools. Calcutta actually finish term today but they intend to send some as well. When I went in to Louisiana this morning we talked about the Buddies' adventures. The children here are very excited at the idea that their own Jose Luis (Pronounced Hosae Lewis) had stayed with English children, visited their homes, met their parents, neighbours and friends, been on outings and etc., etc. and been cold. We were sorry to hear about the accident to Jose Luis but he was quick to tell us how well he was looked after. Actually, we weren't too surprised because he isn't used to skateboards and he wouldn't have told you that. He is brilliant on roller blades but had never tried a skateboard before. (George usually walks or rides his bike - when he can't catch a bus). I was in La Immaculada School yesterday. They were busy packing their parcel for 7G so you should receive that shortly. There will be a Buddy in the parcel, coming back with Spike. You will have to be quick with email if you want them delivered before the end of term. Certainly, the children here would like to hear from you by that means, especially as it will prove the advantage of being able to use it. It has been quite difficult explaining how email works because many children (and staff) simply have no idea about it. Most children have never used a computer and will have only seen them in use in shops and businesses. To combine that idea with sending written information electronically requires quite a lot of imagination on their part. You are in a position to prove all that by writing quickly. I have offered the same email facility to the other three schools. Obviously, there is no reason why you shouldn't write to them first and I expect, at least for some, it could continue through the holiday. I will be working with staff from all but La Immaculada School every day for the next four weeks of the school holiday and I can make contact with many of the Immaculada students anyway. On Wednesday I was a guest speaker at the Graduation Ceremony at Calcutta School. My address was based on the effort which you and they have made at establishing the link between Belize and England and the way that effort has resulted in the grant being made for the school to have a computer and to use email to communicate with you so much more easily. The theme was 'Making Friends' and 'Learning from Each Other'; quite an emotional experience for me. You might like to imagine the circumstances and begin to work out why that should be so…'

And from and for children still in UK primary…

'…I was really pleased and excited to receive your email - it was the first I had had. The email is a good system and works effectively! The linking system between the two schools sounds good…'

'…We have contact both ways! I thought that I would send straight back to tell you that because I shouldn't be surprised if you are looking for an answer when you come home from school (or even before you go). It is pleasing and exciting even to an old codger like me!! Also, I was particularly pleased to have sent you your first email. Tell your Dad I could do with a decent pint…'

Fathers' Day was celebrated in church this morning. All fathers including me were applauded and wished a happy Fathers' Day by a female member of the congregation. It rained this afternoon and produced the most wonderful storm which lasted for about an hour. You can hear the rain coming in the trees of the forest, there is a rush of wind and down it comes; great heavy drops and plenty of them; rain absolutely pouring off the roof. Although there is a sharp drop in air temperature, the rain is warm and those that have to be out in it just get wet and seemingly without complaint. There was no visible lightning but heavy thunder just continued on with one long peal running unbroken, into the next. The air was suddenly fresh and the smell of it most invigorating. Perhaps the rainy season really has come at last.

'…Your 'Wall to wall Belize' set me thinking. How easy it is to miss the obvious. When your children come in to your room it must hit them and it will do that at regular times. That is a great stimulus to keep the action going. Here the children remain in the same classroom for the times when they are doing so many other things and they do not have the displays we are used to in England. We will need to think more about tangible stimulus. Also, it is difficult to demonstrate what is happening to their parents. Calcutta is the school which has been most successful at this but that is not through any kind of display but more because it is a village and because I have got to know many of the parents as well. Belize schools are big on ceremony as I have found out by attending several Graduation ceremonies, but there is little visual aid; something to think about. I am sure that the key to success is direct communication with staff and fast mail to supplement the more 'concrete' packages going back and forth. Perhaps one way that sponsors could help would be in funding resource material coming from England so that schools could mount Wall to Wall UK with SMCC at its centre.

I had supposed from what you have said about not having had Buddies from St Pauls and Calcutta, that the parcel from Calcutta was lost. I see in your last letter that Uncle Albert has returned. That means that you have received their parcel and their Buddy. The Buddy 'Bingo' is a little dog sent from Calcutta School with Uncle Albert in their parcel…'

'…Thanks for your last email, and a huge thanks also for your package which arrived on Friday 19th. It had actually been opened by customs - I wonder what they made of the contents? Perhaps they even tested the sauces! I had my last group of year six pupils in school on that day, so I haven't really properly explored the contents yet. One or two nosey pupils were hovering around when it was delivered, and I know they will be keen to share what was inside. Oooooops!!! Sorry about the passports! They are still on show as part of the wall to wall Belize display. Thank goodness for George - sometimes it's good to know people in high places! We are all looking forward to receiving a parcel from La Immaculada. I cannot overstress how important the actual buddies are themselves.

My immediate targets are to: a) get as many emails sent off to you as possible before our term ends on July 17th. I am aiming to get some to you before your term ends; b) start putting together materials/written work to support a 'Wall to wall Belize' display; c) seek sponsorship from local charity groups; d) plan my course of attack for the next school year. Obviously, we will keep in touch in the meantime. I now have things clear in my head - thanks to you. A constant exchange of 'tangibles' via snail mail, supported by a regular contact (pupils mainly) through email. The foundations for an exchange project are now firmly in place…'

A letter for the class teacher at St Pauls was included in the email for rapid delivery…

'…I don't mind acting as postman at all. That, after all, is what this equipment is for. The curriculum planning that I have to coordinate over the next four weeks is taking place in Corozal Town so delivery tomorrow is easy. Also, the Principals of St. Paul's Anglican, Calcutta Government and Louisiana Schools are part of the planning team so lines of communication remain open to them. All the participating schools in the pilot stage are working together - located at Corozal Methodist School. It is quite a challenging project and one which demands a degree of (apparent!) confidence and assertiveness while giving full opportunity and encouragement to all of the seventy teachers and principals who are doing the actual planning. Mrs Vega of La Immaculada lives not far from me and the Burns children next door go to that school so that is no problem either. I'm ever so pleased that the package has arrived in good time. I have been putting it together for a long time and it was always a problem to decide when to send it. Do with the contents as you will. I hope they give inspiration and also hope that they will stimulate requests. I will do what I can to obtain anything you ask for.

I expect the customs will have had fun and games trying to open the parcel. ALL the box flaps were glued down before being taped and bound with string. Also, you will see that the glass bottle and jars were in polythene bags as a precaution against low pressure as well as corrugated paper for shock. I trust the contents didn't leak? Did the posters travel undamaged? If they did, everything else should be okay. It is quite a journey when you think about it. Do keep up the flow of email. I think that will be great for developing ideas. It is difficult to deal with the thoughts I have through the post and you must find the same. As it becomes a dialogue, the ideas can bounce off each other; the sum being greater than the parts and all that. It will give me an opportunity to give you a better picture of reality here as well. I am aware of many things about life here which I take for granted now (live with!) and there must be much more that I haven't thought about. One thing we must discuss soon is the influence of politics and the quest for control (power). Both have a great influence on every-day life and schools do not escape (They are always one of the first in line it seems to me). One aspect which is very significant for the project is that of staff appointments. Don't let me forget to enlarge on that. There are a number of other schools who are interested in becoming involved. I haven't advertised the project in any way but those who have got to know about it, in and out of school, are showing considerable interest. I don't necessarily think that anything needs to be done about that just now but you should be aware of it and it may become an active part of the dialogue. The immediate targets are great. I look forward to the emails too. Are there children, as well, who would be able to develop that through the holiday? …'

Schools do not all close for the summer holiday at the same time and the final week for the remainder was just as busy. The District Planning Workshop in Corozal Methodist School began on Monday morning and continued through the week.

In the evening Pedro Sanchez called round to bring an invitation to their school Graduation and to his birthday celebration. We had managed to charter a bus which meant that we were able to leave, sharp, at 3:45 and I was home by 5:00 just as heavy rain started again.

I stayed on after the planning for the Graduation at Corozal Methodist School on Tuesday. It was a very moving occasion with good quality recitation and singing. The voices of Belizean children have a particular quality which is most apparent when they roll their 'r's and stretch out the sound. It poured with rain coming home on the bus such that it was impossible to see out even with interior lights switched off as they generally are in between the villages.

All the celebrations were a great distraction from the heavy demands of the workshop and on Friday I returned on the bus at 12:00 as planned and went on to the Graduation for Louisiana School. Ricardo and Marbella came round at about six with their youngest and, after a few beers took me on to the staff party at Chapel School. This was good fun. After a few games, we sat down to an excellent meal and I was brought home by Julian Chi at 11:00pm. A great end to the term – almost…

'…I have just collected a parcel from the Post Office, for Randy Cassanova of Calcutta Government School. The school is now closed for the very long summer holiday but Orvin Rancheran, the Principal, is on the Planning Course I am running and he will certainly deliver the parcel to Randy; how exciting for him and very pleasing for me. I must say I would love to know what is in the parcel but I'll have to wait until the report comes back as I don't have the opportunity to go to Calcutta myself just now. Randy and many of the other students you have linked with at Calcutta have graduated to High School now, but I am sure that they remain in touch as I have said previously. It is a small and lively village. Also, the school should be on email early next term as the purchase of a computer is in now hand following the VSO grant (It all takes time!). There are still the students remaining in Standard Five who will be joined by the next lot next year and a few who will repeat Standard Six…'*

'…I expect this will be my last letter to you as Year Seven but I will be writing to you again next year. My last letter was two weeks ago which was not intended to be so long but it was then that a Planning Workshop for fourteen Principals and sixty Teachers began. As I am running it, I have been pretty busy and will continue to be as it doesn't end until the 17th July which, I believe, is the end of your term. The workshop involves fourteen schools across Orange Walk and Corozal Districts, who are piloting the new curriculum for 5-7 year old children. Three other workshops are taking place across Belize and ours is being held in Corozal Town, thirty miles away. Each workshop is planning one area of learning. Ours is Language Arts which is effectively English (Reading, Writing, Listening, Speaking and Viewing) and Spanish (listening and speaking). We have a charter bus for Orange Walk which picks everyone up individually. As everyone knows everyone else here (more so than in South Molton!) that is the way it works. I set off at seven in the morning and return at five in the evening. We spend the entire day together including lunchtime when Belizean (obviously) food is served. When this is over, the Coordinators from each workshop gather together in Belize City for three weeks (when you are all on holiday) to bring together all the work that everyone has done and turn it into what is called a Divisional Scheme and Units of Work which are designed to cover the three years. Even then, there is much to be done because the schools have to spend the week before the children come back making sense of it all even before they think about their Lesson Plans. Before that, the Coordinators will spend a week preparing for that. My 'summer' has dwindled to one week as far as I can see! Is any one of you considering being a Teacher? Right now, it is very important that as many of you as possible send end of term communications to your partners here. Schools here have already been closed for a week but I expect that I can find ways of making sure your mail reaches the right person and I may even be able to arrange some replies, using email.

For next year, I see no reason why you should not continue to be involved in the 'Link' as well as the next Year Seven. After all, you have been the ones to set it going and you have been the ones to experience the greater frustrations of delay. You know that Calcutta, at least, will be able to use email themselves next term and communications all round should be much better now that it has all started.

One thing that I think is very important is that the School to School links are developed. The personal relationships are important but it will only work properly if they are built up on the School to School ones and not the other way round. You have (all??) played an important part in that and that is another good reason for you to continue. One difficulty is that children here mostly move to another school at age thirteen and some of the ones you have been linking with move this year. I don't think that problem is insurmountable as this is a very small country with a small population and there are ways in which young people can remain involved. We need to attend to that while I am still here to help it along.

While on the subject of my being here, I have to say that I have had very few (count on the fingers of one hand) personal letters from any of you. This is a pity. My enthusiasm for your 'Linking' doesn't come out of thin air or by magic; it results from knowing so many of you and all of the young people you are linking with. That is exciting. Helping to make it possible for you to learn from each other is very worthwhile and very rewarding and I can assure you, having been here for nearly a year, there is much to learn and in doing so you learn a great deal about yourself. It would give an enormous lift to all that to hear from more of you. I always reply straight away to all letters so go for it! I am almost certain now, that I will be here until the end of April next year. Then I will be home for some time but I am in the process of considering the application for another posting after that. This means that we have two more terms to secure the linking; to try to ensure that all the schools here have a computer and email; and to provide for continued growth. Much will depend on you. Put simply - 'If you are waiting for a letter, send another one'. I have been on my own here long enough to know the truth of that.

I have been to several Graduation Ceremonies. You would be amazed. They are very formal, moving and valued occasions indeed. It is quite obvious that it is a special time for every one of the young people involved and, of course, their parents. It is also very British in the way that we used to do things only more so. The Graduates (or is it Graduees at this stage) enter the hall and process to the stage to the sound of Sir Edward Elgar's Pomp and Circumstance (Land of Hope and Glory) which is always played at the Albert Hall for the Last Night of the Proms. Stirring stuff! You should listen to it if you don't know it. Then imagine the students coming in, one by one, very smartly dressed; the boys with white shirts and black trousers; the girls in long dresses all of the same colour (usually pink, white or silver-grey); and all carrying a single rose. The appearance alone must in many cases break the family budget except that the 'family' is so extensive as to spread both the cost and the pride. As they come in, there is a long, slow, patterned movement of the feet which (as those of you who know how awkward I can be, will understand) I couldn't possibly achieve but only marvel at.

The National Anthem is sung when everyone is ready. You have a copy of it and I will send a tape when I have one. Suffice to say for now, that the national pride in singing it sets the seal of the solemnity, the emotion and the joy of the occasion, all at once in a way that I cannot properly describe except that I have experienced it as a boy, long ago. There follows the speeches, poems, stories, advice and memories you might expect before the certificates and awards are presented. At the end of the ceremony, the Graduates recessional is the same as the start and after that, the food for everyone present. To have been one of the two guest speakers (and the only non-Belizean) at the Calcutta ceremony is an experience I am unlikely to forget. I am left with the feeling that we have much to learn - or maybe, re-learn!!!

Last Sunday I set off on my bike to San Estevan to arrive for nine o'clock at Pedro's house. It is six miles to San Estevan over fairly reasonable road and it was a very pleasant ride. A little later Chino arrived with his bus to take us off to the lagoon just before Progresso where we were to have a barbecue to celebrate Pedro's birthday. The bus stopped at all the family homes through the village to pick people up on the way. Neria and Tabo had come up from Belize City with Miguel and Mariami. In all, there were thirty people on the bus including children. We turned off the road before Progresso to a private frontage by the lagoon where there are open cabanas with a centre pole and a circular table on which the food was set out and prepared. The bus was unloaded of everything needed and within minutes the barbecue was set up and the charcoal getting hot ready to cook the lamb steaks and chicken quarters which had been well marinated and seasoned Belizean style. Needless to say, there was rum to drink as well as the usual soft drinks and fruit punch.

I really can't remember whether we all went into the water before the food or afterwards but it doesn't matter because it was that sort of day; plenty of very pleasant company; good conversation; lively games in the water which was incredibly warm and clean; and a continuous supply of food and drink. It was also the first time I have ever gone in the water intentionally with my clothes on! They didn't take long to dry! I hope you all have a good summer holiday...'

Chapter Four:
A Belizean Summer

The only notable difference with the last weekend of June and the beginning of the school summer holiday amounted simply to children not being at school - unless work being even more frenetic counts. At least, I didn't find work difference significant since any increase in overall pace was more than offset by the reduction of frustration through availability of staff by default as it were; not that the enforced activity and negligible leisure was universally appreciated at first. I believe that learning should be fun however, and it was FUN!

Arranging almost anything had become quite novel compared with the world I had known, even to the matter of purchasing and making payment for gifts with which the weekend began. Karen, one of the volunteers who worked in the central library in Belize City also had access to rather special textiles and so it was that I went to the library early in the morning to arrange with my librarian friend in Orange Walk to take a cheque to her and to bring the garment back so that I could pick it up at the Library; also, for the librarian to arrange for a parcel to be collected for me from the Post Office so that I could pick that up at the Library on Monday night. The library is close by the Post office and I would not be able to go there at all during the week, being in Corozal every day at the workshop. These arrangements coincided quite naturally with my reading group.

Teachers and principals were great. It didn't take long to set up working groups set the tasks and debate the options. All resources (and refreshments) were easily accessible; a note of group competition was introduced and any requests for help (especially beginning with 'Mr Max') were met only with questions. Thus we can say 'We did it ourselves.' By Friday the Divisional Scheme for Spanish was finished and English Units of Work were almost completed for one full set. It was a most satisfactory start looking forward to a relaxed weekend even if it did involve catching up with correspondence once more. Acting as postman in the holiday also involved writing so that children's snail mail from England could be passed to the school Principal for delivery…

'…I hope you are fit and well and making full use of the long holiday you have stretching before you. Like Mr Rancheran I am still working, planning for the new curriculum in the Lower Division, and I can't see much holiday for me, this side of August. Your parcel arrived from England and I collected it from the Post Office today. Exciting!! - And I would love to know what is in it. Perhaps you could let me know somehow. I guess that it is actually from Ben although it has been sent by the school. I hope that all of you who have graduated (I enjoyed the ceremony very much) will be able to keep the link going that you have started. If you do it will get better and better. Also, I hope you will continue to share with your friends both at your old school and their new ones. It is easy at the English end because all the students there have another four years to go before they leave…'

A note to VSO…

'…The cheque for the computer for Calcutta School has arrived in the District Education Office and they will evidently deal with payment. I am told that the school has been promised that purchase and installation will take place during the holiday. However, the holiday is nearer the length I remember as a child (as you will know from your children) and I don't imagine that there will be much to report for a while. For your interest, an individual parcel arrived from one student in England to one student at Calcutta this week which gave rise to great excitement all round as it was sent from the school (the sender is not exactly well off) to me, passed to the Principal at the Planning Workshop I'm running in Corozal Town and delivered by him that evening. To be in the position of knowing everyone involved - especially the two students - is quite a feeling! Much has happened but perhaps the most telling is that email is up and running from here and it has been used by my typing letters from La Immaculada Students. Would you please advise how I go about applying for a new posting when I have finished this one and supply whatever forms are necessary if that is appropriate. I have almost certainly made up my mind but don't misinterpret that. Things have continued to be very rewarding on all fronts and more than I had dared to hope…'

As I was getting ready for church this morning, Jorge Cawich came to see me to tell me that Rudi

Novelo had been to see the Catholic General Manager to try to get the job at August Pine Ridge that had been offered to him. There are also two Teachers on the Planning Workshop and Curriculum Trial Workshop who are likely to be moved and therefore lost to the programme. I also learned that all staff in Government Schools is personally vetted by the Minister; hey-ho!

This next morning got off to a poor start. I believe that this is following a combination of events: It is Monday, of course, beginning the third week of the four weeks allotted time for the present workshop; a substantial number of teachers have gone on to Belize Teacher Training College (BTTC) for the next part of their Training which has disturbed the remaining teams and there is a feeling going about that we have almost completed the task with a great deal of time to left. This latter is the most serious and, up to a point, it is true. It accords with a view I have held for a long time and expressed at EDC when adjustments could have been made. However, there will be a serious shortage of time at the beginning of next term when the prototypical plan will be nowhere near adequate to put before children in the classroom. The one week set aside for orientation is wholly inadequate as was also pointed out. The more we can do now, to prepare teachers for that time the better. Therefore, some of the remaining time will be used to do just that. The approach to the task was much improved in the afternoon after meeting with the Principals. One teacher who comes from Corozal but works at St. Peters in Orange Walk has a house in Orange Walk where she usually lives. During the workshop she and her three young girls have been living with family in Corozal Town. At the end of last week she was contacted by a neighbour to say that someone had been in her house. It had been lived in while she was away, turned upside down and completely ransacked - even to her children's toys. She no longer wants to live there but had spent her stipend on next month's rent. I discussed this with Principals who agreed to take it to their own staffs to make a discrete collection to help carry her over the difficult short term period. In the evening I walked down to the Library in the rain only to find it closed and returned in heavier rain to get soaking wet and phoned Jack to ask him to send me an email to check my system as I have been waiting for news from SMCC for ten days.

On Wednesday we started on units of work for Spanish using our same programme of key ideas used for English. Vocabulary was seen to be a problem which may be greater in some topics/key ideas/units than others. However, there will be themes within each unit which will be more suitable than others. Also, such a full programme would not be required anyway.

The collected monies were presented to the teacher whose house had been ransacked to help her out of the present position. Two people from Louisiana School also brought full bags of household items and food for which she might otherwise have to go shopping. This was very pleasing. It was reported to me that her husband was a drug addict and had also been found by the police, having sex with another man on the beach. Apparently the drug habit was the cause of the youngest child being in hospital for a long time. They are living apart and police have been called before to remove him from outside the house in Orange Walk. The view was expressed that it may well have been him or one of his associates who had been in the house and that money could be passed on to feed the habit. I don't think that any of that is any business of ours. None of us can judge and it doesn't diminish the need in any way. On the contrary it may make the need more acute. The contributions were made in good faith and I gave them to her in company with her Principal, having asked in private for the teacher to be supported for as long as necessary afterwards.

It seemed appropriate to start off the next morning with 'I like youngsters' from Michel Quoist and the singing of 'Peace, Perfect Peace'. It was quite a feeling to be leading that singing as Belizean female voices especially, are so incredibly rich and moving.

I went to the library as usual on Saturday, did some shopping, cooking and reading but not much else. Elena at the library had paid my electricity bill for me and gave me the receipt. I actually went three times as Elena was out doing some fund raising for the Children's Activity Week. I waited a while the first time and watched a beautiful bright green lizard which was about six inches long, for about ten minutes. The lizard was exactly the same colour as the lush greenery about. Maybe it was because it relies so heavily on its camouflage that it seemed transfixed by my presence and I was able to get extremely close such that I was using the close focus of my glasses to look at it. In return, the lizard barely moved at all except to swivel an eye to inspect, apparently, this intruder in detail. At one point it turned its head towards me and seemed to scrutinise with both of its eyes, first one and then the other. I made no attempt to touch it and was rewarded by being able to move away without putting the creature into panic. It simply tilted its head and watched.

There were only four people in church including Barbara Blades and myself. It turns out that the priest who is temporarily on loan - from the services, I think - is leaving Belize shortly and going to a parish in, of all places, Dorset - where friends of mine have gone to live.

The final week of the workshop was one of happy, confident industry ending as a job well done with time to spare. Principals were invited to make decisions about using the remaining time to the greatest effect with the result that the end of the week was extremely useful: videos on classroom management and planning led to debate on what should a classroom look like, sound like and feel like; A&R the book supplier gave a display and singing was led by Mr Rancheran and his lively guitar to finish the working week on Thursday, leaving Friday free which I filmed and provided text to go with it as usual…

Closing Day of Principals' and Teachers' Workshop. 17th. July, 1998

The four week workshop was absolutely brilliant. I ran it in the same way as I used to do the Leader Training for Scouts and it worked very well indeed. People here are not used to working in those teams and they liked it. The two districts have welded together wonderfully well and a lot of friendships made which will all be to the benefit of children when the new curriculum goes before them in September. We finished the work we had to do in the middle of the third week so the rest of the time could be used to prepare the way for classroom practice and to further integrate the teams.

On the last day we 'socialised' completely. The Orange Walk staff and I travelled to Corozal Town thirty miles away every day on a bus which we managed to charter so it wasn't difficult to pick up the Corozal staff on that morning and continue on to a small leisure centre by the lagoon a few miles further on close to the Mexican border. There are cabanas there by the waterside, boats, volleyball, pool, food etc. And of course, the sun was shining. We started with what are called devotions here. I started it off on the first day but I didn't dream that it would take off so well. Every day has been voluntary, including this last one where it was conducted in what is, after all, a public place. There is nothing strained about it at all; just an open expression of joy and fellowship. At about eleven fifteen we returned to Corozal Town as all the groups had arranged (and booked) a meal out together and we returned to the school we were using for a closing ceremony at one o'clock. The closing ceremony lasted about an hour and a half in which all the eight groups made a 'cultural presentation' which I have on film. They were brilliant. It was really only then that I realised the extent to which I had been privileged to lead the work. I had felt fully a part of them right through the month and before, during the preliminary Principals meetings which I had arranged to bring the two districts together - but this was the icing on the cake for me (and a film to treasure).

The devotions were led by the Lower Division Staff of Louisiana Government School and introduced by Jorge Cawich, their Principal. The traffic noise faintly filtered through in the background, coming from the Northern Highway which joins Belize City, ninety miles south, with Chetumal just across the border in Mexico and not very far away. The guitarist was Orvin Rancheran who is Principal at Calcutta Government School; the venue a Leisure Centre at Four Mile Lagoon; water and palm trees; birds singing. After devotions, everyone spent their time around the leisure area; some rehearsing for the closing ceremony in the afternoon; others occupying the cabanas to talk and eat; some trying a little dancing; others played volleyball and pool.

At one o'clock the closing ceremony began with the National Anthem. Belizeans are very serious about singing their National Anthem. The country is only sixteen years old and national pride is important. All the groups giving presentations were teams from the workshop. I had put teams together who don't normally work with each other and from across the two districts. Right through this workshop I have felt very much a part, a belonging with teachers and principals, Belizeans as they are, and felt this to be an incredible privilege. Yes, it was only during the closing ceremony that I began to appreciate more fully, the extent to which this had happened…'

News came that mail had arrived for South Molton and a reply sent…

'…*Thanks for the mail. I'm pleased that the parcel from La Immaculada has arrived and I will pass that information on. I must repeat, however, that THREE Buddies have been sent so something has happened there. I will ask the Principals of Calcutta and St Paul's to try to arrange for one to be sent in time for next term anyway. I think I can deliver the messages without too much trouble but it would have helped if the full name of the students and their school had been put on the letters.*

I have had to look them up and I have no record of Steven (but I will find Elvis). Are you now using the school email? I will need to know the address. It is a bit late to send children's replies but I will try to get something from the Principals tomorrow. If you can send me the school address immediately, I can use that - it will be more exciting for the four who have sent messages if they can see it for themselves. I will find ways to deliver the contents of the next parcel during the school holiday. There are other schools wishing to take part. I would like your thoughts on this. There will be sufficient knowledge of the scheme (and lots of enthusiasm) for any arrangements to be made direct but we will need to discuss it before any action is taken. One of the many other things which we will have to discuss for its possible influence on 'Linking' is the effect which the exercise of politics has on schools. The rights and wrongs of this is a matter for Belizeans to work out of course but you will need to be aware of what happens in order to maintain proper contact with the four schools and any others that might become involved. The way in which appointments are made is quite different from the UK. To follow it and to be aware of its implications it is necessary to forget about Boards of Governors, Local Management taking account of interested parties, advertised vacancies and even applying for jobs. None of that happens here.

The 'system' also, is a Church/State System which is quite different from ours. I will start with the Government Schools. Each District has a District Education Officer. He (or she) is the Local Manager. The District Education Officer is responsible to the General Manager who is also the Deputy Chief Education Officer! The Local Manager (in this case the District Education Officer) is responsible for appointments in all Government Schools in the District. It doesn't take much imagination to work out how much control this represents or in how few hands it rests. At this time of the year, every Principal and Teacher knows that they could be moved to any school without consultation or warning other than the length of the summer holiday. The Church Schools may be seen to be a refuge from the rigours of this process but they operate the same 'system' leaving control, ultimately, with one person. Politics intrudes here also. In Belize, everyone is perceived (at least by the political parties) as being for one or for the other. This is applied even to people who either have no interest or keep their affiliations to themselves. Each party aims to have in public office, only those persons loyal to itself and the method of achieving this is to change their opponents' employment to one where they might have little or no influence or one which causes them maximum personal inconvenience (presumably in the hopes that they will leave). Teachers are included in this process - in fact they seem to be first in line.

This year is election year. If there is a change of Government and things run true to 'form', there will be a great deal of change in school staff around the country. Change is already taking place for next term in the 'regular' way but also, seemingly, in anticipation of the election (Destabilisation?).

In the Education Development Unit, we have been assured that all staff involved in the piloting of the new curriculum will remain in post next year in order to put into effect the planning which is currently being undertaken. I believe that will be the case for two reasons: a key figure has a foot in both camps; and more importantly, the project is currently funded by the Overseas Development Agency (British) and the World Bank. The weakness is that this funding, as far as I am aware, applies only to the first introduction and two little chinks known to me, have appeared in this assurance.

Three of the schools involved in the 'Linking' are involved in the piloting of the curriculum and the other school is a Catholic one which seems to have a stable management. This means that the Principals of all four should remain in post and, probably, the staff. So there may well be nothing to be concerned about just now. In any case, I will be here through the most uncertain time. Our interest is in young people learning from each other. We have to operate in the system as it exists but to be sure of making the Link work and continue to work we need to know what happens, be prepared and find as many ways as possible of securing the momentum. This is why I think it is so important for you (the school as well as personally) to be in direct and regular communication with the schools here. During the time when communication has been building up, I have avoided offering excuse when things have not gone as smoothly as they might. What I can say now is that schools are very much up against it here in ways which we have long forgotten. If my understanding of the drive for 'power' and 'control' is getting anywhere near the mark, I suspect that something of the sort (or worse) will be happening in all developing countries. It doesn't just happen in Education.

I think that we must be patient and keep trying at all levels and never give up on young people whom I have found to be very deserving. You know me well enough to know that word 'deserving' covers much. I came here with very specific intentions with regard to the 'Linking'. It is not only working; it has its own reward which goes far beyond any expectations I might have had. That parcel for Randy Casanova is just one little example of that. I can guess what went into sending it at your end (I know Ben and his family and I know you pretty well too, in respect of children) and I know something of the good it will do here. I was choking back some emotion when handing it over. We will need to keep possible pitfalls firmly in mind now. I cannot paint a complete picture in one go but it will happen if it becomes a discussion and we now have the means to do that…'

Four lots of mail had arrived for Calcutta School and one for St. Pauls. One of the letters was read to teachers on the course who have been very interested in the linking and its progress.

There was an unfortunate incident on the bus coming home on Wednesday as the driver had been drinking.

When he went off the road, the teachers from Louisiana went to get off. Fortunately the driver's daughter was able to take over. Difficult for both of them! I hope he learns from the experience. It was more a pity because he had served us so well.

With the workshop over, the schools all closed and the staff trying to take some leave, the next couple of weeks were left without form although there was still plenty to do. On Saturday, most of the early morning was spent waiting for Coca Cola and Belikin beer also in bottles. These are supplied by the crate yet in this climate tend not to last too long. In any case Jack was coming to stay for the weekend and there would be much to talk about. I finally went to the library and People's Store at about eleven. The library was actually closed for preparations for Children's Week but I was let in. Unfortunately it looks as though it will be closed for books next week although my part time presence would be needed. Jack arrived at about twelve o'clock. The beer held out and the evening was cool (a relative term) for a walk around the town in the evening; quite the opposite next morning for a walk to Palmar, down by the river and out to Tower Hill by the BSI sugar factory. It was very HOT and there are rumblings about a tropical storm; it is about the right time. Jack left on the five o'clock bus. Emails and letter writing generally, along with helping out at the library and domestics lasted right up to Friday when it was briefly all-change as I collected a parcel of remaining word processing to be done from the Workshop, the story of which is as follows:

I had originally decided that I might do the word processing in the evenings during the workshop although I didn't want to. Margarita had announced that she was going to do it and I hadn't been able to find anyone else - so okay. After the workshop had started, I was informed by Margarita that she was unable to do the typing and Ellajean had forbidden her to do so (Heaven knows why). Once again, it looked as though I was going to have to do it. Margarita then found a professional (a friend in Corozal) who would do the job. The friend didn't complete by the end of the workshop although there had been plenty of time. Louisa who had taken over from Onelia was to oversee completion as she is a friend of the professional as well, and had been working with her to ensure that the copy and corrections were right. Then I received a call from Margarita yesterday to say that the typing wasn't finished and would I do it. I arranged to go to Corozal to do that and to meet Louisa there to make sure that we would be able to pick up the work and get it right between us. The computer in Orange Walk is down which is another reason for going to Corozal (Unless Ms Dominguez' machine is used which would be very inconvenient all round). Margarita phoned again to say that the work was to be done in Belize City because Ellajean didn't want to meet subsistence for going to Corozal. That is why I had the parcel to collect. I also found that Ellajean had phoned Orange Walk afterwards to check that the computer was down; politics; another example of how it is to be preferred to keep people idle rather than pay the small subsistence which is actually part of the Government's own system. So I did the word processing, gleefully really as it would be entirely in my ownership and being voluntary would have other advantage; something to do with itchy backs! All was ready to be taken to EDC on the six-thirty bus on Monday morning beginning another week back and forth on curriculum at the office but also affording other opportunities. I went to the bank at lunchtime to order a new cheque book and to get some cash, finding that the card wouldn't work and that it would take three weeks to get a new one. I did try my cash card at the bank next day however and found that it worked. Such things often occur...

Midweek and the washing completed before catching the 6:30am bus such that the very heavy storm lasting about fifteen minutes from 6:10am meant a brisk run. Such storms were becoming threatening and I began to wonder about the warnings. I called in on the family before going to the bank to pick up my cheque book and tell them that my card was working and how it was made to work; it might have been helpful.

Being well into my placement by now and having had thoughts of Zimbabwe 'what next?' was looming more in the back of my mind to discuss with the family; at least I intend to stay until the end of April and then maybe go home but not come back; also that I am looking for another posting and that I may be able to come back for a holiday. I was told that I would always have a home with them.

Being now seriously short of memory in by elderly 486 I was helped again by Norah and Stanley who rooted around to find me an extra four megabytes; Stanley merely asking for some Modelo in return! Modelo is a Mexican beer not available in Belize (by dictate) but I could easily go to Chetumal with friends. Regular trips over the border for goods were commonplace for Belizeans. Still trying to keep on top of things I talked to the Chief and found that he had done nothing about the computer for Calcutta so I left it with Stanley to arrange directly with Corozal District Education Officer, Pedro Cucul.

Now that the rainy season is in full swing the frogs are even more in evidence. They are everywhere after dark. The ones you mainly see are little ones which are all in the grass now as well as the swampy bits, but there are many others - including toads - which are very big indeed; anything up to ten inches long.

I went to exchange my voucher for subsistence and stipend for part of the Workshop. This was worth $860 which, together with the $360 already received, makes a total of $1220. My expenses were $100 for meals and $120 for travel so that makes $1000 clear, which will be very useful for the schools' 'Linking'. Of course, I only got a cheque and not the money, the bank was packed out and I shall have to wait until Monday so I am still short of cash. I fitted the four megabyte chip in the computer. Works okay. Also went to the Library and did just a little shopping before Henry arrived for the VSO twelve month visit and review. I had arranged for him to meet with Orvin Rancheran at Escuela Secondaria Mexico where Orvin was attending a computer course as a result of the computer grant made to Calcutta Government School to help with the linking. We met there for lunch so that Orvin could tell Henry about the linking, the Curriculum Programme and the month Workshop just completed as well. Afterwards we had a look at the school and surroundings at Calcutta and went on to Corozal to see the schools there and to visit the Mayan Ruin at Santa Rita. That was very interesting. In the evening I went out for a meal at the restaurant just off the San Estevan road, about a mile out of town, which I like so much. Poc Pol with venison instead of pork was excellent. Tabo and Marco called this morning, Saturday, with a relative from Orange Walk whom I recognise but do not remember his name. Neria had gone on to Chetumal. Had a pleasant couple of hours with Modelo, Belikin and rum and coke!

There was rain in the afternoon on Sunday and plenty of water about in the evening. As I went down to have a look around outside the amount of movement was amazing; frogs; lots and lots of regular size black frogs all over the concrete immediately under the balcony and the overhang of my main room round at the side. Further investigation revealed that the grass was running with them and, surprisingly, they do run as well as hop. I believe natterjack toads do that so maybe… When they stop and freeze they are extremely difficult to see. I have often listened to them calling to each other, which they do just like crickets, right through the nights and early morning before the sun is too hot. But I have not known them in any number in the garden because there are no wet patches there. It must be that the numbers are now so great that they are spreading out beyond the regular wet and boggy patches - of which there are many.

There was a wonderful storm during the night which picked up again this morning. All thoughts of going out were banished. The rain doesn't last all that long each time and the sun comes out in between, during the day but the thunder rumbles on. At one stage this morning, one centre was right overhead and the house shook for the second time since I have been here. During those times I shut the computer down as the power supply goes off often enough without inviting trouble. I don't like to trust too much to the surge protector.

'…We need to establish a dialogue in order to be in a position to make the most of the 'Linking' right from the start of next term. I am sure that there are many little things which will add up to a more successful operation which can be sustained, developed and even expanded. Also, there will be aspects of life in Belize (Development Education if you like) which it will help you to know in guiding children to make the most of it. I have a lot to learn too, as every new day shows; it would help me to have that dialogue as well. I think that short and regular (almost daily) 'conversation' would be best…'

'…We return to school on September 3rd, how about you? I have been thinking about where we go next, and you are right to say we should keep in touch. I will do my best. The year seven pupils who started the link certainly want to continue their involvement, but it is essential at my end that I also work with the new intake. We must learn from our first attempt and see if we can improve things second time around. My first job when I return to school will be to start some background work on Belize - much easier now with all my resources - and then go through the election procedure for some new buddies. If we are going to try to establish a link with the new pupils, the buddies are going to be vital. It will be essential that our buddies are returned promptly along with the Belizean counterpart. This gives the work so much momentum, and I think it was the make or break point of our first experience. Do you anticipate any problems with this from your end? Without a doubt, the most successful part of the last link was the exchange of buddies between SOME of the classes. I know I keep harping on about this point, but I think it is essential to the success of the project. I would like to think that the email link will run more smoothly next time around. I have just put an envelope in the post containing some work from the end of term. Many of the jobs were done when I was absent, so it might seem rather 'bitty', but I hope it will be of some use. Much of it relates to a 'Wall to Wall UK' display that we were trying to get together - but were beaten by the end of term bell. This is another area I think we could work on next time…'

'…I expect to return home at the end of April. That will give two full terms. The summer term here is even less use for *new initiative than in England because of BNSE. That gives ample time to secure the whole operation, given that we have got as far as we have. You know of the grant that has been approved for Calcutta Government School. They should be on line at the start of next term. I am certain now, that the key to growth rests there - not merely because of the computer but because of the community, the staff, the children and the Principal there. The possibility of further funding is looking increasingly likely and I have in mind a combined thrust centred on Calcutta and St Pauls - but more of that later. I am as firmly convinced as you are that the 'Buddy' is the key to success. That is as close as we can get to a real student making an exchange. What we need to do now is to think of the 'Buddy' as a real person and ask ourselves how would that person make the most of the opportunity to share his experiences? One thing that stands out a mile is that it is not productive to sit and wait for the ambassador to come back (or even arrive) before taking action or further action. The 'Buddy' needs support to make the most of the experience - I can vouch for that and my own experience may be useful there. The sharing has been a vital part of the whole venture for me. I know that three Buddies have been sent. However, you should receive two more (from Calcutta and St Pauls) ready for the beginning of next term. The only school that hasn't sent one is St. Pauls. We must get started right at the beginning of next term which is 31st August for us. I will be taking steps to ensure an early start here; again, more of which later. As I have said before, I see no reason why links shouldn't continue as new ones begin. After all, the work in Year 7 and Standard 5 can form the groundwork for a new bunch just as well as the first one (better!). That is how I see it - a form of development education and international understanding at peer group level (and the best teaching is that which taps into what young people already do and are interested in - doesn't it?). There are a lot of ideas and comments in previous letters which need a reply. I guess the best way to do that is to start the dialogue. You mention the 'Cooke's Letters'. I am very happy to send those as an additional source and interest for year seven but they will be much better for a response now and again from one or more of the forms; much better to write about things that children want to know. Back to the dialogue again! I am currently putting together another parcel of resources for you. My aim is to ensure that you have enough to provide a good base for the future. I have to be limited to what I can afford but things look quite healthy in that department at the moment...'*

The next week was back and forth to EDC again checking everyone's curriculum documents for consistency and grammar and planning for the week of the 17th August which will be used for bringing principals up to date with the rest of the curriculum; also planning for doing the same with teachers during the week of the 31st August. I left at lunchtime on Friday and returned to Orange Walk for some shopping and Elena at the library had asked for some help with a promotion application which I had discussed with our VSO volunteer. There is a small library in the District Office as well, from where I managed to get some Tolkien for the fifteen year old who spends so much time working in the town library and enjoys reading; also borrowed a travel book from the library covering Yucatan, Guatemala and Belize. I intend to use this next week for a short excursion into Mexico as there is no work and I have decided that I should start to move around more, although in the sense of seeing rather than travelling. I went out to buy a street barbecue just after seven in the evening. I have had my eye on that for a long time but I have always cooked for myself at home so far. Now that funds are much easier I intend to eat out or buy out more. However, this first excursion was disappointing - just food, not well cooked and bland. At six dollars it was not a good buy either. Pity!

I intended to go out on my bike today, Saturday, but there were storms about this morning so I finished up going for a walk in the town (and getting wet), doing a bit of shopping, washing and housework; and making escabeche which was the best one I have made so far.

Sunday morning I cycled out through Palmar, past BSI and on to a point some way beyond Guinea Grass towards Shipyard. I should think that was about twenty-six miles and it gives encouragement to explore that road further. Also, Crooked Tree (The Three Crooks!) should be within reach. It certainly would in one direction to stay overnight. This would be using the Northern Highway but it might be possible to go round by Backlanding if I can find the road beyond Carmelita. After coming home and having a bit of a rest I then went for a walk down by the river and spent a very pleasant time sitting by the bank down by the bridge, returning home by about four thirty after checking on the Batty bus as I intend to go to Bacalar in Mexico tomorrow. While cycling, I saw lots of birds and butterflies and some good sized iguana lizards. I really must get some books. They could be sent to year seven and I could perhaps identify a few species as well. Later on, I saw lots of kingfishers and kikadee down by the river and a couple of humming birds (one from the veranda). There is a little tiny, very black and shiny bird which I see quite often, darting in the low scrub by the roadside.

Chetumal to Bacalar

5:45am Heading down the main road past 'D* Victoria' (a hotel) to catch the Batty Bus for Chetumal, hopefully at six o'clock; 'Eliza's Fast food', opposite the gas station is doing steady business already. Many Belizeans seem to have their breakfast out: burritos, tostadas, salbutes, tacos, and garnaches; mostly tacos at this time of the morning; in fact that is probably the most common on the stalls at any time; some do beef burgers. I wonder what a nine or ten year old boy is doing out on his bike just now; many are engaged in selling and it is always boys except in the main part of the day when a few girls appear.

5:50am the bus is ready and waiting. It is the election on the 17th August and there are posters everywhere; PUP 'Johnny for Central', 'Vote Johnny - Together We Can'; 'UDP, Fred Martinez - Our Choice in 98'; and a notice in Spanish - 'Imaginate $7.5 milliones de pasportes; $3.4 milliones del seguro social; tu dinero desaparecio y todavia quieren mas idile - no al PUP' - next to the Tai San Restaurant! On the bus, I am offered a return ticket for $7 and, as I was expecting to pay $6 each way, I readily accept!

Arrived in Chetumal at 8:20am and am now heading for 'Combi Corner' as described in 'La Ruta Maya' and so called because of the number of VW Combi that have been used as mini-buses. As I was the only Gringo at the border it meant that coming into Mexico involved my being the only passenger to have to fill in the immigration form and this meant catching the bus up as it didn't wait as it does for everyone else but went on to the vehicle customs. Fortunately I had noted exactly which bus I was on and knew where to look.

Found Avenida De Los Heroes which is my focal point when coming to Chetumal, and as I walk along it I am looking out for Avenida Prima de Verdad where I turn left for two blocks. Combi Corner should be on my right. It is very hot already. Chetumal is in any case, a hot and sultry place. A bus is parked - not for me. But what is this? A covered bus departure place! Wonderful! And a bus for Bacalar is waiting; 8:50am and the bus leaves at 10:00. Allowing for the time difference there is only ten minutes to wait - and in comfort too. This is a mini bus of a larger variety than a Combi; rather more like the size of the Red Bus at home; more dilapidated than Red Bus but also more comfortable.

9:40am Belize time: arrived in Bacalar which is a sleepy little place - at least today. The town square which looks more like a market centre just now and overlooks the lagoon from the top of a little hill, is lovely. It is a sort of town square cum park cum market; a real Mexican centre of activity; the fort alongside with cannon pointing out from the corners; there is a fair here as well, a jumble of inactivity in the heat of the day.

The fort was built in 1729. It doesn't appear to be open at the moment. A notice at the entrance declares that it opens at 11:00am local time; only a few minutes to wait? Perhaps I will go and find something to eat and drink... so I make my way back through the huge collection of fairground activities, familiar yet subtly different in the arrangement of attractions, captions and the mess of wires and temporary structures - cut poles instead of machined timber. That was good! Melon con leche and a nice hot dog. The melon was served in a huge glass with ice and a straw after having been prepared with a large portion of fresh fruit, sugar and milk and whipped into a thick consistency resistant to sucking even through a jumbo size straw. Pity the hot dog was the product of a microwave but it was hot, well cooked and generously filled with a greater variety and quantity of trimmings than I have come across before. Sixteen pesos is about four dollars in Belize money - around one pound and ten pence.

10:30am still no action at the fort; might be unlucky. It is very quiet. A check on the notice; it definitely says 11:00am until 6:00pm. I wander off to try to gain some information but with little hope as speaking in English isn't something practised in Mexico. The place where is the most action seems to be some sort of civic building made of the inevitable concrete, two story and unbelievably ugly except for the bright colours, where queues of people form in a seemingly haphazard fashion; policemen with a practised swagger make their presence felt and a boy is filling a huge plastic container with water drawn in a hand-held bucket dipped through a hole in the concrete floor outside. I spy a man with a conference case who looks official and certainly overdressed for the heat. Sympathy, "Wait a minute" and a halted conversation was all I got. I tire of 'waiting a minute', decide that was the limit of his command of English (greater than my Spanish) rather than concern for the predicament and wander off to see if a miracle has happened at the entrance to the fort. It hadn't!

The book says 'The fortress was built over the lagoon to protect citizens from raids by pirates and Indians. It served as an important outpost for the Whites in the War of the Castes. In 1859 it was seized by Mayan rebels who held the fort until Quintana Roo was finally conquered by Mexican troops in 1901. Today, with formidable cannon on its ramparts, the fortress remains an imposing sight. It houses a museum exhibiting colonial armaments and uniforms from the 17th and 18th centuries.' The moat, if that's what it was, has plenty of plants growing in it and no water. Plants establish themselves here and grow so quickly that it would be wrong to form a judgement of any sort of neglect. In fact the fortress has the appearance of being well kept. The entrance is through the little gateway on the left which is just as locked as it was when I arrived in Bacalar, despite the small board on the wall which declares 'Fuerte de Bacalar' open. The main part of the interior building of the fort is built on a small hill overlooking the lagoon and is the highest point.

The lake shore of Bacalar has balneario, or bathing facilities. Small restaurants line the adjacent avenue and surround the balneario which is very busy at weekends. I wandered about the bathing area, had a couple of drinks and moved into the town. Neither the mango I had nor the iced drink I had down there were anything like as good as in Belize and such places do not rate highly on my list of attractions. The fortress was still closed and there was very little going on in the town so I made my way back to the bus, pleased that I had come but glad that I hadn't booked accommodation in Chetumal for a late stay; also resolved not to visit the Mayan site at Tulum which is not the easiest of destinations by bus; and certainly not the tourist mecca at Cancun. Rather, I would like to take the time to visit Campeche on the other coast of the Yucatan and the Mayan site of Chichen Itza if I can organise it.

Back on Avenida des los Heroes was very pleasant. It was good to mingle, have leisurely refreshment and wander by the sea at the end of it before making my way back to the Batty bus via the two bustling indoor/outdoor markets. The shop selling binoculars was closed but looking in the window, it doesn't seem as though they have what I would like anyway. Perhaps I'll do without now. There is a bronze statue of a fisherman on the shore of the bay leading to the Caribbean Sea in contrast with a green building to the left which I believe is part of the university but, whatever, it is some sort of assembly hall which demonstrates the generous use of concrete in this part of the world. The bronze fisherman is drenched at night from a fountain with many jets lit by flood lights looking extremely effective. Just now the tide is out for what difference that makes - just a couple of feet - but the water is clear and very shallow so that the fish can be seen darting around in great numbers.

An obelisk at the end of Avenida des los Heroes is nicely framed by trees but neither this view nor any other can do justice to the amount of shady space that there is available here for families who gather in large numbers in the cool of the evening. There is a sculpture in the concrete façade forming the front of the old market. The Mexicans are heavily into concrete (was it really invented by the Romans or did the Mayans, a much older civilisation, get there first?) and the detail is really quite superb. To the right of the market is the Museo de la Cultura Maya which is absolutely wonderful but such a boring looking red concrete box on the outside; a shame really; let's go for the Batty bus.

Today is Nomination Day for candidates for the Election. The town was very lively this morning as the candidates for the two main parties have a procession through the streets with their supporters to the Courthouse where nominations are made. Afterwards, the processions continued to a rally. UDP were first and held their rally up on the Battlefield - colourful in red and with their drums sounding and flags flying. PUP held theirs in the Town Square or Park as it is called. Their colour is blue and just as bright and their number seemed to be the greater of the two. A parcel arrived containing work from year seven for various schools which I'll have to find a way of using in all four schools to help start things off next term.

'...The latest package from year 7 arrived about a couple of hours ago. Brilliant! It will be difficult now, for me to match names with schools and deliver to individuals (some have changed schools) so what I propose is that each of the four schools has the benefit of the whole package by turn - perhaps for a couple of days each at first and then for a longer period. I will number the pages clearly so that they don't get mixed up through so many people using them. This will help to get things moving right away on 31st August when term starts. I expect to be sending email on specific subjects now. Anything more rambling will be supported by letter...'

Two days were unexpectedly busy around the town and with writing. The letters from year seven included Elijha, over the road from me, Miss Carballo of Immaculada and a girl at Louisiana. The stamps were given to the young son of the Postmistress as he collects them, after being removed with an almost impossible pair of scissors. The library was closed again in the afternoon and I got caught by rain. Sheltering there, I got into conversation with an eleven year old girl who knew me and addressed me as Mr Max. This was unexpected as she goes to San Francisco School and I have never been in there. She also introduced me to her thirteen year old brother and eleven year old cousin. I was able to give Elijha his letter direct. He was very pleased as he had been waiting a long time. More stamps were taken to the Post Office and the Postmistress given a new pair of scissors which I didn't need at home. She was delighted but she wasn't going to use them there as I expected - she said she was going to take them home and keep them so that she could remember and say that she had been given them by Mr Max. What can you say about that? Of other letters, one went to Delilah Reyes who would pass it on for Louisiana and she was able to tell me where to go to meet a family member for another one. She was a Carballo before getting married too. At the next house, the saga became more complicated as the girl was not the daughter of the teacher, Elizabeth Carballo, at Immaculada as I had thought, nor a daughter of the Carballo house at which I had called but another relative who lives on the BSI estate a long way away. Anyway, it was to be delivered! Calling at that house involved and being barked at by three large dogs it was eventually Mr Carballo came out and who was going to talk to me from the house some distance away as well as through the gate so I asked him if I could talk to him where I was. He came down but there was hesitation before doing so. He was helpful in the end.

'...I have been invited to make a bid for a VSO international grant for the project. This could amount to as much as twelve thousand pounds or $Bz40, 000. That would make a big difference. It is very much a World competition but... if you don't ask... What I have in mind for the purpose of making a bid is to centre on Corozal i.e. Calcutta and St Pauls because I know that I can get the staff and the two Principals working together. Ideas then become a team effort in developing links and in determining the material support which would help that. I also intend to involve the District Education Officer in a more proactive way in suggesting that there may be fringe benefits for other schools in the District. Both expansions would provide for a realistic bid. Reaction please! In order to be successful, it would be best to demonstrate the success of the venture so far as decisions on this one would be made in London. Would you please give thought to ways in which we can put on the best show? Your 'Wall to Wall Belize' springs to mind straight away! If you are planning to approach Rotary, I understand that if the two clubs here and there get their act together, Rotary International will double any funds raised. What do you think? Your small package also arrived. One youngster (Elijha) who lives just along the road is very pleased to have a letter from Samantha. He has been waiting ages. If you can find a way of telling your children, the accuracy of spelling here is high. What is weak is creative writing. Schools generally only teach grammar. I have had lots of fun with children and creative writing in my spare time...'

I set off for Belize City at about two o'clock to stay overnight with the family in preparation for the visit to Hill Bank tomorrow. Hill Bank is a research centre in the forest as part of the Rio Bravo Reserve managed by Programme for Belize: jaguars, crocodiles, jabiru storks, toucans, howler monkeys etc. - oh, and mosquitoes; should be fun. The morning had been spent doing some washing and clearing up, going to the library, shopping and writing. The evening with the family went on into the night with the usual rum and coke and I didn't get to bed until gone two in the morning but I had been round to see Karen in the early evening and we arranged to walk to the Programme for Belize Office together in the morning.

I forgot that Neria and Tabo would be going to the market as usual at 5:30am and I didn't feel comfortable raiding Miriam's food store for breakfast so I made my way over to Karen's just after 6:30am, at least to be sure of a cup of coffee! We arrived at the Programme for Belize Office in South Park Street in good time for a 7:30 start but didn't leave until 8:20. Then Nick realized that he had left his wallet behind by the time we got to Brodies shop so most people went in there while a few of us returned on the bus to retrieve it. By the time we finally left, we were an hour and a half late. The route was out along the Burrell Boom Road, through Double Head Cabbage; down and around by the cattle ranch into Rio Bravo Conservation Area. There is a warden's house at the entrance and a barrier to prevent unauthorised entry and another checkpoint which was unmanned, on the way in. This last part of the journey to the centre took about an hour: past orange plantations; open pine savannah; an incredible variety of trees in the thick forest; and dense vegetation such that the ground was exposed only by track which passes for a road. We arrived about eleven o'clock and were first shown our accommodation. There are six dormitories, each named after a local bird, with five bunks in each dormitory - four down below and one up in the pyramidal roof space. The whole block and its contents are made of hardwood timber, beautifully constructed; cool, with a breeze blowing through constantly. All the windows are covered with screens; very comfortable and quiet. We were warned about tarantulas and scorpions dropping from the roof and hiding in beds and shoes. The toilet block, one side for the men and one for the women, is constructed in the same way. There are basins, four showers, urinal and two toilets with a completely bio-degradable and recyclable disposal system. My understanding of the term programme for Belize wobbled! Various buildings are dotted about in what was originally a lumber camp. The Programme had its own water supply and solar powered electricity and excellent meals.

Our introduction started with a talk about Hill Bank and the Rio Bravo Conservation Area, what it stands for and what its history is and then we went for a walk through the forest to have a look at the different kinds of trees, vegetation and insects. A good stand of teak was at the start of the trail. This had been imported from India during the logging period. I hadn't expected the huge leaves the tree has. Life in the raw: a monster anthill may well have been termites; a large strangler vine, well named, has killed the host tree and huge caterpillar-like creatures of a variety unknown to me are packed closely together in an amazing number congregating all the way up one side of the trunk of a tree. The only reasons I can think of for being only on one side are the limited shade and that they are on the lee side away from the breeze coming off the lagoon. I guess they like the bark of the particular tree for some reason too (or, at least, the butterfly/butterflies did, if that's what they are). The number and variety of butterflies and moths in Belize is wonderful. Many of them are very large indeed and I wonder how they are able to fly; also, despite appearing slow and somewhat ungainly, they can move along at 20mph without much effort. A small locust is found in the ground; they do grow a good deal bigger and are not often dozy enough to be caught. They come in large numbers and are responsible for much of the forest noise in daylight and in the night-time. The cicada starts with a slow, heavy clicking which rises in pitch and frequency to an almost unbearable scream when they are in particularly large numbers - as they are around Cayo. A collection of epiphytes and bromeliads are on a fallen tree in the open space of the Bank above the lagoon.

Two banks of solar panels together with batteries provide all the energy used at the Station.

It was time for a siesta which didn't suit me particularly but it seemed to be the thing to do and I fell asleep in my hammock under the thatch. Unfortunately I had changed into shorts and didn't use repellent on my legs. Maybe that was how I came to be severely bitten on the right leg which swelled rapidly. The 'bite' was actually a sting right in the groin aided no doubt by the wide legged tropical shorts and had been the result of a scorpion dropping from the thatch. It is not to be recommended and very painful.

By the end of a slide presentation the leg was twice its proper size, walking was difficult and the night walk for me was in jeopardy but I was determined to go as we were to be spotting crocs which I didn't want to miss. Huh; there were none to be seen! At least the boat ride next morning was peaceful and the swelling had chance to go down a bit.

The site is an open one on a rise overlooking the New River Lagoon; hence the name Hill Bank I suppose. It is approached from the South and has the open lagoon of the New River on the East side. The other three sides of the site are bordered by forest which is penetrated only by a few tracks and narrow access points for the sustainable management of the timber resource. Several buildings are dotted about including individual quarters for staff which are like little houses, and the magnificent dormitory block in which we stayed. The field station manager's house stands on stilts down by the edge of the lagoon and so has a very pleasant outlook indeed and what is probably a perpetual breeze. Despite the heat, there is a steady breeze blowing across the whole site almost all the time and I would think that this is pretty constant in view of the proximity of the lagoon and the open swamp either side of it (The lagoon doesn't have ends as it is effectively a hugely swollen part of the river).

There are many birds even during the day. I am sitting here quietly watching a small bird with a brilliant scarlet head, perched on a low and shady branch of a small tree perhaps twenty feet away. Occasionally it drops down into the grass and catches an insect which it consumes on return to the branch. Satisfied, it flies off and finds a bigger tree further away. (It has a scarlet under body and chest in flight, which is lighter towards the tail - I later found this to be called a vermillion which is a very descriptive name). There are several very shiny black birds also with a scarlet collar and bright red bars on the inner part of the upper surface of the wings. These are called Redwing Blackbirds (surprise!). They spend a great deal of time in the grass rather than in the trees, all in the heat of the day at something after two.

The next week back and forth to EDC was to be followed by another week off before the next workshop week was due to start at the end of the month. Poor management had been simmering in Belize which was not helped by the city being also in Belize District with all the potential to and fro and in-fighting being freely exercised. Two days began usefully enough with preparation for orientation of Principals to the other three parts of the Divisional Schemes and Units of Work. After that it was largely downhill.

The next day started with an update of the programme for Health Education in schools as that was how the two days were funded. The work from Toledo came first which was introduced by Jayne who had found she was making the presentation at the last minute as Geraldine from Belize District had resigned. The presentation of Languages came next which was seriously threatened by the complete inadequacy of the documents prepared at EDC for the principals to use. The work from Orange Walk/Corozal was well presented by Bertha but suffered from the aftermath of the reaction to Toledo and the poor documents. All of the documents had to be page numbered by all the participants in order to gain some semblance of uniformity of approach, use and understanding. The officers for the other three areas rushed off to try to avoid a repeat performance the next day. Some of the team members joined in an attack on the work done on Language and showed little inclination to understand it - or to recognise that it had been produced by teachers and principals themselves. Orientation of principals went well enough but Ellajean conducted a 'witch hunt' at the end of the day to deflect blame from the lack of management from her on to team members. This further aggravated the divisions which already existed; not Bertha, Louisa, nor I became involved in this. We walked out and went home.

Back again on Thursday to make preparation for the Teachers' Workshop 31st Aug/4th Sept, I discovered that Jayne and Oscar had been accused of "Not knowing what you are doing..." by Ellajean at the previous afternoon meeting after I had gone. Rarely incensed, I delivered my view of the disunity in the 'team' without restraint to a remorseful audience and set about strengthening the position of Languages in general and Toledo in particular; managed to give credibility to Jayne and moved to adopt her plan of action for the first day of the coming workshop - then took her out to lunch. All seemed to be settling down with the safety net which had also been proposed for her although there was the outstanding matter of the insulting behaviour of Ellajean. Jayne went in to see her after lunch and emerged to say to David that she had resigned. She left and did not return; all so sad and so unnecessary. I like Ellajean and even now was only beginning to understand the hidden pressures of politics. Friday's effort was subdued: no Jayne, no Louisa and Geraldine resigned. The light note was 'Home is the Belizoo' recorded for me by Helen Rock who is a Creole Belizean.It was a good time to write my second report for VSO here in small part...

'...Belizeans are so polite that the cues and mannerisms which usually indicate understanding in the UK can often confuse. Even after six months, I have left teachers thinking that what has been said has been understood when it hasn't at all. In school and in the classroom teachers are very caring as one would expect but there is a large gap in accounting for the child's point of view. Indeed, there is little expectation of such in children too. Most teaching is at present, a matter of rote; very much telling, listening and remembering with lots of repetition in between. In the face of the rate of change of plans it would be all too easy to 'react to the last command' but, happily, initiative is appreciated, generally accommodated and always acknowledged with thanks by recipients.

There is an amazing level of bureaucracy and duplication. As an example, expense forms are filed and kept with all receipts even after being checked four times and have to be written with a ball point for durability. Fountain pen ink is not enough. This I discovered after a meeting had been told by a high ranking official that the British always write everything down. Perhaps that is from where the practice grew. Time often has little significance. 'Right now' has no more immediacy about it than 'In a minute' would have. It could be anything from soon to never. Start times are similarly flexible and it is difficult to have meetings start on time although the politeness of Belizeans will often find a response if you persist in being on time. An indulgence perhaps but appreciated nonetheless...'

My week off started with making resources for the start of the 'Linking' for this year - eight pocket folders of resources; some sent by year 7 and others by friends at home: Letters; Lundy Island and South West England; Fashion; Food and Flowers; England; Wildlife; My first year at Senior School; If I had Three Wishes; and My Town/Village. Each item of the contents is numbered, identified and listed on the cover. While I was at it, I have produced a ring binder containing twenty pages of postcards, photos etc. and Town Plan, Parish Magazine, Old English Fayre Programme, Fairthorner Magazine, Wizard of Oz Programme and a copy of a letter from PM Blaire to Phillip; a scrapbook of 32 pages (18x12inches) full of cuttings of South Molton News from The Journal, the report of the coast walk from the Western Morning News and The Eclipse Countdown from the same paper; and two books - Exmoor, the Country Magazine and North Devon, Photographs to Remember Her By.

Next week I am running a workshop at which three of the Principals (Louisiana, Calcutta and St Pauls) will attend. I intend to show them the collection on the first day and deliver it to Immaculada close by, to keep for a week. After that, each of the other three will have a week and then a revisit for perhaps a longer time. I will be suggesting campaigning and election of 'Buddies' right away as well as ways of sharing experience and learning across the Atlantic.

Went to the library and posted letters. The cost of materials for the scrapbook and card for the ring binder only came to $5.25 which was very good. In the evening, Pedro phoned to suggest a visit to Lamanai tomorrow - leaving at 7:30am on his motorbike, the whole day being filmed and photographed and supported by the story as always for the new year-7. The ride on the pillion of Pedro's tiny motorbike was part of the film but that's another story...

Maya at Lamanai

The walk in, along the jungle path to the Lamanai archaeological site from an open parking space was wonderful and we first visited the museum filled with artefacts of which there are so many jumbled up together almost in denial of the exquisite nature of the work and leaving one in amazement that they should have lasted perhaps a thousand years or more. The tools on display are all flint. That seems to be a universal material of ancient mankind throughout the world. How did an igneous material come to be in the middle of a vast expanse of flat sedimentary limestone, I wonder?

A short walk through some of the forest leads to the first ruin. There was a wonderful Guanacaste Tree not far from the small museum building which was embraced by a strangler fig vine, making a huge girth together. The Maya (or Mayans) use timber from the Guanacaste for building canoes. Mosquitoes are ever present with their dreary drone, often too close. There are many right through the day and not merely at dusk, evening and night. I had covered myself well - with joggers, long sleeve lightweight top, socks and trainers and knowing that I very rarely get bitten on the hands and face, I hadn't bothered to use any jungle strength repellent. This was a mistake! Every time I tried to take a picture or shoot a piece of film swarms of mosquitoes homed in crazed hordes. Mosquitoes and once, sadly, caught by a doctor fly on the left hand which became very swollen; hands and face bitten all over by mosquitoes and ears as well. As if this was not enough, some insects managed to bite right through my top and ants (which are quite ferocious) worked their way between socks and elasticated jogger bottoms to bite around the lower leg.

The first ruin is the smallest one. These ruins are excavated to an extent but largely only cleared of vegetation and are in no way restored; perhaps not so interesting to the casual visitor but certainly much more realistic in the setting of the forest as it is today (or jungle as they call it round here). Also, the ruins that can be seen are only a part of a huge civilization. This particular part at Lamanai is one of the many great cities which would have housed thousands of people. At the height of the Mayan civilization, the population of the whole of the Yucatan and particularly Belize was considerably greater than it is today. So, looking around this area, as it is flat limestone laid down as sediment through the action of water heaven knows how long ago, it is naturally flat. The many small hills and hillocks are almost certainly man made and part of Mayan remains, underneath the vegetation. Many other remains, too, must lie at lower level and not so readily apparent. It must have been a mammoth job building and maintaining a city in such a place. To find it again in this huge and dense area of vegetation would in my view, be an even bigger job.

Now that vegetation has been cleared a carved face is protected by a simple structure made of thin timber logs for supports and a corrugated iron roof so that it isn't further eroded by rain while it is being decided how best to preserve, protect and restore the monument as a whole.

The view from the top is quite spectacular - with a clear view out across the lagoon through a gap in the canopy of the forest. Here are the first sounds of the Howler Monkeys heard again and again in short patches during a walk through the forest which took us round one of the larger mounds, parts of which can be seen from time to time.

The second ruin visited is the largest one. There are steps at the bottom, leading up to the second level and then the rather less well restored rise up to the third level and the top. We climbed up around the side along a path and steps made for the purpose. The steps are about twice what we would call normal height. I believe that at some stage young men had to run down them at full speed and in a straight line down - not at an angle! That, I reckon, must be about the nearest thing to flying without wings or any other equipment, from which one could survive! When we got to the edge of the second level the focus of interest changed abruptly. We had wonderful luck: a family of Howler Monkeys eating fruits and leaves from the Trumpet Tree, totally unconcerned by our presence or by the camera. They simply got on with their daily business of feeding and remaining together as a family; three youngsters, mother and father. There were no other visitors on this day and I think that this must be the main reason for our incredible luck. At times the monkeys were no more than six or eight feet away. They could not possibly be reached of course, as they were up medium tall trees and I was standing high up on the edge of the ruin so that there was a great drop between us. But I never thought to be as lucky as this, especially in filming, and know of no-one else that has. Pedro, who is Belizean and lived here all his life, has seen nothing like it before despite spending a lot of his time out in the forests and having a considerable interest in the wildlife around. These Howlers are separate from the noisy troop of Howlers which we had been walking around earlier on and who were at the top of a mound that had not been uncovered. I believe by the sounds that they were making, the howling and the softer sounds which followed the howling, that they may have been mating. This family obviously don't need to.

The prehensile tail could be seen in use. Howlers will often hang from the tail alone while they concentrate on gathering food below them. They are in wonderful condition; sleek, beautiful creatures, looking cuddly but their teeth, I imagine, could inflict a serious bite; their mouths are large and the animal is extremely aggressive if threatened. This was something of a risk. I could not reach them but it would have been very easy for them to reach me as they proved by swinging branches over to drop down on the edge of the ruin five or six feet away from me to head off for another tree. On reflection, that was probably the most dangerous time because it was the three youngsters that did this, one after the other. The adults swung round, leaping from tree to tree. Any move towards the youngsters might have been disaster. As it was, I was transfixed in amazement at that point anyway and even forgot to film. Pedro was somewhat further back - sensibly perhaps.

In the woods, away from the steps at the bottom, is a large round stone which is a centrepiece of some of the games that Mayans played. Beyond that is an even more special one upon which Mayans have recorded their main events in intricate detail which is quite meaningless to me just now. This stone, like the earlier carving, is protected from rain erosion by a similar wooden structure covered with corrugated iron. It is located in front of the smallest of the uncovered ruins but one which must have had considerable significance for this stone tablet and its record of events to be located here.

When we returned to Orange Walk we went into the 'White House' Chinese Restaurant for a meal. This is the most expensive meal I have bought and the first that I have gone out to buy in Orange Walk. As we settled down to eat, a young boy of no more than nine or ten came in and asked for food. He then tried the only other two in the restaurant and came back to us to sit down and wait as we had indicated that we could help when we had finished. The boy was clearly not starving but not well fed either; he hadn't asked for money and it must have cost him to sit and watch. I decided that the best course was to feed him so I called the waitress over and asked her to do that to the value of about five dollars for which he gave what can only be described as just the right amount of thanks. He was given his food as a takeaway and turned to give thanks again as he went out of the door.

I enquired afterwards with the help of Pedro's Spanish and found that the boy had been in before. He didn't appear to go to school as he was hanging around in term time, and his mum was said to have left him and gone to Cayo. I determined to keep my eyes open for him. It is eight weeks since the end of term when he could have been seen mitching from school so he must have been 'on his own?' for a long time. If he is in need that need will be great or he will end up on the wrong side of the law. Perhaps, if he could be got into school (which involves fees) he would have a better chance of at least being fed more regularly. Also, having some education might give him a better chance of fending for himself later.

Family Fortune

It was a thoughtful George that listened to the boy's story. He listened in a way that didn't happen too often. He was thoughtful in a way that didn't happen too often either but lately that thoughtfulness had been forced upon him rather more often. He didn't like it much! One thing that troubled George was how he had come to be listening to the story. Here he was, sitting in a Chinese restaurant enjoying a favourite meal that didn't come his way more than once in a blue moon as they say. Snails don't get to eat much in the way of Chinese meals. They normally have to be satisfied with salad stuff. George wasn't keen on salad stuff. He supposed that too, was unusual but he didn't care much about that. For one thing, he usually managed to find something more solid to eat and for another thing, he was enjoying his Chinese. This was a once in a blue moon meal because George had chosen the Chow Mein which was the house speciality. It had lots of seafood in it and George especially likes seafood when he can get it. It was a bit expensive. More than that, he was sharing a meal with his friend Pedro and it was George's treat. That was why George was troubled about how he had come to be listening to the story of the boy telling he was hungry.

It was so unusual for George to be eating out like this. He had been, he was, enjoying the meal so much and sharing the conversation of the day with his friend. And now he was listening to the boy's story. And the boy was hungry. George stole a glance at Pedro. He didn't seem to know what to do either. Pedro continued to eat but George could see that he was thinking hard as well. The boy had fallen silent. From the corner of his eye George could see him sitting sideways on a chair to the right. George and Pedro were sat at a table for two by the wall. Snails think best in heaps. All sorts of things piled in at once. George had already noted that it was unusual, strange even, for him to be here in the first place; strange too, for him to have decided on eating out - and in the evening; and a rare sort of meal; now he was thinking how he came to be here. It had all started with a phone call the day before. "How would you like to go out for the day on the motorbike?" said the voice. It was Pedro, of course.

"Love to," George replied without hesitation.

"Where would you like to go?"

"Oh, anywhere; there are so many interesting places which are difficult to get to on my own. Let's go somewhere you like."

"How about going to Lamanai?"

"Great," George had replied, "I've been trying to go there for ages."

Lamanai, as George knew, means submerged crocodile. The very name conjured up exciting ideas. It was once a great centre of trade in The Mayan civilisation; surrounded now by tropical forest on all but one side which was halfway along an eighteen mile lagoon. He knew also, that nothing had been added. Only three mounds had been uncovered. It was what the archaeologists first see and that too, was exciting.

Listen to the boy; he's hungry!!!

"Let's go man, let's go!" George had never ridden on a motorcycle before and was especially excited by that. He couldn't see much. Pedro, coming from the North of Belize, seemed almost as wide as he was short. You didn't notice until you were sitting behind. But it didn't matter. George travelled in comfort in a special carrier and could see just as well to the side.

The route had taken them a few miles south on the Northern Highway before branching off just before the bridge over the New River, to take the road through Guinea Grass and Shipyard where there is a large Mennonite Community made up of ten or twelve 'camps'. George wondered how Shipyard got its name but no-one seemed to know. It certainly didn't do justice to the well-kept appearance of the whole farm area which George could see was beautiful as well. The other main industries of the busy Mennonites could be seen but without the usual mess you might expect to find: furniture making, building and mechanical construction and repair; anything, in fact, generated by the need to maintain their community.

Listen to the boy; he's hungry!!!
(Do Mennonite children go hungry?)

The transport that Mennonites use is the horse and cart. They do have machines but they are owned by the community. Mennonite children passed by, where they had stopped a few minutes before. Children drive just as well as adults. They gave a friendly wave, even though the community is a closed order and they like to keep themselves very much to themselves.

The journey on the motorbike was an interesting one to say the least. The road was rough and Pedro had to weave about quite sharply to try to miss the potholes. They stopped a couple of times to take in the scene and once at a village shop in San Felipe, for a Coke. George kept thinking that he should give up drinking Coke but nothing else seemed to match it in the tropical heat. Ninety-five degrees again!

Listen to the boy; he's hungry! Is he thirsty too?

Beautiful countryside was passed by for two or three hours altogether and it was very peaceful as there was almost no other traffic and what little there was proved to be Mennonites with their horse and cart going about their daily lives...

Some way along the road from Yo Creek to Blue Creek Village and the crossing into Mexico, at San Felipe, they turned back on to a track again for another twelve miles. The Mennonites were left far behind and they had entered a much more remote village but another one with a very friendly feel about it. A sign read 'Welcome to Indian Church, home of the Xochiley Butterfly.' There is an Educational Centre there - part of the butterfly farm - and a restaurant for tourists who rush in and out again. Most of the few facilities are newly built, including a small quay. The village school was still closed for the summer holiday but George was pleased to see the important message painted on the end of the building

'Today's children, tomorrow's future; educate them all.'

Miles from anywhere, across tropical forest and best reached by boat on the lagoon, Indian Church is a very remote little village but there is plenty of space and the community obviously lives and works together well.

'Lamanai Outpost Lodge' is quite a swish place - being the only point of contact with the outside world for most visitors who come as tourists. From there they had first walked the short track down to the lagoon. A little boy was coming back from swimming; lively, happy and carefree. The water was beautiful; the day was warm; the water was warm; children and adults alike enjoyed the swimming as and when they felt like it, or had the time.

Listen to the boy; he's hungry! Does he go to school?
He can't be more than nine years old.

The walk in along the jungle path from an open space where they had parked had been wonderful and they had first visited the museum. It wasn't a large exhibition but big enough to give some idea of the amazing civilization that must have existed at Lamanai, throughout the whole of the Yucatan Peninsula and Guatemala and into South Eastern Mexico.

Listen to the boy; he's hungry!
Where's his mum? Where does he belong?

A short walk through some of the forest led to the first ruin. There was a wonderful Guanacaste Tree not far from the small museum building which was embraced by a strangler fig vine, making a huge girth together. The Mayans used timber from the Guanacaste for building canoes. Their descendants still do today. They also use cedar.

George was fascinated by the vegetation and insects and listened carefully to the sounds. You could even hear those dratted mosquitoes, of which there were many. The first ruin is the smallest one. It should be remembered that these ruins are excavated to an extent but largely only cleared of vegetation and are in no way restored; perhaps not so interesting to the casual visitor but certainly much more realistic in the setting of the forest as it is today (or jungle as they call it round here). Also, the ruins that can be seen are only a part of a huge civilization. This particular part at Lamanai is one of the many great cities which would have housed thousands of people. George wondered why he still felt guilty. How is it that some children are so much more fortunate than others, thought George?

The town was surprisingly quiet on Election Day 27th August, even for a Thursday which is early closing day, although almost all the movement was somehow connected with the election. I am amazed at the fervour and polarization of the electorate. I have never advertised a political party in any way in my life (I don't think anyway) but here, almost everyone seems to do it. If all the money spent on flags, posters, stickers, tee shirts and gasoline was spent on feeding hungry children the country would be a much better place to live in. And if all the hot air, expounding mostly rubbish or personal abuse was directed into manufacturing energy, perhaps it would go some way towards restoring the country's worrying balance of payments deficit. It will be interesting to see what the outcome will be when the dust settles. I have long thought that there will be a change of government and the indications on the radio seem to confirm that as a big win for the PUP.

It was indeed a big win for the PUP with 26 of the 29 seats taken. Clearly, the people have made their feelings about the government they have had very clear. I hope the new one gets the message too, for the same could happen to them. The corruption which is political favour has to come to an end.

When I went for a walk and did a little shopping this morning I called at the District Office to see if any of the essential documents had arrived for Monday's workshop, from EDC. The door was locked but the secretary was inside working. She let me in and told me that both District Officers had been working all night at the polling station so she was on her own trying to catch up with work as the office had been closed for the election. She had been working until eight o'clock herself yesterday. As it is also the last weekday of the school holiday, many people had left the buying of books until today but she had to close the door to complete essential work. A sad but telling incident occurred as a result. A group of people gathered outside and shouted abuse including the threat that this was to be the last day of her job now that the PUP had been elected. That is the true state of affairs in the minds of many people in this country and I hope for all their sakes that it changes for the better.

I met Elijha who told me that he will be starting at the Agricultural College on Monday. When I asked him how he was going to get there he told me that he would go on the bus and stay with his aunt in San Lazaro during each week. I would like to try to find a way to help him as he didn't look too happy about it and his bright and open greeting and chatter has always been a great encouragement to me.

I had intended going to Santa Rita, the small Mayan ruin just outside Corozal Town today. The guide there had said that I could film his outline of the history when I visited there with Henry Gill. He was very interested then and more than willing when I told him that the film would be for year seven at home. This would have finished off the film taken at Lamanai on Tuesday. Unfortunately it rained all Friday night and the ground was very wet this morning so the visit will have to wait for another day. As I write it is 6:30pm and raining just as heavily again. One benefit is that it has been much cooler today and I have a top on now where I would normally be wearing shorts only. That is not to say that I wouldn't be warm enough without the top - I would. Rather, it is more bearable! A weekend indoors is good for writing, sending all the 'holiday' stories for the next year 7 and making plans…

'…I suggest that it would be a good idea for you to take on two new schools: 7D link with Standard 5 at Calcutta Government School, 7G with a new small school, 7H with St Paul's Anglican School and 7R with a new small school; Year 8 continue their links. I am suggesting this course of action because I see now that it is better for one class at SMCC to link with a small school here rather than a large one. This is because the contact is between two whole classes and thus becomes part of the normal work rather than something undertaken on the side by a group selected from a larger number. I had originally chosen the four schools to give as wide a variety as possible - including being spread far apart. However, not only would it be unfair to lose Louisiana and La Immaculada at this stage, I think it is best to have as many irons in the fire as you can until the continuity is firm. Assuming the four small schools are taken up and continue the link that would mean a pattern of full linking between Year Seven and Standard Five, development between Year Eight and Standard Six and Pen Friends after that.

I have two new schools in mind that would be able to work in a cluster over a relatively small area in Corozal. All four Principals are working together on the New Curriculum Programme so I have no difficulty with contact over my remaining time. Another possible advantage is that their working together, sharing ideas etc. and being in one District would enable a stronger case to be put for funding. There are other considerations which have to do with staff being changed which I will explain as a subject in another letter. The small schools are stable and ready to start based on the question "If one of your class (a Buddy) was to go to school and live in England for a while, what would each of you do to learn as much as possible about life there and share as much as possible about yours?"

The pack of resources I put together, referred to earlier, has gone to St. Paul's Anglican School who started back today. This is to give them a flying start. The pack will go on to Calcutta Government School next week (their computer is not yet installed - this is Belize! - but it soon should be). A teacher at St. Paul's has email at home so I hope you will soon hear from her direct…'

'…Your suggestions sound fine to me. I will get my year 7 geography groups working on their election of buddies, and initial correspondence. This aspect will receive most attention, as I feel we can build on our first attempt and learn from problems experienced last year. My first package will contain a buddy (still the vital ingredient), passport, diary, and introductory work about individual pupils and the school. I will prepare a full programme of packages for you so you know what to expect. I would like to develop the computer links, so please compile an address list of all access points at your end. I also intend to get more departments involved this year. I will speak to the Head of Year Eight to discuss how best to approach the follow up there…'

'…I will go ahead with the two new schools and send details by the end of the week. A wider spread across the curriculum would be much better as you are dealing with Primary Schools here. They are working as a class all the time and it is clearly much better if the 'Link' is a normal part of learning and not an 'add-on'. I know it is a large part of the curriculum for you (You could be the only school in the UK using Belize!) I have nearly finished another parcel from me. These are expensive. That doesn't matter to me because it is what I want to do. But children shouldn't imagine that the Belizean artefacts are valued as, say, those from the Philippines are seriously undervalued. Items sent are all hand-made and cost as much as they would if they had been made in England...'

No documents arrived from EDC for planning but monitoring documents and some material on assessment did arrive for the afternoon at the start of a workshop week for all the teachers and principals involved in the trialling of the New Curriculum. Most of the plan for Monday, the first day of term, was completed however, with some creative thinking and presentation.

164

Documents for Social Studies should have arrived Wednesday afternoon but did not. All of the process had been covered by then and there was even less value, interest or product in studying the documents piecemeal than there might have been looking at them as a whole. What was needed was to use them and they were not available. The next best thing was to plan accordingly anyway and to be ready for the coming weeks on Monday and for the term to follow. With this in mind I called the Principals together to discuss how best to use the time so that they would be able to take their teachers along as productively as possible. Further, I asked for one of the Principals to introduce the work next morning. Henry Neal agreed. I also asked the Orange Walk Principals to arrange a closing event. It was discovered that the Social Studies had been sent to Corozal and returned to Belize City. They finally arrived on Thursday afternoon rather late since life subjects integrate most easily. Even so, teachers and principals left on Friday with the planning completed after a lively afternoon with a band, three entertainers, food and soft drinks. A closing reference to my role was very pleasing indeed. Letters were sent to the four past linking schools for continuity in their next year; for example…

'…I am willing to type out some writing from Calcutta Students and send it quickly to Form 8D using email. Mail sent this way will be available to the students in England by the next school day at the latest. Writing can be returned the same way. A copy of what has been sent would be given to you to check. Obviously, this causes a lot of work and means that I have to act as postman as well so please don't stop writing by the regular route. I suggest that much of the creative writing you do in class could be arranged such that it becomes a communication with English students. They would be just as interested, for example, in your stories, reports, instructions (such as recipes, how you play your games, use tools, make things etc.) and descriptions as your ordinary letters. If your link with England is to be successful you must write regularly, not sit and wait for a reply before writing again, make your writing available to the whole form/class, make it FUN. Remember that the English Form (class) is the second year in a Secondary School. They have a different teacher for each subject and have a lot of homework to do every night as well as at the weekend. Last year they were able to 'Link' through their Geography lessons as Belize is part of Central America and Central America is part of the curriculum in Year 7; this year you will have to convince them that it's worth the extra effort and/or can be part of the English Language curriculum…'

While at EDC on Monday I was able to visit the radio station and the Philatelic Bureau. Love FM is prepared to make tapes of the Anniversary Broadcasts (Battle of St George's Caye) for me to send to Year Seven - complete with greetings to participating schools…

'…Thank you for your kind attention this morning. I have made a few notes of the project which I thought you might like. In fact, there is a great deal more to tell as the opportunities for young people learning from each other are endless, but that story will unfold with time…'

Fish for lunch in Corozal at a little restaurant with an open cabana right by the Caribbean is a great relaxation with gently waving palm trees by the open sea; pelicans and frigate birds gliding lazily overhead. Presenting the Linking idea to Henry Neal and then to the Standard Five class who will take it up added to euphoria but trying to do the same with the new class and part of the old class at St. Paul's was not so good. They were so rude I walked out and went in to a second one. By the time I returned, they were ready to be constructive and with the good news for South Molton the euphoria was restored…

'…*The computer is being installed at Calcutta Government School tomorrow. The spark has lit a fire because the ministry are providing secure premises and BTL is providing full internet connections and facilities free of charge. One of your new schools is Corozal Methodist School. Their Principal is Henry Neal. I have been in and discussed the project with the children and they are electing a Buddy and putting their ideas together about what the Buddy will need to take on his/her adventure and what to do so that the two classes can get to know (about) each other. I suggest that you write to Henry without delay via his email. There will be email contact at St Pauls with one of the teachers as well…*'
The VSO Country Director was also in mind…

'…Having just spent megabucks on a new parcel to go to the school in the UK I remembered it had crossed my mind some time ago that a mid-term grant should appear at some time. So as not to jump in with both feet I went first to VSO Handbook 1996/7 page 17 and discovered 'The mid Term Grant is not paid automatically by the Field Office to you but on request'. "Aha," I thought! Please regard this as my formal request for mid-term grant. I will be going down to stay with Jayne for a week (or even nine days) from Saturday 19th September. That will be four days of my holiday as the Monday is a National Holiday. Ellajean is pressing me to take the rest of my thirty days so I will let you know about that. I will need my passport if we decide to cross the border so could you please try to make sure that is processed and sent to me here (Not EDC)…'

Having collected the pile of resources that I have made for the schools during the holiday from St. Paul's yesterday, I took them together with the video camera and went straight to Calcutta School this morning. Stanley Bermudas and Mr Chan were already there with the computer and all its attachments and they were busy setting it up. There was great excitement in the school. Just as I arrived, Orvin Rancheran was about to drive away because BTL had not been inclined to put a phone extension in from his classroom to the Library so he had to get the cable and fittings to do the job. This was done when he returned. Fortunately he was able to call on someone from the village to run the cable from one building to the other, through the classrooms into the library, and to serve the computer. After some considerable delay the computer was set up and working. In the meantime, while Orvin was away, I went into his class and discussed with them where the 'Linking' is and where it might go. Also the sort of things which Students could do to get ready for this year - the main things being to elect a 'Buddy' and decide upon the sort of things that the Buddy might take with him. We discussed the whole idea of Student Exchange and how and what that student would communicate in each direction to enable the two classes to best learn about each other, to get to know each other, and to understand the sort of life each leads.

Maria provided me with lunch which was nice - the more so that I believe that she must have given up her own lunch to do that. During the afternoon the staff had a brief introduction to the equipment while I spent my time between the two classes, Standard Five and Standard Six discussing the Linking and taking some film which included some still pictures of some of the Students who were also trying to announce their names and ages. The computer is a really up to date affair: 32 megabytes, all the latest software including Windows 98, full encyclopaedia, supply protector, battery backup, printer and Internet connection. Calcutta is the first Primary School in Belize to have full Internet connection (or even email) and the first Primary School in Belize to have an IBM computer. The few that have computers have Apple Macs which are steadily breaking down through lack of service parts which are very expensive here, and which do not have modems or modem connection.

As a result of the 'Linking' and, subsequently, the acquisition of the computer BTL have taken a benevolent interest and allowed connection and use of Internet free of charge, certainly for the first three months, which is a very good start. The Ministry of Education are promising the materials to provide a special secure room for the purpose.

Afterwards, I went with Stanley in the Ministry vehicle up to Corozal Town. We then returned to pick up my kit for the rest of the week from home before driving on down to Belize City where I was to be house-sitting for the family until Sunday.

The celebration of the Battle of St George's Caye is a national holiday. Thursday is the 220th celebration as the battle took place on 10th September 1798. I listened to the re-enactment on the radio and then went off with Marco and Miriam and the children to watch the parade come round the corner off North Front Street on to the Belchina Bridge.

The story goes that Belize grew from a settlement of buccaneers on the Spanish Mainland of Central America, early in the 17th century. There was a series of Spanish invasions, one of which resulted in the sacking of St George's Caye, the captured settlers being marched to Merida, Yucatan and from there being shipped to prison in Havana, Cuba. Settlers, who avoided capture, reoccupied St George's Caye and when reports were received of a further Spanish invasion being prepared the Baymen had to decide whether to evacuate the settlement or stand and fight. They decided to stand and fight and preparations were made. Meanwhile the Spanish had amassed a fleet of 32 vessels, manned by 500 seamen, together with some soldiers with which to invade while the settlement had far fewer forces: two sloops with one eighteen pounder and 25 men each; one sloop with one short nine pounder and 25 men; two schooners with six four pounders and 25 men each; seven gun-flats with one nine pounder and 16 men and HMS MERLIN under the command of Captain Moss. Action started on the 3rd September, 1798 when the Spanish tried to force a passage over the shoals. They were repulsed with the shallow water in the Baymen's favour. It ended on 10th of September, 1798 when 14 of the largest vessels of the Spanish fleet came to about a mile and a half distant. Nine of the Spanish vessels moved to attack and the engagement started about 2:30pm as the Baymen opened fire, and lasted for about two and a half hours when the Spanish gave up and left.

The parade followed seemingly endless speeches and made its way to the National Stadium for a jump-up destined to last the rest of the day which was very, very hot. Carnival Day followed, starting with pancakes and sausages at Jack's Place where VSOs had assembled before taking part in the parade. They all went off to the start point at about a quarter to ten. I prefer to watch carnivals and the Belizeans were much livelier.

It was a disappointment on Saturday that the tapes from Love FM are not available. I returned to Orange Walk as Tabo and Neria came back and the family is planning to go to Benque in Guatemala tomorrow. They wanted me to go with them but I chose to return as time is short to do all I want to do before going down to stay with Jayne in Punta Gorda next Saturday.

Posting the Belize Wall map to SMCC was very expensive. It cost $97 to buy even though I had managed to get a reduction through VSO and $27 to post which made a total of $124.

While also paying the water bill, going to the Library and doing some shopping, I phoned in to EDC to take off this three weeks holiday until Friday 2nd October, although I have a Principals' Meeting on that day and I will be talking with Christian Assembly of God Santa Rita parents on Thursday of this week.

I was walking from the Water Authority Office to go to the People's Store, passing just opposite Batty Bus when I felt a tap on my arm. A boy of ten or eleven smiled and said "I am the boy that you gave some food." He was wearing the St Peter's Anglican School shirt and school trousers so he was obviously alright. That was the school that I was intending to try to get him to go to if I saw him again. I was very pleased to see him and said so; also that I was pleased that he had found me and stopped to talk as I had been worried about him. School had just come out. I asked if his Mum was back from Cayo and he said she was. He told me that his name is Bernard, he just eleven and in Standard Five.

As we parted, I went to continue to People's Store but changed my mind, turned back and went in to see Barbara Blades, Principal of St Peter's right away. I found that Bernard is adopted but that his parents had a little girl of their own some three years ago and this turned Bernard dramatically. He had been expelled from Chapel School and taken on this term at St Peter's on probation following a plea from his Mum. I haven't found out how long he was wandering the streets last term. I asked if Barbara thought it would be a good idea if I came in and gave him some time. She was very pleased at this as his difficulties were causing some concern and there had been two boys transferred from Chapel because of problems Bernard was said to have caused them. I said that I would come in as soon as I could.

Tuesday and I have not had much success with Love FM yet and this is wasting a lot of time and unnecessary phone calls. I went in to see Bernard this morning. His teacher was pleased and said this might give him the boost (credibility) he needs. Apparently other children do harass and intimidate him; getting their own back perhaps. Bernard was delighted and talked very readily. First, however, I introduced myself to the class and told them about the sort of things I do and where I come from. I did not give any reason for visiting Bernard.

It was a maths lesson on converting from base ten to base five. Bernard was lost, as I quickly found that he did not know his tables nor had he much idea about place value. We struggled on - he very willingly, wanting to please, and we made some progress although it was clear that he needed concrete practice and one to one. Otherwise, he is clearly intelligent and wanted to communicate. I asked him to tell his Mum we had met (to do it for me) but he made several references to my having given him fried chicken and asked to "Keep that a secret just between us as his Mum would be upset". I didn't press him on that point.

I had to be at home for two o'clock to phone Love FM again (no joy) and on my way there at lunchtime I looked in the shops for some counters. I couldn't find any but I did manage to get a pack of 100 Poker Chips which would do just as well. By 2:30 I was back at the school for the last hour of the day which was very productive. Now I just hope I can give him enough time. I have to go to Calcutta tomorrow (I'm on holiday!) but I promised to see him on Thursday morning before I go on to Santa Rita. Next week I will be in Toledo of course - and I have told him this. On Friday, I have to go to Belize City.

The lightning this evening was fantastic. It was lighting up a whole quadrant of the sky such that you could see the fluffy white clouds just as day with the sun reflecting on them. It was mixed sheet and forked lightning which was almost continuous for about half an hour but it was so far away that there was no sound of thunder. That it should be at such a distance and still have the incredible effect of light is another manifestation of the power being displayed; a wonderful sight. I thought to do some filming but I left that to the less spectacular time as it was moving away and only ran the camera for about a minute and a half because I want to use that bit of film at Santa Rita on Thursday.

'...I need to know today, whether you are receiving attachments okay from me. I am spending the day at Calcutta School tomorrow where they have seventeen letters ready to send to 8D. The computer is installed and ready to go. My role is to enable them to use it. Obviously, letters would be much better sent whole as an attachment. I am currently on holiday for three weeks* *until 2nd October (my first holiday). I will not be available from Saturday 19th to Saturday 26th of September. I expect to be at home the following week which I will be devoting to 'Linking' as well as this week. I posted a Wall Map of Belize to you yesterday. We could use that as an example of the real cost of things here compared with income quite easily if you wish. This would be good for children to know and understand. What I don't want to do is draw attention to the cost of the things I send as that is done because I want to. The big parcel is almost ready to send. I'm just waiting for one or two more bits and pieces. The object is to give you the resources to run an integrated programme with other departments. Is the school on line and are children going to be able to use the computers there and email…'*

The day at Calcutta was not as fruitful as it might have been but we did get the email to work and two children prepared letters to send to 8D. There was still no luck with Love FM having lost the tapes! They have promised recording of the 17 years Independence Celebration next Monday. Not what I would have preferred but it will do the same job.

Working with Bernard in his class next morning went well until he took a piece of work with which he was particularly pleased to his teacher who made corrections of all the spelling errors and wrote on it 'Quite Good'. His face was like thunder when he came back. I was heading home when I decided to turn back and gently tell his teacher of the effect that it had had. He is going to need a lot of patience.

In the afternoon I managed to make the film I wanted at Santa Rita and then went on to the Christian Assembly of God School in the village to talk to the parents about the New Curriculum. It is the first time I have given a talk through an interpreter as some of the parents speak only Spanish - as, indeed, does the Minister and School Manager.

Friday 18th September I went to Belize City to collect my updated passport which Henry had left with Jack; to buy ink for the computer and two books from Angelus Press and to remind the manager there that he was going to look into VHS produced for the UK and the possibility of transposing from American to European format from existing tape (closing ceremony of Teachers' Workshop); to go to EDC to put in my holiday form for this three weeks and collect a voucher (back pay increase still not paid); and to collect my trainers from the family. I also asked Jack if he would pick up the tapes from Love FM as he works just across the road and I will be in Punta Gorda and around Toledo District and maybe into Guatemala all next week.

I set off for Punta Gorda from home at a quarter past six and left on the six-thirty Urbina bus. I had some fun finding the bus that was going to Punta Gorda from Belize City because I thought that it was going to be the James' Bus Line. I knew where that would start from - only a stone's throw from where the Urbina bus stops. As it was, I found that their bus was only going to Dangriga and that the one that I would have to catch would be the Z-Line (pronounced zee line). Again, I thought that the Z-Line bus terminus was up by the market on Cemetery Road but only Novello's was there. I had to double back to find Z-Line which was over by what they call The Park. A taxi driver offered to take me there for five dollars. I never have a taxi in Belize because they are among the worst rip-off I have come across. I knew it wasn't far and walked the distance in about four minutes including checking the way!

The Z-Line buses go from the Venus Bus Terminal (don't ask!) That was fun too! Once I had found the bus - and I was in time for it and it was due to go at eight o'clock - I went to buy a ticket and was told to buy it on the bus. The choice of seats was considerable as there was hardly anybody on board. I sat in a window seat about two thirds of the way back on the near side. The bus set off and eventually the conductor arrived and I paid my fare of twenty two dollars, through to Punta Gorda. The conductor tried to tell me something about seat 6W and that I would have to change buses at Dangriga. As I was already occupying a seat when I paid for it I assumed that the seat allocation was to be from Dangriga to Punta Gorda and settled down to an interesting journey with plenty to look at. Seat 6W was occupied.

There was a long stop in Belmopan. A girl got on, came to where I was sitting and announced that I was in the wrong seat. There were plenty of empty seats on the bus as there had been all the way. I had not been asked to move and my two pieces of luggage were nicely stored on the floor under the seat and between my legs. I stayed put and she went off to find an official. It was a long stop and some fifteen minutes later a rather officious young man got on and made a great fuss about seats much of which I couldn't follow and I couldn't get a word in anyway so I waited until he had finished. At that point he had abruptly turned his back to go when I responded (quite quietly!) that I was not going to move until he escorts me to my seat. As I said, it was occupied so he had to get someone else to move. I believe his seat was occupied too! The change of buses in Dangriga was long winded, also, but I did occupy seat 6W and there was no further problem except for another long wait in Independence. Another long stop at Big Falls ensured that the bus got in on time and not early. Of course, it would have been early at any of the places that it had passed through, where anyone might have missed it but it wasn't early at its destination. Apparently they get into trouble for arriving early. I would have thought that it would be better for the passengers if the emphasis was on leaving on time.

The mountains are beautiful and there are a lot of pretty areas which are passed through, but also quite a lot of open pine savannah interspersed with some more interesting bits.

I arrived at five o'clock which was the time that the bus was due in. No Jayne but I found my way using the directions she had given from St Peter Claver School. She said that she had been up but obviously didn't check whether the bus had arrived or not. And the week doesn't look very promising because the things that she had in mind to do don't look like happening and, frankly, she doesn't seem to know whether she is coming or going.

Sleeping arrangements were Jayne in her bedroom while I used the hammock in the living room. That was okay although my neck, shoulder and arm are troubling me more than somewhat. I have gone out for a walk now. We were fairly late last night and I have to wait of course. I think it was too late for Jayne although it wasn't much after twelve. I was the one who had got up early and done the travelling and she had suggested that I get up and go for a walk before we went to bed. I took this to mean (correctly) that she wasn't going to be up and the key was left out for me to let myself out of the gate, leave on the table and lock the house door. So here I am, having gone down past St Peter Claver School, through the town centre and sitting in the shade by the sea. I chatted with a taxi driver who spends his day with others sitting in the shade under an almond tree right by the water, and a young man who showed me a piece of jade which certainly looked as though it had come from an old necklace. He said that he had found it at a Mayan ruin and he thought it should be worth a thousand $US but that he would take $US by email from anyone that really wanted it! I said that he had better find someone from the US and that I'm English, relatively poor and I don't collect such things. It is in any case, regarded as looting here and properly so.

I walked on along the sea front and watched the birds: frigate birds, pelicans; passed a small promontory of land covered with rough trees and over a girder bridge along the route by which the Z-Line bus had come into the town; passed a place where people obviously congregate under a number of trees at a very pleasant spot and out to where the road turns away from the coast. I did a little loop at this point and returned again, through the trees to the road by the sea. Despite having gone out at seven and not returned until ten-thirty, Jayne was still in bed. The rest of the day was pretty pedestrian as Jayne didn't know what to do and didn't know what she was doing, seemingly. I didn't feel that I could just go off as I had come down to see her and not just for somewhere to stay. I came prepared for something of the sort but I did think that there would be some activities on which we could build. Jayne had gone out of her way to provide for food for the day, which was nice. I look forward to the morning when the parade takes place for Independence Day, starting at eight o'clock. This evening the two fire engines have gone past and toured the town making a lot of noise and followed by a stream of cars.

Having been up since just after six, I woke Jayne up at half past seven because she said that she wanted to go to the parade at eight o'clock. The fire engines had gone past again just before six, making just as much noise as last evening. She seems to sleep through it though. We didn't actually get out until about half past nine. We missed the assembly but we were able to see the start of the ceremony down in the town centre. Jayne misplaced her camera and wanted some video to take home so I agreed to do that but of course it meant that I wouldn't be able to take any video for myself - nor any photographs as it is very difficult to handle two cameras. None of that seemed to occur to Jayne and I didn't say anything. (I wasn't too pleased at the end of the week when she announced that Tony, the VSO working at St Peter Claver School was taking some video film for her but again, I didn't say anything.) There was a parade of the Belize Defence Force and some local cadets to the park; the presentation of the Queen of the Bay, attendants and local dignitaries. All very colourful, with lots of children and I managed to get some very nice pictures. Jayne spent most of her time making a fuss around people to make film and still pictures so I wasn't able to watch all that was going on and she was in a hurry to go once that was done.

We went on to what is called the Beach Party which took place under the patch of trees I noted yesterday, by the sea. It was very hot. I got some lovely film of local children diving into the river and bathing in the sea; obviously a very familiar element. We ate and drank out comfortably and returned about mid-afternoon when Jayne spent the rest of the day packing ready to go home, which I had encouraged her to do. The place is in a mess.

Jayne seems less decisive than ever this morning, except that she clearly wants to be on her own for the next couple of days. She was very late getting up. I am now sitting down where the beach party had been contemplating whether to go home tomorrow. It is peaceful here with the waves gently lapping against the shore. There are lots of birds around: seabirds and birds here on the land. A woodpecker is steadily tapping on a tree just a few feet away and I did bring a book to read. I called in at the Tourist Information Office which is fine if you have transport. By the time I got to the Tourist place all the buses had gone and most places, if not all, would require an overnight stay.

The saga of the lost camera went on all last evening. 'Somebody must have stolen it.' 'I must have left it somewhere.' 'I know I put it in a safe place.' 'I'll have to claim on the insurance.' 'I can't remember where I left/had/used it.' Jayne rejected and seemed resentful of all suggestions. (Jayne jumped on everything I said, then and at other times, as being patronising and treating her like a child when all I was trying to do was be gentle as after picking up an important paper she had left and saying "Would you like to put that somewhere safe?") Late at night she found the camera under the bed! How the heck had it got under the bed I wonder? A whole evening of quiet ranting which made it very difficult and very long for me - so do I go home tomorrow? I had an excellent lunch at the Mangrove Restaurant down by the sea: two large pieces of barbecued chicken, sauté potatoes, coleslaw, lettuce, tomato, Coke and a glass of water. I enjoyed that.

I got back at 4:30pm after spending the day reading in various parts of town where I could find shade which was difficult. Jayne was just about to go out - delivering, as she says. I was pleased to see that she had been getting on with sorting things out a bit which was part of the reason for my coming down but there still doesn't look to be any activity in prospect.

Jayne did seem to get her act together somewhat when she came in; some possibility of visiting schools with the District Education Officer tomorrow. Perhaps she is getting the message without my having to take direct action. She has been extremely self-centred so far, as well as indecisive. There was discussion about her CV.

Jayne and I went to the District Education Office where they were loading up with text books under the free text books for those in need scheme which is turning out to be free text books for everybody so it would have been far better to give them to the schools. I saw and heard Jayne asking if I could go. I don't know whether she had asked before but she came to say that I could go but there wouldn't be room for her. Did she know this? We set off with the books and some invitations which meant calling in to a lot of schools. Three Teachers' Supervisors from BTTC also went along to work with teachers in one or two of the schools. Back in my own element, now among Keche Maya people and schools at Crique Juge and San Jose I was able to take pictures to send to year 7. It was a very pleasant drive through attractive hills all covered in forest with a huge variety of trees and vegetation; some small plantations here and there, mostly bananas and some plantain.

San Jose Roman Catholic School is built on top of a hill. The village surrounds the school on adjacent hills. At present there is thunder rumbling in the distance. The air is not only hot and humid as it usually is, but also very, very sultry and still. An incredible peace, however brief it may turn out to be, with small sounds carrying a great distance. There must be quite a population around judging by the size of the school but all sorts of communication difficulties; dense forest, sharp hills rising several hundreds of feet; poor roads and few foot tracks; a lot of evidence of minor projects neglected, abandoned and overgrown. Now the foothills and the distant mountains are completely dominated by slate grey clouds while I stand in bright sunshine and the other three hundred degrees or so, all around, bright, white, fluffy and very still clouds. Isidoro Peck, Sebastian Mes and Nalu Umca delight in seeing their pictures on the camera screen. I had a lot of fun with these children while their teachers were occupied with the others and went on to have discussion with some Standard Six children as the storm broke but the storm didn't last long.

The village is twelve miles from the nearest road. High quality vegetables are produced; plenty in both quantity and variety of fruit; turkeys and chickens wandering freely in large numbers; all traditional houses in amongst sharply rising and closely packed hills.

We arrived back at the Education Centre at ten past four. I discovered that the leaving party they are having for Jayne is to be next Tuesday instead of Friday so no doubt that will slow things down even more. It is just as well that I am not anxious to do things but it would be nice to feel more as though my being here mattered. It has rained here too but it is dry now and much cooler - even so, we would still describe it as hot in England. For once, though, strolling back to Jayne's place, I am not sweating. Jayne was in a much better frame of mind and had progressed well during the day - all of which was good - and Tony was there when I got back. I recognised his voice from the gate right away. We chatted about this and that. It didn't seem that we had seen each other so little in the twelve months that we had been here and we arranged to go out in the evening for a drink. I went out after Tony had gone, to buy fried chicken for Jayne and I which we shared with Ellsworth, a ten year old boy who brings Johnny cakes for sale every day; that was good. He went after a pleasant meal and we continued in the same sort of way until Tony arrived. Jayne stayed and Tony and I went to the Mangrove but were driven into the Mira Mar Hotel by a sharp thunderstorm first. We came back not too late whereupon Jayne and I sat and talked until about two in the morning.

I suppose I drank quite a mixture last night, slept like a log and felt like one when I got up but I knew that it was the Belikin that threw me and I decided to have a quiet day (is that different? Perhaps I mean a day in from the sun) washing some clothes and reading. I was up at six but Jayne got up late and went down to the office at about half past eleven to work on her CV which has demanded quite a lot of my attention as well. At 4:45pm and after a phone call from Jayne, I went off down to the Mangrove to eat. The meal was tasty but that was about all that could be said for it. Mine was supposed to be Chow Mein but the pasta was spaghetti and there were no noodles. An awful lot of vegetables were mixed in; the spaghetti was cold; the quantity wasn't very good; and there was very little chicken, certainly not for the $24 total. Jayne had sweet and sour vegetable, again with spaghetti! I spent the rest of the evening reading while Jayne sorted out some papers - which I was pleased to see her do but there was no conversation. She went to bed saying that she wanted to go to the office early.

I could open the door from the inside and close it on the latch but not the gate and I had never been offered a key. I got up at six and expected Jayne to be earlier because she had said that she wanted to make an early start. When I called her by offering a cup of tea at 8:00am it was refused. In the end, I took advantage of someone calling for her from outside. Tea was offered because Jayne had complained about the last (of many) coffees I had made. As it turned out, the cause of the bad taste was her having put milk powder in the sugar which had gone off! I did all the washing up and Jayne's food preparation is much reduced!

So, at ten o'clock, I am heading gently south and other than that, I don't know where the road goes. I will need to be back for four o'clock because I said that I would film someone who rides a three wheel bicycle by pedalling it by hand, and who had written a poem for Jayne. She wanted him to read this so that she could have it on film. So here we go with what is left of this day; missed all the buses again. It is hot and not much breeze. I must make sure that I find enough shade and water; crossed over a small concrete bridge which is extremely well built on two large I-section steel beams located underneath. As the heat of the day progresses it is very quiet and the only real movement is the variety of butterflies, mainly yellow and yellow through to white, all with different markings on them and some shades of brown. I guess that the water under the bridge may be part-river, part creek as it is fairly still and deep but it is also a clear brown colour. Quite close to what I take for the guiding lights to the airstrip, the road meets a tee junction. To the left, it must go back to the sea for, despite a left curve in this road a little way back, it is still heading south. To the right it looks as though there may be the airfield - or maybe not. Maybe these are not guiding lights but warning lights. Guiding lights are on the ground and not on masts. As I get closer I can see that there are nineteen tall, slender masts, some with blinking lights on the top. This turns out to be an establishment of the United States International Broadcasting Bureau; the Belize Relay Station. There is a V and an A with a World symbol in between - so VOA - presumably Voice of America. Underneath, Welcome. Visitors by appointment only; a guard hut; a drop gate for vehicles; and a high fence topped with barbed wire all the way round quite a large acreage. The road goes into it and not past it so, obviously, I'm not going that way.

So, left at the tee instead of right, past the 'No Trespassing' notice which applies to adjacent land and which says 'violators will be prosecuted'. Never seen that word used on a notice before. The boundary is planted with coconut palms behind which is a stand of dense hardwood with quite a lot of trumpet trees interspersed. Sadly, this road also turns into private property with the same funny notice. There are quite a number of boats in there as it is right by the sea. A fairly large house on the property with a very large dish aerial of the kind designed for satellite use. The whole estate, if that is what it is, must be quite large. Pity that there was no warning of this earlier on as the only way back is the way I came. Come to think of it, Jayne has made no effort to show me round except to go where she wanted to go. The investment on those two branches of the tee explains the unusual strength and quality of the bridge that I had crossed.

A small track leads off towards the sea back down by the bend in the road so I wander off down that way. It is all grass covered and with only small evidence of vehicle wheels passing occasionally over it. I pass a variety of wooden houses and the end of a number of communicating lanes running north-south. It is very nice to walk here without any concern for safety and I really do think that this is the friendliest place I have found in Belize. I don't think that would be just Punta Gorda but in this part of Toledo as the same friendliness is evident in the villages I visited on Wednesday. There is a nice bit of breeze as I approach the sea and the track reaches the water's edge at about twelve feet above it. A healthy barrier in the event of a hurricane! Brimstone yellow butterflies are fluttering all over the place; water, beautifully clear, gently lapping against the shore; even a small strip of sand. A greater variety of butterflies: orange and black now, ranging in size from tiny to huge. Moving along the coast between there and the houses back towards the town centre, the route takes in the cemetery before reaching the road again where stands the rather attractive Punta Gorda Hospital. Back at the edge of the sea, a good fifteen foot drop. Wild flowers growing as weeds, absolutely beautiful: scarlet and purples and yellows with, of course, a huge variety of trees having leaves anything from a foot across down to needles and from roundish shape and waxy surface like the almond, down to lush brilliant green and limp; leaves grouped like rosettes to those arranged like a single stemmed ladder; deep, dark green through to the bright colour we know in spring. The air is full of scent; a lovely part of the town.

Back on the sea front, in town, a lot of people are carrying fish so I guess that the morning's catch was good. I sat and had a Coke and bought a litre and a half bottle of water in one of the cafes on the main street where I was approached by a little girl who wanted to sell beads. She told me all about her living on her own in Santa Elena and having come into town on her own, have to go back on her own. Sadly, it was a pack of lies and I told her that I didn't believe her story (which changed a bit). I did give her $1-50 but I would have given her more if she had told me the truth. I saw her meet up with the woman she was operating with; interesting that she had blue eyes; also the remains of nail varnish; nice dress and earrings; and a nice little day sack but no shoes. I went in to see Bernie who had returned from Belize City for a meeting with the appropriate Minister and off with the entourage round the villages. Now this one here Minister.....!!

Visited the Mayan craft centre. Bought two nice embroidered pieces and three bookmarks for $59 but left $60. Had fried fish with rice and beans and potato salad for lunch which was very nice indeed followed by papaya juice with milk. I am now walking slowly off to go and find the Z-Line bus station to check on the time for Sunday morning. Punta Caliente Restaurant and Hotel was where I went with Jayne on Monday after going in to town; where we were the only customers and had just gone in for a coke and were being pressurised to buy food. Next is the Travellers' Inn which is a rather snazzy looking place with Z-Line buses beyond. All of this is in fact, behind the hospital where I walked on the other side this morning. Tickets are bought at the office which is evidently situated in the Travellers' Inn. Most odd! It is all closed right now. Who'd be a traveller? So now I will note the route from Jayne's place. I doubt that she is home so I will then wander down to the town and find some shade.

As I pass it is all locked up as I expected. Gosh it is hot. I must find some shade and I am damned if I am going to go and ask for the key; head back for the sea and some shade.

Sitting for a while in the shade opposite the Mangrove there is a lovely cool sea breeze. I am now walking out towards the bridge and on to the little spot where the beach party was and where I can read some more for a while in the shade of the trees. The tide, such as it is, is high and the water is clear. It is very pleasant at the bridge: fish swimming; three iridescent pipe-fish immediately - four - five, and a whole lot more regular shaped fish of different varieties and sizes; quite a few wading birds even in this heat - mostly small ones. Down by where the 'beach' is there are lots of posts sticking up out of the sea on which a great variety of sea birds rest including cormorants which I always like to see, both grey and black. I guess this bit was once an enclosed swimming area for children but all that remains is the posts, some bits of wire netting and stones. Peaceful though; cool in the breeze and shady; fine for reading before I wander back to take the promised film for which I shall start off from here just before a quarter to four. It is now twenty-five to three. I took the film for her and found that the one event which Jayne had been arranging for tomorrow (fishing) was off so I decided to go home in the morning.

I left on the 9:00am Z-Line on which the brakes barely worked and the bus had to be stopped on the engine. I suspect a combination of worn linings or pads and low air pressure.

The journey was very pleasant despite the length and I enjoyed the view from the windows all the way. There was a change of bus at Dangriga which broke down at Belmopan and the journey was completed on a Batty bus. I managed to fit in a visit to the Bank at the Belcan Roundabout by Savu and caught the

Escalante bus for Orange Walk just after six, arriving at about seven thirty. Not the best of weeks but I did what I set out to do - to visit and try to encourage Jayne. Whether it was worth it is barely even questionable.

It was good to have a quiet weekend enjoying being at home, washing clothes and sorting things out indoors; catching up with my journal, doing some more washing, shopping and going to the Library. It wasn't until Tuesday that I went in to St Peter's so as to make sure that Bernard wouldn't expect me too often and to leave him a note…

'Here are two of the books you need. The other two are sold out so I have ordered them. They are Caribbean Social Studies Book 5 and Once a Week Comprehension Book 3. You should have them in a week or so. Do not expect to see me often. I am very short of time but I will not forget you. Work hard, listen and try to understand your lessons. It takes time and a lot of effort - and only you can do it for yourself. That makes you special if you think about it.'

A number of volunteers had expressed concern (that I did not share) that a tragic event had not been acknowledged by VSO, perhaps mainly in consideration of worried relatives…

'I do not wish to be associated with any criticism of VSO action following the murder of a Raleigh Volunteer. I do find it deeply disturbing but, frankly, I believe that it is part of a much bigger problem in Belize which is really a question of the social fabric and I do not see how our local office could be 'proactive' in a way which doesn't place impossible restrictions on movement. No doubt pressure could be brought to bear on responsible authority by HQs of voluntary organisations working in concert but that is another matter. I work in an area where there has been a large number of murders, rapes and robberies but, if all reports and warnings were to result in no go areas nothing would get done, and that is not an exaggeration. I can tell you that international concern is alive. I have had a number of letters on the subject from England and perhaps the appropriate Minister should know that but I still don't see what you could do or have done. If I did, I would have said so long since.'

'…Hi Max: next Wednesday at 1:30 p.m., we will be having the Annual General Meeting of the Corozal Town Branch of the Belize National Teachers' Union at the Corozal Methodist School. About 115 teachers are expected to attend. This is a great opportunity for us to sell the New Comprehensive Curriculum and for other teachers (from about 15 schools) to be aware of what is going on in some classrooms. I am therefore, inviting you to address the gathering and beg that you limit your speech to 7 - 10 minutes. I am presently drafting up the agenda and would be pleased with an early, favourable reply. Thanks in advance, Henry…'

This I did, covering philosophy, goals and specifications; ending with implementation. I met the National President of the union who was enthusiastic and had an enjoyable lunch of traditional rice and beans potato salad and stewed chicken in a local restaurant. Mail again…

'…Sorry to hear that your computer is in hospital and that you will soon be out of what must have been a long and trying time with it. I had the news from Philip. Not having contact couldn't happen at a worse time. No point in going into that but I need to hear from you - and there may well be correspondence (and parcels) on the way. I last heard on 5th September. An email link is essential now. Three of the schools that Year 7 will be working with have email access of one sort or another and I have less than two terms to ensure that the link is enduring and able to grow. What has happened to the school machines and email or internet use? Can I help in any way? Is there another address you could use in the meantime? I daresay Philip would oblige but I don't like to ask him from here. He has homework to do and he writes regularly already. Other children use the post. The whole potential of the project has become so exciting now that delay would be tragic (overuse of the word but the benefits for children could be very great indeed). You suggested in your last mail that you may not have received all mail. I have copies of everything sent both ways so I can help there. Enclosed is a complete email record from 12th August. If you would like details of the first three subjects or any supporting documents mentioned please let me know. The letter for year seven was sent as an attachment. The story 'Hey Buddy Wait for me!' is an encapsulation of the introduction to the new linking classes for year seven. Also enclosed is a copy of the contents of a large parcel which I am posting today. This was referred to in one of the email docs. I hope it will prove useful. All items are to be used as you see fit except to keep the video after copying and one or two more personal items identified in the list…'

On Friday I went to Corozal on the Chell bus leaving Orange Walk at 7:15am. As they know me well now it was a great welcome on the bus and I was dropped off right opposite the entrance to Santa Rita and the Christian Assembly of God School. After their assembly outside I worked with Standard Five and Six who will be linking with Year Seven. The introduction to the linking actually took over an hour and was based on the story 'Hey Buddy Wait for me!' I left copies for all the children and their teacher to give them a start for ideas. After that I spent some time with the teachers who are working with the new curriculum and head teacher Tomas Zetina drove me into Corozal Town.

My first call in the town was to St. Francis Xavier Parish Office to obtain 100 copies of 'Hey Buddy Wait for me!' for the children. I then went on to Corozal Methodist where I had lunch and talked with the linking children there, also leaving copies of 'Hey Buddy'. Then it was the meeting of principals and teachers involved in the new curriculum. This would have been a much better meeting if the document which should have been available six weeks ago had arrived. I was able to give copies of 'Hey Buddy' to Orvin Rancheran and Valerie Rogers for the two other schools linking with Year Seven - that is Calcutta and St Pauls. I am still at a loss to know properly what to do about Louisiana and La Immaculada because I haven't heard from SMCC for five weeks following their computer breakdown.

Hey Buddy! Wait for me!

Imagine.....
…if a friend in your class is to travel to England to go to school there for a few weeks, make new friends, live in a different environment and see new places…
What would you do?
How could your friend help you to share in the experience and what would you do to help him or her to get ready to go?
Imagine......
…if that friend came back with a friend from England to live here and go to your school for a while…
What would you want the English friend to take back home to England? What experiences would you share? How could you make it so that all your class can take part?
Imagine.....
…if it could be done … It is expensive for children to travel so far and it is too much to ask a twelve year old to live so far from home. But it is possible to have the experience.
What you need is a Buddy.
Imagine.....
…a special soft toy making the journey as your friend; all the same arrangements could be made; all the same experiences; all the new friends; all the new places; returning with an English Buddy and then back again as many times as you like. The only difference is that the Buddy's friends would have to do all the arranging. Buddies don't write; they don't make things; nor do they collect things - well, not very well!
Imagine, your Buddy.....
…needing a letter of introduction, a passport, travel tickets, some knowledge of the journey, a book to read, a diary, money, baggage and personal items.
You might like to send descriptions of yourselves, families etc. personal letters to pupils in the school; photographs and drawings; things that you use which show what life is like in Belize; postcards; maps; drawings of buildings; reports of events and celebrations. There is a whole host of things that help people to imagine what life is like in a different country. Children could take it in turns to take the Buddy home, on outings, to parties etc., entertain him or her as a friend and 'help' to complete the diary!
Imagine, how all of your schoolwork.....
…could be shared in some way from Belize to England and back. Letters and stories come in Language Arts; shopping, measurements of spaces, graphs and charts (pets, interests etc.), maps and the natural world come in Maths and Science; Technology could provide a home for the Buddies while in the classroom or a miniature bed at home; Social Studies is all about your home country which is of interest to others; and Creative Arts is full of possibilities for sharing interests and talent across the Atlantic.
Hey Buddy! Wait for me!
I want to play.
Let's be ready… Elect a Buddy right now and get ready for the journey; make new friends; have new experiences; and learn about each other.

Hey Buddy! Wait for me!

The weekend was mostly domestic and letter writing. I ran out of gas at 5:15pm on Saturday which was a nuisance. I couldn't get an answer from Alonzo's so I tried Belize Gas. They said that they would come round but didn't seem to know where South Main Street is. I rang again at 5:45 but whoever answered the phone couldn't be bothered and put it down. I then asked Elizabeth next door if she had a spare cylinder. She had and Landy brought it round. I left my empty one under the steps out of sight and Landy stayed for a few beers. He was called home and went saying that he would be back. I am sure that I locked the gate when I decided that he wasn't coming, locked the house and eventually went to bed.

It wasn't until late afternoon on Sunday that I noted that the cylinder was missing. The gate was pulled to but unlocked. At first I thought that Landy may have collected the cylinder but he hadn't. It had been stolen. As I am almost certain that I locked the gate someone must have been both watching and had climbed the high wall and fence because that would be the only way of opening the gate without forcing it. My chief suspect is a rather unpleasant character who came round trying to sell models made of wire and to whom I foolishly gave the water he asked for. He was in the house before I turned round and difficult to get rid of. I didn't want to finish up thumping him. Ironically the models were scorpions.

I met with Bertha at the office where I spent all day. No documents arrived and I spent the last part of the afternoon getting the new digital copier working (successfully); had lunch at the Crystal, posted the letters from the weekend and went to the Library for two more books.

The next morning was spent catching up on letters to Year Seven and creating new files and a disc so that they can be sent as attachments to print as written. After that I went down to the office, found that no documents had arrived and went on to the Crystal for lunch. Lunch there is a good deal at $3 for a good meal of rice and beans, salad and meat. Today, I had pork and a glass of cold juice (50c). In the afternoon I went down to the office again to phone VSO about my gas tank and EDC. David had sorted out my budget with Louisa which was one thing that I had to do. He also advised that any holiday not taken for reasons of work could be claimed as money at the end of the posting. It really does sound as though Ellajean has gone.

I wonder what will happen next. Documents arrived for Social Studies and Expressive Arts Units of Works. Shopping was for food and more airmail envelopes as the last 100 are all used up and email news had arrived…

'…Philip brought me your message - that was really nice. There are so many pupils on line now that it would be worth my while compiling a school 'address book'. You should have just returned from your hols - I hope things went well. Let me know what you got up to. I have received a message from Henry Neal (Corozal Methodist School), but unfortunately I was unable to reply promptly. As soon as I have finished this letter I will send him a quick message to let him know I have not forgotten. Hopefully this will be the start of regular links. I am about to start work on this year's link- firstly with the new intake, and then with the pupils who made contact last year. I will send further details in my next letter…'

'…A school address book will be really good. I will also answer any correspondence sent to me. Actually, that would be a great help because it is an indicator of what children really want to know. You should now have a whole heap of email from me to answer. I have sent copies by regular mail but, if you think you are short of anything let me know as it is no trouble to bring you right up to date. I'm very pleased that you got the wall map okay. You can imagine that it was quite a problem to send. I have just posted a very large parcel full of things which I think you will find interesting and which are intended to challenge the ideas you might have. There is also a great deal of film, slides and photos. Also, in respect of ideas I have included an attachment of the sheet I use to introduce the linking to new pupils. You may find it useful. Please let me know if you can read it okay. I may have more trouble reading any attachments from you because mine is the machine Charles Babbage was just getting round to developing when he died...'

The few documents that arrived were delivered which was all such that could be done for the remainder of the week although it was time to write to VSO Country Director again…

'…I have been thinking hard about the VSO Central Project Fund in respect of the 'Linking' of schools. I have reorganised the project in the light of the experience of the last twelve months which would present a much stronger case but I don't think I would be happy even to apply in view of the probable need of some of the other countries that VSOs work. Just a thought: Is there any possibility of a second local grant as a new year has started? I would expect you to say no but I would kick myself, otherwise, for not having asked! The basis of the change is to concentrate on schools which have a stable staff and who are able to involve a whole year group. Stable staff is necessary to maintain continuity and enable the project to be enduring of itself when I go home. Involving a whole year group enables the exchange to involve all parts of curriculum and school life. The two big schools (Louisiana and Immaculada) that do not meet this will be able to continue their contact as pen-pals; one way of ensuring that the youngsters involved don't lose out. Calcutta and St Pauls continue with the link established and are starting new classes this year. The two new schools are Christian Assembly of God at Santa Rita, Corozal and Corozal Methodist School. All of those are stable. The Principals all know each other; I work with all of them anyway and they form a cluster which could, with the growing interest of the District Office, provide some spin-off for other schools. Some staff at St Pauls and Methodist schools have access to email although the schools do not themselves, have computers and Calcutta is well fixed as you know. My interest now, is for Christian Assembly of God. They are all good schools - full of life. Attached for your interest is the introduction I wrote for this year's students taking part…'

I set off for Belize City on the 7:30 Urbina bus with a driver and conductor that I know well; my favourite seat behind the driver, where I can see ahead and all the way round; and plenty of space on the bus it being Friday morning. Just on the edge of the Louisiana area of Orange Walk Town we came up behind a Venus bus and the touting for passengers began; this accompanied by signalling ahead using the air horn, no wonder Belize is so noisy in the towns and along the roadways, and we shot past the Venus bus by bouncing over one of the sleeping policemen at too high a speed and on the wrong side of the road while the Venus bus was negotiating it in the proper manner on the right side (literally). As a result, we picked up one extra passenger and, of course, giving the Venus bus the time to get back in front.

As we approached the junction for Guinea Grass and Shipyard the Venus bus was already there whilst we still had the best part of half a mile to go. That was when our air horn started blaring again to attract passengers away from the Venus bus which was a regular and would therefore stop for anyone who wanted to get on throughout the length of the journey, to ours which was (allegedly) an Express and would take less time by not stopping. No-one did want to get on our bus. The Venus bus got away ahead and after a little hesitation, slowing down and looking round to see if he had missed anyone our driver sought to pick up speed again.

Unfortunately, one passenger who was a Mennonite was waiting at the front of the bus to get off so that he could travel on to Shipyard from there. In his haste to find new passengers, our driver hadn't noticed this; neither had the conductor who was just as absorbed in the game as the driver. This was an embarrassment for the driver of course, and one which he resolved by firmly informing the passenger that this was an Express which is not scheduled to stop and he would have to wait until the next time it does. It was not until we reached the Toll Bridge that the bus stopped which meant that the passenger would have a mile or so to walk back. In that respect, he was lucky because the stop after that would be another forty miles unless it was for a friend of the driver.

Evidently, we could stop for someone getting on (which is more money in fares) but not for someone getting off. This is common practice and, indeed, a policy of the bus operators that the drivers and conductors hide behind and practised by people who are otherwise reasonable and helpful. What makes it even more sad for me is that it should happen to a Mennonite - a member of a hard working community whose contribution to the Belizean economy is second to none and whose life style (albeit somewhat insular) is an example worth following. (Passengers are led to expect that an Express is not supposed to stop at all between the outskirts of Orange Walk Town and the Outskirts of Belize City.) The rest of the journey was interesting but uneventful. I switched buses as usual in Belize City, down by the Belcan Roundabout and Angelus Press, to pick up the local shuttle going in to St John's College, University College of Belize and Belize Teachers' College where the Curriculum Development Centre is located.

I delivered the books which Jayne had asked me to take to Lisa; delivered a book and some cloth which Bertha had asked me to give to Priscilla; returned a book to the Library for Bertha and renewed another one. Otherwise it was catching up with the news and eventually leaving at about quarter to one, and walking over to the family where they were getting ready to go to Chetumal. I had lunch, had a phone call from Jack and wandered over there to pick up the tape he had collected for me from Love FM, a tape for Marco and a set of First Day Covers of the email year Commemorative stamps which he has given me, which is nice and then spent a lazy evening watching television which I enjoyed enormously.

I got up at about six to start my house-sitting which is late enough in this part of the world, and pottered around getting myself ready for the day. Fed the two budgerigars; fed the two parrots; fed the four dogs; had some breakfast and watched BBC World for an hour - a wonderful programme covering the struggle between the Vatican and the USSR through this century called 'A Struggle for Paradise'. At 9:15 I decided that it was time to shut up the house and wander off down into Belize City. I spent the whole morning in the centre of town, first going to the Korean shop to see if I could get a personal cd player which I couldn't, and another shop where I had the same problem. They told me that I could possibly get one in Brodies so I headed in that direction, first calling in to Angelus Press to have a look at their books. $440 was the price in Brodies so I said thank you very much and left it. The bookshop down by Barclays Bank was very depressing by the state of the books they had for sale - still at full price. I was unable to get E45 cream and there was no Food Festival at the Cathedral this year. Disappointment all round so far! I did find the Government Book Store which was very interesting for an hour and then had a pleasant walk back along the sea front to the mouth of the 'river' which is really the exit of Haulover Creek. I returned again from the South side, over the temporary bridge, and went back to Angelus Press where I bought a book for Richard on the flora and fauna of the Caribbean Seas and the Coral Reef, a Belize Cook Book for Janice and a small cook book for myself. Then went back into the Korea shop where I bought a new video tape and a cleaner for the cd drive on the computer. I was pleased with that as it may well solve my playing problem instead of buying a personal cd. The computer drive has been skipping uncontrollably, such that I had to stop using it. It is certainly a lot cheaper at $22 and bought at the assistant's suggestion after explaining the problem. I came back and had $3 chicken from Li Chee, had a lazy hour or so and then went off to buy a bottle of Whisky with a tricorn glass tumbler for Tabo's birthday, a couple of bottles of Coke and some Gillette razors which I have not been able to get recently. Arranged to go to Church with the Coleman family at 6:45 tomorrow morning and then spent a lazy time watching television again. It is amazing how many British programmes there are on. I watched the Antiques Road Show and Top Gear and I am looking forward to watching 'How Green was my Valley' this evening.

Got up at quarter to six and went off with the Colemans at quarter to seven for the seven o'clock Communion Service and Harvest in St Mary's Church; a good service which was about being thankful, acknowledging the things that people do for us and giving people time, especially children. A good opportunity in respect of the children was lost by the Priest as two children were wandering around the whole of the front of the church, in and out behind the altar, and inspecting the fruits and flowers. A practical demonstration might have been a good idea but he really was engrossed in his delivery and I don't suppose such a thing would have occurred to him in those circumstances.

We came back and I fed the four dogs, the two budgerigars and the two parrots, had breakfast and then pottered around for a bit. It is extremely hot still. I have enjoyed watching television but I miss my computer. I wonder what mail there is and, though I haven't done so lately, I would like to go out on my bike. Went out for a walk which took me down to the waterfront, back up along Princess Margaret Avenue and along by BTL to pick up some $3 chicken again, a couple of bottles of Coke and a small bottle of rum to settle down for the evening.

It was a good weekend but it is always nice to get home. I caught the four o'clock Venus and had an uneventful journey arriving back at about five thirty. Mario had arrived back from San Joaquin for his working week in Belize City. I stayed and chatted to him for about an hour before setting off. Tabo phoned about an hour later to say thanks and that they were home safely. Neria's tooth operation was successful but she has to have the stitches out on the 31st.

Sorted out the domestics after the weekend and did some shopping in the morning; arranged to go to St. Paul's on Friday afternoon after the staff meeting in Corozal and to Calcutta tomorrow, Wednesday, both to discuss 'linking' with children and curriculum with staff. I will spend as much time as possible with students at Calcutta, on the computer. On my way back I met with Bernard, or rather, he caught me up and greeted me from behind, having just come out of school for lunch time, and asked when I would be going to 'my school' (good sign). I said I would go in on Thursday so that sorts out this week. This afternoon I went to San Jose Nuevo Palmar RC School for their staff meeting, a mini-workshop on handwriting.

I arrived at Calcutta before the school day started so I was able to get right on to the computer but found that the phone was out of order for some reason so I was unable to pursue the email facility. The real work started with three girls from Standard Six, learning to switch on and off and to use Word for Windows. This was interrupted but I used that time to go through the introduction with Standard Five and Standard Six separately.

Lunch with Orvin and Adelaide was fish which he had caught at the weekend off Caye Caulker. Apparently I had missed the trip as I had set off for Belize to house sit and he didn't phone until Friday evening. After lunch, the three girls continued their practice and were followed by three boys. I suggested that these six be given further time in pairs, preferably boy/girl and then work individually with other members of the class.

Thursday morning started with some washing and finishing off my journal for the weekend which was recorded on tape. This continues to be a very useful way of working as it means that more detail is included and with the accuracy of being closer to the event. Maybe I will write the book. There wouldn't be any shortage of material for detail description to lend authenticity; also arranged with Barbara to go in to see Bernard at 2:00pm this afternoon.

Bertha phoned to say that more documents had arrived and she would be delivering. I arranged to meet her at St. Peter's at about 2:30 after seeing Bernard. In fact, Bernard didn't leave until 3:15 despite the children having been dismissed at 2:30 in favour of a staff meeting. We had an interesting discussion about why I came to see him, families and what he would like to do, all aimed at improving his self-image. He had some homework to do so we worked hard on that. It was a ghastly homework of two exercises, each of ten questions, changing the subject of a sentence from masculine to feminine and from feminine to masculine. There was only one that he could do without some prompting and some of the questions I had to think about myself. Anyway, he went away happy, with the information he needed to do his homework and at that point, of course, he was keen to go and do it. I waited around for a while and, as Bertha didn't arrive, I called at Louisiana on my way home and found her there. The Louisiana teachers are suffering the lack of support and involvement of their Principal or Vice Principal as both have been changed, the Principal twice, since the Workshop. Except for the hard work put in by some of the staff, my inclination is to drop them from the programme. Email…

'…You will be pleased to hear that I am beginning to make regular contact with Henry Neal, and have started work on the link with the new year-seven. You will also be pleased to hear that many of the SM pupils still remember you…'

'…I need to hear from you for many reasons, not the least of which is that I am at a loss to decide what to do for the best for each school, including yours, and I am finding it difficult to know what to write in letters to year seven. You haven't said whether you can read the attachments okay. Until you do, I will go ahead on the assumption that you can. I have letters to send from Calcutta as they are not fully up and running with their computer yet. I would appreciate any time you can manage before going to the Lake District. I hope you enjoy the trip anyway, as I am sure you will. I have heard about it from a couple of youngsters who are going…'

Some things change rapidly so another email was sent to follow…

'I am currently trying to write the next letter to Year Seven; also, a set of letters from Calcutta which they have been trying (unsuccessfully) to send to you by email. When you get the letters they will be in the form of an attachment ready for you to print and copy right away. There will also be some comments from me, about life for children in Belize based on my reading of the letters as I type them. I suggest that my comments and ALL the letters should be read by ALL of the children in Year Seven and Year Eight. This would be a good way of understanding some of the sameness and yet difference of children here and their lives, experience and environment. I also suggest that a letter be prepared for each of the schools by one or more of the children in each of your forms and sent by email to me for delivery. This to make up for lost time. The purpose and content of the letter should reflect what children expect to get out of the link as they see it. Each would need to be a substantial letter for everyone in the receiving school to read. I am quite prepared to get them copied. My time is very limited now. I am coming home at the end of April so we have a term and a half to ensure that the Link is enduring. I will do whatever is necessary. It is important to me but more important is the enormous benefit in young people understanding each other. More and more I have come to see this as important beyond comprehension. The 'Sir' that the South Molton children remember that you mention is somewhat chastened! I came to learn but, as always, my expectations are not only met but enlarged with more questions than I came with! The youngsters here are amazing and have just as much to give as any. Now about some of the questions you asked…

There are books in the parcel I have just sent which will help with the flora and fauna although I would think that Guiana would be little different from Belize as it is quite close. I was a little closer recently as I spent a week in Punta Gorda, way down South in Toledo District. The main difference would probably have to do with the Cayes and the 200 mile Barrier Reef off the Belize coast, and the sea life it supports. (If you find the funds and the opportunity to come out here you will have to get a move on. You can stay here if you want to, or I can fix you up with a family.)

I intend to send a letter about food to Year Seven. For now, tostadas and garnaches are both built on fried (crisp) corn tortillas. Both have peppers, onion slices and sliced salad piled on top but garnaches have stewed chicken as well. There are garnishes as well of course, and sometimes tomato slices.

I often find people asleep on my shoulder on buses but I have to admit that my patience is somewhat shorter with men! I push them off after a few minutes and am tempted to shove them into the gangway. I am only prevented from doing so by the (probably innocent) belief that it means nothing more than a convenient place to rest the head. Even so, I have my own inbuilt English 'complex' to deal with!

178

I expect you are right about the North of Mexico. It is a big country. However, nasty things are going on just now at the border with the US and I expect that the Mexicans at large would in some ways wish it further. My interest ends with the Yucatan Peninsula. I have always been more of a 'liver' in places rather than a 'traveller'. Something my fellow VSOs find difficult to understand.

The Doctor Fly is a nasty brute; quite large, not unlike a horse fly but light brown in colour. It has usually done its business by the time you feel it or spot it. Everyone reacts quite strongly and it is regarded as much the biggest 'pain' of all the insects here. I react more than most to most bites and as you will have read, the affected part swells up very painfully. A few days ago, I was caught in both feet which became very uncomfortable. Fortunately, I killed the beast before it really did too much damage. I expect there is a 'proper name' for it. I will try to find out more but the locals have little use for catalogue names. They already know what they are talking about…'

The District Office was all locked up in Corozal on Friday so Bertha and Louisa and I held our meeting until 11:15 in the Xavier Parish office. Afterwards, as Louisa had to go, Bertha and I went on to Methodist to talk with Henry Neal, Bertha went back on the bus at about twelve and I went for lunch. In the afternoon, I had discussions with Valerie Rogers about the curriculum and then led the two classes, Standard V and Standard VI with some ideas about linking, using the paper 'Hey Buddy… Wait for Me!

The morning dawned bright and sunny after five dull days - the first since coming to Belize. I suppose 'dull' is misleading even now, because there were periods of bright sunshine and the light is strong even when it is dull but there has been a tremendous amount of rain. Today is sunny with the occasional ten minute shower to remind us all that it is still the rainy season and good for a weekend reading, writing and visiting; and to Corozal Methodist School…

'…Hi Henry, Congratulations to you all on your promotion of the canteen programme on Love FM. It came at just the right time in the broadcast and, I thought, would give hope and inspiration to those who would like to become involved. The gentle encouragement of the new administration was brilliant! I could go on but I guess you know what I think of what you have done in your own school already. One thing for certain: the children and staff of South Molton Community College would be very interested; starting with your description on air, the song and poems. It sounds as though there is a great deal more too. South Molton is a very generous town. You never know where that might lead…'

Monitoring began for pilot implementation of the new National Curriculum at lower division in the next week. There will be seven monthly cycles of visits to schools. During each cycle, each Teacher will be visited twice and monitoring will be for a period of one hour per visit. Field Officers Louisa and Bertha, and I would share the visits while mine is an overall role as Coordinator. We determined that our schedule would rotate such that Louisa and Bertha would visit all teachers at some point; theirs would be the responsibility when I go home.

First there was washing and shopping to do on Monday morning and an account to pay at BTL. After that I typed up some letters from Calcutta to send email and sorted out all the Curriculum documents before getting ready to go to Louisiana for a staff meeting to try to get their thinking back on track after their having so many staff changes including the Principal and Vice Principal. That appeared to be successful although I am not impressed by the new Principal (who evidently wanted to be District Education Officer - such is the pumped up view of themselves which people have after their party wins the election!). Then I set up my arrangements for the rest of the week, changed two Library books in the evening and settled down to more typing of letters.

Went to St Peter's as arranged and completed monitoring for Learning Environment and Resources for Infant 1, Infant 2 and Standard 1and discussing the result with the Principal. After that I spent an hour or so with Bernard's class at Standard V; a difficult class which the teacher needs to sit on. All were taking part and behaving properly by the end of the time.

The day at Calcutta Government School was with Infant 1 and a mixed Infant 2/Standard 1. I went to lunch with Orvin and spent the remainder of the morning and the whole of the afternoon working with Students on the computer although I didn't manage to get on line. I did repair the telephone though! St Paul's visit was a repeat of that at Calcutta.

With no schools to visit on Friday I set off on my bike and went to Honey Camp Lagoon. According to Landy Burns this is about twelve miles. If it is, the whole trip must have been nearly thirty as I made a couple of exploratory detours and went on into the Freshwater Forest Reserve. The direction is South East from Orange Walk, first crossing the bridge over the New River and a mile along the San Estevan road before turning right. By then you are in the forest, or at least, a semi cleared part of it but still dense with trees except in the small places where the cane fields are. It really was a beautiful and most enjoyable ride. Fine and sunny as always of course, and the birds and butterflies were about; also, a huge number of lizards of all sizes – big, small, fat, thin, long, short; some standing tall to run, others almost horizontal. Lots of pipefish as well as more regularly shaped varieties where the track passes over Doubloon Bank Lagoon at the neck of its two parts and brilliantly clear water full of small fish by the shore at Honey Camp. I will have to take my costume next time. I did go in for a paddle to cool off all exposed skin as the sun was fierce and I should have used some sun cream - and worn a hat but I had done neither. The water at Honey Camp Lagoon is a pale green and wonderfully warm and both lagoons, though large, have no rivers flowing in to them. The water comes in through the underground limestone from the Maya Mountains eighty to a hundred miles away. The track was almost deserted but, as one or two people do live out there I was able to greet a couple of people and have conversation with a couple more. This is always a good thing to do apart from being friendly, because it means that people know that you have passed by and it adds to the safety. There have been a lot of attacks on lonely tracks and roads. Anyway, if you merely try to be safe you would do nothing, I think. When I got to Landy's place by the lagoon I saw the guy that lives on the other side of the track and looks after it for him. He speaks only Spanish and I speak only English but we managed to converse reasonably well. He gave me water to drink and a bag of tiny and very sweet bananas just picked for lunch. They were just the job. I must have eaten ten of them. Two bites each and delicious. A fisherman poled his way across the water to where I had stopped. How he manages to stand up in an open log canoe which is very narrow and no more than a couple of inches out of the water is a mystery to me but he was so skilled and confident he might just as well have been standing on dry land and not moving at all.

There have been reports for some time, of Hurricane Mitch gathering strength and threatening islands in the Caribbean.

Hurricane Mitch

24th October Saturday

Ready for the weekend, I woke up this morning to the sound of a woodpecker working on the dead coconut tree in the garden outside my front bedroom window. Like all sounds through the windows which have no glass in them it is much louder than I expect and it seems as though it might actually be reducing the house timbers! Also, direction is difficult to determine and it is only through knowledge of the tree that I am able to work out what is going on as I surface out of sleep. The bird is one of those with a greyish brown body and brilliant scarlet head. It is amazing how they vary the speed of their attack on the wood. Sometimes it is so fast that the stroboscopic effect makes it look as though the head has stopped moving. At others, the rate looks slow but the sound belies what the eyes seem to see. Maybe the speed has risen above the stroboscopic frequency like a wheel appearing to rotate backwards. When I went to look later, there was quite a substantial hole already starting. Hurricane Mitch continues to gather strength and is attracting more than the usual attention in Belize. I stayed in, always with plenty to do but with an ear to the little radio I brought with me. Next morning things moved on…

25th October Sunday

Preliminary warning given today for Hurricane Mitch, a category four with sustained winds of 150 miles an hour and strengthening. Current predictions point towards Northern Belize and points further North on the Yucatan Peninsula. If it comes it is likely to be Wednesday or Thursday but there should be a better picture forming by tomorrow afternoon. One red flag is flying over the Police Station and the National Emergency Committee has met. All members of the Belize Defence Force have been called to work. I will have to find out where to go if it hits from the local authorities tomorrow. Your own house is not considered safe in anything over category two so I suppose I had better take notice. Mark Wright, VSO Director, phoned tonight to check which was much appreciated. I hope it doesn't and I am wrong for the sake of Belize but I have had a feeling about this for some time and I am expecting it to come this way. Another day in!

26th October Monday

I went to Louisiana this morning and saw six teachers in their classes which I just finished by lunch time when the school was closed. All schools are now closed until the hurricane emergency is over.

It has just been announced at midday that Hurricane Mitch is now a category 5 hurricane with sustained winds of 170 mph. This is the highest category and Hattie which did so much damage was only category 3; it started to rain again just before midday and it is now coming down in vertical stair rods; very heavy but it is going to be much worse. I don't expect there will be any more school activity this week.

The rain lasted for about an hour and was very heavy with near rivers running everywhere. At four o'clock it is quiet and I have just come back from making a few simple preparations, not the least of which is to make sure that I have some candles. A stage 2 alert has just been announced. The advice at the moment is for people inland and on high ground in a sturdy house to stay put. Anyone else should make their way to a designated hurricane shelter when the call comes. I am still of a mind to stay put. I think I prefer the isolation to the crowd, especially when I couldn't be of much help in the crowd - not in a designated shelter. My house is well above the river level and drainage is good. The Cayes and coastal villages and towns without shelters are being evacuated.

The air is still and the town is quiet, much too quiet. There is an air of expectancy everywhere. The shops are busy but not overcrowded and there is no panic, just an air of quiet resignation.

I posted my letters and parcels. I expect they will be just as safe as I could keep them. And I went into the Library which was still open, and got a couple of extra books. Also put the video camera battery on charge. I hope that isn't morbid but I did come to learn and to share that learning with children. If I get chance, what better way and there is unlikely to be any power if it hits as expected. All the AA batteries are charged.

It has just been announced that Hurricane Mitch has strengthened to 180 mph and is designated a strong category 5. The whole of the coast of Honduras is on full alert. '...capable of causing catastrophic damage... the pressure at the centre is a mere 906millibars.'

Walking down through the town it is very moving to see so many dwellings which are ill prepared for a high wind let alone what is threatened.

5:30pm. Mitch is now the fourth most powerful hurricane ever. It is calm here and the sky is absolutely beautiful as the sun goes down. The light coming from the West is reflected just as brightly on the clouds in the East. How does it do that? There must be some refraction as the sun is very low in the sky and the Eastern clouds are not very high. This has happened many times but not usually as spectacularly and there is a particular poignancy at this time. I wonder what it will be like on Wednesday night. The evacuation of US citizens from Belize by air has just been announced. Bully for them!

5:40pm the sky is dark and I have battened down for the night - shutters unusually closed.

6:00pm just been announced that Belize is unlikely to take a 'direct hit'; I hope that is right for Belize' sake.

27th October Tuesday

At 6:00am the eye of the hurricane is located 200 miles East of Belize City and heading due West at 8mph. It is just as powerful. It is only 90 miles from the coast of Honduras but it should miss there. It is thought that the forward progress should slow and the centre should begin to move a little to the North, hopefully, missing Belize. The whole country is on Hurricane Alert phase 3. Shelters have been open since 9:00pm last night. Belize City is being largely evacuated. VSOs have been moved to Belmopan. I have been instructed not to stay in the house. My house is to be boarded up and I will be going with the Burns family to take refuge in their shop which is all concrete. I am now going to pack up all my things and hope that they are still there when I come back. 10 - 15 inches of rainfall alone is expected in the path of the hurricane. It still has sustained winds of 180mph and gusting higher. My phone isn't working.

7:40am many shelters are already full and Hurricane Mitch is expected to start affecting the country by around six o'clock this evening. Clearing up and packing away is a dismal job. What do you leave, where? Important papers, clothes; personal items, the ones I brought to remind me of people. Outside, the wind is beginning to howl. That would be little to do with the hurricane but it is certainly serving to make the point and heighten the tension. It is still clear and not raining. The wind is not strong but much more noticeable than usual. The dominant sound is that of hammering all over the place; boarding windows.

The phone was working again as I disconnected the computer so I left the phone connected direct after packing the rest of the equipment away.

Landy says that my house is to be boarded up - assuming somebody finds time and material.

Ten o'clock and it is raining very heavily indeed; the urgency increases. I think that the roof will go from this house if it hits because of the overhang, the way the air can get under it and through it and the wind over it; it could take off. I hope not. The best I can do is to pack things that matter most into suitcases which should be reasonably waterproof, and put them into what I hope should be the most secure room in my part of the house. This room is very small, with a window that opens only to the semi enclosed stairway at the back which is protected by a latticed concrete wall on the outside. But I can't do anything about the roof.

11:30am the latest report is that the hurricane is still heading towards Belize City, now at 6mph, and is only 200 miles away. The sustained wind speed has dropped to 165mph but we are warned that it can be expected to go up and down. The movement of the hurricane appears to be following the computer model at the moment. This suggests that it will slow to a stop, hang around and then turn north before affecting the coast, which is what we all hope it will do. If it continues on its present track, hurricane force winds will hit Belize City tomorrow morning at about eight o'clock. If that happens, the tidal rise will be twenty-five feet which will leave almost no buildings and certainly no dwellings untouched. All roads out of Belize City are reported as being extremely busy to the point of being choked. Going for a walk now around the town as it is dry again and there isn't much wind.

Houses are being boarded up everywhere. Extra nails are being hammered into roofs. Where there was a loose shelter roof on the corner of our street, all the corrugated sheets have been taken down, leaving only the frame and the workspace underneath. Louisiana School is open as a shelter and the space outside littered with vehicles unloading into it. Very sad; very moving; but everybody doing the best they can.

The roads and streets are quiet of both pedestrians and traffic. I have just been asked what arrangements I have made by a concerned Belizean friend - not even one that I have spent a lot of time talking to but just having met casually in the street from time to time.

Coming round the 'Boulevard' on to the main Northern Highway where there is a steady stream of traffic but nothing overmuch and all moving at a very sensible speed; an air of resignation everywhere.
A car is being secured into a shop which is part of a concrete building and another one waiting to go into another shop nearby. Many shops have roller shutter fronts just like garage doors, only stronger.

Vehicles are unloading evacuees into D*Victoria.

There is a small queue at the gas station, unlike the only one that is open in Belize City where I understand from the radio, there is a very long queue of people waiting for gas.

So many places are boarded over. A bus load of evacuees stands by the side of the road, close by L&R Liquors. The shops are shut and boarded over with sandbags put in place at the entrances. Drainage ditches are being cleaned out by ordinary people rather than the Town Board. P&P Supermarket, run by East Indians, open as always, and just one or two of the fast food outlets.

Trucks roll by carrying people's belongings. I wonder where they are all going to go with all their furniture.

Five past twelve by the Town Clock. The fire station stands open; one fire engine out; the old Bedford ready. One fresh food stall braves the elements and conditions but all the fast food stalls along by the main road edge of the Square are absent. No doubt their owners have got better - or at least, more urgent - things to do. I have never seen that happen before - day or night! In fact the Square is quite empty - almost, even, of people sitting, there being only four men taking time out including one, a one legged man, whom I have never seen doing anything else.

Tai San Restaurant closed; the Diner II boarded over; Batty Brothers bus park empty for the first time of buses except one small yellow peril, heightened in colour by the strange yellow-grey of the light around us and the even grey backdrop of the sky towards Corozal. Strange dabs of colour are provided by the flowering trees and by the now sad looking decorations proclaiming the coming of Halloween; All Hallows Eve to remember maybe; and wishing everyone a happy time! The irony of the Social Security building which is boarded over more securely than any I have seen so far.

Down by the Police Station a Belize Defence Force truck is taking its members off to do some service somewhere. Two red flags are flying from the flagpole, each with its black spot in the middle, together proclaiming the state of hurricane alert and potential disaster.

Passing the Sandy Hunter Library, I see that the Librarian was obviously not successful in getting the building boarded over but I take shelter there, in the overhang of the roof over the surrounding pathway, as the greyness from the Corozal direction translates itself into heavy rain. The river in front of me is disturbed as I have not seen it before - like frosted glass with patterns on it. On the other side, the fringe of trees above which is a totally featureless sky and a dull light penetrating through a uniform bank of cloud-like fog.

I sit down on the concrete path with my back resting against the wall because it doesn't look likely to stop raining for a few minutes. A few people are milling around the new market building opposite, also taking shelter, but it all looks closed up from here. I hope everyone has the food they need.

A van approaches the bridge from the San Estevan direction, moving slowly, yet in a cloud of spray picked up from the running water on the road. The gentlest of breezes stirs the air.

Surprisingly, the rain stops in minutes and the sky lightens again. The wind speed must be much greater, higher up; and I start to make my way back along Main Street. How high, I wonder, will this river rise?

Sung Wong Chinese is open and doing good business with take-away food. The Chinese never give up. Some customers at least, have come from the St Christopher Hotel opposite, which no doubt is overloaded and I don't think that they do meals anyway.

Quite a few buses are around that I haven't seen in Orange Walk before and the Zeta Purified Water Factory is busy - that's a good sign.

The building occupied by Landy's Store where I shall be going, looks very secure. It is the first time I have looked at it from that point of view.

And so I wander back skirting round the Cemetery as I always do when it is wet or dark. Even today, I have been approached for a dollar or fifty cents - not by people that I have seen in Orange Walk before. I don't generally get approached here as everyone knows me.

Half past two. It has gone pretty dark and is tipping down with rain. I have just finished boarding up as far as we can the outside of the house. Somebody who does work for Landy came along with the materials and we did the job together with occasional help from Landy and the boys. Most of my windows on top are not boarded and that is really where the weakness is but I do have access to downstairs if it gets really rough and the roof goes. I shall try to stick it out as there is not much choice now that Landy has changed his mind about moving out. The only preparation I had made for going to a shelter is an emergency one of picking up my small rucksack and getting out. I am not prepared for a protracted stay because I was not expecting to need to.

Three o'clock and the Karl Heusner Memorial Hospital in Belize City, has been evacuated.

The hurricane has swung west southwest so it is till heading towards land, in fact even more so right now. This is bad news.

4:40pm. the people evacuating from Corozal have arrived to move in downstairs. I just hope this lot is secure. I am supposed to have a room to go to downstairs but I wouldn't bank on it. At least I have made sure that the access door is unlocked. There is also the nagging doubt that Henry, the VSO Programmes Director wanted me to go to a shelter and I said that I would before events overtook that and were again overtaken by changed plans next door. This is a high house and the roof is vulnerable both front and back. Not so apparent at the back but vulnerable nevertheless.

Almost six o'clock and still waiting for the Acting Prime Minister, John Briceno, to give his address to the nation which was scheduled for five o'clock. More interesting, perhaps, will be the update on the hurricane which is about due.

The speech took about three minutes. Perhaps I shouldn't feel like it but it was not inspiring and it told us almost nothing. Currently, the centre of the storm is just around two hundred miles away from here, two hundred and three miles from Corozal and about a hundred and ninety miles from Belize City, heading for a point between Belize City and Dangriga.

"... Consider praying to the Good Lord, hoping for the best but at the same time, preparing for the worst. Keep safe, don't panic and let us move forward as soon as this storm is over." It sounded better when repeated in Spanish.

The six o'clock news is that the hurricane is meandering slowly and hurricane winds are affecting the coast of Honduras. The better part of the news is that the maximum sustained winds have dropped to 150mph with higher gusts and the core pressure has risen to 932 millibars. Nobody seems to know with any certainty what Hurricane Mitch is likely to do.

"Latitude 16.6N and Longitude 85.6 west and in terms of Belize's position is about 170 miles east of the Stann Creek District. Er… it has been drifting slowly at… drifting slowly towards the West and may continue to do so during tonight. A slow south-westward to westward motion is expected in the next twelve to twenty-four hours. However, the hurricane is coming very close to the coast and hurricane conditions are spreading onshore to Honduras and the bay islands."

"Mr Halse, erm... as we continue to monitor the movement of this hurricane, I recall erm… er…

asking you that er... when... when... when I first did an interview with you: when the eye of the hurricane passes... er... let's say it passes as it looks as though it's going to pass erm... er... south of Belize City, what does that mean for Corozal and Orange Walk?"

"Okay. Erm... most of the hurricanes erm... maybe this is not what you are asking but er... most of the hurricanes tend to move towards the North, at least a northward movement. And so erm... because they tend to recall... and this one may not do that er... it... it... The problem for the Northern Districts is that they er... they're more likely erm... to be affected than the Southern Districts. Er... because, somewhere along the way this hurricane will try to recall... the probability is high that... it's like erm... Yucatan more likely to be erm... affected because probably Mitch is likely to move... towards the North."

"So, for the people living in, let's say, Corozal and the villages in that District, what should these people be expecting tonight?"

"Okay. Er... the tropical storm winds are just approaching the country and so during tonight the winds are going to get a little more gustier. However, the... the... er... hurricane force winds won't be arriving until about midday tomorrow and that's if Mitch continues to drift west towards the land."

"So, in terms of rain Mr Halse, erm... what rain can people in the North and in Belize City and in the Stann Creek District expect?"

"Okay. It's a lot o' rain. And erm... the forecast is about 10-20 inches expected when Mitch crosses our country. Erm... this could result in erm... life threatening flash floods on that side - not on the north side but that would be more in Honduras..."

It went on. I could feel for the meteorologist but it wasn't very helpful. Also it was difficult to decipher the words and in transcription I have not included the quite pronounced Creole overtones and inflections.

"Does the current path of the hurricane now... Does it look as though the eye of the hurricane is going to come ashore near Dangriga?"

"Oh no... Erm... I don't know... Erm... but... erm... Mitch hasn't been keeping a steady motion over the past forty-eight hours. It is a little west-northwest, then west, then west-southwest. Erm... where Mitch is going to make landfall is uncertain."

"So the entire coast of Belize is erm..."

"Should still continue to monitor Mitch, Mitch is still strong - a hundred and fifty miles per hour!"

"That's a category four?"

"Yeah! A Category four! Erm... it's just five more miles per hour would make it a category five!"

And so it went on about storm surges, protecting life and property and moving inland.

My thoughts turn towards my own problems and the waiting. I am rather disappointed in Landy Burns and not for the first time. It seems he changes his mind at the drop of a hat to suit him and with little thought for the effect on anyone else. He had said that he was going to go down to the shop and that I would be welcome to go with them. That was the basis upon which I packed everything up in suitcases; put things in what I considered to be the most secure room in the house - only to find that he had changed his mind. What I have done is made sure that I have dropped all the immediate things that I might need in one bag, together with the two cameras and all my computer records on floppy discs, so that I can hop it if necessary. With the number of people downstairs I can't see a retreat working in that direction if the need arises. And believe it or not, they've got eight dogs and two vehicles. So I hope the roof holds and the wind isn't too bad.

7:30pm Trying to read but not terribly successfully; should be okay until tomorrow lunchtime. At least it will be daylight then, to make a decision.

Love FM is doing a wonderful job of linking family members with other family members and with extremely happy outcomes. I hope that remains so for them. It certainly gives heart to the rest of us. In fact, they have moved their entire operation from Belize City to Belmopan in order to safeguard the broadcasts. Indeed, that is where many of the people from Belize City have gone and Belmopan is absolutely jammed, packed. Messages have been going out for some time saying that no more people should go expecting shelter in Belmopan but carry on straight through to San Ignacio or Benque.

Ten deaths have occurred in Honduras already - those being the figures known so far.

Three Refuge Centres in the Queens Square area of Belize City are flooded already. So far, here, there is just a moaning wind and, at the moment, no rain.

"... hundred and forty miles per hour, that's two hundred and twenty kilometres per hour with higher gusts although some further weakening may occur during the next twenty-four hours. Mitch is likely to remain a dangerous hurricane."

That was at nine o'clock and Mitch is thirty-five miles from the coast of Honduras.

28th October Wednesday

6:00am hurricane Mitch has reduced in strength to sustained speeds of hundred and twenty miles an hour with higher gusts and has now been designated category three which is the same as was hurricane Hattie. It is only thirty miles from the coast of Honduras which has taken a tremendous battering along with some of the islands. The hurricane is almost stationary and it is thought that the mountains of Honduras helped to reduce its strength as it is not able to feed itself from the South. I don't understand that but the reported pressure at the eye of the storm is now 949 millibars which sounds much healthier. Still no-one knows what it is going to do or where it is going to go.

7:30am the streets outside the house are deserted; heavy showers but little wind; just an air of waiting. The news, currently, is of concern for the huge numbers of people in hurricane shelters: feeding them; keeping them comfortable. Everyone was asked to bring food and water for three days but the shelters particularly in Belmopan and San Ignacio are heavily overloaded. Shops in San Ignacio are being asked to open as normal for today.

Eight o'clock and it has now been announced that it is unlawful to sell liquor in Belize; the concern being for improper behaviour in the shelters.

At this time I am getting the computer out again as I need something to do as well as read. There would be plenty of time to put it away again should the need arise and in any case if Mitch hits my house will go and the protection I can give the computer seems pointless; better to use the time and get all my recording down on disc that can be saved.

8:30am After an early meeting of the National Emergency Management Organisation the Minister for National Security, Jorge Espat, came on the air to advise that everything is being done to secure the food and comfort in the shelters. He praised the behaviour of people in the shelters. I wonder how far this has to do with the prohibition of the sale of liquor as well as the overcrowding and cramped conditions in many places.

9:00am report given at 9:50am: Mitch pounding relentlessly the coasts and islands of Honduras. The position of the eye is still 30 miles from the coast of Honduras. It is expected now, to remain stationary through tonight and remains a threat to the entire North Western Caribbean for the next two days or longer.

Midday report: Mitch pounding relentlessly, the coast of Honduras; the centre 16.4 North 85.6 West

Not much change and Mitch is likely to remain stationary through the night. Some weakening is possible as the hurricane continues to interact with land. 15-24 inches of rain expected with the sea 8-10 feet above normal levels and accompanied by large and dangerous battering waves.

2:00pm. Finished transcribing the tape recorded from half past seven yesterday morning until I got the computer going again at half past eight this morning.

3:30pm "The update issued as of three o'clock our time from the Miami Hurricane Centre, the National Weather Service in Miami, Florida US - 'The four o'clock (Eastern Standard Time) position of Hurricane Mitch 16.4 North, 85.9 West' - Now this indicates that the storm has drifted westwards somewhat over this past few hours, and when I say drifted, I mean *veeerrry* slowly, estimated at about two miles per hour westward drift. Maximum sustained winds now put at one hundred and fifteen miles an hour. That's down just five miles an hour from the last report but more important than that, central pressure has increased to 960 millibars. That's twelve millibars additional pressure from the last report. We have some distances and vectors from various points in Belize. If you have a chart; if you are a fisherman or a mariner or boatman or an aeroplane driver and you have a chart; I'm going to give you the distance and the azimuth in degrees from the different points in Belize and, this way, from wherever you are, if you have a chart, you can figure out just where the storm is in relation to you. The hurricane is 215 miles from Corozal Town at a heading of 130; 172 miles from San Pedro on a heading of 128; 170 miles from Belize City on a heading of 117; 160 miles from Dangriga on a heading of 185; 123 miles from Half Moon Caye on a heading of 117; and it is 194 miles from Punta Gorda Town on a heading of 83. The maximum sustained winds, as we say, have dropped five miles per hour. Hurricane Mitch now has sustained winds of about one hundred and fifteen miles per hour... Mitch has been drifting westward over the past few hours. This overall motion is expected through tonight and that will keep much of the hurricane over or very near the offshore islands of Honduras. Mitch is likely to remain a threat to the North Western Caribbean for the next few days. Hurricane Warnings remain in effect for the entire Northern coast of Honduras, the Caribbean coast of

Guatemala, the entire Eastern coast of the Yucatan Peninsula including the entire coast of Belize. So this entire corner, the entire bay, continues under hurricane warning. We won't know for several more hours exactly which direction Mitch is going to go, finally. This drift of two miles per hour towards the west may or may not indicate its future direction. Storm tides of 8-12 feet above normal can occur where the storm goes in." Better news!

At about 4:30 I had had enough of the dogs. The family below simply take over without even bothering to make contact despite my giving them welcome when they arrived. I went down my own stairs and was met with eight barking and posturing dogs trying to come for me up the stairs. I only had flip flops on but kicked a few and went for the back door downstairs. The two larger dogs backed off. They came out. A young (to me) woman seemed to be in charge with two men hanging behind her and Nelson (as always) comes to watch. I managed to control rapidly rising temper and asked that we could have a break from the dogs as I couldn't hear the radio (important just now), couldn't concentrate on work and was even finding it difficult to read. Of course, it all sets the Burns' dogs off as well (They have four). I haven't heard anyone else's dogs since the emergency started - otherwise, the self-centred attitude of those downstairs and (let it be said) next door is so strong that I would think that I am wrong. If it were not for the convenience, location and the problem of changing postal address, I have felt for some time that I would move which would be a shame.

6:00pm No significant change except that the central pressure has now risen to 966 millibars.

9:00. "Hurricane Mitch is at a virtual standstill near the Bay islands of Honduras. Little overall motion is expected tonight. Maximum sustained winds have decreased to near a hundred miles an hour with higher gusts. Some additional weakening is likely while Mitch continues to interact with land. Hurricane force winds extend outward up to sixty miles and tropical storm force winds extend outwards for 135 miles. Estimated minimum centre of pressure is 970 millibars; latitude 16.3 north, longitude 86.01; very near the island of Guanaja. This position is about 25 miles east of the island of Roatan and about 25 miles north of the coast of mainland Honduras. The next report will be at 3:00am."

There has been little noise from the dogs.

'…Attached are some letters for Year 7 and 8 with a letter from me which is self-explanatory. They should print out in ready broken sheets. Excuse more now. Belize is in the midst of National Emergency on Hurricane Watch. Hurricane Mitch has been hammering the adjacent coast of Honduras for some time and is expected to come this way. It is not far away. It is weakening, however, and we hope it continues to do so and doesn't recover. I will send you a diary of it all when it is over - assuming I can. I am using email while it is still working…'

'Dear Friends in Year 7 and Year 8,

Together with this letter are some letters written by students in Standard Six of Calcutta Government School. They were 'Linking' with Year 7 last year. As you see, they were written on 9th. September and it was intended that they should be sent by e-mail direct from the school. For one reason or another, this couldn't happen so I said that I would type them out at home and send them for them. Then the Field Trip to the Lake District and your Half Term intervened so they are late. Also, we have a hurricane threatening Belize right now and I am doing this during a quiet period. I discussed these letters with their authors and they agreed that it would be a good idea if you all read all of them. That way you will get a much better overall picture. I am adding some notes below to help with that. You might like to do the same in return. The letters are arranged in pages and sent as an attachment so that you can print them easily…

Ferdinand Both friends and family spend a lot of time with each other especially in the villages. Riding horses in Calcutta comes very naturally and little special equipment is ever used. Going to church is a regular part of life and as all ages go there is no stigma attached. This is not the case, so much, in the towns and Belize City. Saints Days are very widely and elaborately celebrated. The majority of people are Catholic but there are a lot of Evangelical Churches as well. Singing is very enthusiastic!

Kenrick I have typed the letters using the language as written. I believe that the letters were written in a rush and not checked but it is good to see them in the 'raw' state. Normally, the English, especially grammar and spelling, would be very good but it is worth bearing in mind that for all children here, English is not their first language. Most of the children would speak Spanish at home, some speak Creole (which was invented by slaves to confuse the English!) and all will use Creole to each other. How many of you would write so well in another language? Pet pigs are not unusual in Calcutta village but I couldn't vouch for a natural life span! Dogs are not usually so well treated. They are mostly kept to bark and bite. The word Maths is not used. Everyone refers to Maths as Math. I can't (or won't) get used to that. Ages are interesting. Ordinarily, you should expect students in Standard Five to be the same age as those in Year Six but there has to be a level achieved in order to move on to the next year. Many students repeat. A lot of families are large. Eight or ten children are not uncommon but some families, *now, are smaller.*

Pollyanna *Most towns and villages have a Queen of the Bay. Also, raising funds is a major part of school activity, especially at this time of the year, and students are much more seriously involved than they are in England. It is very difficult to establish a routine of learning and schools are nothing like as well funded as they are in England. Students buy all their own books and equipment and pay a fee to attend school. It is expensive.*

Giovanni *Many people round these parts have boats or access to them. It is part of life and not in any way an indication of wealth. People in Calcutta do not have wealth but there is a lot of sharing and helping each other. In many ways it is like a big family of which I have been privileged to become a part and it is thirty miles away from where I live. The abundance of fruit has to be seen to be believed - especially... well, you find out!*

William *Knowing William 'waste' really means 'share'. Mr Berry can tell you the story of the computer but it is worth mentioning that they were given it because of what they are and what they have done (for themselves and each other) not the other way round. The difference in family names between children and their parents is not unusual. Nor does it attract any comment.*

Regino *The colour of skin does not seem to be a cause of concern but it is something of which young people are very much aware. If you see what is called 'clear' skin you would describe it as the most perfect (and desirable?) tan. The name Pena is pronounced Penya. In Spanish there is an accent over the n which gives it that sound. The wish to be friends is very strong. We should try to find as many ways as possible to learn about each other and to communicate as quickly and regularly as possible. But friends will best come from the class to class learning because that will put your special friend in a better context.*

Eugene *Sending a Buddy could be the same as one of your own class making the trip. Then, who knows, a visit (at some time) is not impossible. Football (Soccer) is much the favourite game but a lot of baseball is played and most villages have the facilities. The football pitch at Calcutta has floodlights (important when it gets dark between 5:30 and 6:30 the year round.) and two small spectator stands made from concrete - all built through the effort of the villagers.*

Hardy *Young people are very clear about wanting their families to be proud of them. Also, the value of education is not questioned at all - and yet it opens doors for a much smaller percentage of the population than in England and has to be 'fought' for.*

Dean *Fishing is a regular activity which is more than a pastime. The local fish is extremely tasty and many are adept at catching them. Snapper seems to be about the most common. Not a pretty fish, almost ferocious, but very good eating! There are plenty of small sharks and big ones too.*

Rose Marie *Duties in class might be different from yours. There are no caretakers or cleaners and floors are concrete, windows and doors are open to the outside and yet the schools are clean.*

Nayeli *Another complication for writing is the acceptance of both English and American spelling. Much of this, I think, has to do with the Coca Cola National Spelling Bee which accepts both and is taken very seriously by schools and students because there are serious prizes.*

Richealle *I think that the idea of the Pinta is well known in England but it is one of the many regular traditions here. The paper maché figure is usually quite large and is beaten mercilessly with sticks at the 'appropriate' time.*

Luke *The barrier Reef is about two hundred miles long and very important to Belize. Much of the country is flat and at low level. The reef is a natural protection from the sea.*

Alvin *Parrots are widely kept as pets but the acquisition of new parrots as pets is on the decline with conservation in mind. In some homes (as in my 'family') it is difficult to distinguish the parrot shouting someone's name from the person doing it.*

Amir *Belize is far from being free from drugs and violence. The rate of both is high but you can see that it is an important issue at least. Many young people stay with relatives to access their schooling in one way or another.*

Elvis *Burglar bars are a common sight in Belize. They are strong wrought iron frames (rather like the gates we make) which are fastened in front of windows (and doors, sometimes) to prevent unauthorised entry. Cutting (sugar) cane is a second occupation for people of all ages. It is very hard manual work and the cane fields are a favourite haunt for snakes.*

Tyrone *All good friends! Best wishes, Mr Max...'*

29th October Thursday

3:00am latitude 16.0 north, longitude 85.7 west and a core pressure of 987 millibars and 85mph wind.

6:00am little movement but the maximum sustained wind speed has dropped again to 80mph; hopefully, it is going to keep going down until it becomes a tropical storm and then dissipates. "Mitch is expected to resume a general west to northwest motion later today and if Mitch moves in the direction predicted it is going to come straight for our country, Belize. Mitch is likely to remain a threat for the next few days."

The great danger now is from flooding and mud slides. A great deal of rain has already fallen and the rivers are running very high. The Belize River at Roaring Creek, for example, has risen already to within five feet of the bridge (a depth now, of 30 - 40 feet instead of just a few). If Mitch moves in on top with another ten inches, or more, of rain, there will be extensive flooding and water damage as well as high winds.

9:00am "At nine o'clock this morning the centre of Hurricane Mitch was near latitude 16.0 north, longitude 85.6 west. Mitch continues to weaken along the coast of Honduras. Mitch remains almost stationary and we are expecting a slow movement towards the Northwest later today or tonight. Maximum sustained winds are near seventy-five miles per hour and if Mitch stays close to the coast of Honduras it could weaken to tropical storm strength later today."

Commentator: "What happen is that folks have been calling saying that they want to leave their shelters. What is your advice from the Belize Weather Bureau? What would be your advice to them?"

"I have been saying it over and time and time again. If you do leave your shelter do not venture too far away because if Mitch should turn... if Mitch should venture out into the Caribbean Sea again it could strengthen to... to... to... It could quite possibly be a category two hurricane. So we still have to monitor Mitch - the movement of this hurricane. So don't venture too far from a shelter."

"Er, what could we expect weather wise in Belize now. Is it going to be raining very shortly? Give us information on that."

"It will continue cloudy to overcast with regular outbreaks of showers and heavy rain. Winds will be from the North and the North West and will be around fifteen to twenty-five knots. That should produce some very rough seas so we are still keeping out a warning that all craft should remain in port; not only small ones."

The problems in the shelters are fairly obvious ones. Mostly people want to go home and a lot of people are reported as having done so. Officials, local and central organisers express their concern that this should be so as the threat is far from over but what is not really known is the basis upon which people make their decisions and the organisers generally tend to assume the worst. One report pointed out that people who had left live close by and felt they would be able to control any remaining storm.

Some people have just gone for walks and attracted criticism - yet these have been two long and uncomfortable days and while the immediate conditions allow it there seems to be little harm done.

Other problems reported in the shelters apart from sheer pressure on space, are lack of food and water - which all the authorities, services and local organisations have worked tirelessly to overcome and successfully so - and control of dogs. In Belmopan, garbage was being dumped in the drainage ditches which could cause a lot of problems. Garbage must be a headache. Belizeans are used to dumping it and seem to produce as much quantity as anyone else might do. Toilet facilities (which would most concern me) haven't been mentioned as far as I am aware.

11:00am here in Orange Walk, life seems to be picking up again. At the moment the sun is out although there has been sporadic, heavy rain and gusting wind. Some more people who remained at home (and many have) have come out of their houses; a few people walk along the street; some pass by on bicycles; and there are vehicles about. I am tempted to unpack the cases where things were stored against the possible loss of the roof but I think I will wait a short while. We are waiting for another address to the Nation by the Acting Prime Minister, John Briceno. A sudden, heavy squall drives everyone in again. Love FM, who have been bi-lingual, English and Spanish, have just launched into Chinese. It has been a brilliant service - giving personal messages as well as everything else and the experts unused to giving information as indicated by the transcribed hesitations have been dealt with great sensitivity.

11:30am Address to the Nation by the Acting Prime Minister, John Briceno which was heralded with a few of the opening bars from the National Anthem:

"My fellow Belizeans, the latest report from the Weather Bureau states that Hurricane Mitch remained nearly stationary during the last several hours. The centre of the hurricane is located near the city of Limon in Honduras. The eye of the storm will be over or near the central coast of Honduras for another twenty-four hours although little overall motion is expected throughout today.

Mitch is still a serious threat to Belize and the entire country remains under Red II warning. Hurricane Mitch is located 200 miles South East of Belize City and 210 miles East of Punta Gorda. Mitch is likely to develop a north westerly motion today which would place the eye somewhere in the vicinity of Ambergris Caye late tomorrow, Friday.

Maximum sustained winds have decreased to seventy-five miles per hour. This means that Mitch is now a category one hurricane but winds are likely to increase significantly as the hurricane approaches Belize.

The National Emergency Management Organisation has been meeting regularly over the past few days, assessing the situation and making adjustments to improve our preparedness. Yesterday, I visited most of the hurricane shelters in Belize City. Our people are in good spirits in spite of the hardships they are experiencing. To improve the conditions in shelters, the National Emergency Management Organisation have decided to allow the persons in the hurricane shelters in Belize City and Belmopan to leave the shelter temporarily to allow us to clean and sanitise them. Once these hurricane shelters have been cleaned, people should return to their shelters by 5:00pm this evening. I repeat: return to shelters by 5:00pm this evening. Belize Defence Force and Police patrols will be intensified in the streets of Belize City whilst the hurricane shelters are being cleaned.

Hurricane Mitch will remain a threat to Belize for the next two days because it is moving so slowly. I have been advised that flooding is likely to begin throughout the country and major highways are likely to become impassable. Those persons who return to Belize City and other coastal areas today are warned that they will probably be unable to return to higher ground as Hurricane Mitch approaches.

Ambergris Caye and other islands are in particular danger and we continue to evacuate residents. No-one is to return to any Cayes until the all-clear signal is given. Residents throughout Belize must remain on full alert and continue to monitor closely, the progress of Hurricane Mitch. Listen to the official weather reports and announcements from the National Emergency Management Organisation.

At the moment, the supply of fuel is limited. As a result, fuel will be rationed and people will be allowed to purchase a maximum of five gallons per vehicle. Please refrain from unnecessary driving. Where possible use bicycles and for shorter distances, walk.

We appeal to shop owners to open their shops today, so that people can replenish their supplies.
The Danger is not passed. We ask you to remain patient, calm and cooperative until you receive further information from the National Emergency Management Organisation.

A few moments ago, I spoke with the Prime Minister, Moosa, and gave him an update on the current situation. Mr Moosa has been keeping the International Community fully briefed and he has already secured commitment of assistance if the need arises.

As a Nation, we feel for our brothers and sisters in nearby Honduras and extend our sympathy to them. As soon as conditions prevail we will offer our assistance.

We continue to pray for God's blessing for the safety of Belize and for all people in Belize. God Bless Belize and God Bless Us All."

The speech ended with a few closing bars of the National Anthem.

Midday... latitude 15.9 North, longitude 85.6 West, near the city of Limon, Honduras; Mitch remains nearly stationary. A slow movement towards the west north-west or north-west is expected to begin later today or tonight. On this track, the core of Mitch will be over or near the coast or adjacent islands of Honduras for another twenty-four hours. Mitch is likely to remain a threat to the North Western Caribbean for another two days. Maximum sustained winds are near seventy-five miles per hour with higher gusts. Mitch could weaken to a Tropical Storm later today but re-strengthening is possible if the centre moves away from land. Hurricane force winds extend outwards up to thirty miles and tropical storm force winds extend outwards up to 175 miles. Estimated minimum centre of pressure is 990 millibars or 29.23 inches.

3:00pm... latitude 15.9 north, longitude 85.8 west... with maximum sustained winds of 60 miles per hour; additional rainfall totals 15 to 25 inches and locally higher amounts are possible over the mountains of Honduras and other parts of Central America. These rains can cause life threatening flash floods and mud slides. Storm tides of 2-5 feet above normal astronomical levels are possible near the centre of Mitch accompanied by large and dangerous battering waves. Dangerous coastal flooding due to strong offshore winds and waves is also occurring in other coastal locations in the warning area...

6:00pm Mitch has been inland into Northern Honduras. Tropical Storm warnings are in effect for the Caribbean Coast of Honduras, Guatemala, Belize and the Yucatan Peninsula of Mexico... A hurricane watch remains in effect for the coast of Belize... latitude 15.5 north, longitude 85.8 west, or just inland about thirty miles... The centre of Mitch has drifted a little southward, overland during the last few hours... Little motion is expected through tonight. Maximum sustained winds are near sixty miles per hour... Weakening is likely while the centre of Mitch remains over land but the storm could re-intensify if the centre emerges from the coast... The estimated centre of pressure is 995 millibars... There is danger of coastal flooding due to strong onshore winds and large waves...

Much of the text of updates remains the same. Those parts have been largely left out. Little news has been given of the real effect on Northern Honduras which must have been catastrophic. The hurricane has been close enough for very high sustained winds indeed to be effective and the full effect of 180mph for some of the islands. Also, the centre has been hanging around there for an extraordinarily long time. The fact that so much of the energy has been lost over land surely speaks for itself.

There have been human interest stories coming out all day, calls for help from various organisations and individuals and many messages among families who are separated. A baby has been successfully delivered in a shelter in Belize City. Mother and child (a boy) doing well. I wonder if he will be called Mitch.

Still, we are not out of danger. Most computer models still suggest that Mitch will head back out to sea, gather strength and affect the coast of Belize before making landfall again in the North of the country where I live. Fortunately, Orange Walk is at least thirty miles from the sea. And it looks as though the experience will run right into the weekend. It has been a very long week and the stress level is high for many people.

Love FM Report from Belize City.

"We went down to get reports and get a first time review of the situation in the city and as I said in my report down there, erm... going down I saw quite a number of people driving on the highway. Some were headed out west and some were driving in. In Belize City itself erm… er... we noticed that some of the smaller shops were open and people from the shelters were going in to buy their stuff to take back to their shelters.

And er… one thing I want to say… a pleasant evening to… to a young lady I met at the… er... just off Freetown road by… I think it's by the… apparently headed home… saying that they erm… had to all intent and purpose... had had it with erm… with life at the shelters; and erm… I'm glad I was able to convince them to… to… return to their shelter and stay there because… we don't want the tropical storm to erm... get back into a hurricane and people to be running about in the middle of the night with breeze… with strong breeze and er... driving rain and all that. So good evening to you… and here's a mother and her daughter and I think with her… grandchildren… and we know that they are safely back at the shelter now. Continue to enjoy your Thursday evening and er... All the people in the shelter, you are listening to Love FM; a pleasant goodnight to you and thanks for choosing Love FM.

We drove through some of the streets erm… and some of them were covered with about an inch… two inches of water. We came up the Western Highway… sorry, that's the Northern Highway. We went to Ladyville… and er... there was just a portion of the road that was, again, flooded. It was right by Benny's Wholesale Depot and er... another spot down by erm... Roses..."

"Is it passable?"

"It is erm… er... when we were driving today… that our vehicle was high so we got through…"

"How many er... inches or feet of water would you say?"

"Oh it was inches. It didn't reach a foot yet but er... em... all vehicles were having a difficult time getting through and there was three small cars that erm... I take it that they were gas engines... that they stalled… and er... drivers had to get out, roll up their pants and erm... push! And er... try to get it started again and er... em... a small motorcycle tried to make it through and the rider almost had to er... get off and carry the cycle across the water so that er... for very small vehicles it was er... not a very good thing to try to... to go through that.

Errrmmm... going downnnn... Freetown road... Freetown Road, down by the em... the stop light... that was covered across. And further up Freetown Road it was like 50% in front of Love FM; the studios... that had water as well. Kelly Street was flooded. Errmmm... we went through a street in King's Park... I don't know... I can't recall the name of the street we drove. That was covered. As a matter of fact, I brought back a couple of pictures that I took... er... we dropped off a gentleman and when he got out, er... he stepped right out into the water and he er… had to take off his shoes to get into his yard and some houses there - the yard was completely filled. Er... Let's see... we drove down Central American Boulevard; that's alright; the lights are working; the traffic lights are working. We saw some branches broken on Cemetery Road and er... and so... Belize City... erm... When we left it was drizzling and er every now and then you get erm.,., some.,. some strong winds. And we saw the Police and Belize Defence Force out and showing that er everything remained er... safe. Errrmm... The Belize Defence Force and Police were also up by the... gas station and showing that everything is in order. So erm... by and large... there have been er... there are... not that the erm... there are difficulties. There is no damage at all and erm... everybody... the majority are at the shelters."

Then... "To assist us we have the assistant coordinator of the National Emergency Management Organisation, Mr Stewart Lesley, and he is accompanied by Press Officer Vaughan Gill. Er... On the panel are the people who will be fielding questions to him. We have Ruben Moralis Iglesias, Richard A. A. Merrill and er... Patrick Jones. Now, a pleasant evening Belize and welcome to this special broadcast of the National Emergency Broadcasting Network of Belize; and er... Stewart, the meeting has just concluded; could we hear from you about what went on in that meeting?"

"Absolutely; good evening radio listeners and er... em... as Mr Rene Vianella said er... the... er... NEMO has just concluded its meeting under the leadership of the Prime Minister... the Acting Prime Minister... the Honourable John Briceno. And er... what has happened is that a review of the day's events, an update on the weather and er plans for tomorrow and the near future have been discussed and decisions have been taken. Erm... What I'm going to do at this time, Rene, is just er... er... allow you guys because there are so many issues, to go through the list of questions you have there and then in the end, I'll just fill in the blanks."

"Okay, so we start with the questions and who want to go first then... Ruben?"

"Well, I guess one of the concerns is er when is it going to be declared that everything is over... but er... once that is declared, err... one of the main concerns I guess, is the evacuation... or... not evacuation... getting people back to er... their corresponding city or town or wherever they came from and er... I guess one of the concerns you all had er... must have been how to do it orderly. Er... any decision on that?"

"Okay! There are a whole bunch of questions in there. First of all when is it going to be over? I think that is something Mitch erm... to decide er... but also, the Government of Belize is in consultation with the Met... with the Met Office, with the Chief Meteorological Officer, Mr Justin Halse and the National Hurricane Centre in Miami. Er... these directives come er... through the office in Miami and so they will advise us as to when it is... it is an all clear and erm... through the Chief Meteorological Officer, the Prime Minister will then declare all... will declare that we are in Green Phase. I must re-emphasise at this time that we are still in Red Two. Er... that means that you should be in your shelters at this time; that we are still under a hurricane watch, even though we are erm... experiencing tropical storm-like conditions around Mitch... (Interruption) ...I think I only answered one part of the question. Just one minute please. The erm... the other section was... I think you wanted to know about evacuation - or actually, the movement back into the city. Er... The preliminary discussions have begun and the Prime Minister, er... the Acting Prime Minister, the Honourable Johnny Briceno has asked the... the... the parties responsible for the er... for movement, to go out and do another assessment of the conditions of the road to see how erm... the Northern Highway, the Western Highway, the major highways and roads - the conditions that they are in and er em... to do preliminary predictions as to their... anticipate... get together with the Met people, look at the tides and the rising river levels and er... report to him as to the conditions of the road and er... the possibility of flooding; also other ways that we may be able to move people, especially those who are sick and elderly. So, er em... preliminary work is in place and erm... the Police are going to manage the highways and the traffic departments in the various municipalities will take over once the flow of traffic arrives in those places   but first an assessment... an overnight assessment of conditions will be carried out."

"Er... One of the concerns is, for example when er... er... er... NEMO organised the evacuation of the city and towns er... you allowed buses free of cost to people; would you do that for the... er... for people to go back to their places of origin?"

"You're asking about free transportation? Er... Let me give you a definitive answer on that. Obviously we will not allow anybody to be er... em... er... I will give you a definitive answer on that in my next briefing but obviously we will not allow anybody to be stranded in Belmopan.

"Stewart, as far as the assessment goes... will ermmm... probably you can update us and tell us what's the situation so far as the utilities are concerned?"

"The utilities... telephone?"

"Telephone... electricity..."

"Fully operational; electricity... erm... there were reports that erm... one of the villages and one feeder in Belize City... er three feeders in Belize City... er feeder number three, sorry, in Belize City was down. It has since been restored and er... em the entire country has power.'

"And so far as keeping our international er... partners informed... er... one... when will the Government go through the courses of getting in touch with them and keeping them up to speed as to what's going on here?"

Er... Patrick. We communicate with our international partners through their Missions here and through our Missions - especially through our office in the United Nations. Also, er... the Prime Minister has been dealing with international communications as well, from erm... from Taiwan. The Prime Minister, this afternoon, held a meeting with erm... funding agencies and some members of our local diplomatic corps - where they were informed – er... the Ministry of Foreign Affairs, as you know, is in charge of our foreign relations and at this time, they have been fully activated. We have already been assured and guaranteed funding from a number of agencies and er Mexico, Cuba... er... Guatemala, United States, United Kingdom, Netherlands and other countries have all... standing by for the all-clear for them to start moving in with the aid and assessment. They are constantly being updated. In fact there will be another briefing with the Prime Minister... the Acting Prime Minister... on Saturday."

"We have had reports from San Pedro and some of the other Cayes that some damage has been reported. Erm... What's the situation there?"

"Yes. Well, erm... I recently got off the phone with the Honourable Patti Jose in San Pedro and the situation out there is that a number of piers and dive shops are down and er... damages to some homes, trees... they of course, have taken probably the worst erm... beatings... than any of the other erm... than any other part of the country. Er... the... The Prime Minister tonight er... asked that the military, first thing in the morning, er... do an assessment, despatch a permanent secretary to San Pedro and that area PS Delisle, who is to report at six tomorrow evening as to the er... the preliminary report as to the damages that have occurred in San Pedro and erm... to make recommendations as to the extent of aid that we are going to have to render to that place as soon as possible."

"You touched briefly on the medical services. The Karl Heusner Memorial Hospital was relocated erm... when the threat erm... from the hurricane erm... was imminent. When will the KHMS be fully operational?"

"Okay, the... the Karl Heusner Memorial Hospital is almost fully operation but we've had to split er... the resources there because of the volume of people here in the Nation's Capital. And so, erm... as we move people back to the city we will continue to step up operations and so, by the time this is all over the Karl Heusner... by the time all Belizeans are relocated in their places Karl Heusner Memorial Hospital will be fully operational again. Emergency services are available at this time; ambulance services erm... er... erm... are available... and so, to all intents and purposes the Karl Heusner Memorial Hospital can function."

"Er... What about flooding, especially out West?"

"Okay. We continue to study that. An assessment is going to be done again, in the morning. We have been receiving some reports also we have gotten from you... ha... ha... erm... on what's going on out there in the Districts. Er... We know that there has been er... flooding... some... some... er... flooding in Corozal District; in a couple of villages in Corozal District. Erm... Douglas village in Orange Walk and er... yea... and maybe some parts of PG. As we get that information, the Belize Defence Force... is operational, along with the British er... military... trying to see how to deal with that."

"It was er... a fifteen point er... agenda when you went in to your seven o'clock meeting. At the head of that list is the situation with schools. What er... erm... Update us on that."

"Okay... erm... Assuming that sometime before the end of the weekend Mitch is going to be history as far as Belize is concerned; er... the Prime Minister has decided that we will open schools on Monday. And so, the decision on schools is that tomorrow morning, er... der... pl... erm... the necessary logistical plans are to be made and ready so that as soon as evacuations of hurricane shelters, most of which, as you know, are schools, are completed, work crews er... erm... will go in there - and structural engineers and so on - erm... will go in and will assess damages and will make necessary preparations for those classes - for those classrooms - to be functional as educational institutions again - by Monday morning. Er... Most of this has been turned over to the Municipal bodies. The er... the Mayor and er... Village Council Chairmen and so on... erm... are being contacted as we speak, for them to put together local... er... local expertise to assist with this."

"Erm... Stewart... er... a Love crew has just returned from Belize City. We... we drove around to some streets and... We noticed that erm... there was er garbage and er debris in some of the streets... and... I take it that is the situation in many of the District Towns as well. Erm... How... will you go about getting that cleaned up?"

"Okay; that... that... this... that has been taken care of even... has been taken care of even before our meeting; the first instance... in Belize City. The Mayor of Belize City er... provided City Council trucks and some personnel to... to take care of alleviating the problems er... of garbage in the hurricane shelters. Additionally, the erm... manager of the Waste Management Control has been contacted and erm... if by now you haven't heard, the manager of Waste Control is calling all his workers back to work. By seven-thirty tomorrow morning, all the garbage trucks that were moved in to higher grounds in the city will be fully operational... and... in the Districts. And so, before the mass exodus back to Belize City and the other erm... major places, like Corozal and so on, where people were moved out, er... all the garbage will be taken... the garbage will have been disposed of."

"And er... One other point I want to touch on is the erm... issue of er... the Public Servants and their erm... contribution to this entire effort. Erm... er... certainly their contribution was... is commendable; they gone some erm... above and beyond the call of duty. Er... Some of them... I don't know that they collected erm... their end of month salary yet. When will those people be receiving... be receiving their pay?"

"Okay, from Monday. We've been in shelters since Tuesday. From Monday, the Prime Minister... the Acting Prime Minister, the honourable John Briceno, instructed the Head of the Public Service to go ahead... and erm... em... the Financial Secretary, to go ahead and pay staff. De… erm... Cheques and vouchers were written. The problem for those people who haven't gotten money is because... all the banks have not been fully operational. Many people erm… have accounts in Barclays Bank. I've been meeting one of them. And erm... so salaries - if... if you are banking with Barclays Bank - they have been erm... they have not been operating... and we are appealing to the management of Barclays Bank erm... to open - and I'll speak about that in a minute. But erm... people... The Government of Belize paid its workers. And so, if you... if your account is Scotia Bank, or if you receive vouchers through Treasury or so on... erm... your salary was in the bank since Monday."

"And er... Some more about the bank... is er......"

"Okay. Erm... We would just like to appeal to the manager of er... erm... Barclays Bank. I checked with the Chief Meteorologist... or the meteorologer... the meteorologist on duty at the erm... the... the... erm... the Philip Goldsmith International Airport, Fred Evans - and as well, I checked with the erm... the acting erm... guy in charge, Mr Torres. BTL are... BTL is fully operational; internet services, cellular services; everything is running and erm... Fred Evans assured me that they are not predicting any extraordinary wind patterns tomorrow and so there is no reason why somebody that has to do something like communication would not be able to... to operate. So we are appealing to Barclays Bank people to please, open the bank."

"Okay..... Stewart, I know the... the assessment will start at er... the break of dawn and what have you. Em... but... even tonight as..."

"Erm... erm... Assessments have... have been done er... as... as... like... er... one example - the... the... the shelter. Honourable - the Attorney General, the Honourable Dickey Bradley He went erm... He and I travelled to Belize City on... on Tuesday night. We did an assessment. The following morning, the Prime Minister himself - the Acting Prime Minister - went in to the... to some shelters; did an assessment. The Honourable Florencio Marin, in Corozal, has been doing assessments and calling in. Erm… er... I got an update earlier from the Honourable erm... erm... er Marshal Meeth in Toledo. We got an update from the Honourable Cordell Hyde in Belize City, just this evening. Er... assessments are coming in but... erm... the best kind... the best assessment in many cases, is to go up in the air and... and... look down and... Planes have not been up in the air and so that... that kind of assessment will be done tomorrow; actually getting in there and... and looking at things… er... That will happen tomorrow."

"So erm... what has been the contribution to er... like from other organisations... public spirited organisations; er... public interest organisations such as the Belize Red Cross?"

"Erm tremendous! Many of the organisations and many people are... people who don't belong to any organisations have been showing up to shelters and in places and saying "Listen; how can I help? What do you want me to do? Do you need me to move people here? Do you need me to do this? Do you need me to do that? And so the volunteer spirit is... is great and the... the pla... organisations like the Red Cross and so on... er... have been invaluable and we appeal to those wonderful groups that have always done a lot er... right after this thing is all over - groups like Rotary, groups like the Hospital Auxiliary, the erm... International Women's Group - to erm... assemble as soon as this thing is over and... take an assessment of how you can help us in this situation - erm... because we have suffered some damage... because of water and all this movement and so on."

"The erm... We did not get a direct hit by the hurricane and er thank goodness that did not happen but I... I get the feeling that er... the country did suffer er... major losses: lost time in production; lost time finance-wise. Er... are you erm... able to give preliminarily, without any hard facts in your hands, what, what the erm... the nature of the... of the loss we've suffered in the country?"

"Erm... I can only give you certain figures. It's been... just to feed people in shelters... for a... for a day, has been costing us upwards of $175,000. Er... when you look at... since Monday - because people started to close down businesses and move erm... equipment up to higher ground and so on - Since Monday! It is now Thursday. The last four days - production in this country has come to a screeching halt. Medical supplies erm... due to the amount of time being spent; fuel being consumed - we are damaging... our... the... the... the bill has been well into the millions of dollars."

"And that's without even the hurricane getting here."

"That's right. And that doesn't even... a factor in the damage that erm... the infrastructural damage: for example, San Pedro. Er... the roads and bridges in Cayo - had to do some emergency work on the Hawkesworth Bridge to... to get it ready to fun... the get it erm... sort of functional before a hurricane that was a work in construction... as a construction incomplete. Obviously we are going to have to go back and do some work... again when it is finished work that we've... that... we'll probably have to go... were back two steps so to speak. And so, erm... the... the... People may say "Oooh, well, well say thank God no hurricane no come yet." But erm... the... the amount of money that it has cost... Er... personal families. Let's take, for example, the guy who works as a Dock Worker, who goes out to the dock and gets a job - today - and tomorrow he goes there and he may not get a job, he goes there and gets no job. That guy hasn't earned any money for four days... you know... and erm... Saturday and Sunday he won't earn any money either; so representing up to Monday; and so... Yeah... the...It's been a... the... the. It's been costly!"

"While on the topic of money, Stewart, I have a question here. Erm... there are people who have loans to pay and have maybe spent their money erm... getting ready for the hurricane and what have you. Will there be any influence placed on lending institutions to - sort of - cooperate with er... the public who have had to er... lay out cash er maybe up front, to cope with the situation?"

"Well, erm... we would want to hope that the situation... er... It has not been addressed at this point because we have been dealing with the... the immediate issues, but I am sure that, as we begin to become a little bit more comfortable - because, again, we are still in Red Two - as we begin to become more comfortable with er... with the Mitch situation, we can then address erm... things like well... when ar pi ar phone bill I no like bill de waater bill an yo, yo, yo sin-di-cate an Credit Unyon an t'ngs like dat!"

"And er... I was going to come to things like the utilities because we don't want... as soon as we return on Saturday ("Ha, Ha, Ha") and ("Ha, Ha, Ha") to find that there's ("Ha, Ha, Ha") no light, ("Ha, Ha, Ha") no telephone... because we never pay de bill.

"Ha, ha, ha, well, at least we have a couple of days when... 'till these people get their telephone lines back up and their FAX machines plugged and all their computer systems back up so... At least the... the... the erm... the logistical part of it should delay them a little bit, but if not, I'm sure that somehow we can appeal to government."

"Er... I'm gonna give you a big break now, Richard, but erm... before I go on to that... can't Government sit down and, maybe, work with the utilities and ask them for a grace period, like a week, something so that people can er... work this out - so that there is no cutting of any utility or whatever."

"Erm... Eha... I can't speak entirely for the Government. The Government is an entire organisation. I must admit, at this time, that we have been pressed with, with the issue of feeding people and keeping people safe and so on, so it has not been prioritised. So erm... It is something that I will definitely bring up with the Prime Minister the next time we sit down to talk."

"So, what will be the level of communication with erm... the Belizean community abroad? What brought this up is that erm... word has reached us... and when we were in Belize City er... erm... er... we cross check it and it checked out that erm... CNN news organisation is down in Belize and er... the international press have not been particularly kind about reporting about Belize abroad and... We wouldn't want er... anything negative or... to come out of this whole experience and get splattered across the pages of international newspapers or international erm... television abroad... So what will the Office of NEMO and maybe, the Prime Minister's Office, be doing to get the word out to the other countries that erm... we made it well through this erm... through this emergency period?"

"Okay. Erm... First of all er... the coordinator of NEMO, the Cabinet Secretary, Mr Robert Lesley and myself, have done numerous interviews erm... with ABC, NBC, CNN, Roiters. These are interviews that we have done already... erm... The Washing... I spoke with the Washington Post; I spoke with the New

York Times erm... I was on erm... I gave a telephone interview for Good Morning America... er... Mr Lesley was with Roiters and erm... I spoke with NBC. We have been spea... we have been erm... in touch with the international media, both in English and in Spanish. Some of your Spanish experts have had to help us out; and er... John here, who takes care of our communications, has been disseminating information through the Internet. We have also erm... kept er... the National Hurricane Centre in Miami fully abreast with conditions in Belize and they have also been disseminating information through their erm... through their different er... communication outlets. And so that process has started. Er... We... continue to work with our missions to update er... media houses in... foreign media houses, especially in places where we have large Belize population. For example, in New York, the Caribbean News Association has been fully briefed by our First Secretary Mr Alphonso Begahona. In er... In Los Angeles, we've talked to the Los Angeles Times. In Houston, we've been in contact with people there and in Miami. So, we have been talking especially with those international agencies in municipalities where there are Belizeans."

"What have... what have we as a people erm... learnt or gotten from this entire experience?"

"There have been so many things. We were talking about some of that last night with erm... with Richard and Rene but I'll say it again. For example: this is the first time we had to deal with the fact that we were gonna... we could have had er... water coming into our city twenty-five feet high. It is the first time we've done a mass exodus out of our largest city, Belize City. It er... these things... we think we managed them if not very well, adequately. We have learnt erm... so much about management of food; about management or resources like fuel and water. We have learnt that we have some really brilliant and talented people in this country, who can lend valuable advice. Er... We have learnt to work especially with erm... communications agencies like you guys here in the media, all the media houses. Er... and so, there are so many things; I could go on and on all night. And we have looked at places where we have made mistakes as well, and we are taking note and we are checking stock; and erm... figuring out how to make sure that these things never happen again."

"Basically that was what I was going to ask - was what we have learnt so that you are looking ("Ha, Ha, Ha, Ha"). This is the sort of exercise that we would not deliberately go through, obviously, but now that we have been through it without the storm actually hitting and having gone through the er... the er... We have learnt where the weak spots are, where the strong points are; what we really need to look at - and change - so that next year, if a storm does hit us, we'll be prepared ("Yeah... Erm...") - better prepared."

"Er... One: one thing that hit us that I'm sure nobody will fault anyone for er... Richard is the fact that... We have never had to deal with two, three... or, if worst case scenario, five days in hurricane shelters. How do you prepare to keep people cooped up in barred up buildings for so long? You know erm... and so, that has been a lesson. Two: I think: information management, er... People are very Internet and Television literate and they are out there getting information. So many times, the Honourable Attorney General, Dickey Bradley, mentioned that half the time, or more, the forecasts that we were receiving from the international agencies on the weather were wrong - or at least, invariably incorrect - you know, and yet Belizean people depended on what we were saying here at NEMO. We depended on our local weather forecasters and we depended, especially on you guys in the media. And, with the exception of a few instances of people putting us into a little bit of panic, we commend all of you in the media houses for the fantastic job that you have done... erm... with regards to disseminating information... and especially your own er... demeanour, your own attitude in... in... in... telling people what's going on. You did not allow yourselves to get too excited most of the time because... what we are doing here is er... is one thing but how you tell the Nation can panic them, can calm them, can er... encourage them and I think you have been more than anyth... if nothing else, encouraging."

"Do you think that possibly, though, we didn't panic a few people enough? ("Ha, Ha") In some of the areas that, had that storm come, there were some areas ("You are thinking of the islands, I am sure) I'm thinking of the islands; I'm thinking of the Placencia Peninsula; I'm thinking of areas like that. Er, Monkey River - that is a low lying... on a... on a low lying river bank... er... right on the sea, and thinking of these areas that er... maybe there wasn't quite enough emphasis put on the fact that these areas should have been evacuated. Had that storm come, there could have been real tragedy there. Is there any discussion about a mandatory evacuation order that er... Government could say... In the event that a storm approaches, Government can say these areas will be evacuated; no argument! Is there any discussion of doing so?"

"We were under the impression that that was... that that was the case in the Dis... in the erm... low lying coast and in the Cayes. I think the Prime Minister, when he addressed the Nation, not today but yesterday, said 'I am ordering the evacuation of low-lying coastal areas. Erm... Those people who chose to stay, I think, made a major mistake. Now, the question I think you are asking is should we have maybe, sent some people in there to physically move them. Er... in... if we had gotten a storm and those people had died er... maybe we would have had some serious erm... questions to answer to the Nation. It is something we definitely have to discuss. Erm... what is... what is the extent that we must go to evacuate people? That is a question that we are... that we are to address."

"How far can you go ("That's right!") to make someone leave an area ("without violating their rights")? Right!" Er.........

"This is Love FM. We are coming... this is a National Broadcast... coming to you from Belmopan to you ... Stewart... You were?"

"Erm... If we could just erm... get in touch with erm... Dickey Bradley for one minute. That erm... I have no problem answering questions but I think Mr ... Mr Bradley is on the line if we can erm... okay... erm... if we can go to commercial"

"Ha, Ha - We'll keep it here a while Stewart and erm... continue the discussion here and certainly Ruben has to do the translation for us in Spanish and erm... er...

"... A lot of people still stayed there and from what I remember, I don't know if there was a mandatory er... evacuation with regards to Belize City..."

"There wasn't a mandatory evacuation with regards to Belize City. Er... The contingency was that erm... we provided shelters that we felt could sustain er... an extre... er... a severe wind and... and... and storm surge - and we had both erm... forces trucks and other erm... em... vehicles on stand-by. Er... we er... Should the situation have arisen where we had to evacuate fast. We also had the roads pretty much clear er... for movement out of there if we needed to evacuate more... but erm... it would have been virtually impossible to evacuate 75,000 people. Where would we put them?"

"Are we in danger, now, that next year, if a hurricane approaches, people will not be so ready to move to shelters. People will not be so ready because they will say 'Well, I went to all of that inconvenience last year; went and sat in this crowded, hot, noisy, smelly shelter for four days and there was no need for it; er would there be a problem next year?"

"Excellent question, erm... excellent question and er... I think it's going to be the responsibility of government, through people like Vaughan Gill here, which takes care of our information, to make sure that we continue to inform Belizean public that as arduous a task as this may be, it is a necessity; it is for your life. And er... I think when the time comes people will be willing to move again. But we must make sure that the... that the information mechanism is in place; that we continue to inform people that this is something that must be done."

"Early this morning at about three o'clock or before that... er... minister Bradley was with us and er... he was saying that government has to er... have in mind is that we don't have appropriate shelters and that most of these are schools where there are no er... er... toilet facilities for example and er... that government seriously has to consider that. Er... what if any, er... discussions has cabinet had so far, with regards to building shelters? - Which of course is a... I guess, be a high cost and er... you had to also think about what else you could use these places for."

"We have discussed this issue er... extensively over the past couple of days Ruben... er... there are two arguments in there: the humanitarian argument and the... the financial argument. Er... you know... What do you do? Do you build huge buildings and leave them empty for erm... hurricane shelters. Do you spend er... millions and millions and millions more dollars on... on buildings that should be normally schools and... and erm... and community centres where people do limited activities er... and spend tremendous amounts of money - very needed money for infrastructure and more of it for better education - just so that er... you can house people er... in times of National disaster? Well, maybe yes. The reality of it is that er... right now we had to look at what we had and... and work with that. This new Government came in and in less than a hundred days, it was faced with the possibility of a major National disaster. And so we are... we are admitting, those of us who are working in in National Disaster Preparedness, we are admitting that our shelters, some of them, erm... leave something to be desired... and we must address that immediately."

"Erm... If I may, er... er obviously, that's what I was asking. What else would you do; because to build a building and just have it there, it would also deteriorate? But er... maybe consideration could be made. Schools are those mostly used - and maybe churches and other public buildings. Er...maybe er... the suggestion... it would be that er... that there could be guidelines as to these buildings that toilets must be within the building itself and not outside so that people would be able to access them without having to go out because there's no possibility that under extreme circumstances or these er… er… big winds, you can go out to the toilet or whatever, and if you… there's no facility like that. It's also, after a while, very inhumane to be in a place where everybody has to do their necessity within… which is exactly, what I guess, has happened or happens in other situations."

"There is also one other consideration too, and this one's not just er… er as the situation of a disaster but this was also an extraordinary situation. Erm… Normally, people don't expect category five hurricanes… erm… so many places that we would have erm… used for shelters, we couldn't use. Erm… had it been a category two or maybe in a category three hurricane, many Belizeans have homes sturdy enough that can withstand the wind and could withstand, maybe, up to fifteen feet of water but this twenty-five feet of water, winds up to and over 175 miles an hour - erm… who builds for that? You know? ("Mmm") And so this was an extraordinary circumstance also. So that is also something that needs to be considered."

"Let's go to er… whenever the… the green flag is raised ("Mm Hmm") and the all clear is sounded and everybody heads home. We talked with the Commissioner of Police this morning, and he said that there will be officers on the highways. And of course, the thing that we are facing with now is getting everybody back home safely. It would be a double tragedy now, if we lost a life in getting everybody back, because so far we have come through quite well ("Absolutely") er… without any problem. Are you going to make sure that… government going to make sure that there is adequate patrolling on the highway; that there is enough control there? Er… are you going to do anything as far as to making up convoys to go… or… or strictly regulate the traffic? How is that going to be handled?"

"Tonight, this agenda, that, that we had at this emergency meeting, was - almost one third of the time in that meeting, was spent dealing with two issues. The issue of food, feeding people, and the issue of getting people back to their normal lives - transportation. The Prime Minister is insisting that law enforcement authorities manage, regulate the movement and the flow of people back; even if it means staggering traffic; posting Police vehicles and erm er commandeering certain er… Government vehicles and so on; monitor the highway to ensure that people maintain order. No overtaking; work within a certain speed; having convoys led by… by… by… official people. Erm we are looking at a number of scenarios. Like I said, we have taken the issue of transport and broken it into two sectors. One, transportation on the highways; this is going to be the responsibility of Policemen and Military Officials; and then, transportation within the major towns and in the cities. And so, in Belize City, the Mayor has been er… has been informed that it is going to be his responsibility to have his transport department fully operational. We have looked at alternative roads er… looked at the Vernon Street situation. Erm… we are going to assess there - if any damage was done to Vernon Street. We know most of these people are coming in from the West. Erm… somebody is going to be looking at the Hattieville-Boom road. Er we're looking at the Father's Road route so there… there will be an assessment. The Mayor is going to be responsible for the traffic once it enters… once it enters the city limit. Police will be responsible. Yes, this is something that has been discussed."

"So, what about the possibility of flooding on the Western Highway; I was there at around mile seven, mile eight where there are some very low areas."

"We are currently experiencing a high tide and erm… somebody is on that as we speak. So erm… if we are experiencing a high tide right now er… we are going to make an assessment. Er we keep watching the waters. We have no control over whether we are going to get a flood or not. What… erm… should there be a flood then we won't be able to move people."

"Stewart, again erm… er… a message here… a question here that was er erm… Rene just phoned in… Will there be any kind of regulation to ensure that businesses do not increase the price of goods to cover their loss?"

"Er… We… we live in a… in a free market enterprise and em er obviously, government cannot go to businesses and dictate prices, but we appeal to the humanitarian side of our entrepreneurs in this country - or at least our merchants - to remember, not… the fact that people have not been working for four days; to remember the fact that erm… this is an extraordinary situation where people have had to take - erm… allocate monies that weren't budgeted or planned in their spending for this emergency situation. Er… We are confident that the business community is not going to do that."

"You say government cannot dictate….."

"Well, it is not… This Government… This Government is not in the business of price control and price regulations….."

"But in an emergency......"

"But in emergency, government, what? Can? Maybe? Ought to?"

"Er... sp... perhaps ought to."

"You think our moral responsibility?"

"To... er... to... to... say that prices can't be raised beyond what they were before the emergency to er disallow price gouching on necessities. Er... we still have to eat - everybody does ("absolutely") and we still have to have er all of the other things ("absolutely").

"And again, we are in consultation with the... er... er many of the people er... whom we have relied on for expertise at this time. In fact, government is incurring a food bill, Ha Ha, as we speak, we are buying food at the merchants and they have not been overcharging us, so we are confident that this is not going to be a problem."

"I have here, the latest advisory, the nine o'clock erm... advisory for Hurricane Mitch... Tropical Storm Mitch - I beg your pardon... Mitch over Northern Honduras, moving little... and I'll just read and then we will take comment afterwards...

'Mitch over Northern Honduras, moving little; tropical Storm warnings are in effect for the coasts of Honduras, Guatemala, Belize and the Yucatan Peninsula of Mexico Southward including the offshore islands. A Hurricane Watch is also in effect for the coast of Belize. Small craft in these areas should remain in port. At nine o'clock Belize time, ten o'clock Eastern Standard Time, the centre of Tropical Storm Mitch was located near latitude 15.5 North, longitude 85.5 West or about twenty-five miles or forty kilometres South of Limon, Honduras. Mitch has moved little over the past several hours and little motion is likely through tonight and early Friday. Maximum sustained winds have decreased to near fifty miles per hour or eighty-five kilometres per hour, with higher gusts. Weakening is likely while the centre of Mitch remains over land but the storm would re-intensify if the centre emerges from the coast. Tropical storm force winds extend outward up to 175 miles or 280 kilometres from the centre, mainly over water. Estimated minimum centre of pressure is 995 millibars or 29.38 inches. Additional rainfall totals of 15-25 inches, with locally higher amounts, are possible over the mountains of Honduras and other parts of Central America. These rains could cause life-threatening flash floods and mud slides. Coastal flooding due to strong on-shore winds and waves continues over portions of the tropical storm warning area.'

(The discussion continued in respect of concern and aid for Honduras, especially, at this point; the likely future behaviour of Mitch; and the time when the all-clear might be given. None of the remaining discussion was enlightening in terms of forming a picture of what is happening in Belize.) Then...

"That is the figure that captured my attention first of all, 995 millibars is very, very near to normal pressure and this would indicate that pretty soon we're going to see the circulation break up. Once the circulation pattern breaks up we no longer have a tropical storm. We have a **bad** rainstorm that can still bring flooding but er... once that circulation breaks up then there won't be anything left to develop. Er... if we can see an end to that circulation... so er... that's the key to it, right there."

"Cautiously optimistic!"

"Cautiously optimistic!" "Cautiously optimistic!"

"Because er... the re-intensification will only happen if... if the eye moves back over the Caribbean Sea and er... right now, it doesn't look as though that is going to happen."

"But, then again, Mitch has been unpredictable"

"Yes, yes er... that is very much so."

"This has been one of the **strangest** I have ever seen."

"I'm beginning to put this one into the bizarre category..."

"Yes. Oh I've er... this one has been in the bizarre category for several days... Yes. Yeh... Here's the map that shows er... the Watch Areas and Warning Areas and er... this computer model indicates that the storm could re-emerge, go back out over the sea and er... redevelop. But er... the... the only... the bright spot there... Even if it did that, I don't think that it would have time. It is so close to us that I don't think it would have time to develop a tremendous amount of strength, even if it did that, because it's already over Honduras so, if it came out into the bay, it simply wouldn't have time before it got to us to... to develop into anything really bad. A category one hurricane, I'd say, at the most ("Rene er... em... just...") Absolute most."

"Just... just since you mention it, er... as the Prime Minister said in his speech this morning erm... 'We continue to be concerned about erm... Honduras, especially the coastal areas, and erm... about what's happening there. Er... we are going to... ...our Mission in New York erm... has been in contact with the

Honduran Mission and erm... like I said, the Prime Minister, yesterday authorised the signing of a... erm... of a... of a declaration in the United Nations and erm... as soon as this is all over, and we are able to put erm... an assessment on our house in order, we, of course, will be approaching the Honduraneans to see in which ways we can assist.”

“Of course we’ll be talking to the National Meteorological service a little later on to get their comments on... on er... this er... the position of...”

“They would be able to do a lot better than I would on this...”

Well, what I’m... what I’m noticing... what I’m noticing here, erm... is that the six o’clock erm... update erm... the six o’clock update placed Mitch 15.5 north and 85.8 west. Er... The update we have just read places Mitch at 15.5 north - yes, longitude er... 85.5 west instead of 85.8. Erm... it was... at six o’clock it was 30 miles south south-east of Trujillo, Honduras and this other forecast is saying twenty-five miles or... or... so I think there is some clarification that we need to contact our Weather Bureau...

“I will defer to Fred Evans on that one!”

“Exactly!”

“Are there any more questions?”

“Er... One of the things I understand you discussed is how much longer you will be feeding people at the different shelters and I guess that depends on how long er... they’re gonna be there.....”

“As long as it takes”

“.......as long as it takes. When would er... NEMO declare that it is safe? At what point? Er... When it goes on to what? Twenty miles per hour or when it er...

“When the meteorologists here in Belize and the centre in Miami tells us...”

“That is...?”

“That is when we move - yes.”

“And of course, you’re still going to have the... the… er... problem there with floods and what have you?”

“Absolutely; and we’re discussing that already - How do we deal with that.”

“From a matter of physics, it’s the circulation... not the wind speed. From a matter of physics it’s the circulation that matters. If the storm loses its circulation (“Again, I’ll refer to Fred on that one Ha, Ha, Ha, Ha”) then... then er... then you don’t have a tropical storm anymore.”

“Er… what would er... be the situation now - I mean when does er... NEMO, the National Emergency Management Organisation meet again, considering that that er... this tropical storm is losing its power and er... more or less, what do you think would... would be... er a decision taken at that particular meeting?”

“The Prime Minister has declared six o’clock tomorrow evening for another meeting of the larger group. However, erm... there are a number of us who are always working. The Prime Minister remains in Belmopan and is in control and erm... we have complete access to him and erm......
.....NEMO continues to function...............”

“A concern I have is er... This morning when we started announcing as we got the advisories that er... Mitch was er... getting closer to a tropical storm and during the day we have been receiving reports that people have been moving out of the shelters. Of course you have been insisting that they should stay at the shelters and er... er... because there is a possibility that Mitch could get back to the ocean and re-intensify. That er... advisory stays, right? That people should......”

“Oh we are still under Red Two. We are under Hurricane Watch and er... and it’s very clear by the documents that have come out. We are in Red Two and under Hurricane Watch.”

“And anybody moves does so at his own risk?”

“Yeah… Erm... You know... er... once those reports come out - one of the things I want... I want to say right now is that one of the... is the major issues that we are dealing with is the issue of floods; the fact that we have sustained damages in this country. You know and... and… so... we need time to assess evaluate our damage and so we cannot go back to full operation until we know exactly, how much damage we have suffered. And so we are under hurricane watch.”

“I’d like to say thank you so much, Stewart Lesley, for taking time to talk to us................”

Thus a remarkable response to the powerful threat of horrendous disaster, all too real even in the event; hesitation and tentative response on air representing a tiny country trying to get it right against one of the greatest powers of Nature.

30th October Friday

6:00am the centre of Mitch is located at latitude 15.4 north, longitude 86.1 west; centre of pressure 997 millibars and maximum sustained wind speed 40 miles per hour.

Last Report - now that Mitch is downgraded to a tropical storm:

"9:00am Belize Time, the centre of the Tropical Storm Mitch is located near latitude 15.3 north, longitude 86.2 west. This position is inland over Honduras about fifty-five miles or eighty-five kilometres East South East of La Ceiba. Mitch is drifting towards the west south-west at near two miles per hour or four kilometres per hour. A slow, mostly westward drift is expected for the next twenty-four hours. Maximum sustained winds are near forty miles per hour or sixty-five kilometres per hour with higher gusts. Little change in strength is forecast today. Tropical storm force winds extend outward up to 175 miles or 280 kilometres mainly over waters to the North of the centre. The estimated minimum centre of pressure is 997 millibars or 29.44 inches. Additional rainfall totals of 15-25 inches are possible over portions of Honduras, Nicaragua and portions of Belize, Guatemala, El Salvador and the Yucatan Peninsula. These rains could cause life threatening flash floods and mud slides."

Stewart Lesley - Deputy Chairman of the National Emergency Management Organisation:

"Good morning. The National Emergency Management Organisation has announced the downgrading of Hurricane Mitch to a tropical storm. Tropical storm warnings, then, are in effect for the entire country of Belize. Those persons who are now in shelters may return to their homes in the mainland. Those who (whose homes) are on the Cayes are strongly advised to remain where they are. Persons who were evacuated from San Pedro, Caye Caulker and other Cayes and very low lying areas are strongly advised not to return to their homes until the all-clear is given. Free buses are available in Benque Viejo Del Carmen, San Ignacio and Belmopan to transport people back to Belize City and their homes inland."

"The all-clear will be given only when Mitch causes no threat at all to the country of Belize."

There is still very heavy rain at times; the road outside runs over its whole width with water when it comes down - despite the drainage and run-off being good.

A British Army helicopter landed in Louisiana field just after 11:00am and left at midday. Don't know why - although the weather was atrocious when it landed.

I have just had a phone call from Jayne (1:15pm. Friday, 30th October). She has just come out of hospital in the UK after operations on her eyes. She had a detached retina in both of them. The left eye seems to be okay but she won't know about the right eye for some time. One good thing about her going home, she has been told, is that she would have lost her sight had she stayed. The cause isn't known but Jayne is young for such a thing to happen. On top of all that, the Belgian boy-friend, Eric, dumped her on Monday - at the very time when she 'needed a friend'. Fortunately, her 'Ex' has been supportive. It was difficult for me to get all the details clear. She is very down and was more inclined to talk than answer questions. What is clear is that she would like to hear from her friends here in Belize.

31st October Saturday

Short, heavy rainstorms this morning; went shopping, especially for water and meat which I was now out of. All clear given at ten o'clock this morning as Mitch had been downgraded to a tropical depression.

Mark phoned later and I told him that I was okay and what had happened, also that I had heard from Jayne and gave details. He took her address and email and said that he would make contact. All the other VSOs had been in Belmopan during the emergency and were mostly home or were on their way.

Marco arrived with his cousin about midday which was very nice. Neria had gone to Chetumal to have her stitches taken out and they would all be going home tomorrow. Marco's cousin said that he would give me a call when he was ready to cane harvest as I want to know by doing it, what it is all about. I removed the hardboard from the front windows at about 4:00pm. No sign of next door all day.

1st November Sunday

Only five adults and three children other than the minister and I attended morning service in the Anglican church; even so there was a powerful sense of experience shared and truly, little needed to be said although much was. Real emotion fully surfaces only rarely.

A welcome and indeed 'normal' letter arrived from friends in England, even including news of less than pleasant weather they were experiencing; a deep irony and frankly a relief as any reference to the experience in Belize could take another three weeks to arrive.

Back on track, the rest of the day was spent finishing transcription from my little voice recorder and writing up the record.

2nd November Monday Reflections as observed.

There was a great deal of congratulatory discussion and phone calls on Love FM this morning which was, frankly, sickening. There is no doubt that improvements have been made in hurricane preparedness and many organisations - including NEMO and Government Ministers - did very well with the resources that they had. They are to be given heartfelt thanks. However, in my view, two important issues are being disgracefully played down.

The first is that, if Hurricane Mitch had struck, the measures taken would have been wholly inadequate. Belize City, for example, would have been wiped out. In those circumstances, only total evacuation could have been good enough. A city already in flood, with a 25 foot sustained surge on top and waves 40 feet high as well, right on the coast and much of which is below normal sea level could not survive. It is not good enough to assert that total evacuation is impossible. The question should be 'How are we going to do it?'

The devastation caused by the hurricane on the coast of Honduras and inland, and of the Tropical Storm later, in Guatemala and Nicaragua; unprecedented rainfall, flooding and mudslides costing thousands of lives stand testament to there being no room for congratulation in Belize - only grateful thanks.

The second issue is the reality faced by many families in shelters with inadequate and inaccessible sanitation at all levels. By way of example, on my visit to Louisiana School in Orange Walk this morning, I could smell what needed to be cleaned from the gate. The teachers were busy doing the cleaning themselves. Enough to say that there were cases of Hepatitis B in one of the rooms packed with people.

Let us be grateful; thank those who most thoroughly deserve our thanks. But let us not congratulate; let us not blind ourselves. We were lucky, very lucky indeed.

There were various and developing reports of the strength of Mitch. In the end it was declared to be the most powerful hurricane on record. Winds were gusting up to 220 miles per hour for a long period. Mitch defied the norm by turning south, creating huge damage and loss of life as it crossed to the Pacific where it was given a name change before turning back across the Yucatan and reverting to Mitch to cause havoc in the US and across the Atlantic.

'…We have had the all-clear from Hurricane Mitch which was heading straight for Orange Walk at one point. You will no doubt know of the disaster it caused to Honduras and the offshore islands, and the devastation caused by water also, in Guatemala and Nicaragua. We were very lucky. I will send you a full report of that as it affected Belize, as soon as I have finished it. It will be a good geography resource if nothing else. Right now, my concern is for action with 'Linking'. I had led the schools to expect something soon after the end of September because that was your intention, and I want to avoid a repeat of the slow start we had last year; I know why the delays of course, but that doesn't help…'

Chapter Five:
Back on Track

I wasn't able to profitably go in to St. Peters as it is their first day back but I did spent an hour with Bernard in the late afternoon. After that I went to see Miss Carballo at Immaculada where we agreed that it would be a good idea for them to continue the link but with year eight on a pen pal basis and with her whole class as part of English Language work. I suggested that she might like to use the resources I have put together to start them off so I expect to pick those up from Calcutta tomorrow.

There was a great thunderstorm which started around seven, put out the lights, and lasted all night. I had shut down the computer before it started.

More normal activity started next morning as I went to Calcutta on the 7:15 Chell bus to spend the morning with teachers at the Government School and at Seventh Day Adventist School, also in Calcutta in the afternoon; and went home with Orvin for lunch in between at Ranchito which was brilliant as usual. I could do that every day! His school had started its collection of food and clothes items for Honduras already so I went to the local shop and bought some tinned foods which could be eaten without cooking and in the largest tins they had. This was ever so well received and gave another opportunity to discuss how lucky we are and how responsibility rests with Belize to assist.

Email arrived in the evening, all of which was answered, and from the Community College…

'…I was relieved to hear that everything is OK re Hurricane Mitch. My thoughts have been with you. I have started the ball rolling, and my pupils have completed their first piece of work. Buddies and letters will be in the post next week, and I will write a 'letter of introduction' to each school this weekend...'

'…We were very lucky indeed. At one point, all 180mph of Hurricane Mitch was heading straight for where I live. It was in any case, the fourth most powerful hurricane ever (recorded) (later known to be the most powerful) but had it taken that route which would have been across water, I believe that it would have increased in power. In fact, it hung around the offshore Honduran Islands and then headed inland there (and was expected to re-emerge, which it didn't as you will know). Honduras is said to be 70% destroyed and put back 50/60 years in its development. That speaks for itself. Low lying Belize would have been wiped out. Everyone here is collecting food/clothes etc. The first consignment was sent from Toledo, down South (You can see the coast of Honduras from there on a clear day) the day the all clear was given. You might imagine that it was a pretty stressful week. I believe that you will be receiving reports from children but they will have seen and understood only the response to the threat and not the cause. Corozal was most affected in the North of the country, being by the sea but nothing in Belize can reflect what has happened in Honduras, through the power of wind and water and in Nicaragua and Guatemala through flood and mudslides. You will have more first-hand knowledge of that than I because I do not have television. I have a twenty-four page record of some of the scenes here and transcript from Love FM (Belize Radio) which has many possibilities as a record from a Social Studies point of view. If you would like a copy quickly I will try to send it as an attachment (My little machine should do it, given time.) There will be a fuller story incorporating that text when I have finished it. (I didn't sit and mope!). There may well be children who would like to know that we escaped. Perhaps you could tell them that. Also, perhaps you could get a message to Janice who would tell any of the adults. You have direct email contact with Henry at Corozal Methodist of course. If you want me to print out email for any of the other schools and deliver it, I would most likely be able to do so on the next school day. It would be best to do that for the Christian Assembly of God School at Santa Rita anyway, so that Tomas Zetina can give you the address himself. Please tell me when I should start writing to Year Seven again. I suggest that Year 8 could maintain their 'Link' on a pen-pal basis with children who took part last year. I could arrange that at this end easily. There are children at both Immaculada and Louisiana who would like to keep that up - even though they won't be involved as they were last year. I need to know whether you are getting my mail okay. Also, you should be receiving another (larger) parcel from me with some interesting items in it. Several films, sets of photos and slides are included. If there is anything you would like and haven't got - please ask...'

It was St Pauls turn next in Corozal for me to monitor two classes in the morning and one in the afternoon. I make no bones about having fish soup at lunchtime in a local cafe which was brilliant as always; whole fish - hence bones - tomato, carrot, short spaghetti, rice, onion rings, peppers, garnishes etc. and tamarind to drink in a very large iced glass!

Before going home I spent a very pleasant hour in the craft shop (White Sapphire). Viola Pasos was most helpful - to the point where it was I who had to be 'pushy' to buy anything at all! In fact I got two wonderful wall carvings, one each for the two Leiva families, and four carvings and a cushion cover to go towards the ones to send to England.

Received four emails from SMCC, one from Caroline about a computer for sale and one about a snorkelling and diving weekend but it involves spending the night in a tent which I don't fancy. It means finding one for a start. Mail had always been heavy; I couldn't remember six in one go but all six were answered. One of the ones from SMCC children is testing the school system and another requires a message to be delivered to Louisiana tomorrow. Perhaps we can get started at last. The rest of the evening involved more effort towards the Christmas presents. I expect I will go back to the shop in Corozal tomorrow.

'…A friend of mine is selling a Compaq Contura 430C 486 Laptop computer with 16MB RAM, colour screen. I wasn't able to figure out the size of the HD or if it has a modem or not (I know I'm a computer teacher but laptops confuse me!). It appears to have been networked once so may have a network card in it. It looks nice and apart from a few software errors seems to work well - probably would need to have the software reloaded (it has no CD ROM drive). The asking price is BZ$2000 but I said that was too much (in my great wisdom!) so you could probably make a reasonable offer if you are interested…'

I went to the District Office in the morning to find that the British High Commissioner wanted to come and visit me as part of a familiarisation exercise on Wednesday. He doesn't seem to be visiting anyone else at this time. Thought afterwards, that it would be more useful for him to visit a school rather than sit in the office and, best of all, go to one that is also in the 'Linking' programme - so I will suggest Calcutta which I can set in place this afternoon at the Corozal meeting of Principals and Teachers in the programme at St Pauls; also a good time to go back to White Sapphire to buy the rest of my Christmas presents.

'…Mum was very relieved to hear that you are ok, she had heard about the hurricane (well the news here downgraded it to a tropical storm) and the terrible loss of life…'

'…I'm not surprised that the news was as it was in the UK because, by the time they woke up to what was happening Mitch probably had become a tropical storm. There has never been a recorded hurricane like Mitch which rewrites much of the learning so far. Suffice to say that the offshore islands of Honduras suffered two whole days of sustained winds of 180mph with higher gusts before Mitch moved on to dump 20-30 inches of rain inland. A lower wind speed of such a storm merely means that it covers a wider area. The worst recorded disaster in Central America…'

'…I will write more another time but I just wanted to know if you were all right after the hurricane. We have seen a lot of coverage in the newspaper and on the television. We have had a lot of bad weather but nothing compared to what Central America has experienced. We have received a package of letters from Belize and Drake will soon be replying…'

'…Yes I'm okay; thank you so much for your thoughts. I should have written before but a lifetime seems to have been packed into these last two weeks even though the hurricane week was largely a matter of waiting… Most shelters are schools which are built with concrete and have concrete roofs. That is probably okay but the weak point is the wooden slatted openings which are the windows. Imagine several hundred people crammed into those spaces for four days, with no inside toilets and no washing or cooking facilities at all in most cases…'

'…Glad to receive your email and to know you were O.K. From what you said it sounded quite awful. From listening to the news I think this Country is sending several millions in aid to Honduras…'

'…I've arranged with my pupil to bring the laptop around to me on Sat morning some time, so allowing for Belizean casualness about time perhaps you should come over to my place sometime late afternoon on Sat? Maybe give me a call first just to make sure I'm there…'

I went to Belize City to look at the computer that Caroline's student was offering but it was much too expensive. I might be interested at $1000 although it looks as though Marco might be able to get one through his cousin in the States. There was a very moving service of thanksgiving in a packed church at St Peter's this morning with people 'as one body' more than I have ever known; then a day of letter writing with even more to write about and letters to reply than usual.

'…I have passed on your recent email attachment of letters to what is now 8D. They were met with great enthusiasm… The links have shaken out as follows - 7D/Calcutta, 7G/Corozal Methodist, 7H/St Paul's, 7R/Christian Assembly of God. Each school will receive a personal email from me within the next 2 days via you, but also directly to Henry Neal at Corozal Methodist. Please let me know who else is 'on line'. The pupils here have been working on some background to Central America, and Hurricane Mitch has rather taken over. Nevertheless, a package will be in the post by Friday 13th containing a buddy and personal profiles of each child. As soon as we get a response, the project will really get under way. This is quite

deliberate, and shifts the responsibility to the schools in Belize to reply. In the meantime I hope some emails will be sent to you, but I will await a reply from the schools concerned until I put in the effort to embark on further work. I think the motivation of working to send off information before a reply is received is a valuable one. By the way, your "Buddy - Wait for me!" sheet was brill, and a great start to the process. I hope all schools have one…'

'…I have tried to get schools here to make a start without receiving from you and the batch of email letters for Year 8 was a first contribution. In fact, I have been pushing since the beginning of term. To be fair, like you, they have all had their problems - one of which has been the need to raise funds which schools here have to do for themselves. Mitch hasn't helped! Now I can start writing to year 7 again I will do a profile of each of the schools for you. It will be much easier when I have something in my hand to give. It is part of the Belizean psyche to expect to be given something (Hey mister, Gimme a dollar); a difficult thing to describe without giving the wrong impression, which is why I have avoided doing so. Why not put together a small team of Year 7 to email me direct? I would be quite happy to channel some material that way and respond to their ideas and suggestions; quite happy to communicate with year 8 also. What is the school email address and should I use it? No-one else is on line yet. Calcutta should be but there is a double problem of the availability of the technician (80 miles away) and bringing the computer into full use. I have spent as much time as I can with students and we are making progress. Calcutta is also 30 miles from here. As attachments seem to be a success and 'Hurricane Mitch has rather taken over' there is a twenty four page (you are warned) set of my notes and transcriptions which you may find useful. I have also arranged to get copies of the track and reports from the Internet which was obviously monitored here but they will have to come by post. Glad you liked 'Hey Buddy'. Each student has had a copy here. While I think about it - the British High Commissioner is coming to see me on Wednesday so he will be given a copy before I start angling for another grant…'

I managed to contact the British High Commission. Final arrangements should have been this afternoon, Monday, but the call didn't come through so I will have to phone again tomorrow. Both St Peter's and Calcutta will accept a visit. I spent the whole day at Louisiana and managed to see seven staff in their classes but it is revue week so, again, it is of limited value.

'…I will be mailing the first batch of letters first thing tomorrow morning - from class 7G to Corozal Methodist School. They will be carried in the diplomatic baggage of a rather unusual 'buddy' called Choco-mint! He (or maybe she?) is something of a 'split personality', because he can adopt two different forms - either a turtle or a rabbit. Depending on mood or environmental conditions perhaps? Anyway, he should reach you by 20th November. The letters are basically introduction profiles of the individuals in form 7G, and include a lot of personal photographs. Choco-mint will be carrying a diary, and I hope he will get chance to fill this in over the next week or so to describe his travels. Unfortunately, he left in a bit of a rush, so his passport will have to be sent on in a second package. It would be great if he could return to us at the start of December, along with a Belizean buddy from Corozal and some letters from children there. As this is a 'new' school, perhaps you could give some guidance about what to do. 7G have a number of ideas to work on for future correspondence, but will wait for some sort of response to give them the signal to go ahead. I will send an email direct to Henry Neal to give him advanced warning of the package, but perhaps you could send a copy of this letter to him as well. This is a good group with plenty of enthusiasm, and I hope they get a speedy response in order to get their link up and running…'

'…I look forward to meeting Choco-mint. It sounds as though we have a lot in common. I hope there are no problems with Immigration. They don't care much for travellers having no passport. We all have to show our passports to go shopping in Chetumal! I don't think you need worry about a speedy response from Methodist but your idea of the start of December might be optimistic. Mail has been quite fast lately but it can take three weeks and Christmas is coming up. I'm sure the response will be quick anyway. At least you should miss exam week which is next week. You will be interested to know that term ends on Friday 27th November and the new term starts (for three weeks before being interrupted by Christmas) on the following Monday, 30th November. This idea was thrust upon schools without warning at the beginning of this term. Maybe the Buddies could start their journey to the UK by the beginning of December. The 'guidance' has already been given - long ago, when we were expecting a parcel for the end of September, promised in a rash moment. The British High Commissioner is coming to see me on Wednesday afternoon. He is interested in the work and the project, so you might imagine my mind is working overtime in terms of possible support, assistance and involvement…'

While spending the day in St. Peter's Anglican School I managed to contact the British High Commissioner's office where it was confirmed that he will meet me as arranged and go to Calcutta Government School and finalised that arrangement with Orvin Rancheran.

I delivered two bags of my clothes to St. Peters to be sent through the church to Honduras, bought packing materials and wrapping paper for the Christmas presents and spent the evening preparing papers for Calcutta School Linking and to give to the High Commissioner, Tim David, for both Curriculum and Linking.

Wednesday morning was spent at Palmar, walking both ways which was very pleasant, then showered and got ready to meet Tim David at the District Office. There was a message from Ellajean arrived at the office requesting my attendance at a two day workshop on Monday and Tuesday (two working days' notice) at BTTC. Tasks have been assigned which are non-specific and which will require preparation and without having been discussed with me - yet again! The memos were dated 4th November, five days ago! Children organise their birthday parties more effectively than EJG at EDC.

The visit by the British High Commissioner was brilliant. He came to the office where I introduced him to the District Education Officer and the Assistant District Education Officer for Orange Walk and then we set off in his chauffeur driven vehicle for Calcutta School which took about forty minutes. He met with the Principal who showed him round and was able to give him the background of my work and the 'Linking' which suits me very nicely. During this time, I took a Standard 2/3 class for some revision work. That class had prepared a song for their visitor whom they greeted with the warmth that I have enjoyed so much. They sang well and it was much appreciated. Next was Standard 6 who were in the Library (few Primary Schools have one) where the computer was in full use. They had prepared a topical sketch based on some unacceptable behaviour in which the boys had been involved out of school (stealing oranges from someone else's trees!) We had traditional Belizean refreshments with the staff as it was already well past time when the students should have gone home. Then I was driven back right to my house before he continued on to Belmopan which is another hundred miles away. He had been driven two hundred and sixty miles for that visit so someone must think it is important. Quite a humbling thought. As for me - It was with not a little pride that I was driven in a British vehicle (Range Rover) with the Union Flag, unpretentious in size but not to be missed up front and the CD plates below - and far from home!

'…The next package of introduction letters was posted today - from 7R for Tomas Zetina at Christian Assembly of God. I will send a letter to you for Tomas in the next day or so. Yes, I did receive your last attachment - extremely interesting and also extremely useful. What an experience that period of waiting must have been…'

'…Glad you found the attachment useful. You will get a better one when I have had chance to expand it to include a wider view - possibly as a story. Now I can be sure of attachments it seems to be a good way of getting material to you which you will not have to edit in any way. I posted a very large parcel to you at school on 1st October. Has it arrived please? Please let me know. The contents are of high value anyway but the films and slides are priceless because they can't be replaced. I assume that the parcels are coming to me. There will be no delay in their delivery and it is probably best to do it that way first. Some schools have to collect their mail from the District Office. I will investigate the position for each school although they will probably advise you direct. Your school email doesn't work! I suggested that Year 8 could maintain their 'Link' on a pen-pal basis with children who took part last year, thinking that it is something the English Department might like to take up. The idea came from La Immaculada to develop their written language skills. The visit by the British High Commissioner was brilliant…'

The last two days of the week were spent monitoring at Calcutta SDA and at Chapel after which I set off to stay overnight with the family in Belize City for Marco and Miriam's wedding anniversary and on Saturday, attended the Service of Ordination to the Sacred Order of Deacon at the Cathedral Church of St. John the Baptist in Belize City. This was for Lynda Moguel (Orange Walk), Constancio Perez and Ilona Smiling. The two women are the first to be ordained in Belize. Neria came to the service with me. The church was packed and the service lasted for some two and a half hours; the first time I have been able to sing in Belize with an organ accompaniment which makes so much difference. There was also a steel band so the Caribbean flavour was strong. Afterwards we went back for lunch and I set off for home on the 3:00pm Premier (allegedly).

I had come home to be able to attend Lynda Moguel's first Communion Service this morning at 8:30 but when I got there the church was locked and several people were waiting outside. When I got Barbara Blades up to find out what had happened she said the time had been changed to 3:00pm because the Bishop couldn't come in the morning. This was very disappointing as the 8:30 time had been given out at last Sunday service. The Church is the people and its officers are the servants of the people. That had been the message of the Bishop's address the day before but as so often, it doesn't get translated into practice. In any case, it was Lynda's first service and I believe it would be better without the Bishop holding her hand. I didn't go in the afternoon as there were Christmas parcels to pack.

'…I posted the last two parcels on Friday, which means that the following characters should arrive in Belize: Boxing Bruno (7D) - to visit Calcutta School, Choco-mint (7G) - Corozal Methodist, Ed (7H) - St Pauls, Baby Bunting (7R) - Christian Assembly of God. Passports to follow! I will send off a personal letter to each school before the packages arrive in the post. I have recently discovered a bedraggled Fluffy on my doorstep - from La Immaculada, I think. She must have got lost or been kidnapped or fallen in love with an English boy - who knows? Anyway, I think it only right that she returns all be it

rather late. Yes, your package arrived, and all slides have been developed...'

'...I'm impressed by the Buddies' names. Bit puzzled about Ed though. Ed what! Ed It? You can tell 7R that Baby Bunting will be accommodated at an ancient Mayan site - the original Chetumal at Santa Rita. I will not be able to write to the four classes before next weekend but when I do, I will tell them something about their schools and send the letters as attachments...'

Back again in Belize City and having been asked to extend my placement I had a letter for Ellajean...

'...My posting is due to come to an end on 6th. March 1999. I am able to continue until the end of April 1999. If you wish me to extend the posting for the extra two months please provide written confirmation. To date, I have been able to take only 14 of the 30 days holiday due in the first 12 months of employment with EDC. That period came to an end at the beginning of September. I'm sure that you will remember that five days of the holiday taken was at your request. It also happened that I spent three of those days on EDC business: to address the Corozal Branch of BNTU; to attend the first meeting of Corozal Teachers and Principals involved in the Lower Division Trials; and to speak with parents of children at the Assembly of God School, Santa Rita. I suggest that the remaining 16 days (80% of one month) be remunerated in lieu, since holiday now applies for the current year...'

All of the latter was aimed at raising more funds for schools' computers.

The Orientation Workshop I went down for was specifically for District Education Officers and Belize Teacher Training College personnel and lasted two days. My closing address reflected learning and experience in Belize: awareness of great talent assembled; commitment to Education; all giving the same message but that we now go back to reality; get excited, give the Student the task; we must move towards children's ownership of their own learning.

And being Belize we were able to link hands for the prayer 'The Wire Fence' - Quoist.

The 19th November is another National Holiday, Garifuna Settlement Day. There was quite enough of that on the radio for me and I didn't fancy dragging all the way down to Dangriga to stay up all night and then face coming back again. In any case, I have more than a few misgivings about the way in which ethnic groups are in danger of becoming fractionalised through independent 'cultural' fervour. I spent the day finishing the packing of the Christmas parcels for the UK and sending mail...

'...Today is (yet) another public holiday, being Garifuna Settlement Day. The disruption of school life and children's learning has been horrendous this term. All of these things are important of course, but they do tend to go over the top (understandably, I suppose, as all the groups celebrating are really establishing an identity)...'

'...There are considerable changes going on as a result of the recent election, particularly in Education. At one level, it makes no difference because the curriculum work continues unabated - strengthened even. On the other hand, the director of the Curriculum Development Unit has been removed. I hadn't really said anything about her before because the echoes are too close to home. Suffice to say that she was hopeless (much as I like her) and caused a great deal of damage, being interested only in control! (Where have you heard that before?) She didn't bother me because I came with fairly considerable experience and attacked my work accordingly but she was the reason why I would not consider returning to Belize for a further term. Now the picture has changed. I have made a lot of friends and have been in a position to 'enable' Teachers and Principals across the two Districts who are continually asking me to stay. Also, VSO have an interesting piece of research in mind which they are asking me to undertake in schools. I will be extending to the end of April which is an extra two months and then I will come home. As to the rest of it: I had made up my mind but I am prepared to listen to what is being said to me. I will be meeting with the new Director of the new Quality Assurance and Development Section (QADS) which includes the Curriculum Development Unit, tomorrow. We shall see. Schools in Belize do not have half term but children are only in school for 36 weeks...'

I went to Belize City first thing this morning because I have been asked to stay beyond my current placement. This is to help set up all sorts of exciting things as well as continue to coordinate the introduction of the new curriculum. VSO are also asking if I will undertake a piece of research for them in schools. I hadn't intended to stay because of a poor management regime but all that has changed following the election and the whole thing looks very exciting. As it stands, it looks as though I will be going home for a six week holiday from the beginning of May and then returning to Belize. Fancy going home for a holiday! Anyway, it all looks too good to refuse. My two conditions - namely enabling Belizeans to take on and continue the work rather than a gringo and my having sufficient challenges are met. It would be quite something to be in on the ground floor in the way which is being suggested; must have done something right. Now that Ellajean has gone and the new structure is giving autonomy and responsibility it should be possible to get the job done much more easily and it is a bigger and wider ranging job too.

I went round to see Neria to give the family the news and stayed for lunch before trying to rush back to Orange Walk to deal with my Christmas post. Needless to say, the bus went ten minutes before I expected and I had an hour and a quarter to wait before catching the next one; this involving being whisked down to Belize City to sit in the very close heat in a waiting Urbina bus in case I should happen to be tempted to use the competition.

It was 3:30pm by the time I got in but I was able to post the remainder of my Christmas parcels for the UK - at a cost of $102. With cards, the total post comes to $170. Expensive!

Ricardo phoned to say that he and Marbella would collect me at 3:00am on Sunday morning to go to Caledonia and for the killing of the pig. I phoned Orvin to say that I had got a new cartridge for the school printer ($63) while I was in Belize City. He wasn't in so I asked for him to phone back but he didn't. This has happened before and is a disappointing aspect of his way of working.

'Dear Henry, News, news, news... The parcels for Corozal Methodist and Christian Assembly of God arrived at the Post Office this afternoon and I picked them up when I returned from Belize City. They will be delivered on Monday. I expect that I will go to Santa Rita first as the Chell bus will drop me there. I think that it will be important to send some material off to England this week if possible and not to wait for replies before sending more. I believe that is the only way to keep the flow going. I was in Belize City today because I have been asked to stay beyond my current placement... I will be moving to Corozal on my return so I will be living close by...'

Saturday started with clearing up and doing some washing which had, unusually, built up during the week; this because it has been very wet and nothing would dry. I only have an inside line in the covered space outside the back door which opens on to the stairs leading to the apartment below. The wall of blocks with square holes in gives protection from wind and rain but the space is small. Even though the balcony at the front is so big it only has a roof and that is useless in this weather. Then heartening mail all round...

'...Herewith as attachments, letters for 7G and 7R; perhaps some of the children might like to reply. It would be a useful way of finding the right way to promote a vibrant exchange. I think the two main principles to keep in mind are to treat the Buddies as exchange students and act accordingly, and to communicate as far as possible class to class as a body. There are so many differences to learn about, the mind boggles - and yet we are all the same...'

'...Your Buddy, or should that be Buddies? Choco-Mint arrived in Orange Walk Town yesterday. George the Snail was delighted, especially with the Mint side of things. He decided that Choco-Mint is Gemini which he approves mightily, as well as approving the outside shell. However he is not sure whether to refer to Choco-Mint as he or she so I will use the initials CM for the time being. It is not the sort of thing one asks is it? Perhaps you could solve that problem for us. CM was being looked after by the Post Mistress who was also looking after the luggage. It is difficult to look after luggage when your 'other self' is not properly tucked away although it was good to see all of whom we were dealing with. Anyway, fortunately I have friends in the P.O. so the arrival was quicker and more comfortable than it might have been. I also had some awkward questions to answer over the lack of a passport. Right now, CM is resting in front of my computer gently insisting that I write to you. I see that CM doesn't write very well so someone else will have to do all that and I have made a start until the Buddy arrives in Corozal Methodist School on Monday. Actually, I suspect a superior intelligence which is lurking behind that minty freshness of face and deep black eyes (Choco is tucked up asleep). Perhaps that is why I am doing the writing and the Students at Corozal Methodist School will have to do the same.

I'm sure that the students will find your writing very interesting - I certainly have - and you can expect an early reply. However, you shouldn't wait until you receive a reply before sending more because the mail takes too long. There are plenty of ideas you can use. I'm sure that CM will help and also the Buddy who comes your way. Perhaps they will travel together at some point. Who knows what they will decide when they each get to know students in the other's country? If you wish to send correspondence, stories, any writing quickly, you can use my email address if you wish and I will arrange delivery. If you do this, please keep it to plain text only and it will save me work if you send as an attachment. That is how this letter has been sent. I would like to hear from you in any case. The Corozal Methodist School is 30 miles from here and right beside the Caribbean Sea. The town has about the same population as South Molton but is nonetheless, one of the major towns in Belize. Belize has a total population rather less than that of Plymouth. The students you are linking with are in Standard Five and are the same age as you but you will soon discover that this is a Junior School and students do not move on until the end of Standard Six (Infant1-2 + Standard 1-6). Some students may be older because there is a lot of repeating of years that may not have been successful…'

'…Your Buddy, Baby Bunting, arrived in Orange Walk Town yesterday, arms akimbo and wearing a Pooh Bear bib…'

'…Two things for you: I will be moving to Corozal on my return so I will be living close to all your linking schools and right next to the Caribbean Sea; also, when I come home, I would be pleased to be a resource for your four classes…'

<u>Caledonia Feast</u>

I was 2:15am to be ready for 3:00am to go to Caledonia but the time came and went without Ricardo and Marbella having arrived. I sat reading while I waited but then an awful thought occurred: had Ricardo said 2:00am? At that time the lights would still have been out. "No," I thought, this is Belize and people are rarely, if ever, on time. Even so, it was disconcerting and I did consider the idea of going back to bed before they arrived at just before 4:00am. Ricardo had been asleep in his cruiser after a heavy session the night before - much to Marbella's disgust! We set off and arrived in Caledonia to witness the dawn which was beautiful. Introductions and greetings were made and the business began without delay. The killing and butchering of a pig is a long job and always starts in the cool of the early morning. The despatch of the pig also falls to the eldest son of the family who happens to be Ricardo.

There were two pigs in evidence, already happily rooting round, and two more still unmoving from the night. One of the two was white and the other, larger and black had not long to go! Men and youths appeared from everywhere, each with his role to play so that the animal would be despatched without delay and without undue stress. The two pigs were separated and the black one given attention which she seemed to enjoy. Corn is a favourite food of the pigs and part of the attention was a special feed given by the children who normally look after her almost as a pet.

A quick movement secured the two back legs off the ground and roped them together. This seemed to be the only part which caused the pig distress and she objected strongly but she only had her voice and teeth available now, to make her feelings known and the teeth were rendered ineffective by a well-placed boot which trapped the snout to the ground.

The squealing ended very quickly and didn't seem to be any different at the moment when the knife penetrated the heart. This was Ricardo's job - I assume because he is the eldest of the adult brothers; their father, elderly now, living some distance away in another part of the village. All of this is part of life in the village and witnessed by the whole family but there was a noticeable silence for a few seconds afterwards as though old and young together and as one, observed the passing of an animal from their midst. Interesting too, how animals and wildlife are respected by village people; not at all persecuted as they might be in town by those who do not live with them and know no better.

I took no photos of the actual killing; feeling, rather, that doing so would be intruding on a privacy shared only among those present. The carcass was a different matter and I did take a set of pictures as the butchering progressed to the first sharing of meat and the subsequent barbecue to celebrate the eldest son's eighteenth birthday.

Everyone had a part to play. A table was set up next to an outside covered space, constructed from two piles of concrete blocks and two well used mahogany planks. When this had been washed down, the carcass was lifted by four men, one to each leg, from the place where it lay on to the table ready to scrape off the hair.

Well before we had arrived, a fire had been set, also under the covered space, and a large container of water heated to be ready for the cleaning. Some of this was poured over the body at intervals to enable the hair to be scraped off with sharp knives. More knives were available and one of the men was on hand for more or less continuous sharpening! Apparently, care has to be taken to ensure that the water hitting the hair is not too hot otherwise the white skin would be covered with a thin, black, sticky layer. Quite a long job and hard work but the scraping did not take as long as I expected, even including the great care which was taken around the more difficult parts: the limbs, the head and the tail. Nothing is wasted. Even the discarded hair seemed to be of great interest to the chickens all round, who were also quick to polish off any tiny scraps which came into their view.

Next came the washing. The whole carcass and the 'table' on which it lay, was thoroughly scrubbed using scourers and washing powder. Washing powder is much more effective than soap with cold water.

I have seen that many people use this method to wash pots but they are always well rinsed in clean water afterwards, as was the pig's skin and the table; the result a gleaming white where once had been black as night. I suppose the bacteria in the gut continue to work as the anus too, was part of the cleaning process.

The carcass was held on its back, held by the feet, while the skin of the whole length of the underside was slit right up the middle, penetrating through flesh and bone to reveal the innards. Only once did I note an error of judgement in this team effort as one of its members moved to remove the feet before they were used to hold the body in place; an act delayed by a barely noticeable sign and nothing was said. The carcass had now become so much a poundage of meat, fat, skin and bone with very little to discard. More washing, a removal of blood from the chest cavity, the guts separated from the rest and hands that had done this before set about the meat.

The women went off to deal with the innards in a shining clean zinc galvanised bath and helped in spirit only, by the children who were very much part of the proceedings; not revelling in any way but joyful at the shared activity and the feast in prospect; each fully aware of his and her place. The gut is used to make black pudding together with the blood. Meanwhile, the men removed the skin and its layer of fat which would be rendered down to produce lard for cooking and tasty snacks. The head, removed and lying to one side did not look in any way grotesque as I had expected but somehow a comment on a necessity observed which I am unable to explain. It would not, in any event, be wasted.

At this point I went with Richard (also Ricardo but choosing the English as a mark of independence from his father) to explore the village at its river edge and enjoy the peace there; another physical and powerful sign that life goes on; somehow cleansing of all that is around; the tranquil expanse of water which is the New River from under the bough of a spreading tree, its leaves reflected in the water; then downstream, in direction only for the flow is such to appear a stillness; and up towards the next village on the other side, San Estevan, nine miles away. The water is still in flood by some four feet in the aftermath of rain following Hurricane Mitch in October, which so closely threatened Belize and devastated Honduras particularly, Nicaragua and Guatemala before becoming a storm attacking Florida and making its way as a depression across the Atlantic to promote bad weather in the United Kingdom. The colour is the reflected and deepened colour of the sky on the smooth and slow moving surface; the water itself being heavily brown with sediment washed down by the heavy rains. The village edge too, is beautiful by the river. A single tree dominates the concrete and stone landing recently made for ease of use by boats and providing local people with a communal place to swim mostly in the evening of the day and before the mosquitoes are active; and the palm trees, lush and verdant, reflect almost perfectly in the water.

Meanwhile preparations had been made for the cooking of the meat which was ready to be cut up and jointed. The first taste which was a meal in itself was joints cut from the back along the spine, cooked in its own fat and seasoned only with salt and soon to be ready. The fire is fed with hardwood which starts long and is pushed into the fire as the ends burn away in the manner of the old woodsmen and copied by Scouts whenever they have the chance.

As this first cooking took place another walk in a part of the village by the water, a short distance further downstream where mangroves grow and some cohune which is the straight and hard timber used in the construction of traditional houses.

Not long after came the tasting. I don't think I have ever tasted pork as fresh nor as delicious as that first bite - and of course, I was not alone! The barbecue was set up much in the manner of the butchery table except that it was under the covered space as was the earlier fire, and was topped by a huge barbecue pan and grill completely covered with more than enough meat for everyone. I did have a turn - under supervision of course! In case there should be any wonder about what happened to the head, the removal of the edible parts was recorded before they were cleaned and cooked - a part considered a delicacy as it is in many parts of the UK; but back home, few people seem to know, or want to know, what it is.

Two of the many well fed and satisfied family and friends celebrating the birthday in such a closely communal way are father and son; visitors, as I was, welcomed into the bosom of the family and the village and privileged for an all too brief while, to share in its time honoured life and history; it being said among the elder people that Caledonia was once a camp formed by the British people who came and cut logwood and mahogany. After the British left, the inhabitants remained and worked to make it the village it is today. Among the inhabitants was a woman called Seledonia. She was the oldest among everyone and after she died they wanted to honour her by putting her name to the village which later on, became Caledonia.

Parcels from 7R and 7G were delivered to Corozal with their Buddies, Baby Bunting and Choco-mint and a letter arrived for delivery to all four new classes…

'…Hello from South Molton School! By now, your 'buddy' should have arrived, along with some letters of introduction from pupils in year seven. There was a real mix up in the passport office in England, and this delayed the buddy's departure. Things seem to have been sorted out now, and special permission was granted for the buddy to travel without his documents. His passport has now been prepared and should arrive in Belize within the next week. Please don't forget to send it back with him!

Pupils here are looking forward to receiving a guest buddy from Belize, and hope that you will be able to send one soon. They are already making plans for him, and deciding who will look after him and write up his diary. Perhaps it will be a 'she' though! We will just have to wait and see!

Once the 2 buddies have got used to travelling between our two countries, a regular exchange of work, ideas and questions and so on will be able to take place. Individual pupils can also write directly to each other. I would be happy to receive any email messages at my own address, as this is probably a bit more reliable than the school address at the moment. I'm sure Mr Max would send some from his computer if need be. Perhaps there are some other email addresses we could use?

I have already packed up the next envelope for your school - work written by year seven pupils early in the school year. This is their first year in their new school, and it explains their feelings after the first few days. Most of them joined us from much smaller primary schools, so life in a larger school was bound to seem different. This work was put on display at a recent parents' evening, and I must point out that no spelling errors were corrected! I have some ideas about work to complete for future mailings - but is there anything that you would like us to provide? Perhaps your children would like to think about this…'

'…I delivered the two packages yesterday morning and had a lot of fun with the students and the Buddies. I try to get them to see the Buddy as an exchange student as far as possible – also emphasising that the ones you have sent will have 'grown up' with someone from an early age. I see in your letter to Teachers and Pupils that you refer to the Buddies as 'He'. Perhaps you could check with the owner. I hope that Choco and Mint are both the same (or perhaps on second thoughts, I hope they aren't - I think perhaps I'll stick to the Gemini split personality and treat Choco-mint as one!) At the moment, Methodist is much livelier than Christian Assemblies but I have great faith in Tomas Zetina and once it gets going properly, theirs will take off too. All four schools should be sending a package and a Buddy to arrive before Christmas so you may have to make space in your end of term scheduling to make the best of their arrival. It would be nice for the Buddies to spend Christmas with an English family. Glad the children liked the letters. Do encourage those who so wish to write back. I will do my best to answer all letters and, as I said to them, it will enable me to tell them what they want to know rather than what I think. It is nice to have writing which has not been 'corrected'. I have made a point of drawing attention to this because it is a way of demonstrating that all children are the same which emphasises that differences are in learning - experiences and environment. I have set out your letter to Teacher and Pupils and I will print off enough copies to give one each to all the students. There is a new digital duplicator in the District Office and as I was the one to set it up for them I get preferential treatment! My itinerary as outlined in the last mail is in the process of being confirmed. I have been asked to continue with the curriculum to involve all Lower Division Schools and Pilot in the Middle Division to start with. All of that will involve dealing with a lot more people; also, to have a hand in assessment and the setting up of an inspection system. To have the opportunity to enable teachers rather than strangle them is very exciting - and that is how it has turned out so far…'

'…The mix up in the passport office seems to have been sorted out now, so the official documents will soon follow. The classes enjoyed competing for a t-shirt while designing their passports…'

There is always the unexpected (especially in Belize apparently) and my telling Bertha about staying in Belize led to a discussion about her applying for a grant from the British High Commission to take Master's Degree in England. I said I would provide a reference which I wrote for her next evening. There was a Principals' meeting for Orange Walk at St Peter's from 2:30pm and then, on to show Barbara Blades how to use her computer.

I went in to the office first thing on Wednesday morning to give a reference to Bertha, arrange for BJAT results for St Peter's 1996 to be sent from the Assessment Unit for Helen Terry and to print Paul's letter for each of the students. All week so far, there have been four Teacher Trainers from Belize Teacher Training College working in the District Education Office in Orange Walk Town and today one of them surprised me by saying "I have been meeting Baby Bunting!" We had met and spoken to each other before, smiled and said good morning but that was about as far as it went. This means that she knows me; so many people do! I am the only Englishman around and one of very few white people who are mostly visitors; just a few from the United States. Also, the work I do and the time I spend with Principals, Teachers and Children means that other people take notice because it affects them. On the other hand, I knew very little about her. I am very poor at remembering names and I meet an awful lot of people. This is made even more difficult because all the ways we have for remembering all sorts of things in our own town and country have to be re-learned in a different culture. Imagine my surprise then, when this very pleasant young (to me!) lady follows up a smile of greeting by saying "I have been meeting Baby Bunting!"

My mind went straight into a whirl. 'Baby Bunting,' I thought? I don't think 'Baby Bunting' in Orange Walk District and it took time to switch in. 'Baby Bunting?'... Buddy! Corozal District..... Which School? All this in a flash I suppose. It seemed a long time to me but I don't think she noticed and I have it. I see Baby Bunting in my mind's eye and all the fun we had when BB was introduced to the children (students) of Standard Six in Christian Assemblies of God School at Santa Rita, just outside Corozal Town in Corozal District.

She is speaking. "My daughter is in Standard Six at Santa Rita and she brought Baby Bunting home last night to stay with her." My face must have shown that I was now completely switched in to all that she was saying despite my surprise. Santa Rita is thirty two-miles from Orange Walk. It is early in the morning and she is at work as am I. It always surprises me when I find out how far many people travel to go to work. She continued... "She brought Baby Bunting home last night to stay with her. She hasn't stopped talking to her and telling her all about home and what to do. And they slept together last night. I think the boys have decided that Baby Bunting is a boy and the girls have decided that Baby Bunting is a girl."

I hadn't thought of that. I say "I'm not surprised" but I was because I hadn't thought of it. Do I still have the problem, I wonder? Do I continue to refer to Baby Bunting as BB? Or do I too, go with the boys and decide on 'he'? She for now anyway!

"She is very excited about it all; an English Buddy! Last night she went out and came running back because she had forgotten to take Baby Bunting with her. Then, this morning, she wanted to know what to write about it all." "All of it!" I hear myself say...

Bertha phoned to tell me about a musical instrument making session at Hattieville which had been arranged by Belize City - something which Ellajean had set up. I found that only one person per District had been allowed for and we were to decide which. I never get into that sort of arrangement anyway so I will not be going.

Someone, somewhere, decided that all the terms should be the same length so the new term starts on Monday, to be interrupted by Christmas three weeks later. Having no monitoring to do until the second cycle also starts next week I set about catching up with some writing, washing clothes and housework; sent another email to 7R about Baby Bunting; checked on the Post Office for mail, the District Office for FAX and paid the electricity bill which arrived this morning. Next day I decided to change diet to overcome malaise which has relentlessly increased; also to stop using tap water for cooking except when the water is to be eventually thrown away such as in boiling potatoes: Enriched oat cereal for breakfast, fruit - probably oranges and bananas. Not too keen but there it is. Try to get at least some more exercise as well. Several short walks on Saturday, just around the town; didn't get much work done; sent email to Paul and phoned Marco who is coming (tomorrow morning 8:00am?) to give me details of the lap top computer which he says his cousin can buy in the States. In the event Marco did arrive with Miriam and the children, Tabo, Chino and Manuela at about eleven which was a jolly visit. I'm now waiting to see if he can obtain a laptop for me.

'...Would you like any more tee-shirts? Is there anything else you would like? Please don't hesitate to say. I'm not particularly bothered about funds - I'm doing what I want to do (as usual!) Have any of the writings or resources already sent suggested anything else you would like? I think that the opportunities for young people learning from each other and widening the horizons of their understanding are much too valuable to neglect - so whatever. Some of the points of previous letters and thoughts have been missed. I have a complete documented record. Would you like any part or all of it? Please, that is only meant exactly as written (as always). It is just the way I work and more so nowadays and in trying to make some sense of this experience for myself. I could at least provide you with a list of my files if it would be helpful and you would like one.

I am getting to know a lot of parents as people now, not just as parents. One of the things that I am hearing often from those whose children were involved in 'Linking' last year is the quote "If I don't get an answer this time..." It seems to me that many letters were sent from individual to individual at their home addresses. I think this should be discouraged until the relationship on a class level is firm. That is the chief reason why I suggested a change of two of the schools - they couldn't operate on a class basis because they are too big. I know from my own experience how hard it is to work on the correspondence at a personal level. I have got it right now but that has only been through very persistent writing on my part. I have been down to the Post Office every day this week on the lookout for the packages from 7D and 7H but they haven't shown up yet. My going down to the Post Office direct can save as much as a week. Next week I have to be in Orange Walk schools on Monday and

Tuesday but I will be going to Corozal schools on Wednesday and Thursday so I'm hoping the parcels will be here by then...'
The second cycle of monitoring started with a visit to Louisiana.

'...I have talked with Standard Six at Louisiana today, who linked with 7R last year. Many of them would like to see the relationship grow. Attached is the basis upon which I outlined the way they might continue. I expect to receive some 'writings' from them on Monday of next week which I will word process and send as email attachments so that you can print them straight out. I decided that I would have to make the running in this case but, if you get the chance to make the point without upsetting anyone, the six schools are not on the same campus; they are up to 35 miles apart across Central American lowland! I have deliberately not told you of the horrendous problems that have been faced by Louisiana School (this is not England) but they have tried. I know that some students have written as many as three letters in a row to last year's 7R, without having a reply. I suggest that the most profitable route for those children would be through their English lessons as outlined in the attached notes. The attachment is the gist of my talk with them this afternoon and may be of use to 8R. I expect that they will be starting on some writing in the ordinary way as well but that is unlikely to reach you before the end of term. Immaculada should have some writings already, for 8G when I visit tomorrow - if they haven't already sent them. The arrangement and the basis in English remains the same...'

At the end of a day monitoring at St. Peter's, on visiting the Post Office I found that packages had arrived for St Paul's and Calcutta. I had to be in Corozal next for a day at Xavier and Calcutta being three miles or so back along the main highway, I phoned the School to arrange delivery. First call in the morning was then to St Paul's to deliver their package. Mr Chan's mother collected his son from there at lunchtime and arranged delivery of the package for Calcutta; also visited Methodist and saw some of the contents of their package which was just about to leave for England with Buddy Tookie.

Today, Thursday is the Feast of St Francis Xavier and the school is on holiday so I have tried to catch up with some work at home and in the office and phoned Orvin to check that the package had arrived and that Calcutta packages would be posted this week. He suggested a fishing trip to Caye Caulker this weekend which sounds good.

'...Dear Friends in 7D, Your Buddy, Boxing Bruno, arrived in Orange Walk Town today. George the Snail was beside himself with delight. He had already met Choco-Mint from 7G and Baby Bunting from 7R and here was yet another two Buddies because Ed arrived from 7H as well. Then he looked at the class list and I simply couldn't hold him down! "Wow!" he cried, as he does when he sees something mega-exciting, "Wow! I know him and her and him and... (Counting...) I know twelve of the students. Hey! How about that? Mind you," he added, "I know all the students at Calcutta Government School - and not just those in Standard 5." When George calmed down and began letting his mind wander over all he had seen and read and was talking to BB, he looked at his new friend and said "You know what?" "What?" said BB. "I'm glad you're Bruno 'cos I reckon Bruno's a boy and I like to know whether to say he or she. There was some doubt about Choco-Mint and Baby Bunting and I don't like to ask. Well you don't do you? Boxing Bruno sniggered, waved his red gloves and stuck his thumb up...

...I have to go to Corozal Town tomorrow and someone from the school will meet me there to provide the final transport for Bruno to meet with his new friends...'

'Dear Friends in 7H, Your Buddy, Ed, arrived...'

Also for last year's Buddy friends...

'...Dear Friend in 8G, I'm sorry I don't know exactly, to whom I am writing but no doubt you will tell me. I tried to get it out of Fluffy but she gave me a 'you should know without asking me' sort of look and made it quite clear that she wanted to go to La Immaculada School without delay and report on her experiences in England. Anyway, that is why I am writing to you. Fluffy's diary, which I know you had a hand in writing, is brilliant. I enjoyed every word of it and I know that the students at the school will do as well. Both Fluffy and her diary are safely home and I expect that you and your form will hear from them very soon. I can't tell you about their greeting with Fluffy because the students were all away at lunch and I left her resigned to waiting the time out with the Principal who was reading the diary.

Unfortunately you won't hear from the same students because they have all moved on to High Schools or left school. This is because you were linked with Standard Six, which is the last year in the school. However, I know that the new Standard Six is preparing a lot of descriptions of themselves, where and how they live, stories, reports etc. to send to you and with any luck, you may receive them before the end of term. Be prepared for a lot of questions prompted by your diary. A lot of the things you take for granted in the writing would be unknown or not understood by Belizean Students. This actually makes your diary even more interesting. All writing which promotes questions is interesting; a really good way of getting to know each other.

Actually, I think that there is enough material in your diary to provide ideas for your whole form to be occupied in English for a long time - writing of all kinds - and for you all to gain a lot from doing it as well. Just from the first two paragraphs there are the Milky Way, Trago Mills and Trains. I know about Milky Way but Belizeans don't. Some will have seen something similar on TV or may have been to the States (a few do). Clearly, there is a death slide, another slide with balls at the bottom, a cafe and some animals but you see how it whets the appetite? You could do a whole project on the Milky Way. Even if you used their brochure, there is a lot more to build on from a personal point of view. Even more so, Trago Mills; there is nothing quite like Trago Mills is there? What a great project that would produce - lots of Geography and Social Studies there too. As for trains, Belizeans know about them of course but there are no trains in Belize and very few roads. In your next paragraph there is a massive project called Exeter! As I said - a brilliant diary; something really good to build on and well worth all the effort you must have put into writing it. I was moved to search quite hard to discover its author but I could not and I didn't recognise the writing style although it was quite a while since I was at SMUJS - if I should have recognised it. Do write and tell me.'

'…I saw the material which is coming from Methodist today. It is brilliant; food for thought. They have arranged all of it to be shared by the whole form. I didn't see student details as I hadn't much time. If they haven't done that it would be something to ask for. The Buddy is Tookie, a friend of the Belize National Bird and made by the students…'

The new arrangements for the Education Development Centre were made clear at the first meeting of the newly named Quality, Assurance and Development Section (QADS) which was at Theresa Catering Services, 11, Central American Boulevard from 9:00am to 5:00pm. The roles of each of the five departments were presented in the morning, followed by discussion and the afternoon was given over to a social event. Dinner was excellent; altogether a great starter for the promised weekend with Orvin, his two boys and his cousin on Caye Caulker.

The speedboat left Belize City heading for Caye Caulker at around 10:00am. I was travelling with Orvin Rancheran who is the Principal of Calcutta Government School which links with 7D, and his two sons. Orvin had telephoned the evening before and asked if I would like to spend the weekend fishing with them! Would I!!? The big twin Yamaha outboard motors opened up as we cleared the restricted speed zone at the mouth of Haulover Creek which passes right through Belize City to join up with the Belize River on the North Side. A big building rapidly receding close to where we started is known as the commercial centre but is perhaps better described as an indoor market on three floors. There is a café inside which looks out on the river from above, where scraps from filleting fish are thrown out and it is good to watch perhaps twenty pelicans competing for the food by their twists and dives in the air and combat in the water. The now distant water alongside is where the old swing bridge is still operated by hand. This is a monument which Belizeans have refused to have replaced and it is currently being restored. The day is warm and humid already but the Caribbean has only a gentle swell and the breeze, wind really, from the speed of the boat is very pleasant while, coupled with weaving between lesser Cayes in the shallow water, green and lush, the movement is almost soporific and time passes as in a dream. The jetty of the small island came in sight and it was wake up time as the passengers on the crowded boat moved to be first off and we, being local, took our time. On shore the 'roads' are hard sand and maybe three metres wide, the only traffic being the occasional bicycle and tiny two-seater electric buggies. It doesn't take long to walk the whole island so the latter are more for tourists really. Orvin's cousin had to be found first, going about his business, and then we made our way to the three cabanas which he lets to visitors – one of which we occupied for free.

It was much later in the day when we set off for the fishing. As the temperature is well up in the nineties, Belizeans wait until the sun is on its way down before venturing out on to the water. In any case, the fishing is better by then; not for me though; I can go through all the motions and even get them right but I caught nothing in the whole two days while the other three filled the bottom of the boat in a most respectable manner. My time was better occupied soaking up the whole atmosphere, the clearness of the water and the amazing variety and colours of fish so easily seen. I had wondered about bait though, as we set off but that puzzle was soon solved when 'Plantain' as Orvin's cousin is called, stood in the bow of the boat and spun a weighted net out over the water, drew it closed and hauled in a multitude of small fish, bait size, ready for action. Then, all too soon for two whole days, it was time to leave.

I had thought and still think that four terms of equal length with no half-term break is a good idea for schools but the sudden decision to arrange things with a Christmas break three weeks into one of them, especially while working up a new curriculum was more than one step too far; disruption at best. Finding a gas leak in the cooker first thing on Monday morning which made me late for once didn't help. It wouldn't have been worth starting a monitoring before break so I went down to the office first to print some more sheets, spent the rest of the day monitoring three lessons at Louisiana and decided not to attend the Christmas Pizza Party at the British High Commission on Thursday because it will take two days out and there is too much pressure on the time available for monitoring as it is. I gave up monitoring in St Peter's because of the exams and spent the rest of the week at Xavier. Then it was a weekend of the regular sorting out of mail problems for individual students, finishing many Christmas cards made with pictures I had taken including an armadillo and catching up with mail…

'…*Topsy arrived today - from Tomas Zetina at Santa Rita. 7R were really impressed, and there was a bit of a fight over the letters. I was pleased about this, because I did not think they would react in this way. I hope they will get some letters to their new friends before Christmas. This looks like it could be a solid contact. I hope the other packages arrive soon to satisfy the other groups…*'

'…*I came home from Corozal at lunchtime as I had a meeting in Orange Walk this afternoon to find the good news about Topsy. I phoned the school right away and as you are six hours ahead of us they have had the news of Topsy's arrival the same day! Could you please encourage even personal mail from children to be sent to the schools rather than home address to start with? …*'

'…Christmas is certainly coming. I'm not sure whether it all starts earlier here or not but it might well do. There seems to be always some celebration going on anyway as there are a lot more occasional holidays and, being mainly a Catholic country, any amount of Feast (Saints') Days. I quite often find a school closed because it happens to be their Saint's Feast Day. What is amazing is the elaborate decorations people go in for. I think a lot of them are rather garish but Belizeans love it - especially the Mestizos. The house next door, owned by the family who own this one (Orlando Burns - Landy of Landy's and Sons - is the father), is covered with coloured lights - including the roof; and there is a Nativity group, dwarf size at about three feet high which lights up as well. No one seems to bother that we are only in Advent so that only Mary and Joseph should be around yet. No! We've got Jesus, the shepherds and the Wise men as well. I must try to get some photos of some of the displays this year but it is risky taking a camera out at night.

Yes, the new term date is definitely weird. It came out of the blue and its only merit is that it (allegedly) makes all the terms the same length. Lots of things happen by somebody's decree (common in developing countries) and that someone rarely considers the consequences or (I suspect) is able to. I could go on about that but it is really a subject for debate because just writing could give entirely the wrong impression about what are essentially happy, friendly and caring people. Lots of things have to change but change takes time. I have to keep reminding myself how long it has been since the Romans started giving us some ideas about government. Yes and no to doing the same job as now, when I return. I have been asked to continue to co-ordinate the introduction of the New Curriculum in the North but the job gets bigger. At the moment it is being piloted in the Lower Division (5-7 year olds) in 14 schools for which I have responsibility. In September, the rest of the schools follow on and, at the same time, pilot schools expand into the Middle Division (8-10 year olds); then on into the Upper Division (11-12 year olds) and the Secondary Schools. As the staff increases, part of my task is to work myself out of a job! It doesn't end there because I have been asked to become involved with introducing a new system of pupil assessment and with eventual inspection of schools as well. At the same time, administration is to move away from the centre to the Districts with a pilot exercise centred on Corozal District but including (as far as I'm concerned) Orange Walk. I will be moving to Corozal Town at some time so I will then be living right by the Caribbean! I'm surprised that you don't know about your form parcel. Boxing Bruno arrived safely on 1st December and insisted on meeting his new friends the very next day. I wrote a letter to your form and sent it as an attachment the same day.

The Post Office is about three quarters of a mile away, on the other side of the centre of town. When I walk there the temperature is usually in the nineties so I suppose it takes a bit more effort than you might imagine. It has been 'cooler' for the last week or two, at around eighty six or eighty seven degrees. There are similarities with our Post Office resulting from when Belize was British Honduras. The real difference is in the delivery. There are postmen but no letterboxes at the houses so you miss it if there is no-one in. Most people have dogs which are there to repel intruders so the postman remains at the gate. There are no outside boxes because the contents would be stolen. Most houses also have iron bars on the windows and those that have walls or fences have their gates locked as well as their doors. The Post Office shares a space with the Sub Treasury which is very important as Government monies due to individuals are distributed through a voucher system rather than cheques. Few people use any form of credit transfer. The two offices are in a single story building which also houses the Magistrates' Court. It is made of concrete and has a corrugated iron roof. The Police Station is next door and the Library is opposite (I'm their best customer - at the Library that is!) ...'

I went to a meeting of QADS in Belize City to start the last school week before Christmas. This meeting was much better from a curriculum point of view but disappointing personally as David Price was out of the country so I couldn't discuss the VSO research I had been asked to do or extending my placement in Belize with him. There was one orientation session to run for field testing Middle Division Outcomes in Corozal and a meeting at Orange Walk District Office re proposals for decentralisation. Nothing was mentioned about Corozal being the lead District except that it was made clear that Corozal was better organised, enthusiastic and endowed than any other District in Belize. Otherwise there was a huge mailbag from England which was wonderful and was my sole reason for visiting schools.

A first email from Hal in 7R for Tim at Santa Rita both exposed the difficulties in perception between the schools and started a chain of events in which I became closely involved. This first was hoping for an email from Tim not a reply from me...

'...I expect that part of you will be disappointed at this not being a reply from Tim at Santa Rita School and part of you will be pleased at just having a reply. I live in Orange Walk Town. Santa Rita is just on the other side of Corozal Town, some 32 miles or so away. Term ends tomorrow and I went there for the last time before Christmas this afternoon. However, I will phone the school in the morning (we are six hours behind you) and hang the expense! Tim's teacher is also the Principal. The school telephone is in their classroom so I may well be able to read your message direct to Tim. I will email his reply tomorrow evening so that you will have it on Saturday morning.'

When I phoned Santa Rita all the children had gone home at 11:30 for Christmas. Tomas wrote down an answer and delivered it that afternoon when it was sent; also...

'...*A package arrived today containing the display showing what year 7 children think of South Molton School. That's great! Today is the last day of (this part of) term so it will not go into schools until the week of 11th January. However, that is probably a good thing because it will give time to plan the impact. As all the four schools are now in the same District I will contact the District Education Officer on Monday and discuss with him the best way to get the most out of the display. Maybe we can find some portable boards somewhere such as you have obviously used...*'

The last days before Christmas were much as those days always seem to be: busy, short and not particularly notable. The computer refused to recognise a 4Mb card and started to run slow; photos of some of the Christmas lights at houses around the town in the evenings were jolly. I tried to walk out to Palmar but turned back when it started raining; started washing the front of the house which had become very dirty, the woodwork doesn't take too long but the burglar bars, made of twisted iron, are rather tiresome; delivered presents for Pedro and Benita, Chino and Manuela at San Estevan via Chino's bus; and fixed the computer which turned out to have bad connections at the RAM cards. Pedro came round on Wednesday morning with Daiami on his motorbike. They brought a tee shirt from Neria and Tabo which was very nice. They stayed for quite a while and chatted and Daiami managed well in working out what to do with Tut's Tomb. I delivered the presents for Ricardo and Marbella as well as Raul and Rosie where the boys threw their arms round me in what has become their standard greeting. Phoned Neria to check on names and she asked me to pick up 6lbs of masa from Pablo Reyes Tortilleria. It was essential for her tortillas so I had to check it out first. It was the one I thought in fact, so I could do that on my way to Belize City for Christmas. Lots more post came and went...

'...Ed the Duck has gone to St Pauls in Corozal Town. This can only have happened if Ed and Boxing Bruno swopped luggage before leaving England - indeed, before leaving South Molton. That's what you get for travelling without a passport. I will advise Chief Superintendent Berry of the British Emigration Authority accordingly. In the meantime I imagine that both Buddies will be in homes that wouldn't otherwise have entertained them over Christmas. The hospitality will be just as good I am sure. I have made a note to myself in case your two forms wish to do a switch. If you do, I will have to arrange some sort of ceremony between the two schools...'

Clearing up first thing on Thursday morning in preparation for going to Belize City; went down and collected some more post; changed my Library book and booked a seat on the four o'clock Premier to give me time to check on the Post Office again before leaving.

There was no more post and I left for a comfortable journey, arriving with the family at about 5:30pm. There were no other family staying and a very pleasant evening was spent after a roast ham supper. Neria and I took Miguel and Mariami to the service at St Joseph's at 9:00pm accompanied by David's Mum next door. The laptop computer wasn't available until Marco's cousin had left the States so it will have to come by mail and is now expected in mid-January. Christmas Day was very much a family time and with chilmole at lunchtime which I like very much. In the evening we all went to family friends who have the big Stationery House where we had a 'ricardo' supper and rather too much Belikin - certainly ten bottles - such that I resolved to give up Belikin altogether. It doesn't do me any good as I found out that night and next morning. It upsets my stomach and I have had enough of that.

We all went off to Benque on Boxing Day to visit Miriam's relatives and so that Neria could go across the border to buy children's clothes for a Lions' event. Neria had thought that I might go with them to Maskall but I hadn't got my passport. In the event, I would have preferred not to anyway. Miriam has lots of family in Benque and they all made us very welcome. It would have been difficult to say no to crossing the border had I got my passport and I had never been to Benque before anyway. I saw quite a lot of the town and was able to take a few photographs. Marco still doesn't have his licence so we were driven by their friend who brought his daughter. On the way back a puppy was collected to be grown into the house protection duties. Not something I like but there it is. In the evening we had chilmole supper prepared by Miriam. Two couples arrived who are friends from Dangriga.

Next day Neria went off to Dangriga for a couple of days with the friends and I spent some time going over a school budget with Tabo before coming home. I was asked to stay but at least to go for New Year so I will travel down on Thursday afternoon and come home again on Saturday. As I got home I found another email which had been sent on Christmas Day and the year ended until 4:00pm New Year's Eve with much more email and letter writing…

'…Package arrived today containing a multiplicity of Passports for Baby Bunting, Choco Mint and Ed the Duck; also letters for students at Christian Assembly and a departure diary for Ed and C. M. Int! These will be delivered when school starts on 11th January. Is a similar selection coming for Boxing Bruno? I haven't managed to talk to the District Education Officer about the display you sent but that will be dealt with before term restarts. I need to be advised about Ed and Boxing Bruno. I don't know whether you had time to get a good look at the passports but they are brilliant. There are some excellent ideas and I sat on the veranda laughing for fully half an hour reading them. I will write to each of the Forms as attachments in time for the start of your term but I thought you might like to know now that they had arrived…'

I travelled down to Belize City on the Premier which was a good journey but it was one of the two bendy buses which are nothing like as comfortable as the other ones. Neither the video nor the air conditioning was working. The latter was something of a discomfort as the opening windows, confined to one side only, and high up, are smaller and much less effective than on the regular buses, presumably because the vehicle is supposed to have air conditioning. We had all been invited to the Stationery House for the evening again which was very pleasant but Neria elected not to go and stayed to look after Martin and Mariami. Miriam took Miguel home just after twelve, I think, but I didn't see the going of her. There was plenty of hospitality as before and the main meal was my favourite - escabeche.

I had thought that I might go home tomorrow but Cousin Carlos Chan, the Tour Guide/Courier told me of a trip he was doing to Tikal on Saturday and said that he had a spare seat if I wanted to go. Do I just! Neria pointed out, again, that I should carry my passport to be able to take advantage of any opportunity that comes along so most of New Year's Day was spent travelling to and from Orange Walk for my passport although I did get some email done and we had a pleasant family evening downstairs but finished fairly early. Tikal in Guatemala is a World Heritage site deep in jungle surrounded by lush vegetation and is one of the major sites of the Mayan civilization. There are great temples and palaces in the centre and the remains of dwellings are scattered throughout the surrounding forest as it has overtaken the deserted space. There are artefacts and remains showing a religious, artistic and scientific culture which finally collapsed in the late 9th century. It was an awesome day but not one I would care to try to describe in any sort of whole having been there for so short a time. More modest sites in Belize seem easier to comprehend. Maybe I'll go back one day.

I had the sandwiches which Neria had packed for me when I got back and then went with Tabo and Marco over to Jack's place for a few drinks with him and Gill and Kathryn.

As I was sitting on my own on the 10am Batty Bus for Orange Walk on Sunday for some time, one of the characters who are continually demanding money got on and sat on the seat opposite to try his various methods of what amounts to extortion; certainly not a beggar. First he tried the hard sell on travel guides and notebooks which may well be stolen or obtained through some hard luck story from someone else.

Then the hard luck stories started, followed by attempts at aggression and finally trying to take a bag from the rack which happened to be mine; all of this accompanied by non-stop lies. The sad thing is that some people are in need but I suppose you rarely see them.

Back home next day and after doing the washing I set about organising the Journal for 1999 from January to June to cover going home at the end of April and coming back again mid-June. This enabled work schedules to be better identified as I don't yet have a diary for the current year. There is no other curriculum work to do today and I had lunch at the Crystal.

Off to Belize City again 6:15am I remembered the Government had had some consultations with Urbina and Escalante about scheduling to prevent the competition spilling over into vying for position on the road but I didn't know what the effect would be. It turns out to be fewer buses at that time, which are more crowded. Only Escalante are running so I assume that Urbina goes later. I watched the 6:30 pull out packed and waited for the next one, also Escalante, which came along almost right away but didn't leave until 7:00 - waiting unattended with the engine running the whole time of course.

I arrived at QADS to find that there was to be a meeting about the classroom assessment workshop at 9:30; met with David Price to confirm my extending and met up with Kathryn and Corinth particularly. The meeting determined that there would be one central workshop at BTTC on Tuesday, Wednesday and Thursday next week; Xavier, Calcutta, St. Paul's and St. Peter's are to be invited from the North. No time to waste!

I went for pizza lunch with Kathryn and then went to the bank and on to the Korea shop for some film for a family wedding on Saturday and a video cassette. My legs are still sore from the exertion last Saturday. I really must sort out my exercise (That is my New Year resolution). I returned to QADS to collect materials for Bertha's workshop on Thursday and letters about next week for Urbano Uck and Gilgardo Arcurio and got home about 5:15pm.

Gilberto Novelo called round at 8:00 to suggest postponing a trip to Lamanai tomorrow. I was pleased at this because it really has been most unusual weather today and the forecast is for more to come so there wouldn't be much to see and that would be a shame. At least that gives me another day to catch up with some writing which has really piled up over Christmas. Also I will be able to check on the mail and cash the voucher I received today ($240).

As I walked down to the District Office in the morning to deliver materials for a workshop on Thursday, Wilfredo Novelo called from the Lover's Restaurant to apologise for not running the trip today. The weather is fine and set fine of course although it is windy which might reduce clarity of both the water and the trees. I didn't do very much other than shopping, housework and some writing although I did have lunch at the Crystal. News never stops…

'…I'm not sure if you know that Ed the Duck who is one of the Buddies has arrived in Belize yet. He is mine (well really he was Paul's but he is too grown up to have stuffed toys). We all had fun at home making his passport and working out what inoculations he had to have (these included foul pest)…'

'…*Attached are a letter and a story for each of the forms 7D, 7G and 7R. I haven't received passports from 7H as of the Post Office today so I can only assume that theirs haven't been sent yet. I will write to them when they arrive. The display and the passports probably won't get into school before the 18th. January as our primary schools don't start until 11th and I have workshops in Belize City for the whole of that week. I will try to find a way of beating that! Please would you secure the use of email from your school as soon as possible? Not having that direct contact is now an obstacle in respect of material progress and the publicity I can obtain for the schools. Lastly, could we please establish at least weekly communication (yours doesn't need to be long!) so that I can keep things ticking over. Your whole year display of writing 'showing what year 7 children think of South Molton School' has also arrived and I am wondering what the best way to deal with it is. It is obviously intended to be split into four parts and given to each of your schools but the whole thing would be of enormous interest to other schools as well. Perhaps that can be done after each of your link schools have finished with them; that will give me time to find a way to mount such a large display where it can be seen…*'

'…Dear Friends in 7D, Your Buddy, Ed the Duck, has gone to St Paul's School in Corozal Town, which is the 'Link School' for 7H. Their Buddy, Boxing Bruno, presented himself at your school - Calcutta. This can only have happened if Boxing Bruno and Ed swopped luggage before leaving England - indeed, before leaving South Molton. That's what you get for travelling without a passport! I have advised Chief Superintendent Berry of the British Emigration Authority accordingly. In the meantime I imagine that both Buddies will be in homes that wouldn't otherwise have entertained them over Christmas. The hospitality will be just as good I am sure. I have made a note to myself in case your two forms wish to do a switch. If you do, I will have to arrange some sort of ceremony between the two schools. That should be worth some discussion in Year 7 Geography lessons! Please let me know the outcome and what you would like me to do. Yesterday, passports etc. arrived for three Buddies – Choco Mint (7G/Methodist), Baby Bunting (7R/Christian Assembly) and Ed the Duck (Yours, as I now discover). Passports for Boxing Bruno have not yet arrived. ???Complicated isn't it???

The diary for Ed's departure, written by Stephanie, and the American Airlines ticket (How did he get here without that?) have also arrived. The diary is just as interesting as the passports - especially as it has been so well thought about. Anyway, you produced the five (!) passports for Ed the Duck so those are the ones I am referring to now. I really enjoyed reading them. If the Passport Office displayed as much imagination as that travel would be much less stressful - perhaps! I'm sure Ed will be proud to find himself in possession of such documents so the story which follows on the next page is a bit of fun. (You have to remember the Quacking we used to do when going under a motorway flyover, the anatomy of a duck, the creator of Jemima Puddle duck lived in the Lake District and Gus Honeybun does (did?) birthdays on TV…'

E. Duck Flies In

Or should that be

Ducks Under

The Immigration Officer peered doubtfully over his half spectacles. The visitor before him cut a dashing figure in his black cape - or was it goggles and flying jacket? The officer was having a bad day and it was getting worse. He blinked as both overdressed individuals vanished and standing before him was the broad, hard and thick-lipped grin of a bird-like individual stripped to the bare(ish) essentials and carrying a great deal behind. 'Reminds me of someone I met in the English Lake District,' he mused to himself. He flicked through the five passports again. "You are Ed the Duck?"

Ed shifted his weight from one broad foot to the other, completing a thirty degree rotation of his body each way as he did so. He ruffled his feathers and drew himself up to a magnificent thirty centimetres. "Yes!" he said.

'My God it quacks!' thought the officer, looking Ed up and down in amazement, 'And it wears webbed shoes! - No! - By golly, they're feet! Pull yourself together you fool, and get on with it.' "How do you spell your name?"

"DUCK," Ed replied firmly.

"No your first name!"

"ED"

"It says EDD on this one… and this one… and this one…" A big sigh followed!

"I sometimes spell it like that."

"You're not supposed to….. Oh well…. Why do you have five passports?"

"I had five Passport Agents! It's the luck of the draw!"

"Ask a silly question," mumbled the officer, "What time's lunch?" He straightened himself up and thumbed through the passports, one after the other, to collect his thoughts.

"You seem to have more than one address as well?"

"Got more than one passport!"

"Ah… Yes?   Occupation… Swimmer?"

"Yes… and sometimes. I do a bit for the BBC. I hope you are not going to hassle me. I have a lot of friends in and around the pond: Freddo, Otis, Gordon, Gus Honeybun ('It's my birthday,' thought the officer), Edwina - she's a relative really, Mrs Duck - she is as well, and seven eggs - still to be hatched… so you could get thrown in."

"Well, you're paddling in a different pond here. We have sharks, barracudas and snappers in the Caribbean and crocodiles in the lagoons and rivers: not to mention fifty-four species of snake, jaguars and wild pigs! And I had duck for Christmas! … You do seem to have travelled about a bit. Let's see:

(1) Australia, Spain, America, France, Portugal, Turkey, Holland, Germany or is it…

(2) France, Spain, Greece, Germany, and Turkey or…

(3) Luton, Newmarket (Must be having me on) or...

(4) Brazil, USA, Asia, Turkey, France, China, Spain, and Canada or even...

(5) Where?"

"I told you! I've got five passports!"

"Pass..." The officer sighed.

'I'll show em,' Ed muttered to himself. 'I'll go to St. Pauls!!!!!'

A Case of Uncertain Identity
A. Lien Enters Belize!

The Immigration Officer peered doubtfully over his half spectacles. The visitor before him shifted uneasily; the long ears stood straight up and turned like tracking dishes to catch the verdict and the long bristles twitched as if to snatch the vibrations of his very thoughts. The officer was having a bad day and it was getting worse. "You are Choco, I suppose, from Great Britain, (age: 99? - doesn't look it)? That's what it says here and you look like the picture.

"Yes," Choco replied, somewhat relieved at the simplicity of the question.

"Funny address though; seems to be a school. Is that the right spelling? Shouldn't it be Molten like lead? And what's this Alswear bit? I think that should be All Swear!"

'Poor chap,' Thought Choco and tried to explain about the South town on the River Mole and the nearby village, Alswear, who's name had its origin (as far Choco knew) lost in the dim and distant past.

But the officer wasn't listening. He muttered "Don't care for the signature (spelt 'paw')," and moved on to the second of the passports. "Just a minute," he exclaimed, "It says Choco/Mint here! You can't do that!" He peered closely at the document.

"I've done it," Choco replied, but he was worried now and felt sort of faint as his knees buckled, ears shrank, back hardened and his stomach felt as if it was turning inside out. "Now I have done it..." the voice trailed off into an echo until it strengthened again.

"Hi!" said Mint.

The Immigration Officer immediately did a double-take! What else could he do? He could hardly turn turtle in the circumstances. And there was no doubt about them both-on this passport; before and after, as it were! 'Oh my god,' he thought, 'Just look at the size of those two front teeth,' and he hurriedly moved on to the next passport, reading aloud to himself: 'This is Chocolate, formerly known as Choco - Chocolate Hare. This is Mint the Tortoise..... Oh dear, Oh dear..." He turned the page. "Date of Birth... '87... Not very old. Place of birth... Llandridnod Wells? Ah... that's alright then... He's, She's, It's, They're Welsh; neither of them Bach! ... Next passport! ... Ah! One for Mint!"

Mint, or was it Choco, was a little offended at all this. "I'm British!" he protested.

"Don't care!" replied the officer, "I'm enjoying myself now. Let's see... occupation? ... runner? ... Is that all?"

"I do a bit of jumping and swimming. Don't you want to know where I've been?"

"Hardly dare ask... but you do seem to have moved about a bit... depending on which passport you happened to be using... that contravenes International Regulations you know... Let's see:

(1) Choco's Passport - no record. First time out?

(2) Mint's Passport - no record. Second time out?

(3) Mr Chocolate and Mint (Hare9696Toise - better than TorTare, which would be a sauce, almost!) - Gambia, Hareland, Toiseland (Are they in Rupert Books?)

(4) Choco/Mint - no record. Both time out?

(5) Mr Chocolate-Mint - Brazil, Gambia, Scotland, Madrid, Portugal, Austria, Wales… Belize... Not yet mate!

(6) Chocolate (front) Mint (back) - Malta, Florida, China.

Oh well... At least you've been together. Do let us know if you decide to travel separately! Your tickets are good anyway. That's what we say in Belize 'Let's Go, Man; Let's Go!' Pass!"

"PHEW; phew," echoed the reply.

Boxing Bruno in 'I Wonder' Land

('Will you, won't you? Will you, won't you? Won't you join the dance?')

The Immigration Officer sighed and peered doubtfully over his half spectacles. The visitor before him moved lightly on his feet prodding sharply at the air with his gloved fists. The officer was having a bad day and it was getting worse. He blinked as both fists shot over the counter in quick succession and jabbed at a punch bag, part of the luggage, which (unfortunately) lay on the counter. The guard leapt forward, rifle at the ready, and leapt back again as Boxing Bruno turned sharply, danced out of the line of fire and cuffed him playfully round the ear.

"Sorry!" said Bruno, grinning, "It's in the blood you know - and I come from a famous stable."

The officer heaved himself up on to his elbows, trying to look big as he had become a little hoarse (from a different stable). "Now, about these passports." he said, patiently, "You are only allowed one and you have six. What's more, they are all different. Do you have anything to say for yourself?"

"Yes!" was all the reply.

The officer waited in silence, seeming to expect more.

"It's convenient," said Bruno, "I keep losing them. I think this is the first time they have all come together. That is because I forgot to bring one and my friends had a good search when I found out and sent them all on just to be on the safe side."

"So why are they are all different?"

"Even a punch-drunk out of work boxer down on his luck could work that out! They've been to different places. You don't expect me to go back just to make them all look the same do you? The dates would be different anyway."

The Immigration Officer spotted the flaw in the argument straight away but you can't tell some people anything when they have decided that they are right so he held his peace. "Yes... Well... Let's see what we have here - and here - and here - and here - and here - and here. I think that's it! Now! Let's see! Four Boxing Brunos, a Bruno the Boxer and a Mr B Bruno! Are these you?"

"Yes!"

"Is that all?"

"Yes, yes, yes - yes, yes - and yes!"

"Dear Lord! And it's only Wednesday! - About the number - 097800, 097881, 097899, 097890, 09785608 and 276934. How do you explain that?"

"I couldn't get a matching set."

"That is not what I mean. It's the last two: 09785608 has too many digits and 276934 is out of date. You don't look that old. I mean mega years!"

"Use one of the others. I don't mind."

"You've given me six!" The reply was icy but the officer was also a gentleman and searched on. Nice pictures - all different! One of them is a dog! I mean - well it would be but this is a dog-dog if you see what I mean? How did that come about?... No! No! Don't bother!... Place of Birth - all different!... Address all different!... Visas - all different!... What time is it?... Five o'clock!... Pass!... Take him away Mr Max!"

"I'll show 'em," Bruno muttered to himself. "I'll go to Calcutta!!!!!"

Small Flags for Baby Bunting.

"Next please!" The Immigration Officer was tired. He was having a bad day. First there was the changeling Choco or Mint or Chocomint or any combination therefrom. Then there was that damned Duck - Ed! There's nothing worse than and Educ(k)ated bird! AND they had too many passports! The law clearly states that.... now what does it state?

The Immigration Officer looked up. Standing before him, dressed in a bright red baby-grow was a diminutive figure with (apparently) no hands and ('I don't believe it!') no feet, grinning from eye to eye (It would have been ear to ear but it was a very round grin). Immediately the officer buried his head in his hands, resting upon his elbows, and peered cautiously out from between his fingers. "Oh my god another one," he muttered.

"Name?"

"Bunting. - Baby Bunting."

"I can see that. (Put the flags out) Why are you wearing that yellow bib and bright red baby grow?"

"Don't be rude. It's part of the uniform! And it's a red track suit! Anyway, I thought we were supposed to look like our passport... for identification purposes... you know..."

"Yes I do or at least, I did... five passports!!" corrected the officer and you only look like the picture in some of them. And your address is different, your signature is different, your place of birth is different, your nationality is different and you don't seem to know where you have been. Can you explain?" He sank lower down on to his blotter. Two wet patches were beginning to appear as the wet on his fingers gathered into drops.

"Of course I can," Gurgled BB happily. "I was warned that there would be trouble at Immigration if I flew in without a passport so I got my friend Louise to make me one. Charles, Hal, Eleanor and Luke each made one as well, just to be on the safe side."

A loud sob came from the heap of fingers and hair on the blotter. Behind them shoulders jerked up and sagged back down, slowly fading into resignation and despair. "Do you have anyone who can vouch for you?"

"Of course I have," BB still gurgled happily, "There's Louise, Charles, Hal, Eleanor and Luke. They will..."

"But they... Oh never mind. Why are you allergic to Brussels Sprouts?"

"Weren't you when you were my age?"

"But they're good for you..."

"So say all the wrinklies - but not if you're allergic. That's my excuse and I'm sticking to it. In any case, I've had Chicken Pox and Fluff Disease."

"I'm not surprised but that leads me to emergencies. There are no friends or relatives listed, who may be contacted..."

"No need! BB continued to gurgle happily, "There's Louise, Charles, Hal, Eleanor and Luke. They will..."

"Yes... Well... Are you British or Tommasoman (ese)?"

"Definitely! No need to worry about that."

"I don't, now," sighed the Immigration Officer, "Any distinguishing marks?"

"Stitched at the seams" chortled Baby Bunting.

"I'm bursting at mine," was nearly the last word. "Pass," he said, smiling.

After a District Meeting at Orange Walk District Office at 9:00am on Friday, the weekend was completely taken up with the wedding of Melanie and Aldo at which I was guest as 'family' of the bride, and photographer; thus involved in all the final preparations the day before as well as the celebration. The feast and party were held in the 'Lion's Den', a huge thatched round-house, being the headquarters of the Lions Club of San Estevan right on the bank of the wide and slow-flowing New River with the rainforest on the other side. All is right in the nature of things; a timeless rhythm of nature and natural and nuptial.

The third cycle of monitoring in Lower Division, due to begin on Monday, was delayed by a workshop for Classroom Assessment called at short notice at QADS lasting until Thursday, postponing arrangements for three schools and resulting in a meeting of all Lower Division staff on Friday. The regional representative from the World Bank was in attendance. Maybe that had something to do with the rescheduling but whatever the reasons it did give me an unexpected opportunity to discuss the links project with him; and in reply to a UK student…

'…I am paid in country, a sufficient living 'wage' by the Belize Government. VSO are responsible for everything else. During the time I take to complete the research for VSO and write up the report, the Government will continue to pay that wage so I am officially working for them and there is no break in service. VSO, on the other hand, will still pay for the work done for them. This has been agreed by both parties so that I will be able to use that money to purchase a computer for another school.
It will be enough! I didn't take any holiday last year and I used that to barter the continued 'wage'. Neat isn't it? ...'

I had a film to finish off which had been used outside the church and at the reception at San Estevan last week and so walked along the highway to the fork leading to the sugar factory at Tower Hill and continued on to meet the main road at the fork for Guinea Grass and Shipyard; returned along the highway to where I left it and continued back through Palmar.

It was interesting to talk to some of the cane farmers from Corozal who told a different story about the reasons for the share which they have of the BSI operation and the provision of quotas which was said to have saved the industry. All the administration is through political appointees as are so many things in Belize. It is easy to buy a whole family of votes by awarding shared quotas and in this way, a huge number of votes can be 'bought' in the North. Cane farmers from Corozal enter from a different direction from the Orange Walk farmers. This is a direct result of the 'wars' between them when the Corozal factory was closed and the Tower Hill one took over. The new factory was apparently built by the Briceno family who have figured large in the fortunes and experiences in Orange Walk - one of whom is now Deputy Prime Minister. Interestingly, the cane from Corozal is of much higher quality because the soil is better. The Orange Walk soil is really too sandy.

The walk to San Estevan really happened next day!! And, though tired, I am so pleased to have done it not only because I enjoyed it but because I feel to be back on track towards the sort of fitness I like to have. I did the washing first and had breakfast - eggs, bacon and fried bread. This is the second lot of what is called butt bacon which is expensive in terms of foods I have been buying but very nice. I set off at about 11:00am with an orange to eat on the way back, a banana for the outward walk and water of course.

There was a surprising amount to see for what appears to be a rather dull road and I wished that I had taken my micro cassette recorder. Plenty of birds, butterflies and interesting vegetation where there were no cane fields. A huge black stork appears to live at about mile two. As I walked I fell to reflecting on how I feel about being here. I only came to two firm thoughts of many more fleeting ones. First, much as I love England in all its moods, I will miss all that is here. Second, I feel as though I have been let out to play and not been called back in! Yes I do work hard but it doesn't feel like it. I have always enjoyed what I do but here, there has been such a level of trust, appreciation and friendship even the work is part of being let out to play. Pedro and Benita drew up behind me on their motorbike at mile four.

This meant that lunch would be ready with the family as soon as I arrived! - Rice and beans and chicken in large quantity, water and Coke. Lovely! Neria had been up on Friday as I expected. She returned yesterday but she had delivered the photos I took of the wedding and they were pleased with them. The whole walk was about fourteen miles; pleased with that.

I went to Corozal on Monday and first visited St Paul's where I discovered that students in Standard Five were ignoring the new Year-7 and had the idea that they were to continue with the last year's link which is now Year 8. This seems to have come about through children staying another year in Standard Five when they should have moved to Standard Six, and spreading the idea. I don't yet know whether I have got the message across or fully, what has happened. I then went to Assemblies (Christian Assemblies of God or CAG at Santa Rita) to do some monitoring in the Lower Division and while I was there, had some discussions with Standard Six and delivered the passports for Baby Bunting and letters for four students. I returned to find email waiting but then lost my settings by accidently clicking on 'Get on the Internet' and having to follow through the Connection Wizard to get out of it. Now it doesn't work and I will have to find a way of linking with BTL tomorrow.

It took until about 9:45 to sort out my email. It is working but I have to go through a security screen every time now, which I didn't have to do before. Now it is a rush to get started on monitoring, covering different schools all week.

'…The pupils at this end are very excited about the link - it certainly seems to have worked much better this year. 7D, 7G, and 7R are all looking after their buddies, and there is real competition as to who will have the next turn. Each pupil with the buddy is writing up a diary which should build into an interesting snapshot of everyday life in England. In answer to previous questions, 7H and 7D would quite like you to relocate their buddies. Your idea of a special ceremony sounded really good. The passports for 7H are on their way, and should reach you soon. The parcel for 7G was excellent! The mini projects on different themes made very interesting reading, and made 7G determined to return something similar. The toucan buddy was also something else! The only snag there was that we had no idea of his/her name! Perhaps you could find out? The only thing that disappointed 7G was that there were no personal letters. Maybe these are on their way. If not, they would be really welcomed - this is probably my best group and the one most likely to maintain a link. A number of pupils are now writing independently, although it can be quite difficult to keep track. However, this is by far the best way for things to work. I know also that you have received a number of emails. Email is really my next target now. I have devised a system whereby pupils can work in our computer room as a group and save their letters onto a floppy disc. It should then only take a few minutes to send this off. The school system should be running effectively now. 7H are now the only class waiting for 'communication'. Once that *has been established, I will send all the buddies back in a package for phase 2…'*

'…I thought you would like the parcel from Methodist. You would probably enjoy regular communication with Henry too. He is a great character with an extremely lively mind. I think that the Toucan is called Toucy but I will check and make sure I have the spelling right. I will be delivering the 7G passports on Wednesday anyway, so that will be an opportunity. There were no personal letters to start with so that a full class to class exchange could be established. All that material was sent at the instigation of your Buddy Chocomint who is an exchange student with Toucy. The passports for Assemblies were delivered today and Calcutta's will be delivered also on Wednesday but their Buddy is at St Paul's! As far as I am aware, a package was sent from St Paul's for 7H before Christmas but I will check again…'

I talked with Necetas about the display of first impressions of South Molton School, the passports for Ed the Duck which Orvin has not passed on from last week, and working out some sort of exchange ceremony to put the right Buddies with their schools. Pedro sent an email using the Calcutta computer so that should be running this week.

Thursday morning was spent at Methodist again in Corozal and so I was able to visit St. Pauls where I left Standard Five in no doubt about my disappointment at their lack of action with 7H and left them to produce some thing for me to send by email by the end of the day.

'…Dear Friends in 7H, I found today that your 'Link' class here in Belize had sent you nothing. I was not happy about that and those of you who know me will not be surprised that I left the class in no doubt about it. I'm not going to go into detail because it would not be fair but you will know that things do go wrong in classes sometimes and some children sometimes prevent others from doing things by one means or another. Some of the children dashed off some notes for you while I was visiting another school and, to save time, I have typed them to send by email. You will also realise that, having got into this position, the children at St Pauls will now need some encouragement. I would ask you to do two things. Please send off another package of interesting 'chat', schoolwork, whatever. But, right away, find some means of sending a lively email via me. I will deliver it immediately and you should expect a quick reply, also via me. I will be in Corozal on Tuesday, Wednesday and Thursday 26/8th January so it would help if you could send by Wednesday evening. Standard Six have sent a package to 8H so you may like to talk to them as well - and the other year 7 forms have had packages from their schools. Below is a class list so that you at least know who you are dealing with…'

'…Attached is a set of letters for 7H in respect of St Pauls Anglican School Standard Five which is self-explanatory. Would you please urge a rapid response, via me, by email? This is important! I will give you some idea of how this has come about when I have more time but there are hints of it in my letter to the children. Suffice to say for now that the age range in Standard Five is from eleven to fifteen and the older ones are there by failing previous years. Encouragement is needed desperately, for the others. Note that a package has been sent by Standard Six (last year's 'Link') to 8H addressed to you. You can now communicate with Calcutta (Orvin Rancheran) direct…'

Set off for Belize City (Saturday) to go to San Ignacio for tomorrow's visit to the sink holes on the Urbina at 11:00am. I first called at the family to deliver the rest of the wedding photos and then on to Jack's to give him some photos he wanted of cane trucks and also one of him at the reception. Had a few beers there as Tabo and Marco arrived and we then went back for lunch to which I had been asked. Earlier, I arranged to catch the three o'clock express with Kathryn and Gill but wasn't able to and eventually caught the 4:00pm regular, arriving in San Ignacio at 6:30pm. Apparently it was just as well I was delayed as there were only two available seats on the express. Unfortunately though, Kathryn had walked down to meet me from the earlier bus. Anyway, we went out for a pleasant meal and spent the rest of the evening chatting.

There must have been twenty of us gathered at Donald's house at 9:00am and we left at about 9:30 when those from Belmopan arrived including Nik who had organised the trip.

The first part of the journey saved a lot of walking as we were taken by three vehicles, well beyond Bullet Tree for a distance of six or seven miles before heading off into the forest. There was plenty of wildlife about but we didn't see much as the party was far too big and the Belizean guides set a cracking pace. There were plenty of interesting trees of course, which were identified and described as we passed, especially for their medicinal uses as yet barely tapped. There were lots of parrots about and it is easy to identify their ungainly flight and loud and communal squawking. One very attractive pair of birds in both appearance, display and sound - whose name I have forgotten - went through a wonderful courtship ritual which only the two guides and I witnessed; a series of acrobatic leaps high from the ground and a discreet mating in the ground cover. The whole walk was about three and a half hours so it was much less demanding than I expected but it was really great to be climbing hills again. Of course, here all the hills and even the mountains are completely covered by forest.

Sink holes are caves which have become so huge that the roof has collapsed inwards. The two we saw were absolutely amazing; both around three hundred feet deep and rather more than that across. Only a small part could be covered by the camera which would need a very wide angle lens to do justice to the view, both across and down. The sides were almost sheer all the way round making a striking bowl shape with dense vegetation down at the bottom. There were only a few places where you could get right to the edge and the drop is so precipitous as to look as though the edge is undercut. There is no known way in to either of them other than the obvious and no-one has yet gone beyond having the idea of abseiling down. I think I would be more concerned about what I was descending into than anything else. This part of Central America is one of the most cavernous areas in the World and the stone looks like limestone (I suppose it must be) but it doesn't look to me, as hard as the limestone we see in England. Pamela gave me her story from her point of view…

Hike in the Sinkholes in the Cayo Area

A cloudy day dawned which forebode a good day for hiking guaranteed of coolness and hopefully not rain. About eight of us climbed into the back of a pickup truck and felt like Belizeans - the typical 'ride in the back of a pickup' transportation system. After driving for about fifteen minutes, we came to the turnoff, a small country road running alongside pastureland. Our revelling in the beauty of this pastoral country came to an abrupt halt as we were jolted for the next ten minutes along a deeply rutted and muddy lane. Got as far as the mud would allow us and breathed a sigh of relief thinking our legs would not be the only sore muscle at the end of the day. Applied layers of bug repellent and headed off along the same narrow lane, now a grassy, rocky pathway that is really a dry stream bed.

Soon we came to our turn off, a small hidden path that only Lenny our leader could possibly know. Up we scrambled. This technique became the norm for most of the hike to the sinkholes. Mud caked on the bottom of our boots gave a second sole, thus invalidating the tread of hiking boots. So those of us in runners were now on an even playing field, so to speak, as far as the superiority goes of those most appropriately clad for a hike. Our second sole created a challenge in trying to scramble up the hills and scramble it was, in whatever way we could, to get to the top of small rises in the trail. Branches and thin tree trunks became our allies until we became alerted painfully to the wonderful defence of jungle trees that don't like creepy crawlies messing with their trunks. Spikes!!! In all forms and sizes - needle like four inch long dense spikes, single thick green five inch spikes more widely spread apart and small thin black spikes covering all of a stem, a thick layer of sharp fuzz. So alertness became the name of the game, not only in what we would grab but what we might brush by inadvertently.

Large flat rocks added to the surprise; a great slide to the next section of the path. All dignity or the litheness of a mountain climber left us. Melissa decided that she would be my protector as I seemed to be the leader in this game of sliding. She would stand in front with her arms spread out to catch me flying past, saying "I couldn't protect you from my dog (remember the pit bull that decided to use my arm as a munching bar) but I can help you now!" Found that talking and laughing up a hill added to the strength and skill of scrambling on hands and knees to get to the top of a slippery muddy patch. Could see the sinkhole appearing in front of us and joked about sliding to the edge and carrying on in an arch over the edge. It almost came true.

The sinkhole was quite impressive. Looked like the Grand Canyon except that we were looking down at a jungle canopy far beneath us and enjoying vultures and hawks circling above the greenery, outlined against the limestone cliffs. Sinkholes are made when the top of a cave collapses. So we were looking at the walls of a cave with the roof at the bottom, now the bed for a great jungle.

Getting my 'Parrot Spotting' certificate; finally graduated, I can now recognize a flock of parrots as they fly by. Their squawk is the first clue. They fly like ducks. Their wings stretch only to body level and don't go up past their body - the stroke goes down and then back up to body level. I can even pass the written test. Saw the curve of their beak; can't see the colour as they are silhouetted black against the sky. Saw orchids clinging to trees. Don't know whether they had finished blooming or were ready to bloom. They were lovely nevertheless dangling their long tentacles from their tree trunk perch.

Walked by two sinkholes, had lunch and then headed out on not such a demanding path. Everyone let a hoot when they came to the lovely pastoral lane, another dry creek bed? Giant fronds arched over our path creating a very park like feeling. However, flat broad stones lay in wait and the slipping game started again. One technique that some developed as a way to overcome this challenge was to take small running steps and just keep moving, not giving contact any time to think 'slip'. Our leader Lenny added to the acceleration along one spot of the path when he came back from a reconnaissance saying, "Ants ahead, MOVE FAST!" So high stepping and running we headed out of enemy territory and the invasion of the ants. Inspection revealed that we were clear but the imagination lasted long after one felt safe. Donald had an ant crawling up his pant leg - starting at the calf, making its way up his thigh. Someone suggested spraying because his slapping was having no effect - missing every time. However he felt that spray was not good on soft tissue and declined this procedure opting for invasion rather that extermination.

Mud along the path led to attempts of identification of small jungle animals - observing at least four different tracks. We all stood in a line trying to muster up all the names of small jungle animals that were in our memory bank. Charmaine with outstretched arms swept a length of tracks and said "and there are the homo-sapiens". Soon these tracks gave way to deeper ones and we had to side step these little potholes filled with water that was sucking us into their sloppy depths - cow tracks! Our path now led to an open area, swamp and pasture land. A barbed wire fence created a challenge of how to make it into the next field that looked drier. Some used the army technique of scrunching under the bottom rung, others tried a high wire balancing act of climbing up and over and other Sir Galahads held a section for fair maidens to squeeze through, guided by the coaching of others successful at 'crossing over'. No sooner had we made it to the other side, each person feeling quite satisfied at the success of their particular technique, having brushed themselves off and stood up smugly, when we were met by an audience of a herd of at least twenty five bulls with long horns watching this whole procedure! One brave member that had farm experience went back to the other side and herded them into an adjacent pasture. I must say Gill was brave heading behind the herd before they were all safely in an adjoining field although I don't know what safety meant - the gate wasn't closed and at any time they could have decided they wanted to join in with our line. Soon the cars came into view and the end of our trip; and motley looking crew we were; covered with mud. Max looking like a war victim, discovered blood streaming down his leg. Claimed he preferred his leg to be damaged rather than another part of his anatomy that was in peril when he was climbing through the barbed wire fence.

'…I will enquire again about last year's Buddies but, as far as I am aware - and I have asked before, they all came home. I assume that 7G pestering you for their letters refers to your comment about Methodist not sending personal letters. This was at my encouragement and was intended to involve the whole group at each end, in the experience of their exchange student more properly known as a buddy. I will ask them to send letters this week although I expect that they have already done so. The most important thing is to keep the WHOLE flow going both ways without waiting for replies. There is no part of the curriculum or the lives of students that cannot be included. I will send you a contact email address for Methodist Standard Five Teacher, Gladys Griffith this week. She has it at home and has confessed that only her husband uses it but she is willing to learn given that she would hear from you and from 7G. I am working on ways of getting computers into the other schools as I have told you before and this will be achieved before I finally come home. Could you please get a response from 7H to St Pauls Standard Five to me by Wednesday evening otherwise they would have to wait until next week and I have promised them something this week. Please tell Tricia and Hannah (who I know well of course) that I will ask one of the children to write to each of them but I will write to them both (email) this week. I am pushed for time again after coming back from a long trip to hike to a couple of amazing sink holes over in Cayo. You probably know that this region is one of the most cavernous in the World. The holes were well over three hundred feet deep I would say, and over that across the bowl…'

The last week of the third cycle of monitoring would run right to the end of January. Although there was the usual clutch of delays and rearrangements it continued to work out well and combined positively with all the other activities and events. Father Lowry had closed the school at San Pablo for Mass and a feast day and Assemblies Health didn't happen because their manager had decided against it for some reason. Students' letters from St Pauls were posted and copies of the letters I had sent by email delivered there so that the students could see their work in print and read the letter I had written. After that I went to White Sapphire to enquire about making a special carving to commemorate the Belize/UK link for presentation to SMCC in May. The idea is for some sort of Mayan effigy signifying kinship or belonging. Caught a bus back to Orange Walk (Tillett's!) at about half past three and went straight to the office to discuss budgeting and my being out of operation for three months and preference for keeping the current schools now that a full rotation has been completed. I just managed to make the mile and a half along mud road from San Pablo to Nuevo San Juan without getting wet as I was given a lift over the last half mile or so, as it turned out from the husband of the teacher I was to see in the multigrade class. She gave me a lift to the main road afterwards but I missed the first bus to Calcutta by crossing to the other side of the road to shelter from the rain. I did arrive in time to catch Orvin for lunch which we got at a stall down in San Joaquin. Fitting in with maths back at the school some time was spent with Standard Five and Six and with Orlando writing to Philip, on the computer. The printer wasn't working which presented another problem. Two packages arrived for Calcutta on Friday which I delivered on Saturday when we made much useful if stumbling progress in setting out some of the content of a School Policy as a first step towards producing a Mission Statement. The Village Council were running a barbecue so that was our lunch and I spent some time in between, making a little progress with the computer.

Thoughts sent to a friend…

'…Just made it before we go into another month; January has simply flown by. Yesterday, Saturday, I spent at Calcutta working with staff on their school policy with a view to producing a mission statement!! Actually, I think these are important and I am trying to ensure that none of the stress we had is experienced by the school that, at the moment, are enjoying it for the advantages that it gives. Today, I have spent setting out my itinerary for February; outline planning a new workshop for non-pilot schools that have to start in September and typing up a paper on classroom discipline written by one of the Principals. It has been like that since well before Christmas and with that and all the writing attached to 'Linking' my letter writing has suffered. Anyway, here I am although I am going to cheat by sending you a copy of a story sent to 7G which I think you will find amusing.' Home for a holiday in three months but back on track; I'm certainly not hankering after going home otherwise I wouldn't be coming back but I do want to spend a holiday there and spend some time with all the people who have been writing. There is so much to share…'

1st February, Monday, the start of the fourth cycle of monitoring scheduled, I spent the morning at San Pablo and travelled to Corozal at lunchtime to attend the ceremony for the Inauguration of the District Education Centre due to start at 3:00pm. Even after a leisurely lunch I arrived before two so there was some hanging around; also the Prime Minister was late but that wait was made more acceptable by being able to meet with all the ministry hierarchy from the Minister of Education down. Afterwards I was able to have some discussion with Louisa as well as meet up with Orvin and make conversation with many of the Corozal Staff.

Tuesday morning was spent at Chapel School but I wasn't able to do any monitoring as both teachers were off sick. I finished up taking Standard One for the morning with no preparation or planning! It took most of the morning getting them working as I wanted and one child was sick all over his part of the table and on the floor. He went home and some Standard Six girls did the cleaning up. After that I went to lunch with Julian Chi and his family. The afternoon was the third workshop for Orange Walk 'testing' outcomes. By this time I could feel a cold coming on, my first to take hold in Belize and as I was not really needed, I went home early.

I should have been at Methodist next morning but my mind was not functioning too well with the cold and I had made arrangements to meet with Elaine Parchu and go to San Juan and then on to Calcutta. Had I not made this arrangement I would have stayed at home. In the event, I finished what I had to do at San Juan and then went straight home to bed.

'…Here is the promised letter and story for 7H. Hopefully, the errant Buddies will find their proper place next week. Please let me know how the letters and stories are received. I need to know whether they are pitched about right. The stories are 'read aloud' for preference…'

Feeling a bit better and without the running nose, I went to Corozal Methodist all day, having first called at the Corozal District Office to try to arrange for a speaker for Orange Walk on the subject of identifying children at risk. While there I put the idea of a VSO grant to Henry who will obtain estimates for computer equipment from Angelus Press on Saturday. There is a non-VAT, preferential arrangement which the Methodist Management can access. At the end of the morning I shared a story written for year 7 with Standard 5; also shared at St. Pauls but they were nothing like as responsive. I could have followed up the research for a carving for SMCC at White Sapphire at the end of the day but, not feeling too good, I went to catch the bus and ended up waiting for an hour (again) at Batty Bus Terminal.

The 7: 00am Escalante bus to Belize City on Friday was slow, and I arrived in the office at QADS just before 8:30 for a two hour discussion with David Eck covering a multitude of topics. These included: the need for official requests being made in writing and in good time; prompt reimbursement of expenses; my extension and move to Corozal; the VSO project; and the need to consolidate the present progress in introducing the curriculum rather than lose the impetus with an ever increasing work load placed on a limited staff.

The VSO project was discussed along with associated timings and my holiday in the UK. It was confirmed that my holiday would begin on Saturday, 1st May and continue for six weeks until the middle of June, Sunday, 13th. The six weeks for the project would begin 'in mid-March', Monday 22nd. I pointed out, however, that the school Easter break runs for two weeks in that period (29th March – 9th April) and this would be likely to interfere with the gathering of data. In later discussion with David Price, I was given the freedom to arrange the times myself. This works very well as the end of the coming cycle of monitoring with which I am involved, comes to an end with exactly two weeks grace before the project is due to start. During the whole period I will remain on the payroll for QADS and the budget which includes that is in place. This is important to me because it means that there is no break in service. The time will be offset in large part by holiday which is outstanding from last year. Also, monies paid by VSO, other than direct expenses, would go directly to one of the Belize 'Link' schools for the purchase of a computer - which is my expressed wish; part of a broader intention that all four of the Belize Schools will have email link with the school in England before I leave Belize. The timing of my move to Corozal is flexible, particularly as the job description is effective from mid-June when I return from England.

The current proposal for the introduction of the New Curriculum includes going country-wide from next September in the Lower Division. I have proposed that we confine our activities, at least for another year, with the (around sixty) pilot schools but continue with the plans to extend into the Middle Division from September, with those same pilot schools. This would enable participating schools to consolidate; to include more of their staff in the execution of the process and to begin to demonstrate the results of their labours. That in turn, should increase the desire of non-pilot schools to take part.

With respect to the job description - which is the first I have had other than the original one from VSO - it was agreed with David Price that it is all inclusive in the sense that the range of duties are enabling rather than to be necessarily, fully executed! There is nothing in those duties with which I could not be fully committed given the constraints of time and resources (human and material). One of the objectives extends further into the unknown! That is 'To assist in the operationalizing of the District Education Centre'. However, I don't anticipate any problem with that as I believe that I am quite clear about where my responsibilities lay and the actual duties or potential duties, are quite clear.

After having further discussions with David Leacock and Corinth I had hopes of catching the 1:00pm bus but there wasn't one and I didn't leave Belize City until 2:15 on the Urbina - just in time to have my vouchers processed at the Treasury which had already closed, and cash the cheque at the Belize Bank. By this time it was 4:30 and I was just able to do essential shopping on the way home. This had been delayed by having the cold and lack of funds due to the lateness of the vouchers (again!). My cold is still unpleasant and so another early night.

Mostly a day of work to start the weekend again as much of it was spent in responding to VSO about the extension etc., getting up to date with my journal for the latter part of the week, sending a copy of my response to David Price and Faxing a revised itinerary which will take me right up to mid-June when I come back from England. On Sunday it took until four o'clock to clean the house to my satisfaction: floors, window shutters, bathroom and kitchen, front of house and veranda; all sparkling clean. Much of that won't have to be done again before I go to Corozal; also washed all the bedding before writing letters.

'…Attached is a class list for Corozal Methodist School (7G) and addresses for all four schools. I hope that you will be able to send some email messages for St. Pauls this week. Also, would you please send me an email from school? I have found a way to pick up the address. Then that should work. It is nearly half term for you too. We don't get one...'

'…Dear Hal, Your message for Tim has arrived here okay. Of course, Murphy's Law being what it is, I was in Corozal Town today and now I have to go in the opposite direction to Belize City each day until Friday. Then, on Friday, I have an appointment here in Orange Walk in the morning and several other things crowding into the day. I will find a way of delivering your message somehow this week…'
In writing to friends…

'…My work continues to be both interesting and demanding. Teachers and Principals place a great deal of faith in all that is presented to them and there is no greater spur than that (to me anyway) to try to get it right. My main effort, however, is really directed at finding ways of releasing the expertise and enthusiasm which is already there. This is difficult in a culture/system in which classroom practice boils down to mere 'telling'. There is no tradition of promoting thought, understanding or skills. You might imagine how frustrating that can be - even though it might be quaint (and even attractive) to hear children chorus 'Yes Ma'am' or provide the required answer in unison. I have to be quite blunt: pointing out that my observation shows that the children only have 'one scout out' at any one time. That one triggers the response while the rest are more satisfactorily distracted! And they take it in turns on some sort of agreed basis which is impossible (I think) to target as it, like the scout, is constantly shifting. The choral response (whatever we happen to be doing or thinking about) makes the teacher think that everyone is listening of course.

Anyway, the New Curriculum is written in such a way that there is proper opportunity to make progress and progress is being made, albeit slowly. 'You can only move from where you are' is another constant reminder that I have to make. Through this year sixty pilot schools across the country are working with the Lower Division (5, 6 and 7 year olds). I am responsible for fourteen of them in the two Northern Districts, Orange Walk and Corozal. Each of those Districts also has a Field Officer. In September, the Pilot Schools take the Curriculum into the Middle Division (8, 9 and 10 year olds) and the Lower Division goes country wide. Pilot Schools start to operate the whole curriculum in September 2000 and the whole thing should be in place from September 2001.

When I return my job expands. This is partly because I have been ensuring that the work I do is taken up by Belizeans which is how it should be. That frees up some time and opportunity to become involved in a decentralisation of administration, working on methods of assessment and helping to devise a workable inspection system for schools. You would not be surprised to know where my main concerns lay in ensuring that such a system should be enabling and not disabling!!

There are lots of friends because I have continued to live almost exclusively among Belizeans and only see other VSOs or non-Belizeans occasionally. The family I first stayed with in Belize City have been wonderful. They have relatives all over the country and I often go and stay with them for a day or two or visit one or other of them. Christmas was more of a family affair than I can remember for a long time. I look forward to seeing you all in May...'

I went to Buena Vista on Monday morning and then on to Corozal. Called at St Paul's after lunch, to deliver email and encourage further contacts with SMCC and exchange of Buddies with Calcutta; then went into Methodist to pick up the quote for a computer from Angelus to go with my new application to VSO; checked with White Sapphire about the wall plaque for SMCC which will probably be the Belize National Symbols and spent the rest of the afternoon at Calcutta.

Three days followed at QADS: assessing results, debating where we are and where we are going and making plans. My impassioned plea not to go country wide in September was listened to but with an inevitability bordering on mania and with a spineless lack of support from the curriculum team. I met with Mark Wright at 2:00pm to discuss the points made in my recent email to him in respect of the VSO project, VSO computer grant, using monies paid for the project to buy another computer, my extension and my holiday in the UK. I had the task of presenting the curriculum news for principals of RC Schools in Corozal on Friday.

I took an email from Hal to Tim at Santa Rita but Tim seems reluctant to write. I am almost certain that this is because one or more of his class are getting to him in some way. It happens. I will make sure that he is able to write and the best way Hal can help him is to keep writing to him. The best friendships have to be worked at! I got soaking wet but no matter. The story will help to show that I take it all seriously too. There can be few better ways to learn than to cross the borders of culture and experience - especially at their age.

Next, I was due at Calcutta Government School for a Barbecue lunch arranged for school funds. Calcutta village is three miles south on the Northern Highway and in the opposite direction from Santa Rita and Tim, two miles further north and nearer to the Mexican border. By this time it was pouring with rain but I was given a lift in a pick-up by a friend.

I arrived with a good hour to spare and found myself boring Standard Six to death on the subject of systems of government with particular reference to Belize. The Principal is also their teacher and he took the opportunity to attend to other matters, not for the first time, as I know all the students. Calcutta is linked with Drake at SMCC and Standard Six communicated with what is now 8D while Standard Five have started with 7D.

The business that the Principal went to attend to was an offer of six badly needed tables (schools don't have much in the way of resources - even furniture) but they had to be collected that afternoon. It was still pouring with rain but the barbecue went ahead and was successful because it had been arranged through the earlier sale of tickets. It was during that time that transport was arranged for the tables.

I travelled back to Corozal Town in the truck! Trucks have to be seen to be believed and there is nothing to beat travelling in one. I went in the cab with the Principal and the driver of course, but two students travelled in the open back. It was still pouring with rain but they loved it. The rain here is warm!

As there was no more sign of the rain easing off than there had been all morning I was taken right to the school at Santa Rita before the truck was turned back to where the tables were to be collected. That might sound as though I was home and dry but not a bit of it. To get in to the school you pick your way through mud and pools of water when it is raining and for some time afterwards. Also, each classroom is entered through a door which opens directly to the outside. There is no glass in the window spaces, only shutters, and these like the door, were closed to keep out the rain.

"Good afternoon Mr Max!" No surprise was expressed as I staggered in and everyone stood up in greeting. Nothing out of the ordinary as far as the students were concerned.

It was a good visit but I got really wet walking back into town to catch the bus back home. Unlike the two students who rode in the back of the truck, I was dressed to give a presentation to Principals. I wouldn't change any of it though. The experience is part of a whole which I couldn't possibly have imagined.

After a barbecue with the family in Belize City at the weekend and two days preparing a monitoring report I went to meet with Louisa and Bertha at the Orange Walk District Office to find that Louisa's Son-in-Law had been attacked with an iron bar at the weekend and was in a coma in Belize City, having first been to Chetumal (at high cost) where they can do brain scans. The in-Laws had insisted on moving him but Belize City can't operate. We agreed that I would finish my report and give each of them a copy with space to add to it. In the meantime, they would get on with producing a budget for the initial orientation of non-pilot schools during March/April. I returned and finished the report this afternoon.

On Thursday I set off for Corozal on the 7:15am Chell bus and got off at Santa Rita beyond the town to meet with Mrs Alejandra Noble who has a two bedroom house to let which I was told was next to the Red Cross. It didn't take much finding as I had a good idea where it was and I arrived on time at 8:15am. I hadn't waited long when a Mr Cawich turned up. He turned out to be the brother and had been working on the house which is a new one built of concrete and with glass louvre windows and burglar bars all round. He knew I was coming and let me in to look around; very nice; tiled floor throughout and I wondered what my very minimal furniture would look like inside. It would also need curtains, unlike the wooden slatted windows I have here, but I noted that there are curtain rails. A very nice house with a super kitchen, main room, utility/store and excellent bathroom with a big tiled shower (no bath but I don't use the one that is here except to stand in as there is no hot water. The location is excellent and there would be people moving in rather than out in the event of a hurricane! The drawbacks are the large outside space which would have to be kept under control, no telephone line installed and a bottom price rent of $400. The owner arrived soon after. All the conditions were confirmed and I said that I would let her know one way or the other on Saturday. I have arranged to see the house belonging to Armando Vasquez, Landy Burns' friend on Saturday morning and I had the address of that house which is close by so I moved on to have a look at that. On the way, I called in to Assemblies and collected a letter from Tim in Standard Six to send by email to Hal at SMCC.

'…Dear Hal, Attached is a message from Tim! I have sent it as an attachment because I think it is nicer to read and it will be easier for you to print and keep; computer generated script of course but it is a fair representation of Tim's writing as students are taught to write in cursive here. It is not quite as neat as you see here you will be relieved to know. Also, the table is a fair copy of the one he drew for you…'

It didn't take long to find the house which is also concrete; not as nice as the other one but perhaps more manageable. I will have a better idea on Saturday. There was a builder working there, putting up a fence and a wall around it. It was hot but I noted that there was a breeze at Santa Rita which wasn't noticeable in Corozal Town which is (slightly!!) lower down. Santa Rita is reckoned to be on a hill and I suppose it is but it is a hill which would pass unnoticed in Devon. The Mayans must have thought it useful though, because they built one of their temples and settlements there.

Next stop District Centre where I made copies of my Monitoring Report for Bertha and Louisa to add to. There was a workshop taking place on child abuse attended by teachers and students. It was nice to have a whole stream of both saying "Hello Mr Max." as they passed from one room to another. I got talking to the two organisers, one of whom was from NCH Action for Children with whom I have had connections through Scouts in the past. They were very complimentary about the children taking part from Corozal Methodist who are also "Linking' with SMCC.

I then decided to go and find Arturo Mendez who is a Presbyterian Pastor and whose name had been given to me by Julian Chi at Chapel School as possibly having a house to rent. There was no answer at the phone number I had been given. It was hotter!! I don't know why I stopped to ask of an American who had a bicycle but it turned out that 'Joe' (Well Hi!) not only knew the Pastor but was also working with him as part of their Mission in Belize. I walked with him to meet the Pastor. It was still hotter!! - And it was a long walk, back in the direction I had covered twice already of course. He said he would contact me tomorrow through Julian Chi (Arturo Mendez is the general manager of their schools) and gave me a lift in the back of his pick-up right back to the District Office. I managed to talk with several people who were attending the workshop and then went into town for some lunch.

The next port of call was to be St. Pauls but I decided to go to Methodist first. That was just as well because it turned out that it was the Annual General Meeting of the Belize National Teachers Union (Corozal Town Branch) held at Methodist as Henry Neal is their President. Everyone was there and the schools were closed. I stayed for the meeting which was very interesting for two reasons. First was that the meeting was addressed by the new Chief Education Officer and second because I had the opportunity of gauging undercurrents - always useful! Got home at just before five, very hot and still with lots of writing to do.

Friday was not the most uplifting day. I had a meeting of schools in the pilot programme in Corozal to attend at 2:30 and a house to look at in Ranchito so I caught the midday bus after housework, shopping and answering the phone. Pamela was supposed to be staying tonight. I hadn't heard from her but Mark phoned to say that he had papers for me to be dropped off at Batty bus depot and that she would be joined by Lisa in the morning so that was some news. The house in Ranchito was $600 a month so that was the end of that. It was then a two mile walk to the District Office and another half mile to Assemblies where the meeting was to be held. And it was hot!! However, I am feeling much more myself now so I didn't mind that and I had water. Also, I broke the walk and called in at Paula's shop which I had been intending to do for a long time. Her young daughter was there whom I had known for a long time and I met Paula's Mum since that is where her family live.

The meeting was not well attended and I had to deal with negative attitude which had been picked up from the new Chief Education Officer. Bad news; if Belize doesn't make this curriculum work, I believe it will be decades before the slide in children's learning is halted.

I had just got home at about half past five and had a shower when there was a call from Lisa to say that she was at the bottom end of Main Street which is at the other end of town! I went out to collect her and we chatted for a while but she had made arrangements to go out for the evening with her boy-friend! The good news of the day was from Marco to say that my laptop had arrived but even that was slightly tainted in that there was duty to pay at $225; must remember my cheque book so that I can go straight down from Corozal tomorrow, after looking at Armando Vasquez house. Next morning Lisa went her way to meet up with Pamela and on to Bacalar and Chetumal saying she would take photos of the fort for me.

I met Mr and Mrs Vasquez and agreed to take the house which is nice and he is making a good job of improvements including all round fencing. I will have a better idea of what it is really like after moving in of course but there is plenty of space. Two large bedrooms, a huge main room, large kitchen and bathroom all very clean; and the floor ceramic tiled right through. The windows have glass louvres in them and window bars over the larger parts. There is a phone line in already and a motor mower for the outside which a relative does for them. The area is very quiet. My furniture will rattle round like a pea in a bucket - well, perhaps a couple of peas - and they will provide some for me. The rent is $350. I had hoped to pay a little less than that but it is much better value than anything else I have seen and the rent will be halved when I go away. I expect to move in three or four weeks' time.

Called in to collect some documents from VSO for the research and came home for a shower before going down to the family to collect the computer. That looks a good buy too but it will take some time to get to using it and, unfortunately, it doesn't have Word for Windows. It won't take long to get that!

Corel Word Perfect version 7 is on the laptop and seems easy to use but I don't want to convert any files so I will have to get Word for Windows installed. However, I have installed the printer driver and taken some nice prints from it. This all took about an hour and a half and I have closed the machine down for a while. Better to work in short bursts I think. Also done the washing and prepared the chicken for tonight.

At midday, I have gone back to writing up the news since Christmas in preparation for a big effort to catch up with my letter writing. I also have several lots of photos and a video film to deal with!

'…I haven't been involved in scouting here except on the periphery. I gave the badges off my shirt to a Venture Scout at Christmas '97. The population is very small, Scouts in proportion. They don't need Trainers because Americans from the States see it as their business to spend their vacations 'do-gooding' and I don't think it helps the Leader shortages for a foreigner to run a Pack or a Group so I have spent the time on the many other things I have to do…'

'…I will be coming home for a six week holiday from the first of May - returning by 13th June. From then I will be extending for another year. That will make a total of nearly three years and there are a number of options from that point on. Before I come home I have a 'Tracer Study' to do for VSO which will take six weeks and starts officially on 22nd March. This is to determine the contribution made by VSOs teaching in secondary schools in Belize - In Dangriga, Corozal and San Ignacio which places are spread all over the country…'

'…You may have gathered from the opening paragraphs that work is going pretty well. Progress is slow and that is frustrating but it is progress. I'm managing to pass the work on to Belizeans too, but the job has got bigger now. That is why I was asked to stay…'

'…I'm not sure what I will do when I come home for the six weeks. My house has been let again which is a relief but I had thought to stay there. I will be visiting of course and I may well take up your kind offer and stay with you for a couple of days when it is best for you…'

'…Mum and Dad both said you are more than welcome to have a meal here, in fact several if you would like. It will be good to see you again and catch up on your news face to face…'

'…I'm sure that six weeks will disappear very rapidly but at some time I hope to turn the nose of a car in your direction and visit Fairthorne. I have had good reports from some of the South Molton children who visited you last year (except for the food!!)…'

'…Attached is a letter for 7R from Tomas Zetina at Christian Assemblies, Santa Rita. The original copy will be sent in their next package. I have a letter arrived from April (7H) for Victoria at St. Pauls which I tried to deliver on Friday but schools were closed for the afternoon (Union Branch AGM). A letter arrived yesterday from Jenna (7D) for Jason Mendez and a package from Patricia (7D) for Yanny Jones both of Calcutta Government. They will be delivered this week. The school addresses could be used. I'm told that the mail is generally delivered direct to the school…'

I set off for Corozal on the 7:15 Chell bus on Thursday. It was a bit of a rush first to leave a copy of an email from Tomas Zetina; next via the DEO to take an Open University Prospectus to Ariel Botes, received from Martyn yesterday; on to St Pauls to deliver mail from SMCC; and Calcutta to deliver mail from SMCC. While at Calcutta I reminded Necetas about the exchange of Buddies with St Pauls (as I had reminded Valerie also) and Orvin about a report on the use of the computer for VSO which will help with the application for Methodist. Also, whilst there, re-aligned the connections to the phone so that dial in could work; still problems at the BTL end. I rushed off to Orange Walk to score for the Spelling Bee due to start at 1:00pm. Got a tee-shirt for that! Arranged to take the laptop to Stanley for extra software and setting up email tomorrow. That would be Friday when the 4th cycle of monitoring ends and I'm off to QADS on the 7:30am Urbina taking the new computer with me as arranged with Stanley to have Microsoft Word and email installed and music set up.

Meeting with Belize District Field Officers, I discovered that the Catholic General Manager, Wade, had been discussing me with them and claiming that I was 'telling his manager in Corozal what to do'. Nothing has been said to me. It is also untrue so I have registered a complaint with David Price to have the record put straight. Whether any further action is required remains to be seen. I also discussed the position in general with David Price, in respect of the agendas that seem to be running at all levels; the last people to be considered in the power/control struggle that is going on seem to be children and teachers. Interestingly, the country is really in constitutional crisis having dismissed the Attorney General, Sosa, for reasons which seem to be unaccountable. People are very much afraid. The only opinion expressed seems to be that of the party. Where have I heard that before - in Europe?

There were more letters to write on Saturday with a break to go and collect 'finger licking' barbecue from Chapel School and on Sunday I finished the long outstanding batch of letters and emails - over thirty of them!

'…The school computer is proving terribly unreliable, so best to use me as the contact point to guarantee communication. I am happy to receive letters from the Belize schools - I know some of my pupils have made a connection…'

'…*Attached are some notes of my 'doings' since Christmas. They were written also for some of your Year 7 and 8 who write to me, as part of my catching up with mail. What I do is send part of it to each of those likely to talk to each other. Anyway, I hope you find it a relaxation. When I come home for my holiday I would like to spend some time with each form, especially in Year 7, if you can fit it in with your planning. You already have any resources I'm likely to need (or will have) so I would be the human one. I don't mind how long it takes or on what days. I am trying to arrange to have a commemorative plaque specially carved to place somewhere in your school so you might like to keep that in mind. Also, if possible, I would like to meet with any other interested Year 7 staff. The potential of this 'Link' is barely scratched yet but to make the most of it there needs to be a clear understanding of how things work for children and in schools here. It is not a matter of 'doing things for Belize' as you must understand from your travels. The benefit is mutual. For your students it could provide an experience which invades all areas of their thinking. My being here has certainly influenced mine…*'

'…I will tell Standard Five about Alli the alligator when I next see them. I should explain that the name alligator is what the Belizeans call them. They are crocodiles really, which can grow up to fifteen feet long. I have seen one about twelve feet and several smaller ones. There are no alligators in this part of the World. The same applies to the Howler Monkey which is agile and the most beautiful shiny black. Belizeans call them Baboons for some reason. Babboons live in Africa of course. They are the ones with the big red bottoms. Howler monkeys don't look a bit like that…'

'…Ho! Ho! Another letter; that's nice; but guess what; I've caught up with my letters! I think this is the thirty-ninth (letter or email) in a week but that is how far behind I was. There should have been a flood of them in South Molton alone, by the time you read this. I haven't finished the writing that needs to be done you understand; only the letters but it is good progress. What I am trying to do of course, is clear some space so that I can get on with the VSO study and I am trying more routes for funding for schools' computers. I have been asked to assist The Rotary Club of Orange Walk in making a case for computers in more Primary Schools too. I don't know what will come of that (not much so far) but I can certainly pass on some ideas. I am concentrating on Corozal because that is the focus for decentralisation of Ministry administration but as time goes on there seems to be less and less solid reason for doing so. That uncertainty is a major part of the work experience. The planning is so much altered by experience and reality that the picture changes regularly. It looks as though my responsibility will be spread over just the same area despite the extras centred on Corozal so, in that respect, I could just as well stay where I am. On the other hand, I don't like swopping and changing back and forth and it will be much easier to work with the 'Link' schools as they are all in Corozal now. Also, much as I would miss Orange Walk, it would be good to live in Corozal for a bit and now is the best time to move…'

'…I haven't written many stories lately because there has been so much writing to do one way or another, but I do have a lot of ideas and I have kept my journal up to date. Actually, there is so much to do and so much which is new to learn about that I also need some time and space to digest it…'

I went down to the District Office after washing the bedding and then went on to Corozal to meet with Bertha and Louisa. The budgets for the three lots of workshops coming up are finished. The two big ones will be held in the Corozal DEO and the orientation for going country-wide in the Lower Division will be held in each of the zones. A meeting for Local Managers will be held at the Corozal DEO a week on Wednesday and Louisa and Bertha will attend a briefing for the Minister at QADS on the 12th. March (foreigners not required!)

'…Hi Mark, Your letter re the (VSO) Conference dated February 18th arrived at Orange Walk Post Office today! I would like to go Bird & Manatee Watching in the lagoon please. I have given thought to the twenty minute personal perspective on disadvantage in the classroom. I think I may well tell it as a story. I hope that is okay. I don't usually do that for adults. (What am I saying?) I start on the study tomorrow, having had some curriculum work to do today. Most of the time will be spent on the study until I go home for my holiday but I am making myself available as needed for QADS. There shouldn't be much need really…'

Work now focusses on the VSO study, collating information received and straight away a request to run a session for the Principals' Training Course on the New Curriculum! That needed to be dealt with so I put notes together, with hand-outs and met with Bertha and sorted out how she would make the presentation and I would make notes to comment on it afterwards. The session is tomorrow. Now I have a problem which has arisen with the new computer - which I am using for the VSO study.

I joined Bertha for her presentation on the new curriculum to Principals in training which she did and did very well. I was particularly pleased about that because it is another step towards ensuring continuity.

I spent my time watching the participants and making just a few notes about what might be added and then joining in the question/answer/discussion session at the end. Points I made were: learning to do is body, mind and spirit - not just using the hands; need to make clear exposition of learning to live together, to be, to do, to know; in talking about Goals, giving value to what the child brings (ideas, experience, culture, thinking) needs to be emphasized; what is child-centredness; how does a child learn; children's learning IS child centred. You cannot change Outcomes after they have been tested and revised and the 'Curriculum' is a prototypical one designed by teachers.

Afterwards I went to Corozal Community College and met with the Principal and the Dean. Bertha dropped me there in her car and I walked back to the District Education Office after that, through Mary Hill which Louisa was at pains to tell me was the (very) long way round!

The objective of the study is to determine the impact of long term VSO involvement in maths and science in the secondary school sector of Belize; a first for VSO, I believe. Obviously all data referring to volunteers, their students or others affected must be confidential but initial thoughts focussed on relevant records of students taught by VSOs; names, achievement, subsequent records and addresses; any measures of likely results without VSO; relations with other staff; continuity of teaching provision; placement objectives; indicators of achievement; output/outcomes/impact and how many views might be obtained. Then much writing…

'…Attached are the promised letters, one for each of the Year 7 forms. Each letter is two pages so there will be eight pages in all. They are ready to be printed out. They are all different but there is quite a bit of information, which applies to more than one school so it is copied across so that you have a complete letter for each. I hope they help with the picture of the schools. It would be good if some of your students were to ask me questions so that I know better what to write about...'

I went to Calcutta on Friday to join in with their Children's Day…

Boxing Bruno and Ed the Duck Exchange in Belize

Friday, 5th March dawned in Belize as it almost always does, in a blaze of light spreading rapidly from the east, casting long and dark shadows beyond anything that gets in its way. After exactly eighteen months, George the Snail was as keen as ever to be up and at it. He knew that today, two of his Buddies were to arrive at last among the children that their friends back home in England were writing to.

There had been a number of mix-ups with the Buddies' passports; or should that be a number of passports with their mix-ups? George wasn't sure of the exact details but today was the day that matters were to be put right. Boxing Bruno was to say goodbye to friends and what had been happy times in Calcutta Village and arrive at last in Corozal Town, at St. Paul's Anglican School by the Sea. Ed the Duck was to leave the joys of the Caribbean behind and settle with students and villagers among lush green coconut palms, papaya, mango, banana and orange trees and the brightly flowering varieties led by the vermillion flamboyan tree.

George was excited. "What time are we off?" he asked.

"We're not." said Mr Max, carefully, but there was no way to wrap it up.

"We have to," George exclaimed, "You promised. You said you would go to Calcutta this morning. You were going to film it. You said! You promised!!"

"That's right, I did and I am. What I said was 'We're not'. I'm going. You are staying here. You would only get yourself in on the act and then you'd steal the limelight and that's not fair so you're not going."

There was an argument but Mr Max was adamant and he set off alone on the Tillett bus from Orange Walk Town to travel north to Calcutta village 27 miles away.

Today was Children's Day and there was almost nothing normal about the school day, except, that is, that it started with the raising of the flag and the singing of the National Anthem in the sunshine at the front of the school building. The flag flew straight out in a fairly strong breeze which was pleasantly cooling. Children of Infant One whose turn it was to give a presentation waited on the concrete stage outside. Their own classroom, a solitary building, was to their left; the village playing field with its three small stands and four floodlights, all raised by the village, were behind them. It was a late start; almost forty minutes later than the regular time of 8:30 and everyone was in good spirits; looking forward to a day of games and food, food and games.

Even lusty voices sound small in a place which is so much a part of the surrounding countryside but the combination of voices and spaces, an environment and a being, was so strong that Boxing Bruno found that his normally gravelly voice was all broken up and he had to stop singing at times. It was then that he remembered that it was all very well going where he was supposed to go but he had made friends here as well. He had been here three months after all and he had stayed with a lot of families by this time.

Singing continued as a Baptist Minister had turned up with a cd player and 'sound box', and a guitar. Bruno thought he was really funny and he was making the songs funny too; so much so that sometimes Bruno forgot to sing. When it came to the actions he found them really difficult because he hadn't learnt the words to make them with!

Anyway, everyone was in a really good mood when they all piled into the two vehicles for the three mile journey to St. Paul's Anglican School to meet with their students and Ed the Duck. Over thirty students, four adults and Bruno piled in; most in the Dodge Ram belonging to the Principal and enough to be a squash in the big American car belonging to their Teacher. Big American vehicles keep going for a long time and gas is half the price of that in England; cheaper still if you buy it in Mexico just across the border. Bruno sat so that he would have a good view out of the window.

The journey was not a long one but very beautiful. It was something to wonder at that they passed through three villages in three miles and that they were all joined together, in effect, right into the town. This is because all the homes seem to be a part of the countryside and not separate from it; the wells and the bathrooms being a direct part of the earth itself; a feeling of everything growing together.

San Joaquin, Calcutta, Carolina, Ranchito, Corozal. All names with their-own distinct history. In the last village, Ranchito, they passed the home of Miss Maria who teaches Infant Two and Standard One; hers is a green house on the right; and they passed the home of the Principal, Mr Rancheran, who teaches Standard Six; a house perched on the top of a little hill.

Around a right hand bend, following another car, and the students behind announce the arrival at the Caribbean Sea. A thrill of excitement passes through Boxing Bruno's body and ends as always, in a tingle in his fingers and an involuntary stab in the air which he covers by pushing up his arm with clenched fist and shouting "Yes!!!"

A cane truck thunders in the opposite direction and once it has passed, Bruno is able to see the left hand sweep of the road and ahead, nothing but the sea; the Caribbean Sea; warm and green; lively with little waves; choppy in the breeze and set against a brilliant blue sky with the whitest, brightest, fluffy clouds he had ever seen.

The road swept on beside the sea; palm trees, sunshine, the brightest of light, deep shadows and a cooling breeze. Past the first part of the bay; past the big pictorial map which shows the layout of the town; past the small park along by the sea, a few parked vehicles, people enjoying the sunshine; past thatched buildings and many palm trees. And the students remind themselves - and Bruno - that they came to exchange Buddies and take names of students in each other's school so that the contact will become four-way with 7D and 7H in England.

At last, there it is, 'St Paul's by the Sea', written on the Church which is in the school grounds. Immediately opposite is the sea and just before that, a little park where all the children from St. Paul's are having their Children's Day.

The vehicle stops and everyone piles out. Little in the way of activities had started yet. Most children were milling about while a small orderly queue of them were waiting alongside the sea wall for Ovaltine served from a large two handled pan by their Principal, Mrs Rogers.

Without any sort of instruction, the students from Calcutta met up with their counterparts emerging from the crowds with the restraint of meeting the first time, and the two stars were not sure whether to be more embarrassed than anyone else, or whether to glow at being the centre of attention. Before even meeting, they both settled on a sort of compromise. Ed ruffled his feathers in anticipation; Bruno, ducked his head and hunched his right shoulder to his ear in mock aggression; both clung to the attractive young ladies; their escorts for the day.

Two mixed groups of students gathered round the two heroes at different parts of the wall, the escorts more embarrassed now, until by mutual consent they came together in the same place and sat side-by-side on the wall above the sea. And they are exchanged, one with the other; each to find a new friend with lots more besides.

More smiles with everyone asking questions and Miss Necetas urging a speech; Ed the Duck quacked loudly in all the wrong places and quickly became the centre of attention. His tail end got quite out of control, drawing the eye unnecessarily to the egg-laying department - rather pointless since drakes don't lay eggs; Bruno with his more customary serious face as though profound thoughts were passing through his mind. Those that knew him well, having their own ideas - perhaps nearer the truth. A time for the comfort of welcome when both Buddies made the most of the caresses they received from their new escorts and the friendly attention of so many.

And then it is all over. The exchange is made. The speech "I am glad to be with my rightful owner (for the time being)" is short and to the point, made over and over in case anyone missed it. The many passports are waved by more students - anxious now, to be part of the action. The two exchange students from England, the Buddies, put themselves about a bit before Ed the Duck and his new found (or long lost) friends are bundled into the two vehicles. They set off back to the festivities at Calcutta leaving Bruno and the students of St. Paul's to theirs.

"Hi," called out George as Mr Max got home. He was always a good hearted Buddy who didn't hold a grudge, "How did it go?"

"I filmed it." was the reply.

"Great!" said George "Thanks! I knew you would!"

The weekend was spent writing: records, plans and updating VSO on the study approach; a story for the conference; application for VSO funding for Methodist and to the World Bank again; also letters and email.

Baron Bliss Day, 8th March is supposed to be a day of celebration in Belize and there was a regatta and a service in the park in Belize City but unlike the time in Belize City last year, Orange Walk was dead as it always is on National Holidays. Most attention seemed to have been given at a distance to the end of the four-day Belize River Canoe Race which ended at the Belcan Bridge at 12:00. I wrote letter to the Rotary Club together with an outline of the 'Linking' project (again) and provided some ideas for their proposal to Rotary International for computers for Orange Walk Primary Schools, together with suggestion for three schools: San Juan, Palmar and St. Peter's for which I provided and delivered courtesy copies. That may not have been a good idea in view of political preferences. Preparing new notes for Bertha's next presentation on Wednesday is more likely to be fruitful.

Tim died on Children's Day Friday 5th March 1999.

On Wednesday 10th March there was a meeting with local managers at Corozal District Education Office attended and addressed by David Price and the Management Team from QADS from 10:00 to midday. I learned of Tim's death afterwards from Louisa who had been asked to tell me by Tomas Zetina. Tomas later gave me the letter he had written on Saturday, smudged and marked with tears, still unknown to me now. Part of it tells the story…

'…the infants had sporting events and games while children from middle and upper participated in football. The children enjoyed themselves including Tim. They wanted to continue playing but we stopped at 3:30pm. Even the teachers enjoyed themselves, as they were the goalkeepers. At 6:30pm the campfire started. I gave a short speech to close Children's Week and then the children sang. Marshmallow roasting and other games followed this. At 8:20pm the children were called and given food. The children were then dismissed and teachers stayed behind to clean up. By 9:10pm I was already at home. Shortly after that I heard the ambulance. I commented to my wife, we thought that the ambulance was taking a sick person to Chetumal. Minutes later I was called by a teacher who told me that Tim was involved in an accident while going home (Tim lived on the Santa Elena roadside) and that she was told that Tim died on the spot…'

I had a meeting at Corozal Community College for VSO Tracer (Impact) Study at 1:00pm after which I phoned Tomas and arranged to go to the funeral tomorrow. I didn't do anything else as the news had completely taken over although letters from home helped a lot.

It is good to work. Next morning was spent collating information supplied by VSO for the study which was briefly discussed with Mark on the phone. We agreed to spend some time on it together at the conference next week. When I phoned Orvin Rancheran I found that Calcutta had not got through to the

National Primary Schools' Football Finals so I will not be going to Punta Gorda. They were leading 2-0 at half time and collapsed to a score of 2-3 by the end of the match. Seen that happen before. Unfortunate really, since Libertad should have forfeited the match - having not turned up to play last Saturday! I phoned through to Tony Brian and left a message that he could come and stay as he was coming this way for the Secondary Schools' Finals, and asked for him to contact me in the evening. He didn't. I tried to contact him at home in the evening and couldn't so I guess he must have left already.

I posted snail mail and caught the 12:00 bus to go to Tim's funeral in Corozal. I had some time to spare so I went to look for the house that Onelia and Ariel had told me about but couldn't find. I was looking for a high house which was also a board house. I saw the two of them as I walked to the church and they gave a fresh description which I followed up later.

The funeral given for Tim was so very moving; a deep and simple faith in people coming together, being thankful for his life and praying and singing for peace. The lesson was the life of Job - The Lord gives...

The church is that of the Chinese Community, Christian and caring and located right by the cemetery. The church was full and all the children from Christian Assemblies of God, Tim's school were there, together with all the staff. The coffin rested sideways on, in front of the Sanctuary (which is carpeted in deep red and people take off their shoes to walk there) and a photographic portrait of Tim faced us all.

The service was conducted in Spanish, English and Chinese and all the hymns were sung in both English and Chinese which added a dimension to the harmony which I have never experienced before. Singing was beautiful and the whole service was conducted by young people, other than the reading of Job and the message of comfort to the parents which was given in Chinese. A group of Chinese teenagers sang for Tim; beautiful voices. It is many years since I last witnessed (and joined with) young people singing so openly, freely and passionately in prayer and praise.

The Principal of the School, Tim's teacher, Tomas Zetina gave an address at the start of which I was introduced as a special friend and asked to stand. I cannot describe that feeling. All I can say is that throughout, I was caught completely off-guard at the depth of feeling which had developed in so short a time and with so little and sporadic contact. Tomas' address was this:

'...On January 12th 1995, Tim was enrolled at our institution 'Christian School Assemblies of God'. Tim was at that time, 7 years 8 months of age. He was placed in Infant I because he could not speak or understand English. At this point Jane (a Taiwanese female student) played an important part in assisting teachers with interpretation. Tim soon proved that he was serious and eager to learn. By the end of the school year, Tim was already in Standard I where, again, he proved himself through his excellent performance.

There was something special in Tim which made him outstanding. He quickly made friendship with his classmates and other students. He shared with them and soon adapted easily to the Belizean culture. Belizean food was no problem for Tim.

As time went by, teachers and community members commented that Tim had no problem in communicating with his friends and classmates; he even spoke more Creole than most of them. The school neighbours further commented: saying "Tim is not like the other Asian children. He does everything like a Belizean."

Tim was one of my son's special friends and classmate from Standard II to Standard V, just before the Lord called him home. Because of this special bond between them I knew many special things about Tim.

In a conversation with my son last week, Tim told him that he would soon be a Belizean because he has already been in Belize for more than 5 years. He was very excited about this. On many occasions Tim went to our house to play marbles or football. I had the privilege of being Tim's classroom teacher this school year. From this experience as his teacher, I can say that Tim was indeed an excellent boy. He always tried his best in everything. Just prior to his departure he proved himself in his Maths exam, obtaining 100% and an additional 3 points on a bonus.

March 1st to March 5th was Children's Week. Everybody was excited and enjoyed themselves throughout the week, participating in special children's activities during the afternoons. On Friday March 5th Tim and all the students of Christian School Assemblies of God paraded through the streets of Santa Rita. This was followed by a Sports Day in which Tim participated in 5-a-side games. He had a wonderful time. At 6:30pm children returned to school where a campfire was held to close Children's Week. This event ended at 8:30pm after the children were given a treat of food. Tim left for home. He had enjoyed himself, never knowing that the Lord was about to call him home. From my knowledge of Tim, I am sure he was prepared to meet his creator. For on Thursday morning during our Scripture lesson, the Holy Scripture guided me to speak to the children to be prepared because we know when we were born but we don't know when we will die - for death respects no-one. I saw the keen interest of my students as we discussed this topic.

Tim we miss you. We know that you are now in Heaven; you are now in those celestial mansions; you are now a citizen of the Heavenly Kingdom. Wait for us. We will soon meet - for life on Earth is like the fog that appears in the morning and disappears when the sun shines. Tim was knocked down by a vehicle as he made his way home. The driver was drunk. He died on the spot.'

At the end of the service Tim's Mum spoke her thanks to us all; an amazing woman. I can only attribute the strength she displayed to an incredible faith, especially when she prayed for the vehicle driver asking only that he learn from what he has done and find his own peace.

We all made our way to the cemetery, behind the coffin, and in a simple ceremony Tim was laid to rest at about 4:30pm; the afternoon of the 11th. March, 1999.

After the funeral I simply wanted to walk and there wasn't a bus so I went back along the sea front and found my way back to the house that is to let but not advertised. It was easy enough to find right on the sea front with just a little grassed space and palm trees on the other side of the small road between it and the sea. I soon managed to get some attention and went in to look. It belongs to Ruby Oxley. She teaches at Maryhill and is a friend of Onelia Botes. Ariola Pasos lives just along the road. The house is in the same substantial grounds as the one that Ruby lives in with her mother. It stands on concrete stilts and is itself, a concrete high house. Not large and only one bedroom but with a balcony all round, some furniture and a cooker with an outside gas tank provided. It is not as swish as the house at Santa Rita but much more manageable and cosy as well as being closer to many more of my friends. At $250 instead of $350, how could I not take the opportunity of living for eighteen months right on the shore of the Caribbean Sea? I managed to phone Mandy Vasquez in the evening (he never phones back). He certainly wasn't happy about it and I think that I would have stuck with my agreement with him had he not tried to suggest that he had incurred some expense getting his house ready for me. I can understand that it is disappointing for him but the house isn't ready, I have been waiting for two months during which he failed to contact me at all to tell me how he was progressing, and he was doing the work. So I withdrew to take the house by the sea and phoned Ruby to arrange to visit on Saturday at 1:00pm. It hadn't been a case of my looking for another house but it coming looking for me. I'm never likely to have that opportunity again; a day never to be forgotten.

I wrote to Hal, for 7R, for year 7, and for me...

'...Dear Friends in 7R, Tim Huang died on Friday 5th March, Children's Day. His funeral, which I attended, took place yesterday, 11th. March at 2:30pm. He is, of course, one of the students at Christian School Assemblies of God, Santa Rita, 'Linking' with you and making friends especially, with Hal. I have no doubt that you will wish to give something of yourselves to Tim's family, friends and school but I have no suggestion to make. You are best able to decide that for yourselves. An intelligent and lively boy, I liked Tim very much. I hope the following helps...'

Time for Tim.

This is my time for Tim. I only know him as Tim and this is my time for him. It isn't long. It hasn't been long but that is not a measure of my time for Tim.

Tim is eleven years old. Somehow, I have a lot of friends who are ten or eleven years old - long after my time. I often wonder in how many ways I stuck at eleven myself.

My time began for Tim with a 'Linking' between his class and a class of children, many of whom came from my old school in England; began with an email from Hal using my address to overcome the slow mail on 17th December; many more each way and many trips back and forth to Tim's school to keep the friendship going...

... ...

...Tim will always be eleven years old for me. He died on Children's Day, March, 5th. 1999. Wiser now, than

I. This is my time for Tim. I only know him as Tim and this is my time for him. It isn't long. It hasn't been long but that is not a measure of my time for Tim. My time for Tim lives on; until.......

Thank you Tim

I tried again, to contact Tony Brian before he would have left for school - but no reply. Tony got through to me at about 2:30pm having arrived in Orange Walk. The arrangement then was for me to meet him at Muffles College at 6:00pm as that was where he was calling from. I had to do some shopping and check on the mail so I called round at Muffles to see what was happening. Of course, the football matches were taking place at the Stadium. When the time came, I walked down to the Stadium (paid to get in) to look for him. Needless to say I had just missed him although I didn't know that until I found him waiting at Muffles at about 6:45pm! A lot of walking and hot! Pleasant evening and didn't eat until about 10:00pm.

Tony, who doesn't like walking left by taxi at 11:00am giving me time to get ready to catch the midday bus to go to Corozal. I was just about to go when Tabo, Marco and Chino arrived so we had a few beers and I phoned Ruby Oxley to say that I would be an hour late. I was dropped off at the bus stop as they went on to San Estevan. The two Venus buses had collided with each other which caused some delay while bent parts were forced out of the way of moving parts but I arrived at the house just about a quarter to two which was okay.

I spent until just after three looking at the house and sorting out details. It is small but it is very cosy, attractive and clean, with a good size bathroom, shower etc. There is room to put up a visitor and keep a spare bed. It is also very airy, being built on stilts about twelve feet above the ground like this one. What is really good is the location. It is right opposite where they call The Beach: waving palm trees; thatched shelter for parties; and the Caribbean Sea right there, with its ever restless breeze, the rustle of the leaves and the whispering of the tiny waves; Heaven! A few yards along to the right is a pleasant bar at the water's edge and the sea front stretches away to the left towards the fish and vegetable market. Many friends live close by and the four 'Linking' schools are all within 30 minutes' walk; two of them being within five minutes' walk. Teacher Gladys of Standard Five at Methodist, who link with 7G is the sister of Ruby Oxley, the owner, who teaches at Maryhill. The garden of the house is shared with the house of the owner whose Mum is a keen gardener - quite one of the nicest gardens I have seen. An enormous rubber tree provides complete shade. And to cap all that, the house has a balcony round it, quite wide enough to sit out overlooking the sea.

I walked out to meet Orvin Rancheran and his family at Ranchito in order to go on to the Wedding of Robert and Emma Guy at the Baptist church which was scheduled for 4:00pm. Of course, it didn't happen until well after five but Orvin wasn't ready and in no hurry so we arrived just as it was starting. Robert and Emma had been married for seventeen years and produced six children but their marriage had been in a registry office and they wanted it to be in church. I took photographs which I will be able to give them on Wednesday. Afterwards we all went back to their home by the school in Calcutta for the party and I was brought home by a friend of theirs at about ten thirty. A plastic sheet has been suspended overhead, outside the house where the Guy family live and some light bulbs suspended. As there is so much space around the houses and the country is so unspoiled there is a remarkable feeling of oneness with the surroundings and there is nothing sophisticated to detract from that. The dancing takes place after the all-important meal. Belizeans are very hospitable and no-one is allowed to go hungry in any way (or thirsty!) and always, there is the bouquet to identify the next bride! I forget what was thrown belonging to the groom just relieved to have the camera!

'…What a tragic thing to happen to one so young. His family must be devastated. I can only say that all of us in Hal's family are all shocked and saddened by the news, and at times like this at a loss to know what to say. It does sound as though Tim was very lucky in his short life to have found such great support and good friends around him, no doubt his family will be gaining strength from you all now. Our thoughts are with Tim's family and I hope the knowledge that Tim's contact across the globe has forged a small link, will somehow add to the strength they will need to see them through this sad time...'

'…I was really sorry to receive the news yesterday and am taking the email to Youth Club to pray for his family and friends tonight (Sunday)...'

On Monday I called in at O/W office, did a small amount of shopping and had my hair cut -which was nice; then phoned Tomas Zetina to arrange to visit and talk with Standard 5&6, his class; took in a whole heap of photos to be printed or re-printed; caught the midday bus and called in at the Corozal office on the way to the school. I went through what I had done about Tim with the students; read the emails from Hal and others and gave weight to Hal's suggestion that the 'Linking' might be used as a tribute to Tim. Walked back down to White Sapphire who had the carving made for me for SMCC and then caught the bus back home to arrive just after four ready for the next day's sorting out in preparation for moving. Landy Burns promised to come round and look at the surplus items with a view to making an offer himself. Needless to say he didn't arrive - had to take Nelson to Chetumal (in the evening) to get some glasses as 'he is having trouble with his eyes'. I would be sorry about that if everything wasn't in the same mould and if there weren't perfectly adequate services in Belize which I have used myself. He said that he would come round tomorrow evening.

All of Wednesday was spent at Calcutta with six students using the computer. It is very difficult for them and puts me in mind of some of the slow eight year olds when I first used computers in class in 1980 and I got home tired. Bertha came round to report on progress and to have a print of the QADS letterhead which I was able to do on the new computer. Four nice emails arrived in reply to my one about the house in Corozal, including a very nice one from Hal. No Landy Burns at the time of writing (8:30pm).

'...Dear Friends in 7R, The Buddy from Christian School Assemblies of God has just returned to Belize. As you know, we are getting some help with Immigration from the Post Office to cut down on the cost of flight tickets; not many exchange students travel by mail but it works! Topsi had some fun because he came with three other Buddies and arrived in Orange Walk just as I am moving to Corozal so he has done well to get here in so short a time. Fortunately, I have friends in the Post Office as well and they said "No problem Mr Max". The drop (as they call it here) was made the next day. (When you have a 'lift', as in a vehicle, here in Belize, they call that a 'drop' as well.) However, you might remember that there are four schools 'Linking', not one, and it would help to include a note for me to say where things are going to save me looking it up.

I sneaked a look in the diary and I must say I thought it was great; just right. It gives a very good picture of what Topsi's new friends are really like and what you think about. It seems that Topsi has had a really good time even if he did spend some time in school bags. I suppose that isn't any different from the international travel arrangements he has already got used to. Mind you, I hope you remembered to remove your smelly old PE kit, especially the shoes, and last week's sandwiches. I do wonder where else Topsi has been but he is very discreet, he's not saying, although he may be more open with the particular friend in Belize that you are writing to. I hadn't better pick out any of your writings because it wouldn't be fair. In any case, I found it all great to read; no doubt the students at Santa Rita will too! They will also be pleased with the letters and card. I haven't opened them; that is for them to do.

I expect that you will be pleased to know that all four schools will soon have a computer to use generally and to communicate with you via email or through the Internet. The funds have all been secured one way or another to do it already. Calcutta School already has theirs. When I come home for a holiday next month, one of the things I aim to do is to make sure that it is going to work at your end! I am sure your support and enthusiasm will help with that! That's it for now. Topsi is right by the computer waiting for lunch. I'm sure that he would be asleep because it has been a tiring journey, but lunch is important so I had better get on with it. I have been using lunchtime to write this and I don't think he can quite appreciate the value of that...'

I finished setting out data provided for VSO Impact study on Thursday and caught the 4:00pm bus for Belize City to stay overnight with the family. On Friday morning I was there to catch the VSO charter bus outside Savu supermarket at 6:00am to travel to Placencia. The journey was via the coast road into Dangriga to pick up Simon and Andy and then on to the hotel. Arnold was not well and didn't go. This was a pity from my point of view as I was hoping to talk to him about his teaching at the Ecumenical College.

Interesting as always, the conference mostly covered activities in which I was not directly involved. We went on a boat trip on the one afternoon, looking for birds and manatees; a pleasant trip but disappointing in respect of the wildlife of which we saw very little; also a Garifuna presentation of drums and dancing on Saturday evening; and my contribution...

"Mr Max Says"
A personal View of Disadvantage in the Classroom

Always a pleasant thing to do at the end of a working day, he sat with a cup of coffee on the balcony, some fifteen feet above the ground. The late afternoon sun was sinking behind the house, bathing the trees opposite in a rich, almost tactile light; emphasising their great variety of yellows and greens and browns of leaf and the regalia of flower. The overhang of the roof covered the balcony completely and as always, a fresh and cooling breeze countered the heat of the day. Somehow, the ten boys playing football across the way seemed to emphasise the peace rather than disturb it. They too, were at one with their environment; their youthful voices calling encouragement in a game - the rules of which he had long since ceased to try to understand - save the passing of the ball beyond the keeper and the howls of joy and derision which accompanied that event.

"How is it," he thought, "That boys aged so widely, from seven to seventeen, share their game, their sport, their teamwork, so well; how to give way to lesser strength, weight or skill; when to pass; how to grow together?"

The game is over for a while. The boys sit in a circle; each taking a turn in the middle to make a point or demonstrate some move which is easily understood by all; skills which are a teacher's dream. True there are no girls here but he had noted that they too, made such groups and boys and girls together, would communicate in the same way in the playgrounds of schools - especially the rural schools. "Why is it, then, that the standard of education is so poor among so many at the end of the Primary phase of learning; education, which is probably the greatest advantage a child can have, next to a loving home and good health. Can it be that there is something seriously wrong in schools or even in the culture itself?"

Elijah is one of the players deep in conversation with his friends. He is fourteen. He passed his BNSE but his score was not high. It was high enough to take him into a secondary school but not high enough to give him the status he thought he needed and, worse than that, it was a comment on what was undoubtedly limited attention on his part, in the classroom. 'Hyperactive' his teachers said. His own knowledge of Elijah suggested, more likely, that he was bored. At first, it was thought that Elijah would repeat but the family is large and resources are few. He was accepted at the Agricultural College after the summer holiday. This was some distance away and not easy to reach but he has an aunt living close by the College, with whom he could stay during the week. It didn't last long. Elijah, away from home and friends and not an academic, dropped out. He spends his days making himself as useful as he can, trying to steer clear of trouble and enjoying the company he now shared.

He watched the group disperse as darkness fell. Elijah turned and waved, calling out "Hi Mr Max!" as he always did; a regular greeting accompanied by a broad grin and which would have included some exchange of news or ideas had they been closer. The other boys turned and waved as well, for he knew them all, but it was Elijah who gave voice to the action. So what had gone wrong?

Strange that a new line of thought should disturb him: 'Mr Max' had come to be a form of address and of greeting which had been, and still was, very friendly. It made him feel at home as it was said in a warm and welcoming sort of way and it meant that his Christian name was used, which he liked. Teachers and principals used it in the same way. But it had been at a large workshop, which he had led, when first the little worm of doubt had burrowed its way into his mind; not identified yet, but a seed to germinate later. "Hi! Mr Max!" among them became "What does Mr Max want us to do next? Is this right for Mr Max?"

It wasn't noticeable at all at first. The teachers had lots of good ideas as they developed a sound working curriculum for Language: Spanish as well as English. Obviously, it was the work of teachers. Mr Max has no Spanish at all!

Great things were in store for children. They would be active in their learning. Their ideas and their cognition would be rooted in reality; never to be forgotten; always capable of regeneration and not solely dependent on memory. The Teachers knew what to do and the whole exercise became one of keeping the enthusiasm going. Similar work was gathered up from other Districts until a whole curriculum was formed for the Lower Division and this was taken into the classroom in sixty pilot schools; fourteen in the North where he works. Progress had been made and yet it had been slow in the schools. Still the biggest single problem was 'telling!' It was quite a difficult job for teachers to make change in a culture or system in which classroom practice boils down to mere 'telling'. There was no tradition of promoting thought, understanding or skills. How frustrating that could be even though it might be quaint (and even attractive) to hear children chorus 'Yes Ma'am' or provide the required answer in unison.

And yet, children were just as bright here, as any others anywhere. They proved that in every lesson but not in a way that helped their learning. They only had 'one scout out' at any one time (that is the one who was really listening). The 'scout' was the one who triggered a response while the rest were more satisfactorily distracted! And they took it in turns on some sort of agreed basis - a basis which was impossible to identify. Like the scout, the system of covert selection was constantly shifting. The wonder was they learned anything at all - when the choral response made the teacher think that everyone was listening!

'This is the way we do it' was a 'tradition' which was difficult to break for individual teachers. Everyone was used to working to a prescription; 'being told' themselves. Unwittingly, 'Mr Max' had been put upon a pedestal. He had become the teller even in the face of overwhelming evidence to the contrary. The whole workshop had been non-directive; teachers even pointed that out for themselves; "Tell us what to do!" they said. The whole product was their work. There could be no denying it; and yet.....

Mr Max was not in the classroom. The prop which was not a prop had been removed. Better go back to the old prop. Some would start from there; most of the others would too, given time. Mr Max lowered his profile - a lot!

Most people do not like to stand out from the crowd. Teachers are no exception. Parent expectations of their children's work in exercise books, their observations of classroom behaviour; all children sitting at a desk and facing the front; attitudes of managers (to mention just a few), have all had a part to play. Not surprisingly, then, much of the actual practice in the classroom reverted to 'Telling'. Mainly the small schools had made the greatest progress, perhaps because they were closer to their parents and able to take them with them. Small wonder that children still had so far to go before becoming active learners; able to grasp at opportunity and see some purpose in their lives. Yet, in the classrooms where the greatest progress had been made, that enthusiasm for learning was alive already.

Mr Max had wondered many times what he might do for Elijah; especially since his predicament seemed symptomatic of so many boys and girls in Belize. But Elijah's environment, his experience, is what he knows. There is great danger in detachment from roots in any way. No! The answer has to be in the classroom but how to hasten the change from telling to learning. That is the question.

Unknown to Elijah, he would become a memory in far off England, a hope that he makes it. Disadvantage has many facets. Mr Max carried in his chair, turning to close the door, and sighed at a faint new dawning in the gathering darkness.

We left Placencia at 1:45pm but went all the way round the Hummingbird Highway which made it late getting back to Belize and late evening getting back home.

Mr Mai at Corozal Community College phoned first thing on Monday to postpone a meeting scheduled for 1:30pm. He had not produced the records as he had been 'busy with the Spelling Bee'! Just as well that he doesn't know my view of the Spelling Bee! He was hoping to leave it until after the Easter Holiday but, after pressing hard, he agreed to Wednesday morning at 10:00. Spent the rest of the day making arrangements with Sacred Heart at San Ignacio out west and Ecumenical College at Stann Creek down south, which were both very helpful; sorting out my approach to questioning; and sending email and FAX to the Institutions to guide and aid their preparation.

'…Your messages were very much appreciated by the Teacher and Students at Santa Rita, and would have been taken to Tim's family last Monday after I had read them out and left copies. I also left a copy of my letter to your form and a complete record of all the mail that had gone back and forth. I have attached a copy of that for you...'

'…I didn't get to see Orlando as I was tied up with students on the computer all day. But better news than that, I have received an email from the Principal, Mr Rancheran, so their email must be working. Try sending an email direct. I'm sure you have the address but, just to make certain here it is…'

A day at Sacred Heart was very full and started the whole business of interviews in earnest. This also involved a good deal of walking as volunteers were both past and present and not necessarily at the institution. This followed by a very useful meeting with staff at Corozal Community College. There was some difficulty with University College of Belize but finally I found the right person to contact next morning. One past volunteer who was at UCB now works for Programme for Belize. It turns out that she is at Hill Bank so I made arrangements to go there on Saturday morning, to return on Sunday. Working on the records already provides plenty to do but it would be very pleasant to spend a couple of days there. I could do without it this weekend from the point of view of preparing to go to Corozal. However, it will help to get this study finished, which I want to do before I leave for the UK.

I got up at five and went on down to Magali's, opposite the Fire Station on San Antonio Road, to meet with the transport to Hill Bank Field Station dead on time at six thirty. The truck was a medium size beat up job with an open back and only the programme for Belize sticker on the door to identify it. However, there was no doubt about Derek's smile of welcome, all white teeth in a dark face, as I was the only English (or white) person around, let alone one who looked as though he was going somewhere.

It is a good view from the cab of a truck and the exchange of life experiences was good also, as we bounced along, through Yo Creek and San Lazaro, into Trinidad. There we collected five girls; one, as I discovered, was the Nanny of Nimmi's two children and the other four were students from Corozal Community College who were going to interview Nimmi's husband Alan, a Belizean, who is Field Station Manager. One of the girls sat with us in the cab while the other three hung on to the sides of the truck at the back. Loud screams and shrieks of laughter could be heard above the engine and road sound when Derek was unable to avoid the worst of the potholes!

The journey continued through August Pine Ridge and San Felipe. I knew we weren't going round Blue Creek where I imagined we might enter the Rio Bravo, passing through the La Malpa Field Station, and as we turned towards Indian Church and Lamanai, I thought that there must be a road alongside the lagoon, although I didn't remember seeing one. In fact, we turned off very quickly and headed more or less south right between what turned out to be the Rio Bravo territory and quite extensive Mennonite farms which appeared to be very well managed, most of the current crop being beans. We arrived to a great welcome at about 8:45. The food was excellent; there were trips out which had been arranged for the girls and the interview was very fruitful. We left at about three thirty and I got back home at just before six to start really getting ready to move tomorrow.

I arranged to leave for Corozal at 1:00pm which gave little time to finish cleaning through and getting everything ready to go. Food and drink was a problem as what I had was quickly used up. I was ready by 12:30 and Landy's transport arrived at 1:00pm! Despite the delay, all went smoothly from then on except that BTL in Corozal had been and gone without fixing the phone as they wanted me to be there to make sure it was in the right place. Orange Walk had assured me that this was not necessary but then, they didn't come as promised, to disconnect my phone in Orange Walk either. Most of the evening was spent unpacking and doing just enough shopping to keep me going. The house is great and I spent a very pleasant night lulled by the sound of the sea and the wind until the cockerel woke me at about 3:30am!

I went to the District Centre in order to look in on the Middle Division Orientation. It was going well so I left and went to BTL who told me to go back for news at 1:30pm. The rest of the morning was spent finishing the unpacking and sorting out in the house. When I went back to BTL, I was told that they would be coming this afternoon so I went straight back home. They arrived at about three and took only twenty minutes and I was not only on the phone but back on email as well. Four messages came in including one which took a very long time to download. I will have to find a way of getting over this.

A visit to Atlantic Bank showed that the only way of transferring my account from Barclays is to do it myself. This is a nuisance because it means transferring payment of the monthly stipend from the Ministry. A bit more shopping and sorting out finished all I could do for the day and I finished reading my books from Orange Walk Library.

Wednesday started gently but there is a great deal of writing to catch up on again, including the notes from the weekend for VSO. I managed to find where to buy meat and identify the various shops which are likely to be useful and convenient, joined the library and took out two books. The selection of books is excellent (from my point of view anyway).

'…I have packed up the Belize buddies and sent them in the post, along with a somewhat belated card of condolence. I am planning a piece of classwork to be sent off at the start of our summer term, and I know a number of pupils are writing. There should be an increase now from 7G to Corozal School…'

'...Dear Friends in Year 7, I have moved. If you wish to send mail via me please note my new address. The email address remains the same but that is above also. I received my first mail from England on Monday which was my first (part) day here. You may like to know that it took five days only, from posting. That is a huge improvement on what I have been used to and largely due to being able to have the mail delivered as there is always someone to leave it with when I am not in. To give you a word picture, the next two pages are an accurate description which I hope conveys some of the atmosphere of the place...

Paradise or What?

Even though the temperature nudges ninety in the shade there is always a breeze, often a strong breeze, cooling and comforting, caressing the body and inducing a feeling of well-being. The house is a high one, concrete, on stilts only part filled in to form a store under the bathroom. Around two sides is a balcony, some six feet wide, twenty-four feet long at the front and eighteen along one side. All this adds to the cooling effect although the fabric of the house stores enough heat during the day to enable sleep through the night without bedclothes and with the window slats open just sufficient to stir the air.

There are two sets of stairs and two doors into the house. The one I use most comes up through the side balcony giving a feeling not unlike that of entering the tree houses I used to build (in other people's trees) as a boy. A low balustrade surrounds the balconies and flanks the outer stairs but the stairs that come up through the balcony have no rail, inviting one to almost swing from the edge on going down, adding to the memory of halcyon days.

Inside is interesting to say the least. A layout of which I would never have dreamed, unconventional to the point of being awkward and yet it became thoroughly lived in within half a day much in the manner of Bilbo Baggins although his aspect was under rather than over ground. Angles everywhere, all painted white and with a summery floorcovering so that the light is strong inside as well as outside the house. Two steps lead down into the bathroom which is huge; a pleasure to use. Many extras have been provided which I haven't been used to since coming to Belize. The cooker is very high class, new and easy to use. It is self-lighting (no more of those little matchsticks with no sulphur on the end or what there was falling off), everything works and the flame is readily controllable. There is a comfortable settee and the most comfortable bed I have slept on for nearly two years.

The telephone was installed within twenty four hours of arrival and the first four emails downloaded right away as the computer was already in operation. In that same time, everything had been put away and I knew where everything was.

There is about thirty feet of pleasant garden between the front of the house and the wall by the road which is not heavily used. The garden extends widely to the sides and back of my house and contains a two storey timber house in which the owner lives. There are many plants and bushes but dominant among them are the three trees, orange, coconut and, biggest of all, a rubber tree. I know about rubber plants of course, but I had never thought of them being a tree even though I know that latex is tapped from rubber trees. Such is the difference between knowledge and experience/understanding. Anyway, the rubber tree is magnificent.

When I think of all the trouble people go to in England to nourish the plant and polish the leaves I stand in awe at Nature doing the same job to perfection, in abundance and on a grand scale. Each leaf opens from a slender red tube about a foot long and forms into a perfect evergreen almond pressing for space among the dense foliage around it; so dense that the space underneath is in deep dark shadow and very little grows there. Like the almond, the rubber tree grows with a horizontal habit. But that is only the edge of paradise. That is without being outside; on the balcony first; in the garden; and then beyond. For this is by the sea; right by the sea; by the Caribbean Sea: palm trees and balmy breeze, peace and pleasure.

Beyond the garden wall is a grassy space with an interesting shoreline which is locally known as Miami Beach. Belizeans are as generous in their use of descriptors as they are with their hospitality. The Crystal Palace is in Orange Walk. When I found The Crystal Palace I had walked around the building for about fifteen minutes before asking and being told I was there. The MCC ground is in Belize City - enough said about that!

The shortest distance from the balcony to the sea must be about forty yards, no more, and it seems nearer from that elevated position. I go out there at any time of day 'just to have a look', being fascinated by the ever changing view: the stirring of the trees; the changing colour and texture of the sea, sometimes flat calm and sometimes completely broken with short lively waves, rarely white-topped and never the rolling variety of the Atlantic or the North or Irish Seas. It is Easter time and the children are off school so that there is a small group of them enjoying a swim at any time of the day. At lunchtime and in the evening, adults, and couples especially, of all ages stroll along the sidewalk or on to the grass, often stopping for a while, perhaps to share their lunch or strengthen a relationship. Bliss!

Palm trees fringe the grassy area and are dotted about on it. There are several almond trees and others, and a single fir-like tree with pendulate, hairy 'needles' which are the longest and most delicate I have ever seen, hanging in dense bunches from long slender and very flexible stem-like twigs sprouting from equally slender branches which in turn, grow from longer ones eventually attached to a trunk which itself, looks like a thick cord of twisted stems somehow cohabiting together. The first couple of feet of each trunk is painted with a white (lime I expect) substance to protect the plant from insects.

At one end of the grassy space is a large shelter with no sides, round and thatched in the traditional manner. This week, a smaller one was built right on the edge of the sea and the frame of another one has been built today. At the other end is a bar, also right on the edge of the sea, where food is served as well as drinks. They play music there but you have to go outside to hear it. Little is really heard above the restless sound of sea, the call of birds and the breeze in the trees.

Although it is called a beach which is clearly understood here, there is little or no sand uncovered by the tide for the simple reason that there is little or no tide. I suppose it might make a foot but mostly, it seems to me to be just a few inches although the tide times are announced each day. What is probably important is the current. The water inside the reef is shallow and the distances involved also have to do with the limits of the tidal levels but the flow must be quite great - as it is on a wide flat beach. So there are no great bare patches in a scene which is ever changing and alive with movement.

But that is not all. There is the light! The sun is very bright and mostly, it lasts all day so the first thing to notice is the strong colours and the deep shadows. This light, playing on the water, makes the waves seem livelier than ever; surfaces reflecting in part, like a myriad of tiny mirrors and creating moving pockets of dark - like shadow. And the water is not blue it is green; a whole range of soft greens so that the horizon between sea and sky is clear, distinct, one from the other. In the brief sundown and the short period which passes for evening in the tropics, the shadows lengthen, the sea darkens and the breeze stirs the trees in a different way. A quiet time until the sounds of night take over from those of the day; especially, the cicadas sing. The moon rises, as does the sun just now, dead ahead over a clear part of the sea in uninterrupted view, and the water changes to shimmering silver sighed over by the restless movement of the sea and the trees; nature's lullaby with which to sleep.

'I didn't mention the Frigate Birds in it which can be seen from the house, especially in the morning and the late afternoon. They are amazing. The wing span is about four feet for a body length of only eighteen inches including the legs which form an aerodynamic shape behind the body as they soar on the air currents. They are completely black with very slender crescent shaped wings except for the rather more angular point where the elbow would be. When they fold those wings to dive for fish, the acceleration is terrific. They barely enter the water before the fish is out of it and other frigate birds are in hot pursuit!'

Thursday 1st April. I went to try to open an account with Atlantic Bank this morning and decided against it - preferring to suffer the inconvenience of the Barclays account in Belize City. I had a cheque for $1531 from VSO to pay in, my current cheque book, my passport and my VSO id card. Even with all that, one is treated (nicely of course) as though the intention is to defraud. I was then informed that cheque accounts (which carry a cash card) were not given to non-Belizeans. Neither could my present account be transferred (So the banks obviously do not cooperate since they certainly have the technology). Special dispensation was sought from the lady manager (who was charming of course) and I was offered an account. I then found that there is no cash dispenser closer than Belize City so I would still not be much better off as banking hours are not exactly convenient (they close at 2:00pm). I still persisted (smiling) but when I was told that there had to be a minimum of $500 in the account without attracting charges that was the end. It would be unlikely that I would allow the account to drop below that anyway, but the idea that I have to loan the bank $500 to run a simple account is one that I am not prepared to accept. I said no thank you.

Afterwards, I went to the District Office and was surprised to find Bertha and Louisa working there. They were about to come to blows so some time was spent trying to get them to work together again. I have said that I wouldn't go to the first day of the workshop which starts a week on Monday but I think I will attend for most of the first week. I will try to get enough 'tracer' visits done with students taught by past VSOs to give me enough notes and then take the laptop along to the office and write them up there. I found where to buy chicken and returned home to await the arrival of water and soft drinks and to do some writing.

Next day being Good Friday I went to the service that was at St Paul's Anglican Church at 7:00am. It was very good and there were a lot of things for me to think about but it went on for two and a half hours! It was centred on the seven things that Jesus said on the cross, each a sermon in itself and emphasised by the next three verses of a hymn telling the same story.
The rest of the Easter weekend was spent still trying to catch up.

I went in to the District Education Office again on Monday morning and found Bertha and Louisa about to come to blows again. I managed to defuse that and bring them together (a counselling session wholly inadequate in terms of time because Bertha was very resistant indeed – especially at the start) sufficiently to complete their preparations for next Monday.

Corinth asked me if I would spend the first four days at the Workshop next week as she couldn't be there and she had also noted the atmosphere between Bertha and Louisa. This I agreed to do but I know it will make things very difficult in respect of the study for VSO and I will have to put off my visit to Dangriga which was arranged for next Wednesday.

'…Now that I am near to the end of my second year in post I wish to apply for a VSO grant from the Small Scale Initiatives/Project Support Fund. This is in support of a personal project in which I have been engaged since my post in Belize was confirmed. I am happy to say that it is progressing well. The project is known to you since a grant has already been made to Calcutta - one of the schools involved…'

I travelled to San Ignacio on Tuesday to stay with Kathryn for four days and to visit some of the past students of Sacred Heart College and their families; also one of the past volunteers who is still living in the area - that is until the end of the schools' Easter holiday and a weekend wholly devoted to data records and organisation and mail.

Four days from Monday were spent as promised at the Middle Division Pilot Schools' Workshop when it was also useful to be back in Corozal with many arrangements to make.
I phoned Stann Creek Ecumenical College to change the arranged visit from this Wednesday to the 21st and managed to make it so that it was of advantage to the College as they hadn't yet brought the records together; also phoned VSO, Sacred Heart College and University College of Belize. Not much progress had been made (still) by any of them!

I managed to talk with Pedro Cucul about the problems I am having with email on the laptop and he told me about Douglas Stansmore who works with a small trading company operating in the Free Zone. It was Douglas who installed Netscape for Calcutta Government School. He installed it for me together with a virus protector, some games and Microsoft Publisher.

Caroline arrived to stay overnight as she had a meeting at the Red Cross which is at Santa Rita. The meeting was due to start at 4:30pm. I met her there and arranged for her to be brought to my house afterwards. She arrived a little over an hour later. It seemed a lot of travelling for her for an hour long meeting. Anyway we went out for a meal and spent a pleasant evening, including walking the seafront which she enjoyed. Caroline stayed until she caught the 1:15pm bus so I came home early from the workshop and we had lunch in the Belizean restaurant before she left. Alphonso dropped me off home so we were able to have a beer together before going out.

I went to the District Centre on Friday morning to liaise with Corinth who will remain with the rest of the workshop. She was pleased with the progress we had made and especially that it was still being run by Louisa and Bertha who have buried their differences sufficient to get on with it. I took my leave of the workshop with a few words about how I had found students in Belize and how they were 'Linking' with students at SMCC. I talked about resources and mentioned that the four schools were well on the way to Internet connection but didn't say how this was achieved. Rather, the point was to show the potential in Belize Students and that the teachers present held their lives and the future of Belize in their hands. In the UK the two big bones of contention are teacher/pupil ratios and resources just as they are here. That never solves the problem of education; only the will to change will do that. (There had been too much diversion into those two issues which could not be addressed at a workshop such as this). Anyway, it went down well and I left with the full Belizean handshake – much to the delight of all who probably didn't expect me to know about it let alone how to do it.

Alphonso gave me a lift to Assemblies where I picked up a couple of students' letters to send by email and then went on to the Post Office. A package had arrived with three Buddies so I took this home and wrote letters to the three classes (also sent email) and took the Buddies, with copies of the letters for the three schools. I called into St. Paul's Anglican to wonder why a Buddy hadn't come for them and went on to Corozal Methodist School. Their class was receptive as always. The Buddy for Calcutta was delivered to Necetas who was at the workshop. This caused some amusement as I had said I wouldn't be coming back. I just missed most of the students at Christian School as it was 3:40pm already, but I made the delivery and Tomas gave me a lift back home. Tim's mother had written an extraordinary account of Tim and Tomas had asked me to type this up so I did that this evening.

The move to Corozal meant spending a great deal more time catching up with mail…
'…Before I leave Belize, all four schools will have a computer to use – with all the advantages that brings – and will be able to communicate directly by email or through the Internet. When I come home, one of the tasks I have in mind is to make sure that it happens at SMCC. At the moment those contacts are operating on a personal basis only…'
'…The modern tradition for house building in Belize is to use concrete. Reinforced columns are built on foundations to form corners and any other support that is required. These are generally about nine to twelve inches in square section. The space in between the columns is filled in with hollow concrete blocks. The roof is cast on the top with reinforcing bars set in place and the whole lot is held up with plywood supported underneath by many long thin tree trunks while it sets. My house doesn't have the bottom filled and is effectively built on stilts…'
'…Dear Hal, Here is a letter for you that I collected today, from Christian School Assemblies of God, Santa Rita. I believe that Tomas Zetina still intends to write…'
Unwarranted difficulties with financial affairs back home were ever present…
'…Thank you for your letter dated 15th March. Please note my new address. There are several points of concern straight away. 1) I was not advised of this transfer until your letter arrived. Why 'New Business?' 2) I am not receiving answers to letters sent to Bristol. I can supply copies of all correspondence if you have lost them. 3) The payment of the fee is supposed to be automatic and there should be no delay in your action on that account. 4) I am plagued with demands for payment of tax and forms from the Inland Revenue. Your responsibilities are intended to avoid that. 5) I now have yet another Tax Return which I enclose for your consideration. They have been triplicated so far and one wonders why? 6) You have had all the information that you need if my letters have been acted upon. The management of the account thus far, has been unsatisfactory. I would welcome your comments and your proposal for meeting some of the inconvenience caused to me…'
'…Dear Friends in 7D, the Buddy from Calcutta School has just returned to Belize…'
… That's it for now. Alli is right by the computer waiting for lunch. I'm sure that he would be asleep because it has been a tiring journey, but lunch is important – especially for alligators so I had better get on

246

with it. I have been using lunch time to write this and I don't think he can quite appreciate the value of that…'

'…Dear Friends in 7G, the Buddy from Corozal Methodist School has just returned to Belize…

… Later, I will take him to school for some minor surgery…'

'…I need to know about the Buddy from St Paul's Anglican School that has gone to 7H. The class concerned (and the teacher) at St Paul's is not what it might be and I get conflicting messages…'

Sunday 18th April. I started by catching up on my journal which has not been written up since 1st of the month. I have never left it for more than a couple of days before and that shows just how my routines have been out of gear as well as the extra work since moving to Corozal. The work prospect between now and the end of the month will leave no time for anything else. I managed to sort out some more ideas, make a few phone calls and do one interview before Ricardo and Marbella arrived for a pleasant couple of hours with their family.

All of the effort has been very much worthwhile because the remaining time before the break at home can be devoted to the study. Curriculum development is running very smoothly. The penultimate week started with records and organisation for the study and on Wednesday I set off for Dangriga on the 6:00am Venus bus to arrive in time to go to the bank in Belize City and still catch the 8:00am Z-Line to Dangriga via Belmopan and the Hummingbird Highway.

I was on schedule to arrive by 11:00am but the bus broke down and I was finally dropped off at Stann Creek Ecumenical College for my meeting with the Principal, a few minutes late, at just after 1:00pm. Accommodation is never a problem with volunteers being spread across the country and I stayed with Arnold and Denise which was very pleasant. We went out in the evening and I was able to meet a lot more of the local people – having already done well at the college. Next day was spent data gathering at the College and we went out again in the evening, first to Simon's house and then Stephen's. Simon is a VSO remedial teacher and Stephen is an ex VSO who stayed. Data gathering continued around the town on Friday until the evening when we went to a different bar and ate out as well. We didn't get in until late on any night and I was up again before six so I am getting tired!

I returned from Dangriga on the 8:15am Z-Line bus which took the coast road and went in to Gales point. What a remote and beautiful little village that is. Most of it can only be between 30 and 100 feet wide and perhaps a mile long, sticking out into the Southern Lagoon. I was fortunate in sitting next to the Principal of the Primary School there. She told me of a project the children are doing in conjunction with the Belize Zoo and the Audubon Society. Apparently the experts had discovered that the children were feeding manatees by hand and this was thought to be impossible! I intend to try to find a way in which this 'Link' can be extended to SMCC. The bus arrived in Belize City in time to catch the eleven o'clock 'premier' bus from the Batty terminal and I was home just after one o'clock, tired after a busy week but the journey had been much better than expected and much better than going down.

Time to write to the founder/director at the Belize Zoo…

'…Dear Sharon, I wonder, did you receive my story Home is the Belizoo? I have just changed computers and I don't seem to have transferred the correspondence. A copy is attached in case something has gone wrong. I would be pleased if you could give a brief reaction early this week as I am going to the UK for six weeks on Friday…'

'…I just finished reading the story - very nice! I really am honoured in how you used the signs as an interlocking part of the tale. Thank you so much for putting in a terrific effort; really brightened my day…'

'…Thanks for the kind words. I heard you on Love FM this morning and I thought you did extremely well in difficult circumstances - whatever you might have felt - and I am pleased to have brightened your day…'

'…Thank you for your compliment about Love FM. This issue has been very hard to deal with, but I just cannot state enough how vital that area is to the healthy ecology of Belize, so on I go. I appreciate your remarks. I really think the children's story would be a nice addition to the zoo's collection/library…'

'…It will be fun to do something with the story for Belize children. I have four schools here in Belize already 'Linked' with my past pupils and a school in England. I will see what ideas they have. I will contact you when I get back. I would also like to learn more of the Manatee project with schoolchildren at Gales Point…'

I spent Sunday morning on domestics after having been away, and catching up on mail.

'…Time is absolutely flying by now. I set off for home on Saturday at 2:05pm from Belize City and change from a 737 to a 777 at Houston. Although there is only a very short wait in Houston, I don't arrive at Gatwick (pity it has to be there) until 9:55am. This is because your time is seven hours ahead of ours. (That reminds me to say that you will arrive in the new millennium seven hours before I will!)…'

'…I returned from Dangriga yesterday, after spending four days collecting data for the Impact Study for VSO. I had a wonderful time and met a lot of very interesting people. This is one of the huge privileges I have enjoyed whilst being here and one which the opportunities I have been given have never allowed me to forget. The buzz must have gone round Stann Creek Ecumenical College (which is about the same size as SMCC but the youngest students are 13) because the young people were very welcoming wherever I went around the campus. To be fair to myself, the conversational style I use at interview probably helps and underneath that is a desire to know people…'

Then went out and took some pictures of the view from the house and around where I live in Corozal. This used up a whole roll of film, 25 pictures. I have started sorting things out ready to go next weekend but I realise that I have some films still to write commentaries for.

In common with most houses, there is no glass in the windows of my house just a hole covered with fine net to keep out mosquitoes. The slats work like a venetian blind, permanently down, to close at night or when it rains particularly heavily with the wind blowing in. The view outside is 'Miami Beach' and the Caribbean Sea. Being Sunday afternoon, families are on the beach. In the garden, here called the yard, is a tree as high as the house. This is a rubber plant which is rather larger than people grow in England. A truck which normally carries sugar cane from the fields to the factory has been used today, to transport a family to the beach. The sea is very green and very clean. It always seems to have a different shade every time I look at it. The sun comes up over the horizon in the morning and is almost always bright. Parked vehicles are mostly old and big, from the States.

There is a large thatched 'Round House' which is intended to keep off the sun almost within stone-throwing distance; no-one bothers about the rain. There is a coconut palm in the yard at the front of the house, mature and bearing a lot of coconuts in season, casting an intense shadow in the sun. The rubber tree has adventitious roots like so many of the forest trees. It seems as though these roots develop into new trunks after they have reached the ground and grown into it. There are orchids growing on the trunk.

Orchids are very common in the forest and they have enormous and beautifully coloured flowers. The balcony is where I like to sit in the shade with rum and coke (or two). I catch hold of the balcony as a habit when passing the entrance hole. You never know when that habit might be really useful!

The house next door and in the same yard, belongs to Ruby Oxley who owns the house I have, and her Mum. Another lady, Miss Luce (Lucille) lives downstairs in their house. As I have three ladies in a house in the same yard, I get well looked after!

At the back of my house there is only a small store on the ground which is underneath the bathroom. The roof is flat. There is no great need for a steeply sloping roof because the sun comes out after rain which is usually in short sharp bursts. The roof is dry in no time.

I have one bedroom, a living room for sitting cooking and eating combined, and a bathroom. All of this is on stilts to catch the almost continuous breeze coming in from the sea, and to avoid having crawling insects and mosquitoes in the house.

The sea water is very clean because there is no sewage going into it. It is warmer than the swimming bath would be even in the middle of the night and the heavy salt concentration makes it very easy to float which suits me. There is very little tide, only a few inches, and as the wind is always on-shore it is very safe bathing.

Just along the road is a Zericote-Cordia Dode Can Dea of Mayan name 'Chack Pote' which is a versatile tree treasured in Belize. Just about every part of the tree is used. The beautiful flowers are children's whistlers and necklace. The leaves are very useful scouring pads for pots and pans, chairs and tables. The fruits make delicious juicy stewed sweets. The bark provides a very effective cough medicine and the wood is sought by local craftsmen for producing beautiful carvings and furniture. Also close by are a theatre built for Independence seventeen years ago in 1982 and a play park by the sea opposite Corozal Methodist School.

The park in the centre of town has plenty of shade which is very pleasant for many people at lunchtime as well as at other times. Food, both hot and cold, can always be bought from small vendors stationed around the edge. St Francis Xavier Roman Catholic Church overlooking the park is built of concrete but it is beautiful inside. There are many stained glass windows and all the woodwork is solid mahogany.

There are a lot of very poor houses just outside of Corozal but the town itself is probably the most modern and certainly the cleanest in Belize. This is because it was largely destroyed by Hurricane Janet which I think was in 1953.

On Monday I contacted both UCB and Sacred Heart (again) for records. Both promised to send the information by tomorrow. Afterwards, I spent some time (and money) at White Sapphire finishing my shopping for presents to take home.

On Tuesday I visited all four 'Linking' schools prior to going home and took the Belize wall plaque bound for SMCC to show all but Assemblies before having lunch with Orvin. The new computer arrived and was set up at Methodist. There was a welcome email from the regional representative at the World Bank and I arranged to meet him for lunch tomorrow.

'...I will be in Belize from Monday 26 April to Friday (noon) April 30. I am staying in the Fort George Radisson Hotel in Belize City. Please feel free to contact me. I received your email some time ago, but I thought it would be better to wait responding until we had an opportunity to talk about it. I think your premise is very relevant. I would be interested to talk to you about the school-links with overseas. I am accompanied by Mr Morton Fisker, Danish Consultant. We are both very interested in talking to you about the Science and Environment education curricula at primary and secondary school level in Belize. Links with the information and communication technology are certainly obvious. I heartily support the idea and would be interested to discuss it with you in the wider perspective of providing opportunities to all Belize primary schools, which would satisfy certain criteria. I would also favour of taking the lessons from your project and now expanding the possible contacts with other schools in the UK and even outside the UK. A similar project is running in Costa Rica, financed by the Dutch bilateral cooperation at the secondary school level...'

Nothing arrived from UCB or Sacred Heart. I won't have time to pursue that any further before I go. It will be a big enough task to put some sort of draft together.

After paying BTL to cover the next two months and putting a film in for processing I caught the 9:30am for Belize City and only just managed to get to the Radisson Forte George in time for the 12:30 appointment, by getting a taxi from the Belcan Roundabout – something I have never done before. The meeting was an interesting one. They openly wanted to know about the progress of the new Primary Curriculum. I was happy to tell them but I would not comment on the politics. With respect to the 'Linking', there was a lot of interest. The idea is to open it up to a full blown project involving one or even two Districts and make a proposal. My notes are as follows:

Analysis of what has been achieved. This should be detailed and include the spin off that occurred in the process. There should be report from Belizeans.

Involve DEO and Principals. Define criteria and present costs. Also the process involved, emphasising the community effort. What has happened and what is it growing into. What were the original goals and the unexpected benefits? Does it add to the quality of schools? What are the benefits for teachers? Can it be run and supervised by students? How would it open the school to the community – discuss with students. Costa Rica project – concentrating on environmental issues and is producing a curriculum. Can students design their own curriculum? What would the professional level be of teachers communicating? Define clear goals. Link with what is going to happen in Belize in the longer term; one District or two?

Are there 'Clearing Houses' that can be used? What about setting up a website? Emphasize contacts with Caribbean Countries. What would be the community input, school website? Belize Region needs a theme and working through the Association of Primary School Principals.

... That would definitely be enough upon which to ruminate during a long flight home.

A 41 page email sent to VSO as a preliminary idea of what was coming out of the Impact Study...

'...Attached is the best I can offer right now. The first seven pages are the outline of ideas in draft. I had hoped to 'flesh out' these rather more but I have run out of time. The late arrival of rather vital information from Sacred Heart (not really their fault because their records don't match what was being asked for) and from UCB (has it arrived yet, I wonder?) is a nuisance. Also, there are some more interviews I can do and I am waiting for a response from ... (a past volunteer) in England (Sacred Heart). It will probably be better to tackle the whole thing in one go when I come back. I will be able to 'tinker about' with the structure and presentation over the next six weeks. The next fifteen pages are notes that include interviews with staff, VSO teachers and ex VSO teachers; after that come eight pages of records followed by a page of CXC results from Stann Creek Ecumenical College. Student 'Tracer' notes are four pages from Corozal Community College, three pages from Stann Creek Ecumenical College, four pages from Sacred Heart College and one page from UCB. (That is not all the documents). I will be very pleased to have your comments, especially as this is a particularly good stage to make them. You will see that I could make a lot more Tracer interviews; happy reading…'

I finished packing in time to set off early on Friday morning on the 8:30am Venus bus to stay with the family overnight. Ruby's sister gave me a lift to the bus station. It was a long day but I enjoyed chatting to Neria through the day and playing with the children. In the evening we opened the 'Glenfiddick' that Jack had given me and I went to bed at about 12:30am.

I left Philip Goldson International Airport, Belize City at 2:05pm local time. The whole family turned out to see me off. Miguel didn't want to say goodbye at first but he later came rushing in to the departure hall to put that right. The flight to Houston took about two and quarter hours but seemed longer as I was already tired. I hadn't slept very well and it was a long time to wait in the morning. The aircraft from Houston was a 777. This is apparently, the latest airliner to go in service. It is very large to have only two engines. There are three rows of three seats abreast. Unfortunately, I was in the middle block and over the wings anyway, so I wouldn't be able to see the dawn. That should have been pretty spectacular as we would be flying into it. In any case, the people by the windows pulled down all the blinds. There was a personal video system that was rather fun to mess about with and there were also computer games, including 'Tetris'. Even so, it was a very long night and I couldn't sleep.

The plane landed at just after 9:50am. Going through the passport check was just a matter of waving it and I was able to change American Dollars for Pounds and buy a ticket for the Gatwick Express to Victoria at one and the same time (That was nine pounds fifty for a half hour ride). By then, I was able to collect my baggage straight away. I didn't have to stop in Customs and was on the train for Victoria by 10:30am. It was a struggle from Victoria Station to the Coach Station with such a heavy case full of gifts and the coach through to South Molton was full but I managed to get a connection at Bristol. I arrived at a few minutes after 6:00pm as the bus was due in at 6:15 (11:15am Bz Time).

My house was let and I stayed with my good friend who was an anchor of support and interest throughout and, living on her own, had a spare room and no one else to disrupt. I am so grateful too, to many others who offered their welcome.

Monday 3rd May was Bank Holiday of course so visits to two families which lasted all day were a great welcome relaxation but the gentle pace was not to last. After a visit to my old school which was an interesting experience not to be repeated I went to the bank and arranged for a cash card to be supplied and an update on finances; gave my new address in Corozal and asked for some action to be taken with regard to the tax arrangements. Bought an adapter for the laptop electricity supply and booked a dental appointment to resolve the long neglected issue of the broken tooth on departure. After that the round of visits and repeat visits were punctuated only with talks with classes at SMCC, day visits to more distant friends and the occasional outing.

A meeting with the Year 7 tutors looks quite hopeful that it will be possible to extend the linking into an integrated project. It would be worth looking at a parental input as well.

It was difficult to decide where to start for the first round of discussion time but I managed to cover different ground with each form. 7G (Methodist) took quite a long time to begin to ask questions but 7H (St Pauls) were quicker. I put this down to the same process as the improvement in communication through the day. The youngsters from the first form would have talked with those of the second one and they would have come in more relaxed. In the same way, during the first contact in the school students avoided eye contact whereas by break time and more so by lunchtime they were seeking contact – which was good. I had lunch in the canteen with Paul and then spent some time with him in the afternoon when I copied off the two 'Links' files for him. I outlined my concern to extend to integrated learning (more difficult for a secondary school) and the important computer dimension which is difficult in Belize but his immediate concern was to create some offering from students for me to take back to each of the four schools in

Belize. We thought that something following his school hobbies day might be a good idea. Discussion time with 7D (Calcutta) and 7R (Assemblies) took place next day. Four sessions were spent with each of the four forms in the school library before half term preparing material for each of their schools in Belize. I spent some time with the students on the idea that Belize students and English students are just the same but that their environment, experience and culture are very different and neither would understand without getting to know each other. This is a very good way of understanding and appreciating one's own environment, experience and culture. Three ways in which we are trying to achieve this are: using a 'Buddy' as an 'exchange student'; sharing projects about our environment, experience and culture; and writing personal letters as to a 'pen friend'.

Video tapes were shown including the change of schools of Ed the Duck and Boxing Bruno, the sports day at Louisiana and the visit to the Belize Zoo.

The art teacher works with a group of year 7 students and is quite excited about doing a banner project with them for Belize. This was inspired by the wall plaque and will take the form of the letters of SOUTH MOLTON painted on squares of cloth and decorated with motifs that tell a story. He has taken some of the Belize money notes to photocopy for ideas.

Another teacher is working with some year 7 students to produce a brochure/booklet 'All about me' to send to Belize and the whole project was discussed after half term including the benefits of linking, shifting the initiative to students and possible ideas which will not need too much combined staff planning. It was a very pleasant lunch and a fruitful meeting in the afternoon which should enable the 'Linking' to grow. There is a lot of enthusiasm in the form groups and in Art and English especially.

The wall plaque presented to the school is solid mahogany, 60x38cm, carved with the national emblems of Belize: the toucan, tapir and mahogany tree. Together with resources not already sent by mail and many gifts for friends, this accounted for most of my luggage which is normally light. It would be just as heavy for the return journey, however. There was plenty of material from the school as well as gifts and resources I was now taking the other way. Hal set out all the photos in the albums for me with descriptions using text from my journal which we spent some time putting on disc for him to use.

I had the dental appointments and a crown fitted although the temporary one fell out one tea time. It was also necessary to have a medical for VSO so a clean sheet to return.

Friday 11th June I spent most of the morning packing and left on the Red bus to Taunton at 2:40pm which arrived at 4:35 after taking a tortuous but interesting route through Dulverton. What I hadn't counted on was the two and a half hour wait at Taunton involving dragging my luggage about as there was nowhere to leave it. I had a meal and a pint in the Rat and Parrot but that didn't use up more than half the time and neither was very good. The National Express coach arrived at Heathrow at 10:40pm then another hour wait at what was no more than a bus stop for the connection which arrived at Gatwick at 11:50pm.

The flight time was not until 9:45am so it was a long night. A ten hour flight followed, arriving at the airport for Houston at 1:45pm as there is a six hour time difference. It was a long time before I could raise the courtesy bus from the Howard Johnson Plaza and I didn't arrive at my hotel until about 4:00pm. Then I had to go out to find some food – and what a dump is Houston, at least in that part. Mega-dead! The meal was good though and I got to bed at about eleven having been up and awake for 46 hours!

The flight out of Houston was due to take off at 11:54am but didn't actually depart until after 2:30pm as all aircraft were suddenly grounded because of the weather. We arrived in Belize such that I was at the Northern Highway for another long wait having just missed a bus (Belize time is another hour behind) and I got home rather tired at 7:30pm.

To start the week I went in to the District Office and met with Louisa early on and did some shopping. Otherwise, I just managed to take the mail and mini projects from SMCC in to St. Paul's Anglican and Corozal Methodist schools before giving up and going to sleep! It was good to rest for next was a really good day! I went in to the office first thing and went on to spend an enjoyable time (as yesterday) at Christian School Assemblies of God to deliver their mail etc. After lunch I did the same at Calcutta. All the schools should be sending a return package before the end of term together with Buddy and diary. And there was mail already…

'…I hope you had a safe journey back to Belize and that you are now getting used to the sunshine and heat again! I enjoyed your company over the six weeks and it has seemed rather strange not having someone else in the house over the last few days...'

'...Hope you arrived safely and you had a good flight. Today we went to Landacre Bridge and had a long walk. Paul drove us there. Dad and I had to go in the back, it was very bumpy! I enjoyed playing Jenga and Monopoly while you were here. Did this email arrive before you did? ...'

'...It was really good to find your message on email thanks and yes it did arrive before I did. There were 17 emails on the server and yours was the only one from the holiday and the first one that is getting a reply...'

A workshop at QADS in Belize City filled the three days up to the weekend when Marco and Jack visited as a welcome back and stayed until Sunday which was pretty pedestrian really; quite literally, as we walked most of the town. I cooked chicken for dinner and Jack spent a lot of time trying to fix the email which had started to go wrong. Tomas Zetina came for the morning before they arrived, which I was especially pleased about because we were able to easily express and share thoughts of Tim's death, the funeral, family and friends.

'...Hope you had a good journey and arrived back in Belize safe and sound...'

'...I am back okay as you can see but the journey was pretty tedious and it has been a busy week. I was up and awake from 6:00am (BST) on Friday morning until 11:00pm (local time) on Saturday evening in the hotel in Houston. That is 47 hours. Also, I had a workshop in Belize City on Wednesday, Thursday and Friday which involves a bus journey of three hours each way on each day... Thanks for the welcome. I enjoyed the time spent with your family very much and it is good to be able to picture where you are...'

I went in to the office first thing and started some planning for the district workshops with Louisa. I composed the necessary letters and we started to look at programme. Louisa had to go early and I delivered letters to St Francis Xavier, St Paul's and Methodist on the way home. On Tuesday I had a Principals' meeting at St. Peter's, which was also an opportunity to do some shopping in the town. I found that Bernard's work hadn't been so good this term and that he had fainted a couple of times in school. He asked me where I had been 'this long time'. I had no answer to that of course, since I thought he was okay and would be better off without my visiting. I saw him at lunchtime hanging around opposite Magali's where I stopped to shelter because of the rain, before meeting Bertha at the new office. While talking with Bernard an adult came by. Bernard didn't know more than the man's first name even though the man was behaving in a familiar way. I resolved to visit Bernard in school on Thursday and arranged that with him. I have to be in Corozal tomorrow to go through the programmes with Louisa at the office which I will finish off – especially as she has already done the budget and made, and is making, the domestic arrangements.

Back in Orange Walk I met with Bertha at the office but I had been unable to see Bernard as he wasn't at school but I did discuss his position in detail with Barbara and related the incident of the stranger on Tuesday. She told me that, as well as the passing out, Bernard was passing blood in his urine and he had avoided being taken to the doctor (according to his Mum). I left it that I would do what I could to help but that I wished to work closely through Barbara as his Principal. The rest of the week was taken up almost entirely with mail...

'...The term has now ended here and all the packages from the four schools should either be on their way or be leaving this weekend. I say should because you know only too well how delays can be caused, especially at the end of term. Anyway, I have done the best I can and no time has been lost at all. When does your term end? Would you please let me know as soon as each parcel arrives, from and to whom and whether the form is able to receive it okay? I have access to all the Principals during the holidays and they will want to know as well as I do. I am thinking of a school in Orange Walk District as your fifth 'Linking' school but I haven't made up my mind yet. It is at San Juan Nuevo Palmar which is an interesting village of interesting people on the bank of the New River and adjacent to forest. I know that their Principal will be very co-operative and enthusiastic. The only snag is that it is so far away from the other four. He does, however know all four of the other Principals well as they have all been in the programme for the new curriculum right from the start. Please send me details of the new form as soon as you can; also form lists and form tutors. This year, I think it would be a good idea if form tutors could communicate directly with principals and teachers of their 'Link' schools. There seemed to be plenty of support and it would make it much more interesting for staff...'

'...Hope you had a good journey back and that the weather isn't too hot and sunny for you. We have had two **warmish** days this week. It's raining steadily now, but was only a little damp for the Olde English Fayre festivities this morning. I didn't get to say cheerio and to wish you all the best for your next stint. It was good to see you and share a little of the project and to learn something of what you have been doing in Belize. I hope to be able to find some time to support - if only by doing an occasional display. We have had the year 6 visits this week. The year 7 librarians - Jenna, Katherine et al got involved in the library visits by chance (showing the new year 6 how they issue/return books on the computer. It worked so well (as you can imagine) that it has now been built in to the rest of the visits next week - I just hand over the issue desk to them and there is an immediate rapport between them all - much more effective than if it was just me…'

'…It was really good to receive your letter, thank you. I wish I had been able to visit you both at home because there were many things we could have talked about which time didn't permit at school. I enjoyed the time spent in school as you will imagine – and I only come to do the best bits! Isn't it interesting how much young people really can do? I would that more have (and take) the opportunity. I am convinced that the ones that do (in the main) are those that have retained their interest and enthusiasm against the odds! Many thanks for your interest in 'Linking'. I do believe that it is growing in a way which will be enduring and who knows what young people will do with it all. Please excuse more just now. I am trying to catch up with my mail but I will keep in touch…'

'…Dear Friends in Year 7, It is ten to eight in the evening as I start this letter and, at last I have found time to write. Unlike where you are, it is dark, as it has been for over an hour. Our longest day is only about fourteen hours. It is dry now but the weather has been rough for several days and not good for most of the time since I came back. Last night we had a tropical storm which was exciting to say the least. Even so, it is hot. I am sweating considerably and back to drinking about a gallon a day. Not much comes out at the other end!

The little computer that you have all seen is a joy – my only toy really, as I don't have television and there is not a lot on the radio. As I type it is playing from CD. Two of them have the whole of the Mozart violin concertos; not to the taste of many of you I dare say, but very much to mine. Shortly, when I have finished writing, I will tell the computer to send this letter as an attachment to an email so that it can be printed straight out for you to read. It will dial the server, send the mail and disconnect itself unaided! Such is the power of modern communication. Hopefully, before too long students in your school and students in Belize will be able to do that for themselves. I believe that Corozal Methodist School has sent emails to Mr Berry for 7G today!

Thank you all for making me so welcome in your school. It was good to meet again with those of you that I knew already and to make new friends. All your letters and projects were delivered on the first two days back, Monday and Tuesday a week ago. There will be packages coming from all four schools at the end of this week, together with your returning Buddies and their diaries. Expect them within two to three weeks. I believe that should be comfortably before the end of your term although the holiday here begins this Friday!

It was great fun delivering the mail. I can't describe the feeling of having been with you when some of it was written and then sharing in the excitement of so many here as it arrived and was opened. I hope that most of you will be able to continue on a pen-pal basis next year and onward. Perhaps it would be a good idea to write straight back during the summer holiday. Those letters should go to students' homes of course but most of them will still be at the same school for another year if you want to write to them there or haven't been given their home address. I am happy to answer any letters that you write to me, or to help in any way I can.

It will be easier again for next year's year7 linking with the new Standard 5. There will have been more experience, we have some new ideas and there should be more use of email as all four schools here will have a computer quite soon and your school is having a new system.

Some of you will have been disappointed. Any teacher will tell you that some classes and some year groups are more active than others in just the same way as some students are. I won't tell you which is which (as I see it) either here or there. I expect you can work that out for yourselves. What I will say is that it would be good if those who are successful will share with those who have been less so – in the hope that their friendships will grow as well.

Yesterday, I went to the Graduation of Standard 6 students from Corozal Methodist School. This is for all school leavers and everyone receives a certificate in a very memorable ceremony. I believe that the students of standard 5 will send you a report in their package but the programme is reproduced below for you to think about: …

Tomorrow, I will be going to the Graduation Ceremony at St Paul's Anglican School. Calcutta

Government School are having theirs at the same time but I went there last year. Santa Rita sadly, is not having one. I have some reservations about it all because it is a financial strain on families that their youngsters are made to look so smart, especially when many are poor or very poor. On the other hand, there is a great deal of value given to an occasion to remember. The processional is a sight to see – with each student moving simultaneously into the next step to the main (slow) beat of the music, immaculately dressed in long pink dresses for the girls and black trousers with white shirt for the boys. And the hall was packed! What is really good is that it is something for everyone to focus on at the end of it all and, as I said, an occasion to remember. Now the long summer holiday begins. Students go back on 6th September which is probably the same as you but after a much longer break.

Many of them will be working in order to earn some money – usually to help with school fees! I have a great deal to do as there are two important curriculum workshops to plan for and run during the holiday as well as a study to finish for VSO. We are also into the hurricane season which doesn't end officially, until the end of November. Hurricane Mitch struck at the beginning of November last year and this year's weather, so far, has been livelier…'

'…You may imagine that six weeks wasn't long enough! I had a time to come and see you but it was overtaken by the amount of contact made with South Molton Community College to support the 'Linking' with the four Belize schools. I spent twenty-two lessons with year seven classes! I enjoyed it enormously of course, but it did shunt on a lot of other things…'

'…Yes I did get back okay as you see and it is really good to hear from you so soon. I like giving things especially when they are attached to a time or event and to see where you put it when I am able to come to your home is a bonus. You always seem to get back more than you give too, but that's the great bonus in life. I'm sure that you will be just as pleased to know that I have played the game you made already with young visitors at the weekend…'

'…Do you know what? I get quite cross with this little paper clip that comes up wanting to teach me how to write a letter. This is because I start with the word 'dear' and then put an indent for the first paragraph. I could get over it by simply starting at the edge and leaving out the indent but I don't see why I should! I think that I will have to find a way into the programme and turn 'clippo' (note the small 'c') into a bit of wire! …'

'…I hope you enjoy the enclosed Atlas of Belize. You may have seen a copy at school but it will tell you a lot about life here and the country without going into too much detail. Also, being you, it might give you some extra ideas about presentation in your own work…'

'…Writing at last, later than I intended; two weeks back seems quite odd. There is a sameness, a familiarity, of course (very pleasant!) but it is a sameness with a space in between (very pleasant also). The six weeks I spent partly on the study for VSO (as yet unfinished) followed by the six weeks in England have left a lot of threads that have to be picked up again. This two weeks have been very busy! I suppose that it is a bit like you moving on to Year Eight in a way – except that the work here has moved on and yours will be waiting for you! My getting back into gear seems to have been reflected in the weather as I come to think of it. It has been really wild since I came back, all over the place, until yesterday when it settled down. Today, the sun is shining and the breeze is blowing strongly off the sea – helping with the evaporation and hence the cooling. Never in life have I experienced such a direct and sustained demonstration of that simple fact of physics. When I say the weather has been wild I mean lots of rain and strong winds – tropical storms which have been quite exciting. As the wind always comes in off the sea and my house is right in the way of it this has been pretty spectacular. I don't think I would hang around here under the threat of hurricane as I did in Orange Walk. If I did, I guess that I would be the only one anyway! …'

'…Many thanks for the soccer memorabilia. I wish (silly to do that but there it is) that you could have been there when the contents were exposed, almost one by one, to Standard 5 and Standard 6 at Calcutta Government School. For the girls as well as the boys, English and Scottish soccer teams are the tops but the only contact for them, usually, is through the television – and that nothing like so much as in England of course. As you might imagine, I made the most of the occasion so there was plenty of excitement. A casual observer might even have had the mistaken impression that I know something about soccer! Anyway, you would have been very pleased to have heard the discussion that followed among the students who are mainly 12 – 14 years old. There was no 'I want' and what they finally came up with was a system by which everyone could share in the books in the library and the shirt and scarf would be trophies of some kind…'

'…I'm sorry this is my first letter to you. It has been a very busy time as you might imagine and I started off very tired when I arrived and it has been a rush to ensure that things happen and contacts are made in the 'Linking' before the end of term – as well as the mail! …'
With much and many more, thank goodness for copy and paste!

I went in to the office first thing on Monday as a courtesy, even though I had no work to do there and very little curriculum work to do at home. Joe Martinez remarked that 'a phone call would have done perfectly well'. I went over to talk to Aisha Pasos' Mum. As a result of that I composed a letter for Kayleigh and attempted to send it. By this time my problems with email had become serious and I tried to get some joy with BTL. I found that I couldn't log on most of the time, couldn't send for one reason or another and my computer was becoming repeatedly frozen out which meant shutting down by switching off – not a good idea.

'…Dear Kayleigh, I delivered your letter and 'Buddy' to Aisha's Mum on the first day back in Belize. That was Monday 14th June. The family have a nice shop called White Sapphire where I have bought a lot of my gifts and also many of the things that have come back for use in your school. That is how I came to know them. It was on one of these 'shopping expeditions' that I met Aisha and found that she had heard about the 'Linking' among the four schools here in Belize and your four year 7 forms in South Molton. Aisha goes to a different school as you know. I had to go back the next day and it was then that Aisha's Mum showed me the Buddy you have and said that Aisha would like to have a Pen-Pal (at least) in England and I said that I would see what I could do. I had several ideas but you were the obvious choice because you were so enthusiastic and I know how dependable you are and that it wouldn't affect what you are already doing with Santa Rita School (proper name 'Christian School Assemblies of God' but it is at Santa Rita so that is what it often gets called). When I delivered your Buddy and your letter for Aisha only her Mum was in the shop and the dreadful news was that Aisha's Dad had died, very suddenly, only the week before. He was a lovely man and I liked him very much. Of course, your Buddy and letter arrived at a very good time because it was something else for Aisha to think about but it would be very hard to write back wouldn't it? It takes a long time to look life in the face after something like that happens to us. I have waited until now and I know that Aisha hasn't written but intends to do so. I also know that about now, you will begin to expect an answer. That is why I am writing to tell you. I think that Aisha should say what she wants to say for herself, but there may be a delay. Perhaps you might find the right words to give her a start without waiting. For me, I haven't known quite what to do. Coming on top of the loss of Tim from Santa Rita School it is hard but I will do whatever I can. If you would like to use email, I will deliver anything you send and I'm sure Mr Berry will organise the technology for you. Whatever else, talk to your Mum and Dad. I know you will but I feel better saying so…'

Later in the day, I took a copy of the letter to Aisha's Mum and then went on to see Orvin on my bike. He told me that he was to be transferred to Ranchito Government School and Maria was to be transferred as well; so much for maintaining staff within the curriculum development programme. There are also serious implications for the 'Linking'. However, to make the best of it, Orvin will 'keep an eye' on Calcutta and will take on the fifth year 7 form next academic year. I was presented with a very nice certificate in thanks from the school.

Tuesday 29th June. Not my day at all. It started well enough – early – but then I tried again to use email and without success; once again, got on to BTL with no result. Still very erratic log-on and still being locked out or having my computer jammed on both Microsoft Outlook and Netscape. I gave up and called Douglas Stansmore who came over more or less right away. He tried everything as far as I could see, even to the extent of re-installing Windows 98, all to no avail. It begins to look as though the fault is with the modem; in which case that is most likely to have been caused by surges on the telephone line which I didn't know about until recently and for which I have been trying to obtain a surge protector. Douglas has those so the next step is to fit one and try working with another card modem which he will try to borrow before buying a new one, as they are expensive. While Douglas was here, he had a message to say that his daughter had fallen out of a tree so he had to rush off. I hope she is okay. His day has been worse than mine. That was about 2:00pm and he came at about 10:00am. One good thing is that I was able to check for sure that there were no emails on the server to date, and remembered that many students in year 7 would be on Lundy Island so there would be little to expect until well into next week. The rest of the day was spent messing about although I did bring my address book on the computer up to date.

I managed to use Netscape this morning and send the mail to Paul that I have been trying to send since Monday (That seems an age ago). I tried again on Outlook first, but without success. There was no problem with logging on in either case but I don't think that we are out of the wood yet. (I saw the BTL engineer messing about with the lines yesterday – evidently instigated by the bank manager next door – so you never know!)

Thursday 1st July. Douglas came this morning and seems to have fixed my computer as far as email is concerned but I have lost all sound since he adjusted out the sounds that were interfering with CDs. That is fine except that the warning sounds are now lost for low battery and also the sound from CD ROM so I will have to get that fixed as well. I have tried but unsuccessfully. Douglas finished just before midday and I went to join the staff of Calcutta Government School for a pizza and a few drinks afterwards as a mark of Orvin and Maria leaving the school to go to Ranchito (Orvin as Principal) and Paraiso respectively.

'…It was good to meet up with you again when I was home. Please give my best wishes to Matthew and Elizabeth. This is really only a test to see if I can get through at last. I will know of course, if it isn't returned but I would appreciate a few short words and then I can begin to explore the extent to which students will be able to communicate through their systems here and yours…'

'…As you can see it worked fine although I still have no idea what you are doing differently. We are still waiting for the equipment to arrive for the new computer network I told you about. Hopefully we will be even more efficient at replying to your mail once that is in place. You can send stuff for the kids at any time and I will print it out and pass it on. Until the network is connected, they won't be able to type their replies in school, but it should be in place for September 6th when they return after the summer break. I hope you settle back in to the routine soon. You will certainly be getting more of a summer there than we are here…'

Progress on the link with Fairthorne…

'…Dear Chris, The silence from this end is wholly due to having 'bitten off' too much for a time but I'm coming up for air after rushing about all over the place and trying to do too many jobs at once – and I'm supposed to be retired. First, thanks for your letter of 19th April which was waiting for me when I got back from the UK. Second, I'm very sorry that I didn't call in to see you. I fully intended to. It was a great time. I didn't get to see everyone that I wanted to see but I don't think I could have done any more even if I had been there longer. I spent a lot of time with the youngsters in South Molton as you might imagine, and a lot of work was done to strengthen the schools' 'Linking' programme. I did 22 lessons in the Community College! Only the fun bits of course!

I have just spoken with Nimmi Herrera at Hill Bank and she is very interested in making some contact with you. As you might imagine, the operation is not generously funded so communication is not the best but then, you are only just going electronic! Nimmi will be on holiday in the UK in August. I have given her your address, telephone number and FAX at Fairthorne but she comes from Manchester where she is going to stay, and she is taking her two children. You will know the importance of that. Perhaps, if this letter doesn't take too long to reach England, you might manage to make contact before she goes…'

Saturday: Ruby held a birthday party today, for her three year old niece. I think about fifty adults came with their children. A small marquee (without walls of course) was put up in the 'yard' and the space under my house given over to the production and distribution of food and drink and the playing of loud music. Around lunchtime people started arriving, all women and children except for one man who was attending to the barbecue. The children were mostly girls as well. There were some games played for the children, including the beating of a piñata. (I can't find this in the Spanish dictionary. The nearest is Peña meaning club or piña meaning cone – as in pine cone. Both have the accent over the n, making the 'ny' sound). There were an awful lot of sweets in it. The men arrived in the early evening as their only interest, as usual, is in drinking beer which was made clear by their bringing in two extra cases of cans and sitting in one exclusive group with eyes for no-one else. This is a great shame. The food was excellent and there was plenty to drink anyway, including soft drinks, rum and beer. I think I had about eight cans of lager, each of which was handed to me with the comment that I was drinking slowly. I don't like the beer much (even though it was Heineken) so it was only partly pleasure and mostly social. The food started with a huge conch based dip each and the best tasting fried tortilla chip I have had. The main meal was barbecue chicken, of course, with the usual flour tortilla, potato salad, beans and coleslaw.

Sunday: I went to visit Onelia and Ariel this afternoon and delivered the gift of a ceramic toy shop which she was pleased with. Stayed for the afternoon and was able to have some ideas for a pen pal for their eleven year old daughter who likes writing. She is going to write for me to send email. The rest of the day was spent working on the resources files for 'Linking'.

I caught an early bus and spent Monday with Neria. She was pleased with the table mats and we caught up with a lot of talking and spent a lovely day. Tabo, Marco, Miriam and Tony came home at lunchtime so I was able to give the other two table mats, the pound note and the small collection of British coins. Arrived home again at six and phoned Tony Brian, suggesting he comes up for a few days as he is shortly going home.

Tuesday morning, early; I was clearing and sorting out some computer bits and pieces from a bottom drawer in preparation for passing the 486 over to St Paul's Anglican School next term, when I came across a nest of red ants. They had set themselves up in a CD case containing a lens cleaner! I don't need it for the laptop, of course, but it is needed for the 486. How to get them out without damage to the CD which has digital instructions in it? Can't use spray and can't scrape them off. In any case, it is not a good idea to get red ants all over your hands and they move fast. So I'm afraid that they had to be cooked in the sun! The whole area of access was subsequently spayed with Baygone that dispatches all crawling and flying insects for a long time. Douglas came this morning to deliver six keyboards for schools to practice on. He also fixed the sound on my computer. The rest of the day was spent on the resources for SMCC again, writing and going to the office to try to name some books supplied from the central bookstore. A package arrived from 7R this afternoon, having taken only seven days. I will deliver the contents tomorrow.

'…The package with late letters etc. for Santa Rita arrived this afternoon. I will deliver them tomorrow. I expect that Tomas will be able to get them to the students. Now, where does year-7 go from here, as they become year 8? In three schools, their 'Linking' class will be simply going to the next year; that is Standard 6, so the school address remains the same. The three schools are Calcutta, Methodist and St Paul's Anglican (except that a few students at Calcutta were Standard 4 this year and will move to Standard 5. The problem class is Santa Rita where some of the Students are this year's Standard 6 so they may well move on (only two passed BNSE so, on the other hand, they may not). In that case, your students affected will, hopefully be able to continue writing to the home address assuming they have it. It would have been better to have involved Standards 4 and 5 (Students tend to be over age if anything because of the practice of repeating years) but that would have meant two teachers as Tomas teaches 5 and 6. For most of your students, it would be possible to carry on as a group. I suggest two things. First, could a member of staff (perhaps form tutor or English teacher, say) do some minimal co-ordination and second, and more importantly, communicate with the class teacher here? I am looking to the whole thing being in a healthy state of growth when I leave of course. There is one staff change in that Orvin Rancheran is moving as Principal to Ranchito, closer to Corozal. That seems the obvious choice as fifth school. I will send you a full list of teachers involved as soon as I have all the names. For the new year7, obviously there will be links with (basically) the new Standards 5. I will send you their teachers' names also, and suggest that form tutors might like to write to them. I anticipate that all four of the present schools will be on line during next term and I am working on ideas for Ranchito…'

'…I received a package of late pieces from your form today. It took exactly seven days to get here! I think that is the best ever. Certainly, the mail is a lot faster here than in Orange Walk. George the Snail has become rather smug about it…'

I delivered the package to Tomas this morning. He was somewhat down when I phoned and I set off to walk over. By the time I reached the highway, where the back lane past the Education Office joins, he had arrived in his car to collect me. I met his family, which was nice, and had a coke. He hadn't sent the mail to SMCC so I undertook to do that and sent it off later in the day. I was right about who was the bully in the class who caused so much of a problem with the 'Linking'. What concerns me most is the way he had dominated Tim. I would probably always regret it but I would have enjoyed teaching him a lesson with my fists at least at the time. Apparently he was a rotten little (big really) sod right up to the end. We discussed how next year might operate and young Tomas elected to write a letter for me to send email tomorrow.

I finished the programme for the Lower Division Workshop and had a long telephone call from Corinth who was very pleased with the Guide hat and belt etc. Onelia arrived with a letter from each of the two girls which I sent off to Paul to find pen pals.

'…I have been to see Tomas Zetina, the Principal of Santa Rita School to take the late mail that arrived yesterday. Theirs has not been sent (funds are short!) so I am posting it myself today. Among the letters is one for you from Aner that is not in an envelope so here is the text: 'Dear Hal…' …This is where it would be nice to have a scanner because it looks a lot better as written by Aner. He has folded legal size paper over in book form and written landscape across the open page. The front has star type drawings and a cartoon figure saying "That's terrific. Let's call someone up". The centre pages have the letter on the left and some line drawings on the right of a horse, a frog and a car – and B.F.F. (can you work that out?). On the back is a cut snake with 'join or die' and 'are you' followed by a happy face. I hope it arrives before the end of term. In the meantime, I will take over your email when it arrives and offer him the same facility. I don't understand why he says he 'didn't receive your letter' because I thought you had put something in the package I brought back. Let me know if you did and I will try to follow it up. I must rush now to catch the post...'

The cockerel (Rooster) next door is a continuing problem. I haven't had a proper night's sleep since coming here at the end of March and there have been repeated promises of removing the nuisance. All of which have not been carried out. The latest was to kill the rooster yesterday but that was not done and last night was really bad. I had no sleep from 2:30. I can't understand why they keep a rooster when chickens are readily available and what they keep chickens for is eggs. In my view roosters just spoil the eggs.

Friday 9th July. I have been up since 3:30am because of the rooster next door. I fact, I did what I had threatened to do because I was very tired, very cross and not entirely in 'normal' control…

Roust the Rooster

It was early. It was very early. It would be a long time before the sun came up. He didn't want to get up because he was tired. He didn't want to stay in bed because he couldn't sleep. It had been like that for months. It was not a new condition but that made it worse. There was no comfort in familiarity.

Outside, the rooster continued its ear splitting cries. Not a farm rooster bringing in the dawn with a statement of its dominance of its brood for the day, but a rogue rooster with no comprehension of time or purpose other, it seemed, than keeping him awake.

Sometimes it started just after midnight. At other times it would be around half past two. Those were most common times but there was no pattern; no pattern that could have provided a window of peace. Neither was there a pattern to the cries. Sometimes there would be seconds between; sometimes as much as half an hour and always an infinite variety of random variations.

He would lie there waiting for the next jolt; usually coming just at the point of dropping off to sleep again… and again… and again.

The performance of the rooster took place right under his bedroom window that was located ten feet or so, directly above the yard next door. There was no escape and this was a problem known for the scale of offence only to the occupants of the house on the other side. Yet even they were further away than he was. The previous people had moved out but he wasn't going to do that.

So what to do? It was July, three months after making the first complaint in April and a nightly cacophony ever since. There used to be three roosters. Now there was only one but as each was dispatched another became dominant. This one was king; this was the worst; king of what; half a dozen hens who produce eggs not chickens? Frustrated or what! But this was not funny. "Not funny!" he told himself, as the occasional flash of humour would break through in relief. So what to do?

That night there had been no sleep at all from 2:30. It had become increasingly difficult to go back to sleep because the anticipation of jolt had become too great; the rolling question 'What to do?' supplanting more pleasant images or the emptiness of a mind sinking slowly into peace.

But there was resolve. All reasoning had so far failed. Promises of the rooster's demise or descent into tamales or relleno were repeatedly broken. This night had been the latest in a long line of expectation followed by hopelessness. It was enough. There was resolve.

All day the rooster yelled its defiance, protected by the indifference of its owners, little knowing, either of them, that there was resolve. All day it was not a problem. In any case he was not trying to sleep, he was on the other side of the house and the sound was largely lost in the general noise of the day. And there was resolve.

It was 3:30am when it next started. He got up; gone was the torpor of tiredness; he was cross; in that calm which overtakes extreme anger. There was resolve.

It didn't take more than seconds to dress. In little more time he had been down into the yard and collected some fairly large stones; stones that were called rocks in that part of the World.

Then he went out on to the back balcony that faces the yard next door immediately outside the bedroom. He started to throw the rocks, one by one and with a fair pause between each. He found that he began to enjoy it, a feeling that left no pride but considerable satisfaction.

He couldn't see very well because it was dark of course, also because of the trees and bushes but he could hear roughly where the rooster was.

The first effect of the rock throwing was to alarm the neighbours' dog. The dog promptly became aggressive and barked furiously. The rooster must have been hit because there was a shaking of wings and feathers at the same time as the rock struck followed by the rooster rushing across the yard squawking in terror. That was a much more pleasing sound, almost soothing, but there was no need for further calm. The dog was next. It was either struck or the rock was very close because all the aggression was gone. He could hear it whimpering and then could see it scratching at the back door of the house trying to get in.

In between all this he had aimed the occasional rock at the roof of the hen house or shed, which is made of corrugated iron. There was a loud and satisfying clunk each time that added considerably to the general noise.

It was disappointing that he could detect no sign of movement in the house in response to his actions so the next large stone was aimed at the corrugated roof over what he took to be a bedroom. Still no result - so a shower of stones followed the single one.

A short wait and out came the man. He couldn't shout "Silence that rooster!" in the Spanish that is the only language the neighbours speak but the volume and tone was sufficiently strong.

The man didn't even look up but disappeared into an outhouse. It was some time before the man came out again yet couldn't be heard doing anything. He was sure that he would have heard any movement, being so close. Maybe the man was waiting for him to go away, but having gained the advantage, he wasn't going to go away. No! He wasn't going to go away!

He realized afterwards that he still had stones. The man would have known that and wasn't to know that the thought of using them in that way hadn't occurred to him.

He waited in silence. All was quiet. Eventually the man did emerge and went back into the house.

Having achieved the objective of the man being up and awake as well, he went indoors and set about meeting a new day with new vigour and new hopefulness. The dawn was beautiful with the sun rising brightly over a shimmering Caribbean Sea. The breeze was gentle and cooling; the water was calm; frigate birds soared gracefully overhead.

The rooster had continued its raucous noise for the rest of the night and through the day but, strangely, that didn't bother him. He had decided to wait and see. He made up his mind not to repeat the performance for a night or two. The element of surprise had been a great advantage not to be lost by regular activity. The possibility of a shotgun being aimed in his direction also passed through his mind and he decided that it would be better not to have a known schedule!

It was early. It was very early. It would be a long time before the sun came up. He didn't mind even though he was tired. He was quite happy to stay in bed even though he hadn't slept. It was like that all night, dozing happily; a passing tension that would be resolved in peaceful rest tomorrow. There had been no sound of the rooster. It was gone.

He waited until the sun rose in a blaze of glory.

I can't say that I am in any way proud of what I did. I don't think I have ever thrown stones at anything or anybody before. I don't even throw stones at aggressive dogs as everyone here does. It is not that I don't think I ever will throw stones at aggressive dogs, I think I would, but it is a complex I have grown up with not to throw stones. Anyway, I'm not proud of it and I hope I never have to do it again. The rest of the day was spent coming right up to date with writing and clearing all work so that I can get back to the study and concentrate on it.

'…Talking about friendliness reminds me of 'Roust the Rooster'. What the story doesn't include is the distress that had been caused to others although they were not quite as close as I was. The neighbours on the other side had moved out because of it! What distressed me in taking direct action was that the people are Guatemalan and Guatemalan immigrants are called aliens here! I didn't really want to alienate them any further and I am happy to say that peace has descended…'

Tomas Zetina came with young Tomas around lunchtime and we sent off a letter by email for him.

He typed in a part of it and was really very quick at picking up the idea, his never having used a computer before.

A letter also came in from Kayleigh for Aisha which I printed direct from the email and set out on word as well, using brush script to fill a page and make it look an attractive letter. This was delivered right away and passed to Aisha's older brother who was minding the shop.

'…Dear Aisha, when I heard about your dad, I really felt for you. It must be hard at the moment to think ahead, but I reckon you're strong enough to get through it. I'm sure that the rest of your family are there for you just as you're there for them. I would remember all the good times you had with him and especially the fun times. Perhaps you would like to tell me what he was like and different things you have done. When the time is right I hope you will feel you're able to write to me and you can trust with absolutely anything you say, so don't worry. I don't really know what else to say apart from how much I feel for you and your family…'

Such spirit shared among so young in tragedy, twice now.

There was no sound of the rooster next door, during the night. Hopefully that is the end of it.

We were warned of a tropical wave that produced brief spells of heavy rain during the day and a wonderful display of lightening way out over the sea after dark. It was the kind, mainly, which lights up the clouds from above and behind with the occasional forked lightening breaking powerfully through. I went for a walk along the sea front in the evening and stood out on the shore and, for a while, out on the jetty to watch the display – far greater than any fireworks!

Sunday 11th July. It was a rough night although I did sleep. I suppose that shows just how disturbing the rooster was because the tropical wave was a considerable force driving rain through the smallest cracks and bringing down any branches showing the slightest weakness. There has also been an earthquake that has been felt all over the rocky parts of Belize. The latest news is that it was 6.6 on the Richter scale and was centred somewhere over Honduras. Fortunately, the two did not coincide. Right now, at 10:00am, the wind is so strong that everything is shut. Otherwise things would be blown all over the inside of the house. That makes it dark inside of course, so I have to have the lights on. Onelia has just phoned to postpone the outing we were to have to Chetumal today. We were going to eat in a restaurant by the sea and that wouldn't have been very pleasant. We will go next Sunday instead.

I did go for a walk of about six miles. The sea was wild along the Beach. I can see that of course, without going out, but being in it is quite a different experience. The spray clearing the sea wall was reaching over into the yard of St Paul's Anglican School, making the road along the front impassable without getting pretty wet. I turned inland and followed the Northern Highway out to a point where the Belmonte business is before turning back and returning through Santa Rita and the back route through the town to settle to mail…

'…There has been lots to do since coming back: catching up with mail of course; delivering mail for the four 'Linking' schools and making sure another lot goes off to arrive at SMCC before the end of term. Our term ended two weeks ago as the children have nine weeks holiday. Then there is the curriculum work. I am up to date with that – being ready for two workshops in August to familiarize teachers with the function and use of the New Curriculum. One is for one week involving teachers in the Middle Division of Primary who have been in the pilot from the start. They are continuing with the next stage of the pilot.

The other follows on for two weeks and is aimed at the Lower Division of all the non-pilot schools. Now that work has gone quiet I have some time to finish a Study I was doing for VSO before I came home…'

'…It is Friday morning and I was up very early; early enough to see the pre-dawn and to watch the sun come up over the sea. It is hot but there is a good breeze coming in over shimmering water outside and just a few feathery clouds high in the sky. Frigate birds are soaring in above the shore line. I haven't seen any pelicans yet, today, but I expect they will be around. I bought a pair of ultra-compact binoculars when I was at home. They are an excellent pair of Pentax 8* which will slip in my pocket. They are used quite a lot without my moving from the balcony. There is always plenty to see and they are very easy to use. So life goes on. I have found a fifth school for the 'Linking' as South Molton Community College are going to five forms next year, which is likely to stick. Now I shall have to find a way of funding a fifth school computer. The two installed so far are heavily used and providing for many uses that were not anticipated. Two more will be in use during next term and as SMCC are having a new computer system ready for next term, the email should be up and running well…'

'…In school today (Friday) I received Ed the Duck back from Belize and also a letter from my pen friend. He (Ed) was rather grubby so the first thing Mum did was to put him through the washing machine. I don't know, he travels nearly half way round the world and the next thing is to be spun around a washing machine…'

'…I hope you are well and enjoying the end of term. Today would have been the 'New Intake Day' I expect you remember yours very clearly. What was it like? Can it seem like a year ago? Counting back from September 6th which is almost certainly your new term date and the start of year 8, I guess that your term ends a week on Friday, 23rd July. Is that right? The schools you have been linking with finished on 25th June so getting a response to your packages was a bit of a rush…'

'…It would be nice to get a conversation going rather than write long letters (apart from my occasional story) so I will just tell you that I walked to your 'Link' school at Calcutta, and back this afternoon. Just over eight miles! I was pleased with that. I've got my tan back…'

'…Arriving back means writing to more people than usual in a short space of time; starting with email because delay is not expected with email. That produced its own problem as my email went down. Apparently the modem I have fitted is faster than that used by the server and there was some problem about them talking to each other. All of that used up a lot of time…'

'…I logged on to BTL this morning, not really with any great expectation… How did you do it? It is 9:30am here so it would be 4:30pm there. Either you were mighty quick off the mark when you got home after school or you did it at lunchtime (and they don't let you out much). If it was when you came home that means there couldn't have been any delay on the server…'

'…Dad was working at home yesterday and checks the email each day when he gets home. Because he checked it early yesterday he had printed your email off before I got home. I changed my clothes and we did the message to you (I tell him what I want to say and he types it). Today in the soft ball match our team won 43:11 Drake (that's us) against Grenville. Tonight I am in the school production where we each have a role to play; I am a nutty professor so I wear a white smock and have a white wig to wear…'

A meeting with Louisa had been arranged at the District Education Centre at 8:00am. There was a phone call from Louisa's daughter at 7:00am saying that her mother wouldn't be there and would go to the office at 8:00am on Wednesday. I asked if she was ill but it was clear from corrections and references being given, that Louisa was present in the room. Why didn't she phone herself? I am not at all happy with Louisa's attitude and can see why she doesn't go down particularly well with the Principals. I spent the morning sorting out some ideas for the VSO Impact Study and starting some of the report. This afternoon I had a really good walk. It was only down the Northern Highway but I made it all the way to Calcutta Government School and back with a diversion to go and look at the airfield in Ranchito. That would be eight miles and a whole litre of water consumed! If anyone had foretold that I would drink so much water (five gallons a week of plain, purified water) I would have laughed. It has never been my favourite drink. I certainly feel better for having walked, especially as I am fighting a cold and have had an uncomfortably sore throat all night. I really do need to recover some of the fitness I had when I came to Belize two years ago.

I had a good meeting with Louisa on Wednesday accepting (to myself) that the personal irritation may well have been due to the amount of work to do together with my first cold in Belize; I don't want another one. Otherwise the rest of the week was mainly spent working on the VSO study and I talked with Henry Gill about records for the study and any anecdotes he might be able to supply. He is coming to visit next Wednesday for an exit interview for the original posting and will arrive for an evening meal out on Tuesday.

On Friday, Caroline arrived as she was attending a First Aid Certificate presentation at the Red Cross building in the Santa Rita Layout. Caroline had said 'at the RC' in her email which I had taken to be the church of course. No one knew of any such event at Xavier and it was only when I was talking to the secretary there that I realised that RC could also be Red Cross! No-one calls it that! Anyway, that would mean that I would be late as it is a good twenty minutes' walk out there from Xavier Church and I had timed things to arrive on time. That meant having a taxi. I did arrive in time but that is when it became irksome because 'Belize Time' was seriously in operation and we all waited for a good three quarters of an hour before the presentation started. Caroline came back for a while afterwards and caught a bus back to Belize City Later.

After a Saturday morning on the VSO study, apart from a bit of shopping, I cycled out to the border

- which I enjoyed. It was very hot but it is okay on the bike as long as you keep going to keep the breezes flowing. There were thousands of huge butterflies that were light yellow through to brimstone flying across the road as I came back. I thought there were a lot of butterflies in England when I was young but I am sure that I have never seen so many before.

The Outing to Chetumal with Onelia and Ariel and their family was great. We left about midday and went to a restaurant right by the sea. The fish I had was baked in a wine sauce and served with a variety of vegetables. We had already had a seafood salad and fried tortillas with peppers. The beer was Modelo Especial, the nearest I have had to an English flavour.

Hal wanted Aner's address so that he could send a letter to him. It was fun finding that out! First I telephoned Tomas Zetina. He told me that Aner's title (surname) is Manzanillo and that his address is 'Paraiso Village, Corozal Town, Belize, Central America'. Well, even after two years, I find it difficult to trust the idea of not having a house number and a street name. Many places do in Belize City, and that makes it worse. Also, Hal has had so much trouble trying to get this letter away (particularly with incompatible word processing to send as email attachment) that I wanted to be particularly careful. I quizzed Tomas. He insisted but I still wasn't sure so he agreed to phone someone in the village and let me know. He rang back to say that he couldn't get an answer but that he had looked in the phone book and found Manzanillo without house number or street names. But 'what if' was really working by this time! I couldn't imagine how the postman would find an eleven-year old, who may very well never have had a letter (personally) before, in a whole village. There seemed to be only one thing to do and I hadn't had any exercise today so 'off I went' on my bike. The first person I asked in the village didn't know of Aner ("Aha," I thought!) but he did know of one of the Manzanillo families and pointed me in the direction of their house. A young man of about twenty was very willing to help, especially as he turned out to be one of Aner's brothers. This was not their house but he took me to it and I was able to speak to Aner. Tomas was right!!

'…*Letters to 7R have arrived and have been delivered. Lots of children are intending to write directly to their pals over the break, and hopefully you will get some mail too! The technicians have already started to install our new computer network, so it could/should be up and running by September. 53 new machines on a new network; maybe an email system that works; Belize, we are catching you up…*'

'…*As 7R letters have arrived I assume that is a full house except for the 7R Buddy which is to follow. You could say to Kayleigh that I would like to give her a big hug for the super letter she sent to Aisha and that I know it has done a lot of good even if it takes time to get a reply…*'

I set off down the Northern Highway on My bike at about 1:15pm Tuesday. It was quite breezy and the sky was sufficiently overcast for it not to be too hot. I would have had to put on sun cream if it had been too bright after the recent spate of outings. I wasn't quite sure how far I would go but I had several possibilities in mind after a morning struggling with data and the presentation of data in the Study for VSO. Calcutta, Carolina and San Joaquin came and went okay and I manage to find where Louisa lives on the other side of San Joaquin. The first person I asked happened to be her brother in Law and I was only the width of the football field away from her house. Anyway, that was pleasant. I was given a drink and shown around the house and the outside; even after being in Belize for two years I hadn't imagined it very well from Louisa's description. I had thought the house would have been more of a 'town house' and the location more 'in the country'. The drink was very welcome because I think that I would otherwise have had to start thinking about turning back again as I hadn't brought any water with me. As it was, I asked how far it was to Best corner and Libertad and learned that it was only about two miles and three miles respectively. In fact I went through both and found my way to the riverbank, south of the closed sugar factory at a tiny village (hamlet) called Estrella.

People were very friendly all the way and I found both children and adults to talk to down by the river. Going through Calcutta was funny because of the number of children who called out "Hi Mr Max" as I cycled past on the Northern Highway! What wasn't so good was the attitude of some truck and most bus drivers whose aim in life is to force cyclists off the road, whether they have room or no. Discretion dictates that you take avoiding action because I know their brakes are not good enough to ensure your safety even if they chose to use them. I think those people happen – like disasters. They couldn't have had regular parents.

I think that the river must split before it gets to the Libertad factory because it is substantially smaller than it is at Caledonia, San Estevan or even Orange Walk which is thirty miles or so upstream – probably much further because it meanders so much. I got back at about 4:45pm after another twenty-mile ride, in good time to get ready for Henry coming from VSO.

Henry was late. This is Belize! He can be excused because he was coming from Belize City and says he was held up. However, it seems to be the rule. The only time things have happened on time that I know about have been my workshops. So, instead of half past six which was the arranged time, Henry arrived at 8:15. But the meal in the Chinese restaurant over on the 'boulevard', by 'Caribbean Chicken' was very nice: fried king prawns (They call them shrimps here!) with a tomato sauce and vegetables.

Henry arrived back at about nine and we spent the morning reviewing the first posting. We had lunch at the Jo Mel In. It was nice to have escabeche again, after quite a long time. Next was another attempt to obtain my Belize driving licence. They insist on having an approved doctor's signature on the application document. My presentation of a full, signed and current medical form was not good enough! After that we went to the Free Zone where I bought a bath towel, a bottle of V/X Appleton Rum and a bottle of Chivas Regal Whisky. The VSO vehicle has diplomatic plates and there is no restriction. I didn't know that Stephen from St Peter's Anglican School in Orange Walk is a friend of Henry. Also he lives close by in Corozal, out on the road to the Community College so that's where he stayed. I did manage to get my driving licence today but that is a story in itself.

'...It is quite something to have Ed the Duck back. You will have to feed me some lines and I will write a story about it. The washing machine is a good start but think where he has been as well as nearly half way round the world. The two schools (St Pauls as well as Calcutta) have completely different ethnic populations. Ed has been in the arms of many different people, been in many different homes and had many different experiences. It certainly is something to have Ed the Duck back...'

There was a QADS meeting arranged on Friday in Belize City. I set off on the 5:30am bus only to find that the meeting had been cancelled; in fact, when I got there at about 7:35 the whole place was closed up and I had to hang around for nearly half an hour getting bitten! The weather has been such to produce a huge number of mosquitoes and it is extremely difficult to catch them in time when they are in such numbers. Eventually, the office was opened and I decided to go down to the Government Bookstore to find out the titles of the books I had sent from there to SMCC when I first came. That was quite a successful visit as I also went to the bank to pay in a cheque for my extender's grant and obtain some cash. I then managed to get four videos in PAL format to send in the next parcel, together with two more copies of the Belize Atlas and a map to replace the one I gave to Hal. The videos are 'The Land of Belize', 'The Sea of Belize', 'Belize: The Maya Heritage' and 'From Invasion to Nation: A History of Belize'. I also picked up another copy of the Belize Fact Sheet from the office. David Eck had asked me to go back to the office to collect a long outstanding voucher (another story) which he had to get for me. On the way back a storm broke such that the only shelter I could find was totally inadequate and I got very, very wet and spent the next couple of hours drying out. I called in to see Marco in the Atlantic Bank on the way to the bus and gave him a copy of Hal's letter and picture on floppy disc. I wanted to see if he could print it for me and to pay for the wine I had asked for to give to Neria and Tabo for their Wedding Anniversary. I then discovered that I was expected for the weekend. I couldn't stay because I was wet and because I had arranged to meet Hilary Hunt in Corozal tomorrow so I phoned Hilary and arranged to meet in the morning so that I could go back to Belize later.

My Lot!

It started with the payment vouchers; way back; 'long time', as they say in Belize. They were not big ones but it was for money I had spent on Education Ministry business some time before. One was reimbursement for an ink cartridge, long used on my printer, and the other was for a day visit made to a school some distance away and outside the District in which I live. Forms have to be filled in, checked, signed, checked, signed... and eventually returned to be presented for cash. I was pleased that the total sum was not large because that would avoid an additional trip to the bank with a cheque. This would be money in hand; my money; 'long time!' Little did I know!

I smiled in pleasant expectation at the girl in the Sub-Treasury. She did not return the smile so I tried harder. Still, there was no response. She was busy checking, ticking, stabbing fiercely at the calculator, checking, ticking, sighing….

"Nice day." I said, hopefully.

The jerking of pen and forefinger stopped and the girl looked up. "No good!" she said, triumphantly, "This is wrong. This should be $9, not $18." The forefinger came into play once more as the offending document was pinned down on the counter by its most offensive digit. The rule states that a time off station of five to seven hours attracts a subsistence of $9 and seven to nine hours attract a subsistence of $18. I hadn't noticed that the time on the sheet was written as seven hours. It is pointless to argue that, when you have been away for seven hours then, in Maths, it has to be treated as more than and not less than the given time. In all the checking no one else had noticed either.

"Never mind," I said, brightly, "Just change the 18 to 9." (My loss after all)

"I can't do that; it has to go back to the person who signed it."

I looked dumb I am sure. I was thinking of the eighty-four miles to Belize City where it was signed and the two months it had taken to get this far. I was also realizing that I couldn't make the change myself, even in favour of the Treasury, because the girl had scribed ticks (and a cross) all over it with a ballpoint pen. Her attention now focussed on the other voucher, which was addressed with a flourish as she settled to the task of defacing the neat figures entered upon it. (Is this what children feel as their work is returned? 'You must check your figures' beneath a big, red cross.)

"Ten cents for the stamp" No 'please', I missed that.

"What do you want a stamp for?" I say.

"It's not legal without a stamp!"

I wish I hadn't bothered with all those documents on my machine. I wish I had paid for that ink myself as well. I wish……

I collected part of my money, having paid ten cents for it, at the next counter. There were no queues at either but there could have been. I wonder why? The offending voucher went back to Belize City and I forgot about it.

Some weeks later, I set off on the 5:30am bus from Corozal to attend a meeting at QADS which was scheduled to begin at 8:30am. There had always been a possibility that the meeting would be cancelled but we would be told if it was.

The journey usually takes two hours and a half and I have known the 6:00am bus arrive too late for an 8:30am start. On this occasion I arrived just after 7:30 to find the doors locked; the atmosphere very hot and humid after considerable rain and the mosquitoes were extremely active coming out of the adjacent swamp. Maybe the damage limitation activities shortened the time before the office opened; maybe the need to indulge in them made it seem longer. Either way, getting in behind the screens was a relief – only to be dashed by "Weren't you told?" Ignore the obvious pointlessness of that question and listen instead to all the reasons why I should have been told while thinking how best to use the day. That's when the voucher surfaced again. It wasn't in the office but it would be later in the morning. "Could you come back?" "Okay" I thought. I had a number of other things I wanted to do that day, including a visit to the Government Bookshop. The weather was fine and I set off to walk, as there was now plenty of time where I had expected the day to be tight. I left my curriculum documents and my umbrella behind. The walk is the best part of an hour as the bookshop is Downtown, close by the Education Offices and the City Treasury.

Mission accomplished at the bookshop, four Belize Videos in PAL format for a South Molton Community College in England from Channel Five, a replacement Belize Map and a visit to the Bank and it was time to walk back. The weather was still fine. Buses and taxis were spurned. A pleasant breeze played around the trees and corners.

The most exposed part of the return walk was that between the end of Baymen Avenue and University Drive. There is no shelter other than a few small trees close to St John's College and that is exactly when the storm came. It was probably a mistake to shelter under the trees because the rain was so heavy that it came straight through. It was probably a mistake to dash for the roof overhang to the little security shelter at the entrance to the College drive, closed for the summer holiday because the rainwater ran back underneath in a continuous stream. It was probably a mistake to make a dash for it because, although the downpour eased it soon picked up again. It was probably a mistake even though I wanted to get back to the office before lunchtime in case it should be closed and that time was close. Whatever the mistake, I was really wet for the first time in Belize; wet right through to the nether regions and squelching water with each step. At this point I remember why I am going back at all. Damn the voucher!

I managed to get the washing done before Hilary arrived at about eight and she went again at ten in order to go shopping in Chetumal. I will be able to stay with her on the night of Jack's party. I left on the 3:00pm Premier Batty Bus to go to stay with the family overnight. The celebration was for their 31st Wedding Anniversary on last Wednesday and they were holding a barbecue. They had just finished putting up a covered area outside at the back which provides shelter for the washing machine (and the washing when it rains) and a play area for the children. The whole of the roof of the rooms below is used and a wall has been built right round the edge to make it safe. The roof covers about half of the space and that is where the barbecue was held. Quite a lot of people came, including the family of the man who did the building. I believe they have helped him in the past and this was their way of saying thanks.

I went to bed at about 3:15am and got up at eight to catch the 11:00am Premier back. Before I left, Marco tried to read Hal's email from the floppy disc copy that I brought with me, but without success. We decided that he might be able to read it by taking it direct into Netscape from my Netscape and then trying to change the file type. The bus arrived in Corozal at 1:15pm. The rest of the day was quite slow but I did some writing and sent on Hal's email to Marco to see if he could change the file into one that his computer can read.

I went to Orange Walk for a Principals' meeting at St Peter's on the 7:00am bus that arrived at eight. The meeting didn't start on time either. This is always annoying and there was an hour wait. However, the preparation for the workshops got under way and the necessary decisions were taken for meeting with other pilot school staff tomorrow.

What was really good was meeting with Bernard's Mum and getting his story from her. He really has got himself on the wrong track again so I said that I would write him a letter. I also asked her if she would bring him to the school tomorrow morning.

I returned to Corozal and spent the afternoon catching up with some mail, paying BTL etc.

The Orange Walk Planning Meeting on Tuesday continued until the afternoon. Bernard and his Mum did arrive which I was very pleased about. The next step is for Bernard to think about what I have said and write to me…

'…Dear Bernard, I missed seeing you at the end of last term after travelling from Corozal to your school. I also have to say that I am disappointed to find that after the excellent progress you made in the first two terms of last year, you slipped back again. In fact, you nearly didn't go into Standard Six. It was the first two terms, only, that got you there. If you do want to make some progress and lead an interesting life then there is only one way to do it. You have to work. You cannot get anywhere by running away from things that you don't like doing. It is the 'boring' bits that make the whole thing really good. I don't want to go on about it. You know better than I, what you need to do. You also know what you should not do and the worst of those is mixing with older people who are 'hanging around'. They will not teach you anything that will satisfy your life. One way or another, they will use you.

Now the better bit. I will be leaving Belize for good at the end of June (or thereabouts) next year. I will not be coming back even for a holiday unless I have very good reasons to do so. What I would like to do is to go home (or to another country) knowing that you are settled and succeeding. That might become one of the reasons to persuade me to visit here again.

I am not going to tell you "If you will do this I will do that". That is a sort of bribery. What I will do is simple. I will make sure that you can go to college if you get a place there. This would be done by an arrangement with your Mum and Dad. They are your family and what you have comes from them. They know what you need if you are honest with them.

The rest is up to you. There is no one in this life that can do your work for you; there is no one that can do what is right for you in your place. It wouldn't help you for me to spend much time with you in school. I would like to but life doesn't always follow what we would like. I will see you occasionally but there are others you could work with easily if you ask them properly and if you stick with it. I wish you well. I will never forget our first meeting and I am sure you won't. My address here is at the top of the page and it will be nice if you will write once in a while. I will certainly write back if you include your home address…'

On Wednesday I went to the Sub-Treasury to obtain some information for Nik and Jack at FMDP. This was really an amusing sequel to the whole saga of my dealings with that department. Maybe things will be easier now. This is how the correspondence went…

'…Hi Max, Hope you had a good time back in England, I am quite envious, this job really gets to me, and I probably get on Jacks nerves! Anyway I was hoping you could possibly help us out down here. We need to make a trip up to Corozal to install a computer and Router in the Corozal Sub Treasury. The last experience left me with a bitter taste in my mouth and the urge to strangle the idiots here. I was sent to Dangriga to install a computer. I found that they had not wired the electricity to BEL, the Phone lines were on the wrong side of the building, they had no table to put the computer on and the location just happened to be the spot where the roof lets in water! I would appreciate if you could take a look at the treasury there and just see if 1. A fresh line from BEL feeds in to the building. 2. BTL has placed phone lines into the building. 3. The location for the computer has air conditioning, BTL phone jacks (x2) and 4 power sockets. 4. Building work has finished and no structural changes to be made. If you don't mind doing this I will inform them that you will make a visit and I will provide more details…'

'…Hi Nik, Good to hear from you especially as I am so poor at contacting VSO people; I don't think anyone here would believe how many letters I send to the UK - all part of the extended experience! Sorry to hear that you are all screwed up with the job but it may help if I tell you that I don't mind going in to the Treasury at all; no problem! If you want me to do it this week it will have to be tomorrow as I have the misfortune to be travelling down to Belize City for the day on Friday…'

'…Hi Max, I don't know if Nik got a hold of you but probably not. If you could check on the treasury tomorrow and email me I would appreciate it…'

'…Hi Jack, I have been to the Sub-Treasury and met with the District Accountant who was very helpful. Taking each point as listed: 1. The BEL line into the building appears to be new and I am told that the whole building has been rewired. There certainly looks to have been a lot of electrical work done. 2. Obviously, there are BTL lines going in to the building but I cannot say more in terms of the number or newness of line. What is evident is that new sockets have been provided. 3. The location for the computer has air conditioning that applies to the whole of the Sub-Treasury by the feel of it. The space has been entirely separated from the Post Office that is now 'next door'. The space in which the computer is expected to go is in the office of the District Accountant where there is plenty of room. In that area there are three double electricity sockets and three new telephone sockets conveniently located in one place. There are four other double sockets in the room and there is another telephone socket in the cashier's office close by the entrance where the members of the public go in. 4. All building works are completed. Mine is a highly skilled service for which there will be a payback…'

Typing up history notes for Corozal and to send to SMCC took a long time and I met with Louisa for the first part of Friday morning to be ready for the workshop next week.

'…I'm fine thanks. A bit bored because I haven't enough curriculum work to do in this part of the holiday. I suppose that sounds a bit silly because I have more than enough to do to finish the Impact Study for VSO but that is too much of one thing and I have been doing less of it than perhaps I should. Do you recognise that feeling? I know that I will do more towards it when I have less time available. The weather here is fine and hot. We have had a lot more rain this summer than in the last two summers but that could be very misleading for you because it doesn't last long each time. A whole day of rain is unusual and more than one day of rain is rare. Otherwise it is clear skies and bright sunshine. That is where I live of course. They have some dull weather in the South and West, close to the mountains. It can be cold there in the night too. Right now, I can look out of the front door across the sea, with a cooling breeze coming in just as I am writing to you. It is a nice break from writing up the study. The mail in Corozal is pretty good so I imagine that Aner should get your letter in about ten days and the return should be the same from the day of posting. This is because mail comes to Corozal from Belize City by air. That was not the case in Orange Walk as there is no airstrip there. Mail goes back down to Orange Walk from here even though it is a much bigger town. The reason is that Corozal used to be much the more important. I don't have any particular reason to see Aner again until he is back at school next term unless there is anything you would like me to do. I do see people around town of course, and the numbers who stop and chat is growing rapidly. One of the things I am doing is collecting some of the history of Corozal. It turned out that one of the two attendants in the Museum is the Dad of a student in the same class as Aner. George is fine. He is sitting on the sideboard on the other side of the door with his back to me. He has had quite a lot of interesting experiences that should be written down and is waiting patiently for the action. Next week is the start of three weeks of workshops that I have to run so he won't have long to wait…'

I went back to the Study for most of the day on Saturday with a break at about 4:00pm when I went to

A & R in the hope of getting a BC02 cartridge as I had just gone on to reserve supply; also a second library book. In fact I got neither. The girl in A & R was addled and the Library was shut. On the way back I had resolved to fetch my binoculars as the coast on the other side of the bay was so clear. I poured a coke and went out on the balcony to find Tabo standing outside the gate. He had gone with his brother and friend to Chetumal for the day. It turned out that the friend is Ruby's brother whom I had met when I first came. That cleared my fridge of beer. A very small world in Belize! Anyway, it made up for the abortive walk, the trouble I had had with my printer before that and set me up for Sunday on the study. The workshop for Pilot Schools in the Middle Division ran for the whole week at the Corozal District HQ with very pleasing results…

<u>In the Name of Your Children</u>

We ask for your help, Lord, in the name of your children.

We know that you want all your people to develop fully, not only spiritually in your son, Jesus Christ, but also physically, intellectually and morally. We know that you want your children to have an education; one that increases as the learning in our society increases.

We know that you have given different talents to your children such that together, they may make up the parts of the body of your people. We know that it is your wish that each should play his or her part to the full; that each should have a learning that is integrated - all one piece that fits neatly with the next.

We are here, Lord, to take a new step in providing for children's learning. To develop a fully rounded curriculum - planned and put into place with children at its centre. To match our teaching with the needs of each individual child's learning as part of a team. To watch over their progress, provide encouragement and variety; to learn from their mistakes and from our mistakes, in our new planning. To provide in the best way we can, the resources and the environment with which to grow.

We ask for your help, Lord, in the name of your children; for they are your children, Lord. Your children go to school. Your children grow and become adults. But how many of them will never develop fully? How many of them will be permanently damaged?

You don't want this to happen to any of them, Lord. We don't want it to happen either.

That is why we ask for your help, Lord - in the name of your children.

'…I hope you are still enjoying your holiday and the weather has remained fine. I am waiting for the Batty Bus to arrive from Belize City which I will shortly go and meet as another VSO is coming to stay for the weekend. She comes from Canada and she is writing Training Material for the Pre-School Unit. Being the only VSO in the Northern half of the country, I don't see much of the others but they are much more inclined to make the journey since I moved here. The last week has been a busy one during which I have run a workshop for Teachers and Principals in the Middle Division of the (Pilot) Primary Schools. That would be your year 4, 5 and 6. On Monday, a two week long workshop starts for the Lower Division. That workshop is for all schools in the District. I think that Aner should get your letter this week. I may hear about it because I know that he sometimes sees Tomas Zetina and Tomas' Dad is one of the participants in the workshop. The school is making plans to provide a secure space to put the computer as soon as possible next term. When that happens and it is all up and running, you will be able to use email direct. Of course, you know already that there can be many unforeseen difficulties on the way and things don't always happen how or when we want them to. But I don't give up. We will get there…'

Pamela arrived just after one on Saturday and wanted to drop her bags and sit around on the balcony for a while having had a rough time with her placement. She didn't want to eat out so I did a roast chicken dinner with what I had. We did some wandering around and looking at the town before returning with a heap of bananas and melon which Pam bought and which I expected to be largely wasted. I don't like waste – more so here because of the insects that it attracts. In the late evening we went to Black Orchid which was very pleasant even though the drinks are expensive. As it was very hot on Sunday we didn't go far; just around part of the town and the whole of the sea front, taking in the museum. Pamela resolved to come again to visit the Mayan Site at Santa Rita. She left on the 3.00pm bus.

'…Pamela has just gone back to Belize City. She had a lot to say about where I live and spent a lot of time out on the balcony. Out and about she was very impressed by the number of people I know here and their friendliness so it was nice to share some of that. She also wanted to talk about her work that isn't going particularly smoothly. I start the second workshop tomorrow. This one is much bigger than the first one and goes on for two weeks. After that there will be a quiet period for about a month before monitoring of progress in the schools begins. I should be able to completely finish the VSO Study during that quiet time...'

The workshop for Non Pilot Schools in the Lower Division ran for two whole weeks at the Corozal District HQ also with very pleasing results. I delivered the whole picture right from the start and resolved to unpick the confusion that is always in the mind when being asked to think for oneself! Suggested that the time given was far too great merely to work the 'process' and plan for a mere two weeks. Started to encourage thinking about how the time might be used more profitably. The lack of documents is a serious problem yet again. Phoned QADS and demanded that copies of the Lower Division Outcomes be sent immediately.

I invited debate on the first Thursday on how the workshop was going so far so that the Teachers could deal with their frustrations and steered that to the objectives I had in mind on Monday. These have to do with extended planning (at least a term), making decisions about topics across the Division, Lesson Plans etc. I managed to maintain the focus on Teaching and Learning Strategies into a second day. Teachers really do have to give a lot of thought to the matter. There is little appreciation of what is meant by 'Child Centred' in practice.

The course numbers held up even for Friday. The walkabout and sharing of ideas was very good although there was still little debate afterwards and the summing up was left to me for the second time.

Saturday was a quiet day pottering about, reading and restocking. It is very hot, as it has been all week. The sea this Sunday morning is as flat and shining as a mirror. There is no wind even up here on the balcony and by the sea. A few children have splashed about excitedly in the water but there is otherwise, little movement of any kind.

Corinth, Vanlee and Ariola came on Monday and gave presentations all day and into next morning so there was little to do for most of the time. I went to the Library to change two books afterwards as it wasn't open on Saturday and I ran out of reading! Over the remaining time the workshop continued to run smoothly with the planned work completed. We had a full house pretty well all the way. 107 on the last day, which was the same number we started with. The closing of the workshop started with a barbecue and went on to the entertainment. The last item indoors was a rendition of Cecil, a favourite of mine, well used and a 'leveller'. This followed by a song and maypole dancing outside. The closing prayer was 'The Fence'.

'...My workshops are becoming rather known for their entertainment and social bits at the end. I don't like lots of speeches in opening and closing ceremonies that are the norm here. The idea is to weld together a group of people who will support each other through what is likely to be a difficult time. We were also extremely well fed by the efforts of a family known to Louisa, the Belizean Field Officer I work with in Corozal District. They have a small catering business at the border that they closed down for the three weeks to attend to our needs. We try to work as friends...'

I had long discussions with David Eck and made it clear that the suggestions made about the work I would do on extending hadn't materialised and all I could see stretching away into the future was monitoring. I reminded him of the promises made in respect of assessment, inspection and setting up the QADS function at the District Office.

After another quiet Saturday, Sunday is again an incredibly still morning! It is so peaceful and has been since the dawn around five and the sunrise about half an hour later. The sea is like glass and the sun rises over it in line with the coconut tree, the front door and just to the right of where I sit with the computer; the light and the colours of the sky and the sea change subtly with the ascending sun and muted birdsong scratches at the air as individuals call to each other. The occasional dog barks. These mornings are rare. The coconut tree with its hanging leaves up to ten feet long, barely stirs, even at their tips. Usually there is a wind.

'...We are all very sorry to hear about Mr Pasos death. Although we obviously never knew him we feel that he will be a part of our family because of the shell ornament he made; it gives it an even greater sentimental value for us and will always have a place in our home as well as our hearts...'

'...I collected your parcel from the Post Office yesterday morning and it was delivered to Mark by lunchtime! You may like to know the process by which that happened so that you can picture a bit more of life here. Parcels are not delivered to homes here although letters are. What happens is that a form arrives with the regular mail telling of a parcel that you then go to collect. The form arrived on Tuesday afternoon after the Post Office had shut so I was not able to collect the parcel until the next morning. According to the receiving date stamp it arrived in Corozal at the weekend. I can't remember the date stamped in England but I am sure that it was August so it hasn't taken very long. It is a good idea to put the date on your letter and keep a note of it so that you can track back if you have to. At the moment I am in the middle of running three weeks of workshops for Teachers and Principals of Primary Schools in the District. Mr Zetina, the Principal of Santa Rita School, is attending the current workshop and he made the final delivery. You can expect a reply without delay – perhaps close to this one. A bonus was that we were looking at some of the things that young people will do if given the opportunity and that sometimes a little help is needed. Your gift was a good example shared by 120 Teachers and Principals in Belize…'

'…The VSO Study is getting there but I haven't touched it for two weeks because of the workshops. The remainder of the work is just hard slog in pulling it together. I have it all set out so it is just a matter of writing now. I started off having difficulty because it was the only worthwhile thing that I had to do as there was so little curriculum work. It became too much of one thing. Now, the workshop requires such careful steering to make the most of it that I get home exhausted and don't want to do anything else! It has also been (and is) very hot and humid. I was supposed to go to a party this weekend at Jack's new place in Belmopan (150 miles each way!) but I decided not to go on Friday. I'm not very keen on parties anyway. I have only been to one and that was his early on in Belize City. So I have had a nice quiet weekend by the sea…'

'…It is now Sunday. The time flies. I had to abandon writing on Tuesday because we had a granddaddy of a thunderstorm just as I was about to comment on tropical storms! Sometimes the thunder crashes on for ten or fifteen seconds, right across the sky. Obviously, the sound will start at the point where the lightning was nearest so one wonders what the lightning was really like…'

'…We have had very heavy rain last week with flooded villages and 85 evacuated families. That storm west of the Yucatan heading for the coast of Mexico, threatening to strengthen to a hurricane. The news tonight is that it did become a hurricane and is now heading for Texas. We are well into the season now, which becomes more active over the next couple of months and ends at the end of November…'

'…A lizard has just run up the wall as I type. The house lizards are not very big and that one was only about two inches long. The biggest I have seen is about five inches. I don't mind the lizards because they are clean, they do not try to get at food and they eat insects. They can be a bit tiresome when they start 'clacking' during the night but that doesn't happen very often…'

'…This morning I was cooking and defrosting the fridge. The fridge has to be done every two weeks or it doesn't work. I was having roast chicken today. I thought it was about time to cook a proper Sunday dinner. I usually only cook like that when I have a visitor. The two activities go together because it is a big chicken and you can't leave food out in Belize. There are too many opportunist creatures about and it is too hot. The lady who lives next door brought over a hot dinner of chicken, rice and beans, fried plantain and tomato while I was still cooking. She would be very hurt to have been refused so I will have to rearrange plans that were already becoming complicated. Never a dull moment unless we make it ourselves! I was busy marinating all the giblets, neck and fatty bits with some lentils as well. You may like to know that includes the feet! Everyone here eats the feet of chickens. They are regarded as a delicacy and 'When in Rome do as the Romans do!' Actually, they are very tasty but they always look like feet. I first met one when it stared at me as I bit into tamales…'

'…What you do with the chicken feet is put the bits in your mouth and suck the flesh off the bone. When it has all gone you eject the bone and the funny little worm-like sinews carefully with the lips and tongue. Belizeans make something of a ritual of it with smiles and gestures and succulent sound effects. It would be sibilance if they made poetry out of it. I hope you are not about to have your tea…'

'…Here are some stamps for your family collection. I don't know how I missed them at the time but they would have been issued just after my arrival on September 6th 1997. Anyway, I spotted them in the display cabinet in the Philatelic Bureau. They have been withdrawn from sale but they had a couple of sets left. I was in Belize City yesterday and I go into the Bureau when I am down that way to check on any new issues. Will you please check which definitive stamps you have so that I can get the ones that are missing. Also, it would be worth checking the others to let me know if you don't seem to have a full set. Would you like a mint set of definitive stamps? The Workshops are over and I have some spare time that is why I was able to go to Belize City. I had to go anyway because I was running out of cash. The bank and the cash machine are both 85 miles away! I went on the regular bus on the way down. That is the way I usually go because I find it interesting with all the stops and the great variety of people getting on and off with their goods and going about their business. It was even slower than usual, however, and I had quite a tiring day so I came back on what is called the 'Premier' which is not supposed to stop except in Orange Walk. I could write several books about 'supposed to' and 'actually' in Belize. It took three hours to go down and two and quarter hours coming back…'

'…A bird has just flown in the open door and I have spent a few minutes clearing a way for it to fly safely out again. It was one of the pigeons that are smaller here, no bigger than a blackbird, and very pretty with dashes of red and brown on the breast and wings. My favourite regular birds are the bright yellow kikadee and the woodpecker with a scarlet head. The most spectacular birds soar around overhead. They are the frigate birds and the pelicans spotting fish. There are a lot of tropical storms and hurricanes about but the weather right now, is perfect. As I look out of the door the sea is untroubled, the sun is shining and a gentle breeze keeps me cool…'

'…I don't think you're going to forget those chicken feet. I certainly won't but I do eat them. I even cook them when I forget myself and buy a whole chicken. You open up the packaging. Then you ease open the back end of the chicken and there they are, staring at you and 'first out' as they say. Alternatively, you go to the little shop that is much more exciting. There, the nice lady will open a big plastic drum about two feet high and twenty inches, or so, in diameter. The drum used to hold lard that would have been scooped out with the fingers and put into a plastic bag for you to cook with (the lard, not the plastic bag). That's just the drum; when her hand comes out after groping around inside, a chicken or part of a chicken, would be hanging from her fingers, all limp and white and very dead. This is then slapped on a board and threatened with a cleaver until you tell her what you want. I generally have all of what is there out of kindness or respect for the dead chicken but what I really like is I don't get the feet. I don't mind her chopping those off because my respect for dead chickens doesn't stretch that far and my kindness for those who come to ask for feet overwhelms (I tell myself) any other feeling I might have. I smile as she wipes her hands with a satisfied look and enquires "What else?" every time. I never buy my vegetables at the same visit; I never buy lard at all; I don't like the way it runs back off the fingers into the drum because it is so hot. I hope it isn't your tea time…'

The rest of the week was devoted to the VSO Impact Study, punctuated only by an evening visit from Onelia and Ariel and the three children and posting a new package to SMCC to arrive ready for next term.

Saturday 28th August 4:00pm the wedding of Onelia Botes' youngest brother took place at St. Francis Xavier Church. It didn't start on time and Onelia and Ariel and family still hadn't arrived when it did so I sat at the back where I could take some photos of the couple coming out. Onelia arrived later but I had already seen the two girls acting as bridesmaids. It was nice to see the bride go in and the couple come out between a guard of honour formed by twelve teenaged boys and girls, six of each. They all carried roses, red for the boys and white for the girls, and there was no suggestion of hiding the flowers in any way when they came out into the street. It is all quite ordinary for them. I took a lot of photos on account of their photographer having left before they had finished with the pictures. The reception was at a family farm on the outskirts of Chan Chen that is a little village some miles out of the town. I saw the meat being taken out from its pit in the ground where it had been cooking all day and the previous night under a fire built on corrugated iron sheet. There were three huge pans of prepared meat and spices. The meat was from a freshly killed young cow from the farm and was certainly one of the most delicious meats I have tasted in Belize. It was a very happy occasion in good company and I was brought home at four o'clock in the morning.

Billy

The middle of a hot sultry morning is not the most inspirational time. The temperature close to a hundred degrees in the midst of the hurricane season and at sea level leaves the mind wondering 'when' rather than 'how'. Not the time to expect a simple human contact to lift the spirit but that is what happened when I met Billy again, for the first time in well over a year. I had often wondered how he is getting on because of the way he engaged with people when I knew him in school. I hadn't seen him since he graduated at age 13 from Standard Six at a village school four miles away, in July 1998, when he was given an award for Most Outstanding Student. I knew that he lived somewhere in Town because he travelled to the village on the bus each day. We would chat as I waited for my bus in the opposite direction. I knew too, that Billy's family only had their Mum and he would spend his spare time selling the meat pies his Mum made around the town. The bond between them was remarkable and Billy would spend much of his spare time keeping the family income going. I had often wondered how they would fare with the great expense of going to High School. I found out that morning.

Billy saw me and it was his "Hi Mr Max" that was the first contact. Even after so long his enthusiasm was the same as ever and he was carrying the inevitable bag of pies. We found some shade to catch up with our news. "I'm working!" was among his first words. His face lit up as he expressed his view of the positive side, as always, of what he is doing. There was no resentment that he had to drop out of college because the family couldn't afford it. There was no complaint that he had to work, more now, to keep up with the cost of their living. He showed instead, simple pride that he was able to help his Mum and his sister make the pies which his brother-in-law 'makes good money' selling at the border. The temptation to simply pay for his schooling is strong but that is a long-term commitment and one would need to be here. Also, it is not merely a matter of fees and books now. There is also the problem of lost income. He has strong ties and a happy disposition and he appreciates just stopping for a chat and the sharing of past times.

One sad thing is that his wish to get to know an English Student is frustrated. He has written several times to Richard (whom I don't know) who would now be in 9D and has received no reply. This is really sad because I am certain that the greater benefit from that 'Link' would be Richard's. As a character and a well-rounded individual, Billy has a great deal to offer. While we talked, he called on his friends, whom I didn't know because they went to a different school, to come and say 'Hi' as well. That their response was perfectly ordinary as we exchanged greeting says a great deal about their friend, Billy Melgar.

I went to the office on Tuesday morning to meet with Louisa. We worked out the budget for all of the Monitoring to be done between October and June. I came home and set it out properly and loaded the 'Cheyenne Bitware' software. It was working okay but the receiving FAX was 'busy' into the evening.

The weather overnight was violently wet with plenty of thunder and lightning overhead and all around into the morning and a whole day was spent after doing some washing, on the VSO Study.

I went to Belize City on Thursday to get some money. It was not a good journey again. The conductor on the Venus bus tried to charge me $7-50 so I insisted on a $3 fare to Orange Walk so as to pay the $3 the rest of the way. In the event, I got off the Venus bus and caught an Urbina express which gets there much more quickly and still for the $3 fare. It was also a very slow journey to Orange walk and it rained heavily all the way from there to Belize.

Chino and Manuela Medina were on the Urbina bus. They were also going to visit the family. That part of the day was good. It is always a pleasure to chat with Neria although she has her work cut out looking after her three grandchildren as well as everything else.

I elected to return on the three o'clock Batty Premier but I will be slow to do that again. It took an hour to get to Ladyville and it stopped in all sorts of places to suit the friends of the driver and conductor. The express at regular fare is a much better bet as the Premier costs $8-50. I was reading a book so it didn't matter to me that the video broke down but I was very hot. The air conditioning was ineffective and, as you can't open the windows this is very uncomfortable. I was sitting at the front where I could see and get some benefit from the driver's fan but that broke down as well. It was tipping down with rain again – just in time to get off – but I was ready for that this time. I had taken my umbrella.

I sent off sections 1-5 of the VSO Impact Study this afternoon and have spent all day working on section 7. It wasn't until evening that I went out and then only to go to the Library and to buy some bacon and eggs. Hopefully, section 7 will be finished tonight or early tomorrow morning and the whole thing will be finished sometime next week. I certainly hope so because it has been difficult to become as absorbed in the writing as I was before going home. I rather think that the ineptitude of the Managers of QADS has a lot to do with that.

Most of the weekend has been spent on the study. I have had an email from Jem to say that she would like to write to Francine Pena so I phoned Louisa to check the address ready to send it to Jem later. As I write, I am cooking dinner and Miss Lucile has just brought hot Johnny cakes that are delicious.

Chapter Seven:
New School Year

The beginning of the schools' first term coincides with the second anniversary of my arrival in Belize, not that it would be noted, nor would I wish it. I simply met with Adolpho Matus at the District Education Centre at 8:00am to acquaint him with what will be required of him to take over from Bertha who has left to go to Trinidad. He came back here for a while afterwards and we had lunch in the Jo-Mel-In before he left to go back to San Estevan.

I am extremely disappointed in Bertha that she went without any contact at all after all I have done for her. That is now at an end; not personal though; there was no contact with anyone.

Caroline phoned to say that she would like to stay over on Wednesday. That will be very pleasant. A large attachment from Philip containing 'Home is the Belizoo' which he has illustrated would not completely download and a letter arrived for Joanna Gilharry at Santa Rita, from Louise in 8R.

'…This morning I got up at 4:00am. I wanted to try to download a big email again while it was quiet, but without success. The problem appears to be the phone lines and I had to ask BTL to delete the whole thing – which was 6 megabytes. I then sent another email to ask for it to be sent on floppy discs by regular mail. As I was up, I watched the sunrise. That was beautiful. Unfortunately, my battery went dead in the camera at the point of taking the first picture so I will have to get up early again tomorrow. The rest of today was spent on the study for VSO with the exception of delivering mail to Santa Rita for one of the girls and buying a new battery at $34! I expect that Mr Berry will pass on the message that her package has been delivered but you could tell her as well if you like. I have no Curriculum work for a couple of weeks and I hope to finish the study tomorrow or Thursday. When I get the money for doing that I will be able to buy a computer for Santa Rita which will be great. Also tomorrow, a VSO is coming to stay over. She comes from Zimbabwe and works for the Red Cross looking after their publicity. So it's out for dinner tomorrow evening…'

'…I should be back in regular touch again - and don't fall over in surprise, but the school computer system should be ready in a week or so! Office 2000 and Windows NT with a 50 machine network, no less. This could really be something for our link! Thanks for your letter re Richard - I spoke to him on the first day, and says he will write to Billy. Thanks also for the parcel that arrived with books and T shirts galore. I will use that to get this year's link up and running. Could you confirm the names of the 5 Belize schools for me please? Term started today, so as you can guess, I have got a million and one things to do. Speak with you soon - hope you and all your friends are keeping well…'

'…Please tell Louise in 8R that her package for Joanna Gilharry at Santa Rita has arrived and I delivered it on Tuesday, 7th September 07. Joanna now goes to High School. Her home address is…'

'…Unfortunately, the phone line has beaten me! I tried four times but the rate of transmission is too slow and it shuts down. The best I could do was about 2.5 of the 6 Megabytes - and it has to finish of course. I even got up at 4:00am to make best use of the server and telephone lines. I had to ask BTL to delete it this morning. Maybe it would be best to mail floppy discs. Ordinary floppies would be most convenient to me but I have friends who have zip drives - I don't know anything about those. I don't need to see what has been done before copies are made here. What I will do when I get it is have two or three bound copies made to give to the Zoo and probably some for schools, depending on the cost. I have friends who can do that. Please make sure that the illustrator is credited on the frontispiece, title page etc. …'

At the end of another day on the study I discussed the layout with Mark and decided that the main body of it is too long and I will have to find ways of putting much more reference material in the appendices. Caroline arrived unexpectedly early in the afternoon. I had just started taking a shower (as always). She later went off for a four o'clock meeting and came back at about 5:30. We ate pizza at Marcello's and afterwards went to the Black Orchid.

'…Richard brought me this message today on disc. I have pasted it, and sent it as written. I will confirm contacts for Zoila & Sheyla Botes as soon as possible. Two years in Belize! Waaaaaaaaw…'

'…To Billy, I am terribly sorry about the fact that you are disappointed with the 'link' we have tried to keep up. Mr Berry (our Geography teacher, and 'parent' to the links) gave me an email from Mr Max which said about when he met you, when you were selling some of your mum's pies. I am extremely sorry that you cannot contact me. I have written to you, quite often. I have recently written to both you, and Jeffery Hall. I haven't sent them yet, so you will receive this before you will receive the letter. One key problem about the letters I sent to you is that I sent them to Calcutta Government School, because I don't have your address. The letter I will be sending to you is going to be sent to your home address. Well done on the award at school for being Most Outstanding Student at your school…'

Another casualty of 'all change at the election'; Orvin would have delivered the mail himself.

'…*The attachment is for Richard. There is a letter for him and a copy of what was given to Billy…*'

Caroline left at about 10:15 on Thursday for a meeting in Orange Walk, after dropping me off at the District Centre to plan the coming month's curriculum activities with Louisa. I returned home and spent the rest of the day documenting the work we had done. A package arrived with photos for Ricardo and Marbella and a CD of Welsh Male Voice Choirs. I first looked to find Myfanwy and put the CD on right away! Miriam and Marco phoned (late – I was in bed this time) to say that they will be arriving tomorrow for the day and 'bringing everything packed cold'.

'…Dear Richard, Your message to Billy has been delivered. Billy wasn't at home but I had a long talk with his Mum and his sisters, which was very pleasant. I took the liberty of setting out your writing in brush script because an email print out is rather cold, and I made one or two minor alterations in spelling. Sorry! I had done that before I realized what I was doing. I hope that is okay. With this letter is an exact copy of what was given for Billy. I put it in an envelope and took a blank aerogramme for him so that there should be no delay in writing back. I liked your letter very much and I am sure that he will too. I told his Mum that I would send any quick message if he wants me to do so. I will do that for you too, but there is nothing like doing it for yourself. You could send your own attachment through me as another alternative. Billy doesn't have other access to email as he has now left school. The whole point is for you to find out how different life can be and thereby make friends in a way that you wouldn't otherwise. That helps to put things in perspective in your own way. However, there may be things that puzzle you that you think I can help with. If there are, I will be pleased to help. But it is better to answer your questions than to try to imagine what they might be (and choose the wrong time). The 'Link' has not been easy to set up and you were in the first year. I thought that I was pretty good at anticipating likely problems and that I had catered for them. Not so! That was one of the many parts of my learning in coming to Belize; thank you for 'sticking with it' and for responding so quickly. Billy is a very thoughtful young man. I hope that you become good friends…'

10th September, 99
The Battle of St. George's Caye Day.
(Public Holiday in Belize)

I hadn't expected the whole family to arrive but that is what they did. A great shout came up from the gate on the beach side of the house and out of their big Dodge vehicle poured Grandmother Neria, Grandfather Tabo, Father Marco, Mother Miriam, Uncle Antonio and children Miguel aged five, Mariami aged four, and Martin aged two. Thus, there were six adults and three children in my little house, including me!

I should explain that my house is fifteen feet by eighteen on the inside. This makes a living space and a sleeping space. The sleeping space takes seven feet by eleven feet out of the living space, laid out (if you pardon the connection) in the same direction (but it makes most sense to actually lay down the opposite way in bed or more accurately, on the bed). There is a door on the opposite wall of the living space from the bedroom that leads into the bathroom that was clearly added as an afterthought; the whole space being altogether too small for such large numbers.

As always, Neria had thought of pretty-well everything so that my not knowing they were coming until after I had gone to bed last evening and that the day is the Battle of St George's Caye Day and therefore a Public Holiday seemed not to be too much of a problem. I had very little food in the house!

We all settled down to a good chat while the children enjoyed the space in the yard and my attentions in between bouts of conversation. They were fascinated by the 'boy dog' and the 'girl dog', and wanted to stroke them or better still, play with them. I first had to explain that the 'girl dog' is nasty tempered and wants to bite. The 'boy dog' is okay but the 'girl dog' is very jealous when he is given any attention. The children's Mum asked which was which! I laughed at the direct question and simply said that the 'boy dog' rolls over on his back because he likes his tummy tickled. I carried each one of the children down into the yard to make the introduction to the 'boy dog' without too much fuss and to put myself in the way of the other one. She doesn't go for me. Both dogs were on long chains but they were in the same space and could easily get to each other. The 'boy dog' and the 'girl dog' remained a topic of interest, questions and conversation for the children until they went home (even though they have dogs of their own). The other thing that interested the children here is the space. There is very little space around their house in Belize City and nowhere else for them to go. I was (willingly) dragged into the games and used as a sounding board for their ideas.

Being the Battle of St George's Caye Day the makings of a monster beach party came together throughout the morning and we could all watch the progress from the balcony. We had a barbecue lunch from one of the stalls run by a friend of mine and then we all went down to the beach to join in.

Did I mention the drinking? No, I didn't! Perhaps that is because it is such a part of the scene that it is overlooked in description. Belizean men don't celebrate anything without drinking to it and it was that which first provoked the idea in my mind that the intention was for all to stay overnight. I began to wonder where I was going to put them all. I soon forgot about this because I had withdrawn from all responsibility and turned the house over to the women when they arrived. Belizean men are totally incapable in the house (the way English women – mostly – imagine their men to be) and it seemed expedient for me to play dumb. To the extent that I didn't know what was going on, I was dumb! So the party on the beach developed. A nice little place was found for the children to go into the water – fully clothed as most people do – and I joined them without the need to do more than paddle. They had a whale of a time (not deep enough or cold enough for real whales). The adults continued as part of the fun and the men continued to exercise their right arm as they were all right handed. The beer tent was close by.

There was a band in the round house – well, singers, keyboard, mixers, and huge speakers belting out the usual Caribbean rhythms (at least the ones they like most in this part of Belize which is Spanish speaking and mostly Mestizo). There was also dancing. Bodies gyrated entirely unselfconsciously and are always fascinating to watch. I dare say that, if I went and did it, there would be a talking point forever more but I didn't think that anyone was in the need of that! It was gone 6:00pm when we returned and had more food.

Early in the morning Miss Lucille, next door, had invited me to join them for relleno this evening and I had said that the family were coming and I didn't know what time they would be going home again so we left it that I would join her party afterwards. Well, when we got back, relleno was sent round – enough for all to share and one way and another we ate well. The beer drinking continued! I thought that the two cases I had in stock would leave me with plenty over but it was beginning to look a bit sick by this time, despite that I don't drink much of it.

Of course, I hadn't expected the whole family to stay overnight but that is what they did. It was just as well that I had withdrawn from the domestics for the duration because the women soon got things organised. There are two mattresses on my bed that is four feet wide. One of these was removed and placed on the floor in the bedroom (part of my plan for more than one visitor). They had brought a hammock that was put up in the bedroom for Martin and two small, thin body-mattresses one of which also went on the floor in the bedroom.

Mum and Dad, Grandmother and the children all shared the bedroom with the fan going all night. Grandfather, Antonio and I slept in the living room. I had my folding bed that I also keep for visitors, Antonio slept on the couch which is a lot shorter than he is, and Grandfather slept on the floor on the other diddy-mattress. I think that is everyone. If you want to know how it all fitted, work it out for yourself. I do have some small items of furniture, a sink, cupboards built out as a worktop, a fridge and a cooker. All the chairs went outside for the night and all the windows were left wide open. Everyone slept well. There was no choice. Grandfather slept especially well, as his consumption had been much the greatest. He gave a memorable demonstration of how to snore unbelievably loudly, whilst yet sleeping on his stomach. We all breakfasted, most remarkably, on scrambled egg with tinned meat and bread. The whole place was cleared such that only a few items had migrated into new hiding places and the family departed, triumphant, at about eleven o'clock! I finished writing the VSO study through the weekend, reorganised it on Monday and sent it off.

I met with Louisa, Suzanne and Adolfo in the District Education Centre to pull back some of the cooperation between Orange Walk and Corozal Districts that had been lost since Bertha had assumed responsibility for

Orange Walk. Also, she had left nothing behind which would help Suzanne and Adolfo in their job so Louisa and I did our best to help them with what they need to do first and an overall picture of the coming year. Having all our documents on computer meant that I was able to provide some examples. Suzanne, who is a Peace Corps, and I spent some time for her to take in some of the flavour of Corozal as she is new, and went to lunch in the Jo-Mel-In. She lives in what Peace Corps have designated a Hurricane Safe House so there is one place I can go if I have to evacuate. After she caught the Batty Bus back to Orange Walk I returned to do some letter writing and to catch up on paper work from the morning. At the end of the afternoon a phone call revealed that Andy West was in town with a Belizean colleague, nicknamed Max, also from Dangriga. They were doing some investigation of the small citrus growing areas up here. I went out and collected them from the square and we spent a pleasant evening, first with a couple of beers here at my house, then a nice Chinese meal followed by a few more beers at Nestor's.

Wednesday started with a knock at the door and Andy asking to leave some gear until tomorrow when they would be giving a lecture at the Education Centre. I then joined Louisa for some more planning and prepared the documents afterwards.

Andy and Max collected their gear and I arranged to go to Belize City with them afterwards, to get some more money from the bank. Andy also agreed to drop my passport off at VSO as it is now out of date. I spent the rest of the morning answering email letters.

On the way down in the afternoon, we stopped off in Orange Walk for lunch at Juanita's and at the NAAFI where I stocked up with two bottles of whisky, one of Appleton's Rum and one of tequila. It was fun bringing those back on the bus. I didn't get home again until 7:00pm.

'…I am about to start on the 'big push' for this year's new 'Linking' students as well as doing what I can for the last two years'. I'm hoping that the money I get for doing the study will buy the computer for Santa Rita School and leave enough over to put a computer for Ranchito School within reach. I think I have saved enough to make up the difference. St. Paul's School had my old 486 and Corozal Methodist and Calcutta Schools had theirs through VSO grants…'

'…My really busy period for curriculum starts at the end of this month as there are several workshops to run before the end of the year and all the Primary Schools have to be monitored for progress which means four visits to each over the coming year. That will be a really good way of getting about because I am hoping to be able to go to most of them on my bicycle. For the town schools I can walk of course…'

A quiet day had started with writing but that was interrupted and enlivened. The primary school children gave 'cultural presentations' in the Civic Centre, which is like a big sports hall with a concrete floor. Our notion of a civic centre is quite different. Afterwards the children paraded through the streets. I took some film and made notes for year 7…

'…The 'band' from St Paul's Anglican School who link with Hawkins at South Molton Community College, is leading the carnival parade. They have been practising daily, for a couple of weeks or more. The result is entirely their own effort, for there is no one to teach them. I noticed one youth trying several times to use a cornet in practice, but they were obviously not satisfied with the result. What comes over is the natural rhythm that people have here, and are able to express in beat and movement.

People are continually experimenting with beat and rhythm too, which probably explains why there is such a rich variety. There is not much emphasis on melody or variety in lyrics. Corozal Methodist School is following immediately behind. They link with Grenville. They do not have a band but it is one of the few schools that have a music club and an enthusiastic teacher. They have a number of good keyboard players.

Immediately behind Corozal Nazarene School comes Ranchito Government School. Ranchito are new to the linking and will partner the new 'form' at South Molton. There is a close shot of the Principal Mr Rancheran who has moved from Calcutta Government School who link with Drake. Calcutta School and Christian School, Assemblies of God from Santa Rita (Raleigh) are not taking part in this parade as they are both out of town and will be taking part in their own celebrations. The dancers from Ranchito won a prize of $500, when all had assembled at the 'Civic' for cultural presentations. The next school, Maryhill, is where Ruby Oxley teaches. She is the owner of my house and lives in the other house in the yard. Following them is another set of drums, resting. They come from St. Francis Xavier Roman Catholic School, which is the largest Primary School in the town. Roman Catholics are the dominant group in Belize – much larger than the Government schools…'

But many things don't run smoothly for long…

'…Hi Mark, I have been at the office over the last two days but I will be at home this morning and all day tomorrow catching up with some of the things I haven't done towards this year's 'Linking'. You may remember that I asked for a Small-Scale Initiatives Fund application form. I am at a bit of a loss as to how I should fill it in and go about it altogether. The attached copy of a letter to Pedro Cucul will tell you my intentions but he doesn't seem keen on operating on behalf of Non-Government Schools. I thought we were dealing with children. I still think that even after two years in Belize! The problem, of course, is item (1) on the form: Name and Address of Organisation Requesting Grant. It is easy to cover one school directly, myself, but there are three Church Schools and in two cases their need is greater than the two Government Schools. I would say that about the third Church School as well really. They only appear to be doing well because of their own enterprise. What is your advice? Please tell Henry that my passport, which is out of date, will be dropped off at your office by Andrew West on his way back to Dangriga...'

'...The Link between four Primary Schools in Belize and a Secondary School in the United Kingdom, involving 11-12 year old students, is entering its third year. The project has progressed steadily and it is my hope and intention that it should be secure in itself by the time I leave Belize. A growing number of students are remaining in contact after the year in which the link operates. One of the difficulties encountered by the schools is the high cost of mail. Many children in the Belize schools have a particular problem in this respect although you will not be surprised to learn that the same problem exists in the UK also. Relative resources only become relative when juxtaposed! Herewith are documents referring to the VSO Small Scale Initiatives Fund with a maximum availability of up to one hundred pounds per year in local currency. I propose to make application on behalf of the Belize Schools and request that you undertake the role as representative of the 'Organisation Requesting Grant'. There are four schools involved, only one of which is a Government school. These are: Calcutta Government School, Corozal Methodist School, St Paul's Anglican School and Christian School Assemblies of God Santa Rita. A further school, Ranchito Government School, is likely to join this year. It is my intention to make up the total sum if the grant is given, to $500 thereby providing $100 for each school and I would hope that you would be able to provide a 'summary breakdown of how the grant was spent' in due course. Having schools involved from several managements, I believe, enriches the whole project. It would be most helpful that support and co-ordination should come from the District Office...'

'...*Attached is a letter for Year 7. If you would like copies of anything else please ask. I have done resources lists but I would like to explore some ideas with you for making them more accessible to students...*'

'...Dear Friends in Year 7, Welcome to Belize! You are not all going to arrive in person of course (I wish!), but we can do our best. Your 'Buddy' will be able to make the trip and a 'Buddy' from your 'Link School' here will be coming to visit you. The idea is that the Buddies are treated as exchange students. Your Buddy will go to school here and 'work' in class just as you do. Your Buddy will go to parties and jump-ups, go on outings (even into Mexico) and stay with friends on 'stopovers'. He or she will be able to join in celebrations, learn a bit of Spanish and Creole and enjoy the delights of the Caribbean with new friends.

Perhaps your Buddy will wonder if one of the hurricanes will come close this year. There will certainly be lots of other things to do that students think of. The Belizean Buddy will be able to do the same sort of things (only different) in and around South Molton and perhaps even further afield. As the Buddy is a soft toy, the travel costs will be kept at a minimum.

However, there is a problem with writing and drawing, collecting pictures and artefacts and dealing with the mail. Buddies are not very good at communication generally but they do want to share their experience among their new friends with those friends back home. The only way they can do this is by asking their host at the time, to do all that for them. Actually, this is a very good arrangement. Imagine a human exchange. That one student would have to do all the writing and drawing and collecting and posting – and hardly have time to enjoy the experience at all. This way there are about thirty friends to do all that instead. Of course, there are all sorts of things a whole form or class can do that will be of interest to friends on the other side (nearly) of the world. The Buddy could travel along with that sort of project to ensure its safe arrival and present it to everyone personally, back at home.

There will also be introductions to individual students. Just as you make your own particular friends at home, you would want to do that with a Belizean. If you write personal letters asking someone to write back and telling them about yourself, your family and school, the Buddy can make the introductions for you.

This is the third year of 'Linking' and it has developed in many ways but it is not an easy thing to do. Many things can go wrong when people try to get to know each other and about each other from so far away. It is no good just doing something and then waiting for something to happen. You have to keep going. If you make it a regular part of the pattern of life it will work very well. An example of keeping going has been the determination that all the schools should have an email facility to enable rapid communication to take place. Obviously, that would be a great help to keep the enthusiasm going. It was thought that would happen in the first year but there were problems at both ends which have persisted. Happily, South Molton Community College have a new computer system and two of the schools here each have a computer and internet connection. The other three schools should be on line by the end of this term. I will continue to act as an email post box for those who wish to use it. Do not imagine that the life of students at your 'Link' school is better or worse than your own. It is different, very different, but the quality of life is what you make it. It is far better to measure life by what you **do** than by what you **have!** The school is also different. Students in Belize go to Primary School until they are thirteen if they are fortunate enough to be still at school. The years are Infant 1&2 and Standard 1-6. Your 'Link' class is Standard 5. The students will mostly be the same age as you are but some have to repeat years so they may be older. You should be able to communicate with your new friend through the school until the end of next year. After that, he or she will move to High School or leave school altogether and you would need to write to the family home if you haven't already started doing so. If you wonder what to share when you are writing to an individual, entertaining a Buddy or working on a project to send, just include what seems to be ordinary. What is ordinary for you in your own country is not so in other's. On the contrary, it is of great interest. It is also interesting to find out about things that seem to be the same.

It is worth mentioning the mail. If you know how it works in Belize it helps. When a package or individual letter is sent to a school it will either be delivered or the school will be advised that it needs to be collected. My mail is delivered to the house but this is not always the case. Sometimes, if the family has a telephone, they are advised but many families only get their mail when they check in at the Post Office. And it will not often be a simple matter of walking up the road. It will be much the best way to get to know your friend through school first. When you know more, you will know what to do and how you should do it. Always make sure that your letters have the necessary information on them!

If any of you wish to write to me for any reason I will be only too pleased to reply or to help or both. If you use my address by regular airmail it will take 7-10 days (from posting!). You could expect a reply in three weeks by regular airmail or in two weeks if I write to you via Mr Berry's email. If you write to me by email, either from home or school, you would normally have a reply the next day. This is my last year in Belize so make the most of it…'

'…Just a quick note to say Mum sent the story by post today. Thought if I emailed you, you would know then to look out for the postman. Apologies for the delay but I could not send it by email - don't know what went wrong…'

'…Thanks to Mum. George is delighted that you referred to Pigeon Post. He says that he is fed up with the usual term – especially when I use it. He says snails are much more sensitive than pigeons and more easily hurt. I hadn't thought of that but when you realise how quickly they go back into their shell it makes sense! I suppose that it is worth remembering that email is really in its infancy. It probably doesn't fail as much as the early mail coaches so perhaps we shouldn't grumble…'

'…As I sit here writing I can look up and slightly right to see straight out of the door and across the beach and the sea to the horizon. The coconut tree in the yard frames one side of the view and the trees on the beach the other. There is little breeze. I have the fan on and no shirt. The air has been very humid, hot as usual and uncommonly still for about a month. We have been in the wake of several hurricanes that affect the weather in this way when they are to the North and East of us. I think that the whole of Belize is holding its breath after Mitch last year. There is still October and November to go in this hurricane season and there is talk of extending the official time. Last month we had a period of very heavy rain that caused considerable flooding in the district. Eighty-five families were evacuated from the villages for a time. The biggest problems for people in the villages when the rain is heavy are water supply, getting rid of waste and cooking. Obviously pits become flooded and wells become contaminated but we wouldn't readily think that most cooking in the villages is done on open fires, outside. I suppose this is a backward move in some ways because the ancient Maya had a cooking fire indoors. The smoke was able to escape and preserved the thatch…'

I have just finished the Impact Study for VSO and I am waiting for the VSO Director to go over it to determine whether any changes in presentation need to be made. He knows best how he wants to use it. Three sixth forms at A-level and Bachelor's Degree at the University College of Belize were involved. As the subjects would not have been offered without VSO that aspect is easy to assess but effectiveness is not as easy as there are no previous results to compare. I used the students' results but added a lot of anecdotal data to fix the position from several directions. There are Volunteers reports that were useful but the main information came from interviews with schools' staff, Volunteers still in post or still in the country doing other work, past students and their families. I designed questionnaires for my own benefit but I didn't use them directly. All the interviews were conducted in a conversational style and most answers were given without asking the questions! It was fun and acknowledged in the introduction: 'A great friendliness has been encountered which itself has been an education.

Taking refreshment in a distant home after a long walk; meeting with grandparent, mother, father, sister, brother; engaging in the staff room banter; being shown, with pride, how Maths and Science have developed; chatting with students on the campus; joining a group of students for lunch outside the cafeteria'.

My being here is very difficult to describe and impossible in a few words. The extension is certainly different and it is obviously best to build on that. From the job point of view the reasons for my extending haven't materialised at all but I knew that no administration (or administrator) in Belize is to be trusted so that is only a disappointment rather than anything else. And I can turn it to advantage in terms of what I came for, which is what I am doing and intend to continue to do. This extra time should be enough and I reckon that I will be applying for another posting somewhere else, to start after a time back home.

It may be a couple of months before Santa Rita has the computer. At the moment they are making a secure space to put it in the appropriate classroom (burglar bars etc.) and arranging a separate phone line. My next move is to decide where to get it. We have some experience already but it seems that VSO could arrange a good deal for me as they have a close association with Angelus Press (the biggest supplier in Belize). I'm hoping to be able to buy two, one for the new school. That should help as well.

Monday 20th September I met with Louisa this morning and we worked out the details for the Workshop on Saturday. Afterwards I prepared the Budget for the workshop and a letter to Principals concerning monitoring. Louisa collected them later.

The carnival procession took place this afternoon and I went out to film it. It really was quite funny because I was playing a game of 'guess the route' and 'guess the time'. I had an idea that it might be coming along the beach road, past the yard but I wasn't certain and nor was anyone else. Also, the word was that it was due to start at 2:00pm which eventually became 3:00pm (officially!). The good news was that there were to be no speeches – otherwise you might as well come back tomorrow. At about 2:30pm I picked up the video camera and a letter I had to post and set off for the square. Lots of people were waiting there making the best of the shade, as it was very hot. No one knew when the procession would start or which way it was to go. What I was reasonably certain about was that it would start from the 'Civic' – the Civic Centre that is really a big sports hall with a concrete floor. I posted the letter and walked up fourth, past the Batty Bus to find an empty space where the assembly should be. Inside the 'Civic' the Gilharry Seven were getting ready for the night's gig which would start with fireworks at 10:00pm. I set off back but got no further help at the square. Everyone was milling about trying to work out from where they could hear the band. For some reason sounds are tantalisingly deceptive in this part of the world. Eventually, it became clear that the whole thing would take the route I had first thought and pass right by the yard. I was just in time! In the early evening there was a power cut which shut everything down. It was wonderfully quiet so I went to sit out on the balcony in the dark, to listen to the night sounds and to watch the fireflies that were in abundance.

The power came back on before too long and the town got back to normal. I stirred at about 9:30pm and walked once more to the 'Civic'. The crowds were far greater than I expected, everyone milling about and chatting. Many youngsters were about, some riding their bikes, some playing games known only to themselves, some running after newly dead rockets falling from the sky after making their splash of colour, and some aping the adults by standing round to wait or chat. The 'Civic' was taken over by the Gilharry Seven setting up the great speaker system and their sound equipment. Their big yellow bus stood outside; empty now, having disgorged its load. Round the other side, on the big open space ordinarily given over to outside sports, the floodlights were on and several areas were roped off in readiness for the various activities. A central covered stand would be the focus of the activities but some of them, needing much greater space, were to take place on the grass. In front of the stand and the grass space a large number of white plastic stacking-chairs had been arranged, about half of which were occupied. It was better to stand behind them as the whole area is as flat as almost anywhere in this part of Belize. The fireworks were being set off at the far end and all around the space were the inevitable supplies of hot food and cold drinks.

There were plenty of activities: bands, marching, dancing, singing and other presentations that were lively and jolly. I particularly enjoyed the punta-rock display and a surprisingly well structured and choreographed dance performed by a group of about twenty youngsters. Activities were to go on through the night, centred on dancing to the music of the Gilharry Seven. A burst of fireworks welcomed Independence Day at midnight but I left when the speeches started. No one else left but this was one time when I didn't want to stay on my own and all my friends were elsewhere. I would estimate that well over three thousand people remained. That is half of the population of Corozal.

Independence Day (18 years) I walked up through the town at the end of the afternoon, beside the sea in front of St. Paul's, through the market and out on to the end of the jetty to watch the sun go down. The effect was amazing. The celebrations were coming to an end at the roundhouse and on Miami Beach which, from that viewpoint, were central to the scene across the water. The sea was still as it had been all day. There was very little breeze and the clouds were thin and at varying heights – enough to make the colours of day at its end. It doesn't take long. I sat there on a bollard on my own, listening to the punta beat and the sound of voices across the bay. The light changed from white, through all the warm colours of yellow orange and red, to a glorious blend of shades and streaks across the sky and reflected faithfully in the water. Between sea and sky the shapes of Miami Beach, the few trees, the round house, the stalls and the people darkened into silhouette. The colours, the sounds, the occasional small bird passing by, the whispering of the wind; all separate and yet all in harmony with the setting sun. The glow swelled and deepened as might the sound of a great organ and slowly died as a veil was drawn over the glory of light.

The music stopped. Celebrate Belize for this millennium had come to an end.

Since arriving in Corozal I have gone 'Willingly' to have my hair cut. That is not a mistake; true, I have gone willingly but I have gone to 'Willingly' for that is his name. It may be his nickname of course; an English word he happens to like; one to attract the few only English speaking people that are about or maybe he cuts hair willingly and that is the name of his shop. I have no way of knowing because there is no name over the shop which is a wooden hut anyway (just inside a garden gate) and he is Mexican, speaking only the Yucatan version of Latin American Spanish. My ability to learn another language is hopeless, having it seems, been left behind when I left school. So our animated conversations were carried out in grunts and gestures depending on the closeness of his scissors or whether he happened to be using the cutthroat razor, always freshly sharpened. Somehow it seemed quite unnecessary to determine whether or not he is 'Willingly'. Anyway, he is a brilliant barber and was recommended by my Belizean friends; I suspect as a joke, knowing my inability with Spanish. I like the joke for we became friends, willingly!

The 'Linking' programme was started off with students of the new Standard Five at Corozal Methodist School where I took all their photographs to send to Year 7. This was done with all five schools and all were sent as prints to the UK.

I Met with Louisa to prepare for the Day Workshop, tomorrow, Saturday, and then cycled down to Ranchito Government School and talked with Standard Five there about 'Linking' especially as it is their first year. Afterwards I spent an hour as requested with Standard Six with some ideas for creative writing. This is not a chore; the fact that their school is in such a mess with all the building going on was a gift to be enjoyed by all; a new view of creative writing among the students apparently. The first focus was a big hole in the classroom wall where a new concrete beam was to be cast and the second was that the Principal's office was full of builders' junk. The first of the two stories we got out of that centred round the idea that the clock used to be where the hole was. (First thing on a Monday morning – time out as it were). The second was built around the idea of a visitor asking a student for directions to the Principal's Office. Any good student would give the directions of course, but the result would be worth watching. I stayed for some lunch as some of the girls were having a party in celebration of winning a prize for dancing in the Independence Celebrations then cycled on to Santa Rita for 1:00pm Standard Five to start off their 'Linking' programme.

The Saturday workshop for Lower Division Teachers and Principals who did not attend the Non-Pilot Schools Workshop went very well and proved my thinking that a series of short workshops for no more than four working groups of six would have been far better than the two week monster for over a hundred.

The first three days of the next week were taken up with time spent in the link schools, mail, curriculum with an infant one teacher and a principal and the AGM of the Corozal Town Branch of Belize Teachers' Union. The illustrated story 'Home is the Belizoo' arrived from Philip. I took it to Henry for his opinion and later, for Ruby's opinion. They both feel that it would make a good text in schools. Tomorrow I will take it to Corinth to see what she thinks.

'…Five files are attached to use as lists of the resources that you have. You may remember that I thought it would probably be easier for me to do than for you. In the event it wasn't as it took ages to search through all the files. I have lots! … The only things that are returnable are the few papers listed and the original videocassettes. All the rest I would like to be used as much as possible. If anything needs to be replaced or extra copies needed please ask. You have nine months to the end of my posting. If you agree, I think that a lot of the resources could be made available in the Library. That would please me and I know that Pam would be happy to facilitate that. If you could arrange for the videos to be copied on to regular tape they could be available on loan as well…'

'…Attached is a list of contacts for the schools involved in the 'Link'. You will see that Orvin Rancheran is now Principal of Ranchito Government School so that is the obvious choice for the fifth school. Would you please provide similar information for the forms so that I can add them in the right places for each school? Also, we need to know how to address email to identify forms or individuals. I assume that the name and form at the school address should be sufficient. The two schools with email are up and running. Hopefully, the other three schools will join them by Christmas. That is my Christmas present to them! I will have talked with each of the new groups (Std 5) to link with your year 7 forms by next Tuesday and they are ready to start. I have delayed this far to avoid all the celebrations that take place in September. They are all very keen to operate at the three levels: exchange student (Buddy), projects and personal letters. To support the individuals getting to know each other I am taking photos of each of the 150 or so students individually. This will be finished next week and I will send them straight off when they are printed. This year I am trying to invest as much as possible in the minds of everyone involved because I will not be here to do so next year. (I did before but it is more urgent now.) I hope to leave it where the five schools are not only working with you but are also working together and each with their own computer…'

'…Attached is a revised list of contacts involved in the 'link'. I had forgotten to put the SMCC forms against the Belize Schools. I have been in to all of the schools and they are all starting to put their first packages together, elect their Buddies and arrange for their travel. In future years you will have to 'light the fuse' early in the term and directly with each school. It might be a good idea to think about setting aside any text that you might use from now so that it can be done without undue effort at the beginning of the autumn term. It would not work to depend on initiation from Belize. There are several reasons for this: 1) There is a culture of dependency (I call it the gimme a dollar syndrome!) 2) Belize schools suffer a great deal more extraneous demands on their time than you do which delay the start of proper routines 3) Most 'teaching' is 'telling' so the nature of the 'link' is more demanding (as the new curriculum works its way through this should improve) 4) Most serious is the way in which the various managements move staff around from school to school. Teachers also tend to move class. Calcutta has the same teacher for Standard 5 but has a new Principal. St. Pauls has the same staff but the Principal is now taking Standard 5 (thank goodness!). Last year's Standard 6 teacher is taking Standard 5 at Corozal Methodist. The wife of the Principal is now taking Standard 5 at Santa Rita. Passing on information from one year to the next is not part of routine (yet). Once the fuse is lit it is okay but it will need to be done (early). September is the month of National Celebrations but I think that is a reason for sharpness rather than delay (or even sharpness plus a prompt). Ranchito is very keen so that was a good choice as I think, are all the schools. A lot of students in Standard 6 at Ranchito are also interested so they would make good partners for those in year 8 who were disappointed last year…'
Then, back to the Belizoo…

'…The script arrived this morning. Well done! I don't know what else to say. The style of the drawings is perfect and the way you have printed them made me put on my closest glasses to see if you had sent the original! The first thing I am going to do is to show it to a couple of Belize friends who write. After that, I will be doing some scouting around because I think that we could do more with it than the original idea of a couple of copies in the Zoo. We shall see… The cut and paste on the front relates very nicely with the content. I think that the whole thing balances very well. George is very pleased. He says that his home is properly valued and you have got his smile right. I thought you had flipped the image for the last picture but George pointed out the differences and told me not to be so silly…'

'…Attached is a document called 'Photo'. It has a list of the first six films that were sent to your school (everything is documented!). Film 2 picture 17 is the male tapir. Film 4 picture 19 is April. It occurred to me after I last wrote to you that you may not have seen those photos. Sadly, none of you have seen very much of the resources that have been sent (I don't think that is anyone's fault and I am gently working on ideas that might help)…'

280

All 'Cards' at the Bank.

At the end of the month, September 1999 there was to be a QADS meeting in Belize City. QADS is the section of the Ministry of Education I work for. The acronym (one of many in Belize) stands for Quality Assurance and Development Section. The meeting was to be a two day affair. Normally, I would travel from home each day even though it takes so long but there was to be an evening out with VSO to welcome the new regional director. The evening happened to coincide with the first day of the meeting so I decided to stay the night with the family. Also, I needed to be certain of obtaining my new cash/credit card at the bank.

The last day of the month dawned. Well, not yet! I had to be up long before then and I left the house soon after five in the morning.

Venus Bus Line is on strike! The general rule is that Venus runs south in the twelve hours between midnight and midday and north from midday to midnight. Batty buses run the opposite way. This has been complicated by an increasing operation of other bus lines, at least one of which has cooperated with Batty to undermine Venus. Batty has also been operating buses in Venus time themselves. Mr Gilharry, owner of Venus is fed up with this. His buses are losing money and he cannot replace an aging (aged really!) fleet. He has gone on strike. Belize has achieved yet another first! I have witnessed or heard of workers going on strike many times before. Never have I heard of a company going on strike. Worse than that: Venus is a public service company.

Anyway, I knew there would be problems getting to and from Belize City but I had been told of an Escalante (cohort of Batty) bus leaving Corozal at 5:30am and I made sure that I would be out on the road to catch it. What I didn't know was what size bus it would be. Mostly, I can recognise an Escalante regular bus as I have ridden all of them, but they do have smaller ones and most of these are unmarked. It was a smaller bus that came along.

I asked an identifying question but most drivers lie through their teeth so I couldn't be sure and I was the only passenger. My doubt was confirmed when the driver announced that he was 'just going to take another turn' and zipped off back around the town. The bus I wanted to catch must have been coming up behind!

The journey to Orange Walk (as I would now have to change buses) was very, very slow. There is no problem with buses from there in the morning so I made sure that I transferred to a waiting Urbina bus which was an express (doesn't stop – theoretically) and managed to get into the office by about 8:30am ready for a meeting to start at nine. Thank goodness I wouldn't be going home that night because I had already arranged to go to a dinner with VSO, to welcome the new Regional Director and I would be staying with the family.

The meeting took place at a new venue nearer to the Belcan Bridge and concerned QADS management reports. It was a very dull day; nothing to do with the weather. It was good to spend time with the family and then a pleasant evening with VSO colleagues whom I rarely see. The meal at 'Memories of India' was enjoyable but not outstanding. Being a Yorkshire man I have never liked picking from dishes being passed up and down the table. I expected a proper Indian meal but it wasn't. I had coffee at Caroline's new house in Newtown Road before returning home to the family. They were all in bed as expected but I had a key.

The affair at the bank was another story. What is it with banks and me? My cash card was due to expire today. I have had it in mind for a month that I could pick up the new card while having to come to this two-day meeting in Belize City. That is the nearest branch of my bank and they will not send the card through the post. Also, the pin number has to be attached using a separate machine inside the bank. The ATM machine outside will not do. I have tried to transfer my account to another bank in Corozal Town but it is such a performance that it is more convenient to leave it where it is – 85 miles away! I had already checked with the bank that the card would be available. Despite there being no branches in the North, Barclays have two branches in Belize City. The main branch is downtown and the one I use is at the Belcan Roundabout on the way in to my office at QADS. That is where I had previously checked the availability of the new card. The afternoon session of our meeting concerned security at our main office. As I am rarely there I felt this to be a reasonable time to excuse myself and I walked the twenty minutes or so to the Belcan branch of the bank. It was very hot.

"I'd like my new card please," I said, smiling hopefully (I've travelled these roads before).

"Certainly Sir, one moment please" my card disappeared in the care of an admittedly attractive young lady. She returned. "I'm sorry Sir. Your card is at our main branch downtown!"

I took a deep breath and explained the inconvenience of living in Corozal (again), the bus strike, the walk in the hot sun and the need to be able to use my card in the ATM machine, as the bank is rarely open when I get there. The point of the card is for my convenience and to enable me to obtain money. "What can you do for me please?"

"We can have the card here for you tomorrow Sir."

Rapid mental gymnastics are required here. Should I, for example, reveal that I would be in town tomorrow? It obviously hasn't really impinged on her mind that I live in Corozal. And I **have** been down these roads before. I adopt a delaying tactic and a quest for more (reliable) information. "What time tomorrow?"

"The card should be here in the afternoon."

Aha! I had the information that I suspected. The word 'should' in Belize means 'may be' or 'probably won't', in the same way that 'right now!' means anything from 'sometime' to 'never' or 'get off my back!'

"I'll go down and fetch it myself," I said, resignedly.

The walk to the main branch of the bank, downtown takes about half an hour. I have an in-built resistance to taxis (which are expensive) and the bus (if I could find one) meanders all over the place and takes just as long as walking. Belizeans don't mind the time taken and they hate walking. I arrived in the air-conditioned bank wet with sweat.

There is no sense of urgency in any movement and private conversation takes precedence over service. Once I had gained undivided attention I repeated my request. "I would like my new card please," I said.

Again, I smiled hopefully.

"Certainly Sir, one moment please," my card disappeared in the care of an even more attractive young lady. She returned. "I'm sorry Sir our pin machine has broken down!"

I took a deep breath and explained the inconvenience of living in Corozal (again, again), the bus strike and the walk in the hot sun to the Belcan branch. I pointed out that they had not been able to supply the card despite my checking early in the month and my long walk to this branch. I emphasised the need to be able to use my card in the ATM machine, as the bank is rarely open when I get there. The point of the card is for my convenience and to enable me to obtain money. "I am now very hot and very cross. What can you do for me please?" I was surveyed with an appropriate degree of alarm. The wet shirt was sufficient evidence – and warning!

"You could take your card Sir, use it in shops and come in for your pin number when the machine is working."

"Keep calm," I thought. Once again I took a deep breath and explained the inconvenience of living in Corozal (again, again, again), the bus strike and the walk in the hot sun to the Belcan branch. I pointed out that they had not been able to supply the card despite my checking early in the month and my long walk to this branch. I emphasised the need to be able to use my card in the ATM machine, as the bank is rarely open when I get there. I do not use it to buy goods in shops. Few shops accept them! The point of the card is for my convenience and to enable me to obtain money. "I am now very hot and very cross. I have not the slightest intention of travelling 85 miles in each direction to come back. What can you do for me please?"

Something close to panic flickered momentarily across her face. (Just as well. I have the business card of the boss of the bank in my wallet but I don't want to have to use it.) She went away again and returned with the new card. She smiled (hopefully?) and said "You could take your card and have the pin number put on at our Belcan branch." My face told all in an instant as she hurriedly added, "We won't have you walking. We will give you the money for a taxi."

There comes a point when resistance is pointless. I took the one remaining opportunity to make a stand. I refused the taxi fare and set off to walk back to the Belcan branch with the new card. That could have been the end of the story but it wasn't. The pin number was attached to the card and supervised (warily) by the same girl as before but I then wanted to be sure that the card worked! I also wanted some money. Outside, I found the card opened the door of the ATM with no problem. I put it in the slot of the machine and followed the usual procedure. "Your card is not yet valid," it said. I sighed and went back into the bank.

"Did they give you your old card back?" said the girl, "You would need to use that today as it is the last day of the month."

"No," I replied, "They didn't."

"Just a moment, do please take a seat." She disappeared and returned with a set of keys and went through a whole security routine to get into a door nearby. I wondered what she was doing but didn't bother too much about it. A little while later she came out again looking somewhat harassed, went off to fetch more keys and returned to go through the same routine. Satisfaction at having rocked the establishment a little mingled in my mind with pity for the girl but, slowly, this was displaced by a new idea. I knew that the door she had gone through is the service door to the ATM. It amused me but the thought had to be acted on. I caught the attention of the other girl who deals with these things. She was working with another customer. "She isn't looking for this?" I said holding up my new card.

"Yes!" came the reply with a hint of shared amusement (always a means of relief) and she knocked urgently on the door. The other girl had somehow thought that the machine had swallowed my card. I couldn't see how but she was harassed and 'all's well that ends well', as they say. There was humour in it. She made out a cheque for some money and I went on my way. Of course, I was able to try the new card the next day but they weren't to know that!

The return journey was straight through but that was all that could be said for it. The Escalante bus left Belize City already packed, shortly after four in the afternoon and after the usual twenty-minute walk. It stopped in the same manner as the regular bus might, despite being classed as express. I didn't mind that too much because people had little choice if they were to get home (there being no Venus). However, the bus was packed to start with. It was stopped by the BDF (Belize Defence Force) but allowed to continue despite being insanely overloaded. The way the driver went down through his gears each time we stopped was testament to the poor state of the brakes and that there was no reserve for emergency. I did think that there would be some relief when a considerable number of passengers got off in Orange Walk but the bus was refilled in exactly the same manner - being the only one going on to Corozal. It wasn't improved by two men, one young, being worse for drink and taking a dislike to each other. I got home at almost eight o'clock!

Mission accomplished. I had attended the meeting and the dinner as well as obtaining the new bank card but the latter would have taken just as long regardless. There is no doubt about it.

They are all cards at the bank!

I left the copy of 'Home is the Belizoo' with Corinth. She will return it with comments.

Mail continued to flow unabated but there was no longer a rush to get everything back in order after the break in the UK. Life was once more the same in many respects making the order easier than when I first arrived in Belize but different in others; in ways that demanded change. My role in development of the new curriculum had certainly moved on to a new phase but mail and writing generally continued with the new cohort adding to the old…

'…Thank you for writing. It will be good to hear more about you too! Perhaps the best way to tell you about the project would be to give you a copy of a piece I wrote called 'Hey Buddy, Wait for Me!' I have attached it for you so that you can print it out as written. If you haven't done that before, just click on the paper clip or the little square on your email and follow the on screen instructions. If that works, I can send you other pieces of writing and stories, which would include quite a lot about Belize. Please tell me if you can receive more than one attachment at a time and whether there is a size restriction on your server. If you don't know, don't bother about it. We will go for it anyway! You will be able to use your school system if you ask. You will see that the project is wide ranging and gives you the opportunity both to make friends and to understand a little of their lives. In that way we begin to understand more about ourselves. Mr Berry has had copies of nearly all that I have written on the subject but you will appreciate that there is only one of him and lots of you. He also has a lot of books, pictures and films that I expect you will be able to share. Don't let that stop you writing to me. You could help by sharing with your friends – and feel free to do so. The school you will be linking with is Corozal Methodist School, which has only a narrow road separating it from the Caribbean Sea. I have just taken photos of all the children and a few of the school so you will see them soon. The children are exactly the same as you. They have the same hopes and worries, the same imagination and the same abilities. They are also at odds with their family at times! What is different is their experience. It is not better or worse, it is different. What you find 'ordinary' in South Molton would be wonderful for them. In the same way, what they find 'ordinary' in Belize would be wonderful for you. There are a huge variety of ethnic backgrounds but those just make it all the more interesting. A lot of people are poor but that is a complicated issue and could mislead you at this stage.

I speak English. People in this part of Belize mostly speak Spanish so your ability will add to the fun. The languages are varied for such a small country (total population slightly less than Plymouth in a country the size of Wales). English is the official language as it is a Caribbean country but the most important language for the nation is Creole because that is the speech that unites everybody. It is no surprise that you hadn't heard about Belize but I am impressed that you have written on the very same day…'

My main involvement in curriculum next was with nineteen of the schools in Corozal District for which preliminary visits took place on every weekday through October. These were a different experience both for the members of staff involved and for me. Others at times were also observing. It was necessary to move from a rigid regime focussed on teaching to one given just as much structure but one in which each child could learn from present understanding. Clearly there had to be even more a relaxed feeling in which all of us share. Arriving on my bicycle helped enormously right from my first visit to Libertad RC about eight miles away. It was fun to ride down to the school on my bike but it was very, very hot and it took a couple of hours to cool down after arrival. I was given an ice-cold coke right away which was a nice thought and helped a lot. I was also fed at lunchtime. I had to stop and shelter from the rain at Calcutta on the way down and just missed the rain on the way back. It poured just as I got home. The welcome at Libertad Methodist was just as good but the school is incredibly hot. It will be much better when the new school building is in use. The old wooden building is also falling apart and there is a real risk of going through the floor to the ground three or four feet below! On the journey back there was heavy rain in sight to the west all the way home. Another friendly visit was made at Libertad SDA with Calcutta Government and Ranchito on Thursday and Friday. I walked to schools in town.

'…I can see that I am going to enjoy your letters if you would like to keep it up. Remembering also, that you have homework and you need recreation and exercise… …You are on the right lines with your ideas for things to send to Corozal Methodist School and it is much better coming from you. If you are building an understanding and, hopefully, a friendship it will take time anyway… …You are seven hours ahead of us during the summertime. I find it amusing that you will be in the next thousand years ahead of me despite your youth!'

'…Ranchito Government School sent their first package for 7S yesterday. They decided to do things a little differently. I think you will find thirty 'Buddies' arrive, each with a letter to a friend!! I don't know about passports etc. I took their photos in today so you can expect another package soon after the first with photographs of the students, each with another letter. Their teacher is writing to you this weekend…'

'…This week I have been in schools all day – a different one for each day of the week. This goes on for nineteen schools and is to be repeated four times. I have done a hundred miles on my bike, getting there and back! I save the money for buses and taxis towards the next two computers for schools…'

There was a Spanish Course for Teachers at the District Centre starting at 8:30am on Saturday. I was particularly cross to find when I arrived at the course that David Eck had given a message to Louisa that I needn't attend. Well intentioned no doubt but this is another example of the appalling bad manners and lack of consideration by people who at best can be described as unprofessional. I had set off early and been unable to do my washing as planned. I had also missed the delivery of drinking water, coke and Belikin. In the present programme of monitoring Saturday is the only day I can do this. I spent the rest of the day catching up with writing and getting ready to go away tomorrow.

Sunday was the party for Tabo's birthday. I set off for Belize City early, leaving home at 6:45am to catch the seven o'clock bus. At least, I was told that it would be seven o'clock by the staff at Venus Bus Line. It left at 7:30am so that was a lot of time wasted – again! The journey wasn't too bad other than the cramped seat and I arrived with the family just after ten. It was a really good day and I went to bed in my old room around midnight as Pan American Day followed which is a Public Holiday in Belize.

I caught the seven o'clock Regular Batty Bus home for the celebrations. I had just missed an extra Premier that had been put on but that couldn't be helped as it wasn't advertised in any way. This was a slow journey and I didn't get home until gone ten. Part of the rush was to meet up with Jack and Kevin who had been to Sarteneja on Saturday. As I got home I found that they had called yesterday and left the pick-up they were using in the yard before going off to Chetumal to stay overnight. They arrived at about eleven thirty just as all the world and his brother were milling round the beach setting up stalls and things – many of whom I know. Robert Guy and his family from Calcutta were just opposite and I managed to talk with them.

The procession was more on the Columbus theme than on anything else. It was small but of good quality and a lot of fun. There was a lot of activity and games as well as the food and the group in the Round House. There were lots of swimming races and competitions and the great attraction of the greasy pole, which was a vertical telegraph pole - well greased.

'...Thanks for all the messages. I think you may have had a few surprise calls from one or two year seven pupils who have just started their Belize work. It was really great to see them take up the initiative so quickly. Samantha received your address from me during a lesson on Monday, and in her next lesson the following day, she came in with a reply! Top marks to the pair of you. She was rewarded with 5 credits, so I think I owe you 5 as well! I will post the buddies and first letters from 7D, G, H, and R this week - and hopefully 7S as well. I will make a special effort here as things have already got going at your end.

My problem is that I do not teach that group, and I know I won't be able to leave it to the teacher concerned. There has been a delay at the British Passport Office again this year, so the buddies may have to travel with special diplomatic papers until the passports can be forwarded. Sean Pavey will also be sending on his art work now. It looks really impressive, and might inspire some sort of similar response. Once initial contact has been made, we must talk about how to develop the link this year. The pupils at this end are more enthusiastic than ever...'

'...I am looking forward to sharing the arrival of Buddies and to the artwork from Sean Pavey. It would be good if you could find a way of increasing interest from other staff. The overwhelming impression I had was the difficulty of having to work within one subject and trying to work the 'Link' with all the forms on your own. (The difficulties here are quite different. I will go into them in detail presently – as promised. Many are cultural of course.) I'm quite pleased at the delay in the British passport office as I suspect the Belize Office is the same and that would be embarrassing after my stories last year! I'll get an update on students' letters and let you know. It takes time because it means a visit to their homes...'

'...When I sent you the list of contacts I don't think that I had put on the connecting forms. They remain the same as before except that 7S links with the new school at Ranchito. Attached is a new list of Schools Involved...'

Preliminary visits continued. I set off to arrive just as assembly finished at Santa Rita where I spent time with the Principal to set up the day and in Infant 1, Infant 2 and Standard 1 until break time. Then returned to do some record keeping and have lunch before attending the staff meeting for Monitoring in the afternoon. I delivered the photos for Corozal Methodist Standard 5 and Standard 6 during this time and took the ones out to Santa Rita Later.

Billy Melgar had been round several times during the day and he caught me in when I came home in the afternoon. He wants me to help him learn to use a computer so I gave him a keyboard on which to practice the keys and said that he could come round on Saturday morning at 8:00am. He has got a job 'learning to be a mechanic' at Venus Bus Depot, starting on Monday. That is pleasing. He has also written to Richard in 9D. I followed this up in the hope that a direct email might be set up between the two of them as part of Billy's practice.

In the evening I went to the Rotary Club meeting at Hokul Kin to give a presentation on the new curriculum. That went very well and led to a lot of questions and lively discussion from the members and guests. The meal on the other hand, was not at all exciting. The fare at the 'Jo Mel In' is far better.

'...Dear Richard, I went round to Billy's home today and found him in. He hadn't written to you but now he has! He sat down and wrote right away and delivered the letter to my house for me to send. I think that he has mixed up the idea that I would send a quick message if he wanted me to with my posting it for him but it is just as well that he has. I can feel a photograph inside and you are not supposed to send enclosures so I have put it in an envelope. It also gave me the opportunity to write to you. I hope you persevere with writing to Billy. I know it would be very good for him and I have no doubt at all that it should benefit you. You will realise that I have gone in for learning from another culture in a big way. I have not regretted it and the rate of learning has been and is amazing. I could easily tell you a great deal about Belize and its people. I could also tell you quite a lot of what it is like to be Billy but I would only do that in answer to your questions. Suffice to say, for now, that writing to you is a bigger problem for him than it would be the other way round. The life of young Belizeans is different from yours. Do not think, however, in terms of 'better' or 'worse' for that would be misleading...'

On Saturday I cycled to Consejo, Consejo Shores and Smugglers' Den. That was about twenty miles in all and was a most enjoyable ride except for the dogs! A whole pack of aggressive dogs met me as I entered the village. There are only two things one can do in those circumstances, as far as I can see. Either, you pedal on and hope or you attack. I attacked! I got off my bike and went for the obvious leader. The other dogs took their lead from this one as it turned tail to bark its defiance from a safer distance. I am pleased about this because it is also safer for me but that is not the end of it. The next step is to grab a stone and run at the dog, making sure that it has somewhere to go. I missed with the stone as I don't throw very well but I didn't miss with the shower of small stones that followed. The bark changed to a howl. All of the dogs quite obviously belonged to the houses nearby and I still find the casual attitude to the safety of others in this way, among some communities, highly offensive as well as dangerous. I went to the nearest house as the dogs backed off and enquired quietly, whether anyone was at home. I was cross to the point of calm so that, when the owner of the lead dog came, I simply pointed out that I would like to ride my bicycle in peace. And by the way – this I indicated with a twist of my two hands and a cracking sound, understandable in any language – if the dog goes for me I will wring its neck. On my way out of the village all the dogs were gone. I don't like doing things like that and this is not my country but there are limits. It is very noticeable that the aggressive dogs on the streets are not strays. Lots of people get bitten and rabies is not far away.

I found some very interesting prints in some drying mud. They looked like the prints of a big cat, not as big as a jaguar but big enough; the size of the average dog perhaps. They were not dog prints. Very sharp claws were clearly marked in one patch. I would have thought that this would be at odds with cats as they sheath their claws so completely. A mystery!

The birds were wonderful. It was a pity that I had forgotten to take my binoculars. I must get a saddlebag next week. I would like to know more about the birds. The kikadees and the parrots are easy, also the kingfishers and doves (very pretty and tiny). One huge bird I saw was one that spends its time on the ground. I have forgotten its name but there are some at Belize Zoo and they appear in my story. Another group of birds is like a huge jay and just as colourful. They have much bigger and more rounded tails than the jay but just as raucous cry.

'…I told you that I had posted a letter to you from Aner. You should get it next week. When I quizzed him about it at his school I found that he had it in his bag! He hadn't posted it because no-one in his family had been into town. What he should have done was to give it to his Principal or his Teacher to post. Anyway, it illustrates one of the many difficulties in a life where communicating beyond the village is unusual. Also, there is little sense of urgency in many aspects of Belize life and in Belize communities. Is that a good thing or a bad thing or can't that question be answered by a simple choice; something for you to think about. I am sure that your Mum and Dad would like to join in that one…'

'…I have given a lot of thought to the story. What I think is the best thing for you to do is to produce some more pictures and send them separately on disc after scanning. I am waiting for the copy you sent to come back from Corinth whom I mentioned to you. She is going to comment on layout and classroom use in Belize as well as suggest other pictures. Marco and Miriam (of the family) are involved with production of cards, leaflets and pamphlets. The business has a powerful laser colour printer and we can either stick edges of sheets or fold and staple. I am thinking of either A4 or A5. You have done a super cover and the drawings are great. I have the text. All that is needed are some more drawings on disc and the whole thing can be laid out and assembled here. My thinking is to provide the zoo with their copies which was the original intention, and the schools that I deal with. A copy could go to potential printers at that stage. The reason for all this is that there is a general expectation in Belize that others will provide. This extends to book printers here, who do not take risks, especially with school books. That is one reason why there are so few of them. At the point of sending copies to them they would be able to take it or leave it. I don't mind paying for the cost of the ones going to the zoo or in to school but I am not here to support businesses or a creaking system! Obviously, there would be some coming to you but I think that they would be unlikely to be in time for family Christmas presents this year (You can use the text yourself if you want to)…'

'…Dear Richard, This is ground breaking communication with your school so you must write back the same way as quickly as you can. I sent a note to you to expect a letter to arrive (at your home) from Billy Melgar towards the end of next week. I posted it for him today. Since then, Billy has been round to my house asking if I will help him to learn to use a computer. There is a long story attached to all this but doing that represents huge enterprise on his part that should be rewarded. I don't have a lot of spare time and he has never used a computer! So I have given him an old keyboard to learn something of where the keys are and he is coming to use my computer at eight o'clock on Saturday morning. You may begin to see the connection. Creating email to send to you will be a wonderful carrot for his learning…'

'…The news here is that I have a cheque coming this week for the balance paid for the Impact Study I did for VSO. I will then have enough for a computer each for the last two schools. All five schools will then be able to communicate by email with each other and with SMCC – as well as the other benefits. I'm quite pleased about that…'

It was a rather more adventurous outing on Sunday with a ride of 28 miles. This took me to Chan Chen from where I turned South on the Old Northern Highway. Passing through Patchacan, Yo Chen, Cristo Rey and San Pedro, I joined the main road between Louisville and Concepcion. The journey back was via Concepcion, Best Corner, San Joaquin, Calcutta, Carolina and Ranchito, which I know well. That means that I could easily tackle the ride to Caledonia provided I didn't come back straight away. The wild life was pretty good. I was especially pleased to see an armadillo and a fox, both running across the road. The armadillo was quite a long way off but near enough to be quite distinct and he was a well grown adult. The little fox was much closer and I had a very clear view of this beautiful little creature which is much smaller than the European fox. When I came through San Joaquin I enquired for and found grandfather Puch. He is Mario's Grandfather and I had been told that he does cross-stitch pictures on crocus bags. What I was not prepared for was the wonderful garden that he was proud to show me. The range and beauty of the plants is amazing. He will work a picture for me, to be picked up in three weeks. Preliminary visits to schools continued through unreliable weather.

It had been very wet indeed overnight on Monday and continued to rain in the morning. I waited to see whether it would change as there seemed to be some clearing of the sky taking place but it was still raining when I got a taxi out to the school. When I saw the state of the road beyond Mary Hill it was obviously the right decision. It was a good morning. I was taken by a member of staff to have lunch at his home which had become the pattern. He introduced me to his family in a traditional house with a huge outside kitchen.

Mark Wright from VSO arrived late on Friday having had a puncture by taking the route through Maskall on the Old Northern Highway. He arrived at about 11:45. It was a pleasant visit and we discussed all the things we needed to. My C.V. will be sent to London with a request for another posting as soon as one comes up after this one. I have asked for Africa, with particular favour for Kenya. The money for the study has been paid into the bank and I requested the small grant to help with postage for the five 'Link' schools.

We went to the Jo-Mel-In for lunch where we also went through the last details of the study. He seems pleased with it especially as it puts Belize up front in VSO in respect of carrying out Impact Studies and in a realistic way. After that we went to the Free Zone as he is entitled to use it with Diplomatic Immunity. Three bottles of whiskey, two bottles of Appleton's Rum and a bottle of brandy should keep me going for a long time. After that I went back to St Paul's, followed by a quiet evening as usual and a weekend of catching up once more; that is after meeting with Louisa in the office on Saturday morning to discuss progress and to plan for the field testing of the Upper Division Outcomes at the beginning of November.

The new curriculum is progressing very slowly. This is because education in Belize is all 'telling'. Learning is treated as solely knowledge. Even language (English and Spanish) is taught as though it is a knowledge-based subject. The use of language for example, is almost wholly a skill but students do not have the opportunity to practise it for themselves. There has also been no provision for developing research skills or problem solving right across the board. Students are expected to listen, not to think! There is no development of a wholesome attitude to learning. As teachers were themselves taught by 'telling', you might imagine that it is very difficult for them to change but working alongside teachers to facilitate that is very exciting and rewarding. All the non-directive training I have done for the Scout Association has been very useful indeed. As a result, I enjoy a privileged position in friendship and I have to be very careful not to think too much of myself. They do the work, not I'

The tenth hurricane of the season has just passed us by. None of them have caused any alarm in Belize and none of them have been devastating like Mitch last year but there has been a lot of damage caused. The ten so far are Arlene, Bret, Cindy, Dennis, Emily, Floyd, Gert, Harvey, Irene and Jose. The season ends officially, on 30th November.

'…Hi Douglas, I now have the money for two computer sets, one each for Christian School Assembly of God at Santa Rita and Ranchito Government School. This is from my own funds so I have an extra reason for looking for the best value (not necessarily price)…'

'…Hello Mr Max, We're currently out of stock at the Free Zone but an order is coming in this week. Due to the earthquake in Taiwan, the price of memory has increased dramatically and we were waiting to see if the price would level off after a while. Anyway, I should be able to quote you a price by the middle of the week and at that time give you all the specs on the system. I know our prices will be competitive and being a local company, our response time on warranty calls and technical support will be a lot faster.

Something else to consider is that maybe since the systems are for educational institutions, the government may grant you permission to purchase it in the Free Zone and bring it in to the country without paying the sales tax. I'll give you a call later today or tomorrow to discuss this further...'

'Hi Richard, I downloaded your two emails yesterday morning before leaving for one of the schools. It was one of those times when I received mail several hours before you sent it! We are seven hours behind you – one of the quirks in the way we organise things. I printed off your letter to Billy, put it in an envelope and delivered it at lunchtime. Billy was working, selling food at the border, so he would have got it last night...'

'...I sent off a package to you including 4 buddies and a letter of introduction from pupils in each form. The passports will follow on, along with a few odd letters from absent pupils etc. You will also see a letter from Kelly in year nine, who caught the post! I wonder if you can deliver her letter please. I have kept the names of the buddies a secret (well, that's my story!) but in the package you should find a) Lamb Chop from 7D for Calcutta School b) Ben (small bear) from 7G for Corozal Methodist School c) Tigger from 7H for St Pauls School d) Harry (the hedgehog) from 7R for Santa Rita School. I will gather together the buddy and letters from 7S for Ranchito as soon as I get back after the half term holiday. Along with these, I will pack the passports and stray letters. That seems to have got the ball rolling from this end - we will now await replies before starting our next piece... I intend to send emails to Calcutta and Corozal, and hope to write letters for the other schools as well...'

'...I can start delivering Buddies tomorrow. The package arrived at the post office at the same time as your email. I know that Ranchito sent their first package some time ago but that may be the only one at the moment. Schools are having a difficult time with too many interruptions (not curriculum!) Could you please encourage starting on next pieces before receiving replies. The mail is too slow otherwise. I know this from my own experience. I look forward to receiving the banner... I will do what I can for Kelly but there wasn't much to go on – not even her form! I looked her up in my files and find that she is in 9H which would be St. Paul's Anglican School. All things being equal, her partner will have moved on to high school or left. As she starts her letter 'Dear Friend in Belize' that will be difficult. Perhaps one of the younger children will remember her name...'

The last week of preliminary visits followed and the usual domestic activities took up most of the day on Saturday. I went to meet with Louisa at the workshop this afternoon and collected the documents I needed for Monday. My voucher had arrived which surprised me, and Corinth had sent back the story 'Home is the Belizoo'. What annoyed me was the message from David Eck that I mustn't use my bicycle to visit the schools. Now that he knows that I am doing it I suppose he has no choice because of the perceived danger involved (drivers on the main roads and violence on the others). What is most annoying is that someone (his sister-in-law at Chan Chen?) has to poke their nose in. He knows that I use spare money for schools. (I resolved that later and continued riding!) I took my small Sony recorder over for Ariola to use on Sunday morning and stayed there for breakfast. That was rather pleasant, especially as I had run out of eggs at home. Then more mail...

'...Attached is my up to date list of children and of letters received. Letters have not been received from those marked in italics... I have had a note from Mark, which I answered, but there was no letter for anyone at Calcutta School. Richard (7H) was not on your class list. I have retained your original and I am supplying schools with copies as attached. I hope to eventually have a list of who is writing to whom. St. Paul's Anglican School have had their letters and Buddy. The others will have theirs by Tuesday. I will write to each of the forms during the next week. Have you found partners for Zoila and Sheyla? They have not received anything. Is Hartley your own Buddy? We noticed the injury to his neck (rugby?). St. Paul's students are arranging surgery...'

'...I have been very busy with the new curriculum so my adventures have been fewer recently... The schools' 'Linking' is now in its third year and the last two of the five schools here will have their computer before Christmas. The email dimension of the link should be fully operational next term. Children still write to me from England as well, and I have the occasional letter from one that I haven't met...'

'...Thanks for the long email last week. I can never find so much to write. As far as the dogs you saw on your ride, I think I would have cycled as fast as I could! You had a busy weekend if you did two long rides on the same weekend...'

'...Our clocks don't change, as there is very little difference in the length of daylight through the year. When you read this we will be only six hours behind...'

'...We have had another tropical storm this week but the week has mostly been taken up with curriculum work that is on-going. The storm didn't develop into a hurricane, which is just as well because it came our way. The centre was over land too long for it to gain momentum. You probably know that the energy required for a hurricane to develop comes from the heat in the sea. Other conditions have to be right too, but that is where the energy comes from. Today, the weather has cleared after an unusual twenty four hours of rain…'

'…In fact the latest batch of mail has arrived for the Belize Schools from the new year 7 at SMCC. As this first package was sent to me I got to read the letters. Wonderful! Some of them are an absolute hoot and they still write about their teachers…'

'…I have some top quality passports to send on - will do so on Friday, along with Tigger. Yes, Hartley has seen some wars! I did find a writer for your 2 girls, but obviously they did not keep their promise to me! I will try again with some different ones. I should be getting everyone to write their own emails in the next week or two now that our system is ready. Some pupils have taken your and the schools' email addresses, and I am encouraging them all to write on their own initiative. I have had some work brought in to send in SPANISH!!! - So look out for that in the next parcel. I will 'fill in the gaps' from the 4 forms, and also send on work from 7S. Please encourage schools to send something from Belize…'

'…I cannot understand why you have not received a package from Ranchito Government (the new) school. I know that one was sent at the end of September and they will have sent their photos and more letters not long after. Perhaps it is in your school office as it is the first day back. The rest of the schools have been rather tardy. The biggest problem seems to be getting the package into the mail! I have even taken photos of all the students this year, quite some time ago, as I told you… Spanish is an interesting dimension; something else that I can write to year 7 about…'

November began with the first week of field testing Upper Division Outcomes, first at Santa Rita and Calcutta and the at the three Libertad schools. Travelling on the bus quickly became very tiresome. I had to go to the bank to cash a voucher cheque the first morning at Libertad and visit the Post Office. I went on to Libertad afterwards but I had to wait for an hour for a bus to the cut-off. I was lucky enough to get a lift with a local cane farmer from there and I joined with the Libertad taxi on the way back; arriving home just after five. The travelling was very tiresome again on Thursday when I had to go in to Corozal Nazarene School first. I was held up there because the Principal wasn't exactly early and I missed the 8:30 bus, thus having to wait over an hour for another one. Already, I am determined to go back to using my bicycle. Then for the third day running I had to wait for an hour for a bus despite being in time for the 7:30 which had gone early.

It had also become very clear in the first week that monitoring and all the necessary records for worthwhile assessment and feedback would be hugely demanding of time. This first round of visits to schools would last until the 3rd of December and be immediately followed with a two week curriculum workshop in Language Arts for the Upper Division. This side of Christmas there would otherwise be time only for the schools' link and correspondence.

I delivered Caledonia photos for Ricardo and Marbella and did a bit of shopping on Saturday but as this was a very wet day I travelled on the bus and declined a trip to Chetumal. Whether it was the rain which continued or my mood, I started Sunday by spilling my breakfast all over the floor but this was soon cleared up and I was able to get on with some writing. The first activity was to catch up with the monitoring notes for the week thinking that I must get back to completing my journal each day as much is being missed out – and always mail…

'…Yes I am busy and I am well thank you, although I have been unduly tired over the last couple of weeks. I am now trying to catch up with some of the things I have 'left undone'. The whole business of encouraging nineteen schools into progress and development by their own initiative is pretty demanding…' – but there is a big plus on the computer front…

'…Hello Mr Max, Please excuse the delay in getting these prices to you. Also, please note that if you pay for the system in U.S. currency, it will be a little cheaper. This is due to the fact that transactions in the Free Zone are done in U.S. currency & the businesses have to pay a high exchange rate to get this U.S. currency. It might benefit if you got the U.S. yourself…'

'…Hi Douglas thanks for the prices. It looks fine to me and there shouldn't be any problem. Financially, I need only sort out the details of sales tax and exchange rates. I will be able to check how far the building security arrangements have progressed at the two schools next week… It may be possible to buy three sets, given favourable conditions with regard to exchange and tax. I have St. Pauls Anglican School in mind. They have my old 486 as you know. In any case, that machine would benefit from some attention…'

New energy stirred into a four page email letter; the first to the new year-seven and combining the experiences and exchanges previously learned adding a word picture of Ranchito as the fifth school.

Monitoring continued with a first such visit to Calcutta. The weather cleared up sufficiently for me to take my bicycle which meant that I was able to go along to San Joaquin at lunchtime to collect the cross-stitch from Grandfather Puk, destined as a gift to send home, and get back to riding my bike to schools. This was important as I had reached agreement that allowances would still be paid for transport and meals away from Corozal Town to be used towards funds for computers. Many such journeys would otherwise have to be by taxi and friends at the schools provided meals; they all knew!

I returned home from San Antonio Government School on a very wet Wednesday which decimated the school population, to find an email from Paul in answer to my one of this morning. He had an immediate answer to that!

'7S buddy is in the post - and is called 'Andrex'; also enclosed are a few stray 7S letters, plus another Spanish offering from Rachel…

'…must be a puppy dog; they won't get the point of that here but I'll tell them if it is… Cathy Alfaro who was at St. Paul's and now at High School wishes to re-establish contact with (your) Cathy and needs her address...'

Later in the afternoon I talked with Louisa and found that the date of the Upper Division Workshop had been changed. There had been some complaint from Pilot School staffs that it was not fair especially to Standard 6 students that they should be sent home and miss two weeks schooling from 6th-17th December.

As a result, the Permanent Secretary, Minister of Education and Chief Education Officer together have decided that the workshop should be held from 27th –30th Dec and 3rd – 8th January! The staff would be given the last two weeks of the summer term in lieu so the students would still miss two weeks of schooling and now have a twelve week summer holiday. The more I see of the decisions taken and the manner in which they are taken, the more convinced I am that the country is out of rational control. Also, there had been no Spanish Workshop last Saturday. It was just as well I didn't go because no-one bothered to tell me again. Apparently there was no money for it. This week money has been found and all the schools have to be told once again that the workshop will take place next Saturday.

On Thursday Christian School, Assemblies of God at Santa Rita had been broken into and all sorts of things thrown around. This included the package for 7R and the contents spoiled so letters etc. had to be done again. The class produced a letter of explanation, which I sent for them by email at lunchtime. Early this morning I had discussions with Joe Martinez to engage his help in the purchase of the three computers through the Free Zone, without paying taxes. I will now write a formal request. It was announced today, that we have had ten inches of rain in five days across Belize.

I had again forgotten that the out of town Government schools all have a half day on Friday; Paraiso now. This meant that I could only use the morning for classroom observation and the meeting was held from 10:00am until 10:30am. Of course, schools could also be proactive in making arrangements, particularly because I have made it quite clear to everyone that meeting times are to suit the school and not to suit me. I returned home in time for lunch.

'…Dear Friends in Year 7 All your packages have now left Belize; well, Corozal at least! 7S are the lucky ones because the third package has just left and the class at Ranchito have all sorts of plans for more. Ironically, they are the only students here, that haven't yet received a package from you. I guess that is Murphy's Law. Together with this letter are three sets of notes about Corozal that you may find interesting.

My file names for them are Corozal Town, Janet Town and N Corozal History. Acquiring the material is a story in itself. The museum is right by the sea between St. Paul's Anglican School and Corozal Methodist School, which are about five minutes' walking apart. The site is right on what is probably the most historic spot in the town. There is a stone pier right by the building where ships used to come and go from Mexico and the area had a number of important buildings around in the Colonial days. Many of these are now ruined or at least dilapidated but the area remains very attractive and the museum building is splendid. The structure is typical Victorian cast iron pillars and roof in the style of English fish markets. It is much less ornate but I was immediately reminded of the Barbican market in Plymouth when I saw it. The walls have long been built to fill the space and enclose the building but it is very attractive and its copper-green roof is a landmark from the sea and right along the coast. I had a lot of fun retyping the information because the language was rather quaint and I didn't want to change too much of it as the way it has been written has a history of its own. The current Librarian, who put the notes together from a collection of other notes, is a Spanish speaker and her English is different anyway. If one of you would like to do something for Corozal Town, it is thought that the libraries in England must have information on the birth of Corozal Town and the wars hereabouts. It would make a nice little project and would earn the eternal gratitude of the people of the town. I have tried to do it from here and failed...'

'...Hi Douglas, It would best suit Ranchito Government School to have a system installed by the opening of their Library on 24th November. I will try to hurry up the proceedings with regard to charges and exchange rates...'

I tried cycling out to the river estuary in the middle of the day on Sunday. I believe that I must have got fairly close but I didn't go all the way. I turned back where the forest really starts to thicken and the track narrows right down. At this point I felt particularly uncomfortable because the whole area is very remote and gives cover for anyone lurking every inch of the way. I had seen no one for several miles but I could see tracks recently made in the mud. In fact, I felt more vulnerable in this area than anywhere I have been and it is the first time I have turned back for that reason – although there are other places that I wouldn't go to a second time. The experience was otherwise very rewarding and interesting.

Animals are not obviously active during the middle of the day but there was a lot of movement in the bush. Much of this would probably be birds or larger lizards. What I did see were a lot of butterflies and large flying insects, storks and egrets; also orchids and lizards.

Part of the route crosses a very flat area with water flowing across it in what appear to be drainage channels. There are plank bridges across each of these that are not easy to negotiate on a bicycle. It also looks as though there must have been attempts to make some sort of facility there for bringing things in from the sea although this only amounts to hard, straight areas on the ground and openings stretching out towards the sea. There has been a plan to open up the route this way, to Sarteneja, via a ferry at the river mouth. I don't know whether this would come to anything. It is a long way and would be an expensive project. It would be an even more dangerous route to take if robbery was likely to be a more attractive prospect.

'...When do you think I should send Aner's Christmas present to get there on time...'

'...I would give a good four weeks for the mail coming this way for Aner. It is only people in town who have their mail delivered. Someone from Aner's family would have to go to the Post Office and that adds to the delay, especially at a busy time. I think that the lack of delivery is one of the ways mail gets 'lost'. The Post Office only keeps things for a limited time if a family doesn't check regularly. On the other hand, there are a lot of Manzanillas in Paraiso and some have a telephone; the Post Offices use that when they can...'

'...Many thanks for the Universal Postal union stamps that arrived yesterday...'

'...I'm really pleased about the stamps. If any more are issued before I leave Belize I can use the same system. I got the form from the Post Office here in Corozal and then phoned Belize City to see if it can be done. I don't often go down there as it is not easy to get to and you can have a lot of hassle in the streets 'Downtown'. (That is not too much now as I guess I look as though I 'belong' by now.) The bonus is that it must be a nice way to receive them...'

'...So the end is in sight for your Belize adventure. It sounds as if it has all been a great success both as regards the work achieved and on a personal level. And with the links you have established with South Molton, it will be an on-going affair even after you have left. You say that you have applied for another posting. What are the options this time?' ...

'...I went out to Santa Rita today but Aner has gone to stay with relatives in Orange Walk for the week. I spoke with one of his sisters who said that he has only had the one letter that I took out for you. It would seem that no-one has been to the Post Office as I feared. Hopefully, they will now. I'll let you know. I don't mind delivering at all but it is obviously better to get your mail going independently. Mail is collected regularly by the school...'

I am having considerable problems with the charges levied on buying the computers in the Free Zone. District Education Officer, Joe Martinez tried the Treasury in Belize City and drew a blank with the exchange of dollars but is working on the taxes and charges. Mark Wright suggested that I might try for dollars for holiday at the Treasury.

'...There were some delighted Year 7's yesterday - keeping very close to their buddies...'

'...The school that sent the whole class of Buddies is the new one, the fifth. Actually, it is a pretty exciting time with the 'Link' for all sorts of reasons, not the least of which has to do with computers, Internet and email. I have managed to earn some extra money while I have been here and am about to purchase computers for each of the remaining schools that don't have one. Before Christmas, all schools should be talking to each other direct! I'm sure that you will imagine that there have been many obstacles to overcome in enabling youngsters to become friends and learn about each other. Hopefully, by the time I finish here in June the project should be enduring. Isn't it fun to imagine that those Buddies came from young people so far away in culture and lifestyle as well as distance and handled through life just as your own?... Lastly for now: I have a really splendid sailing ship made locally from zericote hardwood. I had to buy it because I like it so, and now it wants a home. I thought that it might go rather well with the plaque and your periodic display in the library. The ship is about two feet high and about two feet six inches long. It has three masts and sixteen sails all magnificently carved. If you think the school would like it you can have it and I will send it right away. (I will make a drawing and number all the parts for you to put it back together again – all push fit!)...'

The Treasury idea didn't work. Marco is trying Atlantic Bank to support Education. I arranged to purchase three sets including printers anyway.

Thursday: Orvin Rancheran called in the evening with my invitation to the Inauguration Ceremony at Ranchito Community Library when I will be presenting a computer to the school. Part of the rest of the evening was spent writing the few words I intend to say.

Friday, being Garifuna Settlement Day is a Public Holiday. Apart from a walk round the town, I spent most of the day pottering about and writing. The weather has continued to be cooler, in the low eighties and much less humid. This is due to a cold front that is also keeping Hurricane Lennie at bay, at the other end of the Caribbean and heading north.

I started Saturday by doing some washing and shopping and waiting for water and beer. The wonderful weather has continued but shortage of time demands preparation so no outing. I wrote up 'A Story for Christmas' and packed some of my Christmas presents.

The story was inspired by The Beach Boys' 'I Get Around' and the Tetley advert for their round tea bags, originally written for the children at my old school, and to be read while listening to the music...

A Story for Christmas

George the Snail was so pleased. He was so pleased that he couldn't remember being quite so pleased ever in his life before. And the reason he was so pleased was because he had been asked to do a very special job. He had been asked to do a very special job by a Very Special Person. That Very Special Person was none other than Father Christmas and the very special job was to deliver presents on Christmas Eve.

George wasn't quite sure how it had come about that he was talking to Father Christmas, or how it was that Father Christmas had come to need his help. What he did remember was that he had written down his present list, put it in an envelope, sealed the envelope down, put 'To Father Christmas' on the front, and tucked it under the plate of mince pies he had left with a nice refreshing drink for his very special visitor in the night. After that he had felt all warm and comfortable – as if life had always been like that. And then, there **He** was smiling in **front** of him. The Very Special Person was asking him to do the very special job.

And what was the very special job? You may well ask; George did. And this is what the Very Special Person said:

"George my boy, I have got a very special job for you. I have heard from my Christmas Present Scouts that some children are planning to stay awake to try to see me deliver their presents. This will not do. No! This simply will not do! I need your help!"

"Gosh!" said George. Then George said "Gosh!" and then "Gosh!" again.
When George had stopped saying 'Gosh' for quite a long time and it looked as if Father Christmas was going to speak again, George suddenly had a thought.

"Gosh!" said George (again), "How can I help? If children stay awake to see you - and you are so quick, they will surely see me. I am a snail. And I am – OOOH – so – slow!"

"That's the whole point!" said Father Christmas, "You've got it in one. They **will** see you **because** you are so slow!"

"Oh!" said George, "I see!"

Well, George didn't see of course. In fact George didn't see at all. But, fortunately, Father Christmas went on to explain. "You see George," (and George at this point, did his best to see, to look intelligent and opened his eyes – very, very wide) "You see George the children who stay awake **will see you** George, and then… And then… You know what they will think, don't you George?" Father Christmas waited.

"No!" said George.

"Yes you do!" boomed on the mighty voice, before George could answer, "Yes you do! They will think that Father Christmas is a **SNAIL!"**

At this point Father Christmas started to shake. First it was his boots. Next a quiver up his legs, which spread until his body wobbled. His shoulders heaved up and down. His neck swelled. He threw his head backwards, opened his great mouth wide and gave out the most tremendous laugh. It was a gale of a laugh that went on and on. Father Christmas put his hands on his hips and laughed and laughed and laughed. He rolled his body round and bent double with the joy of it, and rocked and rocked and rocked on his heels.

When he could speak again and the tears of laughter had rolled away down his cheeks so that he could see George once more, he went on….

"And you know what will happen then don't you my boy?" he giggled, "They will go and tell their friends – **FATHER CHRISTMAS IS A SNAIL!"**

Now it was George's turn to laugh. A real belly laugh it was. So much so that his shell leaped up and down and back and forth violently, making a booming sound which joined with Father Christmas' voice until it sounded as though they were a wild orchestra making gales of mirth and music together. George spluttered - and through tears of merriment, managed to say "And all their friends will think them daft!" At this, Father Christmas became suddenly serious. "Serve them right," he whispered.

"Now George, we'd better be getting on; lots to do my boy, lots to do. You can use the mini-sleigh and some of those small plastic sacks (bags really) that the supermarkets put frozen food in. We don't want to give those children much anyway. Oh! – There are no spare reindeer. See what you can find in the workshop. There are plenty of tools and materials. Help yourself. I'll call at **your** house myself of course. 'Bye for now." And with a cheery wave, Father Christmas was gone.

George went into the workshop wondering what to do. Now fortunately, George was a very practical snail and had a lot of common sense. He had a special kind of common sense that doesn't seem to be common at all.

What he wanted was something to get around on; something strong and reliable; something different; something imaginative; something fitting to the idea that Father Christmas was a snail. It would have to be able to pull the sleigh of course, and it would have to be able to go in all directions as well as up and down; something like a jump jet but not so big and certainly not so noisy. No, certainly not so noisy! It had to be silent. Something to get around on… George stood in the workshop and thought. Something to get around on… George turned his head around, looking for inspiration. Something to get around on… George looked around. "What am I doing?" he thought. "Around… yes that's it… Around! I don't know why no one has thought of it before. It needs to be a round… A round, round rider… around the houses… Getting around… **Getting around!**

Oh the joy of it; the getting around started right away. And the giggling and laughing came back. George was really getting around now. He was rushing around. His shell leaped up and down and back and forth violently, making a booming sound again, which seemed to join with Father Christmas' voice in the distance - an echo of delight.

The final creation was delightfully simple. It was round like a saucer and bulged out underneath and on top. It was much like two saucers fitted edge to edge in fact, - only smaller. It was snail size!

In the top and bottom surfaces were holes; lots of holes; lots and lots of holes; but an exact number of holes. It had to be right. And the holes were all the same size, exactly the same size – and round – absolutely round. It was a very finely engineered piece of work!

George filled the inside of the 'Getting-Around Round Rider' – as he called it – with his special fuel. It was a very precise amount of specially prepared fuel. And he tried it out.

There was a brief pause and then, issuing from each of the holes, came a powerful jet of steaming brown liquid. It had to be liquid to be as quiet as it needed to be. Everyone knows that holes with gas coming out are noisy. They are far too noisy for comfort. George operated his thought lever. Immediately, the jets were controlled and the 'Getting-Around Round Rider' shot off and then back again as George used his thought lever in reverse.

All was ready. George loaded up the tiny, yucky plastic sacks and hitched up the sleigh. And off he went into the dark blue, starlit sky. What fun it all was! Zooming round! A round, round rider! Around the houses,

Getting around! **Getting around!**

Each of the visits to the wide-awake children was much the same. The only difference was the way they pretended to be asleep. Some peeped from underneath the bedclothes. Some hid behind their fingers or squinted between their eyelids. It was the squints that were the worst. George could see a squint from fifty megastars distance away. Of course, there were also those who wriggled about so that you can't see their eyes.

"Silly children," thought George. "If only they knew what I know!"
Each of the children saw him. Each of the children saw him leave the awful plastic sack. Each of the children gave a little, muffled shriek. Each of the children fainted.

George had really got around at last. His shell leaped up and down and back and forth again, violently, making that booming sound, which seemed to join once more with Father Christmas' voice in the distance - the echo of delight.

Then the sound faded; became confused. A new sound filled the air; a steaming, gurgling sound. George turned – around and around – until he saw, there beside his bed, a shining new machine with a clock on it, and a little bird shrieking cuckoo, cuck**OO, CUCKOO**, as loud as it could go. Steam was rising. The air was filled with the feeling that something terrific was about to happen. A strange object approached, zooming and hovering by turns. It was round like a saucer and bulged out underneath and on top. It was much like two saucers fitted edge to edge in fact, - only smaller. It was snail size!

In the top and bottom surfaces were holes; lots of holes; lots and lots of holes; but an exact number of holes; very precise. And the holes were all the same size, exactly the same size – and round – absolutely round. It was a very finely engineered piece of work!

The object stopped over the machine and dropped right in. There was a pause and there it was; just what George had always wanted when he first woke up in the mornings.

He laughed and the laughter came back at him. Father Christmas was laughing too. Children were shouting and a merry tune was heard. Words and music floated on the air.

"Father Christmas, Father Christmas is a snail! Father Christmas is a snail and he rides around. Father Christmas is a snail and he rides around **ON A TEA BAG!**

"Don't be daft!" said George, quietly, "And go to sleep!"

I splashed out and bought some 'deer meat' for Sunday. They don't call it venison here. Similarly, mutton and lamb are lumped together as 'sheep meat'. Anyway, I thawed it in the fridge overnight and started it in a fruit base marinade with a range of herbs and spices and plenty of finely sliced garlic, from early this morning. Around lunchtime I put it in the fridge to make it cold and added a bottle of beer with the intention of cooking for a dinner at about eight this evening. It is cooking right now and smells gorgeous.

The pulses are breaking down in a separate pan so as not to muddy the flavours. That was the plan. However, the ladies in the other house have taken it into their heads to feed me on Sundays! I don't know how many times it has happened now but I had just put the beer into the pan and it was frothing beautifully when a voice called up "Mr Max!" There was my dinner again, at about half past one! Pork and rice and beans with creamed potato, sliced tomato and plantain. Good Belizean fare and Lucille is an excellent cook.

The plate was well loaded so my present cooking will have to be cooled and saved for tomorrow because I couldn't eat any more. I don't get any warning. It just arrives. I think that I am supposed to expect it but it is very nice to be like that and much appreciated. (I have just had a taste of the meat. I wish I was hungry!) Writing would be a good distraction…

'…I have received the rest of the money for completing the study and I have managed to put together a larger sum than I expected. The whole thing has grown steadily since I first decided that it would be good for me to have email and I scratched around to buy the 486 computer. I intend to buy three computers so that all five schools will have new, powerful and up to date machines… I have managed to short cut all the funding problems in respect of Ranchito School, because I know the supplier. Their equipment will be installed on Monday or Tuesday in time for the inauguration of the Community and School Library on Wednesday. All the local 'big wigs' will be there and I am to make what Belizeans call 'Remarks'. Three Ministers and the Principal Education Officer will also be making their 'Remarks' and one of the Ministers is the Guest Speaker. These things usually go on forever. Belizeans are great talkers and this especially applies to Ministers or any other speakers when Ministers are present. The speeches always start with a great long list of acknowledgement of those present!

I didn't attend the VSO conference. That was for VSO Directors. But Mark was very pleased with his presentation of my Impact Study. He says that they were all discussing a possible approach to the research that VSO are looking for, before his presentation. Then he was able to get up and say "We have done that in Belize!" Anyway, people took copies away with them and it has gone to London so I suppose it is getting spread about a bit. It was fun…'

'…I don't think that I told you that there are bananas and papaya growing in the yard as well as coconuts. The bananas are delicious. They are yellow and creamy tasting. Plantain, by the way, is like a banana but it is much harder and you cook it. That is delicious as well. Oranges, melons of different kinds and mangoes are very plentiful, with a whole string of other fruits eaten fresh or turned into drinks. What Belizeans crave for is apples. They are obtainable, from the States, but they are very expensive and tasteless. You buy them one for a dollar (I don't!)… …The computer position at your school has been frustrating but access from so many with only two schools on line here might have brought its own problems. It is also difficult for schools here when there is only one keyboard and the computer is not in the classroom. As it is, it should all be up and running for next term…'

I started off by going to the District office before going to Corozal Nazarene School on Monday morning to find out how Joe Martinez had got on with customs and the computer charges. Now I have to have a letter from each of the three Principals stating that the computers would be used solely for educational purposes and some sort of notary declaration. Crazy! I went on my bike and brought back a big box for packing Christmas presents to send by post. I then phoned QADS and left David Eck in no doubt about my feelings over his total lack of communication (even Ellajean never had that problem – just late), messing about with dates that upsets all our arrangements with schools, the total absence of all the promised tasks that brought me back on extension and his lack of courtesy over riding my bike. Package arrived containing Tigger, passports and new letters for all schools but Assemblies.

'…Here is the promised ship! I have enclosed a diagram to help with assembly but here is a written description as well… Tomas Gilharry is the carver. He lives in San Antonio village, which is just out of town. It is the next village to Santa Rita where the school is that links with 7R. Children of the same (huge) family are in the three years that have linked. Anyway, he had discovered the times when I sit out on my balcony, enjoying a rum and coke and gazing out beyond the beach across the sunlit Caribbean Sea, feeling at peace with the world. A soft touch! I had already bought several carvings from him for presents when he obviously decided it was time to go for the big one! He 'sailed' by on his bike, waving it in the air, and that was it…'

'…I am pleased to report that all 5 forms have now received a package. Great stuff! The only immediate problems are… If you could do anything to help, it would be much appreciated. Pupils are already writing back - either to you, to the schools, or to individual addresses. I will post a package on Friday…'

'…I will check on the various shortages. I have had to jolly Calcutta (7D) along this year but I expect it will settle down. In the meantime, I will write to those who haven't had letters myself when I can… Now the bad news: your own Buddy, Hartley has met with an accident. The boy who took him home will tell you about it himself. He was distraught and initially didn't come to school. I believe Valerie Rogers had to fetch him. I have opened all of that up with him and his class so that he knows you would most appreciate hearing from him and how he feels and in that way giving of himself. That is how friends are made. I'm sorry it happened but I guess you will feel for the kid much as I do – and he had taken Hartley home and was caring for him…'

It was interesting talking with Florencio Marin at Ranchito Community Library Inauguration Ceremony. I told him about the problems I am having with taxes and changing money for the computers. He simply said "When you are ready to buy, come to me and I will fix it!" Of course, that is not what I wanted him to do. I have no wish to be even in that kind of debt to him. Ministers here like to be 'fixing' everything because they like to have all the 'control'. What I wanted him to do was take steps to ensure that others would not face the same problems that I have done. In consequence, I will continue to try to find a way for myself.

Ranchito Library

Friends, a Library is a window on the World. It is a means of sharing the thoughts of mankind, not merely the thoughts of today but thinking over thousands of years. Without those thoughts we have no future. A Library is a means of learning from each other. It was with the same idea of learning from each other that I came to Belize over two years ago.

On a professional level, I have continued to make friends and learn with teachers and students - as a Volunteer - throughout that time. On a personal level, it has been my great joy that over one hundred and twenty Belizean youngsters each year, and an equal number in England, have also been making friends and learning from each other. Four schools in Corozal have been involved for two years. In this third year Ranchito Government School has become the fifth. That is a total of over four hundred youngsters across the World!

Regular mail is rather slow and it was obvious that communication would be enhanced through the use of email and the Internet. The same technology provides a revolution in the access to information, word processing and data handling. A great bonus in the facility enjoyed by any School or Community Library – or both! With those thoughts in mind it is my great pleasure to present their first computer to Ranchito Government School.

It took some time to make sure that everything had been done ready for the weekend and to pack and post the gifts. I had to delay my departure until the 6:00pm Premier, which got me into Belize City at about 8:15. Actually, the bus was more like a regular bus except that it had more comfortable seats and it only stopped in Orange Walk. Needless to say, there was food and welcome when I arrived.

Las Cuevas

'Las Cuevas', the caves in English, seemed almost the stuff of legend. There was an exciting visit in prospect that I had almost given up. Access is difficult and expensive, set against limited resources. The prospect opened up when an ex VSO friend announced that he knew the manager of the 'Field Centre'. A visiting party was being arranged with transport provided, and at a modest cost. There would be two whole days and nights in the Rainforest.

The idea was that just five of us would travel in to the site on Friday to be joined by the other sixteen, making a party of twenty-one, late on Saturday. Our five would consist of two ex VSO friends, two Belizean friends and me. The others would all be VSO or ex-pat, all non-Belizeans anyway. I have mostly avoided the VSO excursions because I came to live in Belize with local people and have made many friends that way. In company mainly with other Europeans I feel somewhat detached from all that I came to learn, to do and to share. Jack and Nik, the two ex VSOs have been here a long time, they are taking Belizean Citizenship, and Marco and Miriam are of 'the Family' wherein I am 'adopted'. As Belizeans do not arrange such visits for themselves, this one was ideal.

A meeting that I was to attend had been arranged at the Ministry of Education on the Thursday. This is in Belize City where the Family live, eighty-four miles South of my home in Corozal Town. I arranged to stay with the Family overnight and travel on to visit the VSO office in Belmopan on Friday. Belmopan is on the way to Las Cuevas and combined with having to be in Belize City on Friday, this gave good reason for effectively taking the day off. All went well until the Tuesday previous, when a message came to say that the meeting on Thursday had been cancelled and there would be a second one on Friday! (How can there be a second one when the first one hasn't happened?) This sort of thing happens with monotonous regularity in the Ministry I work for and invariably coincides with some arrangement of mine so I was less than pleased, cross even! When I checked what the meeting was all about I found that it was more to serve the power games that go on rather than advance the work I do so I was morally as well as materially prepared to resist!

"I can't come!" I said on the phone, "I have to meet with my VSO Director". I explained all the arrangements I had made to connect my meeting with him with the Thursday meeting, now cancelled; all this into a silent 'phone.

"But we need your input!" 'I don't need your output.' I thought, but replied, "Sorry!" "Well, come for the beginning of the meeting." "Okay!" I said. I had expected more negotiation than this before reaching the planned outcome but there it was, back in business!

I travelled down on Thursday almost as planned, but later, and stayed over with the Family. Marco, Miriam and I arranged to travel to Belmopan and meet with Jack, leaving at 10:00am. I was at the office for 8:00am and the 8:30 meeting started at 9:15 and I left at 9:45 after carefully avoiding making any input. I was back in time but needless to say, Marco was not ready (Belize Time is an interesting phenomenon, a subject in itself) but that gave me time to go to the bank to get some money and to order a new chequebook. We left just after eleven!

To be fair, I was at fault here. I hadn't thought of what it would mean to Marco and Miriam to have never made a visit of this kind before. They were concerned as to what to pack and I should have anticipated that. Anyway, the journey of 54 miles was very comfortable in Marco's first and recently acquired vehicle; a Chevvy of generous proportions and a lively 'personality' complete with armchair seating. Arriving in Belmopan, we met up with Jack and Nik. My calling in to VSO only took a few minutes (It had to be done though!) and we left for Las Cuevas with Chapal, a member of their staff who picked us up at about 1:30pm, with a Land Rover. In San Ignacio, some fifteen miles away, we met with the Manager of Las Cuevas at his house and then began the long and rough journey to the site in the Chiquibul Forest in a big, four-wheel drive pickup truck. There were five seats in the cab. Chapal drove with his wife beside him. She was cook for the weekend. Marco and I sat behind with Miriam between us, and Nik and Jack sat in the open space at the back. It must have been a rough ride for them. I often turned round to see them hanging on for dear life or ducking to avoid tree branches or flung mud as we bounced and slithered along. The four-wheel drive had to be engaged quite frequently, especially when we penetrated deeper in to the forest. It was the first time I had encountered a four-wheel drive automatic! That part of the journey was over fifty miles of very rough territory made up of the Mountain Pine Ridge Forest Reserve followed by Broadleaf Rainforest. The River Macal neatly separates the two areas of flora. We stopped on what in Devon might almost be a Clapper Bridge to gaze in awe at the contrast of one side with the other, the stark then softened beauty of so many trees. The whole journey from Corozal had been over two hundred miles. We passed through Cristo Rey, San Antonio and Douglas Da Silva Camp before dropping down to cross the Macal River and arrived to find welcome food prepared in advance, and good accommodation. Chapal's wife then set about preparing the evening meal.

Las Cuevas is a research centre deep in the Chiquibul Forest Reserve, operated jointly by the Natural History Museum in London and the Government of Belize. The objectives have as much to do with sustainable management, conservation and natural development together.

The visitor centre has to be self-funding. The British Army built the accommodation block complete with showers. It is of timber construction with a galvanised roof and obviously built to last. As with most such buildings it is constructed on timber struts some eight feet above the ground. With only two sets of steps up it is detached from inquisitive or opportunist animals and free of snakes. Tarantulas and scorpions rather like the shelter so it is a good habit to check bags before use and shoes and clothes before putting them on. You don't just jump into bed in the jungle. Netting over the windows helps and it keeps out most of the mosquitos but is by no means exclusive. There is generous accommodation for twenty-four visitors, mostly in twin bedded rooms. The male and female washrooms each have showers supplied with hot water facilitated by an electricity supply generated by a twin Lister diesel set located at a discrete distance in the forest. The whole block has a wonderful veranda all the way round it and the building situated in a large cleared space making observation of the surrounding forest through binoculars, very easy indeed.

It is difficult to describe the peace of just sitting there watching; so few of us in so remote a place. I am not one to sit doing nothing and it certainly wasn't like that. The ever-changing light, the distant sounds clearly carried on the still calm air, the occasional animal, the birds and the insects were a symphony in light and sound, of the life in the trees. The evening was spent watching wildlife. There must have been four or five hundred parrots on the wing at sundown, making a great and glorious din. There were also Scarlet Macaws and the big green parrots as well as a pair of Toucans. The colours were amazing in the dying sun. A jaguar crossed the open site at about 8:00pm, causing much excitement, and the barking sound of the puma was heard. Later, we could hear Howler Monkeys bellowing to each other across considerable distances. Many hours were passed in this all-absorbing way, with occasional comment, good food digesting and a glass of good cheer to hand. We all slept well that night after checking beds for unwelcome visitors that might have resented our arrival, of course!

First thing on the Saturday morning the birds returned. I was up before the dawn, which was at 5:15am. The parrots returned the other way and toucans, green parrots and scarlet macaws all performed during the day. All the big birds obligingly sat on open branches of trees for very long periods so that they could be watched through binoculars at almost any time during the day. I also spent a fascinating half-hour watching a fox, much smaller than ours, with the aid of the binoculars. He was a beautiful dog fox and I watched as he caught a black snake, a racer, and didn't seem to know quite what to do with it.

In the morning we went into the caves, Las Cuevas that had already been explored to a distance of five kilometres or three miles. They are known to go much further than that and a connection has recently been discovered that goes right into Guatemala. (Is this a forthcoming underground customs post?) The caves are enormous. Many of the stalactites and stalagmites are muddy looking but otherwise unspoiled and very large (15-18ft). Some of the colours derived from impurities are quite spectacular. We were not able to go in very far with our limited equipment that amounted to little more than a few torches and reasonably suitable clothing. A string was in evidence right from the start; a testament to the complexity of the system. I didn't take many photographs and I didn't take the video camera at all. The experience and the atmosphere is not only difficult to describe, it is difficult to capture on film as well. The few pictures I did take were an attempt to suggest the majesty of the World that our sophisticated living tends to hide.

The entrance to the cave system is a yawning black chasm emphasised at first sight by two miniscule figures standing on the edge of darkness with their backs to bright sunlight. The whole thing seems to make little sense at a casual observation since the land is quite high, situated as it is behind the Maya Mountains. How, one might wonder, was there sufficient elevation for water to carve out such a huge and invasive space into the ground? Inside it is even bigger, defying the laws of physics and preparing on some geological time scale, to become yet another dramatic 'sink-hole'. Looking back at the cave entrance, the soaring forest trees are made to look small by the near perfect arched rock. Inside, swallows flit silently to and fro, no doubt feasting on an excess of insects swarming there. Even so large a space is soon lost to sight. There are many side chambers and evidence of occupation but the complexity of underground space is not one for modern man without some sort of navigational aid or return markers, and powerful lamps. The Maya used them freely.

New caves have been discovered, which have untouched Mayan artefacts in them. There is restricted and expensive access to these but I do hope to see them. Outside, there is the remains of an ancient Maya road that leads directly to the cave entrance. Obviously this natural shelter was well used although it is a long way from the ancient city of Caracol.

Next we made a short treck through the forest and climbed a hill on top of which is an observation tower that reaches well above the forest canopy. The view was tremendous. Victoria Peak could clearly be seen despite a morning mist that was still hanging around. I didn't take my camera at all at this point either because photos of the forest canopy and forest covered mountains do not give a true impression of their scale. We saw a Brockets deer grazing, close up, and a couple of snakes on the way out and found a tapir print in the mud on the way back. In the afternoon I went on a forest trail with Jack and Nik. This was mostly directed at looking at the enormous variety of trees and other vegetation - all green at the end of November! And it was hot! I was in the lead and keeping a careful look out for snakes, particularly the yellow head Tommygoff. This snake can move faster than a man can run and is able to launch itself through the air. Often around eight feet long it is one of the most deadly snakes in the World and able to hide very well. Mostly, it would keep out of the way like most snakes but clumsiness or carelessness gains no reward. It is said that the first person alerts it, the second annoys it and the third gets it. On that basis, the front was not a bad place to be!

The five of us all felt, and discussed later, the intense irritation at the arrival of the rest of the party in the late afternoon. Nothing against our fellows but like all such groups, they seemed inward looking and nothing like as aware of the surroundings as we felt ourselves to be. All things relative of course! It would take a lifetime to be truly at one with it all. Chapal is Mayan born and has spent much of his life in the forest. He would slip away in a manner known only in your dreams.

At dusk the birds were again on the wing and the howler monkeys started calling to each other. Much of the evening was spent listening to the bark of a puma and the weaker, answering bark of the young that had evidently strayed some distance away. Eventually the barks became one as the family were reunited.

Early on Sunday morning after witnessing the dawn chorus once again, our little party of five set off separately again on a visit to the Mayan site at Caracol and the thousand-foot waterfall. The first part of the route took us inevitably, back towards the river. Before reaching there, we turned left along a slightly less demanding track to the South West and reached the site somewhat shaken up, after rather more than an hour.

Caracol is the largest known ancient Maya site in Belize. The best known, most developed and most visited Maya site is at Tikal in Guatemala, fifty miles away. Caracol was only discovered in 1937 but it is now known that it was larger than Tikal and home to as many as 100,000 Mayan people - nearly half the present population of the country of Belize! It is also believed that Caracol, in its day, conquered Tikal! The name means 'snail shell' in Spanish and was given on its discovery. Like most sites, it is not the Mayan name. There are, however, many snail shells to be found there. The site covers 1,120 acres and the ceremonial centre that I mainly saw is about half that size. Caana, The Sky Palace, is now known to be Belize's tallest building, rising 127ft above the main plaza. The view from the top is equally spectacular. It is only partially excavated and barely restored so that much flora and fauna flourishes within its walls. Nonetheless, some of the detail can be seen. Some parts have been 'opened up' and treasures found that have been placed in the archives in Belmopan for want of anything better to do with them. Little in the way of Stella remains on the site. A model at the entrance to the site shows what the main complex is thought to have been like.

Although Caracol is ten miles to the West of Las Cuevas and more than twice that by the trail we had to use, it is still in the Chiquibul Forest Reserve and National Park. Mammoth cotton trees, the Ceiba held sacred by the ancient Maya, compete with the temples of Caracol for dominance of the jungle landscape.

Only the efforts of archaeologists have driven back some of the conquering trees. Osculated turkeys are common at the site, bands of howler monkeys loudly proclaim their territory and tapirs are known to graze the open spaces and plazas around the great mounds.

Our last journey of adventure was over about forty more miles of Forest Reserve and Mountain Pine Ridge over steadily improving track. There is a left fork before the British Army training area at Cooma Cairn that marks a track that ends abruptly at the edge of a spectacular canyon, Hidden Valley, where the Thousand Foot Fall, as it is known, cascades into the dense rainforest below. There is a small parking space and a viewing platform built out from the precipitous edge. The fall is actually 1,600ft and is the highest waterfall in Central America. Standing gazing out from the platform over the scene, one might imagine the spectacular falls in the Alps but not so. The temperature is in the eighties even up there. The water looks much the same and the spray but what is really different are the trees. Rainforest trees are everywhere. They are at the bottom certainly, but they are at the top as well. And they cling to the sheer rock face all the way up, obliterating most of the rock from view; a great soft green surround to the majesty and timelessness of falling water.

It is pointless to describe the journey back, dominated as it was by experience. I only had to return to Belize City to stay overnight in good company and return home by bus on Monday morning. Monitoring curriculum progress in schools seemed somehow different then!

Having stayed over with the family, I went with Marco to the Atlantic Bank first thing on Monday morning, to discuss changing Belize dollars into US dollars for the purchase of the three computers. I have already paid for the three power units and printers. I went to see Mrs Liliana Lagos whom I already know because I have met her at Lions functions and at parties with the family. That seemed to be successful and I should be able to pick up the money at the end of the week. I returned to Corozal on the 9:00am Premier and arrived at about 11:30am. Apart from unpacking and having something to eat, I had a bit of shopping to do. Having got myself sorted out at home I went to the SDA School and arranged to meet with staff at 2:30pm. The time in between was spent with Pedro Cucul sharing some of the problems teachers are having with the way the curriculum is being introduced. I took another empty cardboard box home and then it was time for the meeting.

When I returned from the school Louisa arrived to say that there was to be a planning meeting in Belize City for the Upper Division Language Workshop that begins next week. There are to be a lot of changes to suit the pressure on reproducing documents (rather than the curriculum). The chief of these is the intention to work one outcome through at a time and find common elements of content before clustering. I believe this will waste a lot of time and lead to more confusion. It is just as well that I am 'taking a back seat' in preparation for finishing at the end of June. There will be Adolfo and Suzanne from Orange Walk, Corinth, Alphonso and Ariola from Belize City, and Louisa from Corozal as well as me so there should be no need for me to run the whole thing as has happened before.

After doing the washing, I started the morning by arranging to go into St Francis Xavier School for 3:30pm today and Methodist at 2:30pm tomorrow. I would not be going to classes. This would give me the day to catch up. I then went to Church of Christ School and arranged to go to them at 2:30pm on Friday. The next stop was Ranchito to pick up a letter for Alba Garcia at customs. I then had the three letters for her from schools and one from the Ministry of Education, signed by Joe Martinez. I should be able to collect the $US on Thursday. Douglas Stansmore brought an invoice for the computers and VDUs this evening when I passed him the letters to take to Customs at the Free Zone.

There was a meeting at QADS on Thursday to discuss plans for Upper Division Workshop and the English and Spanish specialists. As the other districts didn't contribute it could just as well have been held in Orange Walk or Corozal Town. The setup has changed so that the Divisional Scheme for the Upper Division will have a different layout and content from the other two. Also, the Outcomes will be dealt with one by one and clustered afterwards. This will lead to considerable confusion in a situation where teachers and schools are already all at sea. The main problem is that each David regards himself as the authority and accepts no advice despite not knowing what is happening in schools. To support this, they have used Louisa who will do exactly as they say – or try to! I have refused to lead this coming workshop although I will give support when appropriate.

I saw an anteater run across the road as I came back from Orange Walk to Corozal on the 'Yellow Peril'.

The last of the Christmas parcels together with the writing and sending of 40 of the 43 cards to go to England took up most of the weekend – and mail of course…

'…I took a leaf out of your book this year and collected things over a longer period. I enjoyed that very much. Also, the funds have been easier so that the only real restriction has been what I could send in the mail. I will be spending Christmas with the family again. I took their presents down this week to reduce the load later, but I haven't got anything for their three children yet. I am not planning to stay for the New Year. No doubt I will be pressed. Maybe I'll go back again but it is a tedious journey from here…'

'…You said that you are a strong animal lover when you first wrote. There is plenty to tell you about the animals here although you mustn't imagine that they are in view all over the place as they are in East Africa. Here, you have to look out for them as you do in England. Does your interest extend to crocodiles, snakes, scorpions and tarantulas? We have to be a bit careful about some things when we are out in the forest or in the bush. You may not see them but they certainly see you…'

'…The lack of email facility at your school is causing me considerable problems. The computers provided in schools here are being well used but the expectation of purpose for which they were provided isn't there. You will get the picture without my going on about it I am sure…'

'…Dear Friends in Year 7, the last time I wrote to you I suggested that one (or more) of you might like to research information on the birth of Corozal Town and the wars hereabouts. I am quite serious about that! There is no way that the information can be obtained here. As Belize was the colony 'British Honduras' at the time, all records would be in England. The North Devon District Library would be a good starting point and Mr Hayes might be persuaded! You should have the three papers that were sent to Mr Berry to fire the imagination a bit. It should be a very interesting study and a fascinating story as it involves a relatively small area and a small number of migratory peoples (forced migration). It should be an interesting insight into the history of the larger Yucatan Peninsula.

I know that some of you have discovered that Belize resources are becoming available in the Library. They are there to be used! There is also a lot of writing of mine, which should become accessible in time.

Do be patient as it is a very busy time in your library just now. If you think I can provide anything you want, please ask. There is a lot of information in the form of letters like this one. I don't know how Mr Berry will have these filed. Perhaps I will make it a New Year Resolution to edit them all and send them as one document!

Christmas is upon us and I expect you are fully occupied with that and with all the events and activities leading up to the end of term. Also, I have a workshop to run in this last two weeks. So this short letter to you is my last until we are in the new Millennium! Incidentally, you will all be in the next thousand years six hours before I am despite my being a lot older than you. I am going to enjoy those six hours. When we are having our party you will have had it!

A Happy Christmas to you all…'

Monday 6th December was the start of the second school term in Belize and the two week Upper Division Curriculum Workshop, Corozal and Orange Walk Districts Language Arts at Corozal District Centre. The logic of a four equal term year makes a great deal of sense but starting a new term just before Christmas invites many unintended consequences especially when combined with the absence of so many staff at the workshop; also the already mismatch of terms with the UK made students' linking doubly difficult taken together with the huge disruption and delay of communication and season. Thank goodness the workshop started and continued well, both with Spanish in the first week and English in the second. My being more relaxed in consequence helped in making up for some of the deficit...

'...I haven't told you about the Inauguration Ceremony of the newly completed Ranchito Community Library. It went well but the speeches droned on too long as expected. Mine was the shortest by far but it did excite a lot of other comment because it focussed the 'remarks' of the four Government Ministers on the needs of schools. I was pleased about that. It made it worth having to give a speech myself. No I don't like giving speeches. I enjoy entertaining groups of people (especially young people) or sharing ideas enormously but not giving speeches. Best of all, I like telling stories – and they are always based on experience or truth. It was interesting chatting with the Government Ministers afterwards. I can share with you a lot about power, politics and control if you like. At the end I was given a lift home by one of them.

I'm not interested in having the power but I do like wandering about in the 'corridors'! I doubt that you would imagine the scene of the ceremony. It lasted for two hours during which we sat in the hot sun; the invited guests on display in front of the children, parents and villagers. I'm okay most of the time but it is a Belizean ritual for all speakers (including the MC) to go through the whole list of guests including their titles, before they start. That's when I get most twitchy. Why we can't just have it once from the Master of Ceremonies at the start I don't know. You will have noted my opening 'Friends'. People seem to like it. I think they wish they could do it as well! I missed out afterwards. The food for the invited guests was served separately from the crowd. We had tamales served in the new library. I hate tamales. I only eat them out of politeness and it is a struggle. I would much rather have had some of those nice sandwiches served in the tent outside...'

'...The workshops are pretty tough because the resources, funding and Ministry organisation are hardly adequate. Also, teachers are being asked to change dramatically, from a traditional system that has been in operation, seemingly, for ever! Fortunately, I do seem to have the right sort of skills so that what is tough is also very rewarding...'

'...I have almost forgotten what it is like to see a film and I don't even get to see any television except, rarely, with the family and then it is usually in Spanish because that is their first language. I had managed to glean a little World news from the radio and heard something about Northern Ireland.'

'...I'm afraid it is pretty difficult to switch Aner in to writing. I'm sure that he wants to but it is way outside his thinking and experience. One problem is that he is not really allowed outside his village and certainly not down into town (only just over a mile). No one else is likely to take him or go for him and the needs of young people are not high on the adult agenda in Belize. I haven't been able to help much because it would be no good to do it for him and he gets all guilty when I see him. You know how much use that feeling is! I'm sure that your Christmas Present will be well received and I have told his teacher about it. After Christmas, the school should have access to email so that will help. In the meantime, I think that someone else will write to you as well. I don't think I told you that I took photos of all the students this year so that your year 7 can see what they look like. You probably know that anyway. Mr Berry tells me that a lot of people are keen to write to one of the girls at Christian School at Santa Rita...'

Following a request from another volunteer I helped out with a stall for the 'Rights of the Child' on Saturday which turned out to be quite demanding as her emails showed...

'...Many thanks for your help yesterday I enjoyed meeting people I already know in Corozal and these new experiences are all part of the rich pattern of a VSO's life aren't they? By the time I left just after one o'clock there hadn't exactly been a huge crowd - I hope it picked up a bit in the afternoon. I got back to Belmopan at 6.30 and was standing on the platform in my concert gear by 7.05 - pretty nifty work I reckon...'

'...When I got back to the office on Monday I heard all the grisly details of the afternoon at Corozal Fair and how staunch you were in getting things packed up and organized in the rain. I knew I could rely on you - I'm just sorry that it seemed you were left holding the baby alone as I gather the young lady who had been organized by her mother to help all afternoon didn't exactly pull her weight.. I will return the favour whenever and however you want! More than one thing I left to be dealt with in my absence last week went badly wrong and I'm tempted to say my learning is that I will never again delegate things to be done in my absence - as that of course is contrary to development philosophy I suspect I will continue to delegate and continue to pick up the pieces afterwards. Anyway - a big thank you again for your generous support to me...'

'...Thanks for that. I wasn't too happy about it - especially when the VCR went missing. I hope it has been found. I should say that your colleague (I remembered her name earlier) and the good doctor were splendid...'

'...The artwork is on its way! It was packaged in a large cardboard tube so I hope it survives the journey. I will send on a copy of the N Devon journal with the press coverage. There is also a number of letters and cards from 7S, along with some 'odds' from other forms. I am encouraging pupils to write and email direct to the relevant schools, but these pupils took advantage of me while I was packing up the tube...'

'...Good news about the art work; four of the Principals and the Standard Five Teachers are currently attending one of my workshops so I will see them again all next week. We can arrange a joint effort early next term to include the art work. Please send five copies of the Journal. I can deliver the letter for Pollyanna without any difficulty. I have made a hard copy and I will pass it on that way. Ranchito is not a Pilot School and is the only 'Link' School not represented at the workshop. I should be able to find time to go down and see them. I hope the cards and letters arrive in time. Our schools finish next Friday (17th December). Are you receiving my attachments okay now? Have you missed any? If you have, can you identify which ones? Did you receive the three bits of information about Corozal okay? It's essential that we start email right from the beginning of next term. If we don't, it doesn't give me long enough to secure it all before leaving Belize. Then it will surely founder. If the school system can't cope then we must find some other way of creating and sending batches of attachments. Schools here find it very difficult to organise student use of one computer...'

'...Now that I am flushed with success, I have attached several documents. None of them are large. Some things Paul will obviously want to keep to hand and I can't say that the lists are complete as I didn't record everything in one place. (It took some time to put the lists together). The titles are more or less self-explanatory. The attachments are: Artefacts, Photographs, Videotapes, Written Text. All of these are items already in school. There is a full set of photos that I expect Paul will want to hang on to in class but there is a second set (for the Library) in albums...'

The last of the workshop sessions finished early. I had relented over leading it and the conclusion took place on the second Wednesday with social in the morning – lasting until about 1:30pm. A package arrived with items for Methodist, St Paul's, Christian School and Calcutta. The contents for St Paul's and Methodist were delivered right away. I called in at Ranchito on Thursday and delivered the package to Calcutta; tried to deliver the one to Christian School but there was no one at school and the Zetina family was not at home.

'A package arrived yesterday... I can arrange for the Ranchito mail to be delivered when it arrives during the holiday and will meet with the five Principals on Tuesday, 4th January to discuss joint operations and our first publicity in Belize. I hope that the banner and newspapers will have arrived by then...'

'...Glad you enjoyed the story. It is a 'read aloud story really'. I guess the story you enjoyed most of mine would have been 'Edelweiss'. I can remember you and many others lying on the floor in the school hall kicking your legs in the air at that one! Perhaps I shouldn't remind you but we should never lose the joy of good humour and a sense of the ridiculous. There seems to be plenty in your house anyway...'

As the schools break for the Christmas holiday I joined with Calcutta School for the staff lunch at the Maya Hotel Restaurant; a rare treat for me and with friends.

'...My interest certainly includes such animals as crocodiles, scorpions and tarantulas. In some ways I would rather curl up on the sofa with a puppy than a crocodile but then again crocodiles are more interesting to study. I have held a tarantula before in England and actually prefer them to spiders. As for snakes, I nearly had a pet one...'

A letter was sent from the UK to the five link schools...

'On behalf of all year seven pupils in my school, I would like to wish you and your students a very happy Christmas and most prosperous New Year. I hope we will be able to maintain our link in the next century, and continue to learn from each other. We were all very pleased to receive your letters, and we hope that our 'buddies' are enjoying themselves in Belize. We hope they are behaving themselves as well! The buddies that arrived in England have asked to stay on for Christmas and the New Year celebrations, but they tell me that they are also looking forward to returning home. Each one has kept a diary to give you an idea of what they have been doing during their stay. Unfortunately, we have experienced some problems with our email in school, but it should soon be sorted out. As soon as it is, the students here will all be keen to write to you. In the *meanwhile, I am quite happy for your staff and students to write to me at my email address. A number of my students are lucky enough to have access to their own computers, and I am encouraging them to send their own emails. Many others are also writing letters, but of course, these will take a bit longer to reach you. Sometime around Christmas, Mr Max will receive some art work which he will bring to your school to show you. The art teacher in our school has worked with his class to produce large painted letters to spell the name of our town - 'South Molton'. When they are all assembled together, they make an impressive banner display. The decoration on each letter was inspired by the wildlife and colours of your beautiful country. You might like to produce something similar to send to us.*

When the new school term begins after Christmas, all the pupils in year seven will start to prepare for the school 'Hobbies Day'. On one afternoon, everyone brings in a display of their hobbies and interests to show off to the rest of the school in the main hall. With 140 pupils in year seven, we usually have a wide range of things to look at! My pupils are keen to send you some of their work so that you can see what they get up to in their spare time. Mr Max has been to one of our Hobbies Days before, so he will be able to tell you more about it. I hope we can now keep in regular contact, and please do not hesitate to ask if there is any particular information we can provide for you. As I am writing this, the rain continues to fall, and the temperature is around 3 degrees Centigrade. We have snow forecast for the next few days, and it makes me jealous of your warm climate!'

The banner arrived on Tuesday 22nd December from SMCC together with correspondence for children that I arranged to deliver and on Wednesday the package for Ranchito was first delivered to Ana Gomez mother-in law's house. Then I travelled down to Belize City and back to give Marco and Miriam their birthday present, leaving at about nine in the morning and returning on the three o'clock Urbina to Orange Walk. I tried unsuccessfully to get some new flip-flops that I like and then returned on a 'yellow peril'.

'...The hurricane season is over for this year. We have been very fortunate because the Caribbean, generally, has taken a battering from a lively season and a greater number of storms than usual. There have been nine hurricanes. Apparently this increase in activity can be expected to last for the next ten years. I don't know how they can be sure of that. The predictions for Mitch alone were wildly out! I finish here in 2000. I am going through the process of re-volunteering. I don't know where that will lead. I would still like to go to Africa but I wouldn't be surprised if it turns out to be Pakistan...'

Thursday 23rd December: I set off this morning to find Bernard's house in Orange Walk. He was in Corozal with his aunt. However, I did meet with his Mum again, and his Dad. I then had some lunch in the Crystal restaurant and returned to Corozal where I found Bernard and met with his aunt and family. The aunt teaches at Paraiso so she knew me already. I gave Bernard his card and Christmas present and we had a useful conversation. He was pleased.

'...This is my third Christmas in Belize and it is very much a time of contrasts. It is only 9:30am and I am sitting here in shorts and sports shirt with very little on my feet. The door and windows are wide open and the sea is calm. The sun is shining. A gentle breeze stirs the palm trees. (Nothing much disturbs the big rubber tree out front). On the other hand, the evenings are all aglow with the incredible decoration of Christmas lights that people go in for here in a big way. Children look forward to Father Christmas too. Boy, it must be hot for him around the shops! Very different but all the same...'

'...Young people here have much more holiday than you do although that can't be taken as a direct comparison with your life in the obvious way because both demands and opportunities are very different for them. It just means that they have more time on their hands...'

It was a busy day getting ready but I had managed to get a seat on the 3:00pm Premier Batty Bus for Belize City and I was ready in good time. I was glad I had taken all the presents down on the last two visits, and left them with Marco. I knew they would then find their way to the right place under the Christmas Trees and appear at the right family time. They all assume that I know these things as a regular member but I have to employ these devices because I don't! It was a good journey. I arrived in the city around 5:00pm after having had a window seat on a bus without the wretched curtains that the Belizeans like so much to draw shut. They like to sleep. I can't and I like to see where I am going.

The house was full of excitement and anticipation as the three children seemed to be everywhere: upstairs where the grandparents and Marco's brother live and downstairs where the young family live. The whole house was colourfully decorated and had been decorated in the regular way as well. What we do in the spring, Belizeans do for Christmas. It is a huge celebration. Both trees, up and down, blinked their lights randomly, and competed for attention with those outside. Only the family was there for Christmas and the evening was the usual mix of playing with the children and pleasant conversation, fun and laughter over a few drinks well into the night.

The Catholic Church service is not really how I like it because there is much more of a ritual than I feel is appropriate and there isn't time for reflection on the words of the service. It is rather like saying the Lord's-prayer too fast without thinking. However, Neria is Catholic. Also St Joseph's is much closer than St Mary's Anglican, downtown, or the historic Anglican Cathedral of St John even further away on the South side. I have been to both; so no matter.

The present opening was as present opening usually is with young children – chaos! Paper flew everywhere accompanied by shouts of surprise and pleasure and demands that everyone should see. This is difficult with three at once and the young children aged five, four and three humble me by remembering to speak English when talking to me! After that the whole performance was repeated upstairs at the other tree. There was plenty of food with the American traditional whole ham at any time and the very Belizean Relleno for dinner. That is a chicken heavily stuffed with a ground pork and egg mix laced with herbs and spices, onion and garlic and the local black Ricardo. Egg yolks set in the middle add contrast to the white of the chicken and the black of the stuffing. The result is delicious.

The remainder of Christmas Day passed as Christmas Day does, with friends dropping in during the afternoon and evening."How about going to Benque for the day tomorrow?" "Fine," I said, "That would be nice!"

We were due to leave at 6:00am. Neria and I thought that funny but we were ready and thus able to enjoy a leisurely breakfast and a pleasant early morning wait until we all piled into the vehicle and left an hour later. Remembering how I struggle with tamales, Neria packed some ham sandwiches for me to eat whenever they appeared throughout the day. Belizeans eat tamales for a pastime. I like the joke about the tourist who was asked how he liked them. He said, "Fine but the lettuce was a bit tough!" Tamales are cooked and served in a palm leaf! But what I don't like is the corn.

Benque Viejo Del Carmen is almost on the border with Guatemala. To get there from Belize City you travel along the whole of the Western Highway through Hattieville, past the Belize Zoo, missing Belmopan by a couple of miles and on through Santa Elena and San Ignacio where you cross the Mopan River. The bridge in that direction is a temporary one downstream of the famous Hawkesworth Bridge, which can no longer cope with the volume of two way traffic. A little further down, the Mopan River joins the Macal to become the Belize River that joins the sea on the North side of Belize City by Haulover Creek.

It was a lovely day. We visited Miriam's Grandparents and two of her aunts and the children played with their cousins. All the families are large. For part of the day Neria and Tabo went shopping across the border with Guatemala, in Melchior. I had forgotten to bring my passport again (I had taken it to Belize City but left it in my bag) but so had Marco. So we dropped his Mum and Dad off and went and had a few beers with one of his friends, back in Benque. We couldn't have done that in Guatemala because it was Election Day there and the sale of liquor is banned before, during and after the election. I wonder why that time was chosen. The Belizeans were not happy about that so the Guatemalans must have been really put out at holiday time. We returned to arrive back just after dark at around 6:00pm and had a pleasant evening as the previous one but without visitors.

After one of Neria's usual filling breakfasts I made my goodbyes and thanks, and set off for home. First, I wanted to make sure that I had a bank slip showing the present balance as we are so close to the end of the millennium. This, apart from having enough food and water, is my only concession or concern for the Y2K thing. I also wanted to know if my payment for the three computers for schools had been debited. It is a nuisance that the bank and the cash machine are so far from home. There is not a great lot of choice in Belize, one way or another, so I have to take the opportunities as they occur.

Rather than just request a mini statement at the ATM I punched in a request for $100 so as to show a debit on the receipt slip. That was okay and the money popped out as requested. Now, for some reason I decided to put my card away at this point, before picking up the money that was sticking out of the slot. Imagine my surprise when the machine snatched the money back again, gobbled it up and calmly announced on the screen that I hadn't taken it in the time allowed; worse than that it also said that my account had been debited. Today was a Bank Holiday so I would have to deal with it from Corozal. I haven't had much luck with banks this year. I determined to go through the whole procedure again to obtain a second slip in case it was needed for evidence as all the slips are timed and the two were too close together for anyone else to have come into the security booth. Somewhat chastened, I withdrew the next $100, put everything away and set off for Batty Central Bus Station, Downtown, to try to get on the 9:00am Premier bus that goes right through, stopping only in Orange Walk and Corozal on its way to Chetumal. By now it was 8:20am and twenty minutes fast walk to go.

The streets were clear and I thought that the bus station would be likewise but not so. It was chaotic and packed to the doors. Would I get a seat or have to go on the regular bus, taking three hours, or maybe wait two hours for the next one? The ticket office was swamped. As it happened the queue for the North was much smaller than that for the West and South, so it didn't take too long and I got a window seat!

While I had been waiting, I had noted a Creole boy of about twelve hanging around with a shoeshine box over his shoulder. He looked very anxious and I soon saw that he was tentatively approaching waiting passengers with long gaps of time in between, and asking - for what? That was pretty obvious. He carried a piece of paper in one hand and he wasn't having any luck, which made him even more nervous.

As I collected my ticket I was aware that the boy had gone round the back of the two queues and was now close by my side between our queue and the wall. A very quiet, polite and gentle voice said, "Please Sir". I continued. There are many approaches made; would that the ability to make judgements was as easy. Again, "Please Sir". I turned. There was a pleading look and eye contact, which is unusual. "Please help my Mom buy some food." The paper was set out in columns with a few names on it and small amounts of money written down. I could see that there was a message at the top. I didn't read it and I didn't write on it; just gave him all my change and I think I said "Oh dear" (for want of a much stronger word) and moved on leaving his thanks behind. I felt terrible after that. I should have given him more time but it was too late. I should have found a way of letting him know that there is no difference between his worth and mine. All that failed and I have to console myself with the knowledge that he is a little better off and I am a little wiser now.

There was plenty of time to reflect on the bus home. It was a 'bendy bus' and there was clearly something wrong with the coupling. We stopped many times while the driver carried out inspection and made adjustments and crawled northwards. Many buses have radio contact. He was busy on that too. Eventually we met a relief bus that was much smaller. It was quite a squash as we all piled on that. The regular bus had passed us long ago! Needless to say, the five minute stop in Orange Walk stretched to twenty as it usually does, and the engine was left running in an unattended bus as it always is. We eventually passed the regular bus about four miles before Corozal Town but it had left Belize City after us anyway!

'…I don't know what will happen for the Millennium. I have just come back to be with friends here and that's as much as I know. There are two reasons for this. The first is that it rarely occurs to Belizeans that others' expectations or understanding may be different and the second is that probably, they don't yet know themselves. Christmas was very much a family affair, which was really nice. The three children were very excited about all their presents (far too many) and we all had a lot of fun…'

First thing in the morning I rang the bank feeling rather foolish. The girl at first thought the ATM had swallowed my card. It took some time for her to realise that it was the money not the card. I decided the humble approach was better than complaining about the machine and the total absence of warning. That worked! She agreed to check the machine credit my account and send a new statement by mail. She asked for and took my telephone number. There was no call so I guess all of that was okay. Most of the rest of the day was taken up with washing, housework and shopping so it wasn't until evening that I got to the library, returned, finished writing and settled down for a good read.

'…I hope that your family Christmas went well and you avoided the colds and flu that everyone seems to have had. I saw your weather chart on BBC World over Christmas. I should think those isobars would be enough to upset anybody's health. I ought to keep quiet about our weather but I'll tell you just the same. It is about as cool as it ever gets now. If you think of the best of the early summer days when the air is fresh in the morning and the sun shines all day. Well, that's it! The temperature reaches a maximum of about eighty during the day and drops as low as sixty in the small hours of the morning. The sun comes up over the sea directly opposite my house. The sight of some snow would be nice, or a crisp early morning frost but we can't have everything! Belizeans have all the wonderful tropical fruits (my house is full of the smell of ripe pineapple) but they drool over apples and grapes that they can't grow…'

Carving

In the main, I buy gifts from three sources. A shop in Belize City Commercial Centre run by a young lady I know whose family live in Ranchito, which is a village just outside Corozal, a shop on the edge of Corozal Town called White Sapphire and a lone carver who lives in San Antonio just outside Corozal and next to Santa Rita village.

This year I have been collecting model boats made by the woodcarver who lives at San Antonio. His name is Tomas Gilharry. He has a lot of children to support and I believe carving is all he does to support them. Despite the fact that Gilharry children go to Christian School Assemblies of God at Santa Rita I had not found out about his carving until I came to live in Corozal and had come back from England in July.

There are many Gilharry. It is more of a tribe than a family. There are many Gilharry families living in the same area. One family runs the Venus Bus Line (That is a story in itself). The premier rock band in Belize is the Gilharry Seven. So there are quite well off Gilharry. There are also very poor Gilharry and Gilharry who have been involved with the law one way and another. With my connection with the school at Santa Rita as a link school and a pilot school for the curriculum, and with San Antonio School as a pilot school, you can see my dilemma.

This Gilharry seems to be a worker and certainly a skilled carver, so I bought a ship from him when he first stopped his bicycle to hail from the gate one afternoon as I sat on my balcony overlooking the road and the beach. After that, of course, I was a target for further sales!

I didn't mind his persistence because his models would do so well and it would also help his income considerably. I like to try to serve more than one purpose whenever I can and I avoided thinking too much about what else he might be spending the money on. You will eventually see the granddaddy of his boats in your school library and will no doubt spot one that James will have. The latter is for you to know only just now, because I am sure it hasn't yet arrived. It was posted after your present. Of course, you already have a boat so I didn't want to give you another one. The father of the young lady I mentioned made your boat. His great skill is in the lines he creates and the finish. A lot of the things that were first sent to your school were bought at Paula's Gift Shop.

I know all of that is not what you asked but I'm getting round to it! A lot of the more recent things sent to school etc. have been bought at White Heather. I got to know the family there very well too, especially as the eleven year old Aisha wanted someone to write to and her Dad died just two days before I returned to Belize. Their shop is an Aladdin's Cave of high quality crafts from all over Belize. I could spend a fortune in there but what I do is a great joy. Buying is not a quick thing. Mrs Pasos gets all the stock out of similar items to make sure I get what I really like. You will have noted by now that I like to give things that I like!

Wilfred Peters made your mask. He lives in Maskall, which is on the old Northern Highway about halfway between Orange Walk and Belize City near the huge Mayan site at Altun Ha. A lot of his carvings are sold direct to tourists visiting the site. Wilfred Peters (What an English name!) is a Creole from San Ignacio in Cayo, out near the Western Border with Guatemala. He uses no sophisticated tools. All his work is done using a machete and chisels. He is a true artist who fashions his designs straight from the lump of zericote wood.

The mask is of Mayan style, not necessarily an accurate copy of one of their gods but the impression of them on the craftsman. Such masks are not at all common, even in Belize. A lot of masks are made in Guatemala but they are made from much softer, lighter wood (in colour and weight) and are stained in bright colours. The Guatemalan masks are also Mayan Indian and very Indian looking but the Mayan peoples who populated the whole Yucatan peninsula and much of Central America were tribal and there were many of them. The Mayans have made great cities but never a nation. This is as good a reason as any other to explain how the Spanish managed to overcome the Maya, and in the most inhuman ways imaginable.

Really, there are many cultures and connections in that carving. I have yet to meet a Mayan carver. The carvers are mostly East Indian, Garifuna or Creole. But I have met quite a few Mayans, fascinating people who still seem to lack a corporate identity and are still marginalised as a result of it.

Wednesday 29th December came with news to bring me up sharp. Quite a few Christmas cards have arrived late but that is to be expected and it is nice to have them to open having come home from Belize City. Of several today, one of them stopped me short. My old County Commissioner is dead and I didn't know. The note from Muriel reads: 'I am sending this card to thank you for remembering us each year but also sad to tell you Geoff died on 3rd Sept. after a fairly short but distressing illness – primary liver cancer. He was very brave and tried to be cheerful but it was very sad to see all the strength and vitality drain away…'

Geoff was my great guiding light in Scouting. I still see him coming across a huge field of camping Cub Scouts, many yards away, with his left arm outstretched in greeting. I still remember his arm across my shoulder at a Leader training course I was running at South Molton Community College. "I want you to be my Assistant for Cub Scouts," he said. And later, "Would you do a holding operation for three weeks as District Commissioner of Torridge (as well)," he said. I told him it would take longer than that. Three years later it emerged that was probably the most successful job I ever did in Scouting. He would expect the work to go on and it will – not in Scouting now for me, but still with young people and also with their teachers. And much is owed to those days of which he was so great a part for me.

I spent much of the next day on domestic work and writing letters. I don't share the Belizean idea of sitting around even now.

Friday 31st December: I went to call on Bernard's Grandmother today because I had understood that he was going to be there for the New Year. He was not. He had stayed the night when I last saw him on the 23rd but he was at home for Christmas and had been there ever since. I did find that they have a telephone, however, and obtained the number. They were out on the first call but were expected back in the evening. When I called again they had returned but Bernard had gone right out again and was in the town. It was 7:00pm. I can see the attraction, it being New Year's Eve but he should be celebrating that, if at all, with his family. I checked that mail would be delivered to his home and said that I would write to him. Perhaps, if I can get him doing that it will help.

I finally got my statement finished on why I want to re-volunteer. How do you get three years' experience and an elusive prospect into a few words?

'…The outcome has been finding something more of me rather than change. It has been surprisingly easy to maintain my own set of values and be accepted for them. In the face of that appreciation I shrink from 'thinking too much of myself' (curious, that!)

The gain overall is extremely difficult to put into a simple statement but most of it can be included in becoming more at one with the environment, both natural and man-made, and joining with others in our human development. Most of all, it has been fun!

There have been frustrations that have really been inevitable given the point of development of education and administration but none of them have been exclusive. In many ways dealing with those frustrations (together) has been the means of great satisfaction. It would not be possible to become as much a part of the life of people I live with otherwise…'

The welcome to the New Year was very disappointing. I had been led to believe that it would be a get together in the yard but it all suffered the misinformation and lack of information that is so common here. There were a lot of firecrackers around the town but that was about it. I should have gone to Belize City. I know that there are meals planned for tomorrow but that is not the same thing at all.

After the great disappointment of New Year's Eve, today was much better. We had an all-day social in the yard with relatives and friends dropping in and joining in throughout the day; some staying all day. Fausty cooked escabeche for lunchtime and Lucille cooked Relleno for the evening; snacks, music, conversation (dancing if you wanted it!) all day and night. Oh, and rum and coke of course.

Sunday was busy with letters and sorting out my papers and personal effects. The letters were to the bank, to Muriel, to Bernard and for re-volunteering. The re-volunteering letter took me a long time and I had in any case been kicking it to touch for some time. I find questions like 'what have you gained?' and 'why do you want to?' difficult to answer but I was pleased with the result. The South Molton branch of NatWest evidently has a new manager again who wants to use a new broom. The sorting out was with going home in mind. I expect to be taking quite a lot of gifts that will not leave room for excess personal items, especially papers so these have been sorted out ready for burning and stories and writing paper given to Gladys and Ruby respectively.

'…Dear Bernard, I hope that you enjoyed your Christmas. I also hope that your New Year will be a really good one. It will not be easy but I have no doubt that you can do it…'

I spent most of Monday around the town, sending letters and quite a lot of time at the office chatting with Joe Martinez. He told me again of the way computers were distributed by the Prime Minister during his recent visit to schools. The MP who clearly did not properly research any sort of need made the decision of where they were to go. A computer was given to Methodist and St Paul's both of whom already had one. Methodist came from VSO and St Paul's had my 486. St. Paul's are also due for another one from me! A computer was also given to Guadeloupe but the most interesting was the one that went to Maryhill. The MP openly said that he had a daughter there so they would have the computer rather than it go to Corozal Nazarene! None of this upsets my plans although I have to admit some little irritation that political gain is clearly the objective and that the four computers were paid for by Belize and not the Prime Minister. Much the better thought was having started something big!

When I phoned Henry at Methodist about our meeting tomorrow it was no great surprise to find he had forgotten about it, although I was pleased that he elected to remind the other four.

Tuesday 14th January I did the regular washing first thing and then settled down to working out notes for the forthcoming schools' monitoring visits and arranging my diary and journal.

The meeting went pretty well considering that I have never known schools to work together in any way in the time I have been in Belize. To start with, the idea is to have a joint presentation at the Education Centre, probably on 14th January, to share the 'Linking' and present the remaining three computers. The banner from SMCC will form a backdrop together with artwork from Belize and children will make presentations of the 'Link'. In the longer term it is proposed to develop a newspaper to extend and further share the interest and talents of the students. Then response to plans from VSO...

'This year's Annual Conference will run from March 17-19 and will be held at Cahal Pech Village in San Ignacio. We hope to start preparing the agenda shortly and would be interested to know of any suggestions volunteers may have for topics or invited speakers.'

'My choice of subjects: 1. What have we learned from the Mayan sites of Belize? 2. The Chalillo Dam affair. 3. Unity and continuity in Belize (of which political reform can only be a part) 4. The Meso-American Biological corridor - concept to reality.'

Tomas came round today to say that the Minister of Education would be visiting seven schools on the chosen Friday including his school and Ranchito. He does not wish to mix our get together with the visit and I made it very clear that I don't either. I have no intention of being used for any politician to gain kudos from any gift or action of mine.

'...When we had the last workshop in December both Bernard's teachers for Standard 5 and Standard 6 were there. I had received no news up to then and to my dismay, found that he had gone from bad to worse rather than picking up again as I had hoped, since I hadn't had an answer to my letter. He had been sent to a 'corrective' boarding school for a time and would have to go back for another month after Christmas. I am cross with myself for not checking up as you might imagine, but I honestly don't know what I could have done. He doesn't do 'bad' things up to now; I am sure of that but he mixes with the wrong people and stays out at all hours 'messing about' in a most reckless way. He needs some purpose and a much better self-image but his actions will gain only the opposite. For now, I will write to him regularly and see where that leads. At least I can help to secure his schooling when he returns but who else will be looking out for him. One straightforward example of his knowledge of right and wrong, his recklessness in associations and danger is that he has 'shopped' some drug dealers who have now gone to prison. He is only twelve...'

'...You will be interested to know that the card was intercepted in the Post Office in Orange Walk (a town of about 15000) and sent to Corozal (a town of about 8000) with no further address, where it was delivered straight to me...'

'...I hope that you are all better now. Dare I say that we are still enjoying sunshine and what you would call hot weather (and I still do) but Belizeans tend to get colds when the temperature drops. I can't say I notice it much although it is cooler at night. I don't need the fan and I am using a sheet (even a blanket a few nights ago!). I don't know that there is any flu here but the death announcements are much more numerous in the 'cool' period – can't help noticing that because they have them on the radio...'

Thursday 6th January I went to Orange Walk today. It was good just to walk around and chat with old friends and have lunch with the Muffles College Students in the Crystal Restaurant again. I remembered on the way back that I had seen an anteater run across the road around about Louisville on a trip some time back. I also managed to get a new pair of the flip-flops that I like and some new computer discs. The Burns family was all very chatty and their children seem to be doing well. I also spent some time in the Post Office, the Library and the District Education Office. Friday was different...

It was a good trip into Chetumal today. I wanted to secure the layout and the past visits in my mind and that was surely done. It rained for a short while and it was dull for part of the day. The only restriction that caused was to stop me walking the sea front and back around the University. I set off on the 8:15am Premier, which was waiting when I got to the Batty Bus Terminal. Pancho was driving so that was another 'Happy New Year'! The border post was a nuisance as usual but it was the Mexican side and not Belize that was difficult. I filled in a form that I had not seen before. This is not easy to do because there is the pressure of the bus waiting and the knowledge that all the other passengers were Belizean and didn't have to go through this performance (Why not?). I was also last off the bus so they were waiting when I got back. It is just as well that Pancho was driving! On the return I had the form thrust back at me with the accusation that I hadn't paid! All this was in Spanish, translated for me by Ruby who appeared behind me at just the right moment. She had taken her Mum to the doctor in Chetumal. "What charge?" I wondered, and in any case it could hardly be my fault if money hadn't been demanded on my way in! My face must have expressed the rapidly mounting anger despite my keeping quiet as my passport was stamped and thrust back with a grunt. It was the same officer who had stamped it on the way in too! Most of the time during the day, was spent walking but I stopped for lunch in a nice restaurant and treated myself to Ceviche con Pescado, which was very nice with a couple of bottles of 'Especial'.

Both markets were interesting although I didn't buy anything. The shirts I like are $120-150 and I found some paper sculptures/models in a shop right down on Avenida des los Heroes.

As I came back home through the town I met up with Orvin Rancheran who told me of the Education Minister's visit next Friday. I left it that it would be acceptable if he included a visit to our celebration in his schedule but there was no way that I would agree to tack on to his school visits.

It had been raining heavily during the night and the roads were wet but I was able to go for a short ride on my bike in the afternoon. I wanted to explore some of the areas of the town outskirts that I hadn't been through. Most particularly, I wanted to follow the road through from the north end of Fourth Avenue to Paraiso. The mud roads were still pretty sticky so I was only out for about an hour. The only significant event on Sunday was a walk of a couple of miles. I went past the Civic Centre where the PUP was holding a convention. The Belizeans are wonderful for names. I have already described the Civic Centre, which is really like a huge barn. It is useful as it holds a large number of people. It has a concrete floor and a pitched corrugated roof but very little in the way of fixed seating. It is marked out for some indoor games and there is a small stage used mainly for rock bands and pop groups. What was interesting was the convention. It was billed by the loud speaker van yesterday, as the biggest convention of the New Millennium. The question was posed right away because there hasn't been a convention in Belize this century until now. Anyway, it turned out that it was some sort of selection arrangement for PUP (Peoples' United Party) candidates for the Town Board elections. When I went past there were about a hundred people present, mostly in a queue. It was not my idea of a convention! Perhaps, there had been speeches earlier!

'…I hadn't realised that you started school last Thursday. I should have done because our High Schools started on the same day. Primary Schools don't start until tomorrow. Attached is the first letter of the term for year 7. I will try to write regularly. I have one or two things in mind to send to you again and I am in the process of getting them together. If there is anything you would like sent over please let me know. I have some ideas for getting over the video problem so I will be working on that next…'

'Dear Friends in Year 7, all of your letters and cards etc. were delivered in time for Christmas – right up to Christmas Eve! It would be nice to hear from one or two of you myself! I will always answer. The banner impressed me. It will first form a backdrop together with artwork from Belize at a short celebration when Belizean students from all five schools will make their presentations of the 'Link'. In the longer term it is proposed to develop a newspaper to extend and further share the interests and talents of students. We have had problems setting up computers in all the schools (don't we all) but you will be all able to send email to your 'Link' school by the end of this month. You know the addresses we have so far but here they are again… You may have to wait a week or so for St Paul's to come on line. It is important that these addresses are well used without delay; those of you who have access to email please use them. Hopefully, you will be able to do this from school before much longer but please do not wait until then. I will send you the other addresses as soon as I have them. You can always use my email address of course. Many of you have access to a computer, even at school. Why not write your letters in one document, each on a new page and one of you (or Mr Berry) send them to me as an attachment. It is no trouble to me to print them out and drop them into school. That way, the letters would be delivered exactly as you have written them. About now, there will be more Belize resources becoming available in your Library. Remember that they are there to be used. If there is anything else you would like or extra copies of things, please ask and I will do my best to send them. It will be too late after the end of the summer term because my three years in Belize will be at an end. There is also a wooden plaque in the Library, showing the four symbols of Belize and now a wooden model sailing ship. These are intended to support any display you may have. I hope you like them. Local craftsmen using local timber have done the carving. The plaque is mahogany, which should be easy for you to identify but the ship is rather special. That is zericote, a very hard and close-grained wood. The very even texture comes about because there is very little difference in growth through the year in the tropics. Few trees are ever bare of leaves. I don't know for sure, why there is some white in the wood sometimes. I guess that it is heartwood and sapwood. Certainly, the dark wood is much denser. I will write again next week. A Happy New Year to you all…'

'…Holiday times here are far too long, much longer than yours as a rule. My 'holiday' time is even longer because management and administration in Education is not exactly dynamic! I have no professional appointments until 17th January. Fortunately, I can keep myself busy with the schools' 'Linking', writing, reading and spending time with friends. I get out into the country as much as I can as well but this is not as 'free' as it is at home. I have no wish to behave as a tourist, and personal safety is a big problem. You will realise that it must be a problem when you remember that I am not one to concern myself too much (I remember you pressing the advantage of the radio phone, which I never did take up!)…'

'…I thought the packing was good and very secure but it was a little bit hard to get into as it was all sealed tight. Did you mean you're sending a bigger ship into school when you said I would see the Granddaddy of his (Mr Gilharry) boats in the school library? …'

'…Yes the ship is big, as you will see! It has a lot of sails very cunningly assembled. It needs a big space just as your library needs big things to display so the two things went together in my mind. But that was not the start of the story. I had wanted to buy such a ship for a long time and when Mr Gilharry arrived waving it about from the road (and after softening me up with previous visits!) it was really just a question of what I was going to do with it. As I told you, I had a lot of fun with the Christmas presents…'

The most important thing today would be to ensure that the celebration of the five 'Link' schools wouldn't go wrong. This would involve visits to all five schools, securing the computers and getting a clear picture of what the Minister of Education will be doing from the District Office. I set off first, to the District Office on my bike and had a long talk with Joe Martinez. I was puzzled that he was referring to the Minister visiting seven schools when I understood that it was to be five. The five schools including Christian School Assemblies of God and the schools visited by the Prime Minister last term, amounted to all the Primary Schools in the MP's constituency! The extra two schools turned out to be St Pauls and Ranchito and the idea was that I would present the three computers at each school separately in his presence. This is entirely unacceptable to me. The purpose of the celebration was to bring the students of all five schools together to celebrate the 'Link'. The presentation of the computers (or merely the presence of them) to the last three schools was merely incidental. I don't want a lot of fuss about it because it is the 'Link' that matters and not the computers. Also, I don't want to get mixed up with the politics of these visits. There is no educational value in going to five schools in one day. As far as I can see it is a contrary waste of the schools' time in preparation. It would not be possible to continue with our plans as Christian School Assemblies of God would need to be in their own school to receive the Minister of Education. It is interesting, also, that they only have four days to prepare, right at the beginning of term, since no warning was given. I then cycled round all the five schools with the idea that we postpone the celebration to a later date. I first went to Christian School who were most affected, and then went on to St Paul's Anglican, Corozal Methodist, Ranchito and Calcutta – in that order. All were happy with the arrangement. Orvin Rancheran had it fixed in his mind that the Minister would be coming to his school first on Friday morning. I tried to explain that this had only been the idea of the Principal Educational Officer and the MP to include computer presentations but I could see no reason why the school shouldn't have the computer by then anyway, whatever happened.

Later in the evening I contacted Douglas Stansmore and asked him to make his own arrangements for installation at each of the three schools. Ranchito would be for Friday of this week and the other two, St Paul's and Christian School at a time to suit next week. In the event, which suited me very well, there was a delay in supply!

I talked with Orlando Williams at Calcutta to encourage him to continue writing to Philip and then sent email to Philip to tell him what I had done. On the way back from Calcutta, which was my last call, I wanted to get off the Highway so I turned off at Carolina and came back through Xaibe. That was a nice ride. All I had to do then was change my library book again and that would be about it for the day.

'...I was in Calcutta School today so I made a point of chatting with Orlando as you hadn't said anything about hearing from him. What has happened is that he is still in the 'Linking' class because it is a Standard 4/5 mixed and he was Standard 4 last year. He is now writing to your Year 7! I suggested that he write to you as well and I think he will. Orlando is only ten years old but I am sure that you would be okay with that and if you could get him going it would be very worthwhile. You may like to send him email...'

I phoned VSO this morning and found that my application to re-volunteer has been sent on to London so that is good. Mark said the application was fine and went on to say that I was regarded as an ideal volunteer – having the right approach. I needed that!

I spent most of the afternoon at the office. There was quite a lot of wasted time hanging around as always but I achieved several useful objectives. I bought two copies of each of eight textbooks to supplement those on Belize at SMCC at a cost of $227-20. I will send these off this week. Also, in talking to David Eck I find that I am on the budget until the end of August. That being the case, it gives me the option of going with up to two months free time before a post starting in September or staying for the full three years in Belize. That is anytime between the end of June and the end of August. That could be useful as it leaves the options open. There is still my holiday time from last September of course. I haven't taken any of that yet so I could leave it until the end. I can't do any more now, until I have some response from London. I also asked David Eck to send me a copy of the current monitoring instrument by email. I suppose that is living in too much hope but you never know. In conversation I told him yet again, that we ought to discuss the real position of the curriculum in schools. There is to be a meeting in Belize City on the 18th February.

'...Thanks for a super letter that I enjoyed very much after an extremely busy day. I am just making a quick reply and I will write properly later - to show that I am impressed by your use of the technology, to answer one of your questions and to give you something to read, here is an attachment for you. It is called 'Belizing!' and I wrote it about a week ago when some of the 'families' in South Molton were worried that I hadn't written in the usual time. I really have been busy and even got behind...'

<u>Belizing!</u>

In a way, I don't know what has happened to the last two weeks. I hope, now that I have caught up with where I want to be in my work, I can catch up with everything else as well. Next week promises to be a quite a lot lighter so the only risk is relaxing before I get up to date! There are many problems in trying to work with teachers and those in education to introduce the New Curriculum but the problems can all be summarised in one of two headings. One is the present or traditional system of teaching and the other is politics (or control).

The traditional system of teaching treats all learning as the acquisition of knowledge. Understanding is very limited and there is no opportunity to develop skills or personal attitudes to learning. As a result, almost all teaching is rote, "Repeat after me." "Yes Ma'am" and almost all lessons are class lessons that assume everyone is at the same level. Teachers were taught that way themselves and parents as well, so the rote learning and filling in spaces in exercises is what is expected. Change is not only unsettling and threatening, it is treated with suspicion. If the use of language is taken as an example, there is knowledge involved. You have to know what words mean and you have to know how to put them together. But using language is a skill. It can be nothing else. Most Belize students are brilliant at grammar but hopeless at speaking (unless it is memorised) or writing. Worse than that, reading for understanding is poor and there is little ability to disseminate vital information when listening. The latter is very noticeable when you are trying to explain something in a shop or to an official – and even to teachers! Discussion is very difficult and reasoned argument nearly impossible. The personal attitudes mainly have to do with learning how to learn, research skills and solving problems.

The politics is very much about control. There are two main parties, one red and one blue, but I cannot see that they fit easily in the political spectrum. This is a very small country with a population a little less than Plymouth! At the moment there are sixteen ministers. That is a huge percentage in relation to the population. It would relate to about four thousand eight hundred ministers at Westminster! The result is that they control everything – or try to. The jobs that we would normally expect to be done by a permanent staff of Civil Servants, or more importantly, the professionals are usurped by Ministers. (There are 29 Members of Parliament, two of whom form the Opposition. That would be about 8,700 in the House of Commons). There are also Senators that throw their weight about. They sit in the Senate and are appointed – not elected. When the party in government changes as it did last August, much of the work done by the previous administration is rubbished. Building works are left to rot and systems set aside. There is a huge amount of waste of effort. What is really bad is the idea that 'You can't be my friend if you are not one of my gang'. People who are not of the party are relieved of their job and replaced by someone who is of the party. All the experience goes down the drain and many things take a different direction from scratch.

As you might imagine, this has been very interesting and challenging for me (and I have only scratched the surface in explanation). People are people and all of this has to do with the way things are rather than potential ability or intellect. I haven't felt in any way that I know what should be. What has happened is like the best in teaching – when you suffer the learning with the child. Not that there is anything childish about it. I have found myself seriously questioning everything I had taken for granted – or so it seems. Most of it has so far turned out to be sound but it has been questioned. One clear result of all this is the absolute conviction that we (in the UK) do not even begin to appreciate what we have, let alone value and protect it. The effect of the politics on the introduction of the New Curriculum is the pretence. My most eloquent address in the Education Ministry was a plea for a pause to give pilot schools a chance to secure their position before moving on to the next Division and going country wide (at the same time). It gained great applause and approval (and it made me feel better!) but that was all. To compound this, the schools have not been given the authority to prioritise and staff are told to attend (or attend to) this or that with the same abandon as before. On the first day of this academic year, when the curriculum hit the Lower Division of Non-Pilot Schools for the first time, it was announced on the radio that the curriculum was 'fully implemented in the Lower Division of all schools country-wide'. I remember thinking 'Ask me in ten years' time!'

I have been under no illusions about any of this right from the start so I have made sure that the way I work is in accord with VSO to 'tackle disadvantage by realising people's potential'. This is sharing skills, ideas and experience and it is a two way, interactive, process. I spend a lot of time in classes for example, and we share ideas afterwards, about where the learning might go from where it is. So whatever happens to the curriculum, that sharing will remain.

Anyway, the reason why I have been so busy lately is because of the weight of notes I have been making so that the four measly visits to each of the nineteen schools I am monitoring this year can be of maximum benefit to us all. There are also the reports, which I write so that schools can have a copy that they would otherwise not get. The workshops are extra.

I have another use for the notes, which is to make a full report of the task that faces the schools. That will not go unsung. It has been and is a huge learning experience for me and I have made a lot of friends. I value that very much but the effectiveness of what I do has to be nearing its end and that is one reason why I have re-volunteered. After all, one of the functions of a VSO is to work oneself out of a job and there are Belizeans now who can very well do what I do (given chance – and that is not my problem).

Actually, none of the three tasks have materialised that I was asked to extend to do. I rather expected that and I am really doing work that should be done by local people. But that can be made positive as described. Also, it has given the chance to secure the school's 'Linking' programme, which is ticking along very nicely. All five of the 'Link' schools now have a computer. Three of them already have Internet and email addresses and the other two should be 'on line' this month. The acquisition of the computers has been fun and it is a story in itself. I claim no credit for any sort of generosity or anything like that because it is part of what I wanted to do. Together we have done it and it has been and still is a lot of fun.

When I came to Belize very few people were using electronic mail and I wasn't one of them. I brought a cheap, battery operated notebook with me that I had bought second hand so that I could keep a journal and make notes. It was not adequate for the job and I quickly realised that I needed a computer. There was a lot of correspondence immediately in setting up the 'Linking' and all the people I wrote letters to wrote back! Money was very tight. We are paid a living amount and I had brought some money with me but that soon went in setting up and settling down. Even so, after arriving at the beginning of September 1997, I had acquired a second hand 486 that I paid for in two instalments, by the beginning of November. I had already started to explore email through friends that already had it here and I managed to connect for it myself by December. That's another story!

There were four schools joined the Link programme from the start, two in Orange Walk and two in Corozal. The two in Orange Walk were big schools and they found it difficult to cope with but Calcutta and Christian School, Assemblies of God were going 'great guns'. I used a lot of my email to move messages quickly for them, where appropriate. I was visiting the schools regularly in my work and the two things went well together. The programme strengthened and the advantage of a school being able to use email for itself soon became obvious. Money was still tight but I discovered that VSO supported suitable personal projects with grant aid. The VSO Belize Director was impressed with what was going on and Calcutta received their computer two years ago. The slow progress with the facility at South Molton was an obstacle but several people, including Mr Berry, used their personal addresses to help communication. Needless to say, the computer is well used for all sorts of things and it has been fun to share in all of that, especially as Calcutta is a very poor village indeed.

In the second year the two Orange Walk schools dropped out and Corozal Methodist and St Paul's Anglican in Corozal joined. Corozal Methodist was so active and enthusiastic that VSO had no hesitation in funding their computer in the second year. By the third year it was clear that VSO limited funds would have to be considered and I had been having other ideas. None of the approaches to possible providers had been fruitful. The Ministry, while showing great interest and clapping hands from the side-lines, gave no support at all. The British High Commissioner showed great interest and visited Calcutta School but I didn't want any publicity for lots of reasons, so I avoided what is called the 'Small Grants Scheme'.

The first thing I decided for last year was that a laptop would be more use to me and I managed to buy one second hand through a Belize friend whose cousin was studying electronics in Houston. That released my 486, which went to St. Paul's. "Three down, one to go!" I thought, but then South Molton year 7 was increased to five forms! I had saved some money because I rarely go out of Belize and I also get paid subsistence when I go 'Off Station'. That is when my work takes me out of town for the day as it often does. Also, I had been asked to conduct a study for VSO for which I was paid. By making an arrangement with the Ministry over my previous year's holiday that I hadn't had, I was able to take the time to do the job and so had two months extra pay from VSO at a better rate than I normally get. With the expenses that I had already paid out so wasn't interested in, there was enough for a computer. In fact I had enough for two computers with the other monies not spent. That would provide for all the schools except that the 486 at St Paul's no longer looked as attractive in my eyes as before so I set out on a serious saving campaign.

When there was enough money for three computers you would think that would be the end of the story but not so. I could buy the three computers for $2,500 each, from a firm in Belize City. They build the computers themselves, from imported parts. I had also got to know a Belizean computer expert here in Corozal. He has a small business operating out of what is known as 'The Free Zone' (another story). He had provided me with software and finally sorted out my email. Obviously, it is useful for the 'Link' schools to have someone they could call on and I had been introducing him to the few teachers that have computers as well. I understand that a fair amount of business came out of that too, as there was opportunity to make time available at a workshop of 120 teachers. I found that he could supply imported computers of better quality and performance, ready built and for the same price. That would leave schools with the maintenance problem solved. Belize City is eighty-four miles away!

Then I found that there would be $200 import tax on each computer (paid to the Belize Government) and $240 above the exchange rate on each computer to change Belize dollars into US dollars (paid to the Belize Central Bank). The latter is something to do with the way the Government operates the Free Zone. In other words, I was expected to pay Belize $1,320 for the privilege of giving computers to its schools! No way!

The easy way would be to buy from Belize City but I couldn't be sure of what we would be getting and the service (I found) would be close to non-existent - or I could forget the whole thing of course. But it had become a bigger challenge now! The import tax was the easiest to deal with although it was long winded. I had to write a proposal giving all details and I had to get letters from each of the three Principals declaring that the computer would be used solely for the school. Also, a letter had to be obtained from the Permanent Secretary for Education giving authority. All of these had to be presented to the head person at Customs.

The whole process took three months and by that time the head person had been replaced. The original documents were lost and the whole thing had to be done again.

While all this was going on I had occasion to be talking with some Ministers and mentioned the problem to one of them. The purpose of doing that was to emphasise that the procedure may well put people off. That was misunderstood completely and I was told "Let me know when you are ready to buy and I'll fix it!" I should have seen that coming since so many things are 'controlled'. Again – No way! This was now an even bigger challenge!

I wrote directly to the Central Bank of Belize with a supporting letter from The Principal Education Officer and the Permanent Secretary to try to get the exchange charge waived. It was turned down flat. No reason given. Never mind, I thought, I have friends in one of the banks (not the one I use – sadly). I went to them and my application for US dollars was bounced right through and approved to the highest level. Of course, it then goes to the Central Bank who stopped it dead! Fortunately (for my pride as well as my pocket) I have other friends. What happened in the end I don't know (best not to) but it was a matter of trust. I paid over all the money $7,500 in November and the computers were installed at the beginning of February. I have to admit that it was an anxious time but I know for certain now, that those friends will support the use of those computers in schools very well.

The youngsters have given far more to me than I can ever give and I have avoided publicity and politics like the plague, but there have been little ceremonies. The biggest 'danger' was when I was an invited guest to the inauguration ceremony of the Ranchito School and Community Library. What I didn't know was the prominence that the promised computer (his or mine!) was to be given. It rather took over – and there were five Ministers as invited guests as well. Fortunately (in deference to me, I think, because I know the Principal very well) it wasn't reported. The most moving ceremony was last week at St. Paul's. I was asked to attend their morning service in Church and sat sideways on, well in front of the school while their choir sang, facing me and unaccompanied, 'Lean on Me'.

So now I am re-volunteering. Some of the reasons are implied above. I would like to experience another culture and another environment. It wouldn't be the same at all, although the work would be similar I expect. The 'Link' here should carry on. It will be nice to think of that happening at South Molton Community College and at the five schools in Belize, but there are other ways of continuing to share something of a new environment. Without the time spent directly on the 'Link', there will be more time to devote to those other ways. I want to get really serious about the writing and soaking up the environment for one thing (or do I mean two things?). Here are four paragraphs taken from my initial application:

'It has become obvious that my own needs are far fewer than I had thought. This may well be the result of being a Volunteer in material terms, rather than experience of the lifestyle of friends in Belize. In ordinary human terms however, what is important is much clearer – simpler even. I have learned much more about myself, particularly in relation to accepting the validity of the views, practices and beliefs of others. I have made a lot of friends in Belize and even been 'adopted' by Belizean families. The outcome has been finding something more of me rather than change. It has been surprisingly easy to maintain my own set of values and be accepted for them. In the face of that appreciation I shrink from 'thinking too much of myself' (curious, that!) The gain overall is extremely difficult to put into a simple statement but most of it can be included in becoming more at one with the environment, both natural and man-made, and joining with others in our human development. Most of all, it has been fun! There have been frustrations that have really been inevitable given the point of development of education and administration but none of them have been exclusive. In many ways dealing with those frustrations (together) has been the means of great satisfaction. It would not be possible to become as much a part of the life of people I live with otherwise.'

I know that the VSO Belize Director has fully supported the application and I had a reply from VSO London as follows: 'Thank you for your re-volunteering form and your motivation letter. In your letter you mention your desire to go to Africa, preferably Kenya. Unfortunately, we don't have a primary programme in Kenya and also because of the earlier retirement ages in many of the overseas countries in which we work, you would therefore have limited options. The following countries would have possibilities at present, Pakistan (our biggest primary programme), Bangladesh, Cambodia, Mongolia (early years) and Malawi. At the moment, your papers are with our assessment unit. Once a decision has been made, we will look at matching you to a suitable placement for Cycle A, departing August/October. Our matching day will be in April. The placement summaries for Cycle A normally come in around the end of March.'

314

I am very interested in Cambodia but the number one has to be Malawi. It is a small country, not much larger than Belize and at about the same latitude south as Belize is north but there the similarity ends. I know quite a bit about it too, as it is situated at the south end of the Great Rift Valley bordered by Lake Nyasa – or Lake Malawi as it is called there. The population of ten million or so Bantu peoples compared with a quarter of a million mixed ethnic groups in Belize is only one of the many contrasts. So now it is 'wait and hope' but it will be okay, whatever!

'…I have just received email from Mr Berry who says that 'Hal has produced a tremendous set of labelled photos for the library'. Brilliant! That's great - thanks. I know that I haven't said much about it but I have been with you all the way. I knew at the start, probably more than you realised, how much could be involved. What I didn't know then but have learned since, is how determined you can be to do a good job…'

'…It has been a long break as I have no school appointments until next Monday but I have kept busy with writing and with the schools' 'Link'; then starts the run to the end of the posting. Three years is up at the end of this academic year…'

'…Thank you for your prompt reply; also for the sensitive reference to earlier retirement ages rather than my age! The latter is not a problem to me and I 'retired' in order to volunteer. Malawi would be a very attractive proposition I'm sure. After Belize, the contrast in what is also a small country would be very interesting. I suppose too, you could say it is along the Rift from Kenya – albeit a long one! 'Cycle A' departing August/October would also suit…'

'…Garifuna are also known as Garinagu, especially among themselves. They are descendants of African slaves and Carib Indians. The two groups became mixed after a shipwreck on the island of St. Vincent in the Eastern Caribbean during the 17th Century. The local people didn't like their being there and were very cruel to them. As a result and being seafaring people, they migrated throughout the Caribbean. There are now settlements along the coasts of Honduras, Guatemala and Nicaragua as well as Belize…'

'…What seems a long time to me is the waiting to get on with the job; I don't like that at all. It is just as well that I have plenty of other things to do to keep me busy. I expect I will feel it next week as the first three schools are nine miles away at Libertad and the fourth is Calcutta just four miles away. I expect to use my bike and they are day visits. Friday is kept clear for any extra time required by those four schools… … I don't know where for re-volunteering. It is a lengthy process. However, I am now in email communication with VSO London so there will be no delay in that. Also, they advised me yesterday, that there is a possibility of Malawi (and in September). That would be really exciting…'

Saturday 15th January email came for Billy again this morning. Tomas Zetina called round to tell me that his school had been promised a computer as well when the Minister of Education visited on Friday. This was not unexpected and I am quite happy about that because it will mean that the school has two computers so that would improve their lot considerably and could only help the schools' 'Link'; "Fine!" I said. More interesting was the news that the Member of Parliament for Corozal Town who had organised the visit and that of the Prime Minister, tried to divert this computer away from Christian School. He wanted to give it to St Francis Xavier School as Christian School was receiving one from me; 'whisper who dares?' I must write the book! It is also worth noting that all the town schools have now received a computer one way or another, from the Government. Throughout the country, all the computers presented to Primary Schools have gone to the town schools. I know of no rural school that has received one. The Town Board elections are imminent and these presentations in Corozal coincide exactly, with the beginning of the election campaign. I walked to Ranchito to spend the afternoon with Orvin Rancheran. Among many other things, we talked of a trip to the estuary of the New River and a fishing weekend off Caye Caulker with his cousin 'Plantain'.

'…Please can you pass the attached word document on to Billy for me? It is in Word 97 format…'

'…No problem. As your FAO arrived early this morning (We are six hours behind you) I printed it off and delivered it right away. I hope you don't mind my reading it! I had to delete one line space to get it on to one sheet. Most people use letter size here, instead of A4. If you use the same font size your last line to fit on letter size would be line 35. There is no need to change your paper size as it then prints fine. What I did was to put the sheet in an airmail envelope with a stamp already on it and left it with Billy's sister, together with posting instructions, as he wasn't in…'

It was a very windy day today although it was only dull or wet for short periods. I didn't go out but spent time catching up with the outstanding jobs, letters and preparing parcels.

Monday 17th January: This was a long, hard day with the second monitoring visit to Libertad RC! I did the washing early in the morning and got it out on the line before going to the District Office to print copies of forms I needed for monitoring. I had asked David Eck to send an electronic copy or some hard copies but, as usual, nothing had happened. The next stop was the post office to send a birthday present, before cycling down to Libertad.

When I got to Libertad I found that not only had they still not done their Action Plan, but that Louisa had also undermined their position. She had told them that what they were doing was not an action plan and that all schools that had not submitted an action plan had been reported to the Ministry and would be sanctioned. No one has told me this and no one has asked for action plans to be sent in as far as I am aware. In fact there has been no contact from QADS whatsoever, since coming to Corozal – despite my prompting and sitting with David Eck for two hours at a workshop last year. There has been no contact from the school either, despite their having been given my home telephone number and urged to contact me at any time if they needed any help. Only Santa Rita has asked for help and they were given it.

I spent the school day in the three Lower Division Classes and met with the staff to go through the Action Plan again and to complete the report form. We managed to find some time to consider what I had seen in class. The school is clearly moving forward in the manner that had been originally discussed for action. But this had not been formalised and the only real evidence they could produce was what I had seen for myself. Further emphasis was given to the gathering of evidence as well. I made a point of going over to Methodist to make sure that their Action Plan would be ready for my visit tomorrow, as they hadn't done it on my last visit either. Afterwards I cycled back just in time to be home before dark. I then went to the shop and the Library, where I was delayed for a long time by Tom, an American who wants to run a science fair for schools based on the library. This made it very late to prepare and eat some food and write up the day's reports. Some of this was left for the morning.

Early this morning I finished the writing of reports and set off for Libertad again, where I found that Methodist school were in a mess with their Action Plan. A start had been made (since yesterday) in writing it down but discussion with the Principal made it clear that they had been going round in circles finding all the reasons for not doing it although there had been some progress in the school along the agreed lines. They had been offered the same support and contact as the other schools and had not used it. I had not even been told that the Principal would be leaving after lunch and not returning for the rest of the week! I found out that the comment about schools being sanctioned came from David Eck and was delivered at a BNTU meeting in Orange Walk. Such is the level of communication and organisation in QADS that neither he nor anyone else has had the courtesy, even, to contact or advise me! No time was spent in classes. I worked with staff from morning break through lunch time and left them with a clear list of tasks to be completed by an additional visit on Friday 28th January. By late evening, I had caught up with all writing of visit reports of which complete copies are being kept as I have made my own format (again) in the absence of one from QADS.

The cycling is quite demanding just now but I will persevere for that reason. It is very pleasant to be out in the morning sunshine especially, although the buses and heavy truck drivers are often inconsiderate or downright belligerent. I arrived at Libertad SDA just after nine this morning and spent a very interesting day centred on the Infant 1&2 class. The staff meeting to discuss the progress of the curriculum was just as wearing as always because of the need to keep going over and over the same ground and the demands of teachers to be told what to do. This latter often takes the form of "Am I doing it right (especially planning)?" In some ways that is more difficult to deal with because the question can never be answered as yes or no so it can never be satisfactory for the questioner.

I collected the Action Plan from the RC school at the end of the day. They had still counted tasks as things that the children would do rather than the staff but I took it as it was. It will be replaced when I go back to the Methodist school on the 28th January, if the one they've given me hasn't been sent to QADS.

The return ride was pleasant enough. Many children and parents wave anyway but they quickly notice you riding past more than once as well. I saw two of the first batch of Standard 6 students from Calcutta when I passed through that village. I remember both their names (unusual) as Valmar Riverol and Dean Sutherland. Valmar was on the opposite side of the road but I stopped to chat with Dean. He has a horse that he rides bareback! I would think that they must both be fifteen (possibly sixteen) by now. That was a magic class that left me with a lot of friends among the families of Calcutta Village.

I started early in the morning to do the washing for the weekend and to finish the reports from yesterday and set off for a long visit to Calcutta as I had to cover two divisions. There is an awful lot that needs to be done and the Action Plan was not in the required format – leaving serious gaps in its usefulness. I decided that a discussion with David Eck at QADS is essential so I returned home at lunchtime, to arrange it. Needless to say, it was impossible to reach him direct so I eventually left a message with David Price to arrange a meeting for 8:30am tomorrow. I asked that arrangements should be made for someone to take notes or minutes. There is a great deal in the mismatch between what is being asked and reality and the means to bring the two together. I returned to Calcutta for a staff meeting starting at 2:30pm and ending at 5:00pm. On returning home I did the ironing and packing for tomorrow and set about writing the reports. My intention is to go on to stay with Jack for the weekend, from Belize City. Early in the evening, a plea was made for blood for a man in serious condition in hospital in Belize City. As my blood is the right group (A+) I phoned them and arranged for them to contact me at the Ministry of Education from 8:00am tomorrow.

I set off for Belize City on the 5:30am 'Executive' and arrived at QADS at 8:00am. I spent the first half-hour talking to David Price about the programme and found him as inept as ever. Apparently the Minister now wants to reduce the 'Field Staff' by 50%! This is a crazy and wasteful country. The meeting with David Eck went as I expected. He agreed with everything I had to say (but does nothing). The full QADS meeting is changed to the 25th February and he asked me to give a presentation then. I've decided to write it so the details of these discussions will be recorded there.

I walked to the Western Highway via the bank so that I could pick up some money. My account is looking pretty sick after buying the three computers and the Christmas presents but that is how I wanted it to be. The bus journey was not bad at all. I called in at VSO to chat with Angie, leave my kit and check on the location of Jack's office. First I went off to have lunch and returned to VSO to talk over the situation at QADS and re-volunteering with Henry. Jack was very busy so he gave me his key and a disoriented sketch of how to get to his house. I collected some shopping for him on the way and settled down to wait. The evening was largely drink and chat, preparing food and eating it.

After a leisurely start next morning we walked to Guanacaste National Park and followed the whole of the trails. It is not very large and it didn't take long. Unfortunately, it is right by the Northern Highway and the junction with the main Belmopan road so it is almost impossible to get away from the noise of the heavy trucks. Banana Bank was much quieter. It was very pleasant to walk around part of the village and the orange groves where we scrumped a few oranges to be eaten right off the tree. Quite a lot of time was spent sitting watching wildlife on a very shallow little lake. We returned across the small ferry on the Mopan River from whence we came and were saved the long walk back with a ride in a small pickup into Belmopan. Four beers each later, we made our way back for extension of the evening before.

Jack had his birthday gift of a carved walking stick last Friday, as it couldn't be hidden. I can't see him using it but it is a nice piece of carving and it is different! A walk around Belmopan and through the 'park' followed another leisurely start. Four more Belikin accompanied lunch at the 'Bullfrog'. Then it was pack up time and time to catch the bus home. I thought I was lucky to get straight on to a Batty bus for Belize City at 2:45pm but it broke down with about thirteen miles to go. This meant a long wait for another bus to come out and fetch us and my missing the 4:30pm Venus bus for Corozal. The next one (and nearly the last) would be at 5:30. I decided to try Escalante who had a bus leaving at 4:00pm. That was incredibly slow and not a little worrying as the driver was all over the road – at times nudging the edge on the wrong side. It was worst when he decided to eat a packet of chips as he was driving. We made it to Orange Walk okay but then the driver decided that he hadn't enough passengers to go on so those of us wanting to go to Corozal had to get off! I finished up on the Venus bus after all. That wasn't slow. A maniac was driving that one and I was pleased to get off it and reach home just before 9:00pm. I contacted Jack later to say I wouldn't be going to Crooked Tree next weekend as I had had enough of buses for a bit.

The second week of monitoring began well with an enjoyable visit to Ranchito as always. I had lunch with the Rancheran family as usual and was pleased with the progress that was being made. The computer had not arrived so I tried to contact Douglas, unsuccessfully, by phone in the evening.

At San Antonio Government the Principal had been called to a meeting all morning and as she teaches half of the children I have to see in class, this was another setback in a heavy schedule. I sent an email to Douglas that was more terse than I would ordinarily because I am really quite anxious about the computers, having paid for them so long ago…

'Would you please advise when the three computers are to be installed at Ranchito, Santa Rita and St. Paul's schools? I will be home after 6:00pm or use email.'

Again, there was interference with the monitoring; this time at Santa Rita. The teachers were very helpful and we managed to do a reasonable job but they had nonetheless been told to attend the opening ceremony for the skills centre at 3:00pm. We don't normally finish a staff meeting until close to 5:00pm. The news was better in the evening as Douglas phoned to say that the computers would be installed tomorrow.

The computers were installed at Ranchito, Christian School and St Paul's today. That is a great relief very pleasing and more substantial than the Minister's promises and very much a catalyst for action! Douglas came to me in the evening, to upgrade my virus detector and align the FAX driver. While he was here Donald asked if he could come for the weekend. I agreed as I would be pleased to see him but it would put me even further behind with my writing that is already under strain with the monitoring records and reports.

Monitoring at Paraiso was the only unpleasant affair I have had in schools in Belize. A full report was made as usual. I have also reported one teacher's unwillingness to accept that children were being ill served. That would have remained a private comment had she not seen fit to make a big issue all over the school that damaged the work we were trying to do. The report was taken to the Principal Education Officer the next day.

'…Thank you for the parcel of books now safely arrived. I have passed your message on to Paul. The stamps were much appreciated by a number of pupils! Hope your New Year was memorable and that the new term is going well. We were interested to hear of your plans for a new placement; very exciting. Ship still waiting to be glued - I hope to do a display of everything after half term…'

I made an early start for Libertad for the additional visit to the Methodist school there only to find that the Principal wasn't in school after my having made special arrangements to meet her and travelled down for that purpose. I'm afraid my reaction was uncharacteristically ragged after a whole week of interruptions or distractions at the schools. I visited the other two schools successfully and set off back to Corozal much earlier than I expected. In fact I arrived at Ranchito in time for lunch and to find that I was expected there. Goodness knows how. Anyway, Orvin had lunch ready for me and it was nice to chat with staff and students following the installation of their computer. I was fairly late leaving and with a whole heap of writing to do including a new questionnaire from VSO London…

'…We're interested in finding out what people really feel about how volunteering abroad with VSO might have changed them and their opinions of UK society. Can you start off by telling us whether you think you've changed personally since beginning your VSO placement and how? What are the main differences in your lifestyle, attitudes, character, relationships etc. between your old life in the UK and your new life abroad? …'

I think 'change' might be a bit misleading – not that I can think of a better word but I think the seeds of change are already there before volunteering. Some aspects of life have assumed greater importance and others less. Having virtually no family, I have been living on my own since 1988. Many friends have remained in regular contact and part of my being here has been a sharing with them so that too, has its roots back home. There are differences of course, and your title 'Directions' has much to say about that. I maintained the home in the UK from 1988, with great care in all respects. Here in Belize, I find there is little that I need and very little more that I have indulged. The only real luxury in UK terms (if that is what it is) I am typing on right now, although I did bring cameras with me and returned from holiday with a good pair of binoculars. The climate helps since little thought needs to be given to creature comforts, but there seems no great need for many of the other things with which we surround ourselves either. I do all of my own chores and enjoy cooking. All you need for cooking is the ingredients, a few utensils and heat. Surprisingly little is needed in the way of clearing up afterwards! Being where I am and doing what I do is much more in focus. It does not need to be packaged. Nor is there any great need for 'posturing' or status. (Would that be the same if I was a Belizean?) Empathy is very much sharpened. That is in no way feeling sorry for people. It is much more like good teaching should be. That is, getting alongside and 'suffering' with others. There is nothing patronising about it. Rather, I have found myself questioning everything I took for granted. The result of that questioning has been that most ethics, principles and work practices have held firm while the need for material sophistication has not. I don't know about my character. Others would better answer that although I know that I have become much more aware of the issues, both great and small, which affect people's lives. I went to the funeral of a twelve-year-old at a school I work with and which is taking part in a personal 'Linking' programme with a school in the UK. I cried. I didn't realise that I had become so involved. I have experienced quite a lot of life in different parts of Belize and the way that has happened has been a big change. My friends are Belizean. I have friends among volunteers but I don't seek that any more than with anyone else and I don't follow the tourist trail in any way at all (I did in England, although I did a lot of long distance walking as well). Mostly, I have stayed with or visited Belizean families. The nearest VSO is eighty miles away.

'...Recent commentators (such as the BBC's Mark Tulley) have introduced the idea of the Western world being in some sort of spiritual crisis. What is your reaction to this? How does this match your actual experiences of living in another society? In what ways is the culture you are living in 'better off' than that of the UK? ...'

I'm not sure about a 'spiritual crisis' or about Mark Tulley's credentials. One of the things that have happened to me is qualification of opinion that makes one hesitant to express opinion in sweeping terms. I do think there is a serious 'non-spirit' or lack of spirit in the 'Western World' (The UK is East of here!). When I was little, like everyone else I believe I saw things in black and white terms – right and wrong. Then the shades of grey started to creep in. In more recent years that has changed to glimpses of glorious colour. Those glimpses have increased in frequency since volunteering. I can only refer to the UK. What I see is a lack of appreciation of the richness (variety and opportunity) that is there and a lemming-like desire to be all the same (Except that I'm a better lemming than you are!). Witness the family outing on Sunday that now heads for the supermarket. I believe that the UK is way ahead of the US in potential quality of life. It is safer, services are open to (almost) all, freedom recognises the needs of others and the country is compact, rich in variety and accessible. And yet (especially young) people will say there is nothing to do. There is a disproportionate concern with things that don't really matter much – nice if you can get them 'right' as the complainant sees them but not worth sweating over. A similar thing happens in many businesses, institutions, education etc. There is an unwillingness to accommodate 'other(s)' ideas. Responsibility gives way to authority (so people become irresponsible). I think it is a newly developed form of the power or control problem. (You can be my friend if you do as I say). The latter problem is no different here except that it is more obvious. At the moment you can have a job if your colour is blue. The greatest advantage for me in that respect has been to gain a new perspective that has helped to come to terms with reality, perhaps. Maybe people here should seek change but that is for them to decide. What is great is that it does not interfere in any way with the enjoyment of each other's company at times of relaxation. On my wall is a hand-made quote from Emerson. 'Do not go where the path may lead, go instead where there is no path and leave a trail.' It is decorated with a snail trailing joined leaves and made for me by a friend. She probably sees more than I do about my 'reaction' and being 'better off'!

'... What would you say are the benefits of volunteering with VSO? How do they match up with your expectations when you first applied to VSO (if you can remember them!)? Is it all worth it and why? ...'

I had a number of ideas formed in my mind after two careers and having retired from Primary teaching. It has been very interesting to challenge them in a different context and culture. Also, I had reached a point where moving forward together with young people in their learning did not fit comfortably with the prescription (and its protagonists) that was emerging in the UK. It has been a joy to work with teachers within a philosophy that sees education as 'The lifelong acquisition of knowledge, skills, attitudes and values for full personal development and active participation in society.' Nothing is perfect. There are many problems and it may not happen as intended (The intention was much the same in the UK) but it has been very rewarding to share, to learn and to find ways of reaching out with teachers towards children 'learning how to learn'. People, especially young people for me, are the same. We share the same hopes, interests, fears, sorrows, fun and laughter. To find that in another culture is much more the privilege and comfort than was expected.'

"...Have you given any thought to your return to the UK? How do you feel about that? Apart from finding the right job, what do you think you might find most difficult about 'readjusting' to UK society? ..."

I have applied to re-volunteer. There are elements of experience that I would like to take further and in another culture again, and in a different economic environment. When I do return I plan to write after finding a smaller, simpler house in which to work. I am in my third year here and have kept a substantial daily journal with many stories of the experiences I have had and I have written a number of children's stories that need to be arranged if they are to be published. I always enjoyed my free time in the UK before volunteering. Now that I can see so many more possibilities the readjustment should be challenging in a positive way. I always enjoyed walking the wild parts in equally wild weather but I have to admit that I would miss the climate here!

"…If you were in charge of encouraging other people to apply to VSO, what would you say? How would you 'sell' the idea of volunteering abroad? …"

This is a very personal matter. I am sure that there are attractions that would appeal to large groups of people and it is not a job I would care to do. On an individual basis, I would first listen to what is being said and then relate the ideas and expectations to my own experience – suggesting ways of finding more information on aspects that go beyond that. In a small group or with an audience I would quite simply share some of the experience that I have had. It has been so much fun that would be easy. I would shrink from persuasion. In your letter you say that VSO is often misunderstood as being about 'sackcloth and sacrifice' rather than a professional assignment. I'm not sure that matters too much to the volunteer in terms of going to do a job because the assignment is clearly a professional one. That is made very clear during selection. It does matter in the public mind and that in turn would help the volunteer. I have had a great opportunity with the 'Linking' programme involving five schools here and five forms in a school in North Devon. I don't think there can be much doubt in the minds of the three-year's worth of students and their families, so far, that I am here to do a job and that I have enjoyed it.

I tried to get as much report writing done as possible this morning but I had six emails to send as well so I hadn't done too much when Donald arrived at about 11:00am. We went out to lunch at the Jo-Mel Inn (Donald's treat) and followed that with a very pleasant walk through Altamira and Paraiso to Santa Rita where we were shown over the Mayan site by Mr Wilshire, the guide, who has two children at Christian School. After that we walked back around the seaside, looked in at the museum, bought some vegetables and cooked tea. The evening was spent at the Black Orchid and continued until about 2:00am at home.

Sunday morning passed pleasantly with a walk along the sea front and back before Donald caught the midday Batty bus for Belize City. I tried to work for the rest of the day but wasn't terribly successful at it and so went to bed with a great deal left to do.

I was due to go to St Paul's first thing this morning, for their assembly. I only stayed a few minutes because vandals had attacked the school at the weekend and the staff and older children were clearing and cleaning up. I went on to Guadeloupe for their monitoring. The walk takes about half an hour but I arrived at about 8:45am and found that the Principal had gone off sick for two or three months and absolutely nothing had been done either to the Action Plan or to the introduction of the New Curriculum. This has to be the ultimate in having to be told what to do and how and when (Holding hands!). It would appear that the staff could never agree when to meet! I spent the morning in the three classes. One of the classes, Standard 1 is the Principal's class so they had a new teacher. She has three months experience and no training. It is a difficult class. There is no point in regretting the loss of time so I went through the whole process yet again and the staff, including the Acting Principal, agreed to targets set for 18th February when I would visit the school again at 2:30pm. I left at lunchtime to type up records and reports, returned for the afternoon meeting at 2:30pm and set off for home at about 5:00pm. The evening was spent on reports after going to the library.

The visit to Mary Hill was successful but the visit to BTL was not. The bill of over $120 was clearly out of order and I discovered a charge of $53 for metered (local) calls. As I rarely make local calls this has to be investigated. Also, I have not received a bill for four consecutive months although I have insisted on paying according to their records without one. As I have not been able to check any of those bills they are all now open to question. We shall see! I collected two Mayan God carvings from White Sapphire. They go as birthday presents along with the two ships I have but for the time being, they look very good on the wall. My first call this morning, was to St. Paul's for assembly. This was given as a thank you for the computers and help with this and that. The choir sang 'Lean on Me' directly to me at the front of the church. It was as much as I could do to keep a dry eye but I was able to talk reasonably afterwards, along the lines that I can see no point in doing anything unless it is to be shared in some way and young people were learning about each other across the Atlantic.

I cycled out to Xaibe on Wednesday, completed the Monitoring process and spent the remaining time writing reports and notes in the evening.

The cycle ride to Chan Chen, after doing the washing, was quite pleasant except for the traffic on the Northern Highway. The monitoring is all very slow though. It is very difficult for teachers and schools to move from where they are. They do not have the time or the resources and they are given neither the encouragement nor the authority from the Ministry to do the things they need to do to put the curriculum in place. Otherwise, all I did was ironing, go to the library and call in at St Paul's to make sure that they would be ready for my visit next week. I had no energy left for report writing in the evening.

The whole of Friday was spent catching up with notes and report writing for schools although I did go to BTL about overcharging for local calls that I don't make and did a little shopping.
Janice phoned from the UK at about 5:00pm as no one had heard from me for several days. It was quite a surprise but a pleasant one except for having caused unnecessary anxiety.

'…Living here has been a real eye opener. The country is very dangerous, especially if you set the number of muggings, murders, rapes and senseless 'accidents' on the road against the size of the population. It has got much worse in the time I have been here too. Even the dogs are (very) aggressive and yet most people are very friendly in the ordinary way. I get told off for the places I go cycling or walking – although I do take precautions and I try not to do anything silly. There are places I don't go…'

'…Thanks for your letter. I have wanted to write for a week but I'm in the middle of monitoring, action plans and reports for nineteen schools and I had got a little behind with notes on visits and the report writing. If I get too far behind it would be difficult to do what I am trying to do together with the staff of schools. I usually catch up at the weekend but I had a long weekend in Belmopan two weeks ago and then I had an unexpected visitor for the weekend last week. Anyway, I am now up to date – as of the last few minutes…'

Most of the day was spent catching up with correspondence but I did go shopping and I did go for a ride on my bike. The ride started through the town and Altamira to Paraiso. What I wanted to do was to find out about the road that goes beyond the village. It serves cane fields as expected but there is a lot of bush where there are a huge number of parrots, not only the many small yellow ones but the big green ones as well. Eventually, the track joins at a tee-junction where a left turn leads back to the Northern Highway, close to the turn-off to Chan Chen. The right turn just peters out in the bush and cane fields close to the four-mile lagoon but I don't know whether you can see the lagoon as I didn't go that way. Asking the locals was not fruitful. I returned through Santa Rita and on past San Antonio to join with the Xaibe road back into Corozal. That was a new route too.

'…You are right about it being sunny over here. I have got quite used to having sunshine almost every day. It does rain of course, but it doesn't last and it isn't cold. It is 4:00pm right now and I am sitting with all windows and door wide open and just wearing a pair of shorts. I don't think that's bad for February. We get about the best weather in Belize here too. There is almost always a cooling breeze, usually coming off the sea, and we have much less rain than the rest of Belize because the hills and mountains are so far away. There is no shortage of water either because it seeps through the limestone from the mountains in vast quantities. The water table is never far down. I know of no wells that run dry and the town water supply is simply pumped up. There is no need for reservoirs and there aren't any. So there it is. The sun is shining, the birds are singing, the sea is sighing (very noticeable at night) and there is a gentle breeze.

I haven't been here all afternoon. I have just come in from a bike ride and got straight under the shower (I only have or want a cold one!). I only went about ten miles but it was a new ride where there are lots of parrots. I was pleased to see that there are the big green ones as well as the very numerous little yellow ones. I can't remember their names. We have had a lot of migrant swallows recently, too. They are much smaller than the ones that come to Europe. They are very attractive little birds with amazing agility in flight. Even so, I most like to watch our resident pelicans and frigate birds, especially when the days catch of fish is being gutted (heads and tails are left on to be cooked whole – eyes go hard and white!). We also have cormorants of course, and lots of wading birds. The egrets tend to be more inland, especially around cattle. I don't know too much about birds, I just like to see them…'

'…I thought you would like the stamps and my thoughts about them have been much the same as you might expect. I groan every time I see one of these weird things that arrive stuck to the letters from home and wonder what next? What makes it worse is that it is even more of a blur if I haven't got my right glasses on. Maybe it's better without them…'

'…Thanks for sending the illustrations. I will let you know as soon as they arrive. I will be going down to Belize City on the 16th February and will stay overnight, and again on the 25th when I could also stay over. I should have time to sort out the pages beforehand and leave it all with Marco for scanning and printing. Assuming we get far enough, how would you feel about copies in your school? That is entirely for you to decide. They would serve their purpose here. Perhaps I should just send you some copies and leave you to decide what to do with them. I'm not sure how they will be put together yet. Either stuck or with one of those plastic things that go through a row of rectangular holes…'

Lucille brought my main meal round again at lunchtime. That was creamed potatoes, fried chicken leg and salad so my casserole stayed in the fridge. I managed to finish a piece of writing on volunteering and re-volunteering that touches on the problems experienced and the successes in my work and the story of the computers for 'Links'. Many would appreciate that. I also managed to finish all the outstanding mail; always difficult to keep links going…

'…I hope that you are making progress with your study. I have been inundated for some weeks but the attached notes will give you some idea about my re-volunteering as well as one aspect of the point the 'Linking' has reached. It should begin to run itself between schools now but it does need email from your students…'

'…Thanks for your last letter. Good to hear you have been kept busy. I was pleased to hear of your next steps… … The pupils are constantly asking me for letters, but I have heard nothing from the Belize schools for a long time. Many of my pupils are still writing (some direct to home addresses), but I have been waiting for a reply before doing something as a group again…'

'…This weekend has been mostly spent catching up with letter writing but it isn't a chore. I have been right by the door all day. The door has been open, and the sun has been shining brightly. Children have been coming and going on the beach opposite all morning and there were lots of families there this afternoon. A small concrete stand has been built for people to sit when games are being played (why call it a stand?) and this is proving popular because it is in the shade of a tree right on the edge of the water throughout the morning...'

After a whole day on reports and going to the District Centre, mail continued and the illustrations for 'Home is the Belizoo' arrived. ('I thought you would like to know right away; they look good!') Monitoring continued as routine until Friday…

It was a fair rush round today as I had a lot of schools to visit, rounding up late Action Plans. I took my bike and started round Altamira to Guadeloupe, then Paraiso and Santa Rita; from there to San Antonio, Xaibe, Calcutta and Ranchito. On the way out, I met up with Orvin Rancheran taking footballers to the Stadium. I had already been to St. Pauls to enquire about their packages for SMCC and seen their footballers departing on their own as there is no male teacher at the school. At the Stadium the St Pauls boys were all dejected as they had a fee to pay and couldn't play without it. They had no money so I fixed that for them. I also checked on the other four 'Link' schools to make sure that they either had packages to send or were sending them. I managed to get back for lunchtime and was just able to make it at Guadeloupe for 2:30pm. Saturday was another whole day of report writing. I also managed to send off four emails this morning but I still have letters to write and a full report on monitoring – at least for the record.

'…I have checked with all the 'Link' schools this week. Methodist sent a package on Monday and Calcutta sent one yesterday. Christian School (Santa Rita) and St. Pauls will send theirs on Monday (14th). Ranchito sent another package ten days ago. I know that they have sent a huge amount. Ironically, they are the ones who receive least and they have not heard from 7S since Christmas. I agree with you about the need for regularity as you know but not with the tactics. You are not playing on a level pitch. There are many problems here but, if you read between the lines in my last attachment you will see, the biggest problem is lack of initiative. Also, I quickly learned when I came here, that the way to get people to write to me is to keep writing until they do. I have deliberately avoided emphasising the problem of arousing commitment here because it suggests a disparity among peoples and we are no different. It does, however, have something to do with development and all that sort of thing. I call it 'The Gimme a Dollar Syndrome'. No doubt you can work out a lot of that for yourself – confirmed by your travels. I don't like it because it is frustrating on the one hand and demeaning on the other. But I think we are stuck with it in order to strengthen the response; email will help but again much of the initial thrust will need to come from SMCC. If you think back to the effort of trying to get youngsters to use the keyboard when schools first had computers in the UK you will remember how slow it all was. If the schools have a stack of emails to answer I am sure that will galvanise action better than anything. That is why I have been so keen to secure the facility. (Now schools are having problems paying for the server!)…'

I have been extremely busy lately with the monitoring of schools and the days in between have been mostly spent catching up with letters. Even my journal has suffered over the last couple of months although there are plenty of records spread about in other places to make up for that. Today has been no exception although the two 'cooks' have clashed! Ruby came round with a bowl of escabeche and hot tortilla that her Mum had made, just after midday and Lucille came round with rice and beans with fried chicken and salad an hour or so later! Fat chance I have of getting some weight off even though I either walk or cycle to all of my nineteen schools, the furthest being nine miles away; a nice position to be in though. I spent some time on the veranda this afternoon, as there is so much activity on the beach. The new stand under the tree on the shore-line is well used and there are lots of other 'park seats' around now but the big thing is the two poles that people can use to attach their volley-ball net; that livens things up enormously and it is very pleasant to read a book and watch some of the comings and goings at the same time. The last two Sunday mornings there has been a little Gospel group assembled between the big tree and the water. Their singing fits well with the constant sighing of the sea.

This has been a really busy day again. I started off with washing the bedclothes and some small things and then headed for the post office with a fistful of mail; next to the Sub-Treasury to cash a voucher which they did for me without my having to take a cheque to the bank; then the morning at Corozal Nazarene until 11:30am. I managed to type up some notes for the school and have some lunch before going to Corozal Methodist on my bike, to do a session with Standard 4 on Trades Unions at 1:00pm.

They found the presentation quite novel compared with the teaching they are used to! No letting up! I left about half an hour later to go to Christian School Assemblies of God at Santa Rita and San Antonio School for a very short visit at each. The route took me round Altamira and Paraiso to get there, before returning to have a shower and arrive back at Nazarene for a meeting with staff at 2:30pm. Then it was take in the washing, library, shopping, cook dinner and send off a couple of email replies to letters that had arrived during the day – and settle down to read before going to bed.

I decided not to go to the dinner tomorrow night as I would be an hour late arriving and like a wet rag when I get there. The day at Xavier tomorrow is likely to be the most demanding of all because of its size. I sent an email, first thing, to let VSO know.

I went into the District Office before going to school, and talked with Joe Martinez. Apparently he has had a request for appraisal as well but he is refusing to do it because QADS lack of planning, purpose and professionalism has affected him as well. Corinth confirmed what had happened at QADS when she phoned at lunchtime as I was finishing my notes for Christiline Gill School. After the meeting was finished in the afternoon I went to do a little shopping. On the way back I stopped to watch the firemen out practising with their two fire engines just by the market. It was so funny! Talk about Fred Cano's Army! There were firemen running round unrolling hose in circles, kinks everywhere and men rushing backwards and forwards achieving nothing. Still, they obviously need the practice. Perhaps it would be as well to get ready well before a fire starts. Anyway, it was a source of great entertainment for all the onlookers. I phoned Marco in the evening and arranged to go down for the weekend on Friday morning. Then he will be able to use the scanner at work to scan Philip's drawings. On Saturday, he has to go to Orange Walk to do some work on their house there but I can go with him to do that.

Wednesday 16th February the whole day was spent at Xavier School again, except that I managed to get the notes for the Lower Division typed up at lunchtime in order to give them a copy. It was fun going in to Standard 4 where there were three classes, ninety children, located in what was called the garage. I told them of my first visit there two years ago; that I couldn't find it and why. Then I said "You know what? Even to this day I have never found the answer to a simple question." There was a long pause as everyone waited as I looked around all the expectant and curious faces. "How on earth do you get the cars up these stairs?" One girl burst out laughing and I rounded on her and thanked her heartily for laughing at my joke. Immediately the whole place erupted in laughter! Not a bad entrance! The evening was spent cooking, eating and reading. I can leave the remainder of the reports and notes for tomorrow although I will have plenty to do as I have several short school visits to do and I want to go through 'Home is the Belizoo' to be ready for working on it with Marco at the weekend.

I finished right up to date with notes and reports for next week's meeting of QADS. I still have a full report to do for that meeting but I can do that next Tuesday when the Spelling Bee is on in Libertad. I went into BTL again with this this month's bill that is also overcharged. They really are a tiresome lot who still seem to think that they can make no mistake when the whole of Belize knows different. Another angle on the football tournament…

'…With all the schools' visiting I have done now, I can't move without "Hi Mr Max" from adults as well as children. It was really brought home the other day when I went to catch a couple of Principals who had taken football teams to the town stadium for a big tournament. St. Paul's was one of the school teams who were there on their own because all their teachers are female. They told me that they couldn't play because they hadn't got the fee! So off I went with the team to the organiser's tent to pay it for them. This meant crossing the stadium to a constant stream of "Hi Mr Max" from all the star players from the district at up to fourteen years! They are all way ahead of me when it comes to football too! ...'

I went to Belize City on Friday morning to stay with the family for the weekend; spent Saturday with Marco and Miriam scanning Philip's drawings for the story illustrations and returned home after a very relaxing weekend; half term beginning in the UK!

Monitoring at Libertad RC and Methodist was very pleasing but I wasn't able to go to SDA because they had their Spelling Bee, at Concepcion on Wednesday afternoon. What is important I wonder? From My point of view it was useful because I was able to finish my report on the nineteen schools' monitoring such that it is in a condition to give each of them a copy as well. It had been raining hard during the night and I thought that I would have to use the bus or even a taxi this morning but I hung on and it cleared up enough to use my bike although it rained while I was at the school. The Methodist meeting was held at lunchtime because Balthazar was taking the football team to play in the tournament in the afternoon. They were playing Ranchito.

'...I had some great news today. I have been reselected by VSO! That means I will be off again and it could well be for September, which is what I would like. I don't know where yet but I have my hopes and with the time in hand it should give a good choice. Not a great lot of people are offered this second opportunity so I'm pretty chuffed...'

I was up at 3:30am to have breakfast, clear up and get ready to go to Belize City and stay over with the family. When I arrived at the Venus depot I found that the 5:30am 'Executive' had been taken off! This meant catching the 5:45am regular so that I arrived half an hour late at QADS. I would rather that than half an hour early. I was also very tired already. When I phoned Neria, it was to say that I wouldn't be staying over – which was just as well because she and Tabo are off to Punta Gorda tomorrow morning and Marco has to go to caye Caulker.

The meeting was so badly arranged and managed by David Eck that it is difficult to believe even after two and a half years in Belize. However, I was able to present my report and some notes on planning such that everyone wanted a copy.

All the spare time I had at the weekend was devoted to various birthday presents and cards; another extended occupation with limited communication. It wasn't helped when I got as far as printing a card and found that my screen had jammed up and I had to switch off. When I got it back it had reverted to a distorted image that had been appearing between screensaver and the proper worktop since the Windows 98 Plus! was installed. I suppose that it had got fixed in the distorted mould by switching off. Anyway, I got through to Douglas and he is coming to fix it on Monday evening. The computer is rather difficult to use with the display as it is but at least it is still in action as long as I don't look at the screen too much.

'...I imagine that your 'little bit busy' for the Half Term is in comparison with last week – your terms! If that had been me, it would have meant that I had been working my socks off and I no longer knew whether it was morning, noon or teatime. Such is the nature of language that it allows for our nature as well. Actually that has been another interesting aspect of my time here in Belize. The number of different interpretations that are put on the same words is amazing. Also, I notice that Belizeans often don't listen at all (but nod politely or make appropriate noises) unless you are telling them to do something. When you tell them they listen to a point where they can repeat what you have said word for word. I'm certain this is a direct result of early learning in schools and is what I have been trying to help change. If you think about that you will see how difficult running workshops and monitoring really is...'

Monday morning was spent at Ranchito and I returned to the office after lunch to print off copies of my report and notes on planning before going back to Ranchito. After the meeting I arranged to go with Orvin tomorrow evening, to Chetumal to buy some shirts. Douglas came this evening to fix the computer display and reinstall Windows 98 plus! The school had an activity for Children's Week on Tuesday so there was an early meeting at San Antonio Government and I was able to return home to write up my notes and report right away.

The first day of March, a Wednesday, should have been the third monitoring visit to Santa Rita but I was not able to go to school because of the Town Board Elections that pretty well brought Belize to a standstill. I received papers from VSOL for re-volunteering today. This means doing the CV all over again and having another medical, which is a bit of a nuisance.

It was another short visit to Paraiso as the Principal was again outmanoeuvred by members of her staff. I made sure that she was fully informed so that tactic didn't work for them!

Friday 3rd March, Children's Day the Munda Maya canoe race down the Belize River started at 6am today. The start is at the Hawkesworth Bridge in San Ignacio and the finish is at the Swing Bridge in Belize City. It takes four days and covers a distance of 180 miles, finishing on Monday. Monday is a Bank Holiday in lieu of next Thursday, which is Baron Bliss Day.

I started the day by filming a short parade by St Paul's School behind their band and then went off down to Ranchito for their Children's Day celebrations. It always amazes me how children are prepared to sit for so long – as they did even while waiting for food. There is none of the getting it all ready for them while they play games! I was well fed at Ranchito as usual. By the time I had eaten half of a barbecued chicken with two large flour tortillas, beans and salad in the middle of a hot day; it was a bit of a struggle to get home. I met Andrew Rancheran while I was there. He is Orvin's Grandfather. He is 94 years old and he has 450 great grandchildren! That is an average of 7.7 children per family. What a splendid old man!

The package containing the pictures for 'Home is the Belizoo' promised by Marco didn't arrive so I won't be able to do anything to that again this weekend. Next Monday is a Bank holiday too. The PUP supporters are celebrating their victory this evening but it leaves a very unhealthy situation. Because of the voting system there is effectively no opposition in the National Assembly, the City Councils or the Town Boards. As the PUP were put there by only 30% or less of registered voters that means that 70% of registered voters are not represented in any way at all. That is not a good recipe for unity in such a tiny nation. So I don't really see anything to celebrate. Most of Saturday was spent writing and getting ready for Kathryn visiting tomorrow.

'…I have been just as busy and the difficulties created by politicians and financial constraint have increased further. It would take far too long to go into and would leave the wrong impression so I won't do that. What I do is to make sure that the work that is done is effective and enduring. Currently, I'm trying to engage each school in a sufficient vision (Their vision and starting from where they are) to last for a couple of years and find a route to achieve it. It should ease off in three weeks or so…'

Children's Day is as one would expect (and hope) on a Friday and this year was two days ago and the anniversary date of Tim being knocked down on the Northern Highway is today 5th March, Sunday. I find this especially difficult being very much in mind over three days and it is just as well that Kathryn arrived early to stay over. She came by car, with an ex-Peace Corps Volunteer, Pat, who had hired a vehicle. I would have liked to see Kathryn on her own; it was obvious she felt the same but it was good of Pat, especially as try as we might, she was often out of the conversation. We had a good walk around the town and visited the Mayan Site at Santa Rita. Unfortunately, Mr Wilshire, the guide I had recorded, wasn't there so we sat at the top for quite a while and just talked and enjoyed the view. It was a very hot day but the fairly stiff breeze was very comfortable. The route back took in another part of the town as we made our way past the Civic Centre to the park by the sea at the North end of the town. We sat by the sea in the shade of a palm tree for quite a while before walking back along the sea front, stopping on the way to look in the museum. The late afternoon and evening were spent chatting and drinking Belikin and we had a salad and cheese snack when we came in and braised chicken with vegetables later; good therapy, thanks.

Kathryn and Pat left after an early breakfast to visit Altun Ha and see the end of the Munda Maya race in Belize City, on their way back. It being a public holiday in lieu of Baron Bliss Day I had washed the sheets and cleared up completely to be writing email before 10am! Corinth phoned this evening to say that she was doing a half-day workshop at Nazarene tomorrow so I arranged to meet her for lunch.

'…I have been extremely busy trying to keep up with the needs of nineteen schools, monitor their progress, produce notes and recommendations for them and write reports all at the same time. I have deliberately not written to you but time is running out in terms of securing the link as much as possible. I think establishing firm teacher to teacher communication is the only way to do this. Does that all fall on you? I have also sat down several times to write to year 7 but there is not much coming this way, which makes it difficult. I will write to them shortly following this letter…'

'…The present round will finish at the end of this month. Then I have two weeks, which is plenty of time to plan for twelve one-day workshops to be held in May and (as far as I know) that's about it…'

'…I have run into another problem with the story. I didn't stay in Belize City two weeks ago, as I thought I might, because it was a particularly heavy day and there were difficulties with the buses. Also, the Family had a lot on that weekend. I had the scanned pictures on disc and loaded into the computer, as you know, so I cleared the reports and settled down to arrange the illustrations here. Then Murphy stepped in! I was producing a birthday card in Publisher and things like that take a while to print. One of the quirks with a laptop has to do with the screensaver. There is never any problem if you minimise back to the desktop but I had forgotten to do that and the screen jammed. That in turn means switching off and rebooting because there is no way of shutting down properly. When I got going again I found that Corel wasn't working and I couldn't read the scans. Now I am waiting for the originals to be sent back from Belize City so that I can identify the pictures and tell Marco where to put them on his machine! Phew…'

I was to meet Corinth off the 9:00am. Premier and she would be at the Plaza. I thought that the timing would be about right for 11:15 but no Corinth. It appeared that the bus had arrived so I walked up to Batty Bus and was away at the time she appeared at the Plaza! That was sorted out, however, and we had lunch at the Jo-Mel Inn before going to the school. Teachers from Libertad Methodist School and Christian School Assemblies of God were there too. Corinth said she would call round home at the end of the day after my monitoring at Mary Hill and I aimed to be back for 4:30pm. At the end of the day I went to the District Centre for a cardboard box but they didn't have one. I thought I had time to go to A&R where I also got some more brown paper but managed to miss seeing Corinth again. I knew she was to catch the 6:00pm bus so I met her at Batty Bus while out to change my library book. Caroline phoned late to say that she would not be coming tomorrow after all, as she has a cold. That is a pity. She goes back to Zimbabwe next Wednesday and I would have liked to see her before she goes.

I posted various gifts first thing this morning, on the way to Xaibe. As it is Ash Wednesday the whole school went to church for 2:30pm so I was hanging around for an hour and a half but I still managed to get back for 4:30. I didn't do much else.

The Standard 1 class was almost out of control at Guadalupe RC. I went in there first and dealt with one girl particularly, and several others whose behaviour behind the teacher's back needed attention. I then decided that it would be best left to the teacher to settle down and spent the rest of the morning with Infant 1 and Infant 2. Apparently Standard 1 would be doing something they were looking forward to this afternoon. At lunchtime I went home to type up the notes from the morning so that I could leave them when we met this afternoon. I was short of time, of course, and resolved to do without lunch. When I got home Lucille called over to say she was bringing lunch so I did very well with chicken soup with rice.

As I had no schools to visit today I thought I would try to make some progress with the requirements for re-volunteering. I did the washing and then I filled in my part of the new medical form and went off to Dr Garcia early this morning, to arrange an appointment for a medical. There were two problems with this. First there was no Dr Garcia and second, they don't make appointments. I have to go early on Monday morning and asked the receptionist to mention it to him. I had cycled out to the doctor's surgery as it would otherwise be over half an hour's walk. I cycled out through the town and past Santa Rita but decided to go back from Paraiso along the short stretch of bush road to Altamira. I often go that way to avoid the Northern Highway. I was so absorbed by the sight of the small snake that had been run over that I almost missed seeing the live one making its way across the road in my path! It was a case of brakes on and choosing a safer route as this one was over five feet long. I am always surprised at how relatively thin most of the snakes are that I have seen here but this one was a beauty – bright, bright green, tongue flicking and very lively. I needn't have bothered too much though. It turns out that it is quite harmless. Called locally a 'ratania', it lives on small animals such as mice and rats and is not poisonous. I give all snakes a wide birth – especially since I discovered that some of the very poisonous ones are really very small and easily pass unnoticed. It's okay when they pass; forget the unnoticed! I returned home to leave my bike and go to have my hair cut. 'Willingly' was busy; well, busy for him! There was one in the chair and two waiting and he isn't quick! It was about two and a half hours by the time I came out but I had read the paper and had my hair cut for five dollars and I was thoroughly relaxed so it was good! The rest of the day was spent shopping, cooking, ironing, writing letters and reading.

It took all Saturday to finish my CV and write up a story of Three Turtles (Audubon Society) for Year 7 but when I returned plates to Lucille on Sunday morning she announced that she would be sending dinner up so I didn't have to cook and I finished all my correspondence…

'…You might find it difficult to imagine the scene, as so many things are different that you will take for granted and not even think about. Most schools close down completely for lunchtime because the school does not provide meals. In that case, the whole school might be locked up while the teachers go home to eat. Then it is pitiful to see children hanging around for they will have nothing or almost nothing to eat. Children often arrive at school having had no breakfast. A growing number of schools are developing kitchens that they fund in a variety of ways so children are better provided for. Sometimes, as in some of the villages, the school remains open. That is when I notice more of the provisions made quietly, for individual children. Also, that is when food comes in to the school in individual plastic containers prepared and sent by the family of the member of staff concerned. Quite often I eat like that. At other times, I am taken to eat with the family in the village. I enjoy that very much but, again, you might find it difficult to imagine the scene, which varies from an outside kitchen with open fire, through the traditional cohune log hut to a concrete building in a permanent state of construction. It doesn't take long to become part of that scene. There are always children and old people who like to join in and I like to make sure that they do, so it works well and the next visit becomes a continuation from the one before. It is a great privilege. In a village called Xaibe, I have eaten several times with a Mayan family and spent quite a lot of time talking with the grandfather. We talk of the changes we have seen in the last century…'

'…The village schools only have an hour for lunch from Monday to Thursday, and finish at lunchtime on Friday. All schools start at 8:30am and finish at 3:30pm. The 5-8 year-old children finish school at 2:30pm. The contact hours through the year are only about three-quarters of yours because holidays are much longer and more frequent. There are also many more interruptions to the school day and the school routine. I spend the day in classes and generally meet with the appropriate staff at about 2:45pm for about two hours. I have certain set tasks but I put as much emphasis as I can on where teaching and learning is right now and where it might go next; always bearing in mind the ultimate aim of 'the learner learning to learn' and the UNESCO four pillars of learning (Learning to live together, Learning to be, Learning to do and Learning to know)…'

I went for the medical on my way to Chan Chen. The doctor was very helpful but the greatest value of the medical is that the form is filled in, stamped and signed! I went armed with my vaccination record, which I keep religiously up to date, and a copy of the medical I had last year in South Molton. The doctor took my blood pressure but the main part of it was his remark that I am fitter than he is and that was that! I was out in five minutes and that included a chat! It wasn't possible to obtain booster injections at the surgery but I was told that they could be obtained at the Health Centre so I decided to call in there on the way back.

I wasn't expected at Chan Chen (their error). That threw the Principal into a spin because of lunch. It being Monday, the usual cook wasn't available. I told her not to worry as I have a pair of legs and a bicycle but she feels the need to provide. In the event, two lunches arrived and I shared the surplus with her girls and their friend.

At the Health Centre I was told that the Public Health Inspector deals with rabies and typhoid vaccinations cannot be obtained in Belize; that is not out of date yet so it can wait until I go home. The Public Health Inspector would not be available until 8:00am tomorrow and he would be going out soon after.

Having no monitoring to do on Tuesday I met with the Public Health Inspector who was very helpful although he didn't have any vaccine. He elected to check with the authorities in Belize City and would I phone him in the morning. On the way back, I called in at Atlantic Bank to pick up the story boards for 'Home is the Belizoo' and went off home to set out all the illustrations. That took the rest of the day.

After my visit to St Paul's I learned that there is no rabies booster vaccine in Belize City so I can now safely leave all that to VSO whom I have asked before! I managed to write up the report for St Paul's at lunchtime and so remained ahead of the game ready for the weekend.
The children gave presentations at Corozal Methodist as it was my last monitoring visit. That was very humbling and it was good to see the enthusiasm and commitment of children to their task. To be the object of that task was quite something.

I talked with Henry about a possible five school celebration to take place during Education Week and he was very enthusiastic – talking about taking the school learning out into the environment on Miami Beach and taking a theme of communication that would include the absent South Molton Community College. More than humbled now, I went home both emotional and excited.

The VSO Annual conference was held at Cahal Pech Village in San Ignacio over the weekend, including Friday; always interesting and a welcome relaxation that included a couple of visits. Cahal Pech also has a Maya site although that isn't likely to lure visitors with its name, 'Place of the Ticks', derived from the time when it was used as a cattle pasture. It is a small site but being on a high hill surrounded by trees it is amazingly tranquil despite being close to the town. The proposed site of a hydro-electric scheme incorporating a dam at Chalillo in a remote and very beautiful part of the forest is the subject of much national debate, helped no doubt in that the confluence of the Macal and the Raspaculo Rivers is there. Raspaculo means 'Scratchy Bottom' named because of the water being so shallow for canoes.

Third monitoring visits continued. Louisa and I met at the Education Centre first thing on Tuesday, to go over what we might do for the coming one-day workshops and the curriculum workshops. The visit to Corozal Nazarene was fine. I called in to Christiline Gill to put off my visit until next week when they would be installed in their new classrooms.

Louisa and I met again at the Education Centre to continue with plans and proposals. I sent off a letter by FAX to David Price suggesting that the Middle and Upper Division workshops be held at the beginning of the holiday rather than the end of it. I would then stay so that we could work together on them.

'…The finishing time here is still uncertain because the Ministry has got itself into a difficult situation, leaving two big workshops poorly staffed. If I can help with that without delaying beyond July, I will do. Otherwise I would return at the end of June. It would suit me to stay that bit longer because I have taken no holiday this year so that would be added on at the end. I would then have served the full three years in Belize. The holiday would be taken at home like last year but I wouldn't come back. Sometime in the future (when I'm older) I hope to come back here for a holiday…'

'…I know that all schools here have sent packages and received no reply and there has to be a way of securing enthusiasm before I depart…'

'…There has just been a lot of 'banging the drum' centred on the Round House on the beach opposite. I have had some free time this afternoon and Corozal Community College was celebrating taking the National Basketball Championship. People here really do celebrate (noisily). There is none of the English reserve (of which I have far too much but that has softened over the years and much more so since coming here). A whole host of vehicles arrived including five busloads of students. It didn't last long but they will remember…'

'…The monitoring and curriculum work is progressing very well thank you. It is much better even, from a personal point of view, than I could ever have dared to hope – especially in view of the inadequate administration and provision of funds, resources and opportunities for teachers. People express their gratitude in such open and genuine ways that it is difficult to take sometimes. As I keep pointing out, they do the work and I only open up what they already have but there it is. The children are amazing. I felt that I had an extraordinarily privileged position in South Molton but it enters a new dimension here. There are so many children; I go to all their schools; and I can't move for them in the town or in the villages. When I sail into a classroom children stand up and give a choral greeting so you might imagine I take that as an open invitation for fun time! – Not for long but they don't forget. Sometimes I might tell a story or take a lesson (but I never do demonstration lessons). Belize youngsters of all ages are a delightful audience. Come to think of it, the teachers are too. I've had them rolling about as well! The education development team is being seriously cut from September and the workload increased. It would leave Louisa with three major workshops to do on her own in the summer. They are supposed to take place at the end of the holiday so I am trying to get the system into gear so that we can run them together during the first three weeks of July. I can't stay any longer than that but it would set her up for the coming year. What I would do then is take my six weeks holiday afterwards, at home, and not go back. I would then have completed my three years. I have almost finished the monitoring and I'm spending today on records and paperwork. Next week I have to go to Libertad nine miles away on Monday, Santa Rita, which is a 'Link' school on Tuesday and Christiline Gill SDA school in new premises on Wednesday. I went to the inauguration of the new premises yesterday, and cut the ribbon! After that there is a series of one-day workshops in May to prepare for; then the run up to the summer workshops mentioned above and that's it…'

I went to the Education Centre again first thing on Thursday and went through the arrangements for the one day orientation workshops and timetable with Louisa. She will deliver all the letters except two that I took to Christiline Gill yesterday and I sent copies to David Eck by FAX. The inauguration of the new building for Christiline Gill SDA School was at 10:30am. As an invited guest I had an honoured position that I enjoyed very much. It was only an hour and the children sang as well as any I have heard in Belize. The meeting at St Francis Xavier was most enjoyable. I received a round of applause too!

I spent the day on Friday catching up with notes, reports and correspondence before going out to the Post Office, obtaining eight passport photos and booking a seat on the 6:00pm Premier to spend the weekend with the family. Hopefully we will get the book done for 'Home is the Belizoo'. In the evening, Marco and I went out. We met up with Jack and some of the VSOs at his house in Freetown Road but didn't stay and went to join some of Marco's friends at the Biltmore Plaza. From there we went on to a much more interesting and basic place where there were only Belizeans, out on the South side. Marco managed to lock his key in his vehicle (with the engine running) so I was on my own in the place for some time while someone took him home to collect a spare key! He thinks his Mum doesn't know! We were very late back and it is a long time since I have been so affected by drink. I shouldn't have had the two large rum and coke with the VSOs (but I was bored there).

Saturday was very much a family day although we spent a lot of time on the book and got it finished. There were two problems: the programme kept repositioning the pictures and text but we got this nearly sorted out such that it would only be necessary to make small adjustments before printing; and the driver for the laser colour printer had to be reinstalled and aligned. A lot of the day was spent playing with the children. Miguel had asked for a paper aeroplane so I made him a proper origami one that they had never seen before. That led to a lot of fun. The proof copy of the book was printed next morning, after the text and pictures had been checked and reset where necessary. The aeroplanes continued in flight all day. I have never seen the children play with anything for so long and I had to leave spares when I came home. I stayed for lunch and caught the three o'clock Venus bus from the downtown depot to return home.

As we left Belize City the Belize Emergency Response Team (BERT) ambulance overtook us. It was returning in the opposite direction at about mile 28, just before Crooked Tree. At Crooked Tree we passed the two o'clock bus that was parked by the road, still full of passengers. One of the passengers, a lady, had got off to go and urinate and had been knocked down by a pick-up truck on returning across the road to the bus. She was killed. The standard of driving and consideration for others using the road in Belize just now is appalling.

'…Thank you for the 'Post Assessment Day Folder' which I have just received. I have already had a medical as you suggested, and the completed forms have been sent to you through the VSO office here in Belize. My own dentist attended to my teeth when I was on holiday last June and I will be making an appointment with him as soon as I return this year. All that I can see you may require right now, is passport photographs. I will send those in the mail this week. You have my passport details but I will send them with the photos. There has been no change in my circumstances...'

The ride down to Libertad was very hot and the standard of driving is getting worse – such that I often get off the road as a discretionary measure that is very much against my nature! Often, it is very inconvenient and sometimes impossible to go off the tarmac as the edge can be anything from smooth(ish) mud in the villages to extremely ridged and potholed, baked mud or stone; or even bush. How many snakes are in there? The teacher for Infant 1/2 was not in school so my class visit was brief and I spent most of the time in discussion with the Principal. I returned after lunch to exchange my voucher for a cheque at the Sub-Treasury. In the evening I did some correspondence and then called it a day with a book.

'…I am having a meeting with the Principals of the five 'Link Schools' tomorrow. We have rather an exciting idea. I'll tell you more if it looks as though we can make it happen…'

'…Just a quick note to say that I have finished the book and it is part printed. I went to stay with the family in Belize City and finished it then. It is being printed on a laser colour printer so the quality is good and it won't fade. The copies then go off to be bound. I will have to use those plastic binders that wrap round through lots of rectangular holes but it will be a perfectly good book and just right to take to a publisher if I get round to it. I'm having fifty copies made so there will be enough for the schools and a few friends…'

I had an email first thing this morning saying that my papers had been sent to Malawi to see if there was an opening there for September. That is by no means a certainty but it is good news as VSO are trying to get me in. Here's hoping! I went off to the bank to cash my cheque and met with Louisa at the District Office before walking out to Santa Rita where I spent the morning in classes. Louisa confirmed that the three schools that had been left off my expenses claim are 'out of town schools' so I will resubmit the claim for them together with a brief note! I don't particularly want the money except to spend on schools but the attitude that goes with it, is irritating to the point where I feel obliged to push. I came back for lunch and to type up the report and notes for Christian School before returning for a staff meeting at 2:30pm. On the way out there I called in at St Paul's to check that the meeting for 'Link' school's Principals had been called for Thursday. This time I went on my bike. It has been very hot indeed today and looks likely to get much hotter. It is very, very dry this year. In the evening I went to the library but I forgot to take my wallet (again) so I couldn't do any shopping. Later, I wrote up the report for Libertad SDA and sent a copy off by email.

And more washing; there are lots of things that I don't write about as a rule and washing clothes etc. is one of them. It does go on however, three or four times a week. I like to keep on top of it because the facilities are very basic and it takes a long time. The visit to Christiline Gill was good and I got the report done at lunchtime so I was able to wrap all the business of monitoring up by the end of the day.

Louisa and I met this morning but there isn't much to do. I have my final report to prepare and I said that I would type hers up for her when it is ready. Louisa will work out the budgets for the one-day workshops and I will set them out and send them. We are waiting for documents before we can prepare the programme. I gave her my claims forms to send in via Corinth on Saturday.

After that it was a very quiet day except for the meeting with the 'Link' School's Principals at Corozal Methodist School at 2:30pm. Orvin didn't arrive but it was agreed that there would be a 'Celebration of Learning' to be held during Education Week on Thursday 18th May at Miami Beach. Schools would be making presentations, displays, activity bases and communicating with each other. Various organisations will be invited to take part and the whole idea is to take the schools out into the town to communicate their learning with the parents and townspeople. The absent school (South Molton) will be present in the activities shared and it is hoped to set up some sort of email link. BTL will be invited to put on a display and provide Internet facilities direct from the beach. Each school will bring their computer, which can be set up in the Round House.

I received notification of the return of my $100 deposit from BTL this morning, together with $9 interest. That can go towards the celebration! It arrived just as I was about to go and make a holding payment while BTL are sorting out their overcharging that has been going on for the last three months.

While I was out, I went on to see Henry to tell him that 'Friends of the Corozal Library' would take part in the celebration and could supply a video camera. There was a parade of Pre-School children in the town at about 9:00am. People in Belize certainly love to parade and it was quite difficult to concentrate on the children with so many proud parents among them. They must spend a fortune on costumes! I watched the parade with children and staff from Xavier and Methodist by the square and then again with children and staff from St. Paul's outside their school on the beach road. The St. Paul's School Band led the parade. This afternoon I went for a ride on my bike. It was hot, windy and quite hard work but I managed a good ride of about twenty miles of rough road. This was through Mary Hill, Xaibe, Patchacan and Chan Chen and around through the bush to Paraiso and through Altamira to get back into town where I cycled back along by the sea. There wasn't much evidence of wildlife as it was so hot, dry and dusty. I only saw one pair of hawks and a yellow-head parrot of any note. There were plenty of vultures along by the new abattoir though.

'…Attached is a letter for Year 7 that is self-explanatory. Please give it your best shot. The banner has been on display since it arrived and will be used as a backdrop for your contribution…'

'…Dear Friends in Year 7, thank you to those of you who have kept up your correspondence with your partner in Belize at a personal level; collectively all five schools are waiting to hear from you! Now is a good time to share ideas at any level and in any way, and the theme is COMMUNICATION the five schools here are cooperating on a joint activity for Education Week on Thursday 18th May and we would all like the absent partner to take part. The outline of the proposed activity is as follows. (I will be able to tell you more next week but this should be plenty to be going on with!) Venue Miami Beach: – right by the sea (and opposite my house). There are several thatched shelters on the beach and one of them is quite big. The big one is called 'The Round House' and there is electricity available there. The beach is grassed. There is only sand right by the water's edge because the Caribbean Sea has such a small tide. (The islands tend to be sand.)

Resources: as well as power, there are telephone-lines close by. We are hoping to persuade the Telephone Company to provide Internet connection for the day and each school will bring their computer. A large marquee will be sited by the 'Round House' to cut down the effects of the wind. There is no dust there as the wind almost always comes off the sea and that is where bands set up their electronic equipment for beach parties. Display boards and activity bases are being made. There are organisations that can provide video equipment and the Belize Media will be invited to take part.

Active Partners: the activity of the six schools (including yours) in communicating with each other is the focus of course, but organisations that have to do with communicating with young people are being invited. That has to be just about anybody doesn't it? And all they have to do is communicate!

The Idea: The idea is simply to take the school out into the community to share what we do and communicate with them. The schools will be very active in communicating with each other. Miami Beach is very much the activity centre for the town so there will be no shortage of interaction with people and the idea should naturally attract a lot of support from organisations wishing to join in.

What You Can Do: It would be really good if we could establish an Internet link on the day but I think that may be reaching for the moon (a rather apt expression, I think!). A seven-hour time difference presents a major problem anyway – but who knows what ideas you can come up with! There is plenty of time for you to get your contribution together and send it by regular mail. Perhaps each class might design and send a complete activity or information base together with instructions on how to run it? 'Whatever' – your ideas are best. See what you can come up with. I will make sure that you have a complete video presentation and photos arrive shortly after the event.

And Lastly: My time in Belize comes to an end with this academic year. I would rather 'go out with a bang than with a whimper' but that is not the reason for the interest. The reason is the same as it always has been. It would be so good for the South Molton – Belize Link to continue. It is an opportunity not to be missed. If we can learn from each other we learn about ourselves. Have fun (I do)!'

Chapter Eight:
Celebration

The first of April, a Saturday, exactly three years on from my VSO assessment in 1997; the monitoring programme is finished and plans for the schools' link celebration are begun; what a combination! I had an easy day, mostly spent reading – a whole book (Dick Francis, To the Hilt)! Otherwise I only wrote one letter, went out for a walk around the town and the sea front and did a little shopping. I had run out of airmail envelopes so that got me out!

Always the demands of life, there were more letters to catch up on from early morning. I kept the door shut as I have had to do lately because of the strong breeze that blows things all-round the house, but the windows have been wide open. I decided lunch wasn't coming and Lucille had visitors so it was unlikely. Just as I finished eating it was "Mr Max!" and lunch arrived; not the first time I have overeaten on a Sunday.

'…I will miss the children here when I go. They are the same everywhere of course, but I will miss them all the same. I was thinking as I was riding my bike through remote territory where robbery and violence is not uncommon, that it would be a nasty shock for anyone attacking me and pinching my bike (I try not to think of other possibilities). They wouldn't be able to ride it because every Primary School child knows my bike instantly and it is the only American Murray in the district. Walking or riding through town or any of the villages is met with a chorus of 'Hi Mr Max!' or the same as a succession of singular voices. Often, as many as fifteen or twenty dark, darkish or light brown faces will pop up from the back of a pickup and start the chorus until I wave and wave again. I don't think this has very much to do with being foreign; it didn't happen at first. What I notice is that people who come to see 'my teacher' arrive in a vehicle and have nothing to do with the children other than respond to their polite standing up to say 'Good morning' or 'Good afternoon'. I arrive on a bike and my first interest is in them. Professionally, that interest tells me almost all I want to know anyway. Teachers like that too, because we can then spend time working together from the same point. It has been fun - 'big time' - and I want to see what will happen somewhere else, amongst other things…'

'…I thought you would like the ray. I liked the flow of the carving, which uses the natural qualities of the wood so well. I have just looked back over my last letter and I have misled you a bit. Only the ship was carved by Tomas Gilharry, as was the ship in your school library and some others. I should have added a piece about the ray on the end of all that to say that it was made by another carver in Mascal, which is on the old northern highway between Orange Walk and Belize City. He works the same way but I haven't met him. It doesn't matter because your card is a lovely thought and I know Tomas will be delighted. I will probably go and find him tomorrow. Another complication arises out of the ethnic mix in Belize. Tomas Gilharry is of East Indian origin, as are most people in the village where he lives. The zericote tree was and is a useful resource in the Mayan tradition. The Maya are the indigenous people whose civilization goes right back into the ancient world. They built great cities but never organised themselves into a nation, which is one of the reasons why they were routed (just!), by the Spanish invaders. It is thought that the Maya originated in the East as well, but many thousands of years ago…

…Wednesday: I cycled over to Santa Rita this morning. Most of the Gilharry live in San Antonio which is the next village but Tomas lives on the edge of Santa Rita, right by the site of a Maya chief's house (archaeological ruin) that was the centre of the Maya city of Chetumal. I can do this because I have some spare time just now. He was delighted! He was working with two others exactly as I described, out in his yard. A mangy dog was chased away (the state of dogs is very upsetting; they are not pets here) and I went in and explained about the card and gave it to him. He spent quite a lot of time reading and looking at it and then took it safely indoors. I think you can be sure that your card will be shared with a lot of people so you have made ripples in Belize…'

'…You would enjoy the sport here I would think. Basketball is really the national sport although there is great interest in soccer (they scorn American football). The Creole players are especially good at basketball although there are a lot of good Mestizo and East Indian players as well. The shortest players are the Mestizo. Some of them are quite small but most are well built. The Creoles tend to have the physical advantage in all respects, and an incredible natural rhythm, pace and sense of position and space. East Indians are much slighter but often quite tall. I love to watch them although I am hopeless at any game involving a ball, as you know. I also like to watch the youngsters playing a scratch game of soccer as they often do on the beach opposite and did on the ground in front of my house in Orange Walk. I have seen one instance of a youth of about fifteen chase a football at high speed, jump over it, twist in the air and kick it back again before dropping back to the ground; all that in bare feet!...' … Then the next leveller zoomed in…

'…All is not well on the SMCC computing front (what's new?) The emailing is technically possible but has not been enabled for the pupils yet and as this will involve each pupil being set up to gain Internet access (parental permission for Internet/email use is required) I think it is not going to happen very quickly. As you probably gathered, our computer problems are not going to be solved easily in the short term. A great shame for our pupils and yours - let's hope that something can be sorted before you leave. I'm happy to pass on anything sent via the library here if that's a help (but it probably isn't - it's really important for it to be the pupils' experience isn't it? ...'

'…I am more than anxious about the 'Link' because delays are difficult to repair for young people. You don't have a monopoly of Internet problems although it may seem like it. It has been very difficult at this end but for entirely different reasons. Securing a computer for each of the schools was the first problem. That has been overcome but staffs do not have the experience I have had in enabling students to use the computer when they only have one. There is little expertise in any case and only one school has its computer in a classroom. Supervision and expertise both have to come from outside the school.
You can imagine what a difficult problem that gives me to avoid becoming the reason to put things off. Belize Telecommunications are a big monopoly in a small sized pond and are being unhelpful to the Primary Schools which operate up to your year 8. Secondary Schools on the other hand are effectively for the advantaged, having places for only about 20% of the age group. Then there are the on-going expenses. Schools have no money for basics let alone anything else. That is also a problem for me. It is one thing to provide the kick-start but ways of keeping things going have to be found from within. That is an attitude among professional providers that I didn't understand until trying it for myself. Worst of all is getting out of the idea that 'something will turn up' like 'manna from heaven'. I'm not usually into mixed metaphors. I call it the 'gimme a dollar syndrome' (that's the third – or better as one combining the other two) and I wrote about it when I first came. Happily, perseverance has paid off and three of the schools have use of email and the Internet…'

I went down to Ranchito on Monday afternoon and had a long talk with Orvin and with Ana Gomez about the proposed celebration as they had been absent from the meeting. While I was there I learned that Orvin's nephew had drunk a large quantity of Gramaxone that morning, and was seriously ill in hospital. I believe that to be some sort of pesticide – nasty.

I walked down to Ranchito again next afternoon, to take a spare computer keyboard for children to practice finding the keys. Orvin wasn't there. His nephew, Andrew, died this morning and he has all the arrangements to make. Andrew was living with a common law wife who had had a little girl and he was only nineteen. He had gone off the rails in lots of ways and also left for another woman. There had been rows and he had been walking about for several days threatening to take his own life. Young people in Belize are often incredibly confused. It is a terrible waste. On the way back, I called in at Paula's shop and had a long chat with her Mum. Paula has closed up her shop in Belize City, got married to an American and gone off to live in the States. The numbers of young people leaving Belize is rising rapidly and many more would like to. I had a carved figure put back for me at $50 while I was there. Carvings are much more expensive in Belize than anywhere else I have been, including England, but I can only get Belize carvings in Belize!

On Wednesday I went over to see Tomas Gilharry to ask him to make another boat for me similar to a small one I bought earlier, that has lots of sails. He wanted to make it for Saturday but I told him next week. On the way back I went in to see Henry, mainly to ask for the resources sent from South Molton to take on to Ranchito tomorrow. While I was there the two Teachers Union chiefs arrived in preparation for a meeting this afternoon. I had met the chiefs before so took the opportunity to make a plea for strengthening the effort being made to develop the new curriculum. I discovered also, that both the Permanent Secretary and the Chief Education Officer are on their way out to do other jobs so that is a further dilution of the stability that is most important in Belize just now. The funeral for Andrew was at the Adventist Church at 4pm.

I went to Methodist School to collect the resources and then on to Standard 5 at Ranchito to talk about South Molton and answer their questions. It was a disappointing session as I hadn't realised that their questioning and thinking skills are so poor. I cycled there and called in at Paula's on the way back because I had decided that a carving I like there is too expensive.

At about four o'clock in the afternoon I went to see Bernard's Auntie. I hadn't heard from him and I was planning to leave him my bike when I go home. Unfortunately, he has gone from bad to worse and his future is now in the hands of the law. He has continued to mix with men who deal in crime and drugs. He then tells on them. So, apart from his own activities, he is in grave danger of getting himself killed and can't see it. He has been in the habit of only coming home to change in the morning after being out all night. He doesn't eat at home and has continued his practice of going to restaurants. He waited outside for one man who refused him and attacked the man with a machete. He stoned another man. He was sent down from Standard Six to Standard Five. Then the Standard Five teacher refused to teach him. So the police have taken him and he is now in a residential centre of correction in Stann Creek until he becomes an adult. All I can do now is enable him to stay in contact if he wants to. I didn't say anything about the bike. How are children in Belize to learn the attitudes and values they need to survive when they have so little opportunity to think in school and no responsibility at all? How can they value themselves? On top of the death of Andrew Rancheran it is very depressing indeed.

On the way back I saw that dratted woman that lives next door and made a point of pinning her down with just a few words despite the fact that she doesn't speak English. At least she was clear about the venom. She has got another cockerel that crows at all hours under my bedroom window. It is nowhere near where they sleep of course. So they are having bigger rocks hurled at their corrugated iron roof at appropriate times but I choose to do it randomly so that they begin to associate the cockerel with a crash on the roof. If I'm going to be awake, so are they! I believe that it is unnatural to keep cockerels in town because there are lights on all night and they have no sense of time; let's face it, they have no sense at all. And she doesn't need a cockerel for her chickens to lay eggs. I don't mind the chickens.

Miriam phoned in the evening to say that Marco had gone to the US to buy parts for his vehicle so I will have to delay my visit until next week.

The strategy over the rooster seems to have worked again and I haven't used up all the schemes I had in mind yet. The current stock of (larger) rocks is still lined up ready on the concrete balustrade of the back porch and I wasn't kept awake last night; this is because they have penned the bird at the other side of their plot – close to their rooms oddly enough. Anyway, that's okay for now. This morning I set to and finished the final summary monitoring report so I only have the one day workshops and their preparation to do. Louisa is doing the budgets so that is not a problem and there is plenty of time. A meeting with link school principals went well this afternoon and I had a long talk with Mark at VSO about the celebration and about new postings and finishing times. I'm aiming to have my flight booked for Friday 30th June but I will send a FAX to David Price to secure that and my holiday.

For a leisurely weekend that seemed hot there was a lot of reading and several walks. On Sunday morning I went for a walk through the town after catching up with the mail. When I returned Lucille called up with my lunch which was very nice and I set off afterwards on a long walk round Santa Rita and Paraiso. On the way back I met up with Ricardo and Marbella and their family and joined them in a few beers at Marbella's Dad's house. After that we all came back to my house and continued until it got dark. That was very pleasant, as I haven't seen much of them since leaving Orange Walk. I gave them the proof copy of 'Home is the Belizoo', signed, which pleased them.

'…If you have made no arrangements yet can I offer to pick you up from Gatwick on your return to the UK at the end of June? ...'

'…It would be wonderful if you would collect me at the airport. I expect a weekend would be much better for you than a weekday and perhaps it could then be a family outing. I'm sure I can set a time to suit but I don't know whether it would be Gatwick or Heathrow at this stage. Heathrow would be better wouldn't it? Continental goes to Gatwick (as last year), via Houston. Taca (Belize) Airways fly to Miami where British Airways have a connection to Heathrow. It would also be good not to have to restrict what I jam in my cases to bring home. That's a lovely idea – thanks…'

'…It doesn't make a lot of difference which airport; Gatwick strangely enough is easier to get to from here and easy to park near the terminal. Heathrow is still easy to get to but I don't know what the car parking is like there these days. Weekday or weekend again doesn't matter…'

'…Parking apart, I had assumed that Heathrow would have been better for you but that is because I know so little of the location of Gatwick. It is a gap in my learning and doesn't deserve to be, especially as my first (near) contact with Gatwick was as an apprentice; then jobbing crew on a brand new Viscount doing a trial instrument landing approach in early 1957. That was heaven knows what speed a few feet off the ground and with no gear down. I was only 17 at the time and there were no seats in a largely empty fuselage…'

It rained overnight and for part of the morning. That was nice and fresh to start with but the humidity is very high and it became uncomfortable in the afternoon.

I went into the office this morning but that was a waste of time as no-one was doing anything and I had missed Louisa. I left a message for her to phone but she hasn't done so. Part of the day was spent sorting out what I will do for the one-day workshops. That won't take long but I really do need some information from Louisa to make the budget; letters benefitted…

'…Yes the villages are quite different from yours. I suppose the two most striking differences are space and harmony although you have to stop and think about it because you mostly just accept it as being 'how it is'. The roads are generally made from a sort of compacted stone dust that goes quite hard for the most part although some of it can get 'muddy'. There is little demarcation at the edge of the road, which blends into the ground on which houses stand well back. Houses in the villages are a long way apart and are usually made of natural materials, vertical cohune logs and palm thatch, although there is a tendency towards concrete. The whole impression is one of man and nature blending together. There are always people and especially children, chatting or playing or just sitting, and that adds to the feeling of being at one with the natural rhythms. To get somewhere near the feeling in England you would have to find a quiet spot in woodland and sit and listen – although you couldn't reproduce the visual impact. As if to add to the image of the Garden of Eden, the trees bear the most amazing variety of colours and shapes in their trunks and leaves and blossom all the year round. On the other hand – tell all that to the mosquitoes…'

At 10:00am I went to collect the 'Celebration' letters for organisations invited to the Celebration Day from Henry and spent quite a long time there before going on to deliver theirs to Xavier and St Pauls. I am also trying to make some preliminary arrangements and collect names for the forthcoming workshops. After lunch I walked over to Ranchito to deliver theirs letters.

I went down to the Office early this morning, Wednesday, and phoned David about my finishing time. He said it had all been cleared but seemed very offhand and the phone was put down abruptly. Let's be generous and suppose that he was in a meeting or very busy!

Still with concern for the mini workshops, I contacted Louisa and realised that there was to be a meeting with Pilot School Principals about the Middle Division Curriculum at 1:00pm. In the afternoon it took a long time for Louisa to round up the Principals and they went off to make written reports to be handed in by Friday. I arranged to meet with Louisa again at 1:00pm on Friday to make a summary report and some preparations for the workshops. Apparently, no expenses are to be paid so that removes the problems I was having with a budget and all I need to prepare is my own.

I had done the washing when someone came to repair the leaking taps on the shower this morning. I knew exactly that both washers were worn right through and it was now only possible to turn the water off by driving the remains to plug the hole rather than seal it. The taps must be a poor design for such little use. Anyway, he came with a gentle knock on the door at about 8:15, turned off the supply and dismantled the taps. What he found was no surprise but then he had to go off to buy new washers! It took about two hours; another example of the relative value of time here and at home – although, maybe not!

Friday 14th April. It was a bit of a rush this morning, to catch up with letters and get ready for the weekend. I met Louisa as arranged at 1:00pm to discuss the forthcoming orientation days, budgets and the general situation with QADS. Only Buena Vista, St Pauls and San Antonio had done their reports on the content of the documents by the time I left. I included those with Louisa's report and the budgets to take to QADS on Monday.

Orvin came in just as I was leaving and we went to see the new road and ferry that is to go to Sarteneja and is to be opened tomorrow. It was interesting to note that I had reached the river and didn't know it, when I turned back from my cycle ride a couple of months ago.

I managed to get a seat on the 6:00pm Premier. However, it didn't leave until twenty-five to seven and it was just short of 9:00pm by the time I arrived in Belize City to stay with the family. Miriam had fallen asleep with the children when I arrived and Tabo, Neria and Marco were all out so I went round to see Glen and Valerie for an hour. It was just as well that I did because it was Catherine's last night and she was staying with them until tomorrow. She is going on her travels through South America before going home and intends to do the walk through the Andes in Peru. How I would like to do that but I'm afraid the accommodation and washing facilities would not be enough for me nowadays.

We did a little of the printing of 'Home is the Belizoo' later in the evening but it is very slow. I went off Downtown in the morning, to find a birthday present for Miguel. I was really looking for a book of simple origami but was unable to find one. I tried the Stationery House and Angelus Press before looking in lots of other stores for possible toys. I have never seen a balsa wood glider or any other plane in Belize. In the end, I bought a quoits set in Brodies and Miguel played with it for the rest of the day. Tabo and I played with him.

The laser printer was running all day and about half of the printing was completed.

Sunday was very much a family day although the laser printer was going all day again. It was obvious right from the start that the books were not going to be anywhere near finished this weekend. Neria has been making Easter baskets so I bought one for Lucille, one for Ruby and one for her Mum.

Monday, April 17th is the start of the schools' Easter holiday. I went to QADS in time for the eight o'clock start and spent some time talking with David who has begun to build some bridges. He really has been very foolish in being uncommunicative and now wants to discuss some of the ways the best use might be made of remaining resources to support the curriculum. I wonder if his boss is to go and David is to be left 'holding the baby'. Kathryn arrived as I finished with David so I waited for her and we went off for lunch and a very pleasant chat until about 1:00pm when she had to go back to Peace Corps for a medical and dental inspection – as they do when their volunteers leave. I went back to sort out my things and caught the 2:00pm Venus bus, which arrived back in Corozal just before five. There were emails and letters to answer but still nothing from VSO London.

'…I guess that you may not have heard from Billy judging by the way that he takes off in another direction when he sees me. That is very sad because he has no reason to as far as I am concerned although I can imagine his feelings. Anyway, you are very welcome to write to me if you want to, and I will tell you something of life here. You will have to get a move on however, as my three years are up at the end of June and I return home until September when I will be off somewhere else…'

'…I wonder what you would think of the equivalent of a disco here. The music is almost always rock played at earth shaking volume by batteries of huge speakers. The favourite is punta rock, which has a fast repetitive beat all of its own. It is fascinating to watch the women and girls dancing punta. The feet barely move, in a kind of shuffle, but the other parts of the body oscillate in ways I would have thought impossible (especially the more interesting parts). Even the smallest children have the punta rhythm. I think it must be in the genes. (You would never do it in Wranglers!) Another thing that is different is the weather of course. Even at night the dancers would usually be clutching a bottle of water in one hand and wearing clothes that wick away the sweat. But a dance would often be out of doors such as at the 'Round House' on the beach opposite where I live and it is not unusual to combine it with a swim. There is no need to change. You just go in! At the 'Round House' there is access to electricity to drive the amplifiers etc. and anything else that needs power although no-one bothers with light as there is enough from new lights put up along the beach…'

'…The family here wants to have a barbecue for me on Saturday 1st July. That would mean a flight on Sunday 2nd and arrival in London on Monday 3rd. If that is okay I will ask VSO to go ahead and book a flight and give you the details as soon as I have them…'

I sent an email to VSO London and had a reply that there had been no response from Malawi yet so I am still waiting and it looks as though that will continue over Easter. When I was in the Post Office, one of the girls was posting a letter to her buddy; perhaps the World is as small as you make it!

When I went out this morning there were two young boys working for Fausty in the yard. They appeared to be doing some gardening. They were still there when I went out after lunch, in the middle of the afternoon when the temperature must have been close to a hundred degrees. It has been very hot lately. When I returned they were sitting waiting and asked where 'the lady' was. I called for her but getting no reply I could only assume she was asleep so I set the boys up with some iced coke and left them in the shade. Their lot was all very normal to wait upon people in this way in Belize and they would be earning money for their family, not for themselves. There are so many attitudes that have so far to go for much change to take place, even without the need for curbs on control freaks and self-seekers.

I went on a cycle ride to Copper Bank in the heat of the day. And it is really hot just now! We had some rain overnight a couple of weeks ago! That is such an event that you tend to remember it. It must be nudging a hundred degrees at times although it is more likely to be in the low to mid nineties by the coast. Copper Bank is on the other side of the New River and was not accessible from Corozal until last week. A new road has been opened up along the track I explored and turned back a few weeks ago. As it turns out I had reached the river that time and didn't know it! Perhaps it is just as well because it is often difficult to see the edge of a river because of bush and mangrove vegetation and there is a very healthy population of crocodiles. A hand-operated ferry has been built on an old sugar barge to take people and vehicles across the river and the road completed on the other side. Copper Bank is on a beautiful lagoon so I will go off to take some photos next week. Unfortunately, you still have to go right round the lagoon to get to the other side and it is a long way, but that is where I want to go so I am working out some other bike rides to see if I can cope with it. I have more time available as the end of my posting approaches. There were heaps of parrots flying about the bush and the forest, especially later in the afternoon when I was on the way back. One of the many other birds I haven't seen before was an amazing iridescent blue, so bright that I thought it might have been one of the big butterflies at first glance. I think it must have been a humming bird but I haven't seen one as bright as that before. It could be the time of the year because there is a lot of mating going on. The birds know the season even if I hardly notice.

Easter is celebrated much more in Belize than in England. There are activities right through Holy Week from Palm Sunday. Most of the churches enact the 'Stations of the Cross' through the streets on Good Friday. The biggest procession is the Catholic one because most of the Spanish speaking people are Catholic. I watched their procession right to the arrival at St Francis Xavier Church on the edge of the Plaza in the centre of town. The enactment there was in Spanish so I couldn't be sure what was going on but there was a (live) figure of Christ wrapped in the shroud high up over the entrance to the church. It was very pleasant sitting among the crowds on one of the seats, in the shade of one of the trees in the Plaza, before I drifted slowly back home.

Good Friday 21st April. I cycled round Xaibe this afternoon so as not to make too much exertion after yesterday but to keep ticking over for tomorrow, in case I decide to go for an extended ride down to Caledonia. If I can get to Caledonia and back, the next step would be to extend the ride to San Estevan. Then I should be able to return via Progresso and Copper Bank and cross the new ferry again. It would also be a ride equivalent to going round the lagoon to Chunux. Also, on that side of the New River is Cerros and I think I will have to go there via Copper Bank as well. The weekend was mostly devoted to mail…

'…One of the things I'm trying to deal with is bits of paper! I have been quite dismayed by the amount of paper sent by the bank, the tax people, the letting agent etc. when I left things nice and tidy and expected people to just get on with it. We seem to live in a world where people (even professionals) no longer even expect to be trusted! Dealing with paper means destroying it in most cases; I certainly don't want it cluttering up my luggage; another use for the computer, for most of the records I need are in there and backed up onto floppy disc…'

'…Our weather hasn't changed! Although it has been exceptionally hot lately and we had some rain one night a week or so ago. Lots of flowers are out on the trees but that never seems to stop either; and there is a huge variety of fruit. Watermelon is cheap and plentiful and I have a papaya, which I will be cutting up to start eating in a minute. Mangos are just coming into season. There are so many of those that they are left to rot on the ground…'

'…I have been making a start on getting ready to come home. So many things have happened and I want to leave them working if I can. What happens after that is nothing to do with me. Ownership is not something that bothers me over much but I do want to do the best job I can. You are right about the memories of course. There are many of those. What still surprises me is that other people have them too – and the extent to which they have them… … School finishes here, at the end of June which is one of the reasons for my choice of return date. I offered to stay on for three weeks if the dates of the major summer workshops could be brought forward but for whatever reason, I am told the documents cannot be made available in time so I won't stay. That is one of the points where it becomes someone else's responsibility as mentioned above. The documents could be produced easily enough but the gods are at war…'

'…The relationship with children strengthened rapidly with the monitoring of the new curriculum in each of the schools. Most teachers expect people they regard as supervisors to spend time talking to them and scrutinising their plan book (which is usually impeccable). I did neither for the first two visits. On entering a classroom all the children stand up and give greeting. Most visitors answer automatically and then ignore them but for me, it is a gift; open sesame for dialogue before I go and sit down and listen and work with children that happen to be at hand; all good for relaxation! Teachers worried at first and said things like "Don't you want to see my plan book or look at the timetable?" "No!" I would say, "There's no need." At the end of the day we simply came together as a staff and started from where they had been in the classroom. I didn't look at planning until the third visit because I was more interested in the teaching and learning. What is interesting is that at the start, in talking with children, it was a case of having to 'tell' them things like the teachers always did but this quickly changed to being able to ask questions, then to being asked questions and finally, dialogue. The children learn very quickly, given chance…'

'…El señor hombre de mañana. Ask your Mum what that means. Even if she doesn't know I'm sure she will guess. And when you find out (You may have guessed anyway) remember that I am teasing you…'

'…It is just after 7:30am. The Anglican Easter morning service is over, having taken place on the beach outside the church as is customary while the sun comes up over the Caribbean Sea. The morning is as perfect as it (almost) always is, the birds have been a riot and there is almost no wind so the sea is almost flat calm…'

'…Did you manage to make contact with Programme for Belize I wonder? Alan and Nimmi Herrera left Hill Bank in the interest of their children's schooling soon after I last wrote to you. If you haven't succeeded there are other ways but little time left for me to help…'

'…On Thursday 18th May, in Education Week, the five schools (and their absent partner in the UK) are taking their lessons out into the community. (This is 'out with a bang' for me but I have had no part in the organisation.) Schools do not work together in Belize so it is a first from that point of view as well. The theme will be Communication. As well as lessons there will be shared activity bases, displays and presentations; and any organisation that has anything to do with communication or anything positive to communicate to young people (Almost anyone really!) is being invited to join in. The venue is what is locally known as Miami Beach, next to one of the schools and right by where I live. There is a big, thatched, 'Round House' on the beach that has electricity available. Each school is bringing its computer and the local server is invited to provide a temporary access to the Internet. The activity takes place in the morning, so as to include the students in Devon who are seven hours ahead of us. Even so, they will be responding after school hours. It is also cooler in the morning and usually less breeze. Others are providing video facilities and the media will be both present and presenting. Miami Beach is the social centre for the town of Corozal so there should be no shortage of crowds and other schools are invited. Please don't think this is my doing! It is true that I was able to provide the 'spark' but the dream of such an activity was in the minds of friends in the schools. That is how it has been for three years and it has been wonderful to have a part to play – a glimpse of being a part of the world…'

'…I think it must certainly be time to go because I could get too settled here, especially now. Walking or cycling around Corozal now is like South Molton only more so. There it was only one school. Here it is currently nineteen schools and I take time out with the children in all of them. As a result it is 'Hi Mr Max' all over the place and it will continue until you respond otherwise the children assume you haven't heard. Now I find adults giving greeting all the time as well (especially the nice young Mums). Then there are the strangers who see all this going on. Not bad (in Belize) for someone who doesn't even have a vehicle…'

Bank Holiday Monday; I set off for a bike ride at 10:30am having done the washing and not quite knowing where to go but having Caledonia in Mind. In the event, that is what I did! When I set off it was reasonably cool and there was a high haze that was blocking the strength of the sun so that it wasn't too hot. Also, the wind was slight and against me so it would be in my favour on the way back whichever route I chose to take. The ride along the Highway to the Libertad Cut-off was not too bad as there wasn't as much traffic as I expected. Even so, I decided it would be nicer to get off the highway going down and have the advantage of the tarmac road on the way back, so I kept straight on at the Cut-off and went through Libertad, waving as usual at people I know. The distance to the Cut-off is six miles and it would be another eight miles to the point where the road re-joins the Northern Highway at Buena Vista and where I would turn back for the ten miles back to the Cut-off.

It was very pleasant all the way down. Libertad was quiet and the deserted sugar factory deserted. That is where the rough road starts. As it is the dry season, some of the compressed stone and mud is quite smooth but much of it is ridged, rutted, potholed, violently undulating or six inches deep in dust! It is a very remote piece of road. The tiny hamlet of Estrella on the New River is only just beyond Libertad and the old sugar factory anyway, and the only other habitation is at the Santa Cruz Lodge which is closed anyway except for a 'National Pathfinder Camporee' that amounted to about four tents. I shouldn't think more were to come as it is Easter Monday already. The hamlet of Santa Cruz is even more remote along a track of its own, making a cut-off with the road I was on. The only signs of life were the occasional groups of cane workers. Their work never stops in season.

I turned off to cover the three miles into Caledonia and arrived by the river extremely hot because the haze had cleared rather unexpectedly. I passed a Tommygoff of about seven feet long on the way in but it presented no threat as it had been run over. It was a warning though. I am very careful to keep an eye open for snakes but I seem to see them only at the brief times when I haven't been looking and I have got a bit close by then! In Caledonia I spent some time in the shade and chatting with the swimmers. The crocodiles don't come out much at that time of day and there is no cover for them where the locals swim anyway. The water is brown but clear and quite wide. I managed to find the Alcoser family where I had attended the birthday party and barbecue that was the scene of the story of the killing of the pig. I had a welcome half litre of coke there as it was obvious that my water bottle was not going to be sufficient. I suppose I could have asked for some more.

Then came the three miles back to the Caledonia Cut-off and on to the Northern Highway at Buena Vista; by the time I reached there I was very hot. Worse, the wind had backed from south-east to north-north-east and strengthened. It was dead against me all the way back and the last ten miles or so was covered in low gears. I stopped several times and for more coke but managed the whole thirty-six miles in four hours including stops. I was pleased with that but there was no doubt that I was overstretched and still short of fluids. As I left this morning, Ruby had invited me to the family barbecue in the yard and we arranged that I would if I got back in time. I deliberately didn't say where I had in mind to go. It wasn't certain anyway, and she would have probably tried to persuade me not to. I thought I would save the trouble.

When I got back I showered and changed and generally wound down but it wasn't long before a saved barbecue arrived and I went down and joined the family for a little while. Marco phoned to say that the books are finished.

First thing was an email from VSOL that wasn't very informative or encouraging. Apparently there is a problem with accommodation in Malawi. My reaction is to try to solve the problem, if there is a job to be done. I wrote back in a mild way to get some more information before pressing the point harder. I cashed a voucher cheque this morning and went on from the bank to the District Office but there was nothing doing.

As I walked back along College Road I passed a very old lady who was moving very, very slowly on shaky legs and using a stick to steady herself. As I passed I said 'Good Morning'. That or 'Buenos Dias', is the greeting most people seem to favour if they don't know you. The reply was 'Hello', presumably in deference to my English accent. I turned to respond and was met with a most beautiful smile on one of the oldest and most wrinkled faces I have ever seen. All I could think of doing was to smile myself and give a little wave only to find her smile deepen even more, as open as any child!

When I went to the library this evening I met up with Tom's wife (the Americans who have bought a house here and are working with the library). I found that they are in with a senior politician's family and was told that she has the ear of the matriarch. She was working up to poking her nose into education and sited an example of something that was said about the border when she returned with them from Mexico. Apparently it was said and it was done. My comment was that is exactly what is wrong. I hope that finds its mark.

I had a reply from VSO London offering four sample placements for Pakistan and decided that it would be a good idea to go to Belize City and read them on the bus. I caught the three o'clock Premier to collect the books from Marco. I decided to take my flight bag as that would be the best carrier for them and put in a spare pair of pants and a top as well as my pyjama trousers, although my intention was to return on the seven o'clock Venus. In the event I was expected and stayed over while Tabo, Marco and I finished off a bottle of Chivas Regal between us. I left a book for Marco and Miriam, one for Tabo and Neria and a signed one for Liliana Lagos at Atlantic Bank in recognition of her help and for the use of the binding machine.

I caught the bus outside 'White Sapphire' having checked all I needed to check with the girl at Batty Bus this morning.

"Is there a three o'clock Premier to Belize City in the afternoon?"

"Yes!"

"Are there any other Premier buses to Belize City?"

"Yes, there is one at six o'clock."

"Are those the only two Premier buses going to Belize City?"

"Yes!"

"Will it stop if I wait for the Premier down by the Maya Hotel?"

"Yes."

"Are the Premier buses busy just now?"

"No, not busy at all!"

With all that in mind I was at the Maya Hotel (White Sapphire) at 3:00pm. The bus came into sight at 3:25pm. It was hot! I stuck my arm out with no response and had to be quite firm in the indication until the driver finally decided to stop. Out came the conductress.

"Where you goin'?"

"Belize City." I said, having expected to be addressed in that way. People try to get on for short stops and I do have some sympathy with the crews.

"One seat, way to de back!"

'So much for not busy,' I thought and made my way 'way to de back'.

It was 'way to de back'. It was the hot seat where the air conditioning unit directs everyone else's concentrated heat excess at the lower part of your body and by way of 'adding insult to injury', drips condensed water either down your arm or the back of your neck. After giving time for me to begin to sweat nicely in the 'air conditioned' bus, the conductress came to collect my money.

"Is anyone getting off at Orange Walk?" I asked, hopefully. 'This seat is hardly $8-50 worth.' I thought to myself.

"I don't expect so," she replied, and went.

I made some comment to the youngish Creole male sitting in the window seat next to me and he responded by turning his shoulder. Some Creole males consider themselves seriously contaminated if close to a white.

"Oh well, suit yourself!" I said.

A small snack, usually in the form of a bag of chips and a carton of drink are usually served on the Premier bus and in due course the chips arrived. Being by the isle I took one and passed it to the Creole, whereupon he reached across and took one himself. The same performance was repeated with the drink. Creoles also complain that they are not treated with the respect due to them! In my imagination I asked, "Do you speak English?" "Yuh!" (I heard his voice earlier). "Why?" I wondered; but decided discretion to be the better part of valour.

I returned to Corozal on the 9:00am 'Premier' and settled down to sending in my response to four sample posts offered in Pakistan. This was to make sure VSO London had it before the bank holiday weekend in case they wanted anything else.

'…Thanks for your efforts re Malawi and for the very interesting samples for Pakistan. I am not sure how detailed you would like my response to be. The attached has been kept reasonably short, aiming for clarity and to reach you within this week in case you would like any more…' Then more 'artefacts' for SMCC…

'…Here are some more bits and pieces that you might find interesting or useful. The boxes and the towel hanger were made by Standard Six Students of Libertad Seventh Day Adventist School (equivalent to Year 8) to raise funds for the school. You may like to use them as gifts or prizes of some sort. There are also smaller items inside two of the boxes. A teacher at St Francis Xavier RC School makes the crosses from coconut shell, for school funds. All the Link Schools have been very disappointed at not hearing from you since Christmas or in reply to their packages. I know that students are communicating on a personal basis but there is much more to it than that and youngsters need encouragement. There also needs to be communication among staffs. I am managing to get the five schools to talk to each other. That is a major step forward in

The last day of the schools' Easter holiday was Friday 28th April and correspondence once again took up most of my weekend; also parcelling twelve copies of 'Home is the Belizoo' ready to send off to Philip…

'…The book is printed and it looks good… …What I will do is send twelve copies to you and ask you to take the three you would like and look after the rest until I come home. Then we can sit and decide what to do with them together. There is a dedication in the front to all the 'Link' schools including yours. That is mainly for the benefit of the schools I have worked with here. There are not enough copies for all the schools I have worked with (about 80) but there are enough copies for schools I have worked with most since I first came as well as the five 'Link' schools. Two copies will go to the zoo and two or three friends here will each have one – the family and one who writes stories for children…'

'…I forgot to tell you that one of the girls from Corozal Methodist School was busy posting a letter to Mark as I was in the Post Office the other day so he should get it this week. She asked if the address was right (They all think I know everything!) as I think Mark had used some fancy lettering or something, on his letter. I packaged twelve copies of the book together today, ready to go in the post on Tuesday. There is no letter with them. You will have to carefully rip open the package because it is well and truly glued. You will see that as necessary to avoid the books going out of shape. You might like to note how the binders have been locked together to keep everything flat as well…'

'…Apart from my own interest, observation and experience over three years, I have had contact with people and organisations where there is an active passion that you may well like to know about. There is a long-term scheme that is well under way, to establish a biological corridor right up through Belize, to link up the very substantial areas of reserves already in existence. This involves such tracts as the Rio Bravo Conservation Area, The Crooked Tree Wildlife Sanctuary and the Community Babboon Sanctuary. In the latter two, the villagers are becoming an integrated part of the whole. The bird life on the lagoons at Crooked Tree and the animals around are under no threat as is well demonstrated by their huge number and familiarity while remaining utterly wild. You can always see (and hear!) the Howler Monkeys (called baboons in Belize) in the whole area around Bermudan Landing where their habitat is ideal, unthreatened and cheek by jowl with the villages along the Belize River.

Central America has been spoiled of its wild life and habitat like so much of our world (is it ours?) but Belize remains largely untouched and about three quarters of the country is wild. That makes it a vital part in the natural link being established through Meso-America. I went to a lecture about that recently and I will send you a copy of the notes when I get them. There are some amazing things going on. A good example is the Manatee Project down at Gales Point. Manatees are endangered and are also very shy as you probably know. There has been some research in Florida where there is a small population but this has been limited. Gales Point is a remote village on a very long, narrow strip of land jutting north into the Southern Lagoon. There is a healthy population of Manatees around Gales Point as there is at other places in Southern Belize. What is really special is that the children of the little Primary School feed the Manatees by hand at break-time! Anyway, this attracted the attention of the Belize Zoo and the Audubon Society who are now working jointly with the children. Who knows where the interest of young people may lead? I can give you many examples of that. The director of the Belize Zoo is Sharon Matola and the history of the zoo is interesting. I wrote a story for children about the zoo and, with her encouragement, had it illustrated and printed to put in the library and to distribute to some of the schools I have worked with…'

My lunch of rice and beans and baked chicken arrived with a loud "Mr Max" as I finished (I often have to have the door shut because all my papers tend to be blown around by the wind.

On the news this morning, the Prime Minister was talking about trade and buying in Belize and buying Belizean products. He was the 'keynote speaker' at the Lions Annual Convention in Belmopan. He told a story of a store that sold meat. In the refrigerated display all the imported meat was presented at eye level and the customer had to bend down to find the Belize product; okay so far. What was interesting was that the Prime Minister said that he hadn't seen it himself; it had been reported to him; still okay in ordinary circumstances but he went on to say that he will "Certainly have a word with the owner!" Where in action like that is the freedom of the individual? How will people ever make decisions for themselves? And what happens if the shop owner doesn't comply with the Prime Minister's request? Will his licence be revoked? That sort of thing has happened before to my certain knowledge and I believe was behind the recent takeover of Batty buses by Novello and the squashing of the two bus operations from Orange Walk: Urbina and Escalante. Perhaps worse than that is the playground idea it represents "I'm going to tell my Dad of you!" that I come across every day and which strangles enterprise and individual responsibility. Even worse is the obvious fact that the Prime Minister sees nothing wrong in his proposed action and is prepared to tell the nation about it. "If you don't do as I say, I'm going to smack you!" Heaven help Belize!

I spent a long time at the District Centre today. David Eck finally brought the resources I need starting tomorrow. I first asked for these a couple of months ago and have had to keep reminding him. When they arrived, the set of outcomes was incomplete and the National Syllabus was in a mess. There was only one copy and he didn't bring a master roll and ink for the Risograph machine. The machine ran out of master film and printed incomplete copies, all of which could have been avoided. This will mean all the teachers filling in missing words on 25 sheets of paper – and at eleven workshops.

I spent a considerable amount of time again, trying to get David to be decisive and constructive. The two subjects were the meeting at QADS this Friday and the need to leave the Middle Division curriculum alone as written. He had the gall to ask if I would design a workshop for his meeting on Friday. I said no but did tell him what was needed.

The problem with the documents is the tension between the idea of the curriculum being prototypical and the way in which QADS is continually behaving as though it is prescriptive. Wednesday and Thursday were mostly taken up with two one-day orientation workshops of Middle Division Non-Pilot Schools in clusters using one Teacher from each Pilot School; also a meeting of 'Link' schools making preparations for joint celebration. I cycled down to Libertad for the cluster meeting there. The mass of papers still needed to be put in sets because of the shortage of time yesterday. I had almost finished doing this when the wind took the lot. It took me an hour and a half to sort them out. It was then that I also discovered the missing sheets. After the workshop I cycled back straight to Methodist to catch up with the progress on the celebration. There seems to be quite a lot of support and I gave Henry a cheque for $1,000 to help with the expenses for the five schools.

I went to Belize City on the 6:00pm Premier and caught it at the Batty depot! The evening was a 'Thirsty Thursday' session until well into the small hours.

The QADS meeting was quite good and was run along the lines I suggested to David. It took the form of a workshop with eight working groups. Each group was assigned an area of study and asked to consider Capacity of Schools to Deliver the Curriculum, Capacity of Teachers to Deliver the Curriculum, Appropriateness of the Curriculum, Teaching/Learning Strategies and Assessment Strategies. Criteria were offered for each group to use as a standard measure and conclusions were drawn through reports to the whole meeting.

The evening was fairly quiet as I for one, was not wishing to be drinking very much.
I managed to buy some flowers for Benito as she and Pedro came down for Saturday in order to sell ground roasted pig. They went back to San Estevan in the afternoon. I also managed to get a nice bouquet for Neria, which was on prominent display during the party for her birthday, held in the evening. Later, I gave her the discs of British music, Welsh male voice choirs as well; not too sure about that but the choirs could hardly fail to stir the soul.

The Sustainability Workshop at Leo Bradley Library led to some useful recommendations to send to VSO London. I managed to catch the three o'clock Venus bus back to Corozal and arrived at six ready for the mail…

'…I have not been able to contact Programme for Belize, I did write but to no avail, it sounds as if I left it too late…'

'…This is just a (relatively) short reply to keep things going and to give you another contact. First, the contact is Valdemar Andrade at Belize Audubon. You will know about the Audubon Society. In Belize, they are involved in much more than birds and the contact will link straight away with all the other conservation and sustainable management in Belize. Valdemar hosted us at the site of the proposed Chalillo Dam during the annual conference of VSO recently. The VSO Director here suggested him as a contact. I have not discussed the idea directly but that should give you a starting point, especially now you have email…'

'…Now for your question about Jeffery: I have a problem there because well over five thousand youngsters in Belize know me and I have a shocking memory for names. Obviously, he would be a Calcutta student. I think I can picture him but I'm not sure and I am not sure what year he is in or whether he would have left but I will find him in the new term. The Calcutta Teachers will be coming to a workshop on Thursday 4th May and I am free on the Friday so I could go down there then. It is time I did anyway…'

'…The placement we have matched you to is Education Adviser AEP/REACH Pakistan…'

'…REACH (Radio Education for Afghan Children) is a new initiative of AEP (Afghan Education Projects) to meet the educational requirements of out of school Afghan children…'

'…Thank you for your email sent on Friday. I have just returned from a weekend away. There were nine email messages waiting. Maybe I could compete with you! I am pleased to accept the placement offered as Education Adviser AEP/REACH Pakistan…'

'…It is a twelve-month placement with an arrival date set at 11th September 2000. This is the one I asked for of the ones offered in Pakistan and I'm pretty excited about that. It is a challenge that would require just the sort of effort involved in getting alongside 'what is' that I have enjoyed so much here…'

'…I will see if I can find a pen pal for your friend Rose. I will let you know how I got on in a week or so. I was a bit puzzled by your question 'What is your shop called?' until I realised that you got the idea from the workshop. A workshop is a place where people do work. A garage, for example, might have a workshop where repairs are done. A workshop for teachers and principals (head teachers) is where something new is learned or practised. At those workshops I become the teacher (of teachers)…'

After four more days of orientation: I went down to Belize City on the bus at 10:30 this morning in order to be in good time to leave for Belmopan with the family at 3:00pm. It was a regular bus, an old Greyhound coach belonging to Venus. I checked the date of manufacture giving it as thirty-five years old but it was one of the most comfortable and certainly the fastest journey so far. The eighty-four miles were covered in two hours and five minutes mainly because we didn't hang about in Orange Walk. When I arrived I went to the Chinese to buy three dollar chicken, which I enjoy very much and because Neria wouldn't be expecting me for lunch. The family preparations for setting off were hilarious with Tabo constantly complaining how no-one else was ever ready in time and Neria pointing out that she had everything to do and the children to see to as well. Needless to say, it was Tony who disappeared and was last. The pressure was on because the seats couldn't be booked and Neria was determined that the children should be able to sit on seats rather than laps. I cringe! We arrived in Belmopan at about 4:30pm and Jack joined us for the rest of the ride to Teakettle Village where Vicky was waiting to take us the bumpy five and a half miles into the hills to Pooks Hill in the back of a smallish pickup truck. It was well loaded, as there were two girls there as well, who are working on the GAP scheme studying fish in the Roaring River at Pooks Hill. Ray met us on arrival and we were shown to our cabanas before having an excellent meal and spending a very pleasant evening in well-oiled and wide ranging discussion. Ray is a White South African and Vicky comes from Wales but has lived in South Africa long enough to pick up quite a lot of the accent. She says she can't sing and wrongly suggests that only the men sing in Wales!

The cabanas are great! I shared with Jack and the family had a bigger one together. The walls are an oval plan form in concrete with a thatched roof. One end has a screen wall behind which is the toilet, basin and shower. The thatch extends low enough to screen all the windows, which are sited at the two sharper curves of the oval so we didn't use the beautiful fabrics that were there to be used as curtains. There were three beds in the room and muslin sheets stretched high over them to catch any scorpions that might otherwise drop on to the bed during the night. The scorpions like the thatch because that is where they catch the moths that form part of their food. In all the time I have been in Belize I had not seen a live scorpion outside the zoo (I didn't see the one that got me in the groin at Hill Bank because I was asleep; afternoon siesta). Today, I saw two before evening dinner.

Actun Tunichil Muknal

Saturday 13th May 2000: another time to remember and a reach back in time directly to past Maya generations through their undisturbed artefacts reverently protected. Actun Tunichil Muknal is a cave system that stretches for many miles as yet not fully explored in modern times; not in range beneath the hills of the west; not in breadth of importance to human life; nor in change through history. My understanding is taken directly from being there.

The journey from Pooks Hill was as many others had been, heaving about in a four wheel drive and a hike and the arrival was no particular surprise in that before us, after scrambling down a fairly modest river bank was the mouth of a cave with water coming out, the entire supply of the river at that point. Why do we refer to the mouth of the cave I wonder, or the mouth of a river which in this case would be at the other end, both with water flowing out rather than in? Frivolous thought was soon dispelled as the guide announced that the water inside is deep and there is only one way in, you swim; no need to take clothes off, this is Belize, they soon dry. The cave mouth is not large but there is already a presence. The water is cold and deep but so clear that detail of the bottom is seemingly sharper than when dry, appearing only wet, and the flow is slow, emphasizing the silence and depth of the darkness beyond. Inside the sides opened out and we were soon able to clamber out on to rock. We all had helmets on with lamps attached and thus able to see we trekked in single file strangely without talking until we came to a halt arriving at 'Boot Hill'. That is where we were instructed to remove our boots and socks and proceed in bare feet, taking care not to step on any artefact or even broken ones, however tiny; it would have hurt anyway.

Once the domestics were out of the way and focus was on the experience the transport of the mind was almost literally out of this world, a curious impression of space: a Maya pot, almost whole, with the sediment of years built up around it; a plate so old that it is embedded in calcium deposit; a small collection of pottery; the intense white of the calcium deposits; a stalagmite stack of interesting form and flow.

A nice collection of pottery relatively untouched by the ravages of time drew me; the best so far included two complete round pots or jars with beautifully formed lips curling outward, one large and one smaller, and a nearly whole plate surrounded by large broken pieces; all locked into the rock over time's accumulation of calcium where they touched. I became aware of how far involved I had become when I realized that my camera was out of film after trying to take a picture, fumbling while trying to load a new one and becoming mildly irritated as the guide included his finger by pointing to decoration, finely made on the plate. Again, the decoration, even clearer and embossed, was pointed out on finely preserved pot and more until the finger pointed to a well-formed hole in a pot which would have been made deliberately for some purpose and I resolved to listen but wait just long enough…

What was the purpose of the hole so perfectly round near to the base of another vessel; more such wondering with the appearance of skulls long calcified in the rock; and more of them among the remains of broken pottery smoothed out in thick calcium deposits. What can the 'ceremony' have been? Death and disposal and a place of rest; are we so different?

Deeper in, delicate stalactites demand more attention to demonstrate the unspoiled nature of the caves; stalactite 'skirts' that stretch for four or five yards; formations showing some of the range of mineral colours to be found; others hiding pots collected in small spaces in the cave walls.

That finger again – this time making sure that the axe heads are not missed but these are too perfect as though they have been placed and with no evidence of deposit on them of any kind. (The colours and shapes surrounding are incredible.) More decoration – says the finger!

More of dramatic forms of nature were all around; a curiously rounded group of protrusions in almost bizarre formation and the most dramatic so far; a wall of stalactites in the background; glistening falls of bright white and delicate colour sparkling with crystal. Turning to share the sight, I find him there again, standing next to a stalagmite many feet higher than he, grinning and leaning with his elbow on the column, waist width all the way up. What can you say? More of the fairyland! This is real Mr Disney! This is real! There is so much more than posing. A whole skeleton of a female lying calcified there surely says it all if you can listen in the silence punctuated only by the drip of nature's progress.

I returned to Corozal after lunch on Sunday after a morning spent pleasantly lazing about and soaking up the atmosphere of Pooks Hill in the forest.

'…Your friend Rose is in luck. I have a nine-year-old girl here who would like to be her pen pal. She is called

Deborah Rogers and her Mum is the Principal of St Paul's Anglican School, which is one of the schools linking with South Molton Community College. Deborah goes to Corozal Methodist School, which is another one of the linking schools…'

'…Knowing me as you do you will realise straight away that I haven't forgotten Africa. I questioned the accommodation position without being provocative and have got to know the Placement Officer in London as well as one can in London. This placement is only for 12 months (initially, anyway) so the options are still wide open. As for Pakistan – I can hardly believe the luck. The posting fits everything I had hoped for. One of the things putting me off the country is that Pakistan is the biggest operation in education for VSO. I will be the only VSO in the area again so there won't be that distraction and the mountains are very much within reach! As for the job, what a challenge! It fits many other things that interest me and will require a lot of learning on my part to get to grips with where it is all coming from…'

'…There are four copies of the book for you including one for Nicola's project. I counted four for me to use. That leaves four. Those ones are for you to decide. If you want copies to go into school I suggest you talk to teachers about it in the library. I'm sure you will have discussed it at home. It would be much better for you to decide…'

Continuing orientation filled the first three days of the week and continued to go well. There was no distraction from the much anticipated celebration to take place on the day following as the whole organisation was a collaboration of the five participating schools until…

Thursday 18th May 2000:
A Celebration of Learning on a theme of Communication
09:30 – 12:00 at Miami Beach, Corozal

The celebration was absolutely brilliant and was recorded both on film and on videotape. Mark Wright came with the VSO Director for Guiana who is visiting Belize. They were somewhat impressed. I made video film of the arrivals and of the setting up as well as many of the activities, displays and presentations. It just kept coming. I had to get on with the filming otherwise I think I might have burst into tears. As soon as the battery was flat I rushed across home to recharge it and to use my camera in the meantime. In the event, I decided I had enough film and just took a roll of pictures. The celebration ran in full swing from 9:00am to 11:30am.

The quality and scale of the whole thing was amazing. Also, as other schools took up the invitation to come and see what was going on it will have left an impression far beyond expectation or imagination despite the many problems that had to be overcome.

Afterwards we went to the bar at the other end of the beach and Mark conducted his end of placement interview while we had lunch of chicken in the basket accompanied with a few Belikin. It wasn't very easy to fully discuss the placement the way QADS operates and the effect that has with the visitor present as she persisted in just sitting there. I would have gone for a walk and I rather expected her to have an idea to do that as well. I gave Mark a copy of 'Home is the Belizoo' for himself and asked him to drop off copies for the Belize Zoo together with a letter for Sharon Matola.

'Please find herewith, four copies of 'Home is the Belizoo' as promised! The very long delay has nothing to do with neglect of any kind – rather the opposite. Getting to a point where the story was illustrated and printed, both of which caused many problems has taken all the time since my return from England in July 1999! You will know about printing problems in Belize anyway. In the end I had fifty copies printed privately, using a laser printer to maintain quality. I tried students in many Belize schools to find a commitment to illustration and failed. A brother and sister in England eventually did the illustrations. Philip, whose job it was, was twelve years old at the time. If you would like write to them it would be much appreciated… I know that you would get an answer! …'

Celebrating Children

George the Snail couldn't sleep. Actually that was the wrong way to say it. George the Snail wasn't asleep and only just realized he wasn't. He should have been asleep long ago. In fact he would have been asleep long ago. He hardly ever had any trouble sleeping. He would have been asleep long ago had he gone to bed or even wanted to but he hadn't. Right now he was sitting on the balcony gazing at a clear sky full of stars, especially now that all town lights were out. In the stillness of the night only the soft sound of the restless sea, so close on the beach, stirred and caressed his mind. Even Mr Max was silent with his own thoughts, the beer long gone. What a day!

It all started when the sun came up. That never bothered George either; he was always ready for the day. In any case, being near the equator the sun came up later than at home in England just as it set earlier into the night; also it didn't take long about it either way and in the morning that stirred George up big time. This morning Mr Max was already up messing about with cameras and stuff. He was fussing because he said it was an important day and he had to go off to meet the VSO Director for Belize who had come with the VSO Director for Guiana who was visiting Belize. They were staying in a hotel nearby. They had come lots of miles from Belmopan just to see and take part in the celebration and Mr Max said that was important as well. After it was all over they said they were somewhat impressed. Mr Max was ever so pleased – important as well, apparently. Anyway, as far as George was concerned being important wasn't important. What was important was that it was fun just as learning and sharing it all should be.

It wasn't long before things started happening across the road at the Round House; on the beach across the road. And not just at the Round House but all over the grassy part of the beach and all along the road leading up to it in both directions. Trucks were arriving loaded with all sorts of models and equipment, a mass of colourful and exciting objects and banners and flags and streamers, all begging to be explored and investigated. A small army of adults, parents and teachers descended en mass accompanied by a much larger army of children all known to George and it was barely seven o'clock. George couldn't wait for Mr Max and he hurried over to join in the unloading and preparations; not that there was much he could do because it all just seemed to grow together without his help but it felt as though he was busy and there were lots of smiles and greetings and heaps of energy everywhere.

George was amazed when everything was in place and it was half past eight already. Where had all that time gone and yet so little time with so much done. Perfect timing anyway as the first of many crocodiles of children from other schools began to arrive, more and more, seemingly endless until by nine o'clock the whole thing was in full swing and everyone was following their own interest from the huge array of demonstration, information and activity on offer; the Round House transformed from the traditional meeting place into an energy, a gathering of delights, a sweetshop of learning. George was amazed alright.

Outside there seemed to be as many children as inside, perhaps more, but they were not just milling about they were talking about what was going on and directing their friends to what they had been interested in. In any case there were refreshments outside to help the talk and the Belize Defence Force had been invited and had taken over the little Round House close by. A lot of the boys especially had headed over there already. George really wanted to be inside although it was very crowded with all his many friends working the displays and activities and others from the visiting schools looking on, asking questions and trying for themselves. George soon got talking and wondered why the visitors were in class groups and many he knew were missing. It wasn't until a little later that he realized that the groups were coming and going (or going and coming if you see what he means) so that the crowds were much the same for the whole time. There were also a lot of adults not connected with schools who came close to see what was going on, standing in amazement but not quite joining in as adults do (or don't!)

George started to focus more on his friends. At the best of times he couldn't move about very quickly and this was one of those times when that is a big advantage because he was able to feel so much a part of the activity wherever he was and that helped so much in realizing the chosen theme of communication – all down to the schools' link with South Molton in North Devon in England and with each other. Computers were beginning to play a part in making the sharing easier and quicker and all the new ones were on display and in operation as well as model ones that had been made in class to give more children understanding of the idea of using computers through creativity and games and give practise on the keyboard; all serious stuff and fun. Outside George had seen children arriving, returning, standing, sitting, talking, sharing; serious and excited. Inside there was room only to stand so that moving from one base to another meant easing gently among many others doing the same; movement for George being rather more a case of being handed from one friend to the next (his pace low down may well have been disaster). It was only then, after so much close contact that George realized just how much all his friends were the same and yet so different. Quite apart from different interests they were different too. There are many ethnic origins in Belize and they were almost all here: Mestizo (Spanish Maya), Maya, Creole originally from Africa, Mexican across the border, East Indian, Garifuna and (more rarely) European including Mennonites who keep themselves much to themselves as Belize' farmers and workers of wood. Many of the children running the bases wore traditional costume with the Mestizo boys as well as the girls in costume; the boys all in white including their long trousers and smart wide-brimmed hats, excepting only the plain colour neckerchief usually in orange; the girls dresses also white but colourfully decorated in finely embroidered pattern mainly around the neck and shoulders. George was lost in admiration for all the variety in a sea of young smiles all being so much together.

Newsroom, news desk, reporters, newspaper; art and craft and woodwork; health information and maths race; Mestizo food and clothing; making corn tortilla and grinding corn into masa; string art and live interviews; the land of the Maya; understanding science; character development; the evils of society in drugs and guns (BDF display); string art and many more. But what really made George think was a wonderful display called 'Hello South Molton' that reminded him of the huge banner sent from South Molton all about their school sent in greeting earlier in the year that went on proud display first at the District Education Centre and then at each of the five link schools in turn, seen one way or another across the whole district. So what if the hoped for telecommunication link hadn't been provided; Mr Max had said he wasn't very surprised at that. So what if there had been so many difficulties, not the least that different age ranges in the two countries meant crossing the primary and secondary phases; that South Molton had experienced so many unexpected pressures in this last year; that too much may have been expected of too few. It had happened; children had made it happen through interest and curiosity and trying for themselves, discovery and understanding. How far would all the sharing reach? George sighed and muttered softly just before falling peacefully into sleep, "Who Can Tell?"

Friday was Teachers' Day, which is supposed to recognise the importance of teachers who are supposed to arrange events appropriate to that idea but most of them treat it as a day off. There are going to be a lot of clearing up days now, and this is one of them although there is supposed to be the celebration of Lucille's birthday at some point. Is it today or tomorrow? I'm invited but that was all I was told. This is Belize! Only six weeks to go before going home. For about a month now, I have been buying household things and cooking ingredients etc. with how much I need before I go firmly in mind.

There was a workshop arranged for St Francis Xavier today but I discovered last week, that the Government of Belize had changed the holiday for Commonwealth Day to today so it had to be postponed. Once again QADS omitted to tell us and GoB are not free with information either. Xavier had not got in touch! The morning started with Ruby coming to the door as I was working before breakfast. "Did I mind if some workmen plaster her ceiling underneath?" The workmen had already arrived and started work so there wasn't much I could say about it despite having told her before that I don't like living over a building site, so I said okay as enthusiastically as I could. The next thing was bang, bang, bang as they pounded away on the concrete with a hammer and chisel to provide a key. It hadn't occurred to me that anyone would be so daft as to allow concrete to mature before keying for further rendering! I stuck this for over two hours – and it is no joke being in a concrete box with someone hammering away determinedly on the outside. Then I went out and called Ruby and told her that it had to stop, that I would go out until midday and then there would be no more. She somehow suggested that I was being unreasonable! I didn't argue but went. When I came back they continued to work but there was no further noise. The last of the workshops took place on Tuesday and Thursday, both in Corozal, and it was Commonwealth Day on Wednesday which should have been quiet but I had to put a stop to banging against the walls again. So much for a little job to use up the two bags of cement!

The first job on Friday was to sort out the details for my 'Final' report on the placement in Belize. This should be completed during the weekend, ready to go through with David at QADS on Monday. Next I caught up with email as I won't be here for the weekend. The two workmen were still there so I told them how long I would be away which they appreciated.

'…I'm sorry I have been so long in replying to your last messages (thanks). I have had a fair amount of correspondence with VSO London as you might expect and I have been finishing off typing up 'letters received' as I don't want to lose them and I didn't want to carry them home either. That was a labour of love I can tell you! Otherwise the week has seen the finishing off of my workshops. There is only some planning left to do to help the Belizean Curriculum Coordinator to run workshops in August so I should have a lot more time in the last month. Now I am writing because I am off to Belize City for a family celebration weekend and I won't be back until Monday…'

I set off for Belize City on the midday 'Premier', which left at about fifteen minutes past the hour. I sat in the aisle seat of the front nearside pair, next to an elderly American Lawyer who had spent much of his life in Mexico and was moving down to live in Panama with his daughter. As he was taking his time about getting there he wanted to talk and to learn something of Belize so he made an interesting travel companion. Pamela got on in Orange Walk but she had a seat some way down the bus. The rest of the journey was just as lively in conversation but distracted by the violent swerving and strange antics of the driver who also had two near misses through braking too late. From that point of view I was not sorry when the journey was over. The bus reached Pallotti roundabout just before 2:30pm and I made my way to the family via the Chinese 'Li Chee' for three dollar chicken (leg with no ketchup) as I hadn't eaten. Neria had gone to the doctor in Chetumal and taken Miguel with her, leaving Miriam on a day off downstairs with Mariami and Martin.

The social at QADS was pretty good but what was better was the attitude of David who, far from having reaction to the hammering I have given him, was grateful for the pointers and help given. We went for a drink at 'Lindberg's Landing afterwards and I didn't get home until about nine thirty and stayed chatting with Neria and Tabo (and having supper) until about 11:30. One thing I discovered from one of the curriculum officers that had done some marking for the PSE, was that I had figured in one of the essays – I believe, from Libertad SDA. The subject was about someone who had helped! By this time Miriam had gone to bed (Marco was away on Caye Caulker) and I was to have my old room downstairs, which is now occupied by Nellie whom I thought, had gone back to San Estevan for the weekend. As I went down Neria called out that I should leave the screen door off the latch, as Nellie wasn't in yet. The upstairs door was already closed when that significance sank in. There is only the one room to use and that is my old room. The bed was ready and my bag had been put in there so it was a pretty safe bet but there was still the nagging doubt, even though I thought perhaps Nellie would go in with Miriam for company while Marco was away. Also, I sleep with the door open and no fan and I had forgotten to pack my pyjama trousers that I rarely wear! I had not gone to sleep when the light came on briefly but as I remained alone my guess had to be right – as I confirmed in the morning.

I had arranged to take Mariami over to the Stationery House to buy her a birthday present on Saturday; as both she and Miguel had been all over me it was no surprise when Miguel wanted to come as well, or when he indicated he would like me to buy him something too. Mariami finished up with three things so his one definitely wasn't right and he was in a rare old paddy by the time we got home. But he got over it – so another lesson learned.

Jack came for the barbecue in the evening, as did Pedro, Benita and Daiami. It was a very pleasant time that continued until beyond the dawning of my birthday – although I did not know the actual time of course because all the years of those questions were missing in one way or another. Belizean families know all their details. It was a very pleasant family day for my birthday, with plenty of food, drink and happy conversation. Neria cooked escabeche for me as promised, and we went to the University College of Belize graduation ceremony at the Civic Centre where Ricardo received his degree.

I went to see David Eck on Monday as arranged. It was a very cordial meeting when he confirmed his appreciation of the stand I had taken in respect of schools and the curriculum and the work done and ideas and reports given. He says he intends to come up to Corozal and take me out for a meal! He dropped me off at the family as it was raining. I had lunch and was lucky to catch the two o'clock Venus bus after going to the bank. It was one of the old Greyhounds so it was quite a comfortable ride back.

Then came a week of correspondence and final report writing…

'…I haven't heard from Paul and I am completely at a loss to know what is wrong. Would you please ask him two things: one is he receiving my mail and two would he please email me urgently? The five 'Link' Schools had their celebration of learning on a theme of communication on Miami Beach on Thursday 18th May for Education Week. We didn't get a line from BTL but the morning was absolutely brilliant! This is an absolute first for Belize in many ways. The quality was amazing and as all schools had been invited to come and see what was going on it is impossible to even begin to imagine what the benefit is for young people and their teachers. The VSO Programme Director for Belize came and brought with him the Programme Director for Guyana who is here on a visit. He had to do my end of placement interview and chose that day to be able to come to the Celebration of Learning. They were somewhat impressed…'

'…I leave Belize at the end of June and so it is probably a bit late to ask you for a taped performance of your poem in Creole. However, I enjoyed it very much and didn't want to go without saying so. I love to listen to Creole, or indeed any language expressed through the spirit in some way. I can't pretend to fully understand it but there is a level of appreciation that defies knowledge (as hopefully, the new curriculum shows). I did tell you that the purpose for my request was in respect of a thriving, schools' 'Link' among five schools in Belize and one in the UK. It has been an exciting personal project and one that will echo down the years. Do not be surprised to receive the occasional mail from English schoolchildren. I hope you will feel moved to respond…'

'…Thank you for your thoughts and wishes. That was great. The weekend was great too. I really don't know how I'm going to fit in everything that is being talked about. It is just as well I have pretty well finished my work – and that in many things I'm happy to go along with the tide…'

'…I watched three boys chasing around with water pistols at the weekend. In a temperature in the upper nineties it has added attraction of course. One of them was using a 'super soaker' much as I imagine you were doing while the other two had regular size water pistols. They refilled their 'weapons' from a standpipe and it was funny to watch when the one with the greater capacity was trying to fill his. The other two just stood right behind him and their water certainly found parts that other (beers?) can't reach. When his gun was full they ran…'

'…The barbecue for my birthday was on Saturday and attended by members of the wider family some of whom stayed over on Friday night as well. On my birthday proper, we had my requested meal, which was escabeche cooked the proper way. I made it myself yesterday but it isn't as good! There are other outings planned but I don't know that I will get to them all. I expect to go to the cayes for two of the remaining weekends. The cayes are just inside the barrier reef that, unlike the Australian one, is unspoiled – so far. The cayes are tropical islands. The one most favoured by Belizeans is Caye Caulker where I expect to spend the weekend of the Lobster Festival. I love lobster and there will be plenty of it as well as everything else. The other certainty is Tobacco Caye (I don't know why it has that name), which is a paradise island off the tourist trail. You hire a boat specially to get there and it is not very big. Maybe I will go snorkelling and swim with the sharks and rays at last. A lot of water was involved in my going into the cave system I mentioned. The caves are in limestone and formed by water as you know, so there is a river running through the system. You have to swim to get in! Although the water and the air are both warm, it is necessary to wear regular clothes when out of the water so what you do is wear the same clothes when you are in it. I don't remember ever swimming with trainers on before! Anyway, you swim to get in and wade for a long way, on and off, through water that varies in depth from a few inches to neck deep. The water is beautifully warm and unbelievably clean and clear and you can see the occasional cave-fish and freshwater shrimps (eight or nine inches long) by using the underwater lamp. Overhead are the bat dwellings that they create in the limestone by firing up their acid pee…'

'…Please find attached a copy of my VSO Final Report (Placement Review). I discussed Part 1 with David on Monday 29th May and he has seen the last report and Part 2. I'm sure that you will be interested to know that David and I have met socially and will do so again next week but that is not all. He tells me that he met with the Education Committee last week and left them impressed having made full use of the things I have been giving to him one way and another…'

'…I haven't heard from Paul and I don't know what else to do. There is a lot of opportunity for students being missed and all schools here are waiting for mail… … The emails were keeping him up to date, knowing that he has much on his plate and providing some letters etc. for year 7 students. I had one of my stories illustrated and 50 copies printed. The bulk of those have gone to the five 'Link' schools along with a full set of photos from the 'Celebration of Learning' for each of them…'

'…When I come home I will have to find out why mail from SMCC has gone dead and try to do something about it. I was going to buy a video camera in the American format for SMCC to use on my way home but I'm not quite sure what to do about that at the moment…'

'…It is 6:30am. I have been getting up late over the last couple of weeks. The mornings are so amazing that you (I) tend to get up over an hour earlier than that. Anyway, checking the mail is one of the first things on my list of things to do…'

A whole week was spent delivering photos and books to the link schools which involved a huge amount of sharing with classes of students all trying to fit the 'quart into a pint pot'. In between I managed to finish typing up the Posting Pack and notes for Pakistan and had evenings out with friends from the schools' staff before catching the 5:30am bus for QADS on Friday then the 5:00pm boat for Caye Caulker.

The meeting at QADS was disappointing because what was talked about and the way it was discussed were so far from reality. Everyone except Louisa and I wanted to say how well all the schools were doing and yet we have strong evidence to show that Corozal is markedly ahead of everywhere else. I left to catch the boat at about twenty past three in the hopes that there might be one at four o'clock. Alphonso drove me down there in good time for that but the boat had gone at half past three. There was now nearly an hour and a half wait for the five o'clock boat so I spent some time wandering around on the South side of the bridge and the rest of the time watching the traffic on the water.

The ride out was fairly uncomfortable as it was quite windy and the sea was choppy. I sat on the middle of the boat where it takes all the thumps, with its nose in the air. Marco had a table with some friends at 'The Sand Box' when I arrived and I met with Fernando who would be taking us out in his boat tomorrow. The rest of the evening was spent in various bars meeting a variety of people and having spaghetti Bolognese at a restaurant run by the only Italian on the island. It was well into Saturday by the time I went to bed and after a long day, however pleasant in the evening, I was quite glad to get there.

The arrangement was to meet Fernando at eight this morning. We had breakfast in the Sand Box, which was nice but the fry jacks were oily and that added to a discomfort from the night before. The sad part was that Fernando had gone to lay his lobster pots by the time I got there. I went round to the nearest jetty to see if I could see him on the water. I did see him but he didn't see me and I watched him disappear into the distance and around the next little headland – that is if you can use that term for land so little above the water. Marco had to go into the bank and then catch the ten o'clock 'plane so that he could attend a computer course in Belize City. I spent the rest of the morning exploring the entire island – more than once in some parts – it doesn't take long and there wasn't a great deal to hold my interest. The island caters mostly for people who worship the sun, show off, drink and swim. More interesting to me, are the activities on and in the sea. It was good to watch the large number of fishermen making and preparing their lobster traps in order to set them in order to be ready for the opening of the lobster season, next Thursday, on the 15th June.

Jack arrived on the midday boat, at 1:15pm. We got him settled in his room in the hotel and then set off to find Fernando for the afternoon activities. He wasn't difficult to find as Marco had taken me there in the morning and he was back from his laying of the lobster traps. I had met Fernando the night before and his wife that morning (coming out of the loo!) so the first greeting was easily followed by meeting with three of their children and introducing Jack.

I set off with Fernando and his youngest son, aged about nine, and Jack, at around 2:30pm and looked forward to an interesting afternoon and early evening. We went fishing for a while first but all the fish were small at about six or seven inches. This was just as well because I caught my first fish – one of very few in a whole lifetime – and I am very wary of how to hold it in view of the wicked dorsal spines when taking out the hook. It was successful, however, and my fish went back in the water to grow a bit more with all the others. The fishing over in short time because the boat was also dragging its anchor in the current and against the soft sandy seabed, we set off for the reef and 'shark and ray alley'. The water there is about five to ten feet deep and incredibly clear. I could see the sharks and rays from the boat although this is not as good as you might think because of the reflection of the very strong light on the water. You see the shadow rather than the shape.

'…Nurse Sharks are not dangerous (so I am told). I can't say I really cared anyway. My mind was wholly concentrated on what was going on and the struggle to keep seeing. I really didn't want to stop – but having seen I am satisfied. They are images and feelings that will not be forgotten and are easy to recreate in the mind. I like the way you think in terms of intimidation by humans rather than the other way round…'

The side of the boat has to be all of three feet above the water and it occurred to me as I dropped in that getting out would be a problem but "Let's leave that for later"! So I put on the mask, gripped the mouthpiece between my teeth, and in I went. Needless to say, the water was just too deep to stand and get organised. So, when I discovered the mask was leaking like a sieve, my nose was blocked, the tube was full of water and I was getting either washed under or washed away from the boat, I reckoned there were a few problems to be solved and this had to be done now. No way, was I going to get back in the boat. I was 'treading water', which doesn't take much movement for me so I was a bit like a fisherman's float, upended. All of this time I could feel the swish of water past various parts of my body, mostly the legs. I wondered about this of course, and it didn't take long to realise the sharks and rays were the cause of it! I could just see the shadows, less clear now because of the angle of the light on the water. It was amazing and the pressure to see them clearly was enormous.

I don't know how much water I swallowed or how much coughing and spluttering went on but I got there. That was the only object in mind! I float easily and laying on the surface with the mask absolutely clear and the great fish swimming easily below, rays on the bottom and sharks coming very close beat even the imagination. It was an effort of my will each time to break away, check on the boat and struggle back into position. The rays were up to about five feet across in the main, with the odd one slightly bigger, and the nurse sharks were up to about six feet. There were a few other fish but I didn't pay much attention to them. I did notice the fish that swim close with the sharks and feed on the parasites though. I don't know how long I was in the water either, and maybe it was just as well when Fernando signalled time to go. As it was my inside felt as though it was almost part of the sea and I didn't have much energy left to get back in the boat. I have an extremely sore rib cage to show for that part of the exercise and the swimming has found a few muscles that haven't been used much. Would I do it again? You bet! The 'Wow Factor' is one of the greats. But I have done it and I shall be satisfied with that.

We made tentative arrangements to meet with Fernando in 'The Sand Box' and called there several times through the evening but we missed each other. We had a pleasant evening looking round various shops, trying the odd bar and eating well and appropriately on well-cooked snapper. I slept well that night but there were warning twinges in my chest when I came to look back, that I had ignored – foolishly – at the time.

Marco had arranged to come out early this morning but didn't arrive until mid to late morning when we spotted him in 'The Sand Box', having just arrived. Jack and I had breakfasted well on ham and eggs and fry jacks – cooked just right – followed by three good cups of coffee, towards the south end of the island where it is quiet. We all went off to see Fernando where we spent a pleasant time with his family and admiring the shirts and light sports suits he makes. I bought a shirt and ordered one of the suits, which Marco would bring back for me.

Marco was hoping to go out in the boat but there was not enough gas to go to the reef (nowhere open on Sunday) and no bait for fishing. So the chat extended through the day and into the evening when it was back to an Italian meal as Marco's treat. He likes lasagne – and it was very good. Jack and I had breakfast in the same manner (except that I had bacon instead of ham) after Marco had gone to the bank. We spent some time with Fernando and had a leisurely morning before setting off back to Belize City on the midday boat. I was able to go to the bank and caught a bus straight away, at 1:30pm so I was home in Corozal before half past four to find in the mail that a car would be available for me on return home and a quite unexpected experience had been arranged…

'…AEP/Reach will like Max to attend one to two weeks training at BBC London before coming out to Pakistan…'

'…You are right that there was no reference to training with the BBC in London in the Placement Description – and also about the opportunity, I would think. I can go at any time while I am in England except that I would like the first week in South Molton. That means anytime from Monday 10th July until you send me to Pakistan. The only other dates would be VSO ones and I don't know those. If the reference to 'one or two weeks' is being sensitive to me I can tell you that I would opt for two weeks rather than one. I am sure that the whole operation is fascinating…'

I really have hurt my chest on the left side and bruises are beginning to come out. It was difficult to find a comfortable position to sleep and moving was rather painful. When I got up it was even painful breathing and there was a great temptation to do nothing. However, I did the washing, had breakfast and answered the emails. Then I went out to cash a voucher from QADS at the first opportunity – it rained very heavily this morning. The rest of the day was spent pottering about although I went out a couple of times more, shopping for food, and feasted well on chicken and vegetables this evening.

The next two days were spent quietly preparing to return home, mail and sorting more papers; also getting ready for a meeting with Louisa on Monday to plan for the summer workshops and for the meeting with three schools who claim to be struggling with the new curriculum. The schools' meetings will take place on Wednesday of next week.

'…The main thing I missed answering for right now is the very difficult question 'What made you want to go to Pakistan?' There are many reasons. It will be good to talk with you about the more complex ones. On the surface it is the job I am being asked to do. It is quite a challenge and I don't think I could possibly have entertained the idea without having had three years in Belize. Much of my effort here has been taken up in understanding where the learner is in terms of experience and understanding. That applies to the teachers as well as the children and making friends and 'living' together has done much of it. I don't see my being here as 'giving'. I have gained too much for that. You could call it a partnership. Who, really, can tell? The radio programme is aimed at Afghan Refugee children, aged 9-13, who have never been to school. It is therefore about life skills; skills for life. My job is to advise on the learning content and I will have to work very hard to understand where the learner has reached. To also work with the BBC on the project is like a dream. And it is the first time a VSO has worked in this way – with the World Service or with Afghan education…'

'…As you say, my time in Belize is nearly at an end. It is an odd time in many ways. I am psychologically ready to leave. I have done what I came to do and a lot more than I expected. Any giving there may have been is returned many times over in different ways and I think that fits in with what I said about the ideas I had when I was young. On the other hand, there is a lot to do to leave things tidy; I will miss my friends; and those same friends are pressing for the remaining time so all my weekends are taken up one way or another. I guess I will have to come back for a holiday sometime…'

I certainly shouldn't have gone out on my bike this morning. I went to check if the schools had done their captions for the photographs of the celebration day. None of them had of course, but when I got back I was hardly able to move my left side. I think I must have cracked a rib or something. It is strange that I didn't notice anything of the sort at the time although it was a great effort getting into the boat and I dropped on to my side and chest on the edge of the boat. I hadn't managed to get high enough to use my stomach. I slept most of the afternoon in the only position on my right side that gives no pain and now I am forcing myself into an upright position at the computer to give myself something to do. There is a huge row going on over the results of the new Primary School Examination. The scores are very low indeed. Apparently only 48% of students taking the exam got a score of 50% or over. The old exam was scored as percentiles which measures children's performance against other children rather than against the test of course. That means there is no comparison with previous years either! Now everyone will blame everyone else rather than look at the real problem, which is that the whole system is in a mess. No doubt it will make things even more difficult for the introduction of the new curriculum especially as there is no base-line data for that either.

Orvin and Adelaide arrived at about 7:00am to take me to Chetumal so that I could have their help in buying epiles. Their daughter came along too but I never really knew her name, not only because I forget them but also because I cannot discriminate the sounds accurately into written words. The name sounds like Arielle. I must get one or two people to write down their family names so that I can keep in touch properly and so that I can see how close I got to the local language! The Belize customs officer was very positive and even went so far as cracking a joke as all my details were written down in his book – a long procedure that is not given to Belizeans but still makes them wait behind you. Unfortunately, the joke was some forces crack about going off for a day's drinking and I neither expected it nor understood it until he had made three attempts at explanation. It is not a time of relaxed meeting and I commend his perseverance and friendly disposition – a great improvement! Between the two border posts there was more than the usual hassle of the vehicle being inspected etc., and a great confusion of Mexicans trying to get into the Free Zone. That must be a great thorn in the side of the Mexican authorities. Surprisingly, the Mexican customs officers were just as friendly and I was more ready for being treated as a human being so they had better luck despite the language barrier. The form for the day visit to Chetumal was soon filled in and I was sent on my way with a smile from each of the two officers on duty who had combined their efforts. Perhaps it was because the border post was so quiet and I am sure I look at best defensive and at worst apprehensive of potential attempts at humiliation. There was none of that. Little did they or I know that Orvin would announce 'family outing' (in Spanish) as the vehicle was inspected on the return journey, and we didn't even go through the Mexican immigration post. More than that, on the Belize side, I was waved on with a hearty "Go through" as I hauled my bags filled with $500Bz worth of Mexican goods! All of these were gifts to take home but I was nonetheless prepared for a customs duty battle at the border. Was I disappointed about that? – Not a bit!

We had been told that the women from the villages come in to set up their wares in front of the old market in Avenida des los Heroes but they were not there. This was a great disappointment as Saturday morning was 'their time' and this was my last opportunity to buy the 'epiles' that are so special in the Yucatán and that would be enjoyed so much by the women back home. We wandered around the inside of the market and found a few garments that were vastly overpriced and made to the dimensions of the average Mestizo woman – short and amply made! I found myself repeatedly demonstrating with my two palms coming together ("English!") in a horizontal direction and moving apart vertically ("English!") to hoots of Mexican laughter punctuated by words in Spanish from my friends.

I discovered that none of the others had had breakfast so we three went off in search of that while Ida explored along the avenue towards the sea. I had had fish (second breakfast) while Orvin and Arielle had fried chicken, both with all the trimmings by the time Ida came back and she went without as she had found a villager selling just what was wanted on the street. There was a good selection and hopefully enough longer and less full, dresses to come closer to English size and shape. The tops alone would be less of a problem as they may well be modified and in any case would lend themselves to being worn loose and over other garments. Time will tell. Much heartened and well laden, we moved on towards the sea where the villager's son was also selling and added to the collection there.

On return to the big Chevvy we moved off to the new market by the bus station. We found one superb epile and skirt there, the only one of its kind that I had seen, but it would not have fitted anyone and could not be altered. Ironically, it was in very European proportions but it was made for a girl. Most Mestizo girls are slim and it would have fitted an English ten-year-old like a dream. Anyhow, we found some good t-shirts with Mayan designs on them, and two lovely scarves. All but the t-shirts were hand-made and all the garments unique to the area so I was pleased. Then it was off to eat again – tostadas this time – so Ida had her food at last, and we ended up in the big 'San Francisco' store where I found the paper maché figures that I had wanted to buy since first coming to Chetumal nearly three years ago. So the score was five epile dresses, four 'epile' tops, one child's dress, two scarves, seven t-shirts and four paper maché figures. The figures will have to be packed and sent by airmail because they would be crushed in my case. Quite a day!

Once back in Belize we went south of Orange Walk to the scrap dealer just beyond the sugar factory, where Orvin picked up a booster for the brake system on a pickup he was looking after for someone. This was for an American Ford 150, which is quite a large vehicle. I was surprised that it should have vacuum assisted brakes rather than the power assisted ones most of our heavier vehicles use. The rest of the day was taken up with socializing and an excellent meal in the best restaurant in Orange Walk (Chinese) before heading back home.

After church and completing captions for the more recent photos on Sunday and working with Louisa at the District Office on Monday and Tuesday, Wednesday was taken up working with the few schools that were having difficulties.

Thursday has been largely a matter of packing the case which has most of the gifts in it. It is full but there will be plenty of room in the other case for the remaining gifts and my few personal things. I went to White Sapphire and bought four carvings made in Corozal, three tee shirts and a carved tray. Mrs Pasos gave me a wooden map of Belize made by her husband before he died! Otherwise I had lunch in the Jo-Mel-In after having my hair cut at 'Willingly' for the last time.

'…I have finished my work now. The last part was a visit to four schools on Wednesday. I have still to go to all the 'Link' schools for the last time and I know there are some plans afoot. I just hope they don't clash. I have an assembly to do in one school on Tuesday and awards to present in another on Wednesday afternoon. What are really difficult as the time draws near are the greetings I get from children all over the place. I'm sure the greetings won't have changed but the impact has. A disappointment this week is that my video camera is refusing to eject the cassette so I will have to bring it home to have it repaired. It was my intention to leave it with the schools so that they can send video to SMCC that will work on our machines I spent almost all day yesterday packing one of the two cases. I was hoping to get it down to one but that was a pipe dream…'

'…I'm writing (8:15am – I've done the washing and it is on the line) now because I'm off to Belmopan this afternoon (about 130 miles on the bus). I will stay over in Belmopan before going on to Dangriga tomorrow morning, to take a boat ride out to Tobacco Caye. That is right on the reef as I told you, and it is one of the places where you can snorkel with the whole range of tropical fish. It is also very small and few people go there, as there are no shops and no more than basic facilities. I will be back late on Monday…'

I discovered, yesterday, that a bus goes straight through from the Batty Bus terminal in Corozal to Belmopan (and on to the Guatemalan border). It was due to leave at 4:00pm and the girl assured me that it would arrive in Belmopan at 7:30pm. From that I assumed it would be an express and even then, hopping along with fewer delays than usual. The distance is about 140 miles and with Belize City en route. I didn't enquire further as I had plenty to do and it meant that the washing would dry in time as well. I pushed the doubts into the back of my mind and that was wrong! The bus arrived late but left without delay at 4:15. It was one of the oldest regular buses and the only good thing that could be said about it was that the seats were some of the few comfortable ones, well-padded and covered with cloth rather than split vinyl. It stopped everywhere and for everyone wherever they might stand at the side of the road. In Belize, if you are standing waiting for the bus and I am two or three yards away that is how it will remain. The bus will stop twice! I reckon that if the inhabitants of an entire village were to stand shoulder to shoulder the bus would stop for each one. The government introduced bus stops recently, but no one takes any notice of them.

We arrived in Belize City at the time given for Belmopan and the spirits lifted as I saw the conductor (Yes we still have them. They are designed to make the passengers even more helpless) extract the wooden board marked 'Express' and place it in the window. This also served to soften my feeling towards the conductor who managed by demeanour, posture and position, to obstruct as much of the view through the front window as possible. The board didn't help a lot as the bus broke down four times and the driver had to get out and fix the headlights each time. It is a bit disconcerting when all the lights go out on a thirty foot wide highway with no markings when travelling at seventy miles per hour (The speed limit is fifty-five). You have to give the driver credit though, for shining his torch through the window to help decide whether there was a verge to pull on to or a swamp or ditch to fall in. On the other hand, why did he have his torch so ready and how did he know so well, how to fix the lights? I was late for the VSO party!

We set off for Dangriga on the 8:00am bus, which went along the beautiful Hummingbird Highway. That was a lovely run and we arrived at 9:30 to pick up a small boat with an outboard motor shortly afterwards. The ride to Tobacco Caye took about three quarters of an hour instead of thirty minutes as the water was choppy and all the boats of the type are fairly flat bottomed and intended to skate 'bow up', fast over calm water. The bumping on the bottom was harsh and several cases of beer presented a constant threat to my feet until both were jammed as opposing forces. The rest of the day was spent exploring the reef and the shallow water between it and the island. I spent a lot of time looking at different kinds of coral and all the usual sea creatures as well as beautiful young eagle rays using the sheltered and shallow water inside the reef to avoid their predators. Beyond the reef the waves broke and roared over the living coral as an unbroken symphony that soothed and relaxed the mind through day and night. It is a very relaxing way to spend a weekend. The food was good and the accommodation was very comfortable – and there were no mosquitos or sand flies! Also, as there was so much to look at, listen to and think about, even I couldn't find sitting around tedious and I didn't read much of my book.

I decided to miss out on snorkelling on Sunday morning. The wind remained strong and the wildlife is still recovering from the ravages of Hurricane Mitch so I decided that would be better than being disappointed as it would have been a struggle for me to maintain position as well. In the event, I spent most of the day further exploring the reef, watching the fish, the anemones, crabs etc. and the smaller seabirds, many of which I have not seen before. The frigate birds and pelicans never fail to impress me with their display, total control in the air and fishing ability anyway. I even discovered that some detached coral floats!

We left the island at 2:30 in worsening weather and headed back to Dangriga. That journey took about an hour, as the fisherman had to throttle right down repeatedly to avoid plunging the bow of the boat right into the water. I suppose that could have been quite exciting but I don't worry about those things – especially as I wasn't driving and it is not my responsibility. The bus journey back to Belmopan is even more

354

beautiful because you are facing the mountains rather than having them behind the right shoulder. That with the exceptionally lush vegetation after rain and the villages blending perfectly with their surroundings makes it very attractive indeed. We were back before dark to enjoy a quiet evening's chat after a most enjoyable weekend.

This morning I got up nice and early and watched the wildlife in the yard at Jack's house in Belmopan for quite a long time before leaving to call in at the VSO office to say goodbye when they opened at 8:00am. Jack went for his Monday morning run and then we both left his house at about the same time – Jack slightly behind as he went to work on his bike. As it happened, Mark (VSO Director) was about to set off for Belize City anyway, so I had a lift down and said my goodbyes at the same time (after a hug from Angie – VSO secretary).

Mark was taking his wife and two daughters to Belize City as well. That was nice, as I haven't seen much of them. I was dropped off at the bank 'downtown' but, as there had been no movement in the monies I am waiting for, I could do nothing towards closing the account and went on straight away, to catch the Batty bus home. From the choice of the 11:00am Premier and the 10:00am regular I chose the regular as it would give me somewhere to sit and something to look at. Happily, there was only half an hour to wait and even more happily, the Premier failed to overtake us. I arrived in Corozal a respectable three hours later at 1:00pm. The great thing about the regular bus of course, is the action and there was plenty of that. The bus was one of those made for three children on one side and two children on the other. I have written about that before but my seat was one of the ones that slope steeply in from the ends to the middle. I was by the window on the left and two others at varying times occupied the remainder of the slopes. Over three hours it is very hard on the left cheek, especially as all padding has collapsed (on the seat that is) and bone is in almost direct contact with metal frame – with nerve ends screaming in between. One woman, who saw the opportunity to change seat when the bus stopped and lost it, returned to her perch and called out "I am punished!" Full marks for literary comment!

So now my time in Belize is really coming to an end. All being well I have travelled home to Corozal from Belize City for the last time unless I return for a holiday sometime – which is a distinct possibility. The only thing that could upset the timing is if I have to make a special journey to the bank to close my account. As my pay and holiday money hadn't been paid in when I called there this morning, I have decided to leave all that until Friday. I can check the balance when I arrive in Belize City on Thursday. So there it is! I hope to make a brief return visit to Orange Walk during the week (which amounts to Tuesday and Wednesday) and then travel down with Henry (VSO Field Officer) on Thursday afternoon.

A last message for the children, teachers and parents of the five Link Schools in Belize…

'…Tuesday, June 27, 2000 Friends, I did not come to Belize to give anything to anyone. There has been giving but that is not why I came. I came to Belize to share. I came to try to increase understanding among people. But most of all I came to make friends. All of those are two-way things. I also wanted to share my experience with my friends at home in England and most of all with the many children I know. The work here in Belize schools does all of those three things but there was something more. I wanted to find a way for children to do the same thing for themselves. That is why the school's 'link' was born. It was born for children to share, to increase understanding and most of all, to make friends. Those three things are worth working for and I pray that they will continue. Mr Max…'

I went to St Paul's this morning as I was invited to their assembly where I was presented with a memento inscribed with thanks. I then went on to Methodist to say goodbye but the rest of the schools will have to wait until tomorrow as it rained heavily.

Closing the account at BTL was a perfect ending to the long saga of problems I have had with them. I first went to the accounts clerk and said that I wished to pay my account up to date so that I could close it. He looked at it and said that there was nothing to pay as it was over $40 in credit. "Ah, but that is for last month," I said, "I wish to pay for this month so that I can close my account." After some discussion I was told that I would have to go 'to the other end'. I rather expected this and went to see the manager, Mr Acosta.

"I'd like to close my account please."

"Yes sir." I get very good treatment at BTL these days and I have had so much credit given along with the $100 returned deposit for being a good boy and paying my bills on time, that I had made no payment at all for five months. This was to be the sixth month. "When would you like it to be closed?"

"Right now," a succession of expressions chased each other rapidly across his face: surprise, shock, horror, panic; and then the more familiar blank, detached and uncommitted response.

"It takes three days." His voice was quietly triumphant but I hadn't finished yet.

"That's okay," I said, "But I won't be here to pay the bill. It probably won't be more than a few dollars as I am still in credit but if you want to keep the books straight then I am sorry but it will have to be 'Right Now!'"

I had noticed, when I went in to the normally air-conditioned office with all the comforts that BTL affords itself while suggesting that the customer is better served, that all was not well. The door that was normally opened by the armed bouncer for selected people was already open, the windows were open, the whole place was up to normal temperature and the clerk was writing out receipts by hand. So I was ready when the lame and unhappy response came back with no eye contact – "We have no electricity. The computers are down!"

"I can see that," I replied and added, wickedly, "I expect you had the air conditioning too high and blew the main fuses!" It had been rather hot for some time, with daytime temperatures nudging 100°F and very little breeze. I could have been sympathetic.

To my surprise, he laughed. It was a brief, nervous laugh but I had never seen him laugh before and it softened the tone but not the resolve. "You could write it off!"

At that moment, there was a second lightening of his humour as a new girl on the staff, bright, helpful and efficient, intervened. "I'll get on to Belize City," she suggested. After all, the telephones were working! The phone call must have taken all of twenty minutes while the details of my account were worked out and what I owed came to the princely sum of $11, which was rather less than the phone call at that time of day – even without the cost of staff involved. The crisis seemed to be over. The manager smiled and thanked me for coming in. I smiled back. But I hadn't finished yet. "What would you like to do about the instrument?" A selection of the more desperate expressions flashed across his face as he realised that he was going to have to ask a favour. "Er, you will have to…" It ended lamely as he changed tack, "…Do you think you could drop it in for us?"

"No problem!" I smiled gently as I lifted the plastic bag I was carrying and passed the telephone intact, through the hole in the toughened glass screen. "No problem at all!"

After the episode at BTL I went out to Christian School, Assemblies of God at Santa Rita to make the third of my goodbyes to schools. What is happening there is not a happy situation between the management, the acting Principal, and the Principal who is on long leave and his wife. The Acting Principal came to see me in the evening and poured out a story about how his name was being blackened as a drinker when he is a member of the Assemblies of God Church. I found that very difficult as he wouldn't leave it alone and I thought that he would be making any problem worse by making denials and nothing had been said to me by anyone else even though it seemed to involve my friends. Then I went to the library to return my book for the last time. I was sad not to see Dennis who is always there in the evening, as this was still morning time. However, It was really another of the many goodbyes I have avoided making. My many, many Belizean friends will not forget and nor will I.

At lunchtime, Orvin came to collect me for a last meal with his family. As always, Ida had prepared a feast and I am sure I disappointed her a little by not having any of the fried fish that she had bought especially. What I had was the promised escabeche with flour tortilla that was a feast in itself, and the cake to follow. It was a very happy time, not overshadowed by departure but strengthened by the knowledge of always being friends. After I had sorted out the rest of my things to give away and left a message for Louisa to collect a box of useful items and clothes it was time to get ready to go to Calcutta for my last graduation.

Calcutta Government School was where it all started really and I was especially pleased that the students there had asked for me to present their certificates, awards and prizes. I couldn't remember whether the new Principal, Sergio Magana, had said the ceremony was to start at 3:00pm or 4:00pm and I set off early, but even the receipt of that information had been extraordinary so the confusion was hardly surprising.

I had been walking up Fourth Avenue at the beginning of the week, just approaching the 'Chinaman-shop' as I remember when a voice rang out "Mr Max!" This was not unusual but it was an adult voice, which is far less frequent than that of children, and it came from inside a vehicle that was stopping on the other side of the road. I waited as Sergio emerged and crossed the road. "Are you doing anything on Wednesday afternoon?" He asked.

"Yes," I replied, laughing. His face fell. "I'm presenting certificates, awards and prizes at your school graduation."

It took a second or two as his eyes searched my face for clues or confirmation – or something – before he relaxed and said, "How did you know that?"

"One of your parents told me because their children went home and said so." I didn't make any more of that because, in some respects, I probably know the villagers of Calcutta better than he does. The relief that I would be there showed and that was pleasure in itself.

As always when I have plenty of time a bus came along right away for the four-mile ride south along the Northern Highway. I arrived in the village by 2:30pm to find the school all closed up and the village hall where the ceremony was to be held all closed up as well. Everyone would be getting ready. I had not been able to make the promised call on the Guy family so now was the ideal time to be with them as they too, prepared to attend the ceremony and for their daughter to take part. Not the best time to have a visitor perhaps, but that is when I was paid one of the nicest compliments.

"You know what we all like about you?" Whatever my answer was it would have been pretty lame because I had no expectation of such a question and as has happened several times in Belize, was floored completely. I didn't have to wait long. "You just come in as one of the family and belong without looking all round and making judgements."

My view of me is nothing like as positive as that and my feeling for my friends can only be described as love so my answer must have been pretty lame as well; as I fought to control the tears pricking around the eyes, 'Why me?'

The graduation ceremony was just as long and just as moving as always. It started more or less on time with plenty of howls and whistles from the p.a. that was turned up way beyond distortion to the universally approved level (of discomfort to me). The electronic shrieks and feedback settled into the familiar repetition of the theme from Elgar's Pomp and Circumstance March and the students began their slow ritual progress with four movements of each foot per step, in time with the music and with each other. The procession may well have taken ten minutes before all were seated on the concrete stage but the spectacle was impressive with the girls in long, pink dresses, white socks and shoes, and the boys with white shirts, black trousers and shoes. The boys carried a red rose and the girls a white one that, traditionally, is given to their Mum. No ceremony in Belize is without its speeches but they were, perhaps, marginally shorter than usual and the presentations by Standard Five students especially, and Standard Six, were enthusiastic and the time slipped pleasantly by.

My own part was most enjoyable and a great privilege especially as each student at each presentation paused for a photo-call as we shook hands so that more images of Mr Max will find their way into family albums in the village as elsewhere. It was especially nice to be able to speak briefly with each student privately at a milestone in his or her life. My only comment publicly was to quote Emerson on finding your own way through the woods and to emphasise the idea 'I Can!'

Refreshments followed and I made my way back to Corozal for the party in the yard by about 7:30pm. I thought I was going to be late because the arrangement had been for seven o'clock but with the best intentions we were into Belize time and friends were not ready for me until about 8:30pm.

Even after three years I cannot get used to the idea of having so little account of time. My punctuality must almost be a complex so I don't think I would ever change and that results in a tension that is perhaps, not felt by Belizeans. Even so, many things would work much better in Belize, given a proper consideration for people coming together 'one time' instead of over a protracted period that is largely unknown. The party was great. I was spoilt for women, as always seems to be the case, and there was only one other man in the assembled company. It was a very pleasant evening and a great meal set around relleno cooked by Lucille and served by Ruby and her Mum. Pleasant conversation and a fairly late night left another memory secure in the knowledge of always being friends.

Saturday started with Tabo and Neria going to the market at about 6:00am as usual. I didn't get up until about half an hour later as there wouldn't be much to do this morning. I should have gone to the market as well! It was a leisurely start to the day and Neria busied herself with breakfast as always when she came back and just as regularly I wasn't expected or allowed to do a thing. Marco and I went out shopping for food for the evening and the morning soon slipped by. Just as Miriam had lunch ready Corinth phoned and asked if I would join her for lunch and the afternoon. This really suited me because Marco and Miriam were continuing their Saturday computer course and Corinth's husband Victor collected me more or less straight away. It was a very pleasant afternoon and I was driven back for 5:00pm. At the family evening party it was thought that I might have a lot to drink and entertain everyone by dancing. Both of those thoughts were wrong but I did take the floor and tell a few stories including 'Cecil' and 'The Belizean Entrepreneur' known to many back home. They went down well but not as well as usual because Belizeans are not accustomed to stories with punch lines and do not readily share that sense of humour.

It was a long morning on Sunday but everyone did their best to be as 'normal' as possible. I had my lobster tails specially cooked, as there hadn't been enough to share yesterday evening, and I spent much of the time with the children. We had lunch and then the whole family set off in two vehicles (nine adults and three children) to see me off at the airport. Jack took photos that I have no doubt will appear in due course. The flight was delayed and the connection at Houston was tight to say the least but I didn't bother about that as it wasn't my responsibility and was able to watch the flight courier trying to round up her passengers with some detachment. 'What next?' I thought, 'Who can tell?'

Max Grantham (Mr Max)
Born 1939 in Sheffield

Vickers apprentice at Brooklands leading to design, patents and Chief Designer of a medium size engineering company before turning to primary education 'working with live material'. Married 27 years without family, worked with children from assistant Cub Scout Leader to 'Akela Max' for 4,000 Devon Cub Scouts and Leaders, retiring in 1997 to volunteer and follow a dream among peoples of, eventually, five developing countries for which Belize was as perfect a start could be.

First Edition - Published October 2014 in hardback by
Printworkx Ltd, The Old Library, 1 East Street, South Molton, North Devon, EX36 3BU, UK

ISBN: 978-095-761-0941

Copyright © Max Grantham

All rights reserved. No part of this publication may be reproduced, stored in or introduced into a retrieval system, or transmitted in any form, or by any means (electronic, mechanical, photocopying, recording or otherwise) without the prior written permission of the publisher. Any person who does any unauthorised act in relation to this publication may be liable to criminal prosecution and civil claims for damages.

A CIP catalogue record for this book is available from the British Library

Typeset and produced by Printworkx Ltd, South Molton, EX36 3BU

Printed and bound by Advent Colour, Andover